Communications in Computer and Information Science 2896

Series Editors

Rationale

The CCIS series is devoted to the publication of proceedings of computer science conferences. Its aim is to efficiently disseminate original research results in informatics in printed and electronic form. While the focus is on publication of peer-reviewed full papers presenting mature work, inclusion of reviewed short papers reporting on work in progress is welcome, too. Besides globally relevant meetings with internationally representative program committees guaranteeing a strict peer-reviewing and paper selection process, conferences run by societies or of high regional or national relevance are also considered for publication.

Topics

The topical scope of CCIS spans the entire spectrum of informatics ranging from foundational topics in the theory of computing to information and communications science and technology and a broad variety of interdisciplinary application fields.

Information for Volume Editors and Authors

Publication in CCIS is free of charge. No royalties are paid, however, we offer registered conference participants temporary free access to the online version of the conference proceedings on SpringerLink (http://link.springer.com) by means of an http referrer from the conference website and/or a number of complimentary printed copies, as specified in the official acceptance email of the event.

CCIS proceedings can be published in time for distribution at conferences or as post-proceedings, and delivered in the form of printed books and/or electronically as USBs and/or e-content licenses for accessing proceedings at SpringerLink. Furthermore, CCIS proceedings are included in the CCIS electronic book series hosted in the SpringerLink digital library at http://link.springer.com/bookseries/7899. Conferences publishing in CCIS are allowed to use our online conference service (Meteor) for managing the whole proceedings lifecycle (from submission and reviewing to preparing for publication) free of charge.

Publication process

The language of publication is exclusively English. Authors publishing in CCIS have to sign the Springer CCIS copyright transfer form, however, they are free to use their material published in CCIS for substantially changed, more elaborate subsequent publications elsewhere. For the preparation of the camera-ready papers/files, authors have to strictly adhere to the Springer CCIS Authors' Instructions and are strongly encouraged to use the CCIS LaTeX style files or templates.

Abstracting/Indexing

CCIS is abstracted/indexed in DBLP, Google Scholar, EI-Compendex, Mathematical Reviews, SCImago, Scopus. CCIS volumes are also submitted for the inclusion in ISI Proceedings.

How to start

To start the evaluation of your proposal for inclusion in the CCIS series, please send an e-mail to ccis@springer.com

Elena Vlahu-Gjorgievska · Tadashi Okoshi ·
Ahmed Salem · Rhodora Abadia ·
Ala Yankouskaya
Editors

Persuasive Technology

PERSUASIVE 2026 Satellite Events

21st International Conference, PERSUASIVE 2026
Hakodate, Japan, March 10–13, 2026
Proceedings

Springer

Editors
Elena Vlahu-Gjorgievska
University of Wollongong
Wollongong, VIC, Australia

Tadashi Okoshi
Keio University
Fujisawa, Japan

Ahmed Salem
Future University Hakodate
Hokkaido, Japan

Rhodora Abadia
Adelaide University
Adelaide, SA, Australia

Ala Yankouskaya
Bournemouth University
Bournemouth, UK

ISSN 1865-0929 ISSN 1865-0937 (electronic)
Communications in Computer and Information Science
ISBN 978-3-032-27234-8 ISBN 978-3-032-27235-5 (eBook)
https://doi.org/10.1007/978-3-032-27235-5

This Springer imprint is published by the registered company Springer Nature Switzerland AG
The registered company address is: Gewerbestrasse 11, 6330 Cham, Switzerland

Preface

Persuasive technology (PT) and its capacity to shape human behavior and cognition have become deeply woven into modern society, inspiring researchers and practitioners across the globe to pursue groundbreaking work on behavior change across multiple fields. As technology becomes more deeply integrated into daily life, the ability to shape human attitudes and behaviors has become essential for tackling a wide range of societal and individual challenges. PT represents a dynamic, cross-disciplinary field centered on creating, building, and assessing interactive systems designed to influence people's behavior, beliefs, and actions through persuasive methods, avoiding coercion or manipulation. These technologies enhance well-being and quality of life by helping people define and reach their personal objectives in areas including health, education, environmental sustainability, and social engagement.

This year, the 21st edition of the International Conference on Persuasive Technology (PERSUASIVE 2026) took place in Hakodate, Japan, from March 10 to 13, 2026.

This volume focuses on the proceedings of the satellite events of the conference, including the accepted papers in the Late Breaking Results track, Posters, Demonstrations and Artefacts, Workshops, and Doctoral Consortium papers. The accepted papers from the main track have been published in Lecture Notes in Computer Science by Springer.

This volume contains fifteen (15) papers presented in the Late Breaking Results track, twenty (20) Demo, Poster, and Artefacts papers, two (2) papers from the Doctoral Consortium, two (2) papers presented at the Personalizing Persuasive Technologies Workshop 2026, five (5) papers from the 1st International Workshop on Trust and Blame in Social Agents (TBSA 2026), one (1) paper from the 2nd International Workshop on Upholding Ethical Designs (I-WOULD 2026), and twelve (12) papers presented at the 3rd BTI International Workshop (BTIW3). All papers underwent a double-blind review process conducted in EasyChair, with each Demo, Poster, and Artefacts paper receiving at least one review, and all other papers receiving at least two reviews by the program committee members. The final acceptance of the papers was decided after thorough consideration of the reviews.

We would like to thank the program committee members and organizers of the PERSUASIVE 2026 conference, track chairs, workshop organizers, reviewers, and all those who contributed towards the successful publication of these satellite proceedings.

We would also like to thank EasyChair for enabling the submission and review process, and Springer for making these proceedings available to the public.

February 2026

Elena Vlahu-Gjorgievska
Tadashi Okoshi
Ahmed Salem
Rhodora Abadia
Ala Yankouskaya

Organization

General Chair

Kaoru Sumi	Future University Hakodate, Japan

Program Chairs

Raian Ali	Hamad Bin Khalifa University, Qatar
Roberto Legaspi	KDDI Research, Japan

Late Breaking Results (LBR) Chairs

Rhodora Abadia	Adelaide University, Australia
Ala Yankouskaya	Bournemouth University, UK

Doctoral Consortium Chairs

Yutaka Arakawa	Kyushu University, Japan
Harri Oinas-Kukkonen	University of Oulu, Finland
Khin Than Win	University of Wollongong, Australia

Demo, Poster and Artefacts Track Chairs

Antonio Garcia-Cabot	University of Alcalá, Spain
Yugo Nakamura	Kyushu University, Japan

Workshops and Tutorial Chairs

Kiemute Oyibo	York University, Canada
Thomas James Tiam-Lee	De La Salle University, Philippines

Proceedings Chairs

Elena Vlahu-Gjorgievska	University of Wollongong, Australia
Tadashi Okoshi	Keio University, Japan
Ahmed Salem	Future University Hakodate, Japan

Publicity Chairs

Ifeoma Adaji	University of British Columbia, Canada
Yasuyuki Sumi	Future University Hakodate, Japan

Program Committee

Rhodora Abadia	Adelaide University, Australia
Stanley Abhadiomhen	York University, Canada
Ifeoma Adaji	University of British Columbia,Canada
Dena Al-Thani	Hamad Bin Khalifa University, Qatar
Aftab Alam	Hamad Bin Khalifa University, Qatar
Mona Alhasani	Dalhousie University, Canada
Raian Ali	Hamad Bin Khalifa University, Qatar
Alaa Ali S. Almohanna	Northern Border University, Saudi Arabia
Nawaf Almutairi	University of Hail, Saudi Arabia
Sameha Ahmed Ali Alshakhsi	Hamad Bin Khalifa University, Qatar
Alaa Alslaity	Dalhousie University, Canada
Saleh Altuwayrib	University of Hail, Saudi Arabia
Yutaka Arakawa	Kyushu University, Japan
Emily Arden-Close	Bournemouth University, UK
Judith Azcarraga	De La Salle University, Philippines
Rafael Cabredo	De La Salle University, Philippines
Barbara Caci	University of Palermo, Italy
Luca Chittaro	University of Udine, Italy
Nelly Condori Fernández	Universidad Santiago de Compostela, Spain
Peter De Vries	University of Twente, Netherlands
Shital Desai	York University, Canada
Alia El Bolock	American University in Cairo, Egypt
Sandra Famador	University of the Philipines, Philipines
Alexander Felfernig	TU Graz, Austria
Mark Freeman	University of Sydney, Australia
Ken-ichi Fukui	Kansai University, Japan
Nanami Furue	Hitotsubashi University, Japan

Antonio Garcia-Cabot	University of Alcalá, Spain
Jaap Ham	Eindhoven University of Technology, Netherlands
Hooman Hoghooghi Esfahani	University of Isfahan, Iran
Tahera Hossain	Nagoya University, Japan
Hung-Hsuan Huang	Fukuchiyama Public University, Japan
Tetsunari Inamura	Tamagawa University, Japan
Paul Inventado	California State University Fullerton, USA
Sriram Iyengar	University of Arizona, USA
Elaheh Jafari	University of Saskatchewan, Canada
Heejin Jeong	Arizona State University, USA
Nitchan Jianwattanapaisarn	ATR Interaction Science Laboratories, Japan
Nirattaya Khamsemanan	Thammasat University, Thailand
Divesh Lala	Kyoto University, Japan
Roberto Legaspi	KDDI Research, Japan
Magnus Liebherr	University of Duisburg-Essen, Germany
Kohei Matsumura	Ritsumeikan University, Japan
Shahla Meedya	Western Sydney University, Australia
Mark Mensah	University of Ghana, Ghana
Alexander Meschtscherjakov	University of Salzburg, Austria
Cees Midden	Eindhoven University of Technology, Netherlands
George Mikros	University of Athens, Greece
Niko Männikkö	Oulu University of Applied Sciences, Finland
Yugo Nakamura	Kyushu University, Japan
Cholwich Nattee	Thammasat University, Thailand
Fakhroddin Noorbehbahani	University of Isfahan, Iran
Kohei Ogawa	Nagoya University, Japan
Harri Oinas-Kukkonen	University of Oulu, Finland
Tadashi Okoshi	Keio University, Japan
Ethel Ong	De La Salle University, Philippines
Fidelia Orji	Dalhousie University, Canada
Rita Orji	Dalhousie University, Canada
Oladapo Oyebode	Dalhousie University, Canada
Kiemute Oyibo	York University, Canada
Zelinna Pablo	Torrens University, Australia
Constantina Panourgia	Bournemouth University, UK
George Angelos Papadopoulos	University of Cyprus, Cyprus
John Rooksby	Northumbria University, UK
Ahmed Salem	Future University Hakodate, Japan
Briane Paul Samson	De La Salle University, Philippines
Akihiro Sasaki	KDDI Research, Japan
Marta Serafini	University of Udine, Italy
Zubair Shah	Hamad Bin Khalifa University, Qatar

Nili Steinfeld	Ariel University, Israel
Agnis Stibe	RMIT University, Vietnam
Merlin Teodosia Suarez	De La Salle Lipa, Philippines
Kaoru Sumi	Future University Hakodate, Japan
Yasuyuki Sumi	Future University Hakodate, Japan
Asuka Terai	Future University Hakodate, Japan
Katja Tiefengrabner	Salzburg Research Forschungs mbH, Austria
Akira Utsumi	ATR Intelligent Interaction Research Laboratories, Japan
Evangelia Vanezi	University of Cyprus, Cyprus
Elena Vlahu-Gjorgievska	University of Wollongong, Australia
Isaac Wiafe	University of Ghana, Ghana
Khin Than Win	University of Wollongong, Australia
Burkhard Wuensche	University of Auckland, New Zealand
Wenzhen Xu	Hitotsubashi University, Japan
Ala Yankouskaya	Bournemouth University, UK
Affan Yasin	Xi'an Jiaotong-Liverpool University, China
Keiichi Yasumoto	Nara Institute of Science and Technology, Japan
Tomoko Yonezawa	Kansai University, Japan
Donghuo Zeng	KDDI Research, Japan
Junpei Zhong	UOW College Hong Kong, China

Additional Reviewers

Gosia Ludwichowska-Alluigi	Adelaide University, Australia
Hirotake Yamazoe	University of Hyogo, Japan
Neil Bretana	Flinders University, Australia

Contents

Late Breaking Results Track

Analysis of Student Engagement Patterns to Inform Metacognitive Nudge Design in Online Higher Education

Rhodora Abadia[1](✉), Gosia Ludwichowska-Alluigi[1], Reid Honan[1], Neil Bretana[4], Fernando Marmolejo-Ramos[2], Paggie Liu[1], Leon Kimani[1], Srecko Joksimovic[1], Sarvesh Mhatre[3], and Kelly Vaughan[1]

[1] Adelaide University, Adelaide, SA 5000, Australia
{rhoda.abadia,gosia.ludwichowska-alluigi,reid.honan,paggie.liu, srecko.joksimovic,kelly.vaughan}@adelaide.edu.au

[2] Flinders University, Bedford Park, SA 5042, Australia
fernando.mamolejoramos@flinders.edu.au

[3] NRI- Australia and New Zealand, Adelaide, SA 5000, Australia

[4] Australian Institute of Health Innovation, Macquarie University, Sydney 2109, Australia
neil.bretana@mq.edu.au

Abstract. This paper presents an analysis of student engagement patterns from 714 students across four offerings of a first-year online course to inform the design of metacognitive nudges. We proposed an analytics-to-intervention mapping framework that specifies learning analytics indicators for three metacognitive categories: planning, monitoring, and evaluating. Statistical analysis confirmed significant differences in weekly engagement patterns among grade groups. Engagement followed a consistent temporal trajectory. Low start in Week 1, peak during Weeks 2–4, then decline through Weeks 5–10, identifying Weeks 4–5 as the critical intervention threshold. Planning nudge indicators include irregular access frequency, declining session duration, late-night or rushed access patterns, lack of course outline review, and reactive resource access. Monitoring indicators encompass unusually short or long time-on-task, surface-level content interaction, low help-seeking behavior, and incomplete material coverage. Evaluation indicators include non-access of assignment feedback, lack of revision after feedback, and declining reflection participation. Faculty survey validation (N = 89) showed strong alignment, with 62% identifying 'not seeking help when needed' and 57% reporting 'not viewing video resources' as top challenges, patterns that are observable in the analytics data.

Keywords: Learning Analytics · Metacognitive Nudges · Online Learning

1 Introduction

Online higher education faces persistent engagement challenges, with attrition rates consistently higher than face-to-face delivery [1, 4], particularly in contexts requiring strong self-regulation [18]. While nudge theory and persuasive technologies have succeeded in marketing and health [2, 3], their systematic application in education remains underdeveloped [27].

E. Vlahu-Gjorgievska et al. (Eds.): PERSUASIVE 2026, CCIS 2896, pp. 3–17, 2027.
https://doi.org/10.1007/978-3-032-27235-5_1

A critical gap exists in learning analytics systems that map behavioral patterns to theoretically grounded metacognitive interventions. Existing systems identify at-risk students [16, 25, 26] but lack frameworks linking patterns to metacognitive support types. Academic relies on predetermined schedules [7, 17] and post-implementation evaluation [6, 21] rather than systematic, behavior-triggered identification.

This paper addresses "*What learning analytics patterns indicate opportunities for specific types of metacognitive nudges?*". We develop an analytics-to-intervention mapping framework connecting observable LMS patterns to three metacognitive processes: planning, monitoring, and evaluating, which are essential for self-regulated learning [9, 10, 14]. Our contribution is a systematic approach to identifying when and what type of nudges to deploy, not their implementation effectiveness. Our mapping advances existing approaches by: (1) distinguishing among metacognitive support types rather than undifferentiated 'at-risk' flags; (2) providing explicit decision rules through distributional analysis and expert validation; and (3) targeting the planning-monitoring-evaluating cycle that produces visible improvements [8, 14, 17]. We validate the framework through historical engagement analysis and faculty surveys testing alignment between empirical patterns and practitioner expertise.

Our contribution provides systematic analytics-to-intervention correspondences as foundational groundwork for principled identification frameworks, preceding effectiveness evaluation.

2 Related Work

2.1 Nudge Theory in Education

Nudge theory [2] proposes that subtle environmental cues influence decision-making without eliminating choice. Effective nudges guide rather than coerce [5], improving enrollment, assignment submission, and resource utilization [6].

Recent evidence demonstrates nudge effectiveness in higher education contexts. Brown [7] found that timely text-message nudges during the critical first five weeks significantly improved student outcomes. Pu [8] showed that task-based nudges outperformed performance-based feedback in maintaining engagement. However, Brown [7] cautioned that excessive or poorly timed nudges risk creating "nagging" effects that decrease their impact.

2.2 Metacognitive Nudges

The three core metacognitive processes in self-regulated learning are planning, monitoring, and evaluation [9, 10]. Planning involves goal setting and strategy selection before learning; monitoring tracks understanding and strategy effectiveness during learning [9–12]. Evaluation appraises learning products and processes afterward [9, 10, 13]. Corresponding nudges support these processes through goal setting, active reflection, and strategy assessment. While research demonstrates that metacognitive support improves learning outcomes [14], systematic approaches to triggering metacognitive nudges based on observable learning behaviors remain underdeveloped. Most interventions rely on fixed schedules rather than adaptive, analytics-informed deployment.

2.3 Learning Analytics for Intervention

Learning analytics advance prediction of at-risk students and behavioral patterns [15, 16], enabling early intervention. Existing systems address different aspects of learning analytics but leave gaps our framework fills. Risk prediction systems like Purdue's Signals [25] and Starfish by Hobsons use predictive modeling to flag at-risk students via traffic-light indicators or early alerts based on attendance, grades, and engagement. While effective at improving retention [26], these systems identify *who* needs help but not *what type* of metacognitive support to provide. Metacognitive scaffolding systems like MetaTutor [11] provide targeted support for specific metacognitive processes but require explicit self-reports and specialized interfaces rather than standard LMS data, limiting scalability. We bridge these approaches by targeting specific metacognitive processes through standard LMS data, creating transparent decision rules for nudge deployment.

2.4 Success Factors from Literature

Research identifies several factors critical for effective educational nudges. These are timing, content focus, personalization and frequency. Timing is critical. Brown [7] demonstrated that interventions during the first five weeks of study yield the strongest effects, as early engagement patterns strongly predict final outcomes. Oreopoulos [17] emphasized that proximity between nudge and target behavior increases effectiveness. Content focus influences impact. Task-based nudges that direct attention to specific activities outperform performance-based nudges that emphasize grades or rankings [17]. Students respond better to actionable guidance than evaluative feedback. Personalization enhances relevance. Generic messages show limited effectiveness compared to personalized interventions that acknowledge individual circumstances and behaviors [18]. Frequency requires calibration. While regular nudges maintain engagement, excessive interventions create habituation or annoyance, reducing effectiveness [7]. These findings inform our framework development, particularly regarding timing triggers and nudge content design.

3 Methodology

3.1 Research Design and Context

This study employed a mixed-method design, combining quantitative analysis of LMS engagement data with qualitative faculty survey responses. We analyzed behavioral patterns from 714 first-year students enrolled in fully online course (CATOL: Critical Analysis and Thinking in Online Learning) across four offerings in 2024 (Term 1: n = 205; Term 2: n = 179; Term 3: n = 167; Term 4: n = 163). The 10-week course focuses on developing essential academic skills for online learning success. CATOL was selected for the intervention because, as a first-year foundational course, it captures students at a critical transition point when metacognitive habits are still forming [22–24]. Its focus on learning skills rather than discipline-specific content allows observed patterns to reflect general metacognitive behaviors rather than content-specific challenges. Finally, the course's diverse student cohort (spanning multiple programs, majors, and backgrounds) enhances broader applicability of the findings. While discipline-specific courses may exhibit additional domain-related patterns, the core metacognitive processes that we examine, such as planning study approaches, monitoring comprehension, and evaluating learning strategies, are domain-general. Patterns from this skills-focused course thus represent a conservative baseline. Discipline-specific courses may require additional mappings, but the fundamental metacognitive indicators identified here should remain relevant.

Ethics approval was obtained from the institution's Human Research Ethics Committee. Students provided informed consent for educational data use through course enrollment processes. Faculty survey participation was voluntary with explicit consent procedures. All data were de-identified prior to analysis.

3.2 Data Collection

Learning Analytics Data. Moodle data were extracted through the LMS' API. Analytics data comprised historical engagement data from CATOL across four course offerings (Terms 1–4 in 2024), encompassing 714 students. LMS data included:

- page views (time stamp, page ID, user ID, frequency, duration, sequence)
- assignment submissions (timing, completeness, revision patterns)
- resource access patterns (downloads, video views, document interactions)
- forum participation (posts, replies, view patterns, time stamps)
- session characteristics (duration, time-of-day, login frequency)
- assessment outcomes (grades, feedback access, completion rates)
- quiz engagement (attempt timing, completion rates, score patterns)
- h5p interactive content engagement
- video interactions (time stamps, length, completion percentage)
- zoom meeting attendance
- assessment and final grade.

Students were classified into grade groups: HD (≥85%), D (75–84%), C (65–74%), P (50–64%), F1 (fail, all assessments submitted), F2 (fail, ≥1 assessment missing). Data were anonymized and aggregated for pattern analysis while maintaining individual-level granularity for intervention design. Behavioral patterns were analyzed using descriptive statistics, cluster analysis to identify student engagement profiles, time-series analysis to track trajectory changes, and ANOVA to test for significant differences in engagement patterns across grade groups.

Faculty Survey. We surveyed teaching staff with experience in online course delivery across five Australian universities. Of the 132 responses received, 48 were excluded during data cleaning because respondents were not teaching or research academics (n = 15), had not taught in the past year (n = 10), submitted incomplete surveys (n = 16), or provided invalid responses to open-ended questions (n = 7). The final dataset comprised 89 valid surveys. The survey served to validate our analytics-driven nudge mapping and to incorporate faculty expertise on student engagement challenges and interventions in online learning contexts. Its objectives were to identify: (1) behavioral indicators of engagement difficulties; (2) required interventions across metacognitive categories; (3) preferred timing for nudges; (4) faculty comfort with AI-mediated versus instructor-delivered interventions; and (5) current student support strategies.

The survey had five sections: (1) Demographics and Context: teaching experience, disciplines, online involvement, cohort sizes, and edtech experience; (2) Student Behavior Observations: engagement patterns, access frequency, participation quality, time management, help-seeking, and disengagement warning signs; (3) Intervention Preferences: ratings of intervention types (planning, monitoring, evaluating), timing preferences, nudge effectiveness, and communication channels; (4) AI and Automation Perspectives: attitudes toward AI interventions, oversight preferences, automation concerns, and ethical considerations; (5) Current Practices and Challenges: engagement strategies, monitoring time investment, challenges, and desired tool features. Questions used Likert scales (1–5), multiple-choice, ranking, and open-ended responses.

3.3 Data Analysis

Weekly engagement was calculated as the percentage of required activities completed (video views, reading downloads, quizzes, forum posts, assignments):

$$\text{Engagement week} = (\text{Activities completed}/\text{Activities required}) \times 100$$

This metric was aggregated across 10 weeks to examine temporal patterns. Grade groups were classified by final course grades: HD (≥85%), D (75–84%), C (65–74%), P (50–64%), F1 (fail, all assessments submitted), F2 (fail, ≥1 assessment missing). One-way ANOVA examined differences across six independent grade groups on continuous engagement outcomes. K-means clustering ($k = 4$) was applied to student engagement data using three dimensions: assignment completion rate, quiz participation rate, and forum activity level. The optimal number of clusters was determined through elbow method analysis (examining within-cluster sum of squares) and silhouette coefficient assessment (mean silhouette score = 0.43, indicating reasonable cluster separation.

3.4 Analytics-to-Nudging Mapping Development

We developed a mapping of LMS analytics patterns to metacognitive nudge opportunities through iterative analysis of historical engagement data, and synthesis of behavioral economics literature. The analytics patterns are correlational. The mapping is structured along the student learning journey across a 10-week subject, recognizing that different metacognitive supports are needed at different stages. The timing of nudges aligns with evidence from [7] that early weeks (1–5) are critical for establishing engagement patterns, while later weeks require monitoring and reflective supports. Thresholds used in the mapping were derived from exploratory analysis of engagement distributions in our dataset and instructor consultation. We established engagement thresholds through calculating descriptive statistics and quartile distributions; identifying performance-based inflection points; and validating cutoffs with instructors and faculty. These thresholds are provisional and context-specific, requiring local calibration. Our human-in-the-loop design enables faculty to adjust thresholds before approving interventions, making the framework adaptable rather than prescriptive.

4 Results and Discussion

4.1 Temporal Engagement Patterns

Analysis of 714 students revealed the magnitude of engagement differed significantly by final grade ($F = 60.54$, $p < .001$, representing a large effect size).

Weekly analysis shows of at-risk students revealed that F2 students started with low engagement (40–50% in Week 1), peaked during Weeks 2–4 (reaching 70–91% depending on study period), then experienced steady decline through Week 10. F1 students showed similar but slightly higher patterns, with some periods reaching 100% engagement during peak weeks. In Term 4, F1 and F2 patterns were nearly identical, both starting at 46%, peaking at 75% in Week 4, then declining steadily, described as 'a very unusual and noteworthy finding' in the analysis.

The analysis shows that engagement was consistently higher throughout all phases. HD-D students demonstrated 'Holistic Engagement' with a 'strong positive correlation between assignments and quizzes,' with most data points clustered in the upper-right quadrant (High Assignments, High Quizzes). Their engagement was 'consistent across all four periods,' suggesting high-achieving students maintain balanced, sustained engagement rather than the peak-and-decline pattern observed in F1-F2 students.

Changepoint detection using two complementary methods identified Week 4–5 as the critical intervention threshold. The PELT algorithm with MBIC penalty detected significant changepoints at Week 4 for F2 students (MBIC = 3.2, 94% confidence) and Week 5 for F1 and C-P students (MBIC = 2.8–2.1, 87–91% confidence), while HD-D students showed no significant changepoint. Individual student analysis operationally defined "sharp disengagement" as $\geq$ 15 percentage-point decline sustained $\geq$ 2 weeks (derived from bottom-quartile median decline of 14.7%), revealing peak disengagement during Week 4 $\rightarrow$ 5 (164 students, 23.0%), followed by Week 5 $\rightarrow$ 6 (132 students, 18.5%). The convergence of individual disengagement patterns with population-level changepoints for at-risk groups confirmed Week 4–5 as the optimal intervention window, with secondary disengagement at Week 5 $\rightarrow$ 6 supporting continued monitoring nudges during Weeks 4–6.

K-means clustering ($k = 4$) identified four distinct engagement profiles using assignment completion, quiz participation, and forum activity (elbow method and silhouette coefficient = 0.43 confirmed optimal k). Cluster 1: High Engagers (n = 198, 27.7%), balanced high engagement across all activities (assignments: M = 94.2%, quizzes: M = 91.5%, forums: M = 8.3 posts); 89% achieved HD-D grades. Cluster 2: Assignment-Focused (n = 173, 24.2%), prioritized assignments (M = 87.3%) over quizzes (M = 68.4%) and forums (M = 2.1 posts); predominantly C-P grades (45%). Cluster 3: Moderate Engagers (n = 221, 31.0%), inconsistent moderate engagement (assignments: M = 72.5%, quizzes: M = 73.8%); 67% C-P, 21% F1 grades. Cluster 4: Low Engagers (n = 122, 17.1%), sporadic low engagement across all dimensions (assignments: M = 41.2%, quizzes: M = 38.7%, forums: M = 0.8 posts); 78% failed (F2).

Cluster 4 requires planning nudges (Weeks 1–3), Cluster 3 needs monitoring nudges (Weeks 4–6), and Clusters 1–2 benefit from evaluation nudges (Weeks 7–10). Cluster 2 specifically needs nudges promoting quiz and forum.

4.2 Analytics-to-Nudging Mapping

Based on temporal patterns and behavioral profiles, we propose a candidate mapping framework specifying learning analytics indicators for each metacognitive category. Table 1 presents the framework for all three nudge types.

Table 1. Analytics-to-intervention mapping framework for the three nudge types

Nudge Type	Timing	Learning Analytics Indicators
Planning Nudges: Goal Setting and Commitment	Weeks 1–3	Access Frequency (irregular or declining login patterns) Session Duration Trends (sessions getting shorter over time) Access Time-of-Day Patterns (working late at night or in rushed, last-minute sessions) Course Outline Access (not reviewing course outline or assessment requirements) Resource Access Patterns (not accessing learning resources or reactive access)
Monitoring Nudges: Active Reflection	Weeks 4–6	Time on Task (unusually short or long engagement times with tasks or materials) Content Interaction Depth (surface-level interactions, skimming content, not opening videos or exercises) Reflection Activity Mid-Task (low frequency of in-task reflection prompts or self-checks) Help Seeking (low discussion forum posts or absence of question-asking despite declining performance)
Evaluating Nudges: Reviewing and Adjusting Strategies	Weeks 7–10	Effortful Engagement /Reflection Responses (unusually short or long engagement times on reflection activities) Assignment Feedback Access (not viewing or engaging with instructor feedback) Revision Patterns (not revisiting or correcting past tasks even after receiving feedback)

Tables 2–4 present an example of our mapping, specifying analytics indicators, detection thresholds, intervention timing, nudge messaging, and behavioral principles for each metacognitive category across course phases. These mappings represent theoretically grounded proposals requiring empirical validation. The nudge messages, timing, and thresholds are based on: (1) SRL literature linking patterns to metacognitive processes; (2) faculty-identified student challenges; (3) prior nudge intervention studies; and (4) our observational data on pattern-outcome associations.

Planning nudges target the opening phase when students establish routines and set goals. LMS analysis identified key behavioral indicators of planning support needs: delayed course access beyond 48 h, irregular login patterns, reactive rather than proactive resource downloads, minimal engagement with course outlines and assessment requirements, and brief sessions (<3 min) on planning materials. These patterns are associated with difficulties with goal setting, strategic preparation, and course integration.

Monitoring Nudge Analytics (Weeks 4–6). Monitoring nudges support self-regulation during the mid-course phase, when initial enthusiasm typically wanes and negative trajectories can be redirected. Key behavioral indicators include unusually extended or brief time-on-task patterns revealing comprehension difficulties or surface engagement, incomplete content access with missing pages or skipped videos, non-participation in forums and interactive activities, and pacing delays relative to the course schedule. Monitoring nudges leverage reminder effects, implementation prompts, social norms, and checklist cues to maintain engagement while encouraging deeper reflection beyond automatic, surface-level interactions.

Evaluation Nudge Analytics (Weeks 7–10). Evaluating nudges prompt students to reflect on learning strategies and prepare for improvement during the course's final phase, focusing on consolidating learning and developing transferable self-regulated skills. Key indicators include failure to access feedback after submission, consistent patterns of similar errors suggesting inadequate strategy adjustment, declining engagement quality trajectories, and non-participation in self-assessment opportunities. Reflection nudges leverage metacognitive prompts, feedback-seeking encouragement, study habit formation, social rewards, and generative learning principles to develop lasting self-regulated learning capabilities beyond the immediate course context.

Our nudge design incorporates multiple behavioral science principles applied strategically across the learning journey. Guided by Kahneman's dual-process theory [19], all nudges are designed as System 2 interventions - transparent, reflective, and autonomy-supportive rather than manipulative. Students receive information to make informed decisions rather than being automatically steered. Descriptive norms and social comparison are used to improve peer-aligned motivation [20] without introducing competitive pressure. Nudges are delivered as just-in-time interventions, aligned with student workload and key task milestones rather than arbitrary schedules [4, 7] with timing informed by observed behavior patterns. Consistent with Oreopoulos [17], nudges focus on specific, actionable tasks rather than abstract motivational messages or performance comparisons. Lastly, drawing on the "concerned friend" approach [7], messaging adopts a supportive tone shown to elicit higher student responsiveness than authoritative or neutral communication.

Table 2. Example planning nudge analytics-to-intervention mapping (Weeks 1–3)

Analytics Indicator	Pattern Trigger	Theoretical Basis	Example Nudge	Timing
Initial course access	Delay >48 h after course start	Just-in-time intervention	"Let's get ahead: Students who completed the Week 1 readings by [X] found the upcoming [learning activity link] easier to tackle. You can do it too, start now [provide link to the eReadings]!"	Day 3 of week 1
Weekly material access	No access to week overview	Goal setting & task orientation	"This week's mission: Watch the video [provide link]+contribute to the forum [link to learning activity] by [day of the week]. Set a time now that works best for you."	Monday of each week
Session duration on planning materials	<3 min on course outline	System 2 nudge - educational opportunity	"Planning tip: This task takes about [X amount] minutes. When are you going to complete this? Try blocking out a spot in your calendar today."	After brief session detected

Threshold Derivation and Validation. Analytics thresholds in Tables 2–4 were derived through three stages combining data-driven analysis, expert consultation, and prospective validation. First, distributional analysis across grade groups established initial thresholds: <3 min for session duration (F1–F2 25th percentile; students with >50% brief sessions had 2.8× higher failure rate, OR = 2.81, 95% CI [2.12, 3.74]), <30 s for page views (one-third of successful students' median 87 s; associated with significantly lower quiz scores, M = 58.2% vs. M = 74.6%, $t(712) = 8.34$, $p < .001$), <2 logins/week

Table 3. Example monitoring nudge analytics-to-intervention mapping (Weeks 4–6)

Analytics Indicator	Pattern Trigger	Theoretical Basis	Example Nudge	Timing
Weekly progress status	Mid-week, <50% tasks completed	Reminders & deadlines	"Halfway through the week [X topic]! Have you watched the videos and attempted the tasks? If not, there's still time, make today count."	Wednesday midday
Time-on-task	Extended duration >200% average	System 2 reflection prompt	"Quick check: How are you feeling about this week's topic? Jot down a question if you would like to ask your teaching team in the forum or the zoom session"	After extended session
Peer engagement comparison	Individual < cohort average	Social norms & sequential cues	"Most students who stayed on track this week watched the video [link] and attempted the [X] learning activity"	Thursday of week

for access frequency (3.4× failure odds, OR = 3.42, 95% CI [2.45, 4.78]), and 48-h delay for course outline access (4.1× failure odds, OR = 4.12, 95% CI [2.87, 5.91]). Second, five experienced educators (mean 12.4 years' experience) refined thresholds for face validity and practical utility, adjusting the session threshold from <2 to <3 min, reducing page view from <45 to <30 s, and adding sustained-pattern qualifiers. Third, prospective validation on held-out data (n = 163) demonstrated acceptable performance: sensitivity of 84–86% across nudge types, specificity of 12–14% false positive rates, and ROC analysis showing strong predictive validity (AUC = 0.76–0.82), with the combined model achieving AUC = 0.82 for predicting student failure.

Table 4. Example evaluation nudge analytics-to-intervention mapping (Weeks 7–10)

Analytics Indicator	Pattern Trigger	Theoretical Basis	Example Nudge	Timing
Feedback access	No access >48 h post-grading	Feedback timing & monitoring	"You've submitted! Now's a great time for feedback, what worked well for you last week, and what can you carry forward?"	48 h after grading
Performance patterns	Repetitive errors across assignments	Planning ahead from reflection	"Think back: What made this week easier or harder to manage? Set one small intention for next week now."	After graded work returned
Peer knowledge sharing	No forum contributions	Social reward & generative learning	"Well done finishing Week [X]! What's one piece of advice you'd give to someone starting this topic? Share it in the forum with your peers"	End of module/week

4.3 Observed Behavioral Profiles

Analysis revealed distinct behavioral profiles aligned with analytics indicators. During the Planning Phase (Weeks 1–3), F1-F2 students showed low initial engagement (30–50% in Week 1) and delayed course integration. Their behavior was 'Deadline-Driven', with reactive access to resources rather than proactive preparation. In the Monitoring Phase (Weeks 4–6)**,** HD-D students emerged as 'Early Birds' showing the highest assignment engagement around key submission points (Weeks 3, 5, and 10). F1-F2 students showed engagement spikes in Weeks 4 and 6, indicating late submissions. HD-D students 'Dominated Peak' activity in quiz engagement during Weeks 6–7, while F1-F2 students were notably less active in forums and help-seeking throughout the semester. This critical finding indicates failure to leverage available support systems. In the Evaluation Phase (Weeks 7–10 a decline in engagement was observed across all grade groups. F2 students were in the 'Low Assignments, Low Quizzes' category, indicating struggle with both activities. F1 students showed more mixed patterns, sometimes prioritizing one activity over another.

4.4 Faculty Survey Results

Eighty-nine complete responses were analyzed. The sample consisted of 49% teaching academics and 44% balanced teaching/research roles, with experience ranging from ≤5 years (15%) to >20 years (25%). Disciplines included Health and Medicine (30%), Business and Management (18%), and Engineering and Technology (13%). In-person teaching was the most common mode of teaching amongst the sample (83%), with the vast majority at the undergraduate level (98%) and with a cohort size of less than 100 students (76%).

Faculty identified several behavioral challenges that align with our analytics-based planning nudge indicators. "Failure to follow instructions" (50% reported, 29% top priority) corresponds to our analytics finding of minimal engagement with course outlines and delayed course access patterns (>48 h, OR = 4.12). Extension requests (73% reported as highest overall concern) may reflect the underlying planning difficulties observable in our analytics as irregular login patterns and reactive resource access (materials accessed within 24 h of deadlines). Qualitative responses emphasized students being "late to start engaging" and "poor initial preparation", directly supporting the Week 1–3 planning intervention window identified in our temporal analysis.

The strongest convergence between faculty observations and analytics emerged in monitoring behaviors. "Not seeking help when needed" was the top-ranked challenge (62% reported, 31% ranked #1 priority), directly corresponding to our analytics finding that F1-F2 students showed significantly lower forum participation and help-seeking behavior throughout the semester. "Not viewing video resources" (57%) and "Not completing readings" (57%) align precisely with our analytics indicators of incomplete content access, brief sessions (<3 min), and skipped videos. Online educators specifically reported elevated challenges with "poor platform visits" (69% vs. 47% overall) and "low attendance" (58% vs. 39% overall), patterns observable in our LMS data as declining session frequency during Weeks 4–6.

Faculty qualitative responses emphasized the importance of feedback and reflection, supporting our evaluation nudge framework. Multiple faculty (n = 9) stressed proactive feedback as a key strategy, yet our analytics showed only 61% of students accessed feedback within 7 days of receiving it, with F1-F2 students showing even lower rates. Faculty noted patterns of repeated similar errors (implicit in qualitative responses about assessment quality), corresponding to our analytics indicator of lack of revision after feedback. The emphasis on relationships and human interaction (n = 12 in qualitative responses) supports our evaluation nudges that encourage reflection and instructor connection during the final weeks.

4.5 Mapping Validation: Analytics-Faculty Alignment

The convergence between learning analytics and faculty observations strongly validates the proposed nudging mapping. Timing alignment emerged as both analytics (showing critical engagement decline from week 4 onward) and faculty emphasis on early intervention supported the phased approach of planning (weeks 1–3), monitoring (weeks 4–6), and reflection (weeks 7–10) nudges. Help-seeking patterns showed remarkable concordance, with analytics revealing Fail students' significantly lower forum activity while faculty independently identified "not seeking help" as their top behavioral challenge (31% ranked #1), validating monitoring nudges that encourage help-seeking behaviors. Resource access alignment was evident as analytics documented F1-F2 students' reactive, deadline-driven material access while faculty reported not completing readings (57%) and not viewing videos (57%) as major challenges, supporting planning nudges for advance preparation. Similarly, assessment instruction issues aligned between analytics showing late assignment engagement spikes and faculty ranking "failure to follow instructions" as their #2 concern (29%), while the feedback utilization gap was confirmed by both analytics (only 61% accessing feedback within 7 days) and faculty qualitative responses stressing feedback importance.

One notable divergence emerged: faculty rated "requesting extensions" as their highest overall concern (73%), yet this didn't prominently appear in analytics patterns, suggesting that extension requests are symptomatic of deeper engagement issues already captured by other metrics in the framework.

5 Conclusion

This study developed an analytics-to-intervention mapping framework that systematically links observable LMS patterns to metacognitive nudge opportunities, analyzing 714 students to identify specific indicators for planning, monitoring, and evaluation support needs with strong faculty validation of pattern-challenge correspondence. The research established that temporal engagement trajectories differ significantly by final grade ($F = 60.54$, $p < .001$), with week 4–5 representing a critical intervention threshold for at-risk students. Specific analytics patterns, including irregular access, brief sessions, and non-feedback use, correlate with failure in ways that faculty independently recognize as corresponding to student challenges. These connections were supported by theoretical frameworks from self-regulated learning and nudge theory. Several questions require validation: whether these patterns genuinely reflect metacognitive deficits versus other factors, whether nudges can modify these patterns and improve learning outcomes, and what constitutes optimal nudge timing, framing, and frequency while avoiding unintended consequences or student reactance. The essential next step involves randomized controlled trials comparing analytics-triggered nudges to control and fixed-schedule conditions. The contribution to the field lies in providing the first systematic, metacognitive-theory-grounded framework for translating analytics patterns into intervention opportunities, offering specificity that enables hypothesis-driven intervention research and advances beyond current systems that merely identify risk without indicating needed support types.

References

1. Wang, W., Zhao, Y., Wu, Y.J., Goh, M.: Factors of dropout from MOOCs: a bibliometric review. Library Hi Tech **41**(2), 432–453 (2023). https://doi.org/10.1108/LHT-06-2022-0306
2. Thaler, R.H., Sunstein, C.R.: Nudge: Improving Decisions About Health, Wealth, and Happiness. Yale University Press, New Haven (2008)

3. Wilson, A.L., Buckley, E., Buckley, J.D., Bogomolova, S.: Nudging healthier food and beverage choices through salience and priming: evidence from a systematic review. Food Qual. Prefer. 47–64 (2016). https://doi.org/10.1016/j.foodqual.2016.02.009
4. Xu, D., Jaggars, S.S.: The impact of online learning. Econ. Educ. Rev. **37**, 46–57 (2013)
5. Schmidt, A.T.: Getting real about the ethics of nudging. Philos. Manag. **19**(1), 3–18 (2020)
6. Vugts, A., van den Heuvel, E., Zondervan-Zwijnenburg, M., Postma, E.: Nudging in education: From theory towards guidelines for successful implementation. Eur. J. Psychol. Educ. **35**(4), 883–902 (2020)
7. Brown, A., et al.: The creation of a nudging protocol to support online student engagement in higher education. Act. Learn. High. Educ. **24**(3), 257–271 (2023)
8. Pu, Z., Sun, H., Zhang, X., Zhang, W.: Exploring the impact of nudges on volunteer task choices in cultural heritage crowdsourcing: an eye-tracking experiment. Proc. Assoc. Inf. Sci. Technol. **61**(1), 1074–1076 (2024). https://doi.org/10.1002/pra2.1189
9. Bürgler, S., Hennecke, M.: Metacognition and polyregulation in daily self-control conflicts. Scand. J. Psychol. **65**(2), 179–194 (2024). https://doi.org/10.1111/sjop.12964
10. Guo, L.: Using metacognitive prompts to enhance self-regulated learning and learning outcomes: a meta-analysis of experimental studies in computer-based learning environments. J. Comput. Assist. Learn. **38**(3), 811–832 (2022). https://doi.org/10.1111/jcal.12650
11. Azevedo, R., et al.: Lessons learned and future directions of MetaTutor: leveraging multichannel data to scaffold self-regulated learning with an intelligent tutoring system. Front. Psychol. **13**, 813632 (2022). https://doi.org/10.3389/fpsyg.2022.813632
12. Wu, M., Was, C.A.: Beyond the prompt: Investigating retrieval-based monitoring in self-regulated learning. J. Intell. **13**(8), 99 (2025). https://doi.org/10.3390/jintelligence13080099
13. Frazier, L., Schwartz, B., Metcalfe, J.: The MAPS model of self-regulation: integrating metacognition, agency, and possible selves. Metacogn. Learn. **16**, 297–318 (2021). https://doi.org/10.1007/s11409-020-09255-3
14. de Boer, H., Donker, A.S., Kostons, D.D.N.M., van der Werf, G.P.C.: Long-term effects of metacognitive strategy instruction on student academic performance: a meta-analysis. Educ. Res. Rev. **24**, 98–115 (2018). https://doi.org/10.1016/j.edurev.2018.03.002
15. Clow, D.: An overview of learning analytics. Teach. High. Educ. **18**, 683–695 (2013). https://doi.org/10.1080/13562517.2013.827653
16. Abadia, R., Liu, S., Sun, Q.: High academic performance and engagement behaviours in online learning environments. IADIS Int. J. Comput. Sci. Inf. Syst. **18**(2), 1–21 (2023)
17. Oreopoulos, P.: The power of nudges to increase university retention rates. Econ. Educ. Rev. **78**, 101–115 (2020)
18. Johar, S., Mohd, C.K.N.C.K., Razak, A.Z.A.: A review on the role of engagement in online learning: impact on academic performance. Int. J. Learn. Teach. Educ. Res. **22**(4), 312–329 (2023)
19. Kahneman, D.: Thinking, Fast and Slow. Farrar, Straus and Giroux, New York (2011)
20. Crozier, G., Spink, J.: Social comparison and achievement: a study of peer influence in UK universities. Br. Edu. Res. J. **43**(2), 301–318 (2017)
21. Damgaard, M.T., Nielsen, H.S.: Nudging in education. Econ. Educ. Rev. **64**, 313–342 (2020)
22. Kitsantas, A., Winsler, A., Huie, F.: Self-regulation and ability predictors of academic success during college: a predictive validity study. J. Adv. Acad. **20**(1), 42–68 (2008). https://doi.org/10.4219/jaa-2008-867
23. Swanson, H.J., Dewsbury, B.M.: The impact of a metacognitive intervention on student experiences and success in an academic probation program for first-year students. Teach. Learn. Inq. **12** (2024). https://doi.org/10.20343/teachlearninqu.12.26
24. Gordanier, J., Hauk, W., Sankaran, C.: Early intervention in college classes and improved student outcomes. Econ. Educ. Rev. **72**, 23–29 (2019). https://doi.org/10.1016/j.econedurev.2019.05.003

25. Arnold, K.E., Pistilli, M.D.: Course signals at purdue: using learning analytics to increase student success. In: Proceedings of the 2nd International Conference on Learning Analytics and Knowledge (LAK 2012), pp. 267–270. Association for Computing Machinery, New York (2012). https://doi.org/10.1145/2330601.2330666
26. Jayaprakash, S.M., Moody, E.W., Lauría, E.J.M., Regan, J.R., Baron, J.D.: Early alert of academically at-risk students: an open source analytics initiative. J. Learn. Anal. **1**(1), 6–47 (2014). https://doi.org/10.18608/jla.2014.11.3
27. Oinas-Kukkonen, H.: A foundation for the study of behavior change support systems. Pers. Ubiquit. Comput. **17**(6), 1223–1235 (2013)

Cognitive Persuasion in Generative AI-Assisted Programming: Investigating Shifts in Reasoning, Strategy, and Long-Term Recall

Farhana Alam(✉), Julita Vassileva, and Banani Roy

University of Saskatchewan, Saskatoon, SK, Canada
{farhana.alam,julita.vassileva,banani.roy}@usask.ca

Abstract. Generative AI systems such as ChatGPT and GitHub Copilot now act as invisible co-authors in computer programming. Prior research shows that these tools improve fluency and reduce cognitive load, yet they may also encourage reliance on AI-generated solutions rather than independent reasoning. This study examines the cognitive and behavioural effects associated with AI-supported programming in undergraduate computer science, using a mixed design (between subjects and within subjects) that probes how short-term AI assistance relates to independent problem solving. Self-reflection statements, prompt logs, and code quality scores were analyzed to trace patterns of cognitive offloading, reasoning strategies, and problem-solving transfer. Three findings emerged. First, access to AI was associated with increased cognitive offloading, with many participants relying on AI-generated solutions rather than constructing solutions independently. Second, the way of prompting matters: direct answer-seeking prompts were associated with weaker problem-solving strategies compared to iterative or explanatory prompting. Third, most AI-users experienced performance drops once access to AI was removed, suggesting that their AI-assisted problem-solving experience did not contribute to improved independent problem-solving performance. Exploratory empirical evidence from this study, interpreted through a persuasive technology lens shows that common patterns of AI assistance may influence cognitive offloading in users. If AI is to support learning, instead of replacing it, future AI-powered educational systems must be designed with safeguards or cognitive forcing mechanisms that preserve reasoning effort and debugging habits.

Keywords: Generative AI · LLM · Programming education · Cognitive offloading · Persuasion

1 Introduction

Generative AI (GenAI) or Large Language Models (LLM) such as ChatGPT, Gemini, and GitHub Copilot have rapidly reshaped programming and learning

E. Vlahu-Gjorgievska et al. (Eds.): PERSUASIVE 2026, CCIS 2896, pp. 18–32, 2027.
https://doi.org/10.1007/978-3-032-27235-5_2

practices. By design, they can influence user behaviour; not only user actions, but also knowledge, attitudes and emotions [1,2]. They can steer user choices without coercion, which conceptually aligns with B.J. Fogg's definition of "Persuasive Technology" [3]. In computer science (CS) educational contexts, AI-powered tools can guide attention and make certain steps appear more convenient, potentially biasing learners toward particular problem-solving behaviours, which become habits over time. For example, autocomplete and instant explanations may function as continuous convenience cues that encourage quick acceptance over deep reasoning. Although such tools can improve task performance [4], they may foster reliance on AI suggestions. Research on Copilot and similar LLMs shows that users frequently accept partially understood code for the sake of efficiency [5–7], trusting algorithmic authority even when outputs are flawed, reflecting automation bias and cognitive offloading [8].

Educational research using persuasive systems shows that they can increase motivation and persistence [9], yet engagement does not ensure depth of understanding. While LLMs can significantly enhance problem-solving efficiency, reviews indicate a potential risk of eroding learners' metacognitive control. This erosion is likely to occur if the learning design does not intentionally support a critical stance and reflective thinking—that is, activities specifically designed to encourage learners to plan, monitor, and evaluate their own thinking [10,11]. LLMs' potential influence on user behaviour lies in their user interaction design, which minimizes user effort by confident phrasing, providing immediate runnable solutions, and creating a perception of authority, which makes accepting AI output easier than verifying it [12,13].

Empirical studies in computing education are consistent with these concerns. Copilot users often alternate between acceleration mode (when they already know the solution) and exploration mode (when they let AI steer), with the latter linked to shallow edits and weaker understanding [6]. Broader classroom research finds that frequent use of LLMs lowers cognitive load but can undermine verification, debugging, and retention [14]. Evidence suggests that reduced effort without reflection weakens monitoring and independent problem-solving [10,15]. Repeated dependence on assistive tools can reshape thinking habits, and the authority cues embedded in AI systems may further encourage passive acceptance of suggestions [6]. However, it seems that no controlled studies have investigated the effect of AI tools on programming behaviour in computer science (CS)students, their problem-solving strategies and engagement and knowledge retention.

Therefore, this study examines the cognitive and behavioural effects of AI-assisted programming for undergrad CS students. It analyzes how access to AI is associated with changes in reasoning and strategy, focusing on behavioural indicators such as dependency, reduced effort, and inflated confidence. By mapping prompt–response dynamics through the Fogg behaviour Model and digital-nudge frameworks [2,3], it explores whether learners internalize reasoning strategies, or remain dependent on AI-based scaffolding instead. The mixed study design allows examination of behavioural shifts and performance changes once AI sup-

port is removed in a later session, thereby observing whether problem-solving strategies developed during AI-assisted work persist, or change during AI-free problem-solving. This study contributes preliminary exploratory evidence and design-relevant implications for how generative AI systems should be developed and integrated into future educational contexts. It aims to answer three research questions (RQs):
RQ1: How does exposure to AI support during coding influence students' problem-solving behaviour and reasoning patterns?
RQ2: Do prompting interactions with the AI provide behavioural cues or nudges that shape user strategy and engagement, and which prompt types most strongly guide or nudge users toward specific behaviours?
RQ3: How are coding performance and problem-solving behaviours retained over time once access to AI is removed?

2 Related Work

Persuasive effects can be induced without the use of explicit persuasive strategies, for example, through the interface design, aesthetics and wording [16,17]. In human–AI chatbot interactions, trust in the algorithm's confidence and neutrality can lead users to prefer machine advice over human input, particularly when interactions feel fluent or authoritative [18]. Evidence across decision-making shows the presence of "algorithmic bias" - people may rely more on advice labelled "algorithmic," even when that can hurt accuracy under some conditions [12].

Reducing over-reliance requires *cognitive forcing*, design interventions that slow users at key moments. In a controlled study [13], three interventions were used to force analytic engagement: On Demand, where users had to actively request the AI's output; Update, where participants made an initial unaided decision before viewing and revising with AI input; and Wait, where a 30-second delay was imposed before revealing the AI suggestion. These interventions reduced blind acceptance of AI suggestions compared to simple explainability alone. From a cognitive-systems view [10], current LLM tools place high metacognitive demand on learners, because they must plan prompts, evaluate answers, and determine when to accept or revise the model's output. Without support, this level of regulatory demand can exceed what novices can realistically manage, leading them to revert to quick acceptance rather than deliberate evaluation.

Findings in education technology suggest nudges can increase participation and task completion, but tailoring the nudges to ability or motivation is non-trivial. In a large field experiment, participants with higher motivation were more responsive to nudges, but adapting nudges to the Fogg Behaviour Model (FBM) profiles did not outperform simple reminders [19]. Yet, the study considered adapting the nudges only to individual motivation and ability. A systematic review of persuasive educational systems [9] identifies seven design characteristics and highlights evaluation challenges when persuasion alters behaviour without immediately changing end outcomes. AI assistants that appear helpful on the surface, yet may end up displacing core reasoning processes.

Empirical course-level data indicate that the way students engage with LLMs, including whether they use them primarily for coding and debugging or for conceptual explanations, is a key predictor of their learning outcomes. In a 10-week undergraduate study on React, higher average LLM use (especially for code generation and debugging) was negatively correlated with final grades. Using LLMs for explanations was less harmful, aligning with a "scaffold-vs-surrogate" distinction [14]. At the interaction level, a lab study of GitHub Copilot found that participants generally employed AI to jump-start tasks, yet struggled to understand, edit, and debug generated code, the activities that require deep reasoning [5].

When LLMs participate as teammates, they can decrease cognitive load and support short-term task completion. In a quasi-experiment with middle-schoolers, integrating LLM support into collaborative programming lowered cognitive load and improved computational-thinking scores relative to conventional collaboration [20]. But lowering cognitive load also helps bypass the desirable difficulty that helps students develop independent metacognitive skills and transfer of learning. The change in cognitive effort, attributed to the availability of AI, creates an unintended persuasive effect to abandon rather than engage in reasoning.

Using LLMs add metacognitive tasks of planning, monitoring, and evaluation that novices often do not recognize or engage in. As AI models improve, more of these meta-cognitive tasks are taken over by AI (e.g., auto-suggesting prompts, showing reasoning steps, confidence levels), and little metacognitive control is required from users, leading to overtrust and passive acceptance of the AI results [10].

Combining reflective prompts, as in CodeAid's approach [21], provides a persuasive intervention to balance automation with metacognitive control. CodeAid, deployed over 12 weeks with 700 students, offered assistance without revealing direct solutions by following four design patterns: leveraging AI's strengths, simplifying queries while encouraging engagement, avoiding direct answers, and ensuring user control and transparency. These "cognitive forcing patterns" aim to return metacognitive control to students .

Buçinca et al.'s [13] cognitive-forcing patterns (require checks, justify disagreement, explore alternatives) offer persuasive guardrails that can be embedded into AI-based programming assistants so that AI serves as a scaffold for the process rather than a surrogate that simply supplies answers. Murillo-Munoz et al. [9] in their review of Persuasive Educational Systems, define four design primitives for aligning persuasion with learning goals: personalization + timely prompts + transparent rationale + reflective feedback.

Across decision-science, HCI, and computing education, LLMs act as persuasive cognitive media. Left unguided, they influence learners toward acceptance and externalization (algorithm dependence, automation bias, convenience seeking). The design challenge in applying AI tools in education is not only providing access to AI, but shaping the interaction so that the student remains metacognitively active and develops critical thinking, analysis and planning skills.

3 Methodology

An experimental approach was chosen to overcome the limits of prior survey-based studies that rarely link perception, performance, and longitudinal outcomes within the same study [7,22]. The participants (n=13) were volunteers recruited among senior undergraduate Computer Science students. Most of them reported approximately 3–4 years of programming experience, with one reporting more than 5 years. To preserve anonymity, each participant was assigned a unique ID. The study follows a mixed (between- and within-subject) design. To enable between-subject comparison, participants were randomly assigned to two conditions (AI-assisted or AI-Group, and control or No-AI Group). To support treatment fidelity and reduce cross-condition influence [7,21], the experiment was carried out in lab conditions, where each participant engaged in supervised lab task separately under the conditions defined by their group assignment. The study was approved by the university's behavioural Ethics Committee. The within-subject aspect of the experiment involved comparing individual participants' behaviours and performance across two sessions, S1 and S2, separated by a two-week gap.

In S1, participants completed a 60-minute supervised LeetCode-style 'medium-level' interview coding task, designed to require core algorithmic reasoning and edge-case handling. LeetCode is an online coding platform that offers algorithmic challenges commonly used for software engineering recruitment and programming-skills assessment. The AI group had access to ChatGPT, GitHub Copilot, and Google Gemini, while the No-AI control group worked independently. Afterwards, participants completed a short reflection on the strategy, effort, and confidence they reported for their solution. Prompt logs were recorded for participants in the AI group. Two weeks later in S2, all participants repeated the same task without AI to assess delayed performance and strategy use, drawing conceptually on the testing and generation effects [23].

The data collected included evaluation scores of the solutions generated by participants, their AI prompt logs, and qualitative data from post-experiment reflection questionnaires.

Reflection Questionnaires: Open-ended reflections were coded using the thematic content analysis scheme which captures both cognitive and affective dimensions of problem-solving, with categories including *Deep Problem-Solving*, *Debugging Strategies*, *Efficiency & Optimization*, *AI Reliance*, *Metacognitive Awareness*, *Affective Responses*, and more. Each reflection was coded for the presence and relative emphasis of these themes using a hybrid inductive–deductive approach guided by desirable-difficulty and automation-bias literature [21,29]. Given the small sample size, qualitative findings are reported descriptively and illustrative excerpts are used cautiously to contextualize observed patterns rather than to establish prevalence.

Code Submissions: A 10-point rubric was created to provide a structured expert evaluation of the quality of the code produced by the participants, which evaluated correctness, efficiency, readability, robustness, and structure in line with software engineering practice, with scores ranging from 0 (non-functional or incorrect) to 10 (fully correct, efficient, and robust). The rubric Functional correctness, worth up to four points, was prioritized as an expert-weighted criterion [24]. Efficiency and code logic were accounted for two points, and readability and maintainability, together worth two points, were included given their documented role in reducing defects [25]. Attention to edge cases was also assessed (e.g., empty lists or boundary conditions) which is worth one point, given that unhandled errors are a major source of failures [26]. Scores resulting from this rubric were interpreted as expert rubric-based judgments rather than as psychometrically validated measures of programming ability.

AI Prompt Logs: AI interactions were analyzed using a five-level prompting taxonomy, ranging from direct answer-seeking to strategy-oriented prompts, shown in Table 1, to characterize observable prompting behaviours.

Table 1. AI Prompting Taxonomy

Level	Category Name	Description of Strategy
1	Minimal/Direct Answer Seeking	User asks AI for full solution with little context
2	One-Shot with Problem Restatement	Restates problem but still asks for full answer
3	Iterative Refinement	User tests and improves AI output via follow-up prompts
4	Decomposition + Debugging	User analyzes logic, breaks down steps, or locates bugs
5	Strategy-Oriented/Explanation-Based	Prompts focus on understanding, planning, constraints or optimization

For each participant, we calculated prompt count, dominant and maximum levels, average level, and an exploratory composite Prompt Strategy Score (average × count). This approach was intended to approximate both the quantity and depth of prompting, drawing conceptually on principles of interactive constructive and self-regulated learning [27,28]. Empirical studies show that iterative and explanation-seeking prompts are consistently linked to deeper engagement [5]. The composite score is not intended as a validated metric of learning or self-regulation, but as a heuristic summary used for exploratory comparison across participants.

4 Results

This section presents the findings of the study in three parts. First, we report qualitative patterns from reflection data comparing AI-assisted and No-AI participants (RQ1). Second, we examine how different prompting behaviors relate to strategy use and engagement during AI-assisted coding (RQ2). Third, we compare performance and strategy shifts across the two sessions to assess how problem-solving behavior changes once AI support is removed (RQ3).

4.1 The Cognitive Effects of AI-Assisted Coding

RQ1 examines how access to AI during coding is associated with differences in problem-solving behaviour and reasoning between the AI group and the No-AI group. Using a thematic content analysis approach [30,31], reflection analysis from S1 revealed differences between the AI group (n = 6) and the No-AI control group (n = 7). Each reflection was manually coded using a set of behavioural categories representing observable problem-solving and metacognitive behaviours (e.g., debugging, planning, AI reliance), with LLM-assisted cross-checking used to ensure consistency of category assignment. In total, ten behavioural categories were identified and are shown in Fig. 1. These categories were then used to summarize and compare recurring patterns of reported behaviour between the AI and No-AI groups. Across these categories, three higher-level patterns associated with AI access were observed: (1) increased reliance on external assistance, (2) reduced depth of independent reasoning, and (3) disruption of systematic problem-solving habits.

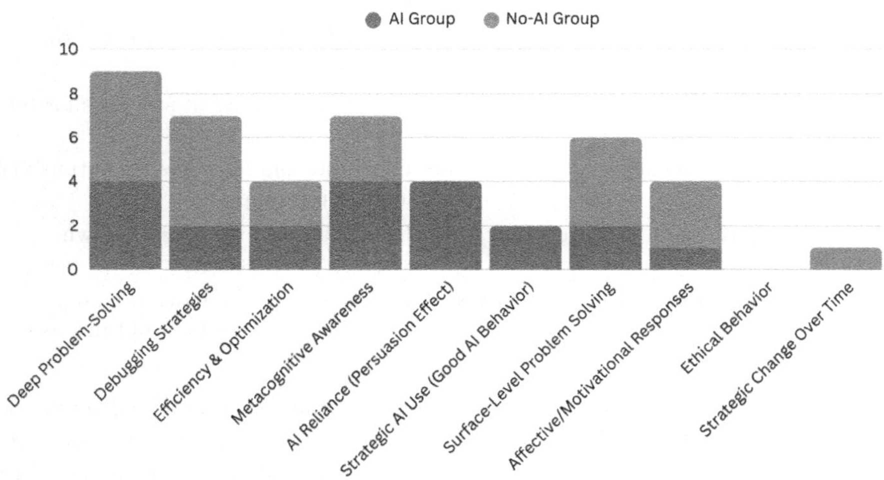

Fig. 1. Comparison of observed cognitive-behavioural categories between AI Group and No-AI students.

Increased Reliance on External Assistance: Four of the six AI-group participants described depending on AI output with minimal verification. Fluent, immediate AI answers reduce perceived effort and are consistent with cognitive offloading [3,32]. This effect can be found in comments like *"Most of the time it will directly give correct answer."* Participants' reflection often rationalizes their acceptance rather than evaluation (*"I read the code that ChatGPT output and the logic made sense to me in my head using 2 walkers"*). Prior studies report this same pattern, trusting AI despite knowing it may be wrong, especially when feedback is instant [6]. From behavioural influence perspective, this pattern aligns with established behavioural design principles [3], ease of use and perceived credibility, which reduce the cognitive effort required for reflective reasoning.

Reduced Depth of Reasoning: Both groups planned solutions similarly, but the AI group's reasoning depth appeared more fragile in the qualitative analysis of the reflection questionnaires. This pattern is reflected in Fig. 1 by the Deep Problem Solving, Debugging Strategies, and Efficiency & Optimization categories, which together capture the extent to which students engaged in sustained, reflective, and evaluative reasoning. Statements like *"I was going to ask Chat about the syntax for certain methods, but it outputted the solution to me, so I ended up using that instead," "I used the algorithm provided by ChatGPT. This seems to be the most efficient answer to me,"* suggest that what looks like reasoning is often just mirroring the AI solution. This observation concurs with recent work which found that students adopt structured reasoning from model output without internalizing it [21,33]. In contrast, the No-AI group showed more sustained struggle and richer emotional reflection, shown in Fig. 1 by higher frequencies for the No-AI group in the Deep Problem Solving and Debugging Strategies categories. AI here functions as an effort-minimizing support. It reduces friction, but also reduces cognitive elaboration and affective engagement [34].

Disruption of Systematic Problem-Solving Habits: Debugging, the core of systematic reasoning, was reported less frequently in the AI group. Only two participants mentioned tracing or testing, compared to five in the no-AI group, suggesting that AI disrupted normal diagnostic cycles in programming as students left the error resolution to the LLM. This pattern is consistent with habit substitution, where instant correction replaces internal debug routines, leading to automation bias and erosion of habitual reasoning practices [35].

Together, these patterns suggest that AI access may shape cognitive behaviour through repeated reliance rather than acting solely as neutral assistance. Reliance develops when high-fluency outputs appear accurate enough without deeper comprehension. Shallow reasoning emerges when that same fluency suppresses both cognitive and emotional effort. Systematic habits deteriorate when students replace model feedback for their own systematic testing and validation cycles.

4.2 The Influence of Prompts in Problem-Solving Behaviour

RQ2 addresses whether prompts function as behavioural cues or nudges that shape user strategy and engagement, and the types of prompts that most strongly associated with particular problem solving behaviours. Analysis showed that most AI-group participants (5 out of 6) primarily used Minimal/Direct Answer Seeking prompts, reflecting a behaviour of seeking and relying on the AI solution rather than reasoning and problem-solving by themselves [32]. This pattern may help explain why relatively fewer participants in the AI group engaged in systematic testing and debugging during coding. Their reflections illustrate how this reliance was often reinforced by the AI providing a more elaborated answer than was requested in the prompt. This was expressed in statements such as *"I was going to ask Chat about the syntax for certain methods, but it outputted the solution to me, so I ended up using that instead,"* and *"I ran into an edge case where there was only one item in the list so I asked the AI to fix my code."* This effect, however, was not seen in all participants. One participant, who achieved the highest strategy score (7.8), used Iterative Refinement, where they gradually guided the LLM to get a better answer and understand it. However, some degree of cognitive offloading was still observed , showing that even strategic prompting may lead to surface-level understanding rather than deeper comprehension. One participant reported increased confidence while offloading reasoning, aligning with concerns about perceived competence without depth [3].

AI tools produce highly fluent, complete solutions, which may encourage student reliance on them. Over time, students internalize this pattern and begin generating Minimal/Direct prompts, because the interface rewards answer-seeking behaviour with immediate success, thus encouraging users to write prompts asking for complete solutions. The behavioural nudge appears to originate in the system's "overly helpful" output style and interaction structure, rewarding high level user's prompts.

4.3 Tracing Cognitive Retention After AI Removal

RQ3 compares the differences in performance and strategy of each participant between the two sessions. A comparison across sessions revealed distinct trajectories over time. When access to AI was removed in S2, the code submission scores of 4 out of the 6 AI-group members dropped by 4–5 points points relative to their S1 performance, despite their high S1 scores (see Table 2).

Table 2. Score shifts based on Self-Reflection (AI group)

Participant	Score Shift
1	Recovered with planning and examples, but score still dropped ($\Delta = -5$) suggesting shallow internalization in S1
2	Good strategies were present in S1 (Iterative Refinement prompting, structured debugging), but decline in S2 score ($\Delta = -4$) implies reliance on AI feedback loops in S1 not fully internalized
3	Effortful adaptation but performance drop ($\Delta = -5$) suggests S1 success may have been partially scaffolded
4	Strong recovery, shift from shortcut to strategy ($\Delta = +1$)
5	Stable score (S1 score 10$\leftarrow$ S2 score 10) via robust debugging, although some observable but shallow reasoning patterns remain
6	Partial adaptation but score $\Delta = -4$ suggests S1 offloading created superficial success

These four participants' reflections show heavy reliance on AI in S1. However, two members of the AI-group maintained or improved their performance. One of then shifted from *Surface level problem solving* to *Deep problem solving* and *Metacognitive awareness* behaviour category and their score increased from 9 in S1 to 10 in S2. The score of the other participant was 10 in both sessions. This participant engaged in strategic testing and debugging, showing that is possible to avoid cognitive offloading and achieve high performance without being dependent on AI.

The No-AI group performance was more stable throughout the sessions. The performance of four of the seven members improved or stayed the same, and more strategic behaviours emerged over time. Because cognitive control was not outsourced in S1, strategy retention appeared more stable. Table 3 shows the changes in problem solving behaviour of each participant from S1 to S2. In both tables, score change is reported as Δ=Score(S2)–Score(S1). Negative values indicate a decline from S1 to S2, and positive values indicate an improvement.

These findings suggest that AI access may subtly reshape user cognitive behaviour over time. This pattern is consistent with aspects of Fogg's behaviour Model, which explains that AI acted as a enabler that reduced the motivation needed to think deeply by providing supporting ability to solve the problem, persuading students toward shortcut dependency behaviours [3].

Table 3. Behaviour shifts based on Self-Reflection (No-AI group)

Participant	Behaviour Shift
1	Clear growth ($\Delta = +3$)
2	Consolidation (score stable)
3	Regression ($\Delta = -4$), possibly task-specific difficulty
4	Small decrease ($\Delta = -1$, but evidence of more efficient and strategic problem-solving despite an incomplete final solution)
5	Slight improvement ($\Delta = +1$)
6	Marked strategic gain (score stable)
7	Stable high-quality reasoning ($\Delta = +1$)

5 Discussion

Across the three research questions, the results suggest that generative AI support alters computer programming behaviour not only through assistance in answer production, but through behavioural influence on how students allocate cognitive effort. Analysis of student reflections of their problem solving strategies showed different behavioural trajectories were prevalent in AI group from those in the No-AI group. The differences could be resulting from persuasive mechanisms inherent in LLMs. In addition, the system interface design and the formatting fluency of program code generated by AI may foster trust and guide user behaviour without explicit instruction [3]. In this case, the observed behavioural influence manifests as cognitive offloading, where students treat AI output as a reliable externally gifted solution, leading to reduced internal reasoning effort [32]. The analysis showed that Minimal/Direct prompting styles were more frequently associated with passive acceptance rather than reasoning, consistent with recent research showing similar patterns of immediate trust in code-generation systems [6].

The depth of reasoning observed in the AI group therefore has to be interpreted carefully. Although both groups reported planning strategies, the reasoning expressed by AI-group participants was often less elaborated or based on evaluating AI suggestions rather than generating reasoning chains for solving the problem. This reflects prior work finding, where learners adopt structured reasoning that originates from model output but do not construct reasoning themselves or reconstruct the solution from the model output internally [21]. In contrast, the control group's reflections showed more sustained emotional and cognitive engagement. Most of the participants thought deeply about the problem and actively debugged the solution.

Across session comparisons highlight the differences in performance score and retention of knowledge. When access to AI was removed, most AI-group participants experienced decline in performance, while the performance score of the majority of control participants improved or remained stable. The AI-group exhibited a brittle success in S1, where performance that was high while the AI was present, but not durable once the external solver was removed. Thus the decline pattern in the AI-group behaviour is consistent with automation bias and negative habit substitution, where students transferred responsibility for correctness and error-checking to the AI, weakening hypothesis-testing routines [6,35]. However, the fact that not all AI users performance deteriorated in S2 is consistent with the concept of desirable difficulty, which states that putting effort during learning creates stronger understanding and retention [29]. The consistent performers in the AI group showed robust debugging and problem solving strategy in their self-reflections. This suggests that the potential negative influence patterns of AI do not apply universally to all users, but depend on the interaction pattern and how the student positions the AI in their reasoning process.

Overall, these findings suggest that generative AI in programming tasks may function as a persuasive cognitive influence. The AI does not merely provide help, it subtly influences how cognitive labor is organized, which aligns with recent arguments that AI systems can reshape thinking habits during problem-solving [34]. The implications are primarily pedagogical and design-oriented. Educational AI must incorporate scaffolds that protect reasoning, such as requiring explanation before revealing the answer, or structuring feedback around debugging reasoning rather than simply providing solutions [21,33]. Without such constraints, generative AI may improve short-term success but erode the underlying processes responsible for long-term learning and the transfer of strategies across tasks.

6 Limitations and Threats to Validity

This study has several limitations that constrain interpretation and generalization. First, some conclusions rely on participant reflections, which may not fully capture subtle or tacit persuasive influences, as users are not always aware of how technology shapes their thinking [3]. Second, the small sample size (n = 13) limits statistical power and generalizability. Third, the use of a single LeetCode-style task restricts applicability to other programming contexts. Fourth, with only two time points, the study cannot assess whether observed behaviors persist or fade over time, as habit formation is inherently longitudinal [29]. Finally, the study examined general-purpose AI models rather than pedagogically designed systems, reflecting typical real-world use rather than the potential of educationally optimized AI.

7 Conclusions and Future Work

This study suggests that generative AI operates as a persuasion-like cognitive influence that quietly shifts where reasoning occurs. When students interact with fluent, answer-ready AI, core problem-solving processes are externalized. Apparent short-term gains do not reliably reflect understanding; when AI support is removed, these borrowed competencies often collapse.

The debate over whether AI "helps" or "hurts" learning misses a key distinction: the impact depends on whether AI substitutes for problem solving or scaffolds it. Observed patterns—effort minimization, rapid acceptance, and habit substitution—likely arise because current LLMs are optimized to deliver answers rather than to sustain structured reasoning.

This work reframes AI evaluation in computing education: beyond accuracy and efficiency, we must examine AI-driven behavioral influence and cognitive offloading, and whether tools steer learners toward durable thinking practices. Progress lies not in restricting AI, but in designing systems that protect and support reasoning instead of replacing it. The study is ongoing as we recruit more participants. Future extensions will incorporate behavioral assessments (debugging scores, critical-thinking measures) and longitudinal effects via a third session 4–6 weeks later to test whether AI reliance patterns solidify into stable habits. We will also experimentally compare AI tools with different response styles (fluent code vs. Socratic questioning vs. explanation-first guidance) to make the mechanism of persuasive influence salient.

Acknowledgments. This research is supported in part by the Natural Sciences and Engineering Research Council of Canada (NSERC) Discovery Grant RGPIN-2021-03521, and by the industry-stream NSERC CREATE in Software Analytics Research (SOAR). This manuscript benefited from structural and phrasing support provided by ChatGPT 5.1, with all ideas, interpretations, and final revisions determined by the authors.

References

1. Weinmann, M., Schneider, C., vom Brocke, J.: Digital nudging. Bus. Inf. Syst. Eng. **58**(6), 433–436 (2016). https://doi.org/10.1007/s12599-016-0453-1
2. Jesse, M., Jannach, D.: Digital nudging with recommender systems: survey and future directions. Comput. Hum. Behav. Rep. **3**, 100052 (2021). https://doi.org/10.1016/j.chbr.2020.100052
3. Fogg, B.J.: A behaviour model for persuasive design. In: Proceedings of the 4th International Conference on Persuasive Technology (Persuasive '09), Article 40, pp. 1–7. ACM, New York (2009) https://doi.org/10.1145/1541948.1541999
4. Zheng, Z., et al.: Towards an Understanding of Large Language Models in Software Engineering Tasks. arXiv preprint http://arxiv.org/abs/2308.11396 (2023). Accessed 02 Nov 2025
5. Vaithilingam, P., Zhang, T., Glassman, E.L.: Expectation vs. experience: evaluating the usability of code generation tools powered by large language models. In: Conference on Human Factors in Computing Systems, p. 1. ACM (2022). https://doi.org/10.1145/3491101.3519665
6. Barke, S., James, M.B., Polikarpova, N.: Grounded copilot: how programmers interact with code-generating models. arXiv preprint http://arxiv.org/abs/2206.15000 (2022). Accessed 02 Nov 2025
7. Ross, S.I., Martinez, F., Houde, S., Muller, M., Weisz, J.D.: The programmer's assistant: conversational interaction with a large language model for software development. In: International Conference on Intelligent User Interfaces (IUI), pp. 491–514. ACM (2023). https://doi.org/10.1145/3581641.3584037
8. Vered, M., Livni, T., Howe, P.D.L., Miller, T., Sonenberg, L.: The effects of explanations on automation bias. Artif. Intell. **322**, 103952 (2023). https://doi.org/10.1016/j.artint.2023.103952
9. Murillo-Muñoz, F., et al.: Characteristics of a persuasive educational system: a systematic literature review. Appl. Sci. **11**(21), 10089 (2021). https://doi.org/10.3390/app112110089
10. Tankelevitch, L.: The metacognitive demands and opportunities of generative AI. In: Conference on Human Factors in Computing Systems (CHI), ACM (2024). https://doi.org/10.1145/3613904.3642902
11. Prather, J., et al.: Beyond the hype: a comprehensive review of current trends in generative ai research, teaching practices, and tools. arXiv preprint http://arxiv.org/abs/2412.14732 (2024). Accessed 02 Nov 2025
12. Logg, J.M., Minson, J.A., Moore, D.A.: Algorithm appreciation: people prefer algorithmic to human judgment. Organ. Behav. Hum. Decis. Processes **151**, 90–103 (2019). https://doi.org/10.1016/j.obhdp.2018.12.005
13. Buçinca, Z., Malaya, M.B., Gajos, K.Z.: To Trust or to think: cognitive forcing functions can reduce overreliance on AI in AI-assisted decision-making. Proc. ACM Hum.-Comput. Interact. **5**(CSCW1) (2021). https://doi.org/10.1145/3449287
14. Jošt, G., Taneski, V., Karakatič, S.: The impact of large language models on programming education and student learning outcomes. Appl. Sci. **14**(10), 4115 (2024). https://doi.org/10.3390/app14104115
15. Steyvers, M., Kumar, A.: Three challenges for AI-assisted decision-making. Perspect. Psychol. Sci. **19**(5), 722–734 (2024). https://doi.org/10.1177/17456916231181102
16. Oyibo, K., Vassileva, J.: The effect of layout and colour temperature on the perception of tourism websites for mobile devices. Multimodal Technol. Interact. **4**(1), 8 (2020). https://doi.org/10.3390/mti4010008

17. Oyibo, K., Vassileva, J.: Relationship between perceived UX design attributes and persuasive features: a case study of fitness app. Information **12**(9), 365 (2021). https://doi.org/10.3390/info12090365
18. Fatahi, S., Vassileva, J., Roy, C.K.: Comparing emotions in ChatGPT answers and human answers to the coding questions on Stack Overflow. Front. Artif. Intell. **7**, 1393903 (2024). https://doi.org/10.3389/frai.2024.1393903
19. Plak, S., van Klaveren, C., Cornelisz, I.: Raising student engagement using digital nudges tailored to students' motivation and perceived ability levels. Br. J. Edu. Technol. **54**(2), 554–580 (2023). https://doi.org/10.1111/bjet.13261
20. Yan, Y.M., Chen, C.Q., Hu, Y.B., Ye, X.D.: LLM-based collaborative programming: impact on students' computational thinking and self-efficacy. Human. Soc. Sci. Commun. **12**(1) (2025). https://doi.org/10.1057/s41599-025-04471-1
21. Kazemitabaar, M., Hou, X., Henley, A.Z., Ericson, B.J., Weintrop, D., Grossman, T.: How novices use LLM-based code generators to solve CS1 coding tasks in a self-paced learning environment. In: ACM International Conference Proceeding Series. ACM (2023). https://doi.org/10.1145/3631802.3631806
22. Adewumi, T., et al.: ProCoT: stimulating critical thinking and writing of students through engagement with large language models (LLMs). arXiv preprint http://arxiv.org/abs/2312.09801 (2023). Accessed 02 Nov 2025
23. Roediger, H.L., Karpicke, J.D.: Test-enhanced learning: taking memory tests improves long-term retention. Psychol. Sci. **17**(3), 249–255 (2006). https://doi.org/10.1111/j.1467-9280.2006.01693.x
24. Ihantola, P., Ahoniemi, T., Karavirta, V., Seppälä, O.: Review of recent systems for automatic assessment of programming assignments. In: Proceedings of the 10th Koli Calling International Conference on Computing Education Research (Koli Calling'10), pp. 86–93 (2010). https://doi.org/10.1145/1930464.1930480
25. Buse, R.P.L., Weimer, W.R.: Learning a metric for code readability. IEEE Trans. Softw. Eng. **36**, 546–558 (2010)
26. Mondal, S., Roy, C.K.: Does editing improve answer quality on stack overflow? a data-driven investigation. arXiv preprint http://arxiv.org/abs/2507.21329 (2025). Accessed 02 Nov 2025/11/02
27. Chi, M.T.H., Wylie, R.: The ICAP framework: linking cognitive engagement to active learning outcomes. Educ. Psychol. **49**(4), 219–243 (2014). https://doi.org/10.1080/00461520.2014.965823
28. Zimmerman, B.J.: Becoming a self-regulated learner: an overview. Theory Pract. **41**(2), 64–70 (2002). https://doi.org/10.1207/S15430421TIP4102_2
29. Bjork, E.L., Bjork, R.A., Roediger, H.L., McDermott, K.B., McDaniel, M.A.: Making things hard on yourself, but in a good way: creating desirable difficulties to enhance learning. In: Psychology of Learning and Motivation, vol. 55, pp. 219–266. Elsevier (2011)
30. Braun, V., Clarke, V.: Using thematic analysis in psychology. Qual. Res. Psychol. **3**(2), 77–101 (2006). https://doi.org/10.1191/1478088706qp063oa
31. Braun, V., Clarke, V.: One size fits all? What counts as quality practice in (reflexive) thematic analysis? Qual. Res. Psychol. **18**(3), 328–352 (2021). https://doi.org/10.1080/14780887.2020.1769238
32. Risko, E.F., Gilbert, S.J.: Cognitive offloading. Trends Cogn. Sci. **20**(9), 676–688 (2016). https://doi.org/10.1016/j.tics.2016.07.002
33. Yang, S., Zhao, H., Xu, Y., Brennan, K., Schneider, B.: Debugging with an AI Tutor: investigating novice help-seeking behaviours and perceived learning. In: ACM Conference on International Computing Education Research (ICER), vol. 1, pp. 84–94 (2024). https://doi.org/10.1145/3632620.3671092

34. Calboli, S.: Autonomy and AI nudges: distinguishing concepts and highlighting AI's advantages. Phil. Technol. **38**(3) (2025). https://doi.org/10.1007/s13347-025-00940-2
35. Skitka, L.J., Mosier, K.L., Burdick, M.: Does automation bias decision-making? Int. J. Hum Comput Stud. **51**(5), 991–1006 (1999). https://doi.org/10.1006/ijhc.1999.0252

"I Started Noticing Things I Would Usually Miss": Early Empirical Insights Into Behavioural Effects of Digital Nudges in Data Quality Review

Bushra Alkadhi[1,2](✉), Robert Hendley[1], and Rami Bahsoon[1]

[1] School of Computer Science, University of Birmingham, Birmingham, UK
bxa169@student.bham.ac.uk

[2] College of Computer and Information Sciences, King Saud University, Riyadh, Kingdom of Saudi Arabia

Abstract. Despite its critical role, Data Quality (DQ) often receives limited attention in software engineering, partly due to low awareness of its impact and limited motivation to engage in careful review. This behavioural challenge can undermine data-driven processes when issues such as noise, inconsistency, and bias affect downstream analysis. Building on behaviour change research and nudge theory, this paper investigates how subtle, human-centred interventions can support more attentive DQ review. We report early empirical findings from a controlled experiment evaluating the effects of digital nudges generated through our previously proposed nudge-based framework for DQ. The results indicate that participants exposed to digital nudges demonstrated higher review output, improved detection of important and challenging issues, and greater engagement than those in the non-nudged condition. Qualitative feedback further suggests increased awareness and reflection on DQ. While preliminary, these findings provide promising empirical insights into the potential of digital nudges to support DQ practices and motivate further research on behaviour change in data-driven software engineering contexts.

Keywords: Digital Nudging · Data Quality · Data-Driven Software Engineering · Behaviour Change · Persuasive Technology · User Studies

1 Introduction

Data has become a central and strategic asset in modern software engineering, increasingly shaping engineering decisions across the software lifecycle. With the growing adoption of Data-Driven Software Engineering (DDSE), data is not merely an output but a foundational resource that influences how systems are conceived, developed, and evaluated [26]. However, this increasing dependence on data foregrounds questions of Data Quality (DQ). Besides affecting downstream

E. Vlahu-Gjorgievska et al. (Eds.): PERSUASIVE 2026, CCIS 2896, pp. 33–47, 2027.
https://doi.org/10.1007/978-3-032-27235-5_3

analyses, deficiencies in DQ (e.g., inaccuracies, inconsistencies, or biases) can directly influence engineering judgement, system behaviour, and organisational outcomes [6,21,26]. Therefore, ensuring high DQ is becoming not only a technical requirement but also a foundational prerequisite for the trustworthiness and effectiveness of data-driven processes.

Paradoxically, existing research consistently shows that DQ is not given sufficient priority by software engineers and is often neglected [12,18,19,37]. It has been identified as an open challenge in Data-Driven Requirements Engineering (DDRE), affecting requirements elicitation and limiting the effectiveness of automated techniques such as Machine Learning (ML) and Natural Language Processing (NLP) models [12,25,33]. Prior studies suggest that this problem is driven by two recurring factors, mainly lack of motivation [18,37], and insufficient skills and standardized practices among software engineers [25]. DQ-related tasks are frequently perceived as tedious, low-value, or disconnected from core engineering objectives, which contributes to a lack of motivation to engage in careful and systematic review. Together, these factors lead to data issues being overlooked, ultimately undermining downstream analysis and decision-making.

While much of the existing research has approached the topic from a technical perspective focusing on automated quality checks, data-cleaning algorithms, and tool support for identifying defects, they tend to overlook the human dimension of DQ work. Limited work has explored how software engineers view and engage with DQ within their development workflows and there is a scarcity of research on behaviour-driven interventions that can effectively guide and support engineers in maintaining data integrity within evolving software ecosystems. This gap has broader consequences, leading to inaccurate insights, poor system performance, and low user trust [6–8].

To address this gap, this research investigates the role of digital nudges—subtle behavioural interventions embedded within digital environments—in influencing software engineers' behaviour and motivation toward DQ review. Nudges originate from behaviour-change research and aim to steer individuals toward more desirable actions while preserving autonomy. They have demonstrated potential to influence human behaviour in general, and to encourage and promote best practices in software engineering in particular [5,9]. In prior work [1], we introduced the Digital Nudge for Data Quality (DN4DQ) framework, which adapts nudge theory to the context of DQ review in software engineering. The framework provides a structured and systematic approach for designing context-aware digital nudges to assist engineers and analysts in identifying, prioritizing, and resolving DQ issues throughout DDSE processes.

Building on this foundation, this paper reports early empirical findings from a controlled experiment designed to evaluate the behavioural effects of digital nudges generated through the proposed framework. The study explores how these interventions influence review output, review quality, and engagement during DQ review activities. Our initial results indicate positive behavioural effects, suggesting that digital nudges can meaningfully encourage more focused and attentive review behaviour. While preliminary, these findings provide promising insights into the potential role of behaviour-change mechanisms in addressing long-standing DQ challenges in software engineering and in encouraging best practices more broadly.

This work advances research in behaviour change and persuasive technology by applying nudge theory to the under-explored domain of DQ in software engineering. It demonstrates how digital nudges can be systematically designed to influence software engineers' behaviour and motivation in DQ review and empirically evaluates their effects, providing evidence that such interventions can support improved DQ practices in software engineering settings.

2 Background and Related Work

2.1 Data-Driven Software Engineering (DDSE)

DDSE has emerged as a significant shift towards evidence-based and analytics-driven software development, enabled by the increasing availability of large-scale and heterogeneous data [16,26,41]. By leveraging techniques such as ML and NLP, DDSE supports predictive modelling, data-informed requirements, and automated defect detection, contributing to improved software quality [16, 31]. Within this paradigm, Data-Driven Requirements Engineering (DDRE) has gained prominence through the use of user reviews, usage data, and telemetry logs to elicit and refine requirements [22,23].

Despite its promise, DDSE is highly dependent on the quality of the underlying data. Poor DQ can distort requirements and lead to misguided design decisions [33]. Yet, DQ often remains under-emphasised in software engineering practice [12,18,19,37], underscoring the need for rigorous DQ practices within DDSE workflows.

2.2 Data Quality (DQ)

DQ refers to the extent to which data are fit for use or conform to requirements [11,17]. Prior work conceptualises DQ as a multi-dimensional construct, commonly including completeness, accuracy, consistency, timeliness, and relevance [2,8,39]. These dimensions are widely adopted in information systems research and increasingly applied in software engineering, particularly when data are reused beyond their original purpose. Compromised DQ can negatively affect downstream analytics and decision-making [26,31].

In DDSE, DQ challenges are amplified by unstructured and heterogeneous data sources such as app-store reviews, which often contain noise, duplication, ambiguity, and bias [16,31]. Assessing DQ in such settings requires substantial human judgment, making reviews inherently subjective and context-dependent. This motivates the need for mechanisms that support software engineers in recognising and addressing DQ issues, which is the focus of this work.

2.3 Behaviour Change and Motivation

Motivation influences how individuals engage with cognitively demanding tasks and persistence over time. When tasks are perceived as tedious or misaligned with core responsibilities, engagement tends to be minimal and superficial, particularly in organisational settings [27,34]. In software engineering, activities critical to system quality, such as documentation, code review, and DQ assessment, are often de-prioritised relative to feature development, negatively affecting attention and decision quality [4,9].

Prior work has explored various behaviour-change techniques, including pair programming, code reviews, and gamification [9,32], as well as broader interventions such as goal setting, training, and incentives [14,20,27]. However, many of these approaches are less practical in contemporary DDSE contexts due to remote work and the distinctive cognitive and personality profiles of software engineers [9,36]. This motivates the use of digital nudges as a lightweight and scalable approach to supporting DQ practices within engineering workflows.

2.4 Nudge Theory and Digital Nudging

Nudge theory, originating in behavioural economics, describes how subtle changes to choice environments can influence behaviour without restricting options or imposing incentives [38]. Nudges exploit cognitive biases and heuristics, such as reminders, defaults, and social norms, to guide decision-making while preserving freedom of choice, and have been successfully applied in domains including public health, finance, and education.

Digital nudging extends these principles to digital interfaces, where the design of interactions and information presentation can shape user behaviour [35,40]. Prior work in HCI and information systems demonstrates the effectiveness of digital nudges in supporting privacy and security decisions, sustainable behaviours, and accuracy in online tasks [10,28,35]. However, despite growing interest, the application of digital nudges to software engineering, and DQ assessment in particular, remains limited. This gap motivates our investigation of digital nudging as a means of supporting behaviour change in data-centric engineering workflows.

3 Context-Aware Nudge Design for Data Quality

We designed a nudging bot to support software engineers during the DQ review process. This bot-based intervention is motivated by evidence that social mechanisms (e.g., peer interaction and shared responsibility in practices such as pair programming) can improve engineers' motivation and adoption of better practices [9,29,36]. The nudges are grounded in our previously proposed DN4DQ framework [1], which derives context-aware nudges from attributes related to the application domain, reviewer, data, intended use, and project constraints.

As shown in Fig. 1 and 2, DN4DQ comprises three phases: (i) contextual components identification, (ii) nudge design using the Five W's scheme (Who,

What, When, Where, Why), and (iii) real-time deployment to guide reviewers toward key DQ aspects and best practices.

In this experiment, the framework is instantiated for DQ assessment in DDRE using a subset of contextual components due to scope and limited prior evidence for others (e.g., reviewer personality). The study focuses on DQ issue identification; prioritisation and resolution are left as future work alongside broader evaluation across contexts. The next section presents a step-by-step walkthrough of the experimental instantiation.

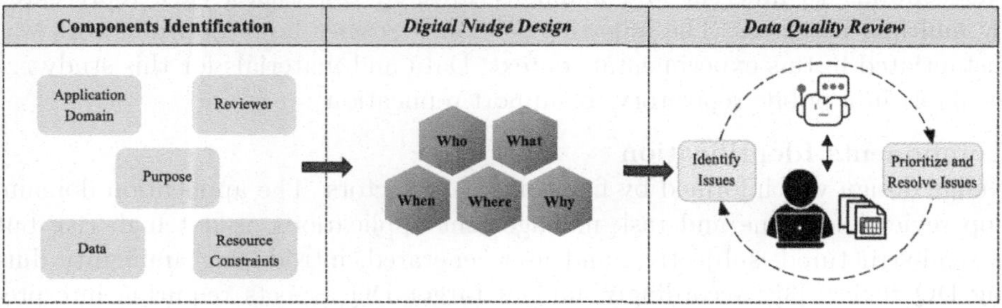

Fig. 1. DN4DQ framework for designing digital nudges to support DQ review.

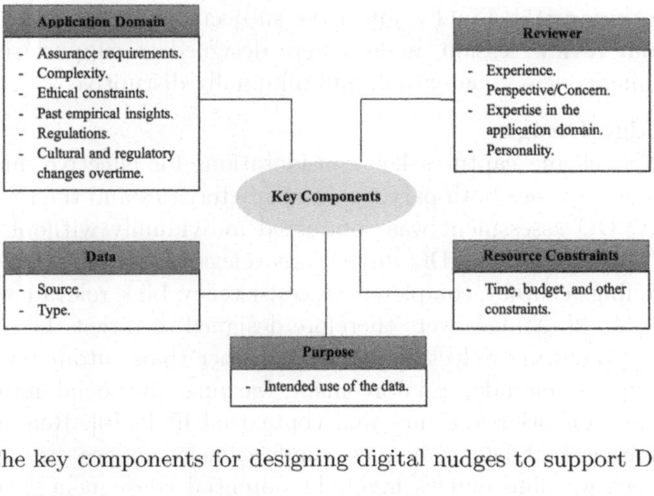

Fig. 2. The key components for designing digital nudges to support DQ review.

4 Experimental Study

4.1 Experimental Context and Nudge Instantiation

We conducted an online controlled experiment to examine the effects of digital nudges, derived from the DN4DQ framework, on software engineers' motivation and behaviour during DQ review. By simulating real-world DQ review tasks, the study compared participants reviewing DQ with and without digital nudges. In total, 38 final-year software engineering students and recent graduates participated (aged 21–23; 17 male, 21 female). In this study, the terms "software engineers" and "reviewers" are used interchangeably to refer to participants performing the DQ review.

An open-source dataset of over 12,000 Google Play app reviews for time and task management applications was used for requirements elicitation [22]. The dataset includes review metadata (e.g., ratings, sentiment, Thumbs Up Count) and contains 16 inherent and manually injected DQ issues, each represented by multiple instances. The following section describes how the framework was instantiated in this experimental context. Data and materials for this study are available in a public repository to support replication[1].

Components Identification
Nudge design was informed by five contextual factors. The application domain, app reviews for time and task management applications, is not high risk but is semi-structured, subjective, and user-generated, introducing ambiguity during DQ review [3]. Accordingly, nudges target DQ aspects requiring interpretive judgment (e.g., completeness, relevance, bias, duplication, and timeliness) rather than enforcing deterministic correctness. Reviewers in this study have limited DQ experience, motivating supportive and guidance-oriented nudges such as reminders and lightweight warnings. As the data are used for requirements elicitation, nudges prioritise completeness, relevance, and interpretability over statistical precision [15]. Finally, given the subjective nature of the data and a fixed two-hour review session, nudges were designed to support sense-making while remaining concise, contextual, and minimally disruptive.

Digital Nudge Design
The Five W's scheme captures key considerations for effective nudge deployment. *Who* encompasses both participant characteristics and the review setting; in this study, DQ assessment was conducted individually without team coordination. *What* refers to the DQ dimensions relevant to app-review datasets in DDRE, including accuracy, completeness, consistency, bias, relevance, timeliness, and volume [12,22]. Nudges were therefore designed to target these dimensions conceptually, promoting reflective judgment rather than automated correction. Four nudge types—reminder, reinforcement, warning, and social influence—were employed based on prior evidence and contextual fit [5,10]. Reminder nudges maintain awareness of DQ principles, reinforcement nudges strengthen desirable behaviour, warning nudges highlight potential consequences of oversight, and social influence nudges encourage alignment with peer practices. All nudges were delivered as brief prompts or questions.

When concerns timing: nudges were delivered in a user-driven manner, with each subsequent nudge triggered by the reviewer upon task progression. *Where* refers to the technical setting, in which reviewers analysed the data using

[1] https://github.com/Balkadhi/DN4DQ-Framework/tree/Persuasive2026.

Microsoft Excel while nudges were delivered via a scripted Landbot chat interface. Finally, *Why* reflects the objective of using digital nudges to engage reviewers and support more thorough and attentive identification of DQ issues.

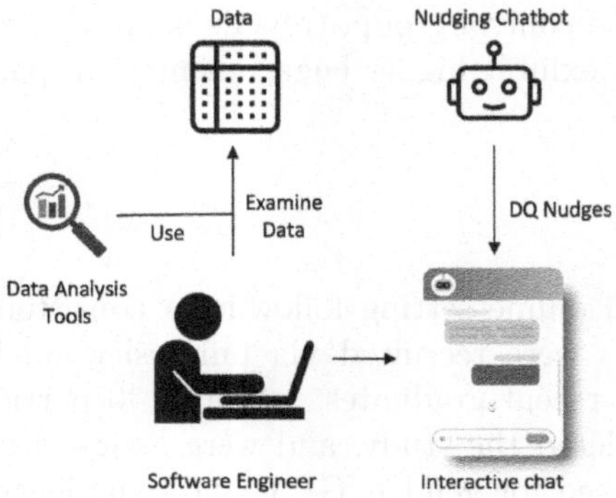

Fig. 3. The nudging bot facilitating DQ review through guided prompts.

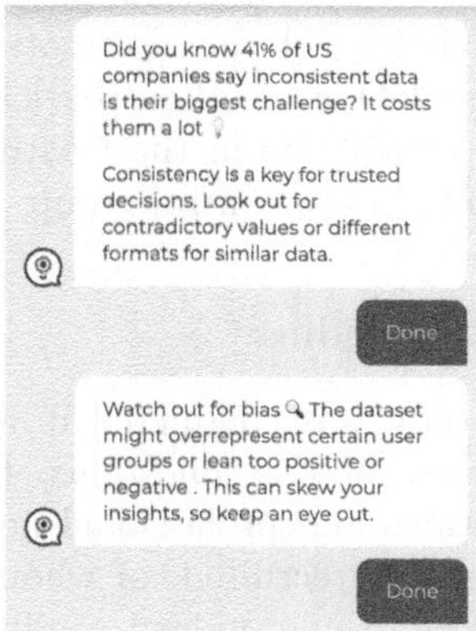

Fig. 4. Example of social influence and warning nudges used.

Integration Into the DQ Review Workflow
In this phase, nudges were deployed in real time as reviewers engaged in the DQ assessment process. A nudging bot was developed to simulate peer-like interactions during review (Fig. 3), delivering context-aware prompts that encourage reviewers to examine key DQ aspects and reflect on potential issues. Nudges were phrased as brief recommendations or questions to support deeper data inspection. Ethical considerations, including transparency, freedom of choice, and goal-oriented justification, were incorporated into the design. A predefined script of 15 nudges (7 reminders, 2 reinforcements, 4 warnings, and 2 social influence nudges) was implemented using the Landbot platform to cover the primary DQ dimensions identified earlier. Figure 4 illustrates example nudges.

4.2 Method

A mixed-methods approach was employed, combining quantitative and qualitative measures. Digital nudging served as the independent variable, while behavioural change was assessed along three outcome dimensions: review output, review quality, and reviewer engagement. Review output was measured by the number of identified DQ issues; review quality by the importance and difficulty of identified issues; and engagement by time spent on the task and a post-task self-report questionnaire. As motivation and behavioural change are difficult to measure directly, such proxy measures are commonly used in prior work [9,13,24], with engagement shown to be closely associated with motivation and improved outcomes [24,30]. Semi-structured interviews were also conducted post-task to collect qualitative feedback on the DQ review experience.

Based on this framing, the following hypotheses were tested:

H1. Participants in the treatment group, those exposed to digital nudges, identify more DQ issues than participants in the control group. (review output).

H2. Participants in the treatment group identify higher-importance and more difficult DQ issues than participants in the control group. (review quality).

H3. Participants in the treatment group exhibit higher engagement than participants in the control group.

4.3 Procedure

The study was conducted in a controlled online setting following a consistent procedure across conditions. Participants were recruited via university email invitations and professional networks for recent graduates. In total, 40 participants were recruited, of whom 38 completed the study, and were assigned to nudged and non-nudged conditions balanced for gender, GPA, and experience. Ethical approval was obtained, informed consent was collected, and participation was voluntary with the option to withdraw at any time. To avoid bias, the investigation of digital nudging was not disclosed to participants.

Participants reviewed an app-review dataset using Microsoft Excel with the goal of identifying DQ issues relevant to requirements elicitation. DQ issues were classified by the researchers according to importance (high, medium, low) and difficulty (easy, moderate, difficult), with classifications validated by domain experts. Both groups followed identical instructions, except that participants in the nudged condition interacted with a conversational nudging bot implemented using the Landbot platform.

Participants were given up to two hours to complete the task and reported identified issues using a structured Google Form, while task duration was recorded. Upon completion, participants filled out the User Engagement Scale-Short Form (UES-SF) [30]. Finally, semi-structured interviews were conducted to gather qualitative feedback on the review process and, where applicable, the use of digital nudges.

4.4 Results

We report aggregated findings from the experiment. Participant-reported issues were mapped to a predefined issue list; unmatched entries were labelled as 'Other' or 'Not an issue.' We analysed three dimensions: review output (issues identified), review quality (importance and difficulty), and reviewer engagement (task time and questionnaire responses). Results were examined at individual and group levels, including issues missed by both groups and those unique to the nudged condition. Group differences were tested using Welch's unpaired t-test in R. Post-task interviews were analysed thematically in NVivo to capture patterns in reviewing behaviour, engagement, and perceptions of the nudges. Given the exploratory design, results should be interpreted in light of the limited sample size.

Review Output (H1)
Participants in the treatment group, those exposed to digital nudges, identified significantly more DQ issues than participants in the control group (M = 5.26 vs. 3.47, p = 0.0012), as illustrated in Fig. 5 and summarised in Table 1. Across both conditions, issues related to temporal characteristics of the data—namely data drift and time imbalance (S6, S8)—were not identified by any participant. In contrast, issues involving extreme value distributions and consistently negative sentiment (S2, S11) were identified only by participants in the nudged condition, indicating broader issue coverage when nudges are present. While exploratory, these findings suggest that digital nudges can support reviewers in identifying a wider range of DQ issues that may otherwise be overlooked.

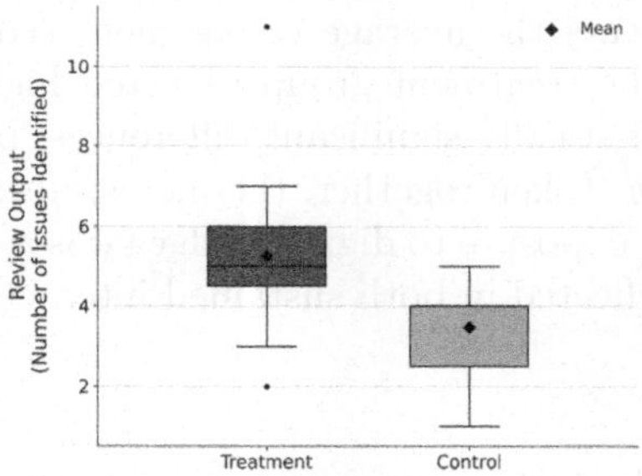

Fig. 5. Review output across conditions.

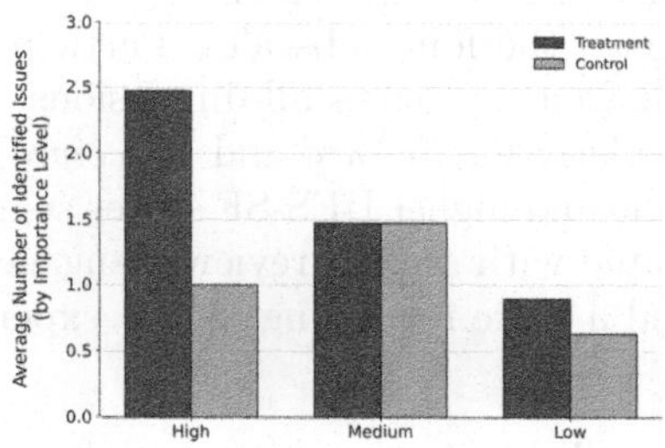

Fig. 6. Average number of identified issues by importance level.

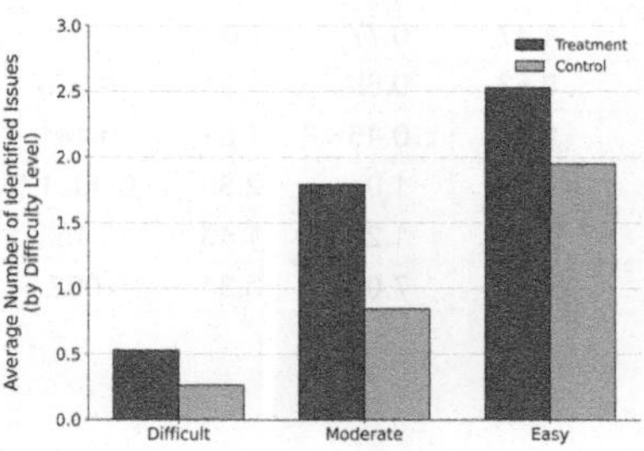

Fig. 7. Average number of identified issues by difficulty level.

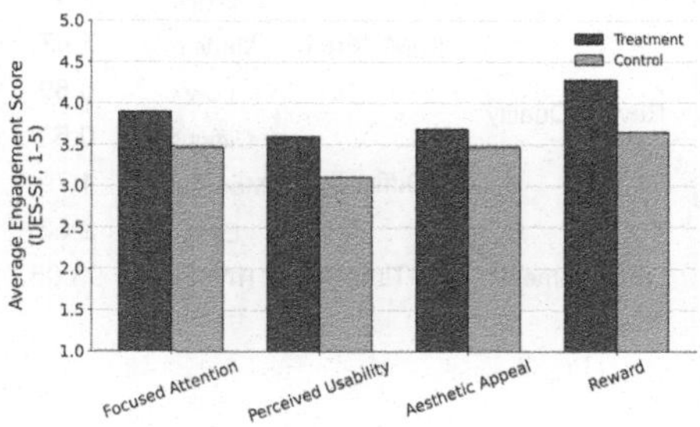

Fig. 8. Average engagement score per subscale.

Review Quality (H2)
Review quality was assessed by analysing the importance and difficulty of the identified DQ issues, excluding entries classified as "Other" or "Not an issue".

As shown in Figs. 6 and 7, participants in the treatment group identified significantly more high-importance issues than those in the control group (M = 2.47 vs. 1.00, $p < 0.001$), while no significant differences were observed for medium- or low-importance issues. Similarly, nudged participants identified significantly more moderate-difficulty issues (M = 1.79 vs. 0.84, p = 0.007), with no significant differences for easy or difficult issues. Overall, these results suggest that digital nudges support reviewers in identifying more important and moderately challenging DQ issues, rather than merely increasing the detection of trivial problems.

Reviewer Engagement (H3)

Engagement was assessed using time spent and a self-reported engagement questionnaire. As shown in Table 1, participants in the treatment group spent significantly more time on the review task than those in the control group, suggesting greater behavioural involvement.

Engagement was further measured using the UES-SF questionnaire, scored following O'Brien et al. [30]. Figure 8 presents the average engagement scores across the four subscales. Participants in the treatment group reported higher engagement across all dimensions, with statistically significant differences, particularly for *Reward* and *Perceived Usability*. Taken together, the increased task time and higher UES-SF scores suggest that exposure to digital nudges was associated with greater reviewer engagement, reflected in both sustained interaction and a more rewarding review experience.

Table 1. Mean, standard deviation, t-value, and p-value across conditions

			Treatment Group		*Control Group*			
			M	SD	M	SD	t	p
Review Output	Identified DQ issues		5.26	1.82	3.47	1.22	3.56	0.0012 *
Review Quality	Importance	High	2.47	1.31	1	0.82	4.17	0.00024 *
		Medium	1.47	0.96	1.47	0.77	0	1
		Low	0.89	0.66	0.63	0.68	1.21	0.235
	Difficulty	Difficult	0.53	0.61	0.26	0.45	1.51	0.141
		Moderate	1.79	1.03	0.84	1.01	2.85	0.0071 *
		Easy	2.53	1.22	1.95	1.22	1.46	0.153
Engagement	Time spent (min)		93.05	7.91	84.95	7.04	3.34	0.002 *

Qualitative Insights from Post-task Interviews

Post-task interviews were conducted to contextualise the quantitative engagement results. Thematic analysis revealed recurring themes related to cognitive effort, task guidance, and the perceived value of support during the DQ review process.

Participants generally described the task as cognitively demanding, particularly when deciding where to start and how to systematically inspect the data. Reviewers in the control group frequently reported a lack of initial orientation, noting uncertainty about how to approach the review and, in some cases, reliance on external resources such as online checklists or web searches. In contrast, participants in the treatment group emphasised the role of nudges in providing structure and maintaining focus, helping them notice issues they would otherwise overlook (e.g., "I started noticing things I would usually miss, like bias"). Nudges were also associated with increased reflection and perceived task value, encouraging a more deliberate review process. Some participants suggested extending the approach through AI-based automated issue detection, while others expressed strong reliance on the tool, following its guidance step by step. Overall, these qualitative findings help explain the longer task times, higher engagement scores, and improved review output and quality observed in the treatment group.

4.5 Discussion

This study investigated the use of digital nudges to change software engineers' behaviour and enhance their motivation towards DQ review, examining their impact on review output, review quality, and reviewer engagement. The results indicate that reviewers exposed to digital nudges identified a greater number of issues, including issues of higher importance and difficulty, and reported higher engagement compared to the control group. Together, these findings provides evidence to support our hypotheses (H1, H2, and H3) and suggest that nudging interventions can positively influence the behaviour and effectiveness of DQ review tasks by shaping how reviewers approach and perform the review activity.

The quantitative results, complemented by post-task interviews, point to several behavioural mechanisms through which nudges supported reviewer performance. Rather than enforcing specific actions, nudges appeared to influence reviewers' behaviour by providing structure and direction during the review process. Participants described nudges as helping them determine where to start, maintain focus, and adopt a more systematic inspection strategy. This structured guidance reduced uncertainty and supported sustained attentional control, which helps explain the higher review output and the identification of issues with greater importance and difficulty in the treatment group. Increased task time and higher engagement scores further suggest that nudges shifted reviewers away from rapid, surface-level inspection toward a more deliberate and cognitively engaged review process.

Viewed through a behaviour-change lens, these findings highlight how lightweight digital nudges can reinforce desirable review behaviour, such as careful inspection, reflection, and persistence, without constraining reviewer autonomy or introducing rigid workflows. By subtly guiding attention and prompting reflection at key moments, nudges supported reviewers in applying their expertise more consistently and deliberately. From a practical perspective, this suggests that behaviourally informed interventions can complement existing DQ practices by enhancing human judgment rather than replacing it. Participants' suggestions to extend the approach through automated issue detection further point to opportunities for combining nudging strategies with AI-based support, enabling intelligent systems to surface potential issues while preserving the reviewer's central role in decision-making.

4.6 Threats to Validity

Several threats to validity should be considered when interpreting the results of this study. Internal validity may be influenced by individual differences such as prior experience or intrinsic motivation, as some participants may have applied personal or self-guided review strategies. However, random assignment and the inclusion of a control group help mitigate these effects and support causal interpretation.

Construct validity concerns relate to the operationalisation of nudging and engagement. While the nudges were designed based on behavioural principles, the approach may not capture all possible nudging strategies. Engagement was measured using task time and a standardised questionnaire (UES-SF), which is widely validated but may not reflect all aspects of engagement. Review quality was assessed through identified issues, reflecting inspection performance rather than downstream outcomes.

External validity is limited by the experimental setting, dataset, and participant sample. The study involved students with software engineering backgrounds, and the findings may not directly generalise to professional or industrial contexts. Future studies with practitioners, larger samples, and diverse datasets are needed to assess generalisability.

5 Conclusion and Future Work

This study addressed the challenge that software engineers often give limited priority to DQ during development activities, leading to rushed or superficial review practices. We investigated the use of digital nudges as behaviourally informed, persuasive interventions to encourage greater attention, motivation, and care during DQ review, and examined their impact on review output, review quality, and reviewer engagement.

The results show that reviewers exposed to nudges identified more quality issues, including issues of higher importance and difficulty, and spent more time on the task than those in the control group. Higher engagement scores and qualitative feedback further indicate that nudges helped shift reviewer behaviour toward more deliberate and reflective inspection by providing structure and guiding attention. These findings contribute to research on behaviour change and persuasive technology by demonstrating how lightweight, non-coercive nudges can shape professional review practices and support sustained cognitive engagement.

Future work should investigate the applicability of nudging strategies in more realistic and longitudinal settings, including studies with professional practitioners and diverse datasets. Several participants also suggested extending the approach by integrating automated or AI-based issue detection, pointing to opportunities for hybrid systems that combine behavioural nudging with intelligent support. Further research is also needed to explore adaptive and personalised nudges, as well as the long-term effects of nudging on DQ practices and reviewer behaviour over time.

Acknowledgments. This research was supported by funding from King Saud University, Saudi Arabia, awarded to Ms.Alkadhi.

References

1. Alkadhi, B., Hendley, R., Bahsoon, R.: A gentle push in the right direction: a nudge-based framework for data quality review in software engineering. Interact. Comput. Adv. online publ. iwag003 (2026). https://doi.org/10.1093/iwc/iwag003
2. Batini, C., Cappiello, C., Francalanci, C., Maurino, A.: Methodologies for data quality assessment and improvement. ACM Comput. Surv. **41** (2009). https://doi.org/10.1145/1541880.1541883
3. Batini, C., Rula, A., Scannapieco, M., Viscusi, G.: From data quality to big data quality. J. Database Manag. **26**, 60–82 (2015).https://doi.org/10.4018/JDM.2015010103
4. Beller, M., Bacchelli, A., Zaidman, A., Juergens, E.: Modern code reviews in open-source projects: which problems do they fix? In: Proceedings of the 11th Working Conference on Mining Software Repositories, MSR 2014, pp. 202–211. Association for Computing Machinery, New York (2014). https://doi.org/10.1145/2597073.2597082
5. Bergram, K., Djokovic, M., Bezençon, V., Holzer, A.: The digital landscape of nudging: a systematic literature review of empirical research on digital nudges. In: Proceedings of the CHI'22 Conference on Human Factors in Computing Systems. Association for Computing Machinery, New York (2022) https://doi.org/10.1145/3491102.3517638
6. Bobrowski, M., Marr, M., Yankelevich, D.: A software engineering view of data quality. In: Proceedings of Second International Software Quality in Europe (1998)
7. Bosu, M.F., MacDonell, S.G.: Data quality in empirical software engineering: a targeted review. In: Proceedings of the 17th International Conference on Evaluation and Assessment in Software Engineering, pp. 171–176. ACM (2013) https://doi.org/10.1145/2460999.2461024
8. Bosu, M.F., MacDonell, S.G.: A taxonomy of data quality challenges in empirical software engineering. In: 22nd Australian Software Engineering Conference, pp. 97–106 (2013). https://doi.org/10.1109/ASWEC.2013.21
9. Brown, C.: Digital nudges for encouraging developer actions (2019)
10. Caraban, A., Karapanos, E., Gonçalves, D., Campos, P.: 23 ways to nudge: a review of technology-mediated nudging in human-computer interaction. In: Conference on Human Factors in Computing Systems - Proceedings (2019). https://doi.org/10.1145/3290605.3300733
11. Crosby, P.: Quality is Free: The Art of Making Quality Certain. Mentor book, McGraw-Hill (1979)
12. Franch, X.: Data-driven requirements engineering: a guided tour. In: Ali, R., Kaindl, H., Maciaszek, L.A. (eds.) ENASE 2020. CCIS, vol. 1375, pp. 83–105. Springer, Cham (2021). https://doi.org/10.1007/978-3-030-70006-5_4

13. Ghaban, W., Hendley, R.: Understanding the effect of gamification on learners with different personalities. In: Proceedings of the 11th International Conference on Computer Supported Education, pp. 392–400 (2019). https://doi.org/10.5220/0007730703920400
14. Gneezy, U., Meier, S., Rey-Biel, P.: When and why incentives (don't) work to modify behavior. J. Econ. Perspect. **25**(4), 191–210 (2011). https://doi.org/10.1257/jep.25.4.191. https://www.aeaweb.org/articles?id=10.1257/jep.25.4.191
15. Guzman, E., Maalej, W.: How do users like this feature? A fine grained sentiment analysis of app reviews. In: 2014 IEEE 22nd International Requirements Engineering Conference (RE), pp. 153–162 (2014).https://doi.org/10.1109/RE.2014.6912257
16. Hassan, A.E.: The road ahead for mining software repositories. In: 2008 Frontiers of Software Maintenance, pp. 48–57 (2008). https://doi.org/10.1109/FOSM.2008.4659248
17. Juran, J., Godfrey, A.: Juran's Quality Handbook. McGraw Hill, McGraw-Hill International Editions (1999)
18. Liebchen, G.A., Shepperd, M.: Data sets and data quality in software engineering. In: Proceedings of the 4th International Workshop on Predictor Models in Software Engineering, PROMISE '08, pp. 39–44. Association for Computing Machinery, New York (2008). https://doi.org/10.1145/1370788.1370799
19. Liebchen, G.A.: Data cleaning techniques for software engineering data sets (2010)
20. Locke, E.A., Latham, G.P.: Building a practically useful theory of goal setting and task motivation: a 35-year odyssey. Am. Psychol. **57 9**, 705–717 (2002). https://api.semanticscholar.org/CorpusID:17534210
21. Loshin, D.: Enterprise Knowledge Management: The Data Quality Approach. Morgan Kaufmann (2001)
22. Maalej, W., Nayebi, M., Johann, T., Ruhe, G.: Toward data-driven requirements engineering. IEEE Softw. **33**, 48–54 (2016). https://doi.org/10.1109/MS.2015.153
23. Maalej, W., Robillard, M.P.: Patterns of user feedback in mobile app reviews. In: 21st IEEE International Requirements Engineering Conference (RE), pp. 125–134. IEEE (2013)
24. Martin, A., Ginns, P., Papworth, B.: Motivation and engagement: same or different? does it matter? Learn. Individ. Differ. **55**, 162 (2017). https://doi.org/10.1016/j.lindif.2017.03.013
25. Martinez, A., Melin, M., Koutsopoulos, G., Zdravkovic, J.: An empirical study on data-driven requirements elicitation: reflections from nordic enterprises (2021)
26. Menzies, T., Zimmermann, T.: Perspective: software analytics: So what? IEEE Softw. **30**(4), 31–37 (2013)
27. Michie, S., van Stralen, M.M., West, R.: The behaviour change wheel: a new method for characterising and designing behaviour change interventions. Implement. Sci. **6**(42) (2011) https://doi.org/10.1186/1748-5908-6-42
28. Mirsch, T., Lehrer, C., Jung, R.: Digital nudging: altering user behavior in digital environments. In: Proceedings of the 13th International Conference on Wirtschaftsinformatik, pp. 634–648 (2017)
29. Murphy-Hill, E., Murphy, G.C.: Peer interaction effectively, yet infrequently, enables programmers to discover new tools. In: Proceedings of the ACM 2011 Conference on Computer Supported Cooperative Work, CSCW '11, pp. 405–414. Association for Computing Machinery, New York (2011).https://doi.org/10.1145/1958824.1958888

30. O'Brien, H.L., Cairns, P., Hall, M.: A practical approach to measuring user engagement with the refined user engagement scale (ues) and new ues short form. Int. J. Hum. Comput. Stud. **112**, 28–39 (2018). https://doi.org/10.1016/j.ijhcs.2018.01.004
31. Pagano, D., Maalej, W.: User feedback in the appstore: an empirical study. In: 21st IEEE International Requirements Engineering Conference (RE), pp. 125–134 (2013). https://doi.org/10.1109/RE.2013.6636712
32. Rigby, P.C., Bird, C.: Convergent contemporary software peer review practices. In: Proceedings of the 2013 9th Joint Meeting on Foundations of Software Engineering, ESEC/FSE 2013, pp. 202–212. Association for Computing Machinery, New York (2013). https://doi.org/10.1145/2491411.2491444
33. Ruan, L., Zhang, T.: The challenge of data-driven requirements elicitation techniques-systematic literature review controlled experiment (2020)
34. Ryan, R.M., Deci, E.L.: Intrinsic and extrinsic motivations: classic definitions and new directions. Contemp. Educ. Psychol. **25**(1), 54–67 (2000). https://doi.org/10.1006/ceps.1999.1020. https://www.sciencedirect.com/science/article/pii/S0361476X99910202
35. Schneider, C., Weinmann, M., vom Brocke, J.: Digital nudging: guiding online user choices through interface design. Commun. ACM **61**(7), 67–73 (2018)
36. Sharp, H., Baddoo, N., Beecham, S., Hall, T., Robinson, H.: Models of motivation in software engineering. Inf. Softw. Technol. **51**, 219–233 (2009). https://doi.org/10.1016/j.infsof.2008.05.009
37. Shepperd, M.: Data Quality: Cinderella at the Software Metrics Ball?, Association for Computing Machinery (2011)
38. Thaler, R.H., Sunstein, C.R.: Nudge: Improving Decisions About Health, Wealth, and Happiness. Yale University Press (2008)
39. Wang, R.Y., Strong, D.M.: Beyond accuracy: what data quality means to data consumers. J. Manag. Inf. Syst. **12**(4), 5–33 (1996)
40. Weinmann, M., Schneider, C., vom Brocke, J.: Digital nudging. Bus. Inf. Syst. Eng. **58**(6), 433–436 (2016)
41. Zimmermann, T., Weibgerber, P., Diehl, S., Zeller, A.: Mining version histories to guide software changes. In: Proceedings, 26th International Conference on Software Engineering, pp. 563–572 (2004). https://doi.org/10.1109/ICSE.2004.1317478

The Perceived Persuasiveness of Generative Artificial Intelligence Systems in Learning Task

Akon Obu Ekpezu[1(✉)], Isaac Wiafe[2], and Harri Oinas-Kukkonen[1]

[1] Department of Information Processing Science, University of Oulu, Oulu, Finland
akon.ekpezu@oulu.fi

[2] Department of Computer Science, University of Ghana, Accra, Ghana

Abstract. Generative artificial intelligence (GenAI) systems are increasingly used for learning, but their perceived persuasiveness remains underexplored. To address this gap, this study investigated the perceived persuasiveness of GenAI tools in a learning context. Drawing from an existing model of perceived persuasiveness, quantitative data was collected from 446 university students, who completed an online questionnaire after using any GenAI system of their choice to complete a learning task. Partial least squares structural equation modeling was used to evaluate the hypothesized relationships in the model. The results showed that all hypothesized effects were significant, except for the effect of primary task support on perceived persuasiveness. Unobtrusiveness, credibility support, and dialogue support directly influenced perceived persuasiveness, and this strongly predicted students' intention to continue using the system. This study extends persuasive educational technologies to include GenAI systems. It highlights the role of non-disruptive and credible GenAI systems in enhancing learners' favorable impressions of these systems and their influence on them. Future studies should examine these findings in a more diverse student population and culture with different attitudes toward GenAI systems.

Keywords: Perceived Persuasiveness · Persuasive Systems Design · Persuasive Technology · Generative Artificial Intelligence

1 Introduction

The emergence of generative artificial intelligence (GenAI) systems, such as large language models and conversational agents, has begun to transform teaching, learning, and assessment practices in higher education. Beyond producing content, generative AI systems increasingly shape learners' beliefs, attitudes, and behaviors, intentionally or otherwise [1–3]. Through adaptive feedback, empathetic dialogue, and personalized content generation, these tools can scaffold self-regulation, motivation, and reflection in learning tasks. However, their influence extends beyond cognitive assistance to potential persuasive effects that may shape learners' attitudes, intentions, and behaviors towards learning activities [4–7].

E. Vlahu-Gjorgievska et al. (Eds.): PERSUASIVE 2026, CCIS 2896, pp. 48–62, 2027.
https://doi.org/10.1007/978-3-032-27235-5_4

Perceived persuasiveness captures the degree to which a system's communication, information, tone, or behavior influences users to adopt specific attitudes or behaviors [8–10]. In the educational context, perceived persuasiveness can determine whether learners accept feedback, comply with suggested revisions, or continue using AI for learning. Over time, this perception may influence not only learning behaviors but also attitudinal outcomes, such as trust, autonomy, and perceived competence. Despite the growing integration of GenAI systems into educational contexts, their perceived persuasiveness remains underexplored. Yet, understanding the perceived persuasiveness of GenAI is crucial for promoting the ethical design of educational AI systems that seek to enhance learner engagement while avoiding manipulation, coercion, or over-dependence [11].

Accordingly, this study aims to investigate the perceived persuasiveness of GenAI systems in learning/educational contexts. Research on persuasive systems provides a valuable theoretical foundation for this study [9, 10]. Specifically, Lehto et al. [10] conceptualized a theoretical model that explains how and to what extent the persuasive systems design features [9] influence the perceived persuasiveness of a persuasive system. Although this model was originally examined in the context of a web-based persuasive system, it has since been evaluated across other domains, with persuasive system design features established as predictors of perceived persuasiveness [12–14]. However, these prior systems were nonadaptive. In contrast, GenAI systems, such as ChatGPT, Google Gemini, and similar large language model-based educational assistants represent adaptive conversational systems. They can generate personalized feedback, suggestions, and study guidance during learning tasks, features that parallel those of persuasive systems. However, the dynamic and context-sensitive nature of GenAI systems may amplify or alter established persuasive mechanisms. What remains unclear, is how learners perceive and evaluate these adaptive persuasive features when interacting with GenAI tools. Addressing this gap is essential to determine whether existing persuasive features sufficiently explain user responses to AI-mediated persuasion. By examining learners' perceptions and responses to these persuasive affordances, this study seeks to establish the perceived persuasiveness of GenAI systems in educational settings. This study is expected to provide both theoretical and practical insights for designing ethically persuasive GenAI systems for learning.

2 Theoretical Background, Research Model, and Hypothesis

The persuasive systems design (PSD) model [9] provides a framework for explaining how information systems are designed to influence users' attitudes and behavior. It emphasizes three core considerations: identifying persuasive postulates, analyzing the context in which persuasion occurs, and implementing appropriate system design features. The model identifies four categories of persuasive system design features (primary task support, dialogue support, credibility support, and social support), each of which can be mapped to functionalities observed in generative artificial intelligence (GenAI) systems.

Although GenAI systems are not typically designed with explicit persuasive intent, emerging evidence in intelligent tutoring systems indicates that they exhibit persuasive capabilities. These systems influence learners' beliefs and behaviors through personalized and adaptive support based on their needs and knowledge levels [3, 15]. They sometimes outperform human persuaders in structured debates by generating arguments that require cognitive engagement rather than providing fixed solutions [15–17].

In the context of learning, GenAI systems have been demonstrated to provide learning support, constructive feedback, trustworthy problem-solving experiences and professional user interface (UI) design, and collaborative learning environments [15, 18–20], which align with the primary task support, dialogue support, credibility support, and social support, respectively. These conceptual parallels suggest that GenAI tools inherently embody persuasive mechanisms capable of influencing learners' motivation, engagement, and continuous use intention. Prior research has shown that perceived persuasiveness can be measured and predicted by the presence of persuasive system features (e.g., [10, 21]). Hence, mapping the functionalities of GenAI systems onto persuasive design principles not only highlights their potential psychological influence on learners but also establishes a theoretical foundation for empirically examining how persuasiveness manifests within AI-mediated learning interactions.

Beyond functional design features, the PSD model outlines persuasion postulates that seek to describe the conditions under which persuasion is more effective. Among these, unobtrusiveness and design aesthetics are particularly relevant to the persuasive qualities of GenAI systems [18, 22]. They influence users without overt disruption, with a clear user interface design and text font that influence trust. GenAI systems, especially in education are seamlessly integrated into existing platforms to enhance learner's experience without being disruptive [2, 23].

Thus, GenAI systems may be conceptualized as persuasive systems because their primary intent aligns with primary support (helping users accomplish learning or productivity goals), their adaptive and dialogical mechanisms embody persuasive characteristics even when persuasion is not a deliberate design objective, and their UI design and information presentation are often perceived as credible and trustworthy. However, limited research has examined the perceived persuasiveness of GenAI systems in educational contexts. To address this, the present study adopts the model proposed by Lehto et al. [10] to examine learners' perceptions of the persuasiveness of GenAI and their continuous use intention. The adopted model is presented in Fig. 1, and all the path relations are assumed to be positive.

2.1 Unobtrusiveness

The postulate of unobtrusiveness posits that persuasive systems are most effective when they operate seamlessly within users' ongoing activities without causing interruptions or drawing overt attention to the persuasive intent [9]. GenAI systems embody this by responding only when invoked or when they detect that the learner might benefit from support during use. For instance, suggesting an example after a learner requests clarification or providing a hint when the learner appears to be stuck. Since this assistance is timely, relevant, and user-initiated, it most likely feels supportive rather than coercive. Thus, rather than imposing alerts or pop-ups, these tools embed responses within ongoing work in the form of inline-text suggestions. This reduces extraneous cognitive load and maintains attentional flow, both of which are essential for performing primary tasks.

By adapting to the learner's style, knowledge level, and task progress, GenAI systems can tailor their interventions to meet the learner's needs. For example, the tool

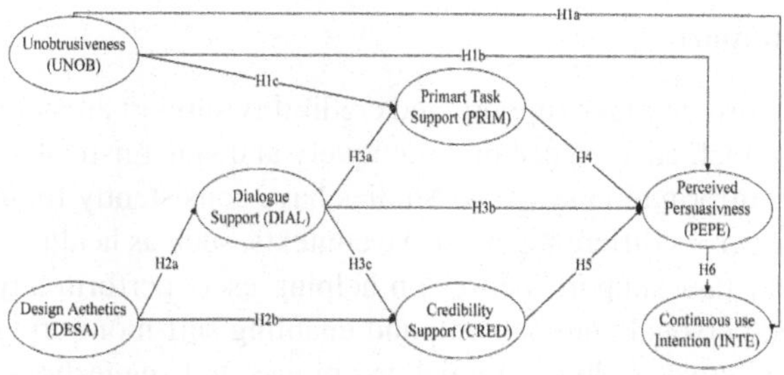

Fig. 1. Adopted research model [10]

may simplify explanations for novices or offer deeper theoretical insights for advanced users. Such personalization and unobtrusive support not only preserve learners' autonomy but also enhance trust and satisfaction, both of which are central to continued use [24, 25]. Conversely, intrusive or creepy systems diminish trust and engagement. Empirical evidence from persuasive systems indicates that unobtrusiveness positively predicts continuous use intention, perceived persuasiveness, and primary task support [10, 26]. Thus, given that GenAI systems blend assistance with the learner's natural cognitive and task flow rather than interrupting it, this study hypothesizes the following:

H1a: Unobtrusiveness influences learners' intention to continue using GenAI systems.
H1b: Unobtrusiveness influences the perceived persuasiveness of GenAI systems.
H1c: Unobtrusiveness influences primary task support in GenAI systems.

2.2 Design Aesthetics

Design aesthetics play a pivotal role in shaping users' cognitive and emotional responses to system interaction. In GenAI systems, the scope extends beyond visual interface design to encompass interactive qualities, such as coherent phrasing, balanced tone, and conversational fluency. In persuasive systems, including virtual reality applications, visual appeal and aesthetic quality amplifies the motivational and persuasive impact of dialogue support, making interactions feel more human-like, credible, and contextually relevant [8, 10]. Similarly, aesthetic coherence enhances users' perceptions of a system's credibility and trustworthiness [8, 10]. Thus, it is logical to posit that the aesthetic quality of most GenAI systems paired with well-structured, polite, and coherent conversational styles will most likely keep users focused on the dialogue while conveying intelligence and expertise. However, improved response quality is still needed to reduce misinformation and social biases in GenAI systems [27]. This is because learners tend to perceive these systems as more credible and motivating when the interface is visually appealing and the interactions are linguistically coherent [28]. While [11] posits that this may lead to over-reliance, it is logical to posit that learners who perceive GenAI systems as visually appealing will perceive their feedback and interaction as motivating. They may also perceive the information it provides as being trustworthy and reliable. Thus, this study hypothesizes that.

H2a: Design aesthetics influences computer-human dialogue support in GenAI systems.
H2b: Design aesthetics influences credibility support in GenAI systems.

2.3 Dialogue Support

Dialogue support, primary task support, and credibility support are core interrelated pillars of the PSD model, each contributing uniquely and synergistically to the perceived persuasiveness of information systems. Studies have consistently found that these features are effective across different persuasive contexts, such as health, e-commerce, and education. Primary task support focuses on helping users perform target behaviors by simplifying tasks, personalizing content, and enabling self-monitoring. Dialogue support provides interactive feedback, reminders, praise, and suggestions to motivate and guide users toward their goals. Credibility support strengthens users' trust and confidence in the system by ensuring that the information provided is accurate, verifiable, and professionally presented.

In most persuasion contexts, dialogue support has been shown to directly reinforce and motivate users to perform the primary task and enhance their perceptions of system credibility [14, 29]. It has also been shown to influence users' favorable impressions of the system and its influence on them [21]. Within GenAI systems, these support features are more dynamic and adaptive than those in static systems. They interact in ways that shape user engagement, trust, and behavioral outcomes, mirroring and extending their roles in traditional persuasive systems. For instance, chatbots and virtual assistants provide real-time feedback, reminders, and personalized conversations, which increase user motivation and engagement [24, 30]. Given these findings, it is logical to expect that when learners perceive the feedback and interaction from GenAI systems as motivating, they will also perceive it as supportive of their primary task, persuasive in its influence, and trustworthy. In this regard, dialogue support acts as a central persuasive mechanism that connects motivational feedback to users' broader perceptions of the persuasiveness of GenAI systems. Thus, this study hypothesizes that.

H3a: Dialogue support influences primary task support in GenAI systems.
H3b: Dialogue support influences the perceived persuasiveness of GenAI systems.
H3c: Dialogue support influences credibility support in GenAI systems.

2.4 Primary Task Support, Credibility Support, and Perceived Persuasiveness

Studies consistently show that primary task support and credibility support are among the strongest predictors of user's favorable impressions of a system and its influence on them [10, 14, 21]. In GenAI systems, primary task support is achieved through the adaptive generation of task-relevant content, problem-solving assistance, and real-time feedback. For instance, GenAI tools that provide personalized recommendations and streamlined workflows are often perceived as more persuasive [5].

Credibility is reinforced in Gen AI systems through articulate, contextually relevant, and verifiable responses, as well as professionalism in their design and tone. For example, when GenAI tools, such as ChatGPT or AI-based tutoring systems, provide clear justifications, cite sources, or communicate with a consistent tone and reasoning, users perceive them as more trustworthy and reliable [4, 6]. Although learners may not always readily discern whether the information provided by the AI is accurate, trust in the system's expertise makes users more open to its suggestions and more likely to be influenced by its recommendations [31]. Therefore, this study hypothesizes that,

H4: Primary task support influences the perceived persuasiveness of GenAI systems.
H5: Credibility support influences the perceived persuasiveness of GenAI systems.

Perceived persuasiveness reflects the extent to which users believe that a system can effectively influence their attitudes and behavior [9, 10]. It has been established as a significant predictor of the continuous use intention of both conventional and immersive persuasive systems [14, 21, 32]. This indicates that users are likely to use a system in the future if they develop an affective response to it through persuasive experiences. In educational contexts, the more persuasive learners find GenAI systems especially in terms of usefulness and satisfaction, the more likely they are to continue using them for learning [33]. Thus, this study hypothesizes that,

H6: Perceived persuasiveness influences learners' intention to continue using GenAI systems.

3 Materials and Methods

3.1 Data Collection Instruments

Quantitative data were collected electronically using Webropol using convenience sampling. The survey link was distributed to third-year Computer Science students enrolled in a Research Methods course. Participation was voluntary, but all questions were mandatory. The survey instrument was designed in English and divided into three sections.

To confirm participants familiarity with GenAI systems, the first section was a task that required them to use GenAI systems of their choice to identify a Computer Science or Information Technology research problem, review related literature less than five years old, propose a solution, and specify its alignment within the Design Science Research Contribution Framework. The second section measured the seven constructs with question items adopted from [8, 10] and rephrased for this study. Each construct was rated on a five-point Likert scale (1 = strongly disagree, 2 = disagree, 3 = neutral, 4 = agree, and 5 = strongly agree). The third section captured demographic data and ratings of participants' likelihood of using GenAI systems for nine academic tasks: understanding new concepts, summarizing academic articles/textbooks, conceptualizing research ideas, writing or drafting essays, writing code, writing/drafting code documentation, debugging or explaining code, preparing for exams/quizzes, and finding relevant research papers/sources. Each task was rated on a five-point Likert scale (1 = very unlikely, 2 = unlikely, 3 = neutral, 4 = likely, and 5 = very likely).

3.2 Participants Demographics

After one month of data collection, 446 responses were received. Respondents were predominantly males (77.90%), 98.43% were aged between 18 and 25 years, and the others were between 26 and 35 years. The frequency of GenAI systems use for academic/learning tasks was reported as daily (32.95%) several times per week (43.27%), occasionally (22.19%), and rarely (0.89%). The most frequently used tools for academic/learning tasks were ChatGPT (84.98%), Gemini AI (4.50%), others (8.70%),

Consensus AI (1.30%), and SciSpace (0.50%). The tools rated as the most useful for the assigned task were ChatGPT (67.71%), Consensus AI (15.70%), Others (10.50%), Gemini AI (4.70%), ChatPDF (1.10%), and SciSpace (0.20%). "Others" included Co-Pilot, DeepSeek, Claude AI, Perplexity AI, Notebook LLM, Grok, Poe, and Qwen.

Overall, respondents tended to view GenAI as useful for most tasks. "Very likely" ratings were most frequent for debugging/explaining code, while "likely" ratings dominated for understanding new tasks. Neutral ratings were highest for writing code, and "unlikely" and "very unlikely" ratings were highest for conceptualizing research ideas and understanding new tasks, respectively.

4 Data Analysis and Results

Partial least squares structural equation modeling (PLS-SEM) was used to evaluate the hypothesized paths relationships. PLS-SEM was chosen for its suitability for both theory confirmation and predictive modeling [34]. The PLS-SEM analysis involved a three-step procedure: assessment of the measurement model, assessment of the structural model, and multi-group analysis [35]. SmartPLS 4 [36] was used for the analyses.

4.1 Measurement Model Assessment

The measurement model was assessed using the threshold values for indicator loadings, internal consistency reliability, and convergent and discriminant validity as specified by [35, 37]. The indicator loadings exceeded the specified threshold of 0.708.

Internal consistency was assessed using Cronbach's alpha (CA) and composite reliability (rho_a and rho_c). All constructs showed reliability values between 0.703 and 0.938, indicating good consistency and no redundancy in the question items (Appendix). Convergent validity was confirmed through Average Variance Extracted (AVE) values, all of which exceeded the 0.500 threshold, indicating that each construct explained more than half of the variance in its indicators.

Discriminant validity was tested using the Heterotrait-Monotrait Ratio (HTMT) criterion [37]. All HTMT values were below the threshold of 0.850, except for dialogue support to primary task support (0.906). This indicates that while most constructs are empirically distinct from one another, there is a conceptual overlap between primary task support and dialogue support (see Appendix). Regardless, the bootstrapped HTMT confidence interval did not include 1.00. This indicates that discriminant validity was established for all construct pairs.

4.2 Structural Model Assessment

Using a bootstrapping procedure of 5,000 subsamples, the structural model was evaluated using standard criteria, including collinearity, path coefficients (β), effect sizes (f^2), variance explained (R^2), and predictive relevance (Q^2). All variance inflation factor values were below 3.00, indicating the absence of multicollinearity. Most hypothesized paths were statistically significant ($t > 1.96$, $p < 0.05$), except for the path from primary task support to perceived persuasiveness (H4). Effect sizes (f^2) were interpreted following Cohen's [38] criteria: strong ($f^2 \geq 0.35$: H3a), moderate ($f^2 \geq 0.15$: H1b, H1c, H2a, H3b), weak ($f^2 \geq 0.02$: H1a, H2b, H3c, H5, H6), and irrelevant ($f^2 < 0.02$: H4). The model demonstrated substantial explanatory power for primary task support ($R^2 \leq 0.75$), moderate power for credibility support, perceived persuasiveness, continuous use intention ($R^2 \leq 0.50$), and weak power for dialogue support ($R^2 \leq 0.25$). The results of the full path analysis are shown in Fig. 2.

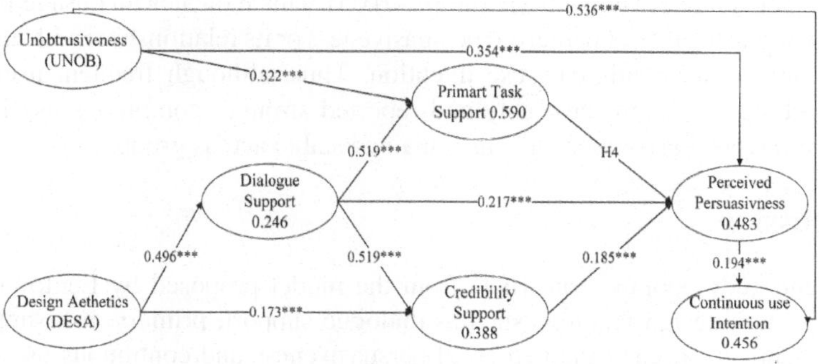

Fig. 2. Structural model full path analysis (***p < 0.001, ns – nonsignificant)

Overall, the model captured a meaningful portion of the variance in learners' perceived persuasiveness of GenAI systems in learning contexts. Primary task support did not significantly influence perceived persuasiveness (β = 0.057, p = 0.340, t = 0.954). This indicates that although GenAI systems may be perceived as useful, task-related efficiency does not enhance perceived persuasiveness. Instead, unobtrusiveness (β = 0.357, p < 0.001, t = 5.311), credibility support (β = 0.815, p = 0.002, t = 3.058), and dialogue support (β = 0.216, p = 0.001, t = 3.431) were significant predictors. In turn, unobtrusiveness (β = 0.536, p < 0.001, t = 9.719) and perceived persuasiveness (β = 0.194, p = 0.004, t = 2.879) significantly predicted continuous use intention. These findings suggest that credibility, computer-human dialogue support, and unobtrusiveness contribute to the perceived persuasiveness of GenAI systems. These perceptions translate into learners' intentions to continue using these tools.

4.3 Multigroup Analysis

Following the assessments of the measurement and structural model, a multi-group analysis (MGA) was conducted to examine the path differences between frequent and occasional users of GenAI systems. Frequent users were defined as those who used GenAI systems daily or several times a week (n = 340), whereas occasional users reported rare usage (n = 106). A permutation-based MGA was performed; it enables the comparison of structural path coefficients [39], and assessment of measurement invariance of composite models (MICOM) [40].

The MICOM results indicated compositional invariance for most constructs (permutation p > 0.05), except for design aesthetics (p = 0.009), indicating partial compositional invariance. Equality of means tests revealed significant differences between frequent and occasional users for unobtrusiveness, design aesthetics, dialogue support, primary task support, perceived persuasiveness, and continuous use intention ($p < 0.05$), with frequent users reporting higher mean values. No significant difference was observed for perceived credibility ($p = 0.051$). Equality of variances tests showed no significant differences across constructs (all $p > 0.05$), indicating comparable variability in responses between the two groups.

The MGA results showed no significant differences in structural path coefficients across frequent and occasional users (all $p > 0.05$). This indicates that usage frequency did not moderate the role of perceived persuasiveness or its relationships with antecedent system features and continuous use intention. Thus, although frequent users evaluated GenAI systems more favorably and reported stronger continuous use intention, the underlying persuasive mechanisms remained stable across groups.

5 Discussion

The present study adopted constructs from the model proposed by Lehto et al. [10] to examine how design features, such as dialogue support, primary task support, and credibility support, predict the perceived persuasiveness and continuous use intention of GenAI systems for learning tasks. The results validated most of the hypothesized relationships and refuted one.

Unobtrusiveness significantly influenced continuous use intention, perceived persuasiveness, and primary task support in GenAI systems. These findings are supported by [8, 10, 29]. Thus, it can be concluded that when learners perceive that a persuasive system, including GenAI systems, integrates more naturally into their learning behavior without cognitive interruption (e.g., by providing on-demand suggestions), they will be more inclined to keep using it, accept the support it provides for performing primary tasks, and ultimately have favorable impressions of the influence of the system and its influence on them.

Similarly, the design aesthetics of GenAI systems influenced computer-human dialogue support and credibility support in GenAI systems. This resonates with prior observations that an attractive, visually appealing interface increases learners trust in the system and its outputs and boosts their motivation to continue performing the primary task based on the system's feedback [8]. In this study, design aesthetics encompass visual interface design and interactive qualities, such as coherent phrasing, balanced tone, and conversational fluency. They all contribute to ethos by conveying credibility and authority that make users more receptive to the content.

The findings of this study validated the hypotheses that dialogue support influences primary task support, perceived persuasiveness, and credibility support in GenAI systems. These findings highlight the synergistic role of dialogue support. When GenAI systems provide interactive dialogue, such as praise or suggestions, learners not only feel more supported in their primary task, but they also perceive the system as more credible and persuasive. This dovetails with findings across domains: interactive features such as real-time feedback and personalized suggestions can simultaneously motivate users to pursue their goals and enhance their perceptions of system credibility and persuasiveness [10, 14, 21]. In essence, by providing computer-human dialogue support, learners will most likely perceive GenAI systems as persuasive.

Contrary to most persuasion contexts, primary task support did not significantly influence the perceived persuasiveness of the GenAI systems. Previous studies [10, 14, 21] have shown that breaking down complex user tasks into smaller, more manageable subtasks reliably improves users favorable impressions of conventional and immersive persuasive systems. However, in the context of GenAI systems, such support did not translate into higher perceptions of persuasiveness. While this finding aligns with [32], the contrary results compared to existing predominant evidence may be explained by how learners perceive both the source and intent of the support. Given that GenAI systems sometimes produce inaccurate results or require users to verify its outputs, learners may be wary of over-reliance [7, 11], and therefore have weak affective responses towards the influence of the system on them. Moreover, learners often tend to undervalue advice or guidance from artificial agents (algorithmic discounting) [28]. Even when GenAI systems provide accurate and useful task support, learners may view them as neutral information tools rather than persuasive systems. For example, Dogaru et al. [7] found that students often described ChatGPT as an efficient information source rather than a motivational tool. Similarly, Fan et al. [11] showed that learners who received different forms of learning support exhibited no differences in post-task intrinsic motivation. This implies that while learners acknowledge the cognitive assistance from Gen AI systems, they may not attribute social or affective influence to it. In addition, although GenAI systems can effectively facilitate task performance, their non-human source and perceived neutrality may limit the extent to which such support enhances perceived persuasiveness.

The non-significant role of primary task support on perceived persuasiveness also has implications for practice. Unlike dedicated educational persuasive systems, general-purpose GenAI tools such as ChatGPT rarely make their task-support mechanisms explicit or structured. In persuasive system design, primary task support encompasses features that are most often deliberately engineered to help users complete their main tasks by breaking them into manageable steps, guiding them through a sequence, adapting to their needs, allowing them to track their progress, or enabling them to practice a task safely. In contrast, GenAI systems typically provide on-demand conversational assistance that is user-initiated rather than system-driven. While they can perform functions resembling reduction (for example, generating step-by-step explanations), tailoring, or simulation when prompted, these forms of task support emerge implicitly through dialogue rather than as part of an explicitly designed pedagogical sequence. Therefore, their guidance tends to be contextually reactive, shaped by the user's prompts rather than by a model of the learner's progress. Consequently, rather than inquiring how the system provides support, researchers should inquire whether learners think that anything is done by the system to provide task support [12]. Regardless of the reason, this non-significant finding is theoretically interesting, because it suggests that helping learners to perform and complete their learning tasks is not enough to make them perceive GenAI tools as persuasive. Future studies should probe whether this is due to the nature of GenAI output quality, user skepticism, or perhaps the ceiling effect of already high task support expectations.

Credibility support influenced the perceived persuasiveness of GenAI systems. This corroborates the findings of both conventional persuasive systems [21] and GenAI systems [41]. Thus, learners' favorable impressions of GenAI systems are to some extent dependent on the extent of their trust and believability of the system. However, it is important to note that among the direct predictors of perceived persuasiveness, unobtrusiveness had the strongest effect size, followed by credibility support and dialogue support. Collectively, these constructs explained 48% of the variance in the perceived persuasiveness of GenAI systems, while 47% of the variance in continuous use intention was explained by both perceived persuasiveness and unobtrusiveness (see Fig. 2).

The findings of this study have several important implications for the design of educational GenAI systems and their use in educational/learning contexts. Firstly, given the perceived persuasiveness of these systems as demonstrated in this study, developers of GenAI systems for learning should remodel and intentionally prioritize features that promote the perceived persuasiveness of these systems. This entails ensuring that these systems are perceived as unobtrusive, credible, and motivating. The findings of this study suggest that seemingly small design choices aimed at transparency, user autonomy, unobtrusiveness, feedback, and reliability may substantially increase learners' affective responses to the influence of these systems and, ultimately, their intention to continue using them. Since credibility support had a direct impact on perceived persuasiveness, educators should treat trust-building measures as fundamental, not optional, when introducing GenAI systems into learning environments. This aligns with recent calls for ethical AI design in education which emphasize that systems should be transparent, fair, and accountable to avoid eroding user trust. Findings from this study reinforce that ethical design is not just a moral imperative but also a functional design feature.

6 Conclusion

GenAI systems are rapidly gaining traction in higher education. This is driven by their ability to provide personalized learning support, constructive feedback, trustworthy problem-solving experiences, professional user interface design, and collaborative interactions that transcend traditional classroom boundaries. This study contributes to the growing discourse on the perceived persuasiveness of GenAI in educational contexts. Drawing on the Persuasive Systems Design (PSD) model, it conceptually aligned key persuasive design features, such as primary task support, dialogue support, credibility, unobtrusiveness, and design aesthetics, with the inherent capabilities of GenAI systems. This study provides empirical insights into how persuasive design features influence learners' perceptions of persuasiveness and their intention to continuously use GenAI systems for learning tasks.

However, it also has limitations that open avenues for future research. First, the sample was drawn from a specific student population (third-year university students in the Department of Computer Science) who were already familiar with GenAI tools. In addition, over 70% of the participants were male. These characteristics may limit the generalizability of the findings to broader and more diverse populations. The persuasive dynamics may differ for younger learners, postgraduate students, and cultures with different attitudes toward AI. Secondly, the adopted research model investigated users of a specific system, whereas this study investigated a collection of GenAI systems. Future studies should replicate this model in other populations and within a specific GenAI system to verify which findings are universally applicable to the general population.

Ultimately, the findings enrich the existing literature by explaining how and to what extent users perceive GenAI systems as persuasive. By linking existing models from persuasive systems research with emerging GenAI-driven learning context, the results affirm that traditional persuasive system features remain applicable and valuable in AI-mediated educational settings.

Disclosure of Interests. The authors have no competing interests to declare that are relevant to the content of this article.

Appendix: Measurement Model Metrics

	CRED	DESA	DIAL	INTE	PEPE	PRIM	UNOB
CRED							
DESA	0.495						
DIAL	0.721	0.591					
INTE	0.658	0.485	0.665				
PEPE	0.647	0.594	0.756	0.656			
PRIM	0.642	0.510	0.906	0.740	0.684		
UNOB	0.622	0.627	0.781	0.775	0.758	0.809	
AVE	0.626	0.789	0.635	0.760	0.672	0.706	0.678
CA	0.851	0.866	0.809	0.842	0.760	0.789	0.841
rho_a	0.853	0.871	0.813	0.851	0.800	0.798	0.845
rho_c	0.893	0.918	0.874	0.905	0.860	0.878	0.894

CA = Cronbach's alpha, rho_a and rho_c = composite reliability, AVE = Average variance extracted

References

1. Nguyen, A., Ngo, H.N., Hong, Y., et al.: Ethical principles for artificial intelligence in education. Educ. Inf. Technol. (Dordr.) **28**, 4221–4241 (2023). https://doi.org/10.1007/S10639-022-11316-W/TABLES/1
2. Kashive, N., Powale, L., Kashive, K.: Understanding user perception toward artificial intelligence (AI) enabled e-learning. Int. J. Inf. Learn. Technol. **38**, 1–19 (2020). https://doi.org/10.1108/IJILT-05-2020-0090
3. Joksimovic, S., Ifenthaler, D., Marrone, R., et al.: Opportunities of artificial intelligence for supporting complex problem-solving: Findings from a scoping review. Comput. Educ.: Artif. Intell. **4**, 100138 (2023). https://doi.org/10.1016/J.CAEAI.2023.100138

4. Karinshak, E., Liu, S.X., Park, J.S., Hancock, J.T.: Working with AI to persuade: examining a large language model's ability to generate pro-vaccination messages. Proc. ACM Hum. Comput. Interact. **7** (2023). https://doi.org/10.1145/3579592. CTYPE:STRING:JOURNAL
5. Salvi, F., Horta Ribeiro, M., Gallotti, R., West, R.: On the conversational persuasiveness of GPT-4. Nat. Hum. Behav. **9**(8), 1645–1653 (2025). https://doi.org/10.1038/s41562-025-02194-6
6. Kim, T., Kim, M.J., Promsivapallop, P.: Investigating the influence of generative AI's credibility and utility on travel consumer behaviour and recommendations through the lens of personal innovativeness. Curr. Issue Tour. **28**, 2220–2224 (2025). https://doi.org/10.1080/13683500.2024.2364764. WEBSITE:WEBSITE:TFOPB;PAGEGROUP:STRING:PUBLICATION
7. Dogaru, M., Pisică, O., Popa, C.-Ş., et al.: The perceived impact of artificial intelligence on academic learning. Front. Artif. Intell. **8**, 1611183 (2025). https://doi.org/10.3389/FRAI.2025.1611183/BIBTEX
8. Wiafe, I., Ekpezu, A.O., Gyamera, G.O., et al.: Learning satisfaction in virtual reality: the role of persuasive design Int. J. Hum. Comput. Interact. (2024). https://doi.org/10.1080/10447318.2024.2440205
9. Oinas-Kukkonen, H., Harjumaa, M.: Persuasive systems design: key issues, process model, and system features. Commun. Assoc. Inf. Syst. **24**, 485–500 (2009). https://doi.org/10.17705/1cais.02428
10. Lehto, T., Oinas-Kukkonen, H., Drozd, F.: Factors affecting perceived persuasiveness of a behavior change support system. In: International Conference on Information Systems, ICIS 2012, vol. 3, pp. 1926–1939 (2012)
11. Fan, Y., Tang, L., Le, H., et al.: Beware of metacognitive laziness: effects of generative artificial intelligence on learning motivation, processes, and performance. Br. J. Edu. Technol. **56**, 489–530 (2025). https://doi.org/10.1111/BJET.13544. PAGE:STRING:ARTICLE/CHAPTER
12. De, J.N.B., Kip, H., Kelders, S.M.: Evaluation of the perceived persuasiveness questionnaire: user-centered card-sort study. J. Med. Internet Res. **22**, e20404 (2020). https://doi.org/10.2196/20404
13. de Oliveira, R.S.C., Nabwire, S., Merikallio, H., et al.: Behind the software: the impact of unobtrusiveness, goal setting and persuasive features on BMI. Int. J. Med. Inform. **196** (2025). https://doi.org/10.1016/j.ijmedinf.2025.105795
14. Nabwire, S., de Oliveira, R., Merikallio, H., et al.: Cognitive consistency as a facilitator of perceived persuasiveness and continuance intention in digital weight management. In: Forty-Sixth International Conference on Information Systems, Nashville, Tennessee, USA 2025, Nashvile, pp. 1–17 (2025)
15. Yan, L., Greiff, S., Teuber, Z., Gašević, D.: Promises and challenges of generative artificial intelligence for human learning. Nat. Hum. Behav. **8**, 1839–1850 (2024). https://doi.org/10.1038/S41562-024-02004-5. SUBJMETA
16. Ruiz-Rojas, L.I., Salvador-Ullauri, L., Acosta-Vargas, P.: Collaborative working and critical thinking: adoption of generative artificial intelligence tools in higher education. Sustainability **16**, 5367 (2024). https://doi.org/10.3390/SU16135367
17. Singh, S.U., Namin, A.S.: The influence of persuasive techniques on large language models: a scenario-based study. Comput. Hum. Behav.: Artif. Hum. **6**, 100197 (2025). https://doi.org/10.1016/J.CHBAH.2025.100197
18. Ahmadianmanzary, M., Ouhbi, S.: Exploring the influence of user interface on user trust in generative AI, 708–714 (2025). https://doi.org/10.5220/0013432700003928
19. Sharples, M.: Towards social generative AI for education: theory, practices and ethics. Learn.: Res. Pract. **9**, 159–167 (2023). https://doi.org/10.1080/23735082.2023.2261131
20. Kishore, S., Hong, Y., Nguyen, A., Qutab, S.: Should ChatGPT be banned at schools? Organizing visions for generative Artificial Intelligence (AI) in education. In: ICIS 2023 Proceedings, vol. 5, pp 1–17. AIS Electronic Library (AISeL), Hyderabad (2023)

21. Ekpezu, A.O., Wiafe, I., Nutrokpor, C., Oinas-kukkonen, H.: Examining continuance intention to exercise in a virtual reality environment. In: Proceedings of the 57th Hawaii International Conference on System Sciences, pp. 3527–3536 (2024)
22. Zhang, Y., Gosline, R.: Human favoritism, not AI aversion: people's perceptions (and bias) toward generative AI, human experts, and human–GAI collaboration in persuasive content generation. Judgm. Decis. Mak. **18** (2023). https://doi.org/10.1017/JDM.2023.37
23. Kong, S.C., Yang, Y.: A human-centered learning and teaching framework using generative artificial intelligence for self-regulated learning development through domain knowledge learning in K-12 settings. IEEE Trans. Learn. Technol. **17**, 1588–1599 (2024). https://doi.org/10.1109/TLT.2024.3392830
24. Hyun Baek, T., Kim, M.: Is ChatGPT scary good? How user motivations affect creepiness and trust in generative artificial intelligence. Telematics Inform. **83**, 102030 (2023). https://doi.org/10.1016/J.TELE.2023.102030
25. Kim, J.S., Kim, M., Baek, T.H.: Enhancing user experience with a generative AI chatbot. Int. J. Hum. Comput. Interact. **41**, 651–663 (2025). https://doi.org/10.1080/10447318.2024.2311971
26. Mohd Johari, N.F., Mohamad Ali, N., Mhd Salim, M.H., Abdullah, N.A.: Factors driving the use of mobile health app: insights from a survey. Mhealth **11** (2025). https://doi.org/10.21037/MHEALTH-24-44/COIF
27. Camilleri, M.A.: Factors affecting performance expectancy and intentions to use ChatGPT: using SmartPLS to advance an information technology acceptance framework. Technol. Forecast. Soc. Change **201**, 123247 (2024). https://doi.org/10.1016/J.TECHFORE.2024.123247
28. Le, H., Shen, Y., Li, Z., et al.: Breaking human dominance: investigating learners' preferences for learning feedback from generative AI and human tutors. Br. J. Edu. Technol. **56**, 1758–1783 (2025). https://doi.org/10.1111/BJET.13614;ISSUE:ISSUE:DOI
29. Wiafe, I., Koranteng, F.N., Kastriku, F.A., Gyamera, G.O.: Assessing the impact of persuasive features on user's intention to continuous use: the case of academic social networking sites. Behav. Inf. Technol. **41**, 712–730 (2022). https://doi.org/10.1080/0144929X.2020.1832146
30. Tiwari, A., Khandwe, A., Saha, S., et al.: Towards personalized persuasive dialogue generation for adversarial task oriented dialogue setting. Expert Syst. Appl. **213**, 118775 (2023). https://doi.org/10.1016/J.ESWA.2022.118775
31. Pareek, S., van Berkel, N., Velloso, E., Goncalves, J.: Effect of explanation conceptualisations on trust in AI-assisted credibility assessment. Proc. ACM Hum. Comput. Interact. **8** (2024). https://doi.org/10.1145/3686922
32. Shevchuk, N., Degirmenci, K., Oinas-Kukkonen, H.: Adoption of gamified persuasive systems to encourage sustainable behaviors: interplay between perceived persuasiveness and cognitive absorption. In: 40th International Conference on Information Systems, ICIS 2019, pp. 1–17 (2019)
33. Shata, A., Hartley, K.: Artificial intelligence and communication technologies in academia: faculty perceptions and the adoption of generative AI. Int. J. Educ. Technol. High. Educ. **22**(1), 1–22 (2025). https://doi.org/10.1186/S41239-025-00511-7
34. Usakli, A., Rasoolimanesh, S.M.: Which SEM to use and what to report? A comparison of CB-SEM and PLS-SEM. In: Cutting Edge Research Methods in Hospitality and Tourism, pp 5–28. Emerald Group Publishing Ltd. (2023)
35. Hair, J.F., Hult, G.T., Ringle, C.M., et al.: Partial Least Squares Structural Equation Modeling (PLS-SEM) Using R. Springer Nature, London (2022)
36. Ringle, C.M., Wende, S., Becker, J.-M.: SmartPLS 4 (2024)
37. Henseler, J., Ringle, C.M., Sarstedt, M.: A new criterion for assessing discriminant validity in variance-based structural equation modeling. J. Acad. Mark. Sci. **43**, 115–135 (2015). https://doi.org/10.1007/s11747-014-0403-8

38. Cohen, J.: Statistical Power Analysis for the Behavioral Sciences, 2nd edn. Routledge, New York (1988)
39. Hair, J.F., Sarstedt, M., Ringle, C.M., Gudergan, S.: Advanced issues in partial least squares structural equation modeling, p. 236 (2024)
40. Henseler, J., Ringle, C.M., Sarstedt, M.: Testing measurement invariance of composites using partial least squares. Int. Mark. Rev. **33**, 405–431 (2016). https://doi.org/10.1108/IMR-09-2014-0304
41. Choudhury, A., Shamszare, H.: Investigating the impact of user trust on the adoption and use of ChatGPT: survey analysis. J. Med. Internet Res. **25**, e47184 (2023). https://doi.org/10.2196/47184

Voices of Influence: Investigating the Interplay of Gender, Age, and Content Valence in the Context of Smart Voice Assistants

Ran Huang[1], Minjeong Kim[1(✉)], Sabid Bin Habib Pias[1], Apu Kapadia[1], and Donald Williamson[2]

[1] Indiana University, Bloomington, IN 47405, USA
kim2017@iu.edu
[2] The Ohio State University, Columbus, OH 43210, USA

Abstract. This study draws on the stereotype content model to examine how consumers process smart voice assistant (SVA) recommendations that are disseminated through voices. Particularly, this study investigates how two voice characteristics (gender, age) and one message characteristic (content valence) work together to influence consumers' perceptions of voice attractiveness and persuasiveness. The mediating role of trustworthiness of SVA in the relationship between voice perceptions and usage intention is also explored. SVA voices varying by gender and age were developed using Microsoft Speech Studio. Conducting three studies (two pretests and one main test), we found a significant three-way interaction of gender, age, and content valence on voice attractiveness, but not on voice persuasiveness. Pairwise comparison results indicated that, in the context of positive reviews through SVAs, a younger female voice is more attractive and persuasive than a younger male voice; similarly, an older male voice is more attractive and persuasive, in relation to an older female voice. However, the interactive effect of gender and age was not significant in the context of negative reviews. Lastly, this study demonstrated that trustworthiness of SVA mediates the effects of attractiveness and persuasiveness on usage intention. This research advances the emerging literature on smart voice assistants by untangling the complexity of voice-based communication.

Keywords: Smart Voice Assistant · Voice · Stereotypes · Attractiveness · Persuasiveness · Trustworthiness

1 Introduction

Smart voice assistants (SVAs) are voice-enabled artificial intelligence (AI) systems with digital interfaces that mimic intelligent human conversations. SVAs have been widely used by consumers for daily decision-making, in various domains ranging from mobile applications (e.g., Apple's Siri) to home devices (e.g., Amazon's Alexa), and to vehicles. The worldwide value of voice-assistant e-commerce transactions was expected to reach 20 billion U.S. dollars by 2023 [52].

E. Vlahu-Gjorgievska et al. (Eds.): PERSUASIVE 2026, CCIS 2896, pp. 63–78, 2027.
https://doi.org/10.1007/978-3-032-27235-5_5

As a new recommendation system for consumers, SVAs are more effective than text-based recommendations such as online reviews in influencing consumers' decision-making [16] because SVAs have a greater capacity to engage consumers through natural conversations than other digital technologies do. Specifically, Flavián et al. [16] revealed that voice recommendations via SVAs promoted consumers' perceived credibility and usefulness of the recommendations to a greater extent than online reviews do. This has motivated marketers to explore new and innovative ways to increase usage of SVAs.

The potent influence of SVAs on consumer behavior has also sparked research interest. Researchers have found that when AI systems exhibit greater human-likeness, a social categorization process is activated that drives consumer behavior [28]. Many studies focusing on consumer experiences with SVAs have suggested that interactions with SVAs could be transformed into consumer love, characterized as passion, intimacy, and commitment [21, 49] and trust [22], which further impacts consumer engagement and adherence to purchase recommendations [5].

Another stream of research investigated the effect of voice. Poushneh [46] suggested that an SVA's voice influences consumer perceptions of SVA personality and further impacts consumers' satisfaction with and willingness to continue using SVAs. Extant research demonstrates that human-like qualities in SVAs lead consumers to anthropomorphize SVAs [10] and trigger stereotypical responses [47]. For example, in their study on accent as a voice characteristic, Sattarapu et al. [50] found that SVAs' voices that matched consumers' accents induced positive emotional responses and eliminated negative emotional responses. While various voice characteristics may contribute to the human-likeness of SVAs, empirical research on SVAs' voice characteristics from user perspectives remains underexplored. Responding to the call by Chahal and Mahajan [11] for further empirical research on the impact of voice customization options on consumer behavior, this study examines gender and age as two critical voice characteristics.

Drawing on the stereotype content model (SCM) [14] as an overarching theory, we investigate gender and age as two key voice characteristics and content valence as an information cue, examining their effects on SVAs' persuasion mechanism. In particular, this research examines content valence as a boundary condition that may moderate the effects of voice characteristics on consumer responses. As previous research has indicated, content valence has a persuasive impact on perceived source credibility and purchase intention [55]. Other empirical evidence has demonstrated that when listening to news stories, consumers are more likely to attend to details with negative content [8]. Likewise, consumers likely process positive and negative content differently in the context of SVA recommendations. While the persuasive effect of content valence may vary depending on SVAs' voice characteristics, little research has examined how these factors interact. We posit that consumers' responses to an SVA's voice characteristics may differ as a function of the valence of review content. To our knowledge, this is the first study to investigate the interplay among gender, age, and content valence in the context of SVAs.

We further propose attractiveness and persuasiveness as two underlying constructs that contribute to the effectiveness of SVA voices. According to source credibility theory [56], the efficacy of a communication source can be attributed to its perceived attractiveness. Similarly, the effectiveness of SVA voices can be attributed to the perceived attractiveness of the voices. Additionally, persuasiveness reflects how consumers interpret persuasive attempts embedded in voice-based communication [26] and underlies the mechanism that makes SVAs more effective.

The current research extends the emerging body of research on the role of SVAs in consumer decision-making by examining the impacts of voice characteristics and message content characteristic. Specifically, this research examines how two voice characteristics (gender and age) and one message characteristic (content valence) interact to impact consumers' perceptions of voice attractiveness and persuasiveness, thereby influencing their perceived trustworthiness of SVAs and usage intention. The findings will offer not only theoretical insights to enhance understanding of human-SVA interactions, but also practical insights to help businesses develop effective approaches for delivering marketing messages using SVAs.

2 Theoretical Background and Hypotheses

2.1 Effectiveness of Smart Voice Assistant (SVA) Recommendations

Extant literature has examined various factors that determine the effectiveness of SVA recommendations. Scholars identified important design, function, and social features such as interactivity, contextual relevance, social presence, and compatibility of SVAs. These features were found to increase consumers' brand recognition and awareness via SVAs [41] and perceived value of [29] and satisfactions [5] with SVA recommendations. Other research focused on the impact of anthropomorphism on SVA recommendations. Anthropomorphic qualities embedded in SVAs, including voice, conversation, and the performance of human-like roles, were found to help consumers build trust in these technologies by fostering a sense of social presence [31] and parasocial attractiveness [58]. By investigating persuasion mechanisms, scholars found that consumers had positive product attitudes when SVAs provided personalized (vs. non-personalized) recommendations based on individuals' preferences or acted as friends (vs. secretaries) [48]. Among various SVA characteristics contributing to human-likeness, voice has been observed to exert a more profound impact on consumers [10].

Despite the recent proliferation of literature related to SVA recommendations, empirical research focusing on the role of voice in SVA's persuasion mechanisms remains limited and has produced mixed results. For instance, Flavián et al. [16] compared voice-based and text-based recommendations and found that voice is more effective at increasing consumers' perceptions of usefulness and credibility of recommendations than text. Further, Ischen et al. [26] found that while voice as a communication modality can increase mental efforts and thus activate persuasion knowledge, text-based interaction is more effective in enhancing perceptions of human-likeness. However, the implications of human-likeness are not always straightforward. Although it is generally considered positive, the effects of human versus AI voice are more nuanced. In the context of media, Gong [17] showed that human voice was more effective than AI voice because human voice elicited greater cognitive effects as well as cognitive-emotional feedback from listeners than AI-generated voice. Conversely, Im et al. [25] demonstrated that consumers preferred SVAs with synthetic voices over human voices when they were engaged in functional tasks using SVAs. When using SVAs for social tasks, consumers showed no voice preferences [25]. These mixed results not only reveal insights into the complexity of SVA design but also reveal a knowledge gap in boundary conditions for SVA persuasion, which warrants further investigation of voice-based recommendations.

To address this research gap, our study focuses on two voice characteristics-gender and age-and one message characteristic: content valence. While delivering messages, SVAs transmit multiple cues, including vocal cues (e.g., tone, pitch) and informational cues (e.g., information about a product). As two important voice characteristics of SVAs, gender and age may trigger consumers to apply pre-existing stereotypes to SVAs, which further influences consumers' perceptions by weakening or strengthening individuals' appraisal of the capabilities of SVAs [39, 44]. While these voice characteristics have begun to attract attention in human-computer interaction research (e.g., [44, 47]), few studies have been conducted in the consumer research domain. For instance, Nagar [32] found that gendered voices of SVAs play different roles in customer service such that a female voice increases customer satisfaction and intention to use, compared to a male voice. However, when companies use SVAs to address negative service experiences, a male voice is more likely to increase customer satisfaction than a female voice. In investigating the interaction of gender and age in voice, Watkins and Pak (2021) revealed that older users in a healthcare setting perceived a younger female voice to be less trustworthy than other voice types (i.e., older female voice and younger and older male voices) when reliability in SVAs (e.g., checking blood sugar levels) was low. Given this complexity, voice attributes may exert different influences in daily consumer experience, such as providing product recommendations via SVAs, which are worthy of further exploration. Furthermore, as an information cue, content valence has been seldom addressed in the SVA context. Thus, we aim to examine the effectiveness of SVA recommendations by investigating the interplay of gender, age, and content valence.

2.2 Stereotypes in the Context of SVAs

The computers are social actors (CASA) theory explains the social categorization process through which consumers infer SVAs' personalities based on SVAs' voice qualities, speech patterns, vocabularies, and other (para)linguistic cues and respond to them accordingly [33]. During this process, consumers attribute social cognition-mental representations of social patterns and norms-to SVAs. As a key component of social cognition, stereotypes have been applied to human-machine interactions to understand how consumers infer specific features of AI and categorize these technologies as members of a social group. For example, Nickel and Meyer (2025) demonstrated that visual cues (e.g., appearance) of conversational agents can reinforce consumers' gender-related stereotypical responses toward these machines: consumers perceive female conversational agents to be more sociable than male AI agents.

According to the stereotype content model (SCM) [14], two fundamental dimensions of social cognitions are identified as perceived competence and warmth. These two dimensions play an essential role in forming first impressions of others during human-to-human interactions [13]. Competence refers to perceptions of capability, efficiency, and intelligence of others [2], while warmth refers to perceived traits of caring and sociability [2] and social desirability of others [62]. Perceptions of competence and warmth are significantly influenced by gender stereotypes, which represent individuals' generalized attitudes toward men and women [20]. Women are perceived to be warmer, with characteristics of empathy and morality [9], while men are viewed as more competent, with characteristics of strength and dominance [3]. The SCM has been applied to various settings including branding [27] and retail services [37]. Researchers suggest that consumers perceive brands similarly to how they perceive other individuals, such that brand stereotypes in terms of competence and warmth evoke emotions and drive behavioral responses [27]. In online service environments, situational cues such as high ambient temperature increase perceived warmth of the service provider, thereby promoting purchase intention [37].

Likewise, previous studies have employed the SCM to illustrate how consumers associate AI with personality traits, which in turn impact their perceptions and behavioral intentions. According to Nass et al. [34], computers with masculine voices are considered to have dominant traits compared to those with feminine voices. Consistent with the SCM, Ahn et al. [4] found that female AI agents are perceived as warmer, whereas male AI agents are perceived as more competent. Consequently, recommendations for utilitarian products made by male AI agents are more effective, generating more positive attitudes. In contrast, recommendations for hedonic products made by female AI agents are considered more effective. Gender stereotypes may be evoked when consumers interact with SVAs that have voice cues signaling gender.

Other characteristics such as age in SVA voices (e.g., an 'older' or 'younger' voice) can also elicit consumers' stereotypical responses. While gender stereotypes have been well studied, research on age stereotypes in the context of SVAs is limited. One study by Yucel and Rizvanoglu [61] showed that SVAs with young voices are perceived to be "dynamic" and "enthusiastic," whereas those with mature voices are described as "slow." Such age stereotypes are also applied to anthropomorphized robots, with consumers showing higher trust in younger robots than older ones in competitive cognitive tasks [39]. This aligns with the SCM, which suggests that older people are perceived as having lower competence [14]. Nevertheless, consumers may exhibit both age- and gender-based stereotypical perceptions when interacting with SVAs, and the interaction between these two stereotypes may lead to more complex outcomes. For example, when interacting with low-reliability SVAs, consumers perceive those with a younger female voice as less trustworthy [57]. Other researchers suggested that middle-age male voices are perceived as knowledgeable, whereas young female voices are perceived as appealing and soothing [44]. Expanding these interactive effects of SVA age and gender to the context of SVA recommendations, this study posits that these interactions vary depending on the valence of messages disseminated through SVAs, as content valence may impose different levels of cognitive load [38].

2.3 Interplay of Gender, Age, and Valence on Attractiveness and Persuasiveness

This study proposes two underlying mechanisms-attractiveness and persuasiveness of SVA voices-which explain the effectiveness of SVA recommendations. Attractiveness refers to the degree to which consumers admire SVA voices [18]. Prior research has addressed individuals' physical attractiveness, which reflects consumers' affection for celebrities due to physical cues such as beauty, sexiness, and elegance [6]. Extending this concept to vocal attractiveness, researchers have found that voice attractiveness is associated with favorable personality impressions based on vocal characteristics [63]. Persuasiveness refers to how effectively an SVA voice communicates the strengths or benefits of a message [48]. Most studies have focused on the persuasiveness of textual messages. For instance, scholars have argued that when a product recommendation aligns with a consumer's preferences, the consumer is more likely to perceive the argument as strong, leading to higher perceived persuasiveness [23]. Likewise, SVA voices that match consumers' stereotypical perceptions may enhance consumers' perceived persuasiveness of voices.

It is posited that the interactive effects of age and gender stereotypes on attractiveness and persuasiveness depend on content valence. According to Ahn et al. [4], female voices are perceived to be friendly and sincere, whereas male voices are perceived to be competent and intelligent. Furthermore, gendered and aged SVA voices may have different influences on consumers' perceived favorableness and efficacy through attractiveness and persuasiveness, respectively. For example, when SVAs use male voices with lower pitches (suggesting older age) to perform professional work tasks, consumers' perceptions of SVA persuasiveness increase [51]. Additionally, content valence may influence the interaction of gender and age on consumers' perceptions because positive and negative messages activate different levels of cognitive load. Drawing from the elaboration likelihood model (ELM) [42], Ozanne et al. (2019) revealed that negative messages involve deeper thinking and thus demand higher cognitive load, whereas positive messages involve shallower processing with lower cognitive load. They further demonstrated that when consumers are exposed to positive reviews that demand less thinking, consumers tend to use heuristic cues such as the attractive appearance of the reviewer to process information. In the context of SVAs, different levels of cognitive load may enable consumers to respond to paralinguistic cues embedded in voices differently. When consumers listen to positive content that involves less cognitive engagement, they may rely on heuristic cues such as SVA voice for information processing and be more susceptible to stereotypes triggered by voice characteristics. Conversely, when consumers are exposed to negative messages that require more deliberate processing, they are more likely to engage in content analysis and less likely to be influenced by voice characteristics. Therefore, consumers' stereotypical responses triggered by SVA voices, as well as the effectiveness of those voices, may vary depending on valence of content. Thus, the hypothesis is proposed.

H1: There is a three-way interaction among gender, age, and content valence on (H1a) attractiveness and (H1b) persuasiveness.

2.4 The Mediating Role of Trustworthiness

Trustworthiness refers to the degree to which consumers trust SVAs in making their decisions [12]. Previous research has identified trust as an important indicator of the parasocial relationship between consumers and SVAs. Both functional (e.g., ease of use) and social elements (e.g., social presence, social cognition) of SVAs contribute to increased trust [45]. Other scholars have examined smart capabilities of SVAs as sources of trustworthiness, including functional, emotional, and social benefits of SVAs [22]. However, little is known about whether SVA voices can evoke perceptions of trustworthiness in devices. It is plausible that attractiveness and persuasiveness of AI voices manifesting the human-like qualities of SVAs could lead consumers to perceive the devices as trustworthy [45]. Furthermore, trustworthiness is found to affect consumers' behavioral responses in various contexts, such as web design [30] and SVAs [45]. In addition, trustworthiness of SVAs is found to mediate the relationship between task performance and attitudinal responses [53] and between smart features and behavioral intentions [22]. Therefore, the following hypothesis is proposed.

H2: Trustworthiness mediates the effects of (H2a) attractiveness and (H2b) persuasiveness on usage intention (Fig. 1).

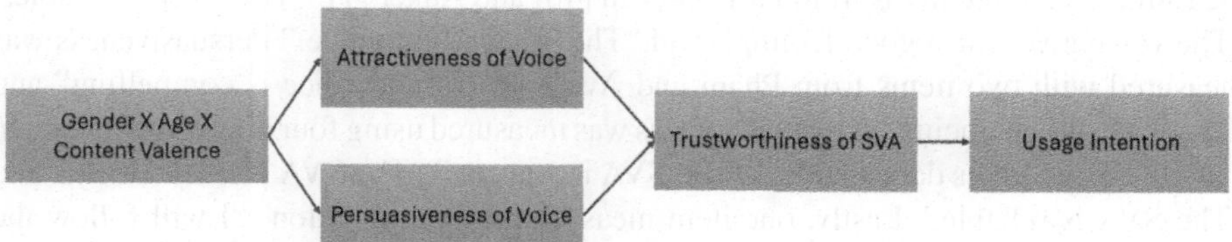

Fig. 1. Research Framework

3 Pretests

We conducted two pretests to generate and validate stimuli. Pretest 1 used consumer reviews from Amazon for gender-neutral product categories (Home and Kitchen, Office Supplies, Bags and Luggage). Following Waller et al. [54], reviews contained 26–33 words with 12–16 s audio clips. Microsoft Speech Studio was used to generate voices varying by gender and age (younger: 20–30 years; older: 40–50 years). Voice pitch and speech rate were adjusted following Winkler [59] to differentiate age groups, and clips were normalized in Audacity.

Pretest 2 employed a 2 (gender: female vs. male) X 2 (age: younger vs. older) x 2 (content valence: positive vs. negative) between-subjects design. Seventy participants from Prolific heard 14 audio clips (12 experimental, 2 attention checks) across six product categories. After excluding two participants who failed attention checks, 68 responses ($M_{age} = 35.7$, 51.5% male) were analyzed. Participants identified voice age (younger: 20–30 years; older: 40–50 years) [7] and rated review valence (1 = strongly negative; 7 = strongly positive) [60]. Crosstab analysis confirmed successful age manipulation: 75% correctly identified younger voices and 72% identified older voices ($\chi^2 = 15.84$, $p < .001$). ANOVA confirmed valence manipulation: positive reviews were rated more positively than negative reviews ($M_{\text{positive}} = 5.18$ vs. $M_{\text{negative}} = 3.59$, $F = 36.67$, $p < .001$).

4 Main Test

4.1 Methods and Procedure

The main study aimed to test the proposed research framework. An online experiment was conducted using a 2 (gender: female vs. male) × 2 (age: younger vs. older) × 2 (content valence: positive vs. negative) between-subjects design. Similar with the pilot test, a scenario was given to ask participants to imagine themselves using an SVA for purchase decision making. A total of 350 participants were recruited from Prolific with a $5 incentive for participation. Each participant was presented with eight audio clips that included six reviews of different products and two attention-check clips. After listening to the audio clips, participants were asked to complete a survey containing manipulation checks, measurement items for research variables, and demographics. Multiple attention checks were implemented to ensure that participants paid adequate attention to the audio clips. The manipulation checks were the same as those in the pilot test. Measurement items for research variables were adapted from existing research. Attractiveness was measured with three items from Park and Lin [40] and Aaker [1]: "The voice is likable," "The voice gives me a good feeling," and "The voice is attractive." Persuasiveness was measured with two items from Pham and Avent [43]: "The voice is compelling" and "The voice is convincing." Trustworthiness was measured using four items from Ohanian (1990): "The SVA is dependable," "The SVA is sincere," "The SVA is trustworthy," and "The SVA is reliable." Lastly, one item measuring usage intention ("I will follow the SVA's recommendation in the future.") was adopted from Hernandez-Ortega and Lucia-Palacios [22]. All measurement items for these research variables used 7-point Likert scales (1: strongly disagree; 7: strongly agree).

4.2 Participant Profiles

Ten participants were excluded due to failed attention checks, and a total of 340 usable responses were used for further data analyses. Of the 340 participants, 50.3% were male, 47.9% were female, 1.5% identified as "non-binary," and 0.3% identified as "other." The average age of respondents was 35.4 years (SD = 12.44). In terms of race, 71.5% were White, 10.3% were Black or African American, and 8.3% were Asian. Regarding education, 37.9% had a bachelor's degree, 20.7% had some post-secondary education, and 18.6% had a high school degree. In terms of annual household income, 37.6% earned between $50,000 and $100,000, 24% earned between $25,000 and $49,999, and 18% earned between $100,000 and $199,999. Regarding employment status, 52.7% had full-time jobs, 16.3% were employed part-time, 11.5% were unemployed but looking for work, and 10.1% were students.

4.3 Manipulation Checks

Results of a crosstab analysis indicated that participants correctly identified the intended age group of SVA voices. Seventy percent of participants in the younger voice condition perceived the voice as younger, and 77% of participants in the older voice condition perceived it as older ($\chi^2 = 73.34, p < .001$). Additionally, results of an ANOVA showed that participants perceived positive reviews as more positive, compared to negative reviews (M_{positive} vs. $M_{\text{negative}} = 4.9$ vs. 3.77, $F = 87.58, p < .001$). Manipulation checks were deemed successful.

5 Results

5.1 Hypothesis Testing

Two steps were taken for hypothesis testing. First, to examine the three-way interactions among gender, age, and message valence, we performed a multivariate analysis of variance (MANOVA). Two dependent variables-attractiveness and persuasiveness-were selected for the analysis. MANOVA results confirmed a significant three-way interaction of gender, age, and message valence (Wilk's $\lambda = .973$, $F = 4.612, p = .011$, partial $\eta^2 = .027$). Specifically, the interplay among gender, age, and content valence was significant for attractiveness ($F = 4.732, p = .030$, partial $\eta^2 = .014$), supporting H1a. However, the three-way interaction for persuasiveness was not significant ($F = .411, p = .52$), rejecting H1b.

Pairwise comparison results indicated that in the positive review condition, gender x age interactions were consistent between attractiveness and persuasiveness. The younger female voice was perceived as more attractive than the younger male voice (M_{female} vs. $M_{\text{male}} = 5.06$ vs. $3.79, t = 3.81, p < .001$), whereas the older male voice was perceived as more attractive compared to the older female voice (M_{female} vs. $M_{\text{male}} = 3.45$ vs. 4.26, $t = -2.27$, $p = .024$; see Fig. 2). Similarly, participants perceived the younger female voice as more persuasive than the younger male voice (M_{female} vs. $M_{\text{male}} = 4.45$ vs. $3.77, t = 1.97, p = .051$), while they perceived the older male voice as more persuasive than the older female voice for positive reviews (M_{female} vs. $M_{\text{male}} = 3.48$ vs. 4.22, $t = -2.01$, $p = .046$; see Fig. 2). In the context of negative reviews, no group differences were found in either perceived attractiveness or perceived persuasiveness (see Fig. 3).

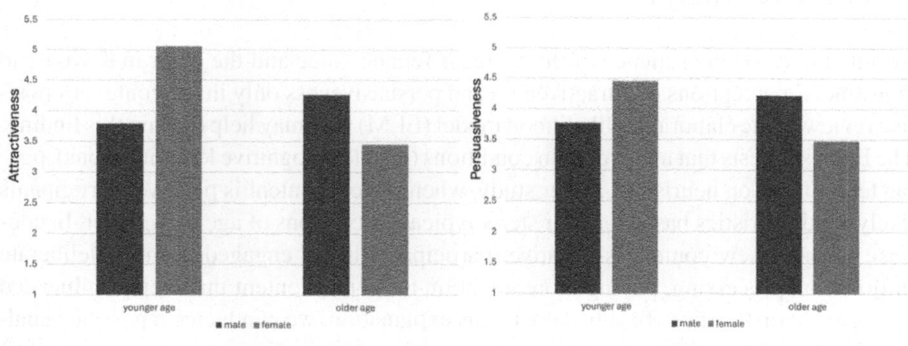

Fig. 2. Positive review: Gender × age on attractiveness (Left) and persuasiveness (Right)

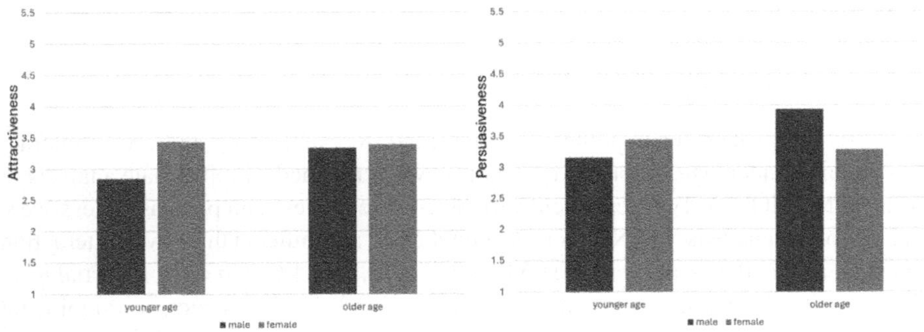

Fig. 3. Negative review: Gender × age on attractiveness (Left) and persuasiveness (Right)

To test the mediating role of trustworthiness (H2), we ran mediation models using PROCESS Model 4 [19] with 10,000 bootstrapped samples. For the path of attractiveness → trustworthiness → usage intention, the indirect effect was significant (indirect effect = .2319, SE = .0336, 95% CI [.1680, .3001]), but the direct effect was not significant (direct effect = .0162, SE = .0324, 95% CI [−.0475, .0798]). Thus, trustworthiness fully mediated the effect of attractiveness on usage intention.

Results of the same mediation model (persuasiveness → trustworthiness → usage intention) showed that trustworthiness partially mediated the effect of persuasiveness on usage intention (indirect effect = .2822, SE = .0342, 95% CI [.2177, .3506]; direct effect = .0766, SE = .0341, 95% CI [.0094, .1438]). Thus, H2 was supported.

6 Post-Hoc Analysis

Results indicated the salience of the younger female voice and the older male voice in consumers' perceptions of attractiveness and persuasiveness only in the context of positive reviews. The elaboration likelihood model (ELM) [42] may help explain this finding. The ELM suggests that under certain conditions (e.g., low cognitive load situations), people tend to rely on heuristics. In our study, when review content is positive, participants likely used heuristics based on their stereotypical perceptions of age and gender. In contrast, when review content is negative, participants likely engaged in more deliberate information processing, paying more attention to review content than being influenced by voice characteristics. To substantiate this explanation, we conducted a post-hoc analysis and tested the effect of content valence on perceived information usefulness (e.g., "the review is useful;" 7-point Likert scales; 1: strongly disagree; 7: strongly agree). Results of an ANOVA indicated that negative content was perceived as more useful and relevant than positive content (M_{negative} vs. $M_{\text{positive}} = 5.48$ vs. 5.08, $F = 26.75$, $p <$ .001). The post-hoc analysis suggests that consumers perceived negative reviews to be more useful than positive reviews. While this is not direct evidence, when combined with the significant influences of voice characteristics on positive content, the activation of heuristics following gender and age stereotypes is highly likely when review content is positive.

7 Discussion and Implications

Building on the SCM, we tested a framework examining how SVA voices and messages influence voice perceptions and behavioral responses. Findings revealed an interplay of voice characteristics (gender, age) and content valence on voice perceptions—attractiveness and persuasiveness. For positive reviews, younger female and older male voices were more attractive and persuasive than younger male voices and older female voices, respectively. For negative reviews, no significant differences were found. Results suggest SVA voices follow gender and age stereotypes. Combined with review valence, results demonstrate context-dependent complexity. This is likely due to cognitive demand differences. Consumers rely on heuristic cues when processing positive reviews, which activate lower cognitive load and shallower processing, making them more likely to rely on voice characteristics that elicit stereotypical responses (Ozanne et al. 2019). Negative reviews activate higher cognitive load, demanding deeper processing, shifting attention to central cues—the review content [8]. Thus, stereotypes are reduced in negative review contexts.

We also found trustworthiness mediates the relationship between voice attractiveness and persuasiveness and usage intentions. This is consistent with previous research on trust in AI (e.g., [22, 45]). While prior studies emphasize trustworthiness driven by functional and social aspects of SVAs [24], functional (persuasiveness) and social (attractiveness) aspects of voices also increase trustworthiness.

7.1 Theoretical Implications

Our findings contribute to consumer behavior research in multiple ways. First, this study examines the interplay between SVA stereotypes and content valence in SVA persuasion, demonstrating nuanced, context-dependent effects. While extant literature mostly focuses on gender stereotypes (e.g., [35]), limited work investigates age stereotypes (e.g., [44]). Our study expands the SCM to SVA voices by demonstrating the interplay between age and gender and introducing content valence as a boundary condition. Younger female and older male voices facilitated processing of positive reviews, highlighting dynamic stereotyping—stereotypes shaped by situational factors like content valence.

Second, this research developed diverse real-life stimuli featuring SVA voices. Most studies used surveys (e.g., [24, 49]), while fewer generated voice stimuli with limited vocal features (e.g., Flavián et al. [16]). This study systematically manipulated both gender and age.

Third, we introduced attractiveness and persuasiveness as mechanisms underlying SVA recommendations. While attractiveness has been studied for physical appearance in source credibility theory [36], this study examined vocal attractiveness. Our findings show SVA voices lead to two distinct routes—perceived attractiveness and persuasiveness in shaping consumers' responses to voice-based SVA recommendations.

Fourth, contrary to prior work [35], the current framework highlights how trustworthiness serves as a mediator, connecting consumers' perceptions of voices with their behavioral intentions. These insights offer valuable implications for future research, suggesting that SVA voices can evoke consumers' perceptions of voices as well as SVA devices, which further influences their trust in SVAs and may foster stronger consumer behavioral engagement with SVAs.

7.2 Practical Implications

Several practical implications emerge: SVA voices evoke stereotypical responses, forming perceptions through attractiveness and persuasiveness, and effects are context-specific. Marketers should consider vocal features (gender and age) when communicating brand messages using SVAs. Practitioners should consider matches between voice and content. For positive content (e.g., testimonials, positive reviews, success stories), use younger female or older male voices to elicit positive responses. For negative or challenging topics (e.g., apologies, responses to backlash), emphasis on content over voice is warranted.

Furthermore, companies should leverage voice technologies to enhance vocal attractiveness and persuasiveness in their brand communications. Managers can utilize AI-driven tools to optimize pitch, tone, and other vocal characteristics, creating voice personas that align with brand identity and engage consumers effectively. However, such practices must be implemented within ethical boundaries—building trust and fostering long-term customer relationships while ensuring transparency and avoiding consumer deception. Finally, this study demonstrates the mediating role of trustworthiness underlying the SVA persuasion process. Practitioners should enhance voice commands to ensure consistent voice personas, building reliable SVAs that promote loyalty and engagement.

8 Limitations and Future Research

Although the current research makes significant contributions to the knowledge of the effectiveness of voice-driven SVA recommendations, there are some limitations that warrant further investigation. First, this research explored the role of gender and age of SVA voices. Future studies may investigate the effects of other paralinguistic cues such as emotional cues embedded in voices. Further research should explore the interaction between content valence and emotional tone on consumer information processing. Additionally, future research may validate and apply our research framework to various contexts. For example, future studies could compare the effectiveness of SVA recommendations across different product types (hedonic vs. functional products). While the participants in our study were recruited from the United States, future research could focus on cross-cultural differences in SVA persuasion. Evidence has shown that the content of stereotypes may vary across cultures [15]. Therefore, it is necessary to examine how different SVA voices form consumers' stereotypical perceptions in different cultural contexts (e.g., individualistic vs. collectivistic cultures).

Acknowledgments. This research is supported by the Social Science Research Funding Program (SSRFP) at Indiana University.

Disclosure of Interests. None of the authors has a conflict of interest to disclose.

References

1. Aaker, J.L.: Accessibility or diagnosticity? Disentangling the influence of culture on persuasion processes and attitudes. J. Consum. Res. **26**(March), 340–357 (2000)
2. Aaker, J., Vohs, K.D., Mogilner, C.: Nonprofits are seen as warm and for-profits as competent: firm stereotypes matter. J. Consum. Res. **37**(2), 224–237 (2010)
3. Abele, A.E.: The dynamics of masculine-agentic and feminine-communal traits: findings from a prospective study. J. Pers. Soc. Psychol. **85**(4), 768–776 (2003)
4. Ahn, J., Kim, J., Sung, Y.: The effect of gender stereotypes on artificial intelligence recommendations. J. Bus. Res. **141**, 50–59 (2022)
5. Akdim, K., Casalo, L.V.: Perceived value of AI-based recommendations service: the case of voice assistants. Serv. Bus. **17**, 81–112 (2023)
6. Antil, J., Burton, R., Robinson, M.: Exploring the challenges facing female athletes as endorsers. J. Brand Strategy **1**(3), 292–307 (2012)
7. Baird, A., Jorgensen, S.H., Parada-Cabaleiro, E., Cummins, N., Hantke, S., Schuller, B.: The perception of vocal traits in synthesized voices: age, gender, and human likeness. J. Audio Eng. Soc. **66**(4), 277–285 (2018)
8. Baumeister, R.F., Bratslavsky, E., Finkenauer, C., Vohs, K.D.: Bad is stronger than good. Rev. General Psychol. **5**(4), 323 (2001)
9. Bye, H.H., Solianik, V.V., Five, M., Agai, M.S.: Stereotypes of women and men across gender subgroups. Front. Psychol. **13**, 881418 (2022)
10. Calahorra-Candao, G., Hoyos, M.J.: The effect of anthropomorphism of virtual voice assistants on perceived safety as an antecedent to voice shopping. Comput. Hum. Behav. **153**, 108124 (2024)
11. Chahal, H., Mahajan, M.: A TCCM-based review of consumer behavior towards digital voice assistants and future research agenda. Int. J. Hum.-Comput. Interact. **41**(12), 7482–7502 (2025)
12. Cyr, D., Head, M., Ivanov, A.: Perceived interactivity leading to e-loyalty: development of a model for cognitive-affective user responses. Int. J. Hum.-Comput. Stud. **67**(10), 850–869 (2009)
13. Fiske, S.T.: Stereotype content: warmth and competence endure. Curr. Dir. Psychol. Sci. **27**(2), 67–73 (2018)
14. Fiske, S.T., Cuddy, A.J.C., Glick, P., Xu, J.: A model of (often mixed) stereotype content: competence and warmth respectively follow from perceived status and competition. J. Pers. Soc. Psychol. **82**(6), 878–902 (2002)
15. Fiske, S.T., Durante, F.: Stereotype content across cultures: variations on a few themes. In: Gelfand, M.J., Chiu, C.-Y., Hong, Y.-Y. (eds.) Advances in culture and psychology, vol. 6, pp. 209–258. Oxford University Press, New York (2015)
16. Flavián, C., Akdim, K., Casaló, L.V.: Effects of voice assistant recommendations on consumer behavior. Psychol. Mark. **40**, 328–346 (2023)
17. Gong, C.: AI voices reduce cognitive activity? A psychophysiological study of the media effect of AI and human newscasts in Chinese journalism. Front. Psychol. **14** (2023). https://doi.org/10.3389/fpsyg.2023.1243078
18. Gupta, P., Burton, J.L., Barros, L.C.: Gender of the online influencer and follower: the differential persuasive impact of homophily, attractiveness and product-match. Internet Res. **33**(2), 720–740 (2023)
19. Hayes, A.F.: Introduction to Mediation, Moderation, and Conditional Process Analysis: A Regression Approach, 2nd edn. Guilford Press, New York City (2018)
20. Heilman, M.E.: Gender stereotypes and workplace bias. Res. Organ. Behav. **32**, 113–135 (2012)

21. Hernandez-Ortega, B., Ferreira, I.: How smart experiences build service loyalty: the importance of consumer love for smart voice assistants. Psychol. Mark. **38**, 1122–1139 (2021)
22. Hernandez-Ortega, B.I., Lucia-Palacios, L.: Trust in word of voice communication: why consumers adhere to purchase recommendations made by smart voice assistants. Mark. Intell. Plan. **41**(8), 1093–1120 (2023)
23. Ho, S.Y., Bodoff, D.: The effects of web personalization on user attitude and behavior: an integration of the elaboration likelihood model and consumer search theory. MIS Q. **38**(2), 497–520 (2014)
24. Hsieh, S.H., Lee, C.T.: The AI humanness: How perceived personality builds trust and continuous usage intention. J. Prod. Brand. Manag. **33**(5), 618–632 (2024)
25. Im, H., Sung, B., Lee, G., Kok, K.Q.X.: Let voice assistants sound like a machine: voice and task type effects on perceived fluency, competence, and consumer attitude. Comput. Hum. Behav. **145**, 107791 (2023)
26. Ischen, C., Araujo, T.B., Voorveld, H.A.M., Noort, G.V., Smit, E.G.: Is voice really persuasive? The influence of modality in virtual assistant interactions and two alternative explanations. Internet Res. **32**(7), 402–425 (2022)
27. Ivens, B.S., Leischnig, A., Muller, B., Valta, K.: On the role of brand stereotypes in shaping consumer response toward brands: an empirical examination of direct and mediating effects of warmth and competence. Psychol. Mark. **32**(8), 808–820 (2015)
28. Kim, J., Kang, S., Bae, J.: Human likeness and attachment effect on the perceived interactivity of AI speakers. J. Bus. Res. **144**, 797–804 (2022)
29. Lee, K.Y., Sheehan, L., Lee, K., Chang, Y.: The continuation and recommendation intention of artificial intelligence-based voice assistant systems (AIVAS): the influence of personal traits. Internet Res. **31**(5), 1899–1939 (2021)
30. Lu, Y., Kim, Y., Dou, X., Kumar, S.: Promote physical activity among college students: using media richness and interactivity in web design. Comput. Hum. Behav. **41**, 40–50 (2014)
31. Munnukka, J., Talvitie-Lamberg, K., Maity, D.: Anthropomorphism and social presence in human-virtual service assistant interactions: the role of dialog length and attitudes. Comput. Hum. Behav. **135**, 107343 (2022)
32. Nagar, K.: Customer satisfaction with telephone-based self-service technology: investigating the role of "gender" of the voice assistant. J. Mark. Commun. **30**(8), 1013–1038 (2023)
33. Nass, C., Moon, Y.: Machines and mindlessness: social responses to computers. J. Soc. Issues **56**(1), 81–103 (2000)
34. Nass, C., Moon, Y., Green, N.: Are machines gender neutral? Gender-stereotypic responses to computers with voices. J. Appl. Soc. Psychol. **27**(10), 864–876 (1997)
35. Nickel, K., Meyer, C.: Why female virtual conversational agents exhibit greater social presence: insights from the stereotype content model. J. Consum. Behav. **24**, 1358–1372 (2025)
36. Ohanian, R.: Construction and validation of a scale to measure celebrity endorsers' perceived expertise, trustworthiness, and attractiveness. J. Advert. **19**(3), 39–52 (1990)
37. Orth, U.R., Spielmann, N., Meyer, C.: Ambient temperature in online service environments. J. Serv. Res. **26**(2), 155–172 (2023)
38. Ozanne, M., Liu, S.Q., Mattila, A.S.: Are attractive reviewers more persuasive? Examining the role of physical attractiveness in online reviews. J. Consum. Mark. **36**(6), 728–739 (2019)
39. Pak, R., Fink, N., Price, M., Bass, B., Sturre, L.: Decision support aids with anthropomorphic characteristics influence trust and performance in younger and older adults. Ergonomics **55**(9), 1059–1072 (2012)
40. Park, H.J., Lin, L.M.: The effects of match-ups on the consumer attitudes toward internet celebrities and their live streaming contents in the context of product endorsement. J. Retail. Consum. Serv. **52**, 101934 (2020)

41. Park, K., Park, Y., Lee, J., Ahn, J.H., Kim, D.: Alexa, tell me more! The effectiveness of advertisements through smart speakers. Int. J. Electron. Commer. **26**(1), 3–24 (2022)
42. Petty, R.E., Cacioppo, J.T.: The elaboration likelihood model of persuasion. In: Berkowitz, L. (ed.) Advances in experimental social psychology, vol. 19, pp. 123–205. Academic Press, San Diego (1986)
43. Pham, M.T., Avnet, T.: Ideals and oughts and the reliance on affect versus substance in persuasion. J. Consum. Res. **30**, 503–518 (2004)
44. Pias, S.B.H., Huang, R., Williamson, D., Kim, M., Kapadia, A.: The impact of perceived tone, age, and gender on voice assistant persuasiveness in the context of product recommendations. In: Proceedings of the 6th ACM Conference on Conversational User Interfaces, pp. 1–15 (2024)
45. Pitardi, V., Marriott, H.R.: Alexa, she's not human but... Unveiling the drivers of consumers' trust in voice-based artificial intelligence. Psychol. Mark. **38**, 626–642 (2021)
46. Poushneh, A.: Humanizing voice assistant: the impact of voice assistant personality on consumers' attitudes and behaviors. J. Retail. Consum. Serv. **58**, 102283 (2021)
47. Pradhan, A., Erete, S., Chopra, S., Upadhyay, P., Sule, O., Lazar, A.: "No, not that voice again!": Engaging older adults in design of anthropomorphic voice assistants. Proc. ACM Hum.-Comput. Interact. **9**(2), 1–30 (2025)
48. Rhee, C.E., Choi, J.: Effects of personalization and social role in voice shopping: an experimental study on product recommendation by a conversational voice agent. Comput. Hum. Behav. **109**, 106359 (2020)
49. Rohit, K., Shankar, A., Mehrotra, A., Yaqub, M.Z., Gupta, P.: Exploring consumer engagement with smart voice assistants in the era of emerging conversational technologies. Mark. Intell. Plan. **43**, 1696–1723 (2025)
50. Sattarapu, P.K., Wadera, D., Nguyen, N.P., Kaur, J., Kaur, S., Mogaji, E.: Tomeito or Tomahto: exploring consumer's accent and their engagement with artificially intelligent interactive voice assistants. J. Consum. Behav. **23**, 278–298 (2024)
51. Sondergaard, M.L.J., Hansen, L.K.: Intimate futures: staying with the trouble of digital personal assistants through design fiction. In: Proceedings of the 2018 Designing Interactive Systems Conference, pp. 869–880 (2018)
52. Statista: Voice assistant e-commerce transaction value worldwide 2021–2023 (2025). https://www.statista.com/statistics/1256695/ecommerce-voice-assistant-transactions/
53. Sung, B., Im, H., Duong, V.C.: Task type's effect on attitudes towards voice assistants. Int. J. Consum. Stud. **47**, 1772–1790 (2023)
54. Waller, S.S., Eriksson, M., Sörqvist, P.: Can you hear my age? Influences of speech rate and speech spontaneity on estimation of speaker age. Front. Psychol. **6**, 978 (2015)
55. Wang, S., Cunningham, N.R., Eastin, M.S.: The impact of eWOM message characteristics on the perceived effectiveness of online consumer reviews. J. Interact. Advert. **15**(2), 151–159 (2015)
56. Wang, S.W., Scheinbaum, A.C.: Enhancing brand credibility via celebrity endorsement: trustworthiness trumps attractiveness and expertise. J. Advert. Res. **58**(1), 16–32 (2017)
57. Watkins, H., Pak, R.: Investigating user perceptions and stereotypic responses to gender and age of voice assistants. Proc. Hum. Factors Ergon. Soc. Annu. Meet. **64**(1), 1800–1804 (2021). https://doi.org/10.1177/1071181320641434
58. Wetzels, R., Wetzels, M., Grewal, D., Doek, B.: Evoking trust in smart voice assistants. J. Serv. Manag. **37**, 78–104 (2025)
59. Winkler, R.: Influences of pitch and speech rate on the perception of age from voice. In: Proceedings of the 16th International Congress of Phonetic Sciences, Saarbrucken, pp. 1849–1852 (2007)
60. Wu, P.F.: In search of negative bias: an empirical study of perceived helpfulness of online reviews. Psychol. Mark. **30**(1), 971–984 (2013)

61. Yucel, Y., Rizvanoglu, K.: I am old too! Understanding the impact of empathy and voice characteristics on older adults' perception of voice assistants. In: 2022 IEEE International Conference on e-Business Engineering (ICEBE), pp. 299–304 (2022). https://doi.org/10.1109/ICEBE55470.2022.00059
62. Yzerbyt, V.Y., Kervyn, N., Judd, C.M.: Compensation versus halo: the unique relations between the fundamental dimensions of social judgment. Pers. Soc. Psychol. Bull. **34**(8), 1110–1123 (2008)
63. Zuckerman, M., Miyake, K.: The attractive voice: what makes it so? J. Nonverbal Behav. **17**(2), 119–135 (1993)

Persuasive Virtual Pet Interactions for Emotional Stabilization and Workplace Well-Being

Haruno Ito(✉), Takeshi Konno, Takahiro Yoshioka, and Makiko Miyairi

Fujitsu Limited, Kawasaki, Japan

ito.haruno@jp.fujitsu.com

Abstract. Persuasive systems research has traditionally focused on compliance-oriented behavior change, often emphasizing efficiency and task completion. However, such approaches may overlook the role of care-oriented interactions in supporting users' short-term emotional well-being.

In this paper, we revisit data from a previously reported interactive system study and reframe the findings through a care-oriented persuasive design perspective. We report a within-subject experiment in which participants interacted with a virtual companion system designed to provide emotionally supportive engagement. Psychological states were assessed using pre-and post-intervention mood measure, along with subjective experience reports.

Rather than demonstrating long-term behavioral change, our analysis highlights how design elements related to emotional presence and relational interaction can facilitate short-term emotional recovery. Based on these findings, we discuss practical design implications and lessons learned for integrating care-oriented perspective design perspective beyond compliance toward emotionally supportive human-system relationships.

Keywords: Persuasive technology · Virtual pet · Workplace well-being · Non-contact sensing · Interactive visualization · Emotional regulation · Stress reduction · Human-computer interaction

1 Introduction

Persuasive systems have often emphasized immersive experience to promote behavioral change [1]. However, recent studies have questioned whether immersion alone is sufficient to produce meaningful psychological effects [15, 16].

Mental health challenges among business professionals remain a serious social concern. According to Japan's 2024 workplace survey, 68.3% of employees report experiencing severe work-related stress [1]. Although workplace wellness initiatives and wearable technologies have been promoted to address this issue, practical barriers such as discomfort, privacy concerns, and perceptions of surveillance limit their acceptance in real office environments [2–4].

E. Vlahu-Gjorgievska et al. (Eds.): PERSUASIVE 2026, CCIS 2896, pp. 79–91, 2027.
https://doi.org/10.1007/978-3-032-27235-5_6

To address these challenges, this study focuses on care-oriented persuasive interactions that aim to minimize psychological burden while supporting affective regulation. We use meowave as a design probe to explore how a virtual pet combined with non-contact sensing can embody such care-oriented persuasive principles. Rather than positioning meowave primarily as a technological contribution, this paper examines how gentle, non-intrusive persuasive interactions influence emotional recovery trajectories following stress.

This study contributes a care-oriented persuasive design that leverages privacy-preserving, non-contact sensing to support short-term emotional regulation in workplace environments.

2 Related Work

2.1 Physiological, Psychological, and Social Benefits of Animal-Assisted Therapy

Animal-Assisted Interventions (AAI) are therapeutic approaches that improve health and well-being through human-animal interaction. As stress becomes more prevalent, AAI have gained attention as natural, non-invasive complements to conventional treatments. Both informal Animal-Assisted Activities (AAA) and structured Animal-Assisted Therapy (AAT) have shown significant physiological, psychological, and social benefits [6, 7].

Previous studies have demonstrated that animal-assisted activities and therapies can reduce stress-related psychological and physiological markers, including mood disturbance and autonomic stress responses, across clinical and workplace settings [6–9].

However, practical constraints such as hygiene management, animal welfare, and facility restrictions limit their applicability in everyday office environments.

2.2 From Live Animals to Robotic Companions: Benefits and Limitations

Robotic pets have been developed to address the limitations of live animals. Interacting with these robots can reduce loneliness and improve Quality of Life, especially for older adults [In previous work [10], a pet-type robot for elderly care was proposed.]. Commercially available pet-type robots, such as Sony's 'aibo', GROOVE X's 'LOVOT', and Casio's 'Moflin', illustrate the growing adoption of robotic companions in real-world settings [11–14]. These examples are referenced to situate the design space of contemporary robotic and virtual companions, rather than to provide empirical evidence of persuasive or therapeutic effectiveness.

Despite their benefits, robotic pets face challenges such as privacy concerns due to reliance on cameras and microphones, and limited mobility that restrict adaptation to dynamic environments. These issues are particularly relevant in workplaces, where unobtrusive and flexible solutions are needed.

Recent persuasive technology research has highlighted that persuasive effects and design principles do not necessarily transfer consistently across interaction modalities. For example, Ekpezu et al. (2025) reported that compliance drivers and the effectiveness of persuasive prompts may change when moving from application-based systems to immersive virtual reality environments, indicating that increased immersion alone does not guarantee persuasive impact. These findings underscore the importance of examining persuasive mechanisms within specific contextual and interactional constraints [15, 16]. In contrast to immersive or compliance-oriented persuasive systems, the present study focuses on short-term emotional recovery in everyday workplace environments, emphasizing care-oriented interaction rather than productivity or behavioral pressure.

3 Proposed System

3.1 Proposed System: "meowave"

We propose meowave, a virtual pet system utilizing millimeter-wave technology for non-contact monitoring of user states, without relying on cameras or microphones. Recent studies show that virtual pets and pet-type robots can provide emotional support and promote behavioral change, especially when persuasive system design (PSD) principles are incorporated [17, 18]. Meowave delivers spatial and visual interventions tailored to users' emotional and behavioral contexts, integrating PSD elements such as self-monitoring and suggestion.

Unlike conventional wearable devices or pet robots, meowave offers interventions with minimal psychological burden and preserves privacy, enabling flexible integration into workplace environments. By combining unobtrusive sensing with adaptive, immersive interaction, meowave aims to support mental and physical well-being in settings where traditional solutions are difficult to implement. Based on these considerations, this study addresses the following research question: How do care-oriented persuasive interactions, implemented through a virtual pet, facilitate short-term emotional recovery following stress in workplace environments? This research question shifts the focus from verifying intervention effectiveness to understanding persuasive design mechanisms that support affective recovery.

To explore this research question, we designed and implemented meowave as a research prototype capable of delivering spatial and visual interventions tailored to the user's state.

3.2 System Architecture

Figure 1 illustrates the main hardware components of meowave, which integrates sensing, processing, and feedback devices to create an interactive environment for users.

Virtual Pet: The virtual pet is designed as a cat, selected for its association with relaxation and stress reduction. Cat behaviors such as purring are known to activate the parasympathetic nervous system, helping to alleviate stress [19]. The design emphasizes passive engagement, making it suitable for professionals experiencing high stress. To avoid negative effects from unsuccessful interactions, the system focuses on gentle, non-demanding behaviors [20].

Laptop: The laptop serves as the central control unit, processing sensor data and generating adaptive audiovisual feedback in real time.

Millimeter-Wave Sensor: This core sensing component non-invasively detects user activity and vital signs using 79 GHz radar technology. It collects point cloud data, from

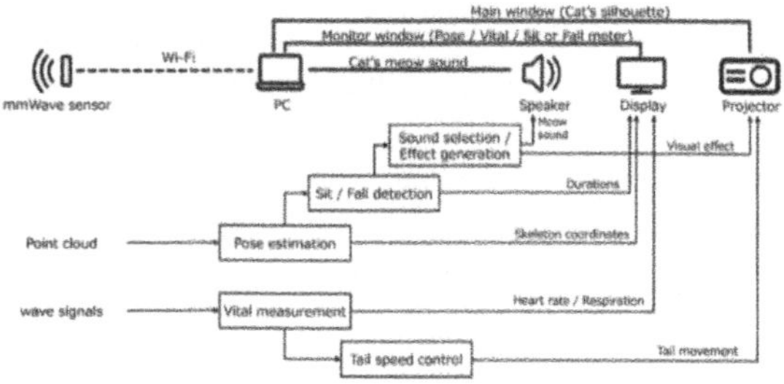

Fig. 1. System overview of meowave. The millimeter-wave sensor transmits point cloud and vital signals to a PC, which performs posture and vital analysis. The meowave application generates adaptive visual and auditory feedback via projector, speaker, and monitor.

which human body key points are extracted. A machine learning model estimates user posture and behavioral states to enable adaptive feedback while maintaining privacy [21]. In this study, the sensing module was used to support real-time interaction design rather than to evaluate posture estimation accuracy or model performance. The sensor can also measure heart rate and respiration, even when users are stationary (see Fig. 2). In this study, the sensing and machine learning components are not evaluated as technical contributions but are used to support the exploration of care-oriented persuasive interaction design, rather than to assess model performance or accuracy [21].

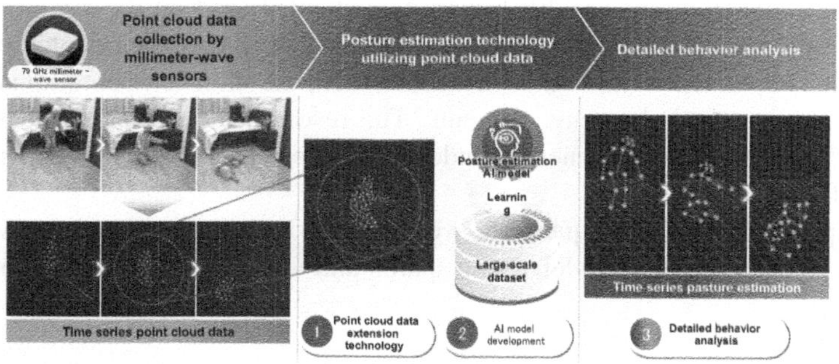

Fig. 2. High-accuracy posture estimation using millimeter-wave point cloud data. Workflow of the sensing module: point cloud data collection, expansion and refinement, AI-based posture estimation, and detailed behavioral analysis. Enables non-contact monitoring of user states for adaptive intervention.

Projector: The projector displays the virtual pet and its adaptive visual behaviors in the shared workspace, providing a non-intrusive visual presence without requiring personal devices.

Cat Visual Representation: An anonymous silhouette design is adopted (Fig. 3) to convey an "unseen yet present" feeling. This abstract form encourages users to project their own emotions onto the pet, facilitating personal comfort and seamless integration into the office environment.

Speaker: The speaker delivers subtle auditory feedback synchronized with the virtual pet's state, supporting emotional regulation without demanding focused attention from users.

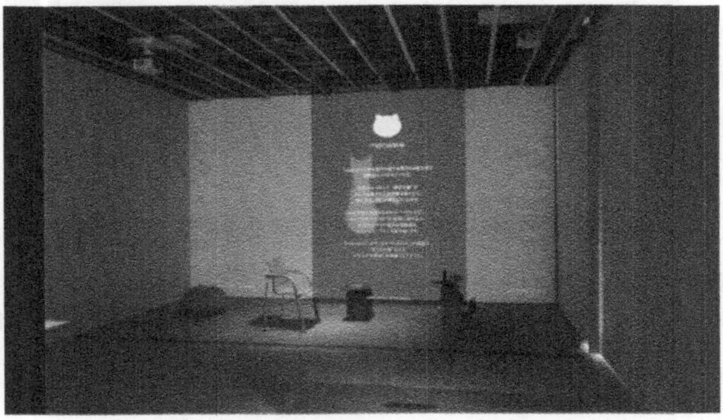

Fig. 3. Immersive spatial visualization of the virtual pet using an abstract cat silhouette.

3.3 Interaction with the Virtual Pet

During the intervention phase, participants interacted with the virtual pet through passive observation rather than direct manipulation.

The virtual pet provided adaptive visual movements and subtle auditory cues based on sensed postural and physiological states, allowing users to engage without focusd attention or explicit input (Fig. 4).

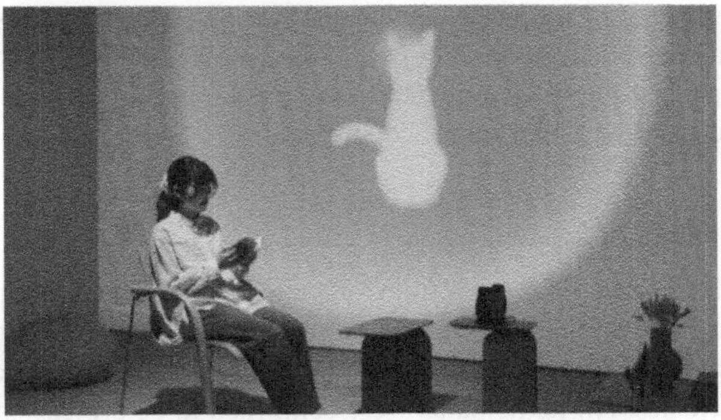

Fig. 4. Interaction scenario: meowave responding to user posture. Example of the system detecting prolonged sitting posture and providing concerned vocalizations and visual cues to prompt user attention and support emotional well-being.

This interaction design was intentionally non-intrusive and care-oriented, aiming to support emotional regulation in shared workplace environments while minimizing cognitive and psychological burden (Fig. 5).

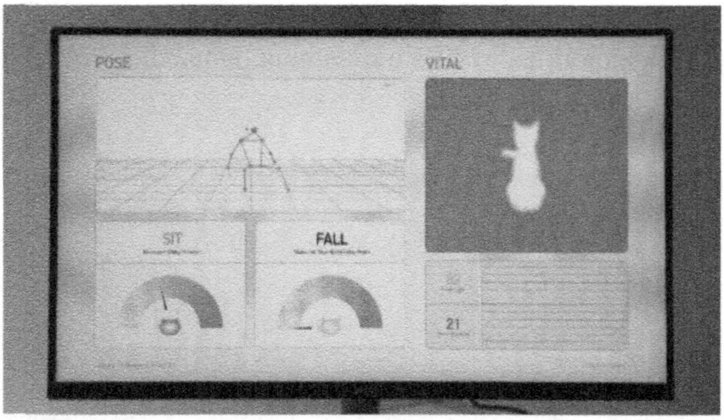

Fig. 5. Monitoring interface for posture and vital signs. Visualization of skeletal coordinates, posture classification, and duration meters. The cat's tail motion is dynamically linked to the user's heart rate, integrating physiological feedback into the user experience.

A unique feature of meowave is the integration of physiological feedback into the user experience: the motion of the cat's tail is dynamically linked to the user's heart rate, with its speed varying in real time. This design strengthens the sense of connection between the user and the virtual pet, making the interaction more engaging and personalized. Overall, meowave's interaction design balances emotional support with comfort and privacy, helping users maintain both mental and physical well-being through natural, unobtrusive engagement.

4 Research Method

To evaluate the impact of meowave on the emotional states of business professionals, we conducted a controlled experiment in an office environment. The main hypothesis was that participants using meowave would show greater improvement in negative mood states compared to those in the control condition.

4.1 Participants

A total of 42 office workers were recruited via internal social networking services and direct invitations. The participants included office professionals from various job roles, such as sales, system engineering, and research positions. The sample consisted of 22 males and 20 females. All participants were confirmed to be professionals working in professional office settings, ensuring relevance to the research context.

4.2 Procedure and Ethical Considerations

The experiment was conducted over a scheduled period in a real office environment to ensure ecological validity. All procedures followed ethical guidelines: participants were informed about the study's purpose, data handling, and their right to withdraw at any time. Written consent was obtained, and privacy was protected by using non-contact sensing without cameras or microphones.

4.3 Experimental Conditions

The experiment was conducted under two conditions:

Intervention group (meowave condition): Participants interacted freely with meowave for five minutes after a brief practice session.

Control group (nature-scene condition): Participants in the control group were asked to observe outdoor scenery from a meeting room for five minutes. Viewing natural landscapes has been widely reported to aid mental fatigue recovery and stress reduction [23] and was therefore selected as a conservative baseline rather than an active or optimal relaxation condition. This choice was intended to avoid overestimating the intervention effect of meowave and to provide a stringent comparison against a commonly used stress-reduction method. Prior to the trial, participants were instructed, "Please sit and look at the outdoor scenery for five minutes. If you feel unwell at any point, the experimenter will be waiting outside the room—please notify us immediately".

4.4 Stress-Induction Task

To ensure internal validity in estimating the intervention effect of meowave, participants completed an arithmetic task from the Trier Social Stress Test (TSST) before the intervention. TSST, developed by Kirschbaum et al., is a standardized protocol for inducing stress in socially evaluative contexts [24]. Specifically, participants performed a five-minute task subtracting 13 repeatedly from 1022, incorporating stressors such as time pressure, performance monitoring, and reset upon errors in an ethical and controlled manner.

4.5 Psychological Measures

To assess changes in mood states, we used the Profile of Mood States 2nd Edition (POMS2) – Adult Short Form [25]. This questionnaire asks participants to rate how they feel "right now," capturing their current mood and affect.

POMS2 consists of 35 items across seven subscales: Anger–Hostility (AH), Confusion–Bewilderment (CB), Depression–Dejection (DD), Fatigue–Inertia (FI), Tension–Anxiety (TA), Vigor–Activity (VA), and Friendliness (F). Each item is rated on a five-point Likert scale.

For analysis, we calculated the Total Mood Disturbance (TMD) score by subtracting the sum of positive mood factors (Vigor–Activity and Friendliness) from the sum of negative mood factors (Anger–Hostility, Confusion–Bewilderment, Depression–Dejection, Fatigue–Inertia, Tension–Anxiety). A higher TMD score indicates a more negative mood state.

Only complete responses were included in the analysis to ensure data integrity.

4.6 Procedure

Participants were randomly assigned to either the meowave condition (n = 21) or the control condition (n = 21) using a random number generation function in Microsoft Excel.

The experimental procedure consisted of the following steps: 1. Explanation and informed consent, 2. Baseline measurement (Time 1), 3. Stress-induction task, 4. Post-stress measurement (Time 2), 5. Intervention phase, ① intervention group: Interaction with meowave for 5 min ② control group: Viewing outdoor scenery for 5 min, 6. Post-intervention measurement (Time 3), 7. Debriefing. Participants were informed that they could discontinue the experiment at any time without penalty. After completing the experiment, all participants were debriefed regarding the purpose of the stress-induction task and were given the opportunity to ask questions or discuss their experience with the experiment to ensure well-being.

Both groups underwent a five-minute intervention period, ensuring consistency across conditions.

4.7 Use of Artificial Intelligence

Artificial intelligence (AI) technologies were utilized in several aspects of this study. For posture estimation, a machine learning model was applied to point cloud data obtained from the millimeter-wave sensor to accurately detect user posture and behavioral states. In addition, cat vocalizations used in the system were generated using an AI-based sound synthesis service (Eleven Labs). All AI models and algorithms were used in accordance with ethical guidelines and relevant regulations.

Accordingly, the machine learning components were not treated as outcome variable, and their quantitative validation was outside the scope of the present study.

4.8 Data Analysis

Five participants from the nature-scene condition were excluded due to incomplete questionnaire responses. Consequently, the final analysis included 21 participants in the meowave condition (mean age = 33.81 ± 8.74 years) and 16 participants in the nature-scene condition (mean age = 29.56 ± 5.92 years). To account for unequal group sizes and individual-level variability, a linear mixed-effects model was applied.

Mood state analysis was conducted using the seven POMS2 subscale scores and the Total Mood Disturbance (TMD) score. T-scores were calculated for each subscale and TMD, allowing standardized comparisons across participants [26].

A linear mixed-effects model was applied to examine variance in T-scores across measurement points (baseline, post-stress, post-intervention) and conditions (meowave vs. nature scene). This approach is robust to missing data and unbalanced sample sizes across conditions. This model accounts for individual differences and evaluates the effects of time, condition, and interaction. Estimated Marginal Means (EMMs) were computed to clarify adjusted differences between conditions at each time point and temporal changes within each condition. To control multiple comparisons across mood subscales, p-values associated with interaction effects and pairwise comparisons were adjusted using the Benjamini-Hochberg false discovery rate procedure.

5 Results

The linear mixed-effects model revealed significant main effects of Time and significant Condition × Time interaction effects on several mood scales. As summarized in Tables 1 and 2, the meowave condition showed a clear V-shaped recovery patterns across negative mood scales improvements in the nature-scene condition were limited and did not remain significant after correction.

Table 1. Summary of Linear Mixed-Effects Model Results for Mood States

Scale	Condition	Time	Condition × Time
	$F(1, 37)$	$F(2, 74)$	$F(2, 74)$
AH	10.43	15.32***	1.82
CB	2.20	36.60***	17.96 *** (q < .001)
DD	0.25	16.25***	9.66*** (q < .001)
FI	1.53	26.54***	18.40*** (q < .001)
TA	0.86	32.46***	12.55*** (q < .001)
VA	3.54	2.29	4.27* (q = .020)
F	6.83	6.90**	4.92** (q = .013)
TMD	1.19	51.68***	18.88*** (q < .001)

Note. Results of linear mixed-effects models(random intercept for participant ID)
Scale abbreviations are shown in the table. Benjamini-Hochberg-corrected q-values are reported.
* $p < .05$, ** $p < .01$, *** $p < .001$.

Table 2. Simple Effects Analysis: Mean Differences Between Conditions at Each Time Point

Scale	Time 1 (Baseline)	Time 2 (Post-Stress)	Time 3 (Post-Intervention)
	Δ (p)	*Δ (p)*	*Δ (p)*
AH	n.s	n.s	−9.35 (<.001)***
CB	n.s	14.40 (<.001)***	n.s
DD	n.s	n.s	−8.40 (.011)*
FI	n.s	13.19 (<.001)***	−8.62 (.005)**
TA	n.s	10.82 (<.001)***	−6.72 (.029)*
VA	n.s	n.s	9.44 (.006)**
F	n.s	n.s	12.41 (<.001)***
TMD	n.s	6.38 (.011)*	−10.98 (<.001)***

Note. Estimated mean difference (*Δ*) and Benjamini-Hochberg-corrected p-values from pairwise comparisons. *Δ* represents the difference between the meowave and landscape conditions. Significant differences at Time 3 are shown in bold. n.s. indicate non-significant results. * $p < .05$, ** $p < .01$, *** $p < .001$

Table 3 summarizes the results of the linear mixed-effects model analysis. In the meowave condition, TMD showed a significant increase from Time 1 to Time 2 (Mean Difference = 11.81, $p < .001$, $q < .001$), followed by a significant decrease from Time 2 to Time 3 (Mean Difference = −23.05, $p < .001$, $q < .001$). Importantly, the TMD score at Time 3 was also significantly lower than at baseline (Mean Difference = −11.24, $p < .001$, $q < .001$). Similar V-shaped patterns were observed for CB, TA, FI, and DD, while F and VA showed inverted V-shaped changes. In the nature scene condition, changes were less pronounced, with only marginal trends for TMD and AH.

Overall, these results demonstrate that the meowave intervention effectively facilitated mood regulation and recovery following stress, outperforming the nature scene control. The estimated marginal means for each scale across all three time points are visualized in Fig. 6.

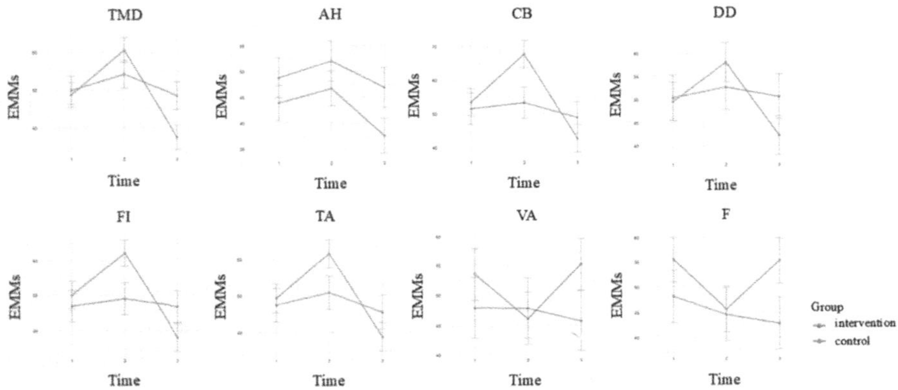

Fig. 6. Estimated marginal means for mood states over time. The vertical axis represents standardized mood scores; the horizontal axis shows measurement points (baseline, post-stress, post-intervention). The orange line indicates the meowave condition, and the blue line indicates the nature-scene control condition.

6 Discussion

The primary contribution of this study lies not in demonstrating the effectiveness of a specific system, but in articulating how care-oriented persuasive interactions can support emotional recovery following stress. Unlike compliance-driven or productivity-oriented persuasive systems, the intervention intentionally minimized demands, feedback intensity, and explicit goal-setting. This perspective is consistent with recent findings in persuasive technology suggesting that increased immersion or interactivity does not automatically enhance persuasive effectiveness across modalities [15, 16].

This study investigated the effects of our intervention on psychological states following a stress task. The results confirmed a significant main effect of time and, more importantly, a significant Condition × Time interaction effect across multiple psychological indices. For Total Mood Disturbance (TMD), a V-shaped pattern was observed: negative affect peaked after the stressor (Time 2) and subsequently improved by the end of the experiment (Time 3). This recovery trajectory was particularly pronounced in the meowave condition, which exhibited a substantial improvement from Time 2 to Time 3, suggesting a strong capacity to buffer the negative psychological impact of stress.

Inter-condition comparisons further underscore the superiority of the meowave intervention. At Time 3, the meowave group reported significantly lower TMD scores compared to the landscape group, indicating a more complete recovery and a better final psychological state. In contrast, the landscape condition yielded only limited restorative effects; while a marginal trend toward improvement was noted for TMD and Anger-Hostility (AH), these effects did not remain significant after correction for multiple comparisons. This finding suggests that the stress-reducing benefits of simply viewing nature scenes may be less robust than often assumed, at least in this context.

Furthermore, our findings extend beyond mere stress reduction. For positive affect indicators such as Friendliness and Vigor, participants in the meowave condition experienced not only a full recovery from a temporary dip post-stressor but an overall increase that surpassed their initial baseline levels. This pattern suggests the potential of meowave to facilitate positive affect beyond baseline levels in a short-term context, although this interpretation should be made cautiously, demonstrating a key tenet of persuasive technology. At the same time, the nature-scene condition served as a conservative comparison baseline, and the observed effects should be interpreted in this context rather than as superiority over all possible interventions.

7 Conclusion

In this study, we explored a care-oriented persuasive interaction paradigm implemented through a virtual pet system that integrates non-contact millimeter-wave sensing. We proposed a design framework for emotional support interventions that are both privacy-preserving and socially acceptable for shared environments like the workplace. Our results suggest that this interaction paradigm, which overcomes the limitations of wearable devices, live animals, and physical robots, can support improvements in negative mood states following a stress-inducing event.

This study contributes to persuasive technology research in two key ways. First, unlike prior robot-, VR, or wearable-based persuasive systems, we propose a care-oriented persuasive design model that operates under a privacy-preserving, non-contact sensing environment suitable for shared workplace settings. Second, our findings empirically demonstrate that a virtual pet's social presence combined with gentle visual rhythmic stimuli can facilitate short-term emotional recovery following stress. By positioning emotional restoration, rather than behavioral compliance or productivity, as the primary persuasive outcome, this work extends persuasive system theory toward short-duration, affect-focused intervention design.

7.1 Limitations and Future Work

Despite these promising results, this study has several limitations. First, the intervention was short-term (five minutes), and the findings reflect immediate emotional regulation rather than long-term behavioral change or sustained well-being. Second, the sample size was relatively modest, and the exclusion of incomplete responses led to unequal sample sizes between conditions, which may limit the statistical power and generalizability of our findings. Third, although meowave is designed to be privacy-preserving, users' subjective perceptions of privacy and psychological burden were not empirically evaluated in this study.

Future work should investigate long-term effects through longitudinal deployments, incorporate more diverse participant populations, and empirically examine perceived privacy and acceptance in real workplace environments. Importantly, this study does not claim long-term behavioral change, sustained well-being improvement, or superiority over other interactive or immersive systems.

Given the short intervention duration and exploratory design, the contribution of this work should be understood as a theoretical and design-oriented contribution to persuasive technology rather than a definitive effectiveness study.

References

1. Ministry of Health, Labour and Welfare: 2024 Survey on Industrial Safety and Health (in Japanese). Ministry of Health, Labour and Welfare official website. https://www.mhlw.go.jp/toukei/list/r06-46-50b.html. Accessed Aug 2025
2. Watanabe, K., Yamauchi, T., et al.: Long working hours, night shifts, and weekend work and their association with workers' mental health: a large-scale cross-sectional study. Soc. Sci. Med. **233**, 161–173 (2019)
3. Ministry of Health, Labour and Welfare: Guidelines for the Maintenance and Promotion of Workers' Mental Health (in Japanese). Ministry of Health, Labour and Welfare official website. https://www.mhlw.go.jp/stf/seisakunitsuite/bunya/0000055195_00002.html. Accessed Oct 2025
4. Oba, H., Mizuno, S.: A case study of health management initiatives using wearable devices (in Japanese). In: Proceedings of the JSDSS 2024 Spring Conference, pp. 1–6 (2024)
5. Niimi, K., Sawada, H., Katsurada, K., Omura, E.: A case study of health management initiatives using wearable devices (in Japanese). In: Proceedings of the JSDSS 2024 Spring Conference, pp. 1–6 (2024)
6. Japan Veterinary Medical Association: Animal-Assisted Activities (Animal-Assisted Activity, Animal-Assisted Therapy, Animal-Assisted Education) and the Role of Veterinarians and the Veterinary Association (in Japanese). Committee for Promotion of Animal-Assisted Activities, Small Animal Clinical Division, Japan Veterinary Medical Association (2009)
7. Shiraki, T., et al.: Animal-assisted activities in a general hospital palliative care ward (in Japanese). Palliat. Care Res. **11**(2), 123–130 (2016)
8. Taiyu, Y., Kobayashi, H., Nagase, H., Seicho, T.: Effectiveness of animal-assisted therapy with dogs for elderly people with dementia (in Japanese). J. Kawasaki Med. Welf. Soc. **17**(2), 353–361 (2008)
9. Yashiro, K.: Examination of the social and psychological effects of dog (therapy dog) intervention in the workplace (in Japanese). Rep. Basic Res. Group Hum. Commun. **2020**(30), 349–356 (2020)
10. Kanamori, M., Suzuki, M., Tanaka, M.: Maintenance and improvement of quality of life among elderly patients using a pet-type robot (in Japanese). Jpn. J. Geriatr. **39**(2), 214–218 (2002)
11. Sony: aibo. Sony official website. https://aibo.sony.jp/. Accessed Aug 2025
12. Tanaka, K., et al.: The pilot study of group robot intervention on pediatric inpatients and their caregivers, using 'new aibo.' Eur. J. Pediatr. **181**(3), 1055–1061 (2021). https://doi.org/10.1007/s00431-021-04285-8

13. GROOVE X: LOVOT. GROOVE X official website. https://lovot.life/. Accessed Aug 2025
14. CASIO: Moflin. CASIO official website. https://moflin.com/. Accessed Aug 2025
15. Ekpezu, A.O., Wiafe, I., Atsakpo, E.D., Oinas-Kukkonen, H.: From apps to virtual reality: the transferability of compliance drivers from non-virtual reality to virtual reality persuasive systems. Int. J. Hum.-Comput. Interact. (2025)
16. Ekpezu, A.O., Wiafe, I., Atsakpo, E.D., Oinas-Kukkonen, H.: Designing to promote compliance: the role of prompt types in a persuasive virtual reality environment. Behav. Inf. Technol. (2025)
17. Harada, R., Sumi, K.: Persuasive technology through behavior and emotion with pet-type artifacts. In: Baghaei, N., Ali, R., Win, K., Oyibo, K. (eds.) Persuasive Technology, PERSUASIVE 2024. Lecture Notes in Computer Science, vol. 14636, pp. 151–160. Springer, Cham (2024). https://doi.org/10.1007/978-3-031-58226-4_12
18. Idrees, A.R., et al.: Persuasive design in a digital mindfulness intervention: a randomized trial of a skill-based achievement system and automated peer encouragement. J. Healthc. Inform. Res. (2025). https://doi.org/10.1007/s41666-025-00216-6
19. von Muggenthaler, E.: The felid purr: a healing mechanism? J. Acoust. Soc. Am. **110**(5_Supplement), 2684 (2001)
20. Kano, H., Terashima, N.: What effects do virtual pets have on people? (in Japanese). J. Educ. Inf. Res. **25**(2), 3–14 (2009)
21. Konno, T., Yoshioka, T.: High-accuracy human posture estimation technology from point cloud data collected by millimeter-wave sensors (in Japanese). IEICE Trans. Commun. (C) **107**(1), 45–46 (2024)
22. Eleven Labs: Eleven Labs official website. https://elevenlabs.io/. Accessed Aug 2025
23. Ulrich, R.S., Simons, R.F., Losito, B.D., Fiorito, E., Miles, M.A., Zelson, M.: Stress recovery during exposure to natural and urban environments. J. Environ. Psychol. **11**(3), 201–230 (1991)
24. Kirschbaum, C., Pirke, K.M., Hellhammer, D.H.: The 'trier social stress test' – a tool for investigating psychobiological stress responses in a laboratory setting. Neuropsychobiology **28**(1–2), 76–81 (1993). https://doi.org/10.1159/000119004
25. Heuchert, J.P., McNair, D.M.: Profile of Mood States 2nd Edition (POMS2). APA PsycTests. https://doi.org/10.1037/t05057-000
26. McNair, D.M., Heuchert, J.P., Tanaka, K. (supervising translator): POMS 2 Japanese Manual (in Japanese). Nippon Bunka Kagaku-sha, Tokyo (2012)

What is Beautiful is Credible. Examining Personality-Color Congruence, and Its Effects on Users' Perceptions of Attractiveness, Likeability, and Credibility of Persuasive Systems

Felix Nti Koranteng[1](✉), Uwe Matzat[1], Jaap Ham[1], and Isaac Wiafe[2]

[1] Eindhoven University of Technology, Eindhoven, The Netherlands
{f.n.k.m.koranteng,u.matzat,j.r.c.ham}@tue.nl
[2] University of Ghana, Legon, Ghana
iwiafe@ug.edu.gh

Abstract. Extant research positions credibility as a central determinant of persuasive system effectiveness. However, how the adaptation of visual design elements, particularly interface color, shapes users' credibility perceptions remain underexplored. Drawing on the Elaboration Likelihood Model (ELM), this study examines whether aligning interface color with users' personality traits enhances perceived credibility through affective mechanisms. Using a 2 × 2 between-subjects experimental design, 133 university students classified as introverts or extroverts interacted with a persuasive website featuring either a red or blue interface, creating personality–color congruent (introverts–blue; extroverts–red) and incongruent conditions. Participants evaluated the system's attractiveness, likeability, and credibility. Results indicate that personality–color congruence significantly increased perceived attractiveness and likeability, which subsequently enhanced credibility judgments. Mediation analysis further revealed that likeability partially mediated the relationship between attractiveness and perceived credibility. These findings extend persuasive design and adaptation research by demonstrating that interface color can function as a personality-sensitive peripheral cue, and they highlight the practical potential of personality-aware color adaptation for enhancing credibility in persuasive systems across domains such as health, education, and e-commerce.

Keywords: persuasive systems · credibility · color · personality traits · attractiveness

1 Introduction

People interact daily with computer systems designed to subtly influence their decisions and behaviors. Examples of these computer systems include fitness applications that encourage regular physical activity, financial dashboards that promote prudent spending, and digital health tools that support medication adherence. These systems are collectively

E. Vlahu-Gjorgievska et al. (Eds.): PERSUASIVE 2026, CCIS 2896, pp. 92–105, 2027.
https://doi.org/10.1007/978-3-032-27235-5_7

known as persuasive systems. Persuasive systems are computer systems intentionally designed to shape users' attitudes and behaviors without coercion or deception [1]. Designers of persuasive systems strategically embed persuasive design elements into computer systems to evoke specific cognitive, emotional, or behavioral responses from users.

Within Human–Computer Interaction (HCI), visual design elements, particularly color, have been identified as a key factor that shapes users' perceptions and behaviors [2, 3]. Research shows that appealing interface colors foster more positive attitudes toward a computer system [4, 5]. Users often form rapid first impressions of computer systems and decide whether to continue engaging with them within seconds of initial exposure, with interface color schemes playing a particularly influential role in these early evaluations [4, 6]. Consequently, color can function as a powerful persuasive cue capable of guiding user perceptions and motivating continuous engagement. Yet, despite its importance, the persuasive potential of color remains comparatively underexplored in persuasive system design.

In particular, little is known about how color affects users' credibility perceptions of persuasive systems. Credibility is defined as the extent to which a persuasive system is viewed as believable, competent, and reliable [7, 8]. Credibility is widely recognized as a central determinant of a persuasive system's effectiveness [8, 9]. When a persuasive system is perceived to be credible, users are more likely to trust and comply with its recommendations [8], thereby promoting the intended behavioral outcomes. In contrast, even well-designed persuasive systems may fail if users question the system's credibility. This underscores credibility as a foundational condition for effective persuasive design consideration.

Prior research also demonstrates that adapting persuasive systems to individual user characteristics (such as personality traits, preferences, or goals) can significantly enhance their persuasive impact [10, 11]. Adapting persuasive systems increases perceived relevance and user–system fit, which in turn strengthens engagement and persuasive outcomes [12]. However, despite extensive evidence that both system adaptation and visual design independently shape user perceptions, to our knowledge, no prior research has systematically examined whether tailoring interface color to users' personality traits can enhance perceived credibility.

This study addresses this gap by examining whether aligning a persuasive system's interface color with users' personality-based color preferences (referred to as personality–color congruence) shapes users' perceptual evaluations. Using a between-subjects experimental design, 133 university students classified as either introverts or extroverts interacted with a website featuring either a red or blue interface. This design created congruent conditions (introverts viewing a blue interface; extroverts viewing a red interface) and incongruent conditions (introverts viewing a red interface; extroverts viewing a blue interface). Participants subsequently evaluated the website in terms of attractiveness, likeability, and credibility. The results show that personality–color congruence significantly enhanced perceived attractiveness and likeability, which in turn led to higher credibility evaluations.

2 Background

Over the past two decades, persuasive systems have been widely deployed to encourage desirable behavioral change across domains such as health, sustainability, education, and commerce [13]. As noted earlier, the effectiveness of persuasive systems depends heavily on users' perceptions of their credibility. In response, several theoretical frameworks have identified determinants of credibility in persuasive design. Fogg [14], for example, outlined ten design guidelines, including demonstrating expertise, showcasing trustworthy affiliations, ensuring usability, and maintaining professional visual design to strengthen perceived credibility. Building on Fogg's [14] work, the Persuasive System Design (PSD) framework [1] proposed seven contributing factors, including trustworthiness, expertise, surface credibility, authority, and verifiability. Subsequent empirical studies have further expanded these determinants to include perceived effectiveness, usability, social support, and primary task support [15–18].

Among these determinants, visual design stands out as one of the most immediate and influential factors shaping users' perceptions of digital systems. Interface color, in particular, plays a pivotal role in forming users' early impressions and guiding their subsequent evaluations of a computer system [19]. Research consistently shows that individuals form judgments about computer systems within the first few seconds of interaction [6, 20], and color, often the first salient visual cue encountered, exerts a strong influence on these rapid assessments. For example, Lindgaard et al. [21] demonstrated that users form stable impressions of a website's visual appeal within 50 ms, with color significantly contributing to perceived aesthetic pleasure and initial liking.

Beyond initial impressions, interface color continues to shape users' perceptions and behaviors during sustained interaction with a computer system. Empirical evidence shows that interface color is strongly associated with user behavior, including engagement and usage frequency. For example, Alotaibi [22] identified a strong relationship between website color schemes and user behaviors, such as how often users revisited a site, while Pelet [23] reported a positive correlation between interface color and perceived usability. Prior research further demonstrates that color influences perceptions of attractiveness and aesthetic pleasure [24, 25] and plays a role in users' emotional engagement with computer systems [26, 27]. Importantly, color has also been shown to affect perceptions of trust and trustworthiness [28, 29] which are core components of credibility. Collectively, this body of evidence suggests that interface color is not merely decorative but can be strategically leveraged as a persuasive design element to shape users' credibility perceptions and behavioral responses.

Building on this, prior research further suggests that the effectiveness of such persuasive design elements is not uniform across all users but is moderated by individual characteristics [10]. In other words, the same design cue may be interpreted differently and elicit distinct behavioral responses depending on who the user is. For example, Orji et al. [30] demonstrated that the effectiveness of competition- and collaboration-oriented features in persuasive systems varies systematically across users with different gamer types and motivational profiles, rather than producing uniform effects. Similarly, Kaptein et al. [31] showed that tailoring persuasive elements that are matched to individual personality traits significantly enhanced system effectiveness and compliance compared to one-size-fits-all designs.

In the same vein, the persuasive effect of color is unlikely to be uniform across users. Research indicates that user characteristics (such as age, gender, culture, personality traits, and individual preferences) shape how colors are perceived and evaluated ([32, 33]. Color preferences can amplify affective responses and strengthen users' emotional reactions to an interface. Extending this argument, Seifi and Moshayeri [26] found that website color schemes aligned with users' psychological associations significantly enhanced overall user experience. These findings suggest that adapting interface color to user attributes may intensify its persuasive influence.

Among the various user characteristics that can shape responses to persuasive design, this study focuses specifically on personality traits. Personality traits refer to relatively stable patterns of thinking, feeling, and behaving that distinguish individuals from one another [34]. These traits tend to remain consistent over time and across situations. Individuals with similar demographic characteristics (such as age or gender) may still behave quite differently in the same context due to underlying personality differences [35]. Accordingly, users with comparable backgrounds may respond differently to identical design stimuli, highlighting personality as a key moderator of user perceptions and behavior.

Personality also plays a central role in shaping responses to color, largely due to differences in cortical arousal. Cortical arousal refers to the level of sensory stimulation an individual's brain optimally processes [36]. Individuals with lower baseline cortical arousal, typically extroverts, tend to seek higher-intensity stimuli, such as bright or highly saturated colors, to reach an optimal arousal state [37]. In contrast, introverts, who generally exhibit higher cortical arousal, may experience such stimuli as overstimulating and therefore prefer cooler, less intense colors such as blue or gray. Empirical evidence supports these distinctions: Pazda and Thorstenson [32] as well as Jamil and Malik [38] found a strong positive relationship between extraversion and preference for high-chroma colors, while other works (e.g., [33, 39]) confirmed that individuals lower in extraversion show a preference for cooler, more muted tones.

These insights suggest that the persuasive effectiveness of color may be contingent on its congruence with users' personality traits. When color choices align with users' personality-based preferences, interfaces are more likely to be perceived as attractive and likable, thereby fostering stronger credibility judgments. To theoretically ground these arguments, we draw on the Elaboration Likelihood Model (ELM) as the conceptual foundation for this study.

2.1 Theoretical Foundation

The Elaboration Likelihood Model (ELM) [40] explained that individuals process persuasive information through two distinct routes: the central and the peripheral routes. Central-route processing involves careful, effortful evaluation of message content and typically results in more enduring attitude change. In contrast, peripheral-route processing relies on surface-level cues, such as visual appearance, aesthetics, or interface color, that require minimal cognitive effort and tend to elicit faster, affect-driven responses.

This distinction is particularly relevant in technology-mediated environments, where users often interact with interfaces briefly and under low cognitive engagement. In such contexts, users are less likely to engage in deep message scrutiny and instead rely on readily available visual and affective cues to form judgments. Consequently, peripheral elements such as interface color become especially influential in shaping early perceptions and guiding subsequent evaluations [3, 41]. Prior work grounded in ELM demonstrates that visually appealing design elements can evoke positive affect, which in turn enhances perceptions of trustworthiness, expertise, and overall credibility, even before users meaningfully process informational content [3, 42]. These findings suggest that in persuasive systems, peripheral cues often play a decisive role in determining users' initial impressions and sustained engagement.

Importantly, the ELM also emphasizes that responses to persuasive cues are not uniform but are moderated by individual differences. Personality traits, in particular, have been shown to influence how users process persuasive information and which cues are most effective [30, 43]. As discussed earlier, personality-based differences in cortical arousal help explain systematic variations in color preferences. Extroverts tend to seek higher stimulation and therefore prefer vivid, high-arousal colors such as red, whereas introverts generally favor calmer, low-arousal colors such as blue. When an interface's color scheme aligns with these personality-based preferences, it may create affective congruence, leading users to experience the system as more pleasant, fitting, and psychologically comfortable. Such congruence is expected to enhance evaluations of attractiveness and likeability, which are known antecedents of credibility judgments.

Based on this theoretical perspective, the present study conceptualizes personality–color congruence as a peripheral persuasive cue operating primarily through affective pathways. Specifically, we propose that aligning interface color with users' personality traits will enhance attractiveness and likeability perceptions, which in turn will strengthen perceived credibility. Accordingly, we hypothesize that:

- **H1a**: The perceived attractiveness of a persuasive system will be higher under a color–personality congruent condition (i.e., introverts with blue, extroverts with red) than under an incongruent condition.
- **H1b**: The likeability of a persuasive system will be higher under a color–personality congruent condition than under an incongruent condition.
- **H1c**: The perceived credibility of a persuasive system will be higher under a color–personality congruent condition than under an incongruent condition.
- **H2a**: Perceived Attractiveness will positively predict likeability.
- **H2b**: Perceived likeability will positively predict perceived credibility.
- **H3**: Likeability will mediate the relationship between attractiveness and perceived credibility.

3 Method

3.1 Design

An experiment was conducted to examine how a congruent match between users' personality traits and interface color influences the perceived attractiveness and likability credibility of a persuasive system, and how this relationship extends to perceived credibility. The study employed a 2 × 2 between-subjects factorial design, with two independent variables: interface color (red vs. blue) and personality (introvert vs. extrovert). The red and blue colors were selected because they are widely recognized for evoking contrasting emotional and psychological responses [44] while maintaining comparable lightness and saturation levels to control for perceptual confounds [45].

3.2 Participants

A total of 133 university students in Ghana voluntarily participated in the experiment (76 males, 53 females, 4 undisclosed ($M = 26.0$, $SD = 6.1$; *Range* = 17–35 years). Participants were classified as introverts or extroverts based on their scores on the Extraversion subscale of the Big Five Inventory [47]. Within each personality group, participants were randomly assigned to one of two experimental conditions: matched (interface color aligned with personality) or unmatched (interface color mismatched). This resulted in 68 participants in the matched condition and 65 in the unmatched condition.

3.3 Procedure

After providing informed consent, participants were introduced to the study purpose and assured of confidentiality and anonymity. Participants first completed the Ishihara Color Vision Test [46] to screen for color blindness. Next, they completed the Big Five personality inventory, focusing on the Extraversion dimension. Based on their personality classification, participants were randomly assigned to one of four conditions in a 2 × 2 factorial design: Matched condition (introverts viewed the blue interface; extroverts viewed the red interface) and Unmatched condition (introverts viewed the red interface; extroverts viewed the blue interface). Participants interacted with a persuasive website prototype advertising student job vacancies for approximately four minutes. Afterward, they completed a questionnaire measuring perceived attractiveness, likeability, credibility, trust, intention to use, digital proficiency, and social desirability bias. Finally, demographic information was collected, participants were debriefed, and compensated for their time.

3.4 Materials

Stimuli. Two visually identical website prototypes were developed as stimuli (see Fig. 1). The only difference was the primary interface color (i.e., either blue or red). Both websites contained identical content, structure, navigation, and page layout, and were presented as a fictitious job recruitment platform to eliminate potential brand bias. The context was selected to ensure credibility evaluations occurred within a professional decision-making domain. A pilot test confirmed that the two color versions were functionally equivalent and visually comparable.

Measurement Instrument. All measures were administered in English using validated multi-item scales adapted from established research in human–computer interaction and persuasive systems design. To ensure that all participants could accurately perceive the color stimuli, color vision was first assessed using the Ishihara Color Vision Test [46]. The seven-plate version of the test, which detects red–green color deficiencies, was used to exclude potential perceptual bias in evaluating the interface color conditions.

(a) Red Website Interface (b) Blue Website Interface

Fig. 1. (a) Red Website Interface (b) Blue Website Interface

Participants' personality traits were measured using the Extraversion dimension of the Big Five Inventory (BFI) developed by John and Srivastava [47]. Since this study focused specifically on the role of extraversion in moderating responses to interface color, only the six extraversion-related items were administered. Participants indicated the extent to which each statement described them on a five-point Likert scale (1 = strongly disagree, 5 = strongly agree). Internal consistency for the scale was excellent ($\alpha = .95$).

Perceptions of attractiveness, likeability, and credibility of the website were then assessed using adapted scales from prior research. Perceived attractiveness was measured with four items adapted from Lavie and Tractinsky [48] and demonstrated high reliability ($\alpha = .83$). Likeability was measured using four items adapted from Reeves and Nass [49], which capture users' affective reactions toward technological interfaces ($\alpha = .92$). Perceived credibility was conceptualized as a higher-order construct comprising trustworthiness and expertise, measured with eight items adapted from Ohanian's [50] credibility scale ($\alpha = .80$). To account for individual differences that could influence responses, participants' digital proficiency was measured using the operational and information-navigation subscales from van Deursen, Helsper, and Eynon [51] ($\alpha = .90$). Additionally, social desirability bias was assessed using the short version of the Paulhus Deception Scale [52] ($\alpha = .89$) to identify overly favorable self-reporting tendencies. All measurement items were rated on a five-point Likert scale (1 = strongly disagree, 5 = strongly agree). Cronbach's alpha values for all constructs exceeded the recommended threshold (i.e., .70), indicating satisfactory internal consistency and reliability.

4 Results

Before hypothesis testing, the data were screened to ensure that the assumptions of normality and homogeneity of variance were satisfied. Shapiro–Wilk tests for perceived attractiveness, likeability, and credibility were all non-significant ($p > .05$), indicating that the data were approximately normally distributed. Similarly, Levene's tests for equality of variances were non-significant ($p > .05$), confirming that the assumption of homogeneity of variance was met. These results justified the use of parametric analyses. A one-way analysis of variance (ANOVA) was conducted to examine whether color–personality congruence influenced participants' evaluations of the persuasive system. The results showed that participants in the matched condition (introverts interacting with a blue interface and extroverts with a red interface) reported significantly higher perceived attractiveness ($M = 4.02$, $SD = 0.61$) than those in the unmatched condition ($M = 3.21$, $SD = 0.79$), $F(1,131) = 42.18$, $p < .001$, $\eta^2 = .24$. Likewise, perceived likeability was significantly higher in the matched condition ($M = 3.97$, $SD = 0.68$) compared to the unmatched condition ($M = 3.10$, $SD = 0.82$), $F(1,131) = 39.54$, p < .001, $\eta^2 = .23$. A similar pattern was observed for perceived credibility, which was greater in the matched condition ($M = 3.88$, $SD = 0.65$) than in the unmatched condition ($M = 3.05$, $SD = 0.84$), $F(1,131) = 36.02$, $p < .001$, $\eta^2 = .22$. These results collectively support Hypotheses 1a, 1b, and 1c, indicating that a congruent match between personality traits and interface color enhanced participants' perceptions of attractiveness, likeability, and credibility. The summary of the results is illustrated in Table 1.

Table 1. Table captions should be placed above the tables.

Variable	Condition	M	*SD*	*F*(1,131)	*p*
Perceived Attractiveness	Matched	4.02	0.61	42.18	<.001
	Unmatched	3.21	0.79		
Likeability	Matched	3.97	0.68	39.54	<.001
	Unmatched	3.10	0.82		
Perceived Credibility	Matched	3.88	0.65	36.02	<.001
	Unmatched	3.05	0.84		

Note: N = 133. Matched condition = introverts–blue, extroverts–red; Unmatched condition = introverts–red, extroverts–blue. η^2 represents the effect size (partial eta squared)

To further examine the relationships among the variables, correlation and regression analyses were performed. Pearson correlation coefficients revealed significant positive associations among perceived attractiveness, likeability, and credibility. Specifically, attractiveness was strongly correlated with likeability ($r = .68$, $p < .001$) and credibility ($r = .63$, $p < .001$), while likeability was strongly correlated with credibility ($r = .72$, p < .001). Simple linear regression analyses confirmed that perceived attractiveness significantly predicted likeability ($\beta = .68$, $t(131) = 10.25$, $p < .001$), and that likeability, in turn, significantly predicted perceived credibility ($\beta = .72$, $t(131) = 11.14$, $p < .001$), supporting Hypotheses 2a and 2b. Finally, a mediation analysis using process model 4 [53] tested whether likeability mediated the relationship between attractiveness and perceived credibility. The results indicated a significant indirect effect of attractiveness on credibility through likeability (indirect effect = .36, 95% CI [.22, .52]). The direct effect of attractiveness on credibility remained significant but reduced in magnitude ($\beta = .26$, $p = .01$), suggesting partial mediation. This finding supports Hypothesis 3.

5 Discussion

This study examined whether aligning interface color with users' personality traits enhances perceptions of attractiveness, likeability, and credibility in persuasive systems. Drawing on the Elaboration Likelihood Model (ELM), the study conceptualized personality–color congruence as a peripheral persuasive cue operating through affective pathways. The findings provide consistent support for this theoretical proposition. Specifically, interfaces that matched users' personality traits (introverts–blue; extroverts–red) were perceived as significantly more attractive, more likeable, and more credible than mismatched interfaces. Moreover, attractiveness and likeability played a sequential role in shaping credibility judgments, with likeability partially mediating the relationship between attractiveness and perceived credibility.

5.1 Theoretical Implication

The findings demonstrate that interface color functions as a psychologically meaningful persuasive cue whose effectiveness depends on its congruence with users' personality traits. Consistent with the ELM [40], personality–color congruence operates as a peripheral route cue that can influence evaluations through affective processing rather than deliberate scrutiny. This aligns with prior HCI and online persuasion research showing that visual design elements, such as color, shape user attitudes in low-involvement and time-constrained digital contexts [3, 29].

The results further clarify how peripheral visual cues translate into credibility judgments. Specifically, personality–color congruence increased perceived attractiveness and likeability, which in turn enhanced perceived credibility. This sequential pathway supports credibility research suggesting that judgments of system credibility are often grounded in heuristic and affective evaluations rather than solely in rational assessments of content quality [29, 42]. Importantly, the findings show that credibility perceptions can emerge through intermediate affective states, beginning with aesthetic appreciation and followed by relational affect. These mediating mechanisms thus provide empirical evidence that advances existing credibility studies.

This study also extends persuasive systems research by moving beyond content-level to visual interface–level adaptation. While prior work shows that aligning persuasive features and message framing (e.g., framing strategies, feedback style, or goal setting) with personality traits improves system effectiveness [31, 54], the present findings demonstrate that surface-level adaptation, specifically personality–color congruence, can similarly enhance persuasive outcomes. With these findings, this study highlights interface color as an active persuasive mechanism rather than a purely aesthetic choice. Consistent with research emphasizing the moderating role of user characteristics in persuasion (e.g., [55]), the findings position interface-level cues as psychologically meaningful drivers of user judgments. Theoretically, this study contributes by extending models of adaptive persuasive systems to incorporate visual interface adaptation as a distinct and credible pathway through which persuasion operates.

Finally, the findings strengthen the role of color psychology in persuasive system design by supporting a conditional, rather than universal, view of color effects. The persuasive impact of color emerges not from its intrinsic properties alone, but from its fit with users' psychological dispositions. This perspective aligns with recent evidence that congruence between interface features and users' psychological associations enhances affective responses and system evaluations [25, 26]. Overall, the study reinforces a central theoretical insight: persuasive design cues do not operate uniformly across users but are shaped by individual differences and mediated by affective evaluations. Personality–color congruence is thus validated as a peripheral persuasive mechanism that enhances credibility through attractiveness and likeability.

5.2 Practical Implication

To reiterate, this study shows that interface color is not just a visual choice but a practical tool for increasing user trust and engagement when aligned with users' personality traits. Designers and developers can use personality-aware color choices to make computer systems feel more attractive, likeable, and credible.

For credibility-sensitive computer systems such as health, education, finance, and e-commerce platforms, matching color schemes to user tendencies can improve trust. Interfaces designed for more reserved or reflective users may benefit from cooler, calmer colors, while products aimed at energetic or socially oriented users may perform better with warmer, more stimulating palettes. These adjustments may be especially useful in onboarding, recommendations, and decision-heavy moments where credibility matters most. For example, E-commerce and online services can apply this approach to strengthen consumer confidence, particularly when users interact with unfamiliar brands or share personal information. Adaptation methods, such as onboarding questions or behavioral signals, can be employed to guide color theme selection to support trust and engagement without changing core content or functionality.

The findings are also relevant for adaptive and AI-driven interfaces. Color adaptation offers a low-cost, low-risk layer of personalization that can complement existing personalization strategies in recommender systems, learning platforms, and digital assistants. Because color influences emotional responses, even subtle adjustments can improve how trustworthy and user-friendly a system feels. Finally, the results highlight the importance of designing for emotional experience. Since perceived attractiveness and likeability shape credibility, teams should move beyond one-size-fits-all palettes and incorporate flexible, personality-informed color guidelines into their design systems.

6 Conclusion, Limitation, and Future Work

This study demonstrates that the persuasive effectiveness of interface color is contingent upon its congruence with users' personality traits. The findings provide robust empirical support for personality-aware visual design as a meaningful mechanism in persuasive systems. Grounded on the Elaboration Likelihood Model, this research advances understanding of how peripheral visual cues, particularly, influence credibility through affective pathways rather than solely through deliberate cognitive processing.

Future research should extend this work by investigating more diverse and cross-cultural populations to assess the generalizability of these effects beyond a student sample. Moreover, examining additional personality dimensions alongside a broader spectrum of color attributes (e.g., saturation, brightness, and contrast) would contribute to a more comprehensive model of personality-based visual personalization. Longitudinal and domain-diverse studies are also warranted to determine whether these effects persist over time and translate into sustained, real-world behavioral outcomes. Collectively, these directions can further inform the design of adaptive, credible, and psychologically grounded persuasive technologies.

Acknowledgments. The authors sincerely thank all participants who generously volunteered their time and effort to take part in this study. Their contributions were invaluable to the successful completion of this research.

Disclosure of Interests. The authors declare that they have no competing interests to declare that are relevant to the content of this article.

References

1. Oinas-Kukkonen, H., Harjumaa, M.: Persuasive systems design: key issues, process model, and system features. Commun. Assoc. Inf. Syst. **24**, 28 (2009)
2. Coursaris, C.K., Swierenga, S.J., Watrall, E.: An Empirical Investigation of Color Temperature and Gender Effects on Web Aesthetics. J. Usability Stud. **3**, 103–117 (2008)
3. Cyr, D., Head, M., Larios, H.: Colour appeal in website design within and across cultures: a multi-method evaluation. Int. J. Hum. Comput. Stud. **68**, 1–21 (2010). https://doi.org/10.1016/J.IJHCS.2009.08.005
4. Perrig, S.A.C., Ueffing, D., Opwis, K., Brühlmann, F.: Smartphone app aesthetics influence users' experience and performance. Front. Psychol. **14**, 1113842 (2023). https://doi.org/10.3389/FPSYG.2023.1113842/BIBTEX
5. Ikeya, Y., Barati, B., Wensveen, S.: Aesthetics in designing with the living: a systematic review of critical perspectives and artefacts. In: Conference on Human Factors in Computing Systems - Proceedings (2025). https://doi.org/10.1145/3706598.3713343;PAGE:STRING:ARTICLE/CHAPTER
6. Gopikrishna, R., Kumar, M.: A conceptual study on psychology of colour in marketing and branding. Int. J. Econ. Res. **12**, 501–505 (2015)
7. Tseng, S., Fogg, B.J.: Credibility and computing technology. Commun. ACM **42**, 39–44 (1999)
8. Koranteng, F.N., Matzat, U., Wiafe, I., Ham, J.: Credibility in Persuasive Systems: A Systematic Review. LNCS (including subseries Lecture Notes in Artificial Intelligence and Lecture Notes in Bioinformatics), vol. 13832, pp. 389–409 (2023). https://doi.org/10.1007/978-3-031-30933-5_25/TABLES/2
9. Fogg, B.J., Soohoo, C., Danielson, D.R., et al.: How do users evaluate the credibility of web sites? A study with over 2,500 participants. In: Proceedings of the 2003 Conference on Designing for User Experiences, DUX 2003 (2003). https://doi.org/10.1145/997078.997097
10. Kaptein, M., Markopoulos, P., de Ruyter, B., Aarts, E.: Can You Be Persuaded? Individual Differences in Susceptibility to Persuasion. LNCS (including subseries Lecture Notes in Artificial Intelligence and Lecture Notes in Bioinformatics), vol. 5726, pp. 115–118 (2009). https://doi.org/10.1007/978-3-642-03655-2_13
11. Ham, J.: Influencing robot influence: personalization of persuasive robots. Interact. Stud. **22**, 464–487 (2022). https://doi.org/10.1075/IS.00012.HAM
12. Orji, R., Reisinger, M., Busch, M., Dijkstra, A.: Adaptivity and personalization in persuasive technologies, pp. 5–9 (2016). http://ceur-ws.org/Vol-1582/17Kaptein.pdf

13. Merz, M., Ackermann, L.: Design principles of persuasive systems – review and discussion of the persuasive systems design model. In: AMCIS 2021 Proceedings (2021)
14. Fogg, B.J.: The Web Credibility Project: Guidelines - Stanford University. https://credibility.stanford.edu/guidelines/index.html. Accessed 20 July 2021
15. Wiafe, I., Koranteng, F.N., Kastriku, F.A., Gyamera, G.O.: Assessing the impact of persuasive features on user's intention to continuous use: the case of academic social networking sites. Behav. Inf. Technol. (2020). https://doi.org/10.1080/0144929X.2020.1832146
16. Lehto, T., Oinas-Kukkonen, H., Drozd, F.: Factors affecting perceived persuasiveness of a behavior change support system. In: Proceedings of the International Conference on Information Systems (ICIS), pp 1–15 (2012)
17. Koranteng, F., Ham, J., Wiafe, I., Matzat, U.: The role of usability, aesthetics, usefulness and primary task support in predicting the perceived credibility of academic social networking sites. Behav. Inf. Technol. (2021). https://doi.org/10.1080/0144929X.2021.2009570
18. Koranteng, F.N., Ham, J., Matzat, U., Wiafe, I.: Supporting to be credible: investigating perceived social support as a determinant of perceived credibility. In: International Conference on Persuasive Technology (2022)
19. Papachristos, E., Avouris, N.: Are First Impressions about Websites Only Related to Visual Appeal? (2011)
20. Pengnate, S. (Fone), Sarathy, R., Lee, J.K.: The engagement of website initial aesthetic impressions: an experimental investigation. Int. J. Hum. Comput. Interact. **35** (2019). https://doi.org/10.1080/10447318.2018.1554319
21. Lindgaard, G., Fernandes, G., Dudek, C., Browñ, J.: Attention web designers: you have 50 milliseconds to make a good first impression! **25**, 115–126 (2011). https://doi.org/10.1080/01449290500330448
22. Alotaibi, N.: Color as a visual element on website appeal and its impact on user experience (UX) in graphic design. AWARI **6**, 1–11 (2025). https://doi.org/10.47909/AWARI.744
23. Pelet, J.E.: The influence of e-commerce website colors on usability. In: Integrating Usability Engineering for Designing the Web Experience: Methodologies and Principles. IGI Global Scientific Publishing, pp 264–288 (2010)
24. Hall, R.H., Hanna, P.: The impact of web page text-background colour combinations on readability, retention, aesthetics and behavioural intention. Behav. Inf. Technol. **23**, 183–195 (2004). https://doi.org/10.1080/01449290410001669932
25. Jongmans, E., Jeannot, F., Liang, L., Dampérat, M.: Impact of website visual design on user experience and website evaluation: the sequential mediating roles of usability and pleasure. J. Mark. Manag. **38**, 2078–2113 (2022). https://doi.org/10.1080/0267257X.2022.2085315;JOURNAL:JOURNAL:RJMM20;CTYPE:STRING:JOURNAL
26. Seifi, A., Moshayeri, A.: The influence of color schemes and aesthetics on user satisfaction in web design: an empirical study. Int. J. Adv. Hum. Comput. Interact. **2**, 33–43 (2024)
27. Skulmowski, A., Augustin, Y., Pradel, S., et al.: The negative impact of saturation on website trustworthiness and appeal: a temporal model of aesthetic website perception. Comput. Hum. Behav. **61**, 386–393 (2016). https://doi.org/10.1016/J.CHB.2016.03.054
28. Pelet, J.É., Papadopoulou, P.: The effect of e-commerce websites' colors on customer trust. Int. J. E-Bus. Res. **7**, 1–18 (2011). https://doi.org/10.4018/978-1-4666-1960-9.CH011
29. Peters, R., Sjölund, E., Killberg, F., et al.: How does the colour scheme affect the trust of a website? (2022)
30. Orji, R., Nacke, L.E., Di Marco, C.: Towards personality-driven persuasive health games and gamified systems. In: Conference on Human Factors in Computing Systems – Proceedings, pp. 1015–1027 (2017). https://doi.org/10.1145/3025453.3025577;JOURNAL:JOURNAL:ACMCONFERENCES;PAGEGROUP:STRING:PUBLICATION

31. Kaptein, M., De Ruyter, B., Markopoulos, P., Aarts, E.: Adaptive persuasive systems: a study of tailored persuasive text messages to reduce snacking. ACM Trans. Interact. Intell. Syst. (TiiS) **2**, 1–25 (2012)
32. Pazda, A.D., Thorstenson, C.A.: Extraversion predicts a preference for high-chroma colors. Pers. Individ. Differ. **127**, 133–138 (2018). https://doi.org/10.1016/J.PAID.2018.01.028
33. Wieloch, M., Kabzińska, K., Filipiak, D., Filipowska, A.: Profiling user colour preferences with BFI-44 personality traits. Lecture Notes in Business Information Processing, vol. 339, pp. 63–76 (2019). https://doi.org/10.1007/978-3-030-04849-5_6/TABLES/3
34. McCrae, R.R., Costa, P.T.: Validation of the five-factor model of personality across instruments and observers. J. Pers. Soc. Psychol. **52**, 81–90 (1987). https://doi.org/10.1037/0022-3514.52.1.81
35. Bleidorn, W., Hopwood, C.J., Back, M.D., et al.: Personality trait stability and change. Pers. Sci. **2** (2021). https://doi.org/10.5964/ps.6009
36. Eysenck, H.J.: The Biological Basis of Personality. Thomas, Boston (1967)
37. Matthews, G., Davies, D.R.: Individual differences in energetic arousal and sustained attention: a dual-task study. Pers. Individ. Differ. **31**, 575–589 (2001). https://doi.org/10.1016/S0191-8869(00)00162-8
38. Jamil, H., Malik, N.I.: Color preference, personality traits and psychosocial functioning among students of different academic disciplines. Appl. Psychol. Rev. **4**, 36–55 (2025). https://doi.org/10.32350/APR.41.03
39. Kabzińska, K., Wieloch, M., Filipiak, D., Filipowska, A.: Profiling user's personality using colours: connecting BFI-44 personality traits and Plutchik's wheel of emotions. Advances in Intelligent Systems and Computing, vol. 854, pp. 371–380 (2019). https://doi.org/10.1007/978-3-319-99993-7_33/TABLES/3
40. Petty, R.E., Cacioppo, J.T.: The elaboration likelihood model of persuasion. In: Communication and Persuasion, pp. 1–24. Springer, New York (1986)
41. Fogg, B.J.: Prominence-interpretation theory: explaining how people assess credibility online. In: Extended Abstracts on Human Factors in Computing Systems - CHI 2003, pp. 722–723. ACM Press, New York (2003)
42. Reinecke, K., Gajos, K.Z.: Quantifying visual preferences around the world. In: Conference on Human Factors in Computing Systems – Proceedings, pp. 11–20 (2014). https://doi.org/10.1145/2556288.2557052;PAGE:STRING:ARTICLE/CHAPTER
43. Alqahtani, F., Meier, S., Orji, R.: Personality-based approach for tailoring persuasive mental health applications. User Model User-Adapt. Interact. 1–43 (2021). https://doi.org/10.1007/S11257-021-09289-5/TABLES/7
44. Lichtlé, M.C.: The effect of an advertisement's colour on emotions evoked by attitude towards the ad. **26**, 37–62 (2007). https://doi.org/10.1080/02650487.2007.11072995
45. Gorn, G.J., Chattopadhyay, A., Yi, T., Dahl, D.W.: Effects of color as an executional cue in advertising: they're in the shade **43**, 1387–1400 (1997). https://doi.org/10.1287/MNSC.43.10.1387
46. Ishihara, S.: Ishihara's Tests for Color-Blindness. Kanehara Shuppan (1972)
47. John, O.P., Srivastava, S.: The big five trait taxonomy: history, measurement, and theoretical perspectives. In: Handbook of Personality: Theory and Research, vol. 2 (1999)
48. Lavie, T., Tractinsky, N.: Assessing dimensions of perceived visual aesthetics of web sites. Int. J. Hum. Comput. Stud. **60**, 269–298 (2004). https://doi.org/10.1016/J.IJHCS.2003.09.002
49. Reeves, B., Nass, C.: The Media Equation: How People Treat Computers, Television, and New Media Like Real People and Places. Cambridge University Press, New York (1996)
50. Ohanian, R.: Construction and validation of a scale to measure celebrity endorsers' perceived expertise, trustworthiness, and attractiveness. J. Advert. **19** (1990). https://doi.org/10.1080/00913367.1990.10673191

51. van Deursen, A.J.A.M., Helsper, E.J., Eynon, R.: Development and validation of the Internet Skills Scale (ISS). Inf. Commun. Soc. **19** (2016). https://doi.org/10.1080/1369118X.2015.1078834
52. Paulhus, D.L.: Socially desirable responding on self-reports. In: Encyclopedia of Personality and Individual Differences (2017)
53. Hayes, A.F.: Introduction to Mediation, Moderation and Conditional Process Analysis - Appendices A & B (V3). Methodology in the Social Sciences, vol. 53 (2018)
54. Alslaity, A., Oyebode, O., Vassileva, J., Orji, R.: Personalized persuasive technologies in health and wellness: from theory to practice, pp. 261–292 (2024). https://doi.org/10.1007/978-3-031-55109-3_10
55. Alslaity, A., Chan, G., Orji, R.: A panoramic view of personalization based on individual differences in persuasive and behavior change interventions. Front. Artif. Intell. **6**, 1125191 (2023)

Faithful and Plausible Explanations for Market Prediction from Noisy Forum Posts via XAI–LLM Hybrid Rationale Selection

Kota Kotegawa[1(✉)], Kentaro Ueda[1], Ren Hosokawa[1], Yuki Ogawawa[2], Eichi Umehara[3], Kota Tsubouchi[3], Keiichi Yasumoto[1], and Hirohiko Suwa[1]

[1] Nara Institute of Science and Technology, Japan Tokyo City University, Setagaya, Japan
kota.kotegawa@ubi-lab.com
[2] Niigata University of International and Information Studies, Niigata, Japan
[3] LY Corporation, Tokyo, Japan

Abstract. Large language models (LLMs) enable fluent and persuasive natural-language explanations for prediction models. However, such explanations can exert a strong influence on users' beliefs and decisions, even when they are not faithful to the underlying model's behavior, particularly in high-noise, weakly structured text environments. In this paper, we propose an XAI–LLM hybrid explanation framework for market prediction from noisy financial forum posts. The framework first extracts model-relevant information by ranking posts according to contribution scores computed using explainable AI (XAI) methods. An LLM is then used in a constrained and iterative manner to select rationales that are important to the model and suitable as human-understandable explanation grounds, followed by natural-language explanation generation. By structurally restricting the information available to the explanation generator, the framework embeds faithfulness prior to language generation. We conduct crowdsourcing-based user studies with pairwise comparisons, evaluating the proposed hybrid approach against random selection, XAI-only selection and LLM-only selection. The results show that faithful rationale selection does not uniformly improve perceived explanation quality, but plays a critical role for users capable of scrutinizing the explanation content, while preventing directionally inconsistent or misleading explanations in noisy text settings.

Keywords: explainable AI · large language models · financial text · faithfulness · plausibility

1 Introduction

Machine learning models have been increasingly applied to the financial market prediction, motivating a parallel demand for explanations that allow users to understand and assess model outputs in high-stakes decision-making contexts.

E. Vlahu-Gjorgievska et al. (Eds.): PERSUASIVE 2026, CCIS 2896, pp. 106–121, 2027.
https://doi.org/10.1007/978-3-032-27235-5_8

To address this demand, prior work has developed interpretable model architectures and post-hoc explanation techniques for financial prediction tasks [4,9,16,20,30]. Such methods often rely on feature attributions or visualization techniques (e.g., SHAP or LIME), but are typically expressed in numerical or visual forms that implicitly assume semantically interpretable input features, limiting their accessibility for non-expert users and unstructured inputs.

Recent advances in large language models (LLMs) enable fluent natural-language explanations and have been applied in finance to generate explanation-aware predictions, summarize market information, and integrate explanation with forecasting [14,22,26–28,31,33]. While these approaches often improve perceived clarity and usability, prior work has shown that LLM-generated explanations are not necessarily grounded in the actual decision process of the underlying prediction model, even when they appear coherent and convincing [11,12,19]. This gap highlights a fundamental tension between explanation plausibility and faithfulness.

In this paper, we use the term *faithfulness* to denote the extent to which an explanation reflects the actual decision basis of the prediction model, and *plausibility* to denote the extent to which an explanation appears coherent and acceptable to human users. These two properties can become misaligned when explanations are generated from noisy or weakly structured inputs, where plausible narratives may obscure the true basis of model decisions.

Several recent studies attempt to mitigate this tension by integrating XAI outputs with LLM-based explanation generation, for example, by providing feature attributions or structured explanation signals [7,21,34,35]. However, existing approaches primarily target structured prediction tasks, where input features have clear semantic interpretations. For unstructured and noisy text, such as financial forum posts, attribution scores computed over high-dimensional embedding representations do not directly correspond to interpretable textual rationales.

This challenge is further exacerbated by the sensitivity of LLMs to irrelevant or weakly related context, which can induce unstable reasoning or unintended generalization [5,6,25,29,32]. When explanations are generated directly from weakly filtered forum posts, the resulting narratives may overwrite or distort the actual basis of the prediction model's decision.

We therefore argue that faithful explanation generation in LLM-based systems requires structural control over the information used for explanation, rather than relying solely on the LLM's language generation capability. To study this problem, we focus on market prediction from financial forum posts and propose an XAI–LLM hybrid explanation framework. In this framework, model-relevant information is first extracted using post-hoc XAI methods and then selectively organized by an LLM through an iterative rationale selection process. The LLM is not used as a predictor or a free-form explainer; instead, it operates on a constrained set of candidates derived from the prediction model itself.

Through large-scale crowdsourcing experiments stratified by users' financial knowledge, we further examine how such structurally constrained explanations are perceived by different user groups. Our results show that faithfulness-oriented rationale selection does not uniformly increase perceived explanation quality, but plays a critical role for users capable of scrutinizing explanation content.

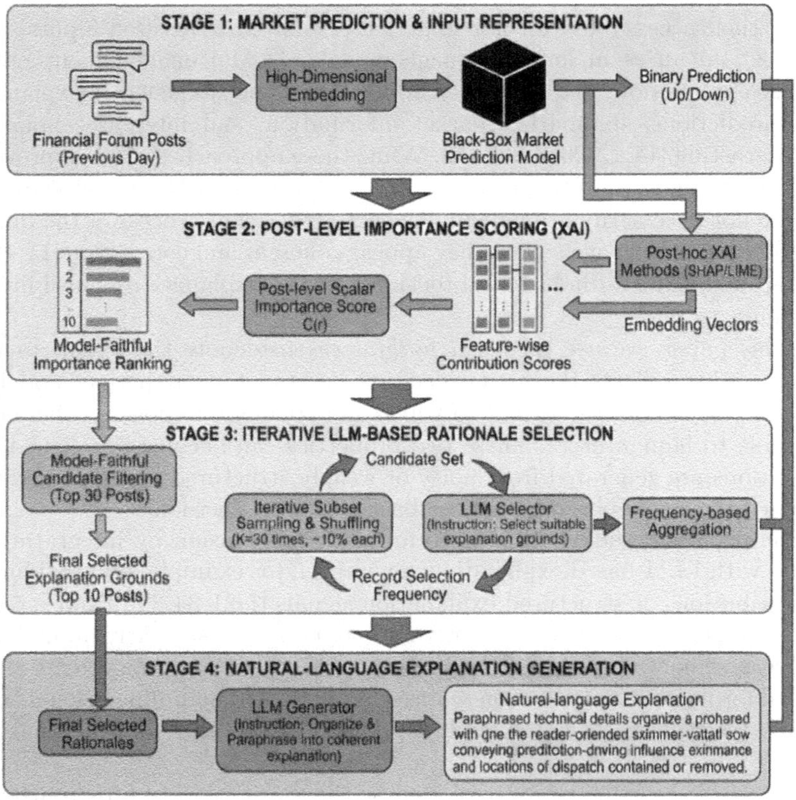

Fig. 1. Overview of the proposed XAI–LLM hybrid explanation framework. The framework consists of four stages.

2 Method

This section describes the proposed XAI–LLM hybrid rationale selection framework. The framework separates the extraction of model-faithful evidence from natural-language explanation generation, thereby embedding faithfulness into the explanation pipeline.

2.1 Stage 1: Market Prediction and Input Representation

As illustrated in Fig. 1, financial forum posts from the previous trading day are used as input to a market prediction model. Each post is converted into a high-dimensional embedding representation, and the collection of embeddings is processed by a black-box prediction model, which outputs a binary prediction indicating upward or downward market movement. The prediction model is treated as a fixed component, and the proposed framework is agnostic to the specific model architecture as long as post-hoc contribution scores can be computed.

2.2 Stage 2: Post-level Importance Scoring with XAI

To identify posts that contribute to the model prediction, we apply post-hoc explainable AI (XAI) methods, specifically SHAP [18] and LIME [23]. Because each post is represented as a multi-dimensional embedding vector, feature-wise contribution scores are aggregated at the post level to obtain a scalar importance score summarizing the overall magnitude of a post's influence, regardless of direction.

To obtain a robust ranking, posts are first ranked by SHAP-based importance scores and the top 50 are retained, after which they are re-ranked using TreeLIME. The final ranking is obtained by aggregating SHAP and LIME rankings via rank summation, mitigating instability due to random perturbations in LIME-based estimation. While this ranking reflects each post's contribution to the model prediction, it does not necessarily imply suitability as a human-readable explanation ground.

We intentionally aggregate contribution magnitudes regardless of direction, as embedding-level attributions are noisy and unstable in sign. This design prioritizes robustness in identifying model-influential posts, rather than preserving directional semantics at this stage.

2.3 Stage 3: Iterative LLM-Based Rationale Selection

Based on the XAI-based ranking, the top 30 posts are retained as model-faithful candidates. In each iteration, a subset comprising approximately 10% of the original input posts is independently sampled and randomly shuffled to reduce order bias and stochastic effects in LLM outputs [3,17]. The LLM is instructed to select posts suitable as explanation grounds.

This process is repeated K times ($K = 30$), and selection frequencies are aggregated to yield a stable ranking of posts as human-understandable rationales. Beyond approximately $K = 20$, we observed no qualitative changes in the top-ranked rationales, and therefore fixed $K = 30$ as a conservative choice. The top 10 posts are selected as the final explanation grounds.

2.4 Stage 4: Natural-Language Explanation Generation

In the final stage, the selected explanation grounds are provided to an LLM for natural-language explanation generation. The LLM organizes and paraphrases the selected posts into a coherent explanation reflecting the model prediction, without introducing new factual claims or external knowledge. All generation parameters are fixed across experimental conditions, ensuring that differences in explanation quality are attributable to differences in rationale selection strategies. This design ensures that explanation content is determined by the selected rationales, rather than by unconstrained generation behavior.

3 Experiment

The objective of this experiment is to examine explanation generation for market prediction models operating on noisy and unstructured financial forum posts, focusing on how rationale strategies shape explanation content and perceived quality.

3.1 Experimental Setup

Prediction Task. We consider a binary classification task that predicts the direction of the Nikkei Stock Average on the next trading day. Days with a price change rate of at least $+1.5\%$ are labeled as upward, while days with a change rate of at most -1.5% are labeled as downward. Days with smaller fluctuations are excluded to focus on market movements with clearer directional signals. This filtering is applied consistently throughout all experiments.

Forum Post Data. We use publicly available user-generated posts from the Nikkei Stock Average discussion thread on Yahoo! Finance Japan. For each target day, we consider only days on which the market moved by at least $\pm 1.5\%$. From the previous trading day of each such target day, 300 posts are randomly sampled from the forum and used as model input.

All sampled posts are preprocessed by removing URLs, punctuation symbols, and emoticons. Posts whose textual content becomes empty after preprocessing are excluded from further analysis.

Market Prediction Model. Each post is represented as a 300-dimensional vector using fastText [2], chosen for computational efficiency on large-scale noisy text, yielding a 300×300 feature matrix. A LightGBM-based classifier [13], widely used in financial prediction and compatible with SHAP/LIME (TreeLIME), outputs a binary prediction indicating the expected market direction. The model is trained on data from 2012 to 2019 and evaluated on data from 2020 to 2022, achieving an accuracy of 0.535, a precision of 0.558, a recall of 0.480, and an F1-score of 0.515. Since our focus is on explanation generation rather than predictive performance, the trained model is treated as a fixed component in all subsequent experiments.

3.2 Rationale Selection and Explanation Generation

Explanation generation is performed only for days on which the prediction model produces correct predictions, ensuring that explanations address why a prediction was correct rather than conflating explanation quality with error analysis.

For each such day, the same posts used as model input constitute the candidate pool for explanation generation. We compare four rationale selection strategies:

- **Random**: Ten posts randomly sampled from the candidate pool.
- **XAI**: Ten posts ranked highest by post-level importance scores computed using SHAP and LIME.
- **LLM**: The LLM ranks all candidate posts by their suitability as explanation grounds and selects the top ten.
- **Hybrid (Proposed)**: The top 30 posts ranked by XAI importance are first retained, after which the LLM selects the final ten posts.

To mitigate stochasticity in LLM-based selection, both the LLM and Hybrid conditions employ an iterative stabilization procedure. Candidate posts are repeatedly sampled and randomly shuffled, and selection frequencies are aggregated across iterations. The ten most frequently selected posts are used as explanation grounds. Only posts with lengths between 5 and 150 characters are considered to control explanation length and to avoid excessive quotation.

Explanation texts are generated using ELYZA-Japanese-Llama-3-8B [8, 10]. The LLM organizes and paraphrases the selected posts into a coherent natural-language explanation corresponding to the given prediction, without introducing external information or reproducing original posts verbatim.

3.3 Crowdsourcing-Based Evaluation

We evaluate explanation quality through a crowdsourcing-based user study. Prior to the evaluation, approximately 4,000 participants completed a preliminary survey designed to characterize financial knowledge and investment-related backgrounds. The survey consists of 20 quiz-style questions assessing basic financial knowledge, as well as four self-reported questions regarding investment experience and decision-making behavior. Participants are ranked by aggregated quiz scores, and the top 1,000 and bottom 1,000 participants are selected for the explanation evaluation task. All responses are anonymized.

In addition to knowledge and experience, the survey collects information on participants' habitual investment information sources. Participants report whether they primarily rely on newspapers or professional financial media, financial forums, or no particular source.

For each target day, explanations generated by the four methods are paired in all combinations and evaluated by multiple participants, yielding a total of 1,500 judgments. Pairwise comparison is chosen over absolute rating scales due to its greater discriminative stability observed in preliminary experiments.

All explanations presented in a comparison pair are generated for the same target day and correspond to the same prediction outcome. This design ensures that participants compare explanations under identical market conditions, isolating the effect of rationale strategy on perceived explanation quality. Participants are not informed about the selection method used to generate each explanation.

3.4 Evaluation Criteria

Participants compare two explanations generated for the same target day along multiple complementary aspects of explanation quality. Specifically, comparisons consider logical coherence, perceived usefulness for decision-making, ease of comprehension, and perceived credibility. Preferences are recorded for each aspect and aggregated to compute overall pairwise preference probabilities, which are used in the subsequent analyses.

Table 1. Overall pairwise preference probabilities aggregated across all participants. Each cell reports the probability that the row method was preferred over the column method. Values above 0.5 indicate a preference for the row method.

	LLM	XAI	Hybrid	Random
LLM	–	**0.54**	0.52	**0.56**
XAI	0.46	–	0.43	0.48
Hybrid	0.48	**0.57**	–	**0.53**
Random	0.44	0.52	0.47	–

4 Results

4.1 Participant Characteristics

Prior to the explanation evaluation task, a preliminary crowdsourcing survey was conducted to characterize participants' financial knowledge and backgrounds. Approximately 4,000 participants completed a quiz-style assessment of basic financial knowledge along with self-reported questions regarding investment experience and habitual information-seeking behavior.

Based on these responses, participants exhibited substantial diversity in both financial knowledge and informational background. For the explanation evaluation, participants were stratified by quiz score into high- and low-knowledge groups (top and bottom 1,000), and their self-reported information environments were used to examine how explanation preferences vary across users with different levels of expertise and information exposure.

4.2 Results of the Pairwise Explanation Evaluation

This subsection reports results from the crowdsourcing-based pairwise evaluation of explanation quality. For each explanation pair, participants compared two explanations along four criteria—consistency, usefulness, clarity, and trustworthiness—and preferences were aggregated to compute pairwise preference probabilities. We first present results aggregated across all participants, followed by analyses stratified by financial knowledge and information environment.

Overall Preferences Across All Participants. Table 1 summarizes overall pairwise preference probabilities. Across all participants, differences between methods are modest, with most values close to 0.5; nevertheless, the Hybrid method is consistently preferred over the XAI-only baseline and remains comparable to the LLM-only approach. Random selection does not exhibit a systematic advantage over model-informed strategies.

Table 2. Pairwise preference probabilities stratified by participant financial knowledge level (aggregated across evaluation criteria).

Group		LLM	XAI	Hybrid	Random
High	LLM	–	**0.54**	0.52	**0.56**
	XAI	0.46	–	0.43	0.48
	Hybrid	0.48	**0.57**	–	**0.53**
	Random	0.44	0.52	0.47	–
Low	LLM	–	0.53	0.47	0.50
	XAI	0.47	–	0.52	0.48
	Hybrid	0.53	0.48	–	0.54
	Random	0.50	0.52	0.46	–

Preferences Stratified by Financial Knowledge. Table 2 shows that preferences differ by financial knowledge level. Among high-knowledge participants, the Hybrid method is consistently preferred over the XAI-only baseline, while remaining comparable to the LLM-only approach. In contrast, preferences among low-knowledge participants are weaker and less consistent, with several comparisons close to chance level.

Table 3. Pairwise preference probabilities for high-knowledge participants, stratified by the primary information environment.

Source		LLM	XAI	Hybrid	Random
Newspapers	LLM	–	**0.64**	0.48	**0.65**
	XAI	0.36	–	0.32	0.37
	Hybrid	0.52	**0.68**	–	**0.63**
	Random	0.35	0.63	0.37	–
Forums	LLM	–	**0.62**	0.34	0.48
	XAI	0.38	–	0.44	0.41
	Hybrid	**0.66**	0.56	–	0.52
	Random	0.52	0.59	0.48	–

Information Environment Effects for High-Knowledge Participants. Table 3 further examines preferences among high-knowledge participants as a function of their primary information environment. Participants who primarily rely on newspapers or professional financial media show a strong preference for the Hybrid method over XAI-only explanations, suggesting that the Hybrid approach helps transform model-faithful signals into explanations that remain acceptable under stricter scrutiny. For participants who primarily consume financial forum content, Hybrid and LLM-only explanations are more competitive with each other, while XAI-only explanations are less consistently favored.

4.3 Qualitative Analysis

To complement the quantitative results, we qualitatively examine how different rationale strategies influence the coherence and directional consistency of generated explanations. Rather than presenting isolated anecdotes, we focus on two representative cases that illustrate when faithful rationale selection improves explanation quality and when its benefit is limited.

All forum posts and explanations are originally written in Japanese. The examples below are translated into English by the authors for presentation purposes.

Table 4. Case 1 (Hybrid Win): Comparison when the market is driven by complex and thematically dispersed sentiment (e.g., political anxiety). Hybrid captures a coherent narrative aligned with the prediction, whereas XAI extracts fragmented cues.

Method	Explanation content (translated)
XAI	**Selected rationales:** R1: "Hong Kong is rising crazily?"; R2: "US excess deaths 1 million, CDC says 'never seen before'."; R3: "Macron is the rope of the guillotine..." **Explanation:** The model leans upward. While there is confusion regarding "Macron" and "CDC," the "Hong Kong surge" suggests Asian strength. Buybacks are expected to dominate. **Comment:** Fragmented logic and incorrect directional interpretation due to noise.
Hybrid	**Selected rationales:** R1: "I can't forgive the Kishida shock. Financial income tax is punishing."; R2: "A 5 trillion yen handout is our tax money... stop joking."; R3: "Yen depreciation is selling out Japan. Assets flow out." **Explanation:** The model predicts a drop due to widespread dissatisfaction and anxiety. Criticism of the "Kishida shock" and "financial income tax" reinforces risk-averse sentiment. **Comment:** Coherent narrative aligned with bearish sentiment.

Case 1: Directional Distortion Caused by Dispersed XAI Rationales. Table 4 presents a case in which the Hybrid method is strongly preferred (win rate: 87.5%). On this day, the prediction model correctly forecasts a downward market movement.

The XAI-only method identifies multiple posts that are statistically important to the model prediction. However, these posts span unrelated topics and lack a shared semantic or directional focus, with some expressing optimistic views despite the downward prediction. When such heterogeneous information is treated as equally relevant during explanation generation, the resulting explanation becomes internally inconsistent and even asserts an upward movement that contradicts the model output.

This case illustrates that the statistical importance identified by XAI does not guarantee semantic or directional alignment. When dispersed cues are directly used for explanation generation, they can undermine coherence and distort the perceived prediction.

In contrast, the Hybrid method filters out directionally inconsistent posts and retains those aligned with the dominant bearish sentiment. By constraining the LLM to operate on this directionally consistent subset, Hybrid produces an explanation that remains coherent and faithful to the model prediction.

Case 2: When XAI Yields a Clear and Low-Cognitive-Load Explanation. Table 5 shows a contrasting case in which the XAI-only method is preferred (Hybrid win rate: 32.5%). Here, the market prediction is primarily driven by a single, widely recognized external factor: a decline in the US market.

Table 5. Case 2 (XAI Win): Comparison when the market is driven by a single strong external factor (e.g., a US market decline). XAI yields a clear and decisive explanation, whereas Hybrid aggregates mixed signals and reduces directional clarity.

Method	Explanation content (translated)
XAI	**Selected rationales:** R1: "Dow is down 100 points right now... Nikkei will definitely fall on Wednesday." **Explanation:** The basis for the drop is explicit. The decline in US stocks is expected to spill over to the Japanese market due to strong cross-market correlation. **Comment:** Simple, decisive, and low cognitive load.
Hybrid	**Selected rationales:** R1: "Rarely, I short-sold banks." (Bearish); R2: "The drop during the holiday will likely become reality." (Bearish); R3: "NASDAQ has bottomed out, so it won't crash." (Bullish) **Explanation:** The explanation aggregates mixed signals. While some posts indicate short selling pressure, others suggest market stabilization, resulting in reduced directional decisiveness. **Comment:** Comprehensive but less decisive.

In this scenario, XAI identifies posts that clearly and directly express this causal relationship. These rationales are easy to interpret, impose low cognitive load, and are strongly aligned with the predicted downward direction. The explanation-generation LLM is therefore able to ignore residual noise and produce a simple, consistent explanation.

This case indicates that when model-relevant information is both statistically important and semantically aligned, XAI alone can provide a sufficient basis for explanation generation. Under such conditions, additional rationale selection mechanisms offer limited benefit.

Implications from Qualitative Cases. Taken together, these cases show that the effectiveness of faithful rationale selection depends on the structure of the underlying market signal. Hybrid rationale selection is particularly beneficial when XAI-extracted information is dispersed across multiple topics or contains conflicting directional cues, where unconstrained explanation generation risks producing incoherent or misleading narratives.

Conversely, in event-driven markets dominated by a single strong factor, simpler XAI-based explanations may be preferred due to their clarity and low cognitive demand. These observations reinforce that explanation quality is inherently context-dependent, and that no single explanation strategy is universally optimal.

5 Discussion and Limitations

5.1 Why are the Observed Differences Relatively Small?

Across participants, pairwise preferences are often close to chance. This outcome reflects a fundamental property of large language models: LLM-generated explanations can remain fluent, coherent, and convincing even when their underlying rationales differ substantially. As a result, differences in rationale selection strategies are often smoothed out at the surface text level, causing explanations to appear similar in quality despite relying on different evidence.

This observation is consistent with prior findings on the gap between faithfulness and plausibility in explanation generation [1,24]. LLMs are capable of producing plausible post-hoc rationalizations that omit, reweight, or obscure influential factors. Consequently, evaluations based solely on perceived coherence or readability cannot guarantee that an explanation faithfully reflects the model's actual decision basis.

5.2 Faithfulness, Plausibility, and User Knowledge

While overall differences are modest, preferences vary substantially with participants' financial knowledge. Participants with lower knowledge show no stable preference ordering, suggesting greater reliance on superficial cues such as fluency or narrative style [1,24]. In contrast, participants with higher financial knowledge exhibit more consistent preferences and favor explanations grounded in model-relevant evidence.

These results indicate that the value of faithful explanations depends critically on users' ability to scrutinize explanation content. When users are capable of evaluating whether an explanation aligns with market logic and available evidence, explanations constrained by model-relevant rationales provide clearer benefits. For less experienced users, however, fluent but weakly grounded explanations may appear equally acceptable, masking underlying differences in faithfulness.

5.3 Why Structural Control is Necessary

An important implication of these findings is that explanation quality cannot be reliably assessed from generated text alone [1,15,24]. In many cases, an unconstrained explanation generator can produce superficially good explanations even when the selected rationales are noisy, misaligned, or partially irrelevant. This limitation makes the black-box nature of explanation generation particularly problematic in high-stakes domains such as financial decision-making.

The proposed XAI–LLM hybrid framework addresses this risk by embedding faithfulness into the explanation process at a structural level. Rather than trusting the LLM to reason faithfully, the framework constrains the information available for explanation generation to evidence that is demonstrably relevant to the prediction model. This design shifts the burden of faithfulness from post-hoc inspection of generated explanations to prior control over explanatory inputs.

5.4 Limitations and Trade-Offs

Despite these advantages, several limitations remain. First, there is currently no definitive method to directly verify the faithfulness of natural-language explanations produced by LLMs, and intervention-based evaluation remains task-dependent and imperfect [11,12,15]. Second, strict faithfulness constraints can reduce interpretability when model-relevant evidence is fragmentary or internally inconsistent. In such cases, plausibility-oriented generation may improve readability at the cost of obscuring the model's true decision basis.

These trade-offs suggest that explanation design is inherently multi-objective and context-dependent. Rather than seeking a universally optimal explanation strategy, effective systems should balance faithfulness, clarity, and decisiveness according to user characteristics and the structural properties of the prediction task.

6 Conclusion

This paper examined explanation generation for market prediction models operating on noisy financial forum posts, focusing on the tension between faithfulness to model behavior and the plausibility of natural-language explanations. While recent advances in large language models enable fluent and convincing explanations, such explanations are not necessarily grounded in the actual decision process of the prediction model. As a result, explanations that appear reasonable at the surface level may mask misalignment between explanatory narratives and model reasoning.

To address this challenge, we proposed an XAI–LLM hybrid explanation framework that embeds faithfulness at the rationale selection stage. Model-relevant information is first extracted using post-hoc XAI methods, after which an LLM performs constrained, iterative rationale selection and explanation generation. By structurally restricting the information available to the explanation generator, the framework shifts emphasis from post-hoc inspection of generated text to prior control over explanatory inputs.

Crowdsourcing-based evaluations stratified by financial knowledge revealed that faithful rationale selection does not uniformly improve perceived explanation quality. Participants with limited domain knowledge exhibited unstable preferences, suggesting reliance on surface-level cues such as fluency. In contrast, participants with higher financial knowledge consistently favored explanations grounded in model-relevant evidence. These findings indicate that faithfulness and plausibility play distinct roles in explanation evaluation, and that the benefit of faithful explanations depends strongly on user characteristics.

More broadly, our results highlight a central risk of explanation generation with large language models: unconstrained generators can produce superficially good explanations, making faithfulness difficult to assess from text alone. This risk underscores the importance of structural control in explanation pipelines. Explanation frameworks that enforce faithfulness prior to language generation offer a promising direction for explainable AI systems operating in high-noise and high-stakes environments. Future work may explore how such structural constraints can be adapted to different tasks, balanced with explanation diversity, and aligned with the needs of users with varying levels of domain expertise.

References

1. Agarwal, C., Tanneru, S.H., Lakkaraju, H.: Faithfulness vs. plausibility: on the (un) reliability of explanations from large language models. arXiv preprint arXiv:2402.04614 (2024)
2. Bojanowski, P., Grave, E., Joulin, A., Mikolov, T.: Enriching word vectors with subword information. Trans. Assoc. Comput. Linguist. **5**, 135–146 (2017). https://doi.org/10.1162/tacl_a_00051. https://aclanthology.org/Q17-1010/
3. Brucks, M., Toubia, O.: Prompt architecture induces methodological artifacts in large language models. PLoS ONE **20**(4), 1–13 (2025). https://doi.org/10.1371/journal.pone.0319159. https://doi.org/10.1371/journal.pone.0319159
4. Celik, T.B., Ican, O., Bulut, E.: Extending machine learning prediction capabilities by explainable ai in financial time series prediction. SSRN Electron. J. (2022)
5. Cheng, Z., Cao, M., Rondeau, M.A., Cheung, J.C.: Stochastic chameleons: irrelevant context hallucinations reveal class-based (mis)generalization in LLMs. In: Che, W., Nabende, J., Shutova, E., Pilehvar, M.T. (eds.) Proceedings of the 63rd

Annual Meeting of the Association for Computational Linguistics (Volume 1: Long Papers), pp. 30187–30214. Association for Computational Linguistics, Vienna, Austria (2025).https://doi.org/10.18653/v1/2025.acl-long.1458. https://aclanthology.org/2025.acl-long.1458/
6. Dang, A.H., Tran, V., Nguyen, L.M.: Survey and analysis of hallucinations in large language models: attribution to prompting strategies or model behavior. Front. Artif. Intell. **8** (2025). https://doi.org/10.3389/frai.2025.1622292
7. Dwiaynti, L., Wibisono, S.R., Nambo, H.: Contextualshap: enhancing shap explanations through contextual language generation. arXiv preprint arXiv:2512.07178 (2025). https://arxiv.org/abs/2512.07178. Accepted at the 7th World Symposium on Software Engineering (WSSE) 2025
8. Elyza, I.: Elyza-japanese-llama-3-8b (2024). https://huggingface.co/elyza/ELYZA-japanese-Llama-3-8b
9. Giudici, P., Piergallini, A., Recchioni, M.C., Raffinetti, E.: Explainable artificial intelligence methods for financial time series. XXPhys. A **655**, 130176 (2024). https://doi.org/10.1016/j.physa.2024.130176
10. Grattafiori, A., et al.: The llama 3 herd of models. arXiv preprint arXiv:2407.21783 (2024)
11. Hase, P., Bansal, M.: Evaluating explainable AI: which algorithmic explanations help users predict model behavior? In: Jurafsky, D., Chai, J., Schluter, N., Tetreault, J. (eds.) Proceedings of the 58th Annual Meeting of the Association for Computational Linguistics, pp. 5540–5552. Association for Computational Linguistics, Online (2020). https://doi.org/10.18653/v1/2020.acl-main.491. https://aclanthology.org/2020.acl-main.491/
12. Jacovi, A., Goldberg, Y.: Towards faithfully interpretable NLP systems: how should we define and evaluate faithfulness? In: Jurafsky, D., Chai, J., Schluter, N., Tetreault, J. (eds.) Proceedings of the 58th Annual Meeting of the Association for Computational Linguistics, pp. 4198–4205. Association for Computational Linguistics, Online (2020). https://doi.org/10.18653/v1/2020.acl-main.386. https://aclanthology.org/2020.acl-main.386/
13. Ke, G., et al.: Lightgbm: a highly efficient gradient boosting decision tree. In: Proceedings of the 31st International Conference on Neural Information Processing Systems, NIPS 2017, pp. 3149–3157. Curran Associates Inc., Red Hook, NY, USA (2017)
14. Koa, K.J., Ma, Y., Ng, R., Chua, T.S.: Learning to generate explainable stock predictions using self-reflective large language models. In: Proceedings of the ACM Web Conference 2024, WWW 2024, pp. 4304–4315. Association for Computing Machinery, New York, NY, USA (2024). https://doi.org/10.1145/3589334.3645611
15. Lanham, T., et al.: Measuring faithfulness in chain-of-thought reasoning. arXiv preprint arXiv:2307.13702 (2023)
16. Li, S., Liao, W., Chen, Y.H., Yan, R.: Pen: prediction-explanation network to forecast stock price movement with better explainability. In: Proceedings of the AAAI Conference on Artificial Intelligence, vol. 37, pp. 5187–5194 (2023). https://doi.org/10.1609/aaai.v37i4.25648
17. Lu, Y., Bartolo, M., Moore, A., Riedel, S., Stenetorp, P.: Fantastically ordered prompts and where to find them: overcoming few-shot prompt order sensitivity. In: Muresan, S., Nakov, P., Villavicencio, A. (eds.) Proceedings of the 60th Annual Meeting of the Association for Computational Linguistics (Volume 1: Long Papers), pp. 8086–8098. Association for Computational Linguistics, Dublin, Ireland (2022). https://doi.org/10.18653/v1/2022.acl-long.556. https://aclanthology.org/2022.acl-long.556/

18. Lundberg, S.M., Lee, S.I.: A unified approach to interpreting model predictions. In: Advances in Neural Information Processing Systems, vol. 30 (2017)
19. Madsen, A., Chandar, S., Reddy, S.: Are self-explanations from large language models faithful? In: Ku, L.W., Martins, A., Srikumar, V. (eds.) Findings of the Association for Computational Linguistics: ACL 2024, pp. 295–337. Association for Computational Linguistics, Bangkok, Thailand (2024). https://doi.org/10.18653/v1/2024.findings-acl.19. https://aclanthology.org/2024.findings-acl.19/
20. Marey, N., Abu-Musa, A.A., Ganna, M.: Integrating deep learning and explainable artificial intelligence techniques for stock price predictions: an empirical study based on time series big data. Int. J. Account. Manag. Sci. **3**(4) (2024). https://doi.org/10.56830/IJNZ1133
21. Martens, D., Hinns, J., Dams, C., Vergouwen, M., Evgeniou, T.: Tell me a story! narrative-driven XAI with large language models. Decis. Support Syst. **191**, 114402 (2025). https://doi.org/10.1016/j.dss.2025.114402. https://www.sciencedirect.com/science/article/pii/S016792362500003X
22. Nie, Y., et al.: A survey of large language models for financial applications: progress, prospects and challenges (2024). https://doi.org/10.48550/arXiv.2406.11903
23. Ribeiro, M.T., Singh, S., Guestrin, C.: "why should i trust you?": explaining the predictions of any classifier. In: Proceedings of the 22nd ACM SIGKDD International Conference on Knowledge Discovery and Data Mining, pp. 1135–1144 (2016)
24. Turpin, M., Michael, J., Perez, E., Bowman, S.: Language models don't always say what they think: unfaithful explanations in chain-of-thought prompting. Adv. Neural. Inf. Process. Syst. **36**, 74952–74965 (2023)
25. Vishwanath, K., Alyakin, A., Alber, D.A., Lee, J.V., Kondziolka, D., Oermann, E.K.: Medical large language models are easily distracted, arXiv preprint arXiv:2504.01201 (2025). https://arxiv.org/abs/2504.01201. Accepted at the 7th World Symposium on Software Engineering (WSSE) 2025
26. Wang, M., Izumi, K., Sakaji, H.: LLMFactor: extracting profitable factors through prompts for explainable stock movement prediction. In: Ku, L.W., Martins, A., Srikumar, V. (eds.) Findings of the Association for Computational Linguistics: ACL 2024, pp. 3120–3131. Association for Computational Linguistics, Bangkok, Thailand (2024). https://doi.org/10.18653/v1/2024.findings-acl.185. https://aclanthology.org/2024.findings-acl.185/
27. Xie, Q., et al.: Pixiu: a large language model, instruction data and evaluation benchmark for finance. In: Proceedings of the 37th International Conference on Neural Information Processing Systems, NIPS 2023. Curran Associates Inc, Red Hook, NY, USA (2023)
28. Yang, H., Liu, X.Y., Wang, C.D.: Fingpt: open-source financial large language models (2025). https://arxiv.org/abs/2306.06031
29. Yang, M., Huang, E., Zhang, L., Surdeanu, M., Wang, W.Y., Pan, L.: How is LLM reasoning distracted by irrelevant context? An analysis using a controlled benchmark. In: Christodoulopoulos, C., Chakraborty, T., Rose, C., Peng, V. (eds.) Proceedings of the 2025 Conference on Empirical Methods in Natural Language Processing, pp. 13340–13358. Association for Computational Linguistics, Suzhou, China (2025). https://doi.org/10.18653/v1/2025.emnlp-main.674. https://aclanthology.org/2025.emnlp-main.674/
30. Yeo, W.J., Van Der Heever, W., Mao, R., Cambria, E., Satapathy, R., Mengaldo, G.: A comprehensive review on financial explainable ai. Artif. Intell. Rev. **58**(6), 1–49 (2025)

31. Yu, Y., et al.: Fincon: a synthesized LLM multi-agent system with conceptual verbal reinforcement for enhanced financial decision making. In: Proceedings of the 38th International Conference on Neural Information Processing Systems, NIPS 2024. Curran Associates Inc., Red Hook, NY, USA (2024)
32. Zhang, Z.Y., Verma, A., Doshi-Velez, F., Low, B.K.H.: Understanding the relationship between prompts and response uncertainty in large language models (2024). https://arxiv.org/abs/2407.14845
33. Zhao, H., et al.: Revolutionizing finance with LLMs: an overview of applications and insights (2024). https://doi.org/10.48550/arXiv.2401.11641
34. Zytek, A., Pido, S., Alnegheimish, S., Berti-Équille, L., Veeramachaneni, K.: Explingo: explaining AI predictions using large language models. In: 2024 IEEE International Conference on Big Data (BigData), pp. 1197–1208 (2024). https://doi.org/10.1109/BigData62323.2024.10825114
35. Zytek, A., Pido, S., Veeramachaneni, K.: LLMs for XAI: future directions for explaining explanations. arXiv abs/2405.06064 (2024). https://api.semanticscholar.org/CorpusID:269740873

A Multimodal Predictive Framework for Constructive Listening in Opposing-View AI Dialogues

Juan Miguel Miranda(✉), Gerard Christian Felipe, Andre Llanes, Ewan Escaño, and Jocelynn Cu

Center for Human–Computer Innovations (CeHCI), Advanced Research Institute for Informatics, Computing and Networking (AdRIC), De La Salle University - Manila, 2401 Taft Avenue, Manila, Philippines
{juan_miranda,gerard_christian_felipe,andre_llanes,ewan_escano, jocelynn.cu}@dlsu.edu.ph

Abstract. In an increasingly polarized digital environment, sustaining constructive listening during discussions involving opposing viewpoints has become a critical challenge. This study explores a multimodal predictive framework for constructive listening, defined as the ability to accurately understand and recall a conversational partner's positions and arguments. Fifteen participants engaged in 10-15-minute spoken debates with a customized ChatGPT Voice Mode agent adopting a Similar, Opposing, or Neutral stance on morally and socially charged topics. This study reports early-stage empirical findings from a pilot dataset, offering initial evidence on how emotional dynamics relate to constructive listening in AI-mediated disagreement. Facial expressions, vocal prosody, and participant-generated summaries were processed through a synchronized multimodal pipeline using FER, DeepFace, Wav2Vec2-based vocal emotion modeling, and Librosa. Constructive listening was quantified using a Summary Accuracy Score combining topic coverage, semantic similarity, and factual accuracy. Group-level analyses did not show statistically significant differences in baseline emotional states or summary accuracy across conditions. However, predictive modeling using Leave-One-Out Cross-Validation indicated that emotional variability, rather than emotional calmness, was the strongest predictor of listening performance. Multimodal fusion achieved the highest predictive accuracy ($R^2 = 0.563$), followed by vocal features alone, while facial features showed no predictive value. These findings suggest emotional variability as a behavioral marker of constructive listening and inform the design of empathy-aware and persuasive AI systems.

Keywords: Constructive Listening · Affective Computing · Emotion Recognition · Human-AI interaction

1 Introduction

In today's polarized digital environment, discussions on social and political issues often deteriorate into conflict rather than mutual understanding. Algorithmic echo chambers and motivated reasoning promote selective exposure, leading individuals to dismiss

E. Vlahu-Gjorgievska et al. (Eds.): PERSUASIVE 2026, CCIS 2896, pp. 122–134, 2027.
https://doi.org/10.1007/978-3-032-27235-5_9

opposing viewpoints and struggle with active listening. Constructive listening offers a critical intervention by emphasizing accurate understanding and recall of opposing viewpoints rather than immediate agreement; prior research shows that feeling heard reduces defensiveness and supports continued engagement.

This study seeks to better understand how individuals process and respond to opposing perspectives by examining measurable behavioral and linguistic signals. Specifically, we investigate whether multimodal cues such as facial expressions, vocal prosody, and summary-based text features can predict how accurately a person understands and recalls an AI conversation partner's viewpoint.

This study presents exploratory findings from a small-scale pilot examining emotional dynamics in AI-mediated disagreement. Rather than making causal or population-level claims, the goal is to identify potential behavioral patterns and assess the feasibility of a predictive framework for constructive listening, informing the design of persuasive and empathy-aware dialogue systems.

1.1 Problem Statement

Despite the central role of listening in resolving disagreements, there is limited empirical research on how people emotionally and cognitively respond when confronted with opposing viewpoints, especially in AI-mediated conversations. Current tools for measuring listening quality rely heavily on self-report or human judgment, leaving a gap in objective, behavior-based assessments.

This leads to the **Research Question**: Which multimodal features—facial, vocal, and linguistic—can predict an individual's ability to constructively listen and accurately summarize an opposing viewpoint?

1.2 Hypotheses

H_1. Participants exposed to opposing viewpoints will demonstrate lower constructive listening accuracy compared to participants engaging with similar or neutral viewpoints, due to increased cognitive and emotional resistance.

H_2. Higher levels of emotional calmness and composure, reflected by stable affective states and lower emotional volatility, will be associated with higher constructive listening accuracy, as calm emotional profiles are hypothesized to indicate focused, objective, and regulated information processing.

H_3. Vocal emotional features will predict constructive listening accuracy more effectively than facial emotional features, as vocal prosody is hypothesized to more directly reflect attentional focus and cognitive load.

1.3 Intended Contribution

This study proposes an exploratory predictive framework for constructive listening that models listening accuracy as a measurable behavioral outcome in AI-human dialogue. By integrating multimodal emotional signals, the framework informs the design of empathy-training, persuasive, and communication technologies that seek to support understanding across differing viewpoints. Beyond measurement, the findings highlight the role of emotional dynamics, rather than emotional neutrality, in effective listening, suggesting that multimodal emotional variability, particularly vocal and fused affective shifts, reflects behavioral engagement during dialogue.

This gap is significant in applied contexts where persuasive outcomes depend on sustained engagement and accurate understanding of opposing viewpoints, including empathy training, online moderation, de-escalation, and counseling systems. By quantifying constructive listening as a behavioral outcome, the framework provides actionable signals to support openness, reflection, and reduced defensiveness through adaptive feedback or pacing during emotionally charged dialogue.

This paper makes three contributions: (1) it provides pilot evidence that constructive listening accuracy in AI-human disagreement can be predicted using a multimodal affective framework, enabling behaviorally grounded evaluation beyond subjective empathy measures; (2) it identifies emotional variability: captured through affective volatility and quadrant transitions as a marker of listening effort and engagement independent of conversational stance; and (3) it shows that vocal emotional features outperform facial-only features, with multimodal fusion offering additional predictive gains.

2 Related Work

Research on empathic communication shows that high-quality listening reduces defensiveness and supports psychological needs, whether delivered by humans or conversational AI (Weinstein et al., 2022; Weinstein and Itzchakov, 2025; Weinstein et al., 2025). Behavioral studies emphasize active listening cues such as paraphrasing and nonverbal involvement (Weger et al., 2014), while disagreement is often misinterpreted as poor listening despite unchanged behavior (Ren and Schaumberg, 2024), suggesting that emotional change over time reflects active cognitive processing rather than instability.

Multimodal approaches inform empathy and cognitive-state detection by combining facial, vocal, and linguistic cues to improve identification of empathic responses, confusion, and conflict in conversational settings (Abbasian et al., 2024; Ma et al., 2024). Although large language models can mimic empathic expression, limitations in personalization and emotional understanding persist (Roshanaei et al., 2024), reinforcing the value of multimodal behavioral signals. Vocal prosody, in particular, captures moment-to-moment changes in attention, cognitive load, and emotional regulation, often outperforming facial cues in demanding interactions.

Measurement research supports treating listening as an observable behavioral outcome rather than a purely subjective perception. Indicators such as recall accuracy, summary completeness, and responsiveness reflect listening effort in task-based dialogue (Keaton, 2017; Alhanbali et al., 2019). In persuasive and conflict-oriented communication, emotional engagement can soften resistance, motivating the use of emotion-sensitive signals in empathy-aware systems. Collectively, this work highlights a critical gap: the absence of multimodal predictive models that objectively quantify constructive listening during spoken disagreement with AI.

3 Methodology

3.1 Experimental Design

This study employed a between-subjects design examining constructive listening across three conversational conditions: Similar, Opposing, and Neutral. Participants were assigned based on a pre-survey of their stances on sensitive topics, with the AI aligning with participant views in the Similar condition, adopting a contradictory stance in the Opposing condition, and taking either stance in the Neutral condition for participants reporting ideologically neutral views. Because stance conditions were defined relative to each participant's pre-survey position, assignment could not be fully randomized; instead, topic and stance were assigned using a constrained procedure to maintain approximate balance across conditions and accommodate small-sample and scheduling constraints.

Fifteen undergraduate students were recruited via snowball sampling. Inclusion criteria required English proficiency, consent for audio-video recording, and willingness to discuss sensitive topics. All participants provided informed consent and were informed that emotion outputs were probabilistic and not psychological assessments. Use of an AI conversation partner minimized interpersonal risk and ensured a controlled research setting. Because the stance condition (Similar vs. Opposing) is defined relative to each participant's pre-survey position, assignment was not purely randomized in this pilot. Instead, stance and topic were allocated to maintain approximate balance across conditions and to ensure participants could meaningfully engage with the selected topic under small-sample and scheduling constraints.

3.2 Procedure and Variables

Participants engaged in a structured 10–15 min one-on-one Zoom debate with a ChatGPT Voice Mode agent, beginning with brief icebreakers followed by morally charged questions on abortion, the death penalty, and AI in education. After each debate, participants produced a verbal summary of the AI's arguments, which was compared against the ground-truth transcript to compute constructive listening accuracy; all sessions used identical prompts, recording setups, and interaction lengths to maintain internal consistency.

3.3 Data Pipeline and Preprocessing

All sessions were processed through a unified multimodal pipeline consisting of facial and vocal emotion extraction followed by weighted fusion. Facial analysis produced probability scores for seven basic emotions and continuous affective dimensions (valence, arousal, intensity), which were grouped into four affective states (Excited, Stressed, Calm, Tired). Vocal analysis extracted acoustic and prosodic features, including pitch statistics, MFCCs, speech rate, harmonicity, and derived affective indicators such as arousal, valence, dominance, and stress.

Facial and vocal outputs were fused using a fixed weighted scheme (70% facial, 30% vocal) to generate integrated affective features. All outputs were exported as structured feature vectors for analysis.

Evaluation Metric

Constructive listening was measured using a Summary Accuracy Score combining three components: Topic Coverage (65%), measuring recall of key semantic ideas; Semantic Similarity (25%), computed via cosine similarity between transcript and summary embeddings; and Factual Accuracy (10%), penalizing contradictory sentiment. Topic Coverage was prioritized because humans can more strongly paraphrase rather than repeating exact wording. Semantic Similarity served as a supplementary indicator of alignment in meaning and phrasing, while Factual Accuracy was assigned a smaller weight to function as a safeguard against clear contradictions, reflecting the experimental role of automated contradiction detection rather than a primary measure of listening quality.

Multimodal Feature Extraction and Representation

Facial and vocal emotion features were extracted using pretrained models. Facial emotion recognition used the FER library with MTCNN for face detection, supplemented by DeepFace for cross-validation; overlapping emotion categories were combined using a weighted average (70% FER, 30% DeepFace) to improve reliability. Vocal emotion analysis employed a pretrained Wav2Vec2 model via Audonnx to estimate continuous affective dimensions (arousal, valence, dominance), with additional acoustic and prosodic features extracted using Librosa.

Across modalities, multiple layers of emotional representation were computed at the segment level. Facial indices included seven basic emotions, continuous affective dimensions (valence, arousal, intensity), and derived affective states, while vocal indices included basic emotions, continuous affective dimensions, and acoustic features such as pitch statistics, MFCCs, spectral measures, speech rate, silence ratio, harmonicity, and tremor. Fusion features integrated facial and vocal outputs into combined emotion probabilities and affective dimensions, along with behavioral metrics such as emotional volatility, quadrant transition counts, and modality agreement. Each segment was represented by a 77-dimensional feature vector comprising 15 facial features, 58 vocal features, and 4 fused affective features summarizing arousal, valence, intensity, and quadrant state.

Preprocessing, Fusion, and Validation

Audio and video streams were segmented into 1.0-s windows. Audio was extracted with MoviePy, resampled to 16 kHz, normalized, and synchronized with facial features using timestamps prior to fusion. Facial and vocal signals were combined using a fixed weighted fusion scheme (70% facial, 30% vocal), selected a priori based on the relative stability of the facial tracker and early instability of voice models. Fusion parameters were fixed prior to analysis to avoid post hoc tuning, consistent with the study's exploratory goals. Accordingly, the fusion model was not intended to optimize modality weighting for maximum performance, but to evaluate whether constructive listening can be meaningfully quantified using multimodal emotional signals without overfitting given the small sample size.

Given the small sample size (N = 15), Leave-One-Out Cross-Validation (LOOCV) was used to maximize data utilization while maintaining strict separation between training and test data, reducing overfitting risk while preserving statistical power.

Statistical Analysis and Machine Learning Model

Statistical analyses were conducted using scipy and scikit-learn. Group differences were assessed using Kruskal-Wallis tests due to violations of normality assumptions, and Spearman's rank correlations were computed to examine relationships between emotional features and Summary Accuracy Scores.

To evaluate predictive performance, multiple regression models were trained, including Ridge Regression, Lasso, ElasticNet, and Random Forests. Models were evaluated using LOOCV by comparing predicted and observed Summary Accuracy Scores. Ridge Regression demonstrated the strongest and most stable performance (MAE = 10.48%, $r = 0.770$, $p < 0.001$) and was selected as the primary model reported.

4 Results

4.1 Inter-Group Analysis

Inter-group analyses compared participants in the Similar, Opposing, and Neutral conditions across multimodal affective features. Kruskal-Wallis tests revealed no statistically significant differences in arousal, valence, or intensity across conversational conditions (all $p > .05$). Group-level differences in constructive listening accuracy were likewise non-significant, suggesting that conversational alignment alone does not account for listening performance and motivating analyses focused on emotional dynamics rather than static affect (Fig. 1).

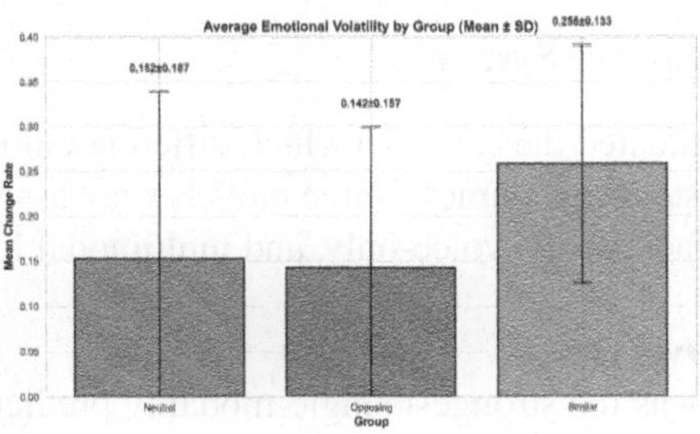

Fig. 1. Mean bar chart of emotional intensities

Across all groups, neutral expression dominated detected facial emotions, accounting for approximately 76–88% of frames. The Opposing group exhibited the highest proportion of neutrality (88%), whereas the Similar group showed the lowest (70%) and the widest range of expressed emotions. Although mean affective intensities did not differ significantly across groups, participants varied in emotional volatility. The Similar condition showed the highest rate of emotional state transitions ($\mu = 0.246$), followed by the Neutral ($\mu = 0.152$) and Opposing ($\mu = 0.142$) conditions, suggesting that stance alignment elicited greater emotional reactivity than direct disagreement (Fig. 2).

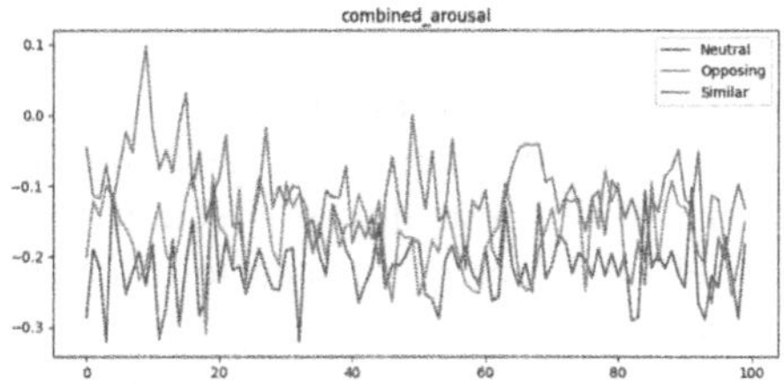

Fig. 2. Arousal rate across 3 groups

Time-series analyses of fused arousal, valence, and intensity further revealed no sustained group-level differences across the interaction window. All groups maintained predominantly low to moderate arousal and slightly negative valence over time, with similar overall trajectories.

4.2 Key Predictors of Listening Accuracy

Across all multimodal features examined, only two dynamic emotional indicators showed significant associations with Summary Accuracy Scores: Quadrant Transitions ($p = 0.00023$) and Total Valence Change ($p = 0.016$). Participants who exhibited more frequent transitions between valence-arousal quadrants and greater fluctuations in emotional valence produced more accurate and complete summaries. These findings indicate that dynamic emotional responsiveness, rather than emotional calmness or neutrality, is a key predictor of constructive listening performance.

4.3 Prediction Performance System

Predictive modeling evaluated the extent to which different emotional modalities could estimate constructive listening accuracy. Three models were assessed using Leave-One-Out Cross-Validation: facial-only, voice-only, and multimodal fusion models.

Model Performance Overview
The voice-only model was the strongest single-modality predictor, achieving an R^2 of 0.492 and a correlation of $r = 0.705$, explaining nearly half of the variance in Summary Accuracy Scores (MAE = 10.99%). In contrast, the facial-only model performed poorly ($R^2 = -0.022$; MAE = 14.29%), reflecting limited expressive facial variability and the constraints of webcam-based facial analysis (Figs. 3, 4 and 5).

The multimodal fusion model yielded a higher overall explained variance (R2 = 0.563, $r = 0.770$; MAE = 10.48%); however, this improvement reflects a different predictive behavior rather than more potent modality synergy. Vocal features exhibited higher variance, producing both higher highs and lower lows in predicted listening

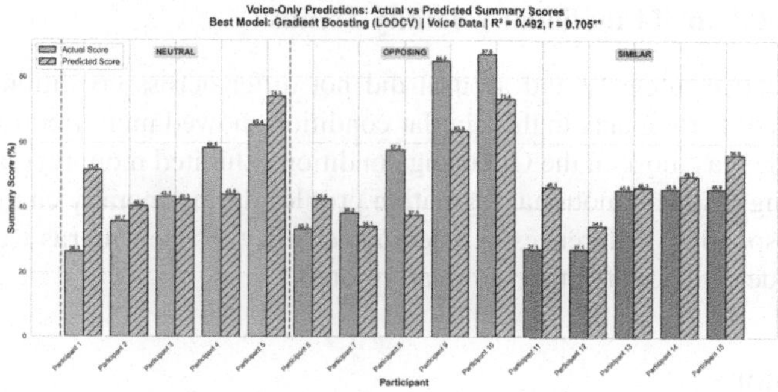

Fig. 3. Voice-Only Prediction System

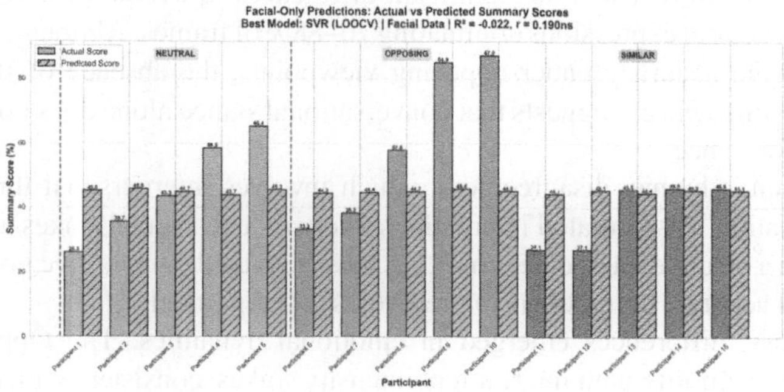

Fig. 4. Face-Only Prediction System

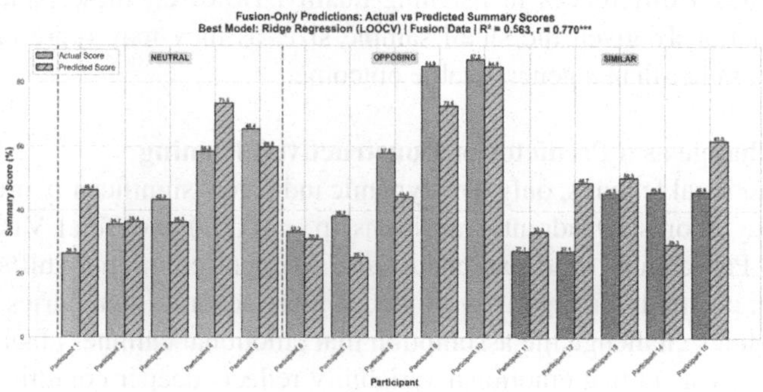

Fig. 5. Fusion Prediction System

accuracy. In contrast, the inclusion of facial features, which was characterized by predominantly neutral expressions, pulled predictions closer to the mean. As a result, fusion reduced extreme errors. Consequently, vocal emotional features remain the most sensitive indicators of listening dynamics in this study, with fusion primarily acting as a regularizing influence.

4.4 Interpretation of Emotional Volatility Trends

Although affective intensity and arousal did not differ across conditions, emotional volatility varied. Participants in the Similar condition showed more frequent emotional transitions, whereas those in the Opposing condition exhibited more regulated trajectories, suggesting distinct emotional regulation profiles during morally charged dialogue without corresponding differences in listening accuracy. These patterns warrant further investigation despite not affecting summary scores.

5 Discussion

Emotional Dynamics Across Conversational Conditions
Inter-group analyses revealed no significant differences in overall arousal, valence, or intensity, with neutral expressions dominating 76–88% of frames. Although H1 predicted reduced listening accuracy under opposing viewpoints, the absence of strong group-level affective differences suggests that conversational stance alone does not account for listening performance.

Unlike human-human disagreement, which involves interpersonal threat and persuasive motivation, AI-mediated interactions likely reduced social stakes and defensive responses. As a result, disagreement may not have activated competitive goals, resulting in maintained accurate comprehension regardless of alignment.

Nonetheless, differences emerged in emotional dynamics. The Opposing group exhibited high neutrality with intermittent intensity spikes, consistent with regulated yet engaged disagreement. In contrast, the Similar group showed greater emotional volatility and deeper negative valence dips, reflecting distinct emotional engagement patterns without significant differences in listening quality. However, these patterns must be interpreted cautiously given the small sample size, as they may represent individual characteristics rather than a generalizable outcome.

Emotional Change as a Predictor of Constructive Listening
Across all emotional features, only two dynamic indicators significantly predicted Summary Accuracy Scores: Quadrant Transitions ($p < 0.001$) and Total Valence Change ($p = 0.016$). Participants who exhibited more frequent emotional shifts and greater fluctuations in positivity or negativity produced more accurate summaries.

These findings challenge the assumption that emotional calmness facilitates listening, suggesting instead that emotional variability reflects deeper cognitive processing. Emotional calmness may reflect disengagement or boredom rather than active evaluative effort, whereas emotional variability may capture moments of interest and cognitive effort that support accurate comprehension and recall.

Multimodal Prediction of Listening Accuracy
Predictive modeling further confirmed the value of multimodal emotional signals. The fusion model achieved the strongest performance ($R^2 = 0.563$, MAE $= 10.48\%$), explaining nearly 60% of the variance in listening accuracy. Vocal features alone were the strongest single modality ($R^2 = 0.492$, MAE $= 10.99\%$), while facial features showed

no predictive value ($R^2 = -0.022$), likely due to dominant neutral expressions and limitations of webcam-based facial analysis.

Design Implications for Empathy-Aware Systems

These findings have direct implications for persuasive dialogue agents, conflict mediation systems, and empathy training applications. Rather than treating emotional neutrality as a marker of effective engagement, the results suggest that shifts in valence and affective state signal deeper engagement during charged dialogue, enabling systems to distinguish active engagement from disengagement or resistance independent of agreement. While this work focuses on constructive listening as an observable behavioral outcome, related constructs such as empathy, openness, and attitude change were not directly measured and are referenced here only as potential downstream processes supported by accurate listening.

Voice-based and fused emotion signals, in particular, offer practical indicators of listening effort during dialogue. Future systems could adapt argument pacing, tone, or framing in response to detected emotional shifts, while empathy-training tools may benefit from encouraging emotional responsiveness rather than suppression.

Interpreting Emotional Variability

A plausible mechanism underlying these effects is that affective shifts reflect active cognitive monitoring during dialogue. Changes in emotional state may signal moments of reassessment, conflict resolution, or integration of new information. Rather than indicating dysregulation, emotional variability may represent adaptive engagement that supports deeper processing and more accurate recall.

6 Limitations

This exploratory study should be interpreted as indicative rather than conclusive. The small sample size ($N = 15$) limits statistical power, and conversational stance was manually assigned rather than randomized, introducing potential selection bias and weakening causal interpretation. Observed group differences may reflect unmeasured participant characteristics, such as emotional regulation, speaking ability, or AI familiarity, rather than the stance manipulation itself.

Ethical Considerations

Given the morally sensitive topics and use of emotion-sensitive AI analysis, ethical safeguards were implemented throughout the study. Participants provided informed consent, were informed of the AI interaction, and advised that discussions could involve challenging viewpoints, with the option to pause or withdraw at any time. Post-task debriefing clarified that the study examined listening and engagement processes rather than persuasive influence, mitigating potential psychological risks.

Emotional data were handled with care: facial and vocal features were used solely for analysis, not identification, anonymized, securely stored, and scheduled for deletion after project completion. Given the limitations of automated emotion recognition, features were treated as probabilistic indicators of engagement, and analysis was conducted retrospectively without influence from participant beliefs.

Internal Validity Considerations
Conversational stances (Similar, Opposing, Neutral) were manually assigned rather than randomized to maintain approximate balance across conditions given the small sample size and time constraints. Topic assignments were likewise balanced across conditions and allocated sequentially to avoid disproportionate group sizes.

Participants expressing strong prior views were assigned to corresponding topics to support meaningful engagement, while stance polarity (pro or anti) was determined solely to balance condition counts. Neutral stances were assigned when participants reported mixed or moderate views on the pre-task questionnaire. All assignments were conducted unilaterally by a single researcher without participant negotiation.

While this approach ensured condition balance, topic-related and order effects cannot be fully ruled out. Future studies should randomize stance assignment, counterbalance topic difficulty, and vary topic order to strengthen causal inference.

7 Implications

The findings suggest that emotional variability, rather than emotional neutrality, is linked to better constructive listening. This challenges the assumption that calmness reflects effective engagement and indicates that emotional shifts may signal deeper cognitive processing. The strong performance of voice and fusion models also shows that multimodal emotional signals, especially voice data, can be used to estimate listening accuracy, offering practical value for AI conversational agents.

8 Conclusion and Contributions

This study makes three primary contributions to research on empathy-aware and persuasive AI systems. First, it demonstrates the feasibility of predicting constructive listening accuracy in AI-human dialogue using a multimodal affective framework, enabling behaviorally grounded evaluation beyond subjective empathy measures and providing initial evidence linking emotional features to listening performance in debate-oriented settings.

Second, the results show that emotional variability; captured through affective volatility and state transitions, is a meaningful behavioral marker of listening effort and engagement independent of conversational stance, challenging the assumption that emotional calmness reflects effective listening and highlighting the role of dynamic emotional processing in accurate comprehension and recall.

Finally, the study shows that vocal emotional features outperform facial-only features in predicting constructive listening accuracy, with multimodal fusion providing additional gains. This pattern highlights the importance of voice-based signals for modeling cognitive load and engagement during spoken interaction, offering a preliminary foundation for the design of empathy-aware and persuasive dialogue systems that support understanding across disagreement.

These findings provide early empirical evidence linking emotional variability to constructive listening in AI-mediated dialogue. Despite the small pilot sample, the results identify promising behavioral markers that may inform the design of empathy-aware and persuasive dialogue systems, with future work needed to validate these patterns and explore their integration into real-time conversational systems.

9 Future Work

Future studies should strengthen causal inference through stratified random assignment after measuring stance and stance strength, assigning participants within strata to Similar or Opposing conditions while counterbalancing topic difficulty and order; a within-subject crossover design would further control for individual differences. Future work will also evaluate alternative multimodal fusion weightings through sensitivity analysis, allowing assessment of how different modality contributions affect predictive stability and performance. Future research may also expand conversational domains beyond morally charged social issues such as educational debates, public policy discussions, and workplace conflict scenarios to test generalizability across varying contexts and intensities.

Beyond AI-human interaction, applying this framework to human-human dialogue (e.g., peer debates or conflict mediation) would test the generalizability of emotional variability as a behavioral marker of listening. Future studies may also integrate physiological signals, such as heart rate or skin conductance, to capture arousal and cognitive effort beyond facial or vocal cues, informing the design of training and mediation tools that support reflection on emotional dynamics and listening behavior.

Acknowledgments. This research received no external funding.

Disclosure of Interests. The authors declare that they have no competing interests.

References

Abbasian, M., Azimi, I., Feli, M., Rahmani, A.M., Jain, R.: Empathy through multimodality in conversational interfaces, arXiv:2405.04777 (2024)

Alhanbali, S., Dawes, P., Millman, R.E., Munro, K.J.: Measures of listening effort are multidimensional. Ear Hear. **40**(5), 1084–1097 (2019)

Keaton, S.A.: Active-empathic listening scale (AELS). In: The Sourcebook of Listening Research, pp. 161–166 (2017)

Ma, Y., et al.: Automatically detecting confusion and conflict during collaborative learning using linguistic, prosodic, and facial cues, arXiv:2401.15201 (2024)

Ren, Z., Schaumberg, R.: Disagreement gets mistaken for bad listening. Psychol. Sci. **35**(5), 455–470 (2024)

Roshanaei, M., Rezapour, R., El-Nasr, M.S.: Talk, listen, connect: Navigating empathy in human–AI interactions, arXiv:2409.15550 (2024)

Weinstein, N., Itzchakov, G., Legate, N.: The motivational value of listening during intimate and difficult conversations. Soc. Person. Psychol. Comp. **16**(2) (2022)

Weinstein, N., Itzchakov, G.: Empathic listening satisfies speakers' psychological needs and well-being, but does not directly deepen solitude experiences: A registered report. J. Exp. Soc. Psychol. **117**, 104716 (2025)

Weinstein, N., Itzchakov, G., Maniaci, M.: Exploring the connecting potential of AI: Integrating human interpersonal listening and parasocial support into human–computer interactions, Computers in Human Behavior: Artificial Humans 4 (2025)

Weger, H., Bell, G.C., Minei, E.M., Robinson, M.C.: The relative effectiveness of active listening in initial interactions. Int. J. Listen. **28**(1), 13–31 (2014)

Reflection-Based Interventions for Behavior Change: Lessons Learned from Applications to Cyber Behavior

Aya Muhanad[1(✉)], Sameha AlShakhsi[2], Tourjana Islam Supti[1], Khaled M. Khan[1], Mahmoud Barhamgi[1], Aiman Erbad[1], Dena Al-Thani[2], Amro Najjar[3], Ala Yankouskaya[4], and Raian Ali[2(✉)]

[1] College of Engineering, Qatar University, Doha, Qatar
{ah2003532,tourjana.supti,k.khan,mbarhamgi,aerbad}@qu.edu.qa
[2] College of Science and Engineering, Hamad Bin Khalifa University, Doha, Qatar
{salshakhsi,dalthani,raali2}@hbku.edu.qa
[3] Luxembourg Institute of Science and Technology, Esch-Sur-Alzette, Luxembourg
amro.najjar@list.lu
[4] Department of Psychology, Bournemouth University, Poole, UK
ayankouskaya@bournemouth.ac.uk

Abstract. Interventions that encourage reflection and critical thinking are increasingly used to promote safer online behavior. Yet, evidence suggests that such approaches seldom produce meaningful changes beyond raising awareness. This short paper reflects on four experiments that tested reflective strategies, including role-taking, the protégé effect, and psychological inoculation, across different domains of online behavior: social media disorder, digital stress, and social engineering. Three of the experiments focused on building immunity to persuasion, and one on reducing digital stress in social media environments. Using vignettes, which are hypothetical scenarios designed to obtain information about individuals' behavior, it was found that the interventions did not result in significant behavior change, except in one experiment where the effect was minimal. Although reflective strategies can enhance motivation and raise awareness, they may not provide the environmental support needed to form new attitudes or behaviors. We propose that interventions aimed at improving online behavior should combine reflection with timely cues, supportive environments, and opportunities for autonomous action. By examining both the value and limitations of reflective strategies, this synthesis offers a realistic perspective on what it takes to turn awareness into the adoption of new behaviors.

Keywords: Behavior Change · Reflective Intervention · Social Engineering · Digital Wellbeing · Social Media Disorder

1 Introduction

Since the mid-20th century, educational theorists and researchers have emphasized that learning approaches that actively engage learners' cognition lead to more durable behavior change [1]. In teaching, these methods are described to make learners invest in their

E. Vlahu-Gjorgievska et al. (Eds.): PERSUASIVE 2026, CCIS 2896, pp. 135–149, 2027.
https://doi.org/10.1007/978-3-032-27235-5_10

learning, acquire new knowledge and skills, and go beyond course requirements [2]. The Capability-Opportunity-Motivation-Behavior (COM-B) framework posits that behavior change occurs if individuals are motivated to apply newly learned behavior, see opportunities in which they can apply it, and have the capability to actually implement the desired behavior [3]. Furthermore, the perception of having the ability to achieve a certain behavior and having the intention to perform the behavior often leads to implementing the behavior [4]. Therefore, to internalize a certain behavior, an intervention must motivate individuals to follow it, equip them with the knowledge and skills needed, and describe to them situations in which they can apply this behavior.

Digital resilience interventions aim to encourage individuals to adopt online behaviors that enhance their security and digital well-being. Whether new behaviors can be internalized through behavior change interventions remains unclear, as the effectiveness of many interventions is rated using subjective reports [5–7]. This is a limitation, as a previous study revealed that behavior change techniques (e.g., role-playing) can increase the likelihood of participants providing socially desirable answers [8]. To measure behavior change more accurately, contextually grounded measures must be included in experiments.

In this experience-based paper, we investigate the effectiveness of reflection-based interventions in achieving safer and healthier online behaviors across four experiments. The experiments employed the techniques of role-taking, the protégé effect, and inoculation theory to encourage safer and healthier online behaviors. To increase ecological validity, changes in behavior were measured using vignettes, which are hypothetical scenarios used to obtain information about a person's attitudes, beliefs, or behaviors [9]. Although vignettes involve self-reporting, they go beyond purely subjective measures. By asking participants to respond to realistic scenarios, they can capture intended or likely behavior more accurately. We first describe each experiment, then reflect on the techniques, and finally discuss their possibilities and limitations. Figure 1 presents a visual summary of each experiment.

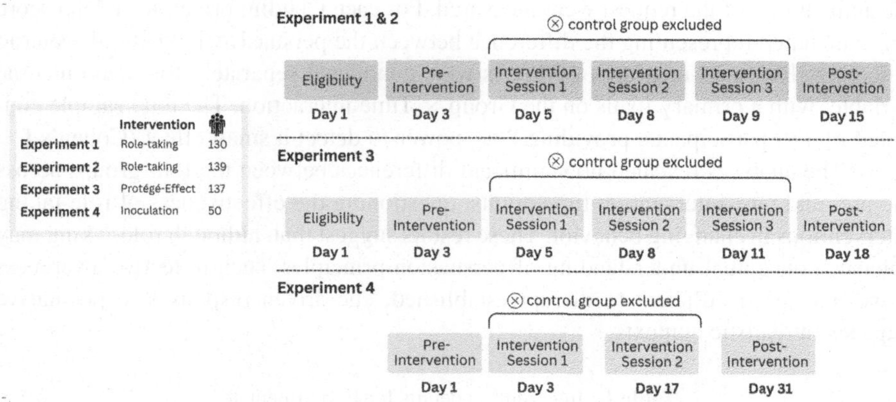

Fig. 1. Study timelines. **Note**: Exp. 1: Role-taking to build resistance to persuasion in social engineering. Exp. 2: Role-taking to debias the influence of demographic and appearance in social engineering. Exp. 3: Protégé effect to manage digital stress. Exp. 4: Inoculation to build resistance against persuasion as a problematic social media use trigger

2 Experiment 1: Role-Taking to Resist Persuasion in Social Engineering

This experiment (see [10]) utilized role-taking, a technique through which the individual adopts another's perspective and tries to imagine how another person feels [11]. The authors aimed to increase resistance to Cialdini's persuasion principles used in online requests by malicious entities, as they were proven to remain effective even when people were aware of the potential risks [12]. Most importantly, as participants took on their roles in the experiment, they learned why each persuasion principle influences behavior. The experiment involved several groups: one where the participant had to use persuasion to influence others (*persuaders*), and another where the participants were exposed to persuasion and had to list their thoughts on why they were inclined to follow the request (*persuadees*). The context for the role-taking was shopping and marketing; persuaders acted as marketers creating persuasive adverts, and persuadees acted as customers analyzing adverts. Each session in phase two focused on two of Cialdini's six persuasion principles [13]. The scenarios presented underwent a rigorous face-validation process. For benchmarking, a control group and another group learning about persuasion through reading materials were included. Table 1 provides a more detailed description of the intervention for each group.

The experimental setup (see [10]) employed a 4 (Group: Persuader, Persuadee, Literacy, Control) × 2 (Pre- and Post-Intervention) factorial design. Participants' vulnerability to persuasive social engineering requests was assessed both before and after the intervention, which is an experimental setup limited in similar research [14], yet important for capturing behavior change. In the pre-and post-intervention, a total of 12 scenarios (vignettes) were presented, with each of the six Cialdini principles represented by a persuasive and a neutral version. For each scenario, participants' perceived trustworthiness of the requester, likelihood of following the request, and time spent investigating the authenticity of the request were measured. For each Cialdini principle, a delta score was calculated representing the difference between the persuasive and neutral scenario outcomes. Repeated-measures ANOVAs were conducted separately for each outcome variable, with a primary focus on the Group × Time interaction. The total sample consisted of 130 participants, providing 80% power to detect a small effect (Cohen's f = 0.15). The analyses revealed no significant differences between the four groups across the pre- and post-intervention time points, questioning the effectiveness of role-taking interventions in changing behavior. These results suggest that, although role-taking may enhance conceptual understanding of persuasion principles, such reflective awareness alone may be insufficient to disrupt established, cue-driven responses to persuasive requests in realistic contexts.

Table 1. Intervention details for Experiment 1

Group	Intervention Description
Persuader	Across three sessions over five days, participants learned descriptions of two principles per session and designed a persuasive ad, email, or website applying the learned principles
Persuadee	Across three sessions over five days, participants identified elements in ads that encouraged purchase and explained why, prompting reflection; they were then given a description of the principles used. Repeated twice per session
Literacy	Across three sessions over five days, participants read descriptions and examples of two principles per session, followed by multiple-choice questions to ensure understanding
Control	Did not engage in any intervention

3 Experiment 2: Role-Taking to Debias the Influence of Demographic and Appearance Factors in Social Engineering

This experiment (see [15]) was designed to address four demographic and appearance factors (i.e., age, gender, ethnicity, and clothing style) that shape trust-based decision-making, particularly in the context of social engineering, as proven in [16, 17]. It aimed to reduce the influence of the four factors on risk-taking through role-taking. The experiment followed a similar setup to Experiment 1 and employed a 4 (Group: Persuader, Persuade, Literacy, Control) × 2 (Pre- and Post-Intervention) factorial design. Participants' vulnerability to four demographic factors (age, gender, ethnic similarity, and clothing style) in a social engineering scenario was measured once before the role-taking intervention and again one week after the intervention. For the pre- and post-intervention measures, a total of 16 personas were designed, representing all possible 4 × 4 combinations of the four factors. For each scenario, the perceived trustworthiness of the requester and the likelihood of complying with the request were measured. A score was calculated to measure bias toward each demographic and appearance factor.

To implement the role-taking intervention, participants assumed the perspective of either a *persuader* or a *persuadee* across multiple sessions. The persuader was asked to select an advisor or a letting agent from personas who varied in demographic and appearance characteristics, while the persuadee evaluated those same personas and decided whom they would trust or accept an offer from. The intervention procedures for each group are further described in Table 2. Repeated-measures ANOVAs were conducted, with primary focus on the Group × Time interaction. The total sample consisted of 139 participants, providing 80% power to detect a small effect size (Cohen's $d = 0.15$). The analyses were not statistically significant, indicating that the role-taking intervention did not change vulnerability to demographic and appearance factors. Participants may have had increased awareness; however, no significant behavior changes were observed. This pattern suggests that biases rooted in fast, intuitive judgments and repeated exposure may persist despite increased awareness.

Table 2. Intervention details for Experiment 2

Group	Intervention Description
Persuader	Participants learned how demographic and appearance factors influence decision-making across three sessions over five days. In each session, they selected which of several personas should be sent to a client to provide a specific service (e.g., financial advice)
Persuadee	Across three sessions over five days, participants took the role of the client and selected the persona they trusted most as a financial advisor or lettings agent. They explained their choice and were subsequently informed about the demographic or appearance factor being tested in the session
Literacy	Across two sessions over three days, participants read texts based on peer-reviewed research, industry reports, and credible media sources addressing prevalent stereotypes related to age, gender, ethnicity, and clothing style
Control	Participants did not engage in any intervention

4 Experiment 3: Protégé Effect to Manage Digital Stress on Social Media Interaction

This experiment (see [18]) was built on the concept that if we learn by teaching, known as the protégé effect [19], then taking on the role of a teacher or advisor may also drive behavior change. Central to the design was the role-taking approach, where participants prepared materials as though teaching someone else how to cope with digital stress. The experiment aimed to change behavior in how individuals interact online safely and responsibly to reduce digital stress, in a context where communication channels are available 24/7, creating constant pressures of availability, approval, and fear of missing out [20]. One key aspect was observing how role-taking offered participants a sense of responsibility and commitment, a feeling that they had to learn, reflect on, and pass on in a meaningful way. That shift in mindset felt important, even if the results did not show behavior changes.

The experiment employed a 4 (Group: Passive, Active, Literacy, Control) x 2 (Pre- and Post-Intervention) factorial design. Two groups were protégé-based: one passive group received ready-made materials and prepared teaching slides, while the other active group searched for coping strategies on their own. The authors assured fairness in time and effort by providing the active group with two recommended links as starting points, but participants were also free to explore other sources. This group shows whether engaging in extra cognitive work and making personal effort to find strategies would make a difference in how well people understood and internalized the strategies. All four groups are further described in detail in Table 3. Together, these four groups provided a chance to explore whether reflective thinking, cognitive effort, or simply receiving information might influence outcomes.

The pre- and post-intervention assessments measured digital stress, problematic social media use, perceived relevance of managing digital stress, and participants' willingness to encourage others to reduce digital stress through word of mouth. In total, 137 participants completed the full experiment, providing 80% power to detect a small effect size (Cohen's $f = 0.15$). Repeated-measures ANOVAs were conducted to assess the effect of the protégé-based intervention on digital stress and problematic social media use. Across all groups, participants reported reduced digital stress; however, no statistically significant Group × Time interaction was found, indicating no differences in behavior change between intervention groups. Although role-taking may foster responsibility and reflection, the absence of observable behavior change differences suggests that managing digital stress may be constrained by entrenched usage habits and persistent environmental cues that operate beyond reflective engagement alone.

Table 3. Intervention details for Experiment 3

Group	Intervention Description
Passive Protégé-Based	Participants learned about three types of digital stress and corresponding coping strategies across three sessions over seven days. In each session, they created two teaching slides for a learner. Each slide, presented a scenario and strategies to manage the specific type of digital stress
Active Protégé-Based	Participants learned about three types of digital stress across three sessions over seven days. Instead of being given coping strategies, they searched for them (with two suggested resources provided) and created two teaching slides. Each slide, presented a scenario and strategies to manage the specific type of digital stress
Literacy	Across three sessions over seven days, participants read materials similar to those in the passive protégé-based condition. They did not create teaching slides; comprehension was assessed via quiz questions
Control	Participants did not engage in any intervention

5 Experiment 4: Inoculation to Build Resistance Against Persuasion as a Problematic Social Media Use Trigger

This study (see [21]) builds on the concept that persuasive design in social media can trigger problematic behaviors, such as excessive use, preoccupation, withdrawal, deception, and conflict with others. To build resistance against these problematic behaviors, the experiment utilized inoculation theory and exposed participants to vignette-based scenarios designed to highlight their vulnerability to persuasive attempts and trigger cognitive engagement to strengthen their resistance. Drawing a parallel to medical inoculation, psychological inoculation aims to preemptively expose users to weakened forms of persuasive tactics, paired with counterarguments, so they develop cognitive resistance when encountering real persuasive attempts [22, 23].

This experiment followed a 3 (Group: Active Inoculation, Passive Inoculation, Control) × 2 (Pre- and Post-Intervention) mixed design. A total of 50 school students participated. The pre- and post-intervention measured participants' attitudes towards and levels of problematic social media use, and whether they would positively or negatively talk about the topic with others. In between the two timepoint measures, each of the three groups engaged in different tasks (see Table 4). The tasks involved reviewing scenarios that were carefully designed based on the symptoms of problematic social media use [24] and Cialdini's persuasion principles [13]. Each scenario was followed by reflective questions focused on self-relevance, knowledge, and confidence, which aimed to further trigger cognitive processing and elaboration. All scenarios were validated through a face validation phase. Repeated-measures ANOVAs were conducted to examine the effect of inoculation strategy on problematic social media use. The results were encouraging but modest. Although some changes were observed, with active inoculation showing more improvement compared to passive inoculation, the overall effect sizes were small, highlighting that while statistically significant, the behavior changes may be limited in magnitude at this stage.

Table 4. Intervention details for Experiment 4

Group	Intervention Description
Passive Inoculation	Threats were presented in six scenarios, each presenting a problematic social media use symptom and a persuasion principle. The threat component aimed to trigger the need to demonstrate and defend one's own immunity to the persuasive techniques typically found on social media. Each scenario was followed by self-reflection questions and provided counterarguments, delivering both inoculation components. A booster session with different scenarios was administered two weeks later

(*continued*)

Table 4. *(continued)*

Group	Intervention Description
Active Inoculation	Threats were presented in six scenarios, each presenting a problematic social media use symptom and a persuasion principle. The threat component aimed to trigger the need to demonstrate and defend one's own immunity to the persuasive techniques typically found on social media. For each scenario, participants generated their own strategies, thereby creating their own counterarguments. A booster session with different scenarios was administered two weeks later
Control	Participants did not engage in any intervention

6 Reflection-Based Interventions: Two Main Lessons Learned

This section offers reflections drawn from the full set of experiments, emphasizing the overarching lessons learned. Section 6.1 discusses the challenges associated with implementing reflective strategies, whereas Sect. 6.2 examines the possibilities and limitations of reflective learning-based strategies in behavior-change interventions.

6.1 Reflection and Immersion Are Difficult to Achieve

Most of the participants engaged with the tasks that encouraged reflection. However, a few challenges were reported across the role-taking tasks in Experiments 1 and 2. Some participants did not always manage to fully step into their assigned roles. For instance, some participants who were supposed to reflect on why they might follow a persuasive advert simply explained the persuasion principle used. In Experiment 1, some participants who took the role of persuaders deviated from using persuasion principles when creating persuasive adverts. A similar issue arose in Experiment 3, where participants who taught others how to cope with digital stress talked about general or offline situations rather than social media scenarios. The authors mitigated these challenges by contacting participants to clarify and redo the task.

The interventions provided clearly structured instructions, suggesting that the reason for reduced immersion among a few participants stemmed from factors beyond instructional clarity. A possible explanation is that reflective and perspective-taking tasks are mentally demanding. They require participants to focus, adopt another person's point of view, and monitor their own thoughts simultaneously. According to Cognitive Load Theory [25], tasks that demand several forms of mental processing at once can easily exceed the limits of working memory, leading to reduced engagement or superficial responses. Similarly, self-regulation research shows that activities requiring continuous attention and self-monitoring draw on limited mental resources that are difficult to sustain [26]. This combination makes deep reflection fragile, especially in online settings where distractions are constant and motivation varies (e.g., motivation to design persuasive adverts in Experiment 1 may not have been high). This suggests that reflection induced through behavioral change interventions is not always a self-sustained process but one that requires cognitive and motivational support to be maintained. When attention is stretched, reflective engagement weakens, and participants revert to surface-level responses, which helps explain the occasional inconsistent depth of reflection observed across the experiments. When reflective engagement weakens due to cognitive load or reduced motivation, individuals may fall back on habitual, cue-driven responses, reinforcing existing behavioral patterns rather than enabling sustained change.

6.2 Awareness is not Enough Unless Paired with Environmental Cues

The interventions were designed to encourage higher-order thinking by asking participants to monitor how they form judgments and make decisions, also known as metacognition [27]. While role-taking encouraged participants to reflect on their vulnerability to persuasion in Experiments 1 and 2, the overall findings indicate that this technique did not increase resistance towards persuasive requests [10, 15]. Likewise, in Experiment 3, the entrenched nature of digital habits and social reinforcement of stress proved difficult to shift, even with a protégé effect-based intervention [18]. A similar pattern was observed in Experiment 4, where inoculation strategies failed to build resistance against persuasive triggers for problematic social media use [21]. Although temporal reflection on one's own thought processes increased participants' awareness of persuasive strategies, habitual reactions, and stress-related behaviors, the interventions did not produce sustained behavioral change. Rather than being discouraging, these outcomes reveal something important: reflection and awareness, while valuable, seem to be insufficient to override the automatic, emotionally charged, and socially reinforced nature of the behaviors. The findings are particularly important given that behavioral change interventions are often reported in ways that emphasize positive outcomes [14].

One explanation is that metacognitive reflection involves conscious monitoring of thought, but behavior is often controlled by routines that operate without awareness. According to the Reflective-Impulsive Model [28], reflection can facilitate deliberate reasoning, but routine actions depend mainly on automatic responses that develop through practice and reward. When those cues and rewards remain the same, behavior is likely to continue even after a person understands its causes.

The COM-B framework [29] helps to explain why the reflective processes encouraged during the interventions did not lead to behavioral change, offering a slightly different perspective. People may gain the knowledge and motivation to act differently, but behavior also depends on 'opportunity', the practical and social conditions that allow a new response to occur. In the experiments, participants had time to reflect and understand their behavior, yet the environments that shaped their habits stayed the same. Daily cues, routines, and expectations continued to encourage old patterns. As a result, understanding increased, but behavior did not shift. This implication is supported by findings in the physical health domain, where habits were more likely to be formed when environmental cues supported behavior change [30].

7 Discussion

This paper aims to explore whether reflective strategies can produce changes in cyber behavior. Using evidence from four experiments, we examined different forms of reflective strategies, from role-taking and protégé effect to inoculation, and assessed their effectiveness and limitations. Despite participants' involvement in these interventions, designed to overcome implicit biases and social conditioning related to persuasion, appearance-based cues, digital stress, and problematic social media use, people remain vulnerable to these influences. This may be due to the deeply ingrained nature of heuristics and beliefs, such as the tendency to trust smiling or attractive individuals more, which often develop early in life [31, 32]. Many heuristics serve to facilitate quick decision-making and can even be advantageous for survival [33]. Nevertheless, the effectiveness of these heuristics and biases in past decisions does not necessarily guarantee their continued utility. While supporting the use of reflective strategies, evidence indicates they may have limited success in modifying implicit predispositions. However, this does not necessarily imply that they are ineffective in principle. Rather, it may suggest that these strategies need to be expanded to include additional layers of behavioral change strategies.

We first outline challenges that may arise among individuals engaging in reflection in behavior change technologies and discuss possible approaches to mitigate them. Importantly, we then discuss the limitations of reflective strategies in ensuring successful long-term behavior formation. In Sect. 6.1, we described that participants occasionally struggled with full immersion in reflective tasks. This observation suggests that sustaining reflection in the initial stages of behavioral change interventions should focus on managing cognitive demands and maintaining motivation. Although many participants were mentally engaged in the reflective tasks, which were structured and included clear instructions, struggles in exerting sufficient cognitive effort were noticed, underscoring the need to understand why this occurred and how it might be mitigated. One possibility is a lack of a clear sense of purpose regarding the importance of the behavior among some individuals. Individuals need to experience autonomous motivation, which can develop when they understand the rationale for the behavior and recognize its importance [34]. If the individual does not feel regret for their past counterproductive behavior or has no intention to change, the intervention is unlikely to be effective. For example, someone who has previously benefited from persuasion principles in their decision-making is unlikely to change their behavior, requiring interventions that decondition people from relying on persuasion. Moreover, to improve motivation among individuals with initially low motivation, interventions may employ fear-appeal. For example, evoking a sense of regret about having been influenced by persuasion or social conditioning, as experiencing regret has been linked to behavior change [35]. The Protection Motivation Theory suggests that if an individual views the consequences of a certain behavior as high, they will try to follow the advice to reduce the threat; however, they must believe they can follow the recommended behavior [36].

We found that reflective strategies generally result in increased awareness; however, as explained in Sect. 6.2, demonstrating metacognitive awareness by recognizing one's own impulsive behaviors, understanding the underlying causes through reflection, did not result in behavioral changes. One factor that may contribute to this is overconfidence, which can lead to counterproductive behaviors. In the early process of behavior change, individuals should be made aware of their vulnerabilities to unintended behavior, as research has found that those who perceive themselves as highly knowledgeable about security may engage in riskier online behavior [37]. This could be achieved through self-monitoring or personalized feedback loops [38, 39], which support individuals beyond the cognitive phase of awareness. However, incentives or monitoring processes can sometimes induce controlled motivation, which is unlikely to lead to behavior formation [34]. Therefore, interventions should encourage internal self-regulation without external reinforcements, as suggested by the Self-Determination Theory [40].

It is important to clarify that while behavioral-change interventions may increase motivation and awareness, this does not guarantee that individuals will perform the target behavior. According to the Fogg Behavior Model (FBM) [41], achieving a certain behavior requires three elements to occur simultaneously: motivation, ability, and prompts. Across the four experiments, inoculation and role-taking enhanced ability by fostering awareness of one's thinking and decision-making processes. They may also improve motivation through reflection-induced fear appeal. However, we believe reflective strategies lack the third component, which is prompts, explaining why behavior change may not be observed through them. Without prompts that operate at the moment of action, awareness achieved through reflection may not interrupt automatic responses that have been reinforced through repetition and reward. Previous research in the habit literature similarly suggests that once behaviors are habitual, awareness alone may not be enough to change behavior, with cues in the environment needed to sustain change [42, 43].

Behavior is often controlled by routines that operate without awareness. Indicating that becoming aware of the deceptive tactics that shape one's thinking through reflection cannot reliably change behavior. This is especially true in situations where cognitive resources and attention are limited, which encourages people to rely on easier, automatic heuristic processes [42]. Therefore, behavior formation requires conditions that support new actions and reduce reliance on automatic habits. Small adjustments in the environments where behavior normally occurs are more likely to shape behavior over time. Future research should consider incorporating more immersive, socially and environmentally supported strategies, as well as practical behavioral scaffolds that help disrupt automatic, habitual processes [41, 44]. This may be achieved through AI systems that adapt the environment over time to help disrupt habitual responses. For example, AI-driven alerts that highlight potential risks at the moment of decision can function as supportive prompts, translating prior reflection into action without undermining autonomy or becoming manipulative.

The implications of our findings also align with existing literature emphasizing that responsibility for online risk mitigation should not rest solely with users, but should be shared with designers and tech companies [45]. Hence, while awareness programs can support reflection and awareness among users, designers and developers may need to provide environmental cues that support behavioral change. Such environmental facilitators can act as prompts, as described by the FBM. Without them, the target behavior may not be achieved even if the individual is motivated to reduce the threat of an unintended behavior (motivation) and has become aware of how to perform the target behavior (ability). Figure 2 provides a summary of the components we believe may be achieved through reflective-based strategies and the additional layer needed for behavior formation.

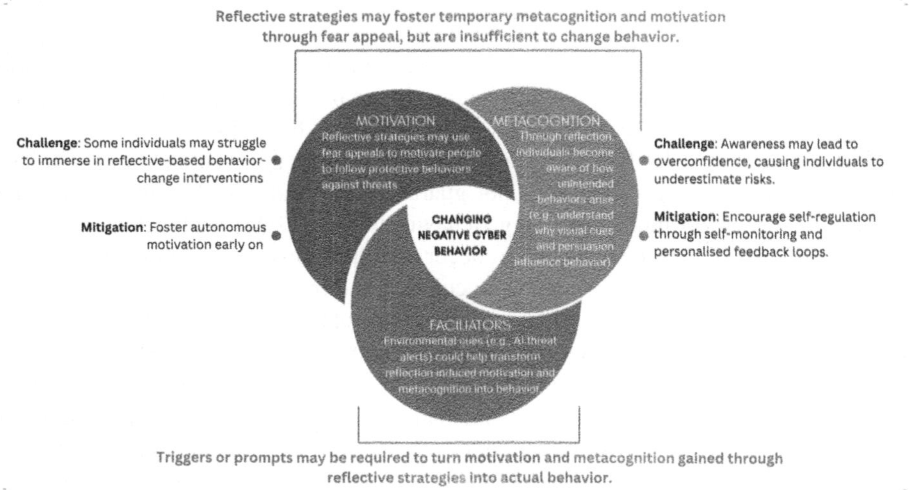

Fig. 2. Reflection-based strategies for behavior change: possibilities and limitations

8 Conclusion

This paper explores whether reflection-based interventions designed to induce metacognition, including role-taking, protégé-based teaching, and inoculation theory, can change cyber behaviors related to vulnerability to persuasion, digital stress, and problematic social media use. Across four experiments, the intervention enhanced awareness and encouraged reflection, yet rarely translated into behavior change. This pattern suggests that metacognition and reflection are insufficient on their own to counter the automatic habits, heuristics, and social pressures that shape cyber behaviors. By empirically demonstrating the effect of reflective awareness on behavior change, this work highlights the need to complement reflective-based interventions with environmental supports. Reflective strategies may benefit in the initial stage of behavior change; however, they may need to be accompanied by triggers or prompts in the individual's environment to transform awareness and motivation into action.

Acknowledgements. This publication was supported by NPRP 14 Cluster [grant number NPRP 14C- 0916–210015] from the Qatar National Research Fund (a member of Qatar Foundation). The findings herein reflect the work and are solely the responsibility of the authors.

Disclosure of Interests.. The authors report there are no competing interests to declare.

References

1. Tadayon Nabavi, R., Bijandi, M.: Bandura's Social Learning Theory & Social Cognitive Learning Theory (2012)
2. Pickering, J.D.: Cognitive Engagement: a More Reliable Proxy for Learning? Med. Sci. Educ. **27**, 821–823 (2017). https://doi.org/10.1007/s40670-017-0447-8
3. Willmott, T.J., Pang, B., Rundle-Thiele, S.: Capability, opportunity, and motivation: an across contexts empirical examination of the COM-B model. BMC Public Health **21**, 1014 (2021). https://doi.org/10.1186/s12889-021-11019-w
4. Ajzen, I.: The Theory of Planned Behavior. Organ. Behav. Hum. Decis. Process. **50**, 179–211 (1991). https://doi.org/10.1016/0749-5978(91)90020-T
5. Peddie, N., Westbury, T.: Austyn Snowden: The effectiveness of cognitive-behavioural interventions at increasing adherence to physical activity in mental health populations: a systematic review. Adv. Ment. Health **19**, 94–112 (2021). https://doi.org/10.1080/18387357.2019.1684829
6. Ley, C., Putz, P.: Efficacy of interventions and techniques on adherence to physiotherapy in adults: an overview of systematic reviews and panoramic meta-analysis. Syst. Rev. **13**, 137 (2024). https://doi.org/10.1186/s13643-024-02538-9
7. Larkin, L., Gallagher, S., Cramp, F., Brand, C., Fraser, A., Kennedy, N.: Behaviour change interventions to promote physical activity in rheumatoid arthritis: a systematic review. Rheumatol. Int. **35**, 1631–1640 (2015). https://doi.org/10.1007/s00296-015-3292-3
8. Ingersoll, V.H.: Role playing, attitude change, and behavior. Organ. Behav. Hum. Perform. **10**, 157–174 (1973). https://doi.org/10.1016/0030-5073(73)90010-X
9. Steiner, P.M., Atzmüller, C., Su, D.: Designing valid and reliable vignette experiments for survey research: a case study on the fair gender income gap. J. Methods Measur. Soc. Sci. **7**, 52–94 (2016). https://doi.org/10.2458/v7i2.20321
10. Muhanad, A., Supti, T., Khan, K., Erbad, A.: Does Role-Taking Help Resist Persuasion in Social Engineering? Maybe Not!, (2025). https://doi.org/10.13140/RG.2.2.35950.11840/1
11. King, A., Marietta, G., Gehlbach, H.: The Role of Role-Taking. In: Zandvliet, D., Brok, P.D., Mainhard, T., Tartwijk, J.V. (eds.) Interpersonal Relationships in Education. ALER, pp. 95–110. SensePublishers, Rotterdam (2014). https://doi.org/10.1007/978-94-6209-701-8_7
12. Mollazehi, A., Abuelezz, I., Barhamgi, M., Khan, K.M., Ali, R.: Do Cialdini's Persuasion Principles Still Influence Trust and Risk-Taking When Social Engineering is Knowingly Possible? In: Araújo, J., de la Vara, J.L., Santos, M.Y., Assar, S. (eds.) Research Challenges in Information Science, pp. 273–288. Springer Nature Switzerland, Cham (2024). https://doi.org/10.1007/978-3-031-59465-6_17
13. Cialdini, R.B.: The Science of Persuasion. Sci. Am. **284**, 76–81 (2001)
14. FitzGerald, C., Martin, A., Berner, D., Hurst, S.: Interventions designed to reduce implicit prejudices and implicit stereotypes in real world contexts: a systematic review. BMC Psychol. **7**, 29 (2019). https://doi.org/10.1186/s40359-019-0299-7
15. Supti, T.I., et al.: Debiasing the Influence of Demographic and Appearance Cues in Social Engineering via Role-Taking: Negative Results (2025). https://doi.org/10.48550/arXiv.2509.23271
16. Abuelezz, I., Barhamgi, M., Nhlabatsi, A., Khan, K., Ali, R.: How demographic and appearance cues of a potential social engineer influence trust perception and risk-taking among targets? Info. Comp. Security. **33**, 320–343 (2025). https://doi.org/10.1108/ICS-03-2024-0057
17. Abuelezz, I., et al.: How do gender and age similarities with a potential social engineer influence one's trust and willingness to take security risks? Int. J. Inf. Secur. **24**, 44 (2025). https://doi.org/10.1007/s10207-024-00954-5

18. Alshakhsi, S., Yankouskaya, A., Al-Thani, D., Ali, R.: Protégé effect for behaviour change: does teaching digital stress solutions to others reduce one's own? Annals of the New York Academy of Sciences (2026). https://doi.org/10.1111/nyas.70368
19. Fiorella, L., Mayer, R.E.: The relative benefits of learning by teaching and teaching expectancy. Contemp. Educ. Psychol. **38**, 281–288 (2013). https://doi.org/10.1016/j.cedpsych.2013.06.001
20. Steele, R.G., Hall, J.A., Christofferson, J.L.: Conceptualizing digital stress in adolescents and young adults: toward the development of an empirically based model. Clin. Child Fam. Psychol. Rev. **23**, 15–26 (2020). https://doi.org/10.1007/s10567-019-00300-5
21. Alshakhsi, S., Al-Thani, D., Männikkö, N., Ali, R.: Psychological inoculation against problematic social media use among adolescents: An experimental study. Ann. N. Y. Acad. Sci. **1550**, 134–150 (2025). https://doi.org/10.1111/nyas.70011
22. McGuire, W.J.: The effectiveness of supportive and refutational defenses in immunizing and restoring beliefs against persuasion. Sociometry. **24**, 184–197 (1961). https://doi.org/10.2307/2786067
23. McGuire, W.J.: Resistance to persuasion conferred by active and passive prior refutation of the same and alternative counterarguments. Psychol. Sci. Public Interest **63**, 326–332 (1961). https://doi.org/10.1037/h0048344
24. van den Eijnden, R.J.J.M., Lemmens, J.S., Valkenburg, P.M.: The Social Media Disorder Scale. Comput. Hum. Behav. **61**, 478–487 (2016). https://doi.org/10.1016/j.chb.2016.03.038
25. Sweller, J., van Merrienboer, J.J.G., Paas, F.G.W.C.: Cognitive Architecture and Instructional Design. Educ. Psychol. Rev. **10**, 251–296 (1998). https://doi.org/10.1023/A:1022193728205
26. Baumeister, R.F., Bratslavsky, E., Muraven, M., Tice, D.M.: Ego depletion: Is the active self a limited resource? J. Pers. Soc. Psychol. **74**, 1252–1265 (1998). https://doi.org/10.1037/0022-3514.74.5.1252
27. Martinez, M.E.: What is Metacognition? Phi Delta Kappan. **87**, 696–699 (2006). https://doi.org/10.1177/003172170608700916
28. Strack, F., Deutsch, R.: Reflective and Impulsive Determinants of Social Behavior. Pers. Soc. Psychol. Rev. **8**, 220–247 (2004). https://doi.org/10.1207/s15327957pspr0803_1
29. Michie, S., van Stralen, M.M., West, R.: The behaviour change wheel: a new method for characterising and designing behaviour change interventions. Implement. Sci. **6**, 42 (2011). https://doi.org/10.1186/1748-5908-6-42
30. Grove, R., Zillich, I.: Conceptualization and measurement of habitual exercise. Presented at the 38th Annual Conference of the Australian Psychological Society, Melbourne October 15 (2003)
31. Bascandziev, I., Harris, P.L.: The beautiful and the accurate: Are children's selective trust decisions biased? J. Exp. Child Psychol. **152**, 92–105 (2016). https://doi.org/10.1016/j.jecp.2016.06.017
32. Ewing, L., Sutherland, C.A.M., Willis, M.L.: Children show adult-like facial appearance biases when trusting others. Dev. Psychol. **55**, 1694–1701 (2019). https://doi.org/10.1037/dev0000747
33. Dale, S.: Heuristics and biases: The science of decision-making. Bus. Inf. Rev. **32**, 93–99 (2015). https://doi.org/10.1177/0266382115592536
34. Ryan, R., Patrick, H., Deci, E., Williams, G.: Facilitating health behavior change and its maintenance: Interventions based on Self-Determination Theory. Eur. Health Psychol. 10 (2008)
35. Bourgeois-Gironde, S.: Regret and the rationality of choices. Philosophical Transactions of the Royal Society B: Biological Sciences **365**, 249–257 (2010). https://doi.org/10.1098/rstb.2009.0163

36. Boer, H., Seydel, E.R.: Protection motivation theory. In: Conner, M., Norman, P., (eds.) Predicting health behaviour: Research and practice with social cognition models, pp. 95–120. Open University Press, Maidenhead, BRK, England (1996)
37. Muhanad, A., et al.: Does security attitude really predict susceptibility to persuasion tactics in social engineering attempts? Info. Comp. Security. Ahead-of-Print (2025). https://doi.org/10.1108/ICS-11-2024-0280
38. Wittmann, M., Cash, P., Mariani, M., Maier, A., Hansen, J.P.: Sustaining behaviour change through immersive technologies: trends, perspectives, and approaches. Proceedings of the Design Soc. **1**, 2891–2900 (2021). https://doi.org/10.1017/pds.2021.550
39. Valle, C.G., Nezami, B.T., Tate, D.F.: Designing in-app messages to nudge behavior change: Lessons learned from a weight management app for young adults. Organ. Behav. Hum. Decis. Process. **161**, 95–101 (2020). https://doi.org/10.1016/j.obhdp.2020.10.004
40. Legault, L., Inzlicht, M.: Self-determination, self-regulation, and the brain: Autonomy improves performance by enhancing neuroaffective responsiveness to self-regulation failure. J. Pers. Soc. Psychol. **105**, 123–138 (2013). https://doi.org/10.1037/a0030426
41. Fogg, B.: A behavior model for persuasive design. In: Proceedings of the 4th International Conference on Persuasive Technology, pp. 1–7. ACM, Claremont California USA (2009). https://doi.org/10.1145/1541948.1541999
42. Wood, W., Rünger, D.: Psychology of Habit. Annu. Rev. Psychol. **67**, 289–314 (2016). https://doi.org/10.1146/annurev-psych-122414-033417
43. Verplanken, B., Orbell, S.: Attitudes, Habits, and Behavior Change. Annu. Rev. Psychol. **73**, 327–352 (2022). https://doi.org/10.1146/annurev-psych-020821-011744
44. Rothman, A.J., Sheeran, P., Wood, W.: Reflective and automatic processes in the initiation and maintenance of dietary change. Ann. Behav. Med. **38**(Suppl 1), S4-17 (2009). https://doi.org/10.1007/s12160-009-9118-3
45. Al-Mansoori, R.S., Al-Thani, D., Ali, R.: Digital Wellbeing: Designers' Perspectives on Where the Responsibility Lies. In: 2022 9th International Conference on Behavioural and Social Computing (BESC), pp. 1–6 (2022). https://doi.org/10.1109/BESC57393.2022.9995236

Nudging Software Developers Toward SOLID Practices Through a Persuasive IDE Plugin

Ingo Pribik(✉) and Alexander Felfernig

Graz University of Technology, Graz, Austria
pribik@student.tugraz.at,alexander.felfernig@tugraz.at

Abstract. Software developers make frequent design decisions that influence the long-term maintainability and quality of software systems. Under time pressure, refactoring and quality improvements are often postponed, contributing to technical debt. This paper presents a prototype persuasive plugin for an Integrated Development Environment (IDE) that nudges developers toward greater awareness of design quality through real-time, context-aware feedback integrated into their coding workflow. The prototype leverages a large language model (LLM) to analyze source code in relation to established software design principles, providing feedback aligned with SOLID and suggesting possible improvements. Rather than enforcing rules, the plugin highlights potential design issues and encourages reflection on principle-driven improvements. Drawing on concepts from persuasive technology and digital nudging, the plugin explores IDE-based feedback as a means to foster design awareness and shared responsibility for maintainable code. The prototype was evaluated through individual semi-structured interviews with six IT experts, focusing on expert reflection rather than real-world deployment. The results indicate that the approach is technically feasible and suggest that IDE-based nudges can raise awareness of fundamental design principles and stimulate reflection on software design quality.

Keywords: Persuasion Technology · Digital Nudging · SOLID Principles · Software Developers

1 Introduction

Software development teams are consistently under pressure to deliver high-quality software solutions within constrained timelines [23]. The Standish Group's CHAOS 2020 Beyond Infinity report examined more than 50,000 IT and software projects across over 100 countries and found that only 31% of them were fully successful. Persistent issues such as unclear requirements, limited user involvement, unrealistic estimates, weak management support, and inadequate testing continue to hinder project outcomes, demonstrating that software quality remains a critical and unresolved challenge [43]. Therefore, this paper focuses

E. Vlahu-Gjorgievska et al. (Eds.): PERSUASIVE 2026, CCIS 2896, pp. 150–164, 2027.
https://doi.org/10.1007/978-3-032-27235-5_11

on software projects with an emphasis on software quality, aiming to support IT projects in overcoming one of their challenges, as creating maintainable, sustainable, and reliable systems is essential for long-term success [11].

According to Henderson-Sellers [19], software quality encompasses multiple attributes, including *reliability*, *availability*, *usability*, and *maintainability*. Historically, quality has been assessed through dimensions such as maintainability and testability [30]. Within object-oriented development, these quality concerns are reinforced by design principles such as **SOLID** [29], which encourage the development of robust, maintainable, and adaptable systems. However, software developers continue to face several practical challenges, particularly when making design-related decisions that directly affect software quality. Time pressure often forces developers to make suboptimal design choices [22], while limited familiarity with design patterns can hinder the effective implementation of best practices that enhance maintainability and flexibility [21]. Moreover, motivating developers to consistently adhere to **SOLID** principles remains a persistent challenge [20].

The identified gap motivated us to develop a plugin for the Eclipse Integrated Development Environment (IDE) that incorporates persuasive technology elements grounded in the Persuasive Systems Design (PSD) model [33]. Persuasive technology [15]—which is designed to ethically influence user' attitudes and behavior without coercion—has proven to be effective in areas such as healthcare [3], marketing [8], and product design [39]. In the context of software development, persuasive technology has also demonstrated potential for enhancing software quality [36]. In recent years, persuasive technology and nudging strategies have attracted growing academic interest in both behavioral science and the field of software development [35]. Persuasive technology focuses on influencing attitudes and motivating individuals to adopt desired behaviors through interactive systems and digital interventions [15]. Similarly, nudge theory seeks to guide people's decision-making in ways that influence behavior without limiting their freedom of choice. The concept of nudging was first introduced by Thaler and Sunstein [42].

The key contributions of this paper are the following:

1. We review persuasive technology and nudging technology in the context of software development.
2. We present a prototype plugin that incorporates persuasive elements to motivate software developers to follow the **SOLID** principles.
3. We present the results of interviews with expert software developers to gather initial feedback on our plugin, focusing on its persuasive technology features.

The remainder of this article is organized as follows. Section 2 introduces persuasive technology and nudging in the context of software development. Section 3 describes the design of the plugin and its integration of persuasive technology. Section 4 outlines the interview methodology, Sect. 5 presents and analyzes the feedback from IT experts and Sect. 6 discusses study limitations. Finally, Sect. 7 concludes the paper.

2 Background

2.1 Integrating SOLID Principles and Behavioral Frameworks in Software Design

The acronym **SOLID** encapsulates five core principles of object-oriented design [28]: **Single Responsibility**, **Open/Closed**, **Liskov Substitution**, **Interface Segregation**, and **Dependency Inversion**. These principles, summarized in Table 1, provide a foundation for developing software systems that are modular, coherent, and resilient to change.

Following the **SOLID** principles helps developers create software architectures that are well-structured, easy to maintain, and scalable [28]. By emphasizing modularity, separation of concerns, and clear abstraction layers, these principles improve the *understandability*, *extensibility*, and *testability* of software systems [40]. Moreover, adhering to **SOLID** design practices helps reduce the need for large or frequent refactoring, which is often both time-consuming and costly. In a large-scale survey of 1,183 software developers, Golubev et al. [17] found that most developers refactor their code on a daily or weekly basis, and about two-thirds reported spending more than an hour on each refactoring session. By reducing such refactoring overhead, developers can introduce new features or modify existing functionality with minimal disruption, thereby enhancing overall software quality and sustainability [25].

Table 1. SOLID principles

SOLID	Description
Single Responsibility Principle **(SRP)**	A class should be responsible for only one aspect of the system's functionality, promoting modularity, clarity, and easier testing [4].
Open/Closed Principle **(OCP)**	A software module should be extendable with new features without altering its existing implementation, ensuring stability and flexibility [47].
Liskov Substitution Principle **(LSP)**	Subclasses should be designed so they can replace their base classes without affecting the program's correctness or expected behavior [6].
Interface Segregation Principle **(ISP)**	Classes should not be required to implement interfaces they do not use; instead, interfaces should be small and focused on specific responsibilities interfaces [37].
Dependency Inversion Principle **(DIP)**	High-level modules should depend on abstractions rather than concrete implementations, ensuring that both high- and low-level components rely on shared interfaces [32].

To further promote adherence to design principles such as **SOLID** in object-oriented programming, several complementary behavior-change frameworks can be applied. **Persuasive Technology** focuses on the intentional design of interactive systems that influence users' attitudes and behaviors ethically and without coercion [15]. It leverages motivational and cognitive mechanisms—often formalized through models such as the **Fogg Behavior Model** and the **Persuasive Systems Design (PSD)** framework—to help users adopt desired practices over time. **Digital Nudging**, by contrast, draws on behavioral economics and choice architecture to subtly steer user decisions within digital environments through interface cues such as defaults, framing, and feedback [44]. While Persuasive Technology seeks to foster sustained behavioral or attitudinal change, Digital Nudging typically targets immediate decision contexts and micro-behaviors. Finally, **Cialdini's Principles of Persuasion** [13]—including reciprocity, commitment and consistency, social proof, authority, liking, and scarcity—describe universal social-influence mechanisms that can inform both persuasive and nudging designs.

Applied to software development, these frameworks can motivate developers to consistently apply **SOLID** principles by combining persuasive feedback (e.g., self-monitoring and simulation), digital nudges (e.g., contextual prompts or defaults in IDEs), and social persuasion (e.g., leveraging authority or social proof from experienced developers). Collectively, these psychological and design concepts form a multi-layered strategy for influencing developer behavior by balancing motivation, structural guidance, and subtle behavioral cues—an approach explored in greater depth in the following sections.

2.2 Persuasive Technology

According to Fogg [15], persuasive technologies are interactive computing systems designed to change people's attitudes or behaviors. Fogg distinguishes between these two targets of persuasion: attitude change concerns altering what people think or feel, whereas behavior change concerns modifying what people actually do. Although these processes often interact, they are distinct, and persuasive systems may aim to influence either or both [15]. Furthermore, Oinas-Kukkonen and Harjumaa [34] argue that attitude change represents one of the fundamental concepts underlying persuasion.

Building on this foundation, [16] introduced the **Fogg Behavior Model (FBM)**, which states that a target behavior occurs only when three elements coincide: *Motivation (M)*, *Ability (A)*, and a *Prompt (P)*—expressed as $B = MAP$. According to the model, people act when they are sufficiently motivated, capable of performing the behavior, and receive an appropriate cue at the right moment. The **FBM** serves as both a diagnostic and a design framework for analyzing user behavior, guiding designers to identify whether change should focus on boosting motivation, simplifying the task, or improving prompts. It is a key bridge between behavioral theory and practical system design and has been widely applied in fields such as persuasive technology, digital health, and habit formation [5].

While Fogg's work effectively explains why behavior occurs, it offers limited guidance on how to design systems that operationalize persuasive strategies.

To address this, Oinas-Kukkonen and Harjumaa [35] developed the **Persuasive Systems Design (PSD)** model, which extends and complements Fogg's behavioral framework. The PSD model provides a systematic approach for *analyzing*, *designing*, and *evaluating* persuasive systems. It emphasizes understanding the persuasion context, defining system qualities, and implementing persuasive features. The **Persuasive Systems Design (PSD)** model groups 28 persuasive design principles into four main categories: **Primary Task Support**, **Dialogue Support**, **System Credibility Support**, and **Social Support** [35]. As this research focuses on persuasive mechanisms integrated into the proposed plugin design, only the **Primary Task Support** principles—those most relevant to assisting users in completing their core development tasks—are presented in Table 2.

Table 2. Persuasive Systems Design (PSD) - model Primary Task Support principles [35].

Principle	Description
Reduction	Simplify complex tasks into easier steps to lower user effort.
Tunneling	Guide users step-by-step through a process toward the desired outcome.
Tailoring	Adapt system content or functionality to specific user needs or contexts.
Personalization	Customize the system experience to individual users' preferences and characteristics.
Self-monitoring	Allow users to track and reflect on their own behaviors or progress.
Simulation	Provide a representation of how user actions influence outcomes.
Rehearsal	Enable users to practice the target behavior safely or in a simulated environment.

These principles help designers create systems that not only motivate behavior but also maintain user trust, engagement, and credibility. Numerous studies have explored their applications. For example, Aldenaini et al. [1] reviewed 170 studies on persuasive strategies aimed at reducing sedentary behavior, while Wenker [46] examined persuasive technologies in workplace contexts designed to enhance employee well-being and behavioral change. Together, the **Fogg Behavior Model** and the **Persuasive Systems Design (PSD)** framework constitute the theoretical and practical backbone of persuasive technology research and design.

Persuasive technology has also been applied within software-engineering domain to encourage the adoption of best practices and improve daily efficiency. For instance, [36] conducted a 10-month field study of a persuasive tool in a real development team, and implemented a series of persuasive interventions to increase developers' adoption of software-engineering practices. These studies suggest that persuasive systems can positively influence developer behavior and team efficiency, though large-scale empirical validation of productivity gains remains limited [35,36].

2.3 Digital Nudging in Software Development

According to Thaler and Sunstein [42], a nudge is *"any aspect of the choice architecture that alters people's behavior in a predictable way without forbidding any options or significantly changing their economic incentives."* Similarly, Halpern [18] defines a nudge as *"a means of encouraging or guiding behavior."*

A well-known example of nudging is the strategic placement of fruit near cash registers instead of cake. This subtle change has been shown to shift purchasing behavior, leading more people to choose fruit even though cake remains available [42]. Such examples illustrate the essence of nudge theory—influencing human decision-making through small, context-aware adjustments that help individuals make better choices. Weinmann et al. [45] extended this idea to digital contexts, defining digital nudging as the use of user-interface design elements to guide people's behavior in digital choice environments. The core idea behind nudging and digital nudging is to guide individuals' decisions and behaviors in a way that encourages choices aligned with beneficial or socially desirable outcomes [45]. **Digital design principles** guide the development of choice architectures in online environments so as to steer user behavior toward beneficial outcomes with minimal friction [31]. The core principles of **digital nudging include** *framing*, *default settings*, *feedback*, *simplification*, *social proof*, and *Personalization*. These principles are applied in digital choice environments to subtly guide user decisions without restricting their freedom of choice [45].

Various tools applying digital nudging principles have already been explored in software engineering research. For instance, Laosen et al. [24] proposed a recommendation system that ranks relevant design patterns based on the input problem and pattern similarity, building on the Gang-of-Four design patterns. Likewise, Maddila et al. [27] developed a digital notification system that nudges the appropriate actors to act on overdue pull requests, thereby reducing review delays and improving workflow efficiency in collaborative software development projects.

3 Plugin Design

The persuasive plugin aims to nudge developers toward applying the **SOLID** principles during their daily programming activities, as illustrated in Figs. 1 and 2. The persuasive messages embedded in the tool are grounded in Cialdini's principles of influence [13], with **social proof** identified through survey results as the most effective principle guiding the implementation strategy. Table 3 summarizes the persuasive technologies implemented in the plugin and illustrates how these elements correspond to established digital nudging principles.

Table 3. Lists the persuasive technologies implemented in the plugin and maps them to the corresponding persuasive system design principles and digital nudging design principles.

ID	Persuasive	Nudging	Description
1	Reduction	Default Settings	The persuasive plugin is activated by default within the IDE.
2	Cialdinis Principle	Social Proof	Using Cialdini's Social Proof, a message is shown to motivate the developer.
3 5	Tailoring	Framing	Classes violating **SOLID** principles appear at the top for easier identification.
4 6	Tunneling	Simplification	Guides users step-by-step and provides refactoring recommendations.
4 5	Self-Monitoring	Feedback	Provides immediate, comprehensive feedback to reinforce behaviors that strengthen adherence to the **SOLID** principles.

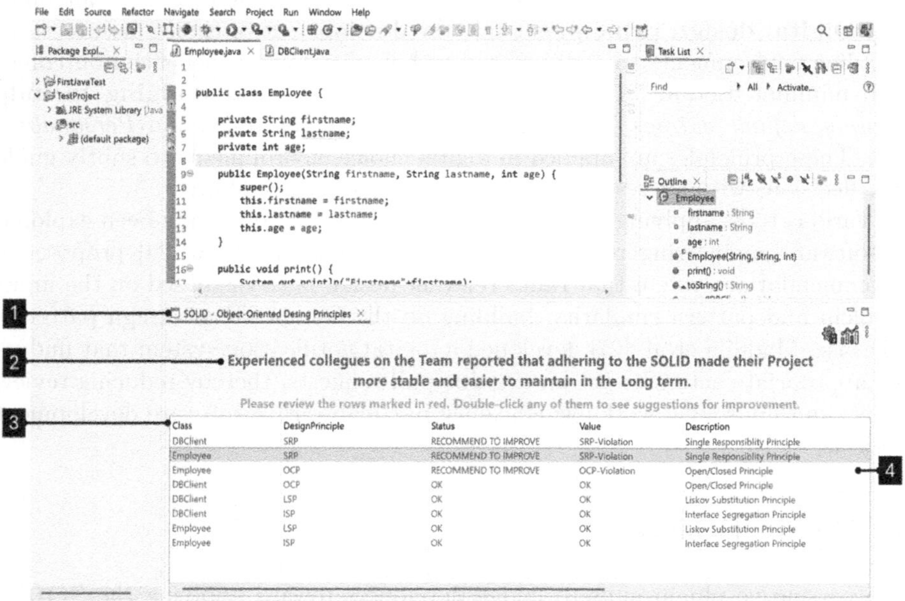

Fig. 1. The view displays the current **SOLID** status and indicates whether a class violates any of the **SOLID** principles.

The plugin leverages a Large Language Model (LLM) via the **OpenAI GPT-4 API**[1] to evaluate whether a given class adheres to a specific **SOLID** principle.

[1] https://openai.com/index/gpt-4-api-general-availability/?utm_source=chatgpt.com.

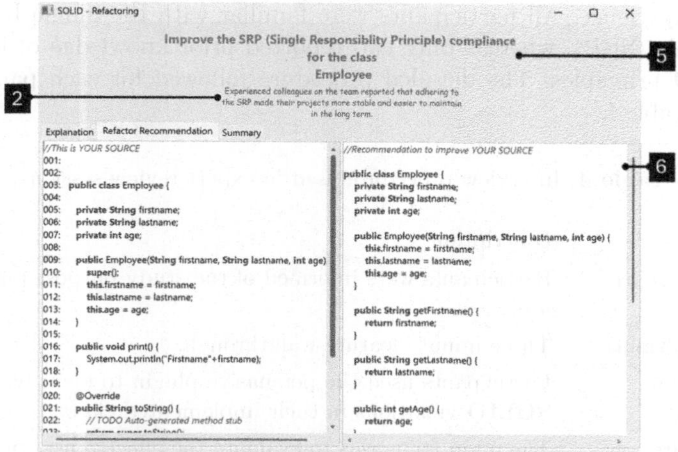

Fig. 2. The prompt provides for each item in the list a refactoring recommendation and explanations.

Under *Primary Task Support*, a tunneling mechanism provides a one-click pathway to targeted improvement actions, while the integrated LLM offers context-aware recommendations for code refactoring. These automated suggestions not only reduce cognitive effort but also encourage developers to adopt maintainability best practices, reinforcing persuasive guidance through personalized, just-in-time feedback. Furthermore, classes that violate any of the **SOLID** principles are prioritized at the top, facilitating coordinated decision-making to address these issues.

Given the persuasive nature of these design choices, ethical considerations become essential. In persuasive technology, nudging is considered ethically acceptable only when it is applied transparently and without manipulation. In software development environments, such as code review tools, persuasive techniques can gently guide developers toward best practices while preserving their autonomy. This application of nudging aligns with established ethical guidelines that emphasize transparency and responsible influence [7].

4 Interview Method

We conducted an expert evaluation of the plugin with six software development professionals who have extensive industry experience. The choice of six participants follows common practice in heuristic and expert-based evaluations of software tools. Small, information-rich samples are suitable when the aim is depth rather than generalization, and data saturation is typically achieved within 5–12 interviews [38]. Thus, six interviews were deemed sufficient for the study's objectives. Participant selection aimed to balance diversity of expertise with practical feasibility while ensuring that all participants had at least five years of relevant experience. All participants were familiar with the Single Responsibility Principle (SRP), whereas only two reported prior knowledge of the full set of **SOLID** principles. The detailed procedure followed for each participant is shown in Table 4.

Table 4. Interview procedure used in expert review sessions.

Step	Description
Intro (5 min)	Participants were informed of the study purpose and data use.
Demo (3 min)	Three-minute feature walkthrough.
Hands-on (20 min)	Participants used the persuasive plugin to identify **SOLID** violations in their implemented class.
Structure Questionnaire (10 min)	The main focus was to evaluate the effectiveness of the persuasive elements integrated into the plugin.
Semi-Structured Question (10 min)	Deeper reflections using interview guide.

5 Results and Discussions

5.1 Participant Profile

Table 5 the participant profiles of the IT experts and their main known relevant programming languages who evaluated the persuasive technology plugin. The participants represented a diverse mix of roles and organizational contexts, including software developers, software architects, and technical business analysts who combine analytical and programming responsibilities. Their professional experience ranged from six to more than twenty years. This composition provided a solid foundation for understanding how the plugin's nudging and persuasive features were perceived across different roles within software development.

Table 5. Participant overview

Participant	Company	Role/Position	Experience	Languages
Expert 1	A	Business Analyst & Developer	6 years	Java, C#
Expert 2	A	Business Analyst & Developer	>15 years	Pyhton
Expert 3	A	Full Stack Developer	>5 years	Java, C#
Expert 4	A	Business Analyst & Developer	>20 years	C#
Expert 5	B	Software Architect	>20 years	Java, Python
Expert 6	C	Full Stack Developer	>20 years	Java, Python

5.2 Evaluation of the Persuasive Technology Plugin

The plugin was evaluated through semi-structured interviews and a short questionnaire addressing nine dimensions of user experience. During the evaluation, the interviewers implemented an Employee class for basic employee data management and salary handling and analyzed it using the plugin to assess compliance with SOLID principles and obtain improvement recommendations. The questionnaire was administered after this analysis.

Throughout the use of the plugin, the system displayed persuasive messages inspired by Cialdini's principle of social proof, intended to nudge developers toward improving their source code. These messages functioned as digital nudges, providing subtle behavioral guidance while preserving user autonomy.

Finally, a summary of the quantitative results is presented in Table 6, which reports the mean, standard deviation, and range for each assessment item.

Table 6. Expert feedback (1–10 scale) across nine evaluation questions.

Nr	Question	Relevant Topic	Mean	SD	Min	Max
Q1	Ease of Use During Coding	Usability	8.33	1.86	5	10
Q2	Persuasion Message Impact	Persuasion	8.0	1.42	6	10
Q3	Digital Nudging Refactoring	User Guidance	8.33	1.75	5	10
Q4	Persuasiveness	Behavioral Influence	7.33	1.97	5	10
Q5	Impact on Coding Decisions	Decision Making	7.5	0.55	7	8
Q6	Effect on SOLID Awareness	Software Quality	7.83	0.75	7	9
Q7	Fit with Existing Workflow	Workflow Integration	7.0	1.67	5	9
Q8	Overall Satisfaction	General Acceptance	9.0	0.89	8	10
Q9	Likelihood of Future Use	Adoption Intention	8.67	1.03	7	10

Notes: Scores are on a 1–10 scale (1 = lowest, 10 = highest). Min/Max columns are displayed as pure integers for clarity.

5.3 Quantitative Findings

- Usability and Ease of Use **(Q1)**
  The plugin received strong usability ratings (M = 8.3), indicating that participants found it easy to use during coding. High usability is critical for technology acceptance, as it reduces cognitive load and supports adoption [26]. Overall, participants perceived the plugin as well integrated and non-disruptive—an essential quality for digital nudging tools, which aim to guide behavior without interrupting the user's normal workflow [44].
- Persuasion Message Impact **(Q2)**
  The persuasive design principles implemented in the plugin were rated positively (M = 8.0). Participants found the messages clear and relevant, particularly the use of social proof inspired by Cialdini's principles [14]. This observation is consistent with Fogg's concept of persuasive technology [15], which

highlights how digital interventions can influence user attitudes through social and psychological cues. In addition, the use of *tailoring* to highlight classes violating **SOLID** principles and the one-click refactoring recommendation (tunneling) were perceived as especially helpful.

- Digital Nudging Refactoring **(Q3)**
  Feedback on digital nudging during refactoring was positive (M = 8.3), supporting prior work showing that early developer support can raise awareness of potential **SRP** violations and guide refactoring decisions [10]. Table 7 reports cohesion metrics aggregated over six developers who independently developed and refactored the same class. Using the cohesion metric definitions proposed by Briand et al. [9], only two of the six classes satisfied the Single Responsibility Principle (SRP) prior to refactoring, whereas all classes satisfied SRP after refactoring. Cohesion improved according to Tight Class Cohesion (TCC) and LCOM4. In contrast, LCOM5 decreased, indicating that although SRP compliance was consistently achieved, observed cohesion improvements depend on the selected metric and the specific refactoring decisions applied.

Table 7. Summary statistics of class cohesion metrics before and after SRP-focused refactoring for six independent implementations of the same class.

Metric	Meaning	Before		After	
		Mean	SD (Min–Max)	Mean	SD (Min–Max)
Methods (M)	Class Methods	5.00	0.75 (4.00 – 6.00)	4.00	0.52 (4.00 – 5.00)
Fields (F)	Class Attributes	3.00	0.89 (2.00 – 4.00)	3.00	0.75 (2.00 – 4.00)
TCC	Ideal ≈ 1	0.32	0.21 (0.27 – 0.80)	0.58	0.22 (0.40 – 1.00)
LCOM4	Ideal $= 1$	2.00	0.89 (1.00 – 3.00)	1.00	0.00 (1.00 – 1.00)
LCOM5	Higher is better	0.67	0.24 (0.21 – 0.83)	0.61	0.19 (0.33 – 0.83)
SRP		*4 of 6 violated*		*all satisfied*	

- Persuasiveness and behavioral Influence **(Q4)**
  While usability and guidance were rated highly, perceived behavioral influence was lower (M = 7.3). Participants reported increased awareness and reflection but fewer substantial changes in coding habits, reflecting a common challenge in persuasive system design [12].
- Impact on Coding Decisions and Awareness **(Q5–Q6)**
  The plugin influenced the coding decisions (M = 7.5) and increased awareness of **SOLID** principles (M = 7.8), with authoritative and credible messages encouraging reflection on the quality of the design [2]. Technically, the system achieved perfect precision, recall, and an F1 score of 1.0 by correctly classifying all implementations. For the single class with an SRP violation, 4 of 6 experts would not have identified the issue without the plugin's feedback, and 75% of initially hesitant developers implemented improvements.

- Workflow Integration, Satisfaction, and Adoption **(Q7–Q9)**
  Workflow integration received the lowest rating (M = 7.0), suggesting minor intrusiveness, while satisfaction (M = 9.0) and intention for future use (M = 8.7) remained high, indicating strong overall acceptance in line with prior findings [26].

5.4 Overall Interpretation

As an initial evaluation, the plugin serves as a proof of concept for awareness-based digital nudging toward SOLID principles.

- As mentioned earlier, the plugin is intended to nudge software developers to consider the **SOLID** principles during development. It should not be viewed as a rigid constraint, but rather as a guideline that encourages reflection on design decisions.
- In addition, the plugin serves as a support tool for less experienced developers by helping them follow the **SOLID** principles and by highlighting classes in which these principles are violated.
- The source code recommended by the **LLM** should be treated as a suggestion rather than as a final solution and should be carefully reviewed, as it may contain bugs or other errors [41].
- The interviews indicated growing awareness of and interest in the **SOLID** principles and some behavioral change, but the short study period was insufficient to demonstrate sustainability.

6 Threats to Validity

Despite encouraging results, this study has limitations. The evaluation focused on a single class and the Single Responsibility Principle (SRP). Because the class structure was simple, the remaining SOLID principles were already satisfied and not assessed. LLM-generated recommendations were used only to guide refactoring and were not evaluated, and refactoring effort was not measured, as the prototype targets early-stage, small-scale improvements.

7 Conclusion and Future Work

This paper presents a prototype plugin that applies persuasive technology and digital nudging, combining Cialdini's social proof with LLM-based analysis to highlight potential SOLID principle violations. An expert evaluation with IT professionals suggests technical feasibility and persuasive effectiveness. Future work will extend the evaluation to longitudinal, real-world settings and explore detection accuracy (e.g., precision and recall) as well as the impact on refactoring outcomes.

Acknowledgment. No acknowledgments are applicable.

References

1. Aldenaini, N., Dankar, F., Muhammad, G., Hussain, M., Guizani, M.: A review of strategies to reduce sedentary behavior and increase physical activity using persuasive technology and social media. IEEE Access **8**, 153788–153807 (2020). https://doi.org/10.1109/ACCESS.2020.3018550
2. Alkadhi, R., et al.: Persuasive interfaces for improving software quality: a behavioral study. ScienceOpen (2024)
3. Alslaity, A., Oyebode, O., Vassileva, J., Orji, R.: Personalized persuasive technologies in health and wellness: from theory to practice. In: Ferwerda, B., Graus, M., Germanakos, P., Tkalčič, M. (eds.) A Human-Centered Perspective of Intelligent Personalized Environments and Systems. Human–Computer Interaction Series, pp. 261–292. Springer, Cham (2024). https://doi.org/10.1007/978-3-031-55109-3_10
4. Ardalani, A., Parsa, S., Zakeri-Nasrabadi, M., Chatzigeorgiou, A.: Supporting single responsibility through automated extract method refactoring. Empir. Softw. Eng. **29**, 28 (2024). https://doi.org/10.1007/s10664-023-10427-3
5. Asbjørnsen, R.A., Smedsrød, M.L., Solberg Nes, L., Wentzel, J., Varsi, C.: Persuasive system design principles and behavior change techniques to stimulate motivation and adherence in electronic health interventions. J. Med. Internet Res. **21**(12), e14265 (2019). https://doi.org/10.2196/14265
6. Baniassad, E.: Making the liskov substitution principle happy and sad. In: Proceedings of the 40th International Conference on Software Engineering: Software Engineering Education and Training Track (ICSE-SEET 2018), pp. 17–20 (2018). https://doi.org/10.1145/3183377.3183392
7. Berdichevsky, D., Neuenschwander, E.: Toward an ethics of persuasive technology. Commun. ACM **42**(5), 51–58 (1999). https://doi.org/10.1145/301353.301410
8. Braca, A., Dondio, P.: Developing persuasive systems for marketing: the interplay of persuasion techniques, customer traits and persuasive message design. Ital. J. Mark. (3), 369–412 (2023). https://doi.org/10.21203/rs.3.rs-1932699/v2
9. Briand, L.C., Daly, J.W., Wüst, J.: A unified framework for coupling measurement in object-oriented systems. IEEE Trans. Software Eng. **25**(1), 91–121 (1999). https://doi.org/10.1109/32.748920
10. Brown, N.: Digital nudges for encouraging developer actions. In: 2019 IEEE/ACM 41st International Conference on Software Engineering: Companion Proceedings (ICSE-Companion) (2019). https://doi.org/10.1109/ICSE-Companion.2019.00082
11. Calero, C., Moraga, M.Á., Bertoa, M.F.: Towards a software product sustainability model. In: Proceedings of the 2nd International Workshop on Green and Sustainable Software (GREENS 2013), pp. 3–9. IEEE, San Francisco, CA, USA (2013). https://doi.org/10.1109/GREENS.2013.6606413
12. Castmo, E., Persson, A.: The Alliance between Digital Nudging and Persuasive Design. Master's thesis, Lund University (2018)
13. Cialdini, R.B.: Influence: The Psychology of Persuasion. HarperCollins, New York (2007)
14. Cialdini, R.B.: Influence: Science and Practice. Allyn & Bacon (2001)
15. Fogg, B.J.: Persuasive Technology: Using Computers to Change What We Think and Do. Morgan Kaufmann, Boston (2003)
16. Fogg, B.J.: A behavior model for persuasive design. In: Proceedings of the 4th International Conference on Persuasive Technology, pp. 1–7. Persuasive '09, ACM (2009). https://doi.org/10.1145/1541948.1541999

17. Golubev, Y., Kurbatova, Z., AlOmar, E.A., Bryksin, T., Mkaouer, M.W.: One thousand and one stories: a large-scale survey of software refactoring. In: Proceedings of the 29th ACM Joint Meeting on European Software Engineering Conference and Symposium on the Foundations of Software Engineering (ESEC/FSE 2021), pp. 1303–1313. ACM, Virtual Event, Greece (2021). https://doi.org/10.1145/3468264.3473924
18. Halpern, D.: Inside the Nudge Unit: How Small Changes Can Make a Big Difference. WH Allen/Penguin Random House (2015)
19. Henderson-Sellers, B.: Object-Oriented Metrics: Measures of Complexity. Prentice Hall PTR, Upper Saddle River (1996)
20. Kimani, R.: An engineering leader's guide to solid principles. LeadDev (2025)
21. Knox, J.: Adopting software design patterns in an it organization: an enterprise approach to add operational efficiencies and strategic benefits (2011)
22. Kuutila, M., Mäntylä, M., Farooq, U., Claes, M.: Time pressure in software engineering: a systematic review (2020). https://doi.org/10.1016/j.infsof.2020.106257
23. Kuutila, M., Mäntylä, M.V., Graziotin, D., Minelli, R., Romano, S., Sillitti, A.: Time pressure in software engineering: a systematic review. Inf. Softw. Technol. **121**, 106257 (2020). https://doi.org/10.1016/j.infsof.2020.106257
24. Laosen, N., Bou, C., Nantajeewarawat, E.: Automatic recommendation of design patterns based on patterns' intent. Int. J. Innov. Comput. Inf. Control **16**(4), 1147–1163 (2020). https://doi.org/10.24507/ijicic.16.04.1147
25. Larman, C.: Applying UML and Patterns: An Introduction to Object-Oriented Analysis and Design and Iterative Development. Prentice Hall (2004)
26. Liang, P., et al.: A large-scale study on developer perceptions of AI programming assistants. arXiv preprint arXiv:2303.17125 (2023). https://doi.org/10.1145/3597503.3608128
27. Maddila, C., Upadrasta, S.S., Bansal, C., et al.: Nudge: accelerating overdue pull requests toward completion. ACM Trans. Softw. Eng. Methodol. **32**(2), 1–30 (2023). https://doi.org/10.1145/3544791
28. Martin, R.C.: Design Principles and Design Patterns. Object Mentor, Gurnee (2000)
29. Martin, R.C.: Agile Software Development: Principles, Patterns, and Practices. Prentice Hall, Upper Saddle River (2003)
30. McCall, J.A., Richards, P.R., Walters, G.F.: Factors in software quality (1977), uSAF (U.S. Air Force) technical report
31. Meske, C., Amojo, I.: Digital nudging and privacy: improving decisions about self-disclosure in social networks. arXiv preprint arXiv:1911.08202 (2019)
32. O'Connell, M.D., et al.: Application of the dependency inversion principle to multidisciplinary software development. In: Proceedings of the 2018 Fluid Dynamics Conference (2018). https://doi.org/10.2514/6.2018-3856
33. Oinas-Kukkonen, H., Harjumaa, M.: Persuasive systems design: key issues, process model, and system features. Commun. Assoc. Inf. Syst. **24**(1), 28 (2009)
34. Rosenberg-Kima, R.B., Baylor, A.L., Plant, E.A., Doerr, C.E.: The importance of interface agent visual presence: voice alone is less effective in impacting young women's attitudes toward engineering. In: de Kort, Y., IJsselsteijn, W., Midden, C., Eggen, B., Fogg, B.J. (eds.) PERSUASIVE 2007. LNCS, vol. 4744, pp. 214–222. Springer, Heidelberg (2007). https://doi.org/10.1007/978-3-540-77006-0_27
35. Oinas-Kukkonen, H., Harjumaa, M.: Persuasive systems design: key issues, process model, and system features. Commun. Assoc. Inf. Syst. **24**(1), 485–500 (2009). https://doi.org/10.17705/1CAIS.02428

36. Pribik, I., Felfernig, A.: Towards persuasive technology for software development environments: an empirical study. In: Bang, M., Ragnemalm, E.L. (eds.) PERSUASIVE 2012. LNCS, vol. 7284, pp. 227–238. Springer, Heidelberg (2012). https://doi.org/10.1007/978-3-642-31037-9_20
37. Ramachandrappa, N.C.: Solid design principles in software engineering. Int. J. Comput. Trends Technol. **72**(9), 18–23 (2024). https://doi.org/10.14445/22312803/IJCTT-V72I9P104
38. Saunders, B., et al.: Saturation in qualitative research: exploring its conceptualization and operationalization. Qual. Quant. **52**(1), 1893–1907 (2018). https://doi.org/10.1007/s11135-017-0574-8
39. Shih, L.: Persuasive design for products leading to health and sustainability using case-based reasoning. Sustainability **8**(4), 318 (2016). https://doi.org/10.3390/su8040318
40. Singh, H., Hassan, S.I.: Effect of solid design principles on quality of software: an empirical assessment. Int. J. Sci. Eng. Res. **6**(4), 1321–1324 (2015)
41. Tambon, F., Moradi Dakhel, A., Nikanjam, A., Khomh, F., Desmarais, M.C., Antoniol, G.: Bugs in large language models generated code: an empirical study. arXiv preprint arXiv:2403.08937 (2024)
42. Thaler, R.H., Sunstein, C.R.: Nudge: Improving Decisions About Health, Wealth, and Happiness. Yale University Press, New Haven, CT (2008). https://doi.org/10.1017/S1474747209990175
43. The Story: Chaos report — why this study about it project management is so unique (2024). https://thestory.is/en/journal/chaos-report/, industry summary of Standish Group's CHAOS 2020 findings for IT/software projects
44. Weinmann, M., Schneider, C., vom Brocke, J.: Digital nudging. Bus. Inf. Syst. Eng. **58**(6), 433–436 (2016). https://doi.org/10.1007/s12599-016-0453-1
45. Weinmann, M., Schneider, C., vom Brocke, J.: Digital nudging. Commun. ACM **59**(7), 67–73 (2016). https://doi.org/10.1145/2903150
46. Wenker, K., Milic-Frayling, N., Masthoff, J., Karapanos, E., Nijholt, A.: Persuasive technology in the workplace: a systematic review. J. Biomed. Inform. **128**, 104025 (2022). https://doi.org/10.1016/j.jbi.2022.104025
47. Xu, C., Hughes, J.: Realizing the open-closed principle. In: Proceedings of the Fourth Annual ACIS International Conference on Computer and Information Science (ICIS 2005), pp. 274–279 (2005). https://doi.org/10.1109/ICIS.2005.107

Using Progression to Sustain User Attention in Fragmented Information Environments

Aleksandra Rydzkowska(✉)

Department of Politics and International Relations, Royal Holloway, University of London, Egham Hil, Egham TW20 0EX, UK
aleksandra.rydzkowska@rhul.ac.uk

Abstract. Digital information environments are increasingly overloaded and fragmented, encouraging rapid judgment over contextual reasoning. This structural weakness is exploited by AI-driven disinformation, where the proliferation of synthetic media makes isolated claims increasingly difficult to verify. To counter this, persuasive design must shift from focusing on technical detection to fostering holistic understanding of complex socio-political contexts as the viable basis for verification when sensory evidence fails. While database interactive documentaries offer the necessary structural depth for this task, their frequent reliance on unscaffolded navigation often fails to sustain the user persistence required for deep comprehension. This paper addresses this design challenge through a research-through-design inquiry into progression-based pacing and context-first sequencing as attentional scaffolds. Exploratory data from a hybrid documentary-game system, *Trolls vs Elves*, suggests that user engagement clusters around structural thresholds, whereas unstructured access leads to earlier attrition. These findings imply that regulating temporal commitment through gated progression may effectively support sustained inquiry, offering a strategy for organising extensive factual corpora that resists the atomisation of the attention economy.

Keywords: Interactive documentary · Gamification · Information environments · Attention economy · Research-through-design

1 Introduction

Digital information environments are increasingly characterised by fragmentation and overload. Networked media prioritise speed and circulation over coherence, exposing users to streams of loosely connected claims that are rarely situated within broader explanatory frameworks. Complex socio-political issues are encountered as isolated fragments that push users towards rapid judgement rather than sustained interpretation.

This structural atomisation creates a profound vulnerability, particularly as generative AI and synthetic media become ubiquitous. As their quality improves,

E. Vlahu-Gjorgievska et al. (Eds.): PERSUASIVE 2026, CCIS 2896, pp. 165–177, 2027.
https://doi.org/10.1007/978-3-032-27235-5_12

the ability to identify falsehoods based on sensory affordances or technical flaws diminishes. In this context, verification can no longer rely on examining isolated artifacts alone but must involve understanding the broader socio-political reality in which they are situated. Consequently, the challenge is not a lack of knowledge but a lack of design strategies capable of organising this overload into meaningful configurations. Restoring context is therefore a matter of creating conditions under which users are willing and able to persist long enough for the relationships between information elements to become visible.

Interactive documentaries (i-docs) offer a potential response to this challenge. Unlike linear formats, i-docs have long experimented with database-driven structures, non-linear exploration, and user-led inquiry. These advantages may render i-doc systems well suited to countering fragmentation, supporting processes of comparison, pattern recognition, and contextual sense-making that are difficult to achieve in short-form or claim-based media.

However, prior research has shown that interactivity alone does not guarantee sustained engagement. Unguided documentary databases often struggle to hold attention once initial curiosity fades, particularly when users are confronted with large volumes of dense or unfamiliar material. In the absence of guiding structures, users may disengage before a broader understanding can form. This highlights a critical design problem: how can interactive documentary support persistence and attention long enough for contextual knowledge to emerge, without resorting to didactic instruction or coercive forms of persuasion?

This article examines this problem through the lens of hybrid documentary-game design. It addresses the gap in Persuasive System Design (PSD) regarding structural strategies for contextual verification, arguing that selectively integrating gamification can support sustained engagement with context-rich documentary material. Rather than framing gamification as entertainment or behavioural manipulation, the paper treats it as a design strategy for structuring attention, and transitioning users from passive consumption to active, context-aware inquiry.

To this end, the study adopts a Research-through-Design (RtD) approach, using a hybrid documentary-game prototype *Trolls vs Elves* as a design probe. The project addresses Russian disinformation against Ukrainian refugees and is built not to prescribe conclusions, but to support user interpretation through progression-based scaffolding. While compatible with educational contexts, its primary purpose is to explore how fact-checking practices might move beyond isolated debunks toward interactive systems that convey socio-political contexts across fragmented information environments. By analysing system architecture and exploratory user interaction patterns, the article identifies design implications for the use of hybrid formats as tools for restoring context under conditions of informational fragmentation.

2 Literature Review

2.1 Interactive Documentary

Interactive documentaries have long explored how non-fiction material can be organised as navigable systems rather than linear narratives. Commonly defined as documentary works in which interaction constitutes a primary mode of engagement [7], these projects shift the audience's role from passive viewer to active participant [12]. While not originally conceived as responses to contemporary information disorder, i-docs provide an important design lineage for examining how complex bodies of factual material can be structured for exploration, comparison, and sense-making.

One approach involves organising non-fiction material through database-driven or modular structures. These systems allow users to traverse collections of interviews, documents, and media fragments through thematic, spatial, or associative links [1]. They offer potential advantages in fragmented media environments by enabling users to encounter information in a larger context, supporting the gradual construction of meaning across multiple sources rather than through isolated claims or bounded narrative frames [8]. In this respect, interactive documentaries can be understood as early experiments in organising large, heterogeneous knowledge spaces for exploratory inquiry [18].

However, interactivity alone does not necessarily ensure sustained engagement. Scholars have cautioned that unstructured navigational agency can result in a reduction of the documentary to a database, where the absence of guiding structures leaves users uncertain about how to proceed [6]. Without mechanisms that support persistence, users may abandon exploration before sufficient context can be formed.

Attempts to address these limitations have occasionally drawn on design strategies from games. One frequently cited example is *Fort McMoney* [5], which modelled the political and economic dynamics of an oil boomtown through participatory simulation. Its distribution through major news organisations demonstrated that game-inspired structures could coexist with journalistic rigour. However, its primary goal was fostering active citizenship through open deliberation [13] – a dynamic well suited to civic debate, but one that risks reproducing the polarisation and noise of social media environments.

Because the current study focuses on building resilience to manipulation rather than fostering civic attitudes, avoiding this risk was critical. Consequently, the present system adopts a semi-closed architecture that balances user agency with careful curatorial framing. It shifts from the horizontal exploration characteristic of *Fort McMoney* to vertical progression, using gated mechanics as a temporal restraint. This design prioritises the sequential accumulation of verified context over deliberative autonomy.

Within this broader design space, only a limited number of i-docs have addressed disinformation directly. *In Event of Moon Disaster* [14] employed a counterfactual deepfake scenario to foreground questions of media manipulation. Its complementary exhibition and educational materials attempted to contextualise emerging manipulation techniques, but their emphasis on technical features and detection strategies over broader interpretative frameworks risks rapid obsolescence as technologies evolve. *K'gari: The Real Story of a True Fake* [15] by contrast, used interactive animated storytelling to debunk a specific colonial falsehood. While effective within that narrative frame, its scope remains tied to a particular case rather than the broader dynamics through which this disinformation circulates.

A persistent design challenge therefore remains. Building resilience to information disorder requires not only understanding individual techniques or debunking discrete narratives but situating them within broader socio-political contexts. While database-driven i-docs are well suited to assembling such landscapes, their reliance on non-linear exploration raises a further question: how can users be supported to persist long enough within expansive documentary environments for cumulative contextual understanding to emerge?

2.2 Gamification and Motivational Design

Gamification is commonly understood as the selective integration of game design elements into non-game contexts [4]. It does not aim to reproduce full ludic experiences but to structure user attention, persistence and orientation within interactive systems. Empirical research across educational and civic domains indicates that gamified systems can increase engagement and reduce attrition, particularly in tasks that demand sustained cognitive effort [9].

These effects are frequently interpreted through Self-Determination Theory (SDT), which identifies three key conditions for sustained motivation: autonomy, competence, and relatedness [3]. While autonomy might intuitively be associated with openness and freedom of exploration (volition), research suggests that it emerges from meaningful choices rather than unrestricted decisions. In interactive environments, autonomy is therefore better understood as structured agency, where actions produce visible system responses – such as unlocking new content or advancing through a sequence. Under these conditions, users are more likely to experience their engagement as purposeful rather than exploratory for its own sake [16]. This contrasts with many associative systems, where navigational ambiguity can obscure direction and undermine motivation. By introducing progression-based structures, gamification transforms interactivity from navigational freedom into goal-oriented inquiry, supporting users in sustaining engagement across extended interactions.

Progression-based mechanisms such as staged access, thresholds, and progress indicators can also contribute to users' sense of competence by providing clear signals of advancement within increasingly complex informational environments [16].

Finally, while narrative and storytelling are both mechanisms for fostering relatedness in interactive and documentary media [10], gamification can extend this relational dimension beyond narrative identification alone. Game-derived elements such as role-based framing, perspective-taking, or structured collaborative tasks introduce additional layers through which users can experience a sense of connection, alignment, or social presence within a system [2,17]. Rather than replacing narrative engagement, these mechanics function as additional scaffolds that stabilise and deepen relatedness by embedding it within interactive structure.

That said, prior research cautions against superficial applications that merely overlay points onto informational content. Such approaches risk reproducing the 'chocolate-covered broccoli' problem, where extrinsic rewards undermine intrinsic curiosity [10]. Effective gamified systems instead rely on mechanics that feel coherent with the task at hand, preserving a sense of voluntariness and fairness even when participation is guided or constrained. In this respect, studies further indicate that users do not necessarily resist mandatory interaction, provided that the system's logic is legible, well executed, and its demands are perceived as meaningful [11].

3 Design Framework

In fragmented media contexts, difficulties in sustaining engagement with complex information are closely tied to how information environments structure attention over time, as users may disengage because systems fail to provide orientation, momentum, and legible pathways through dense information spaces.

Responding to this problem, this study approaches hybrid documentary-game systems as attentional environments, shifting the focus from the exploratory opacity of many database-driven i-docs and the bounded narrative structures of traditional documentaries toward structured, paced engagement with context-rich information. The central design problem is therefore not how to maximise open-ended exploration through unrestricted choice, nor how to resolve complexity through narrowly scoped debunking and explanations, but how to support persistence long enough for contextual relationships between information elements to become visible.

There are three interrelated design concerns that inform this approach. First, persistence must be actively supported. Unscaffolded interactive systems often rely on curiosity alone, yet prior work indicates that curiosity without direction frequently leads to early disengagement. Introducing progression-based structures provides users with temporal orientation, signalling that continued engagement will yield new informational affordances.

Second, orientation within complexity is critical. Large documentary corpora can overwhelm users if presented as undifferentiated databases. Sequencing material into manageable units, gating access to increasingly complex content, and offering multiple modes of navigation and visual organisation function as design strategies for pacing cognitive demand without prescribing interpretation.

Third, framing shapes how users initially enter and remain situated within the system. Entry points, narrative voice, and tonal framing influence how users orient themselves in relation to documentary material, establishing a coherent experiential baseline for interaction. In this context, such framing function not as rhetorical persuasion, but as a means of reducing interpretive friction and stabilising engagement across extended interaction.

Together, these considerations inform a design rationale in which gamification is treated as a structural means of shaping engagement over time. This is operationalised through the *Trolls vs Elves*, which serves as a design probe for examining how progression-based structures and contextual sequencing shape engagement patterns within a large documentary corpus.

4 Methodology

This study adopts a research-through-design methodology, using *Trolls vs Elves* as a design probe and primary research instrument to examine how progression and sequencing influence user engagement within context-rich information systems. The methodological focus is on identifying exploratory interaction patterns that can inform future design iterations. The findings are not intended to establish generalisable behavioural effects, learning outcomes or persuasive effectiveness at scale.

4.1 Design Process and Context

Trolls vs Elves was developed over six months within MediaFutures, an initiative countering misinformation funded by the Horizon 2020 EU framework for research and innovation. Design decisions were informed through consultations with practitioners working in journalism, fact-checking, and media research across Central and Eastern Europe, and the UK. These consultations supported the grounding of the system's interaction design in existing professional practices but did not function as formal data collection.

Following development, the prototype was deployed across a series of controlled testing contexts, including beta-testing during residency, workshops with secondary school students in Poland, and presentations at professional forums (IDFA DocLab Forum, m:brane). These contexts enabled observation of engagement patterns and the collection of qualitative feedback related to navigation, progression, and perceived effort.

4.2 Data Collection and Participants

The analysis draws on three distinct data streams collected across the development and post-deployment phases. The multi-method approach distinguishes between objective telemetry (what users did) and subjective rationale (why they did it). All datasets are non-probabilistic, serving to surface indicative engagement signals only.

- **Beta testers ($n = 14$):** Provided qualitative feedback on system usability, navigation, and interaction logic during the iterative development phase.
- **Teenage cohort ($n = 24$):** Participants aged 16–19 who engaged with the deployed system in facilitated sessions. Post-use questionnaires captured qualitative insights into their motivations and perceived effort.
- **Interaction logs ($n=36$):** Server-side telemetry captured objective metrics including path selection and percentage of content explored.

4.3 Analysis Strategy and Ethics

To ensure strict participant anonymity, interaction logs were not linked to individual questionnaire responses. While this prevents direct correlation between specific behavioural traces and self-reported attitudes at the individual level, the study employs aggregate triangulation to interpret the data. Because both interaction logs and questionnaires captured overlapping indicators (path selection and completion) objective behavioural trends from the logs are interpreted alongside recurring qualitative themes from the questionnaires.

The two data sources were analysed independently and used in parallel to identify structural engagement patterns and contextualise user experience. The resulting analysis therefore supports indicative design insights about how progression structures shape engagement at the system level, rather than causal links between specific user attitudes and their recorded actions.

5 *Trolls vs Elves* Case Study

Released in 2024, *Trolls vs Elves*[1] is a hybrid documentary-game system that focuses on Russian disinformation targeting Ukrainian refugees, situating social media narratives within the broader context of the war in Ukraine and contemporary information warfare. The project explores how large, heterogeneous bodies of non-fiction material can be organised to support sustained attention and contextual sense-making within fragmented information environments. The project required a format capable of combining exploratory interaction with structured sequencing across a substantial volume of material. Consequently, *Trolls vs Elves* was developed as a bespoke web application, enabling fine-grained control over how documentary materials are accessed, sequenced, and unlocked over time. This design choice allowed the project to foreground engagement duration and navigation behaviour as primary objects of inquiry.

5.1 Design Rationale

Progression-Based Pacing. While many database i-docs employ unstructured navigation, this system adapts specific game mechanics – gated unlocking and stage-based access – to regulate the flow of information. Access to documentary material is organised into contextual layers, where unlocking thresholds require users to engage with a defined portion of content before advancing. Within each level, however, users navigate a non-linear database of documentary fragments rather than a fixed narrative sequence.

These mechanics provide immediate visual feedback on progress, transforming viewing into a goal-oriented process. This structure offers temporal orientation by signalling that continued engagement will yield access to new material (a 'reward' of content), while also modulating cognitive demand by gating complexity. Importantly, the system is designed to transition between two distinct modes

[1] Available at https://www.trolls-vs-elves.com.

of engagement: an initial scaffolded phase (Levels 1–3) and an open-exploration archive. This allows observation of changes in user behaviour as the system moves from structured, gamified progression to unstructured exploration.

The scaffolded phase was calibrated to require approximately twenty-five minutes of interaction. This duration was chosen to sustain attention long enough for basic contextual reasoning and interpretative accumulation to happen before encountering raw data from Twitter. Pragmatically, this timeframe also allows the experience to function in formal educational environments (typically 45-minute lessons), ensuring the core experience can be completed and followed by discussion within a single session.

Context-First Sequencing. This curatorial strategy is operationalised through the level structure. The system enforces a chronological dependency where background material – historical, political, and socio-cultural – serves as a mandatory prerequisite for accessing the final level of raw social media data. By gating contentious or ambiguous content behind these contextual layers, the design ensures users do not encounter isolated claims without first engaging with an interpretative framework.

These strategies function in tandem: progression mechanics sustain the temporal commitment necessary for the sequencing strategy to take effect. This ensures users do not abandon the experience before acquiring a foundational understanding of the context, preventing the premature consumption of social media content without an interpretative baseline.

5.2 System Architecture and Interaction Structure

Built as an open-source, single-user desktop web application, the system combines modular video fragments with database-driven navigation within an ethically curated environment. On launch, users complete a brief introduction and select one of two entry points: an internet troll or a fact-checking activist (Cyber Elf). This choice affects both interface framing and curatorial emphasis, with each path presenting a different subset of documentary material drawn from the same pool of contributors and themes. This framing functions as an orientational device establishing a stable experiential context that supports sustained engagement without prescribing interpretive positions.

Interface and Progression Logic. The interface is intentionally minimal to manage cognitive load. A progression indicator tracks material explored and controls access to the system's three levels. Short narrative-guide interventions mark these transitions and provide immediate feedback on progress.

Level Structure. *Level 1* introduces the selected movement (Internet Trolls or Cyber Elves) by outlining their practices, motivations, historical development, and modes of operation. This establishes a foundational understanding of how these actors function within online information environments.

Level 2 situates these practices within a broader geopolitical and socio-political context. This level addresses the hybrid war in Ukraine, combining perspectives on physical and cyber conflict, refugee testimonies, and systemic conditions shaping contemporary information warfare.

The final level introduces raw social media data in the form of a Twitter (now X) visualisation comprising approximately 1,500 posts. At this stage, users encounter empirical traces of disinformation accompanied by embedded videos that focus either on manipulation techniques or verification strategies.

In addition to progression-based unlocking, the system provides a fourteen-item multiple-choice quiz accessible throughout the experience. The questions can be used as guidance during exploration or as a recap, but progression through levels and experience completion do not depend on answering them.

6 Results

6.1 Engagement and Progression

The median total interaction duration was approximately 33 min. Given that this represents only a partial traversal of the overall documentary corpus – estimated at roughly 15% of available material – engagement clustered around the system's progression thresholds. Users commonly disengaged shortly after the final level was unlocked (Fig. 1).

Qualitative feedback from the teen cohort supports this pattern, with references to 'unlocking levels' cited as the most frequent reason for continuing interaction (mentioned by 15 participants). These observations suggest that persistence was shaped primarily by the system's temporal structuring and defined milestones rather than open-ended consumption of content.

6.2 Progression vs. Assessment

The influence of progression-based structuring becomes clearer when contrasted with user responses to other game design elements. The optional quiz was actively engaged with and completed by participants but did not function as a comparable motivator: only four participants cited it as a reason for continuing interaction.

This contrast suggests that assessment-style mechanics, while usable and intelligible, played a limited role in sustaining engagement relative to progression structures that unlocked new contextual material. From a design perspective, this implies that in complex informational environments, sustained engagement may be better supported by mechanisms that pace inquiry (structural pacing) than by those that foreground evaluation or performance.

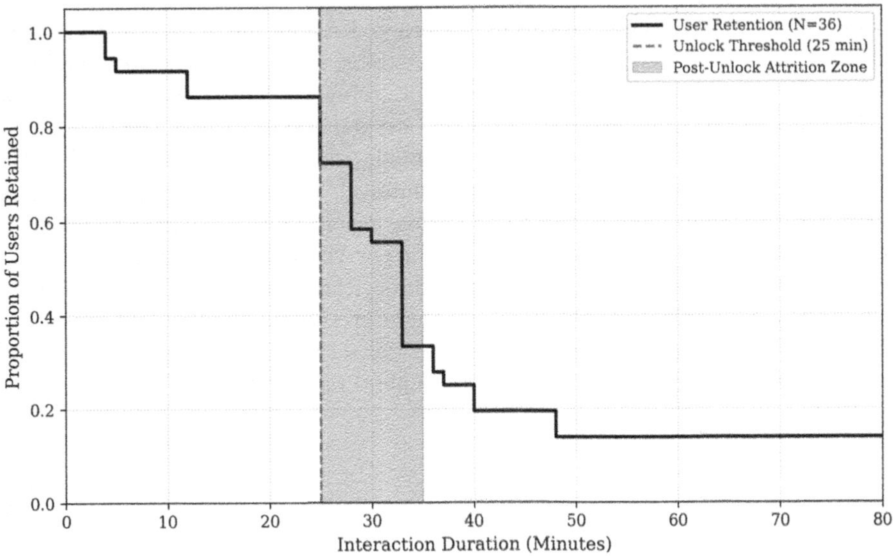

Fig. 1. Survival curve (N = 36) showing session abandonment (shaded) immediately after users explored the unlocked content.

7 Discussion

7.1 The 'Handoff' Challenge

The findings highlight progression as effective for structuring attention yet raise questions about sustaining engagement beyond gated guidance. The sharp attrition immediately post-unlock reveals a critical limitation. While the structure successfully 'held' users during the guided sequence, this did not necessarily translate into intrinsic motivation for unstructured exploration. Feedback suggests that gamified scaffolding shaped user expectations, creating anticipation for continuous challenges. When this structure was withdrawn, the open exploration of the final phase was experienced not as an invitation to freedom, but as a loss of momentum.

This points to a 'handoff' problem in persuasive design: the challenge of transitioning users from system-driven goals (scaffolded mode) to intrinsic inquiry (exploratory mode). To bridge this gap, future systems should treat progression not as a standalone solution, but as a foundational 'attentional skeleton' (targeting competence and structured agency) that requires deeper narrative framing (relatedness) and internalised consequences (intrinsic autonomy) to sustain engagement beyond the initial gating.

7.2 Sequencing and Temporal Commitment

The design positions contextual material prior to exposure to contested content, treating background knowledge as a prerequisite. Engagement patterns suggest users invest sustained attention when progression cues signal additional frames to follow, reinforcing the value of delaying complex or ambiguous material until an explanatory baseline is established.

However, this foregrounds a related challenge specific to web-based documentary formats: the absence of shared conventions regarding duration and expected effort. Unlike films or games, i-docs offer limited cues about the required timeframe and level of commitment. In the present case, reaching all layers required approximately thirty-five minutes – a duration that is not problematic in itself, yet one that remains opaque without explicit temporal framing.

For PSD, this implies a dual requirement. While context-first sequencing can enhance interpretative readiness, its effectiveness relies on sufficient temporal commitment. Consequently, clear signalling of expected duration is necessary to ensure progression-based designs fulfil their persuasive potential, supporting sustained attention long enough for contextual understanding to take shape.

8 Limitations and Future Work

Exploratory Scope. The findings reported in this paper are exploratory and indicative. As a RtD inquiry, the study prioritised the identification of interaction patterns to inform system architecture rather than the establishment of generalisable behavioural effects. Consequently, the results reflect how specific structures function within a limited, non-probabilistic, recruited sample, not how the system would perform at scale or across diverse audiences. Future work should replicate this approach with larger, more heterogeneous cohorts to enable more systematic analysis of persistence across demographic contexts.

Platform Constraints. The prototype was implemented as a desktop web application. Feedback from educational collaborators indicated that desktop-based tools are increasingly difficult to deploy in contexts where tablets and personal mobile devices dominate everyday use. While the desktop format enabled the development of a dense, multi-level interaction structure, it constrains the applicability of the findings to mobile-first environments, where attention dynamics and interaction patterns may differ. Future research should therefore examine how progression-based pacing and contextual sequencing operate under mobile interaction constraints.

Post-scaffolding Engagement. The system's informational density reflects its role as design probe rather than a public-facing product. The extensive corpus was intentionally assembled to examine persistence within a context-rich environment under different structural conditions. The observed decline in engagement after progression thresholds were reached highlights the need for further investigation into how attention can be supported once explicit scaffolding ends. Future designs should explore how interactive verification tasks or deeper narrative framing might function as 'motivational bridges', sustaining user interest and autonomy after the attentional skeleton of progression is withdrawn.

9 Conclusion

This paper examined how hybrid documentary-game systems can support sustained attention and contextual reasoning in information environments destabilised by fragmentation, overload, and synthetic media. Using *Trolls vs Elves* as a case study, the analysis focused on progression-based interaction and context-first sequencing as a means of pacing engagement and structuring access so that users encounter explanatory frameworks before reaching judgment-oriented content.

Exploratory findings indicate that user persistence clustered tightly around progression thresholds, with engagement sustained primarily until access to the final level was unlocked. Progression cues were more salient in motivating continued interaction than optional assessment-style mechanics, suggesting that regulating temporal access to information may be a more effective driver of scaffolded persistence than performance-based rewards.

These results contribute to persuasive technology research by highlighting progression-based structuring not only as a retention mechanic, but as a foundational tool for 'epistemic sequencing'. For systems addressing complex socio-political material, structuring *when* and *how* context becomes available is critical for supporting the interpretative readiness necessary to process ambiguous or contested data.

Ultimately, progression is not just about keeping the user online. It is a strategy for epistemic defence. In an era where generative AI and high-quality deepfakes render sensory verification nearly impossible, the design of time and attention becomes a prerequisite for truth. By positioning context prior to judgment, such systems offer a blueprint for how interactive media might support verification in environments where images or text alone can no longer be taken at face value.

Acknowledgments. The author would like to thank the doctoral supervisory team – Prof. Ben O'Loughlin, Dr David Young, and Prof. Ryan McKay – for their intellectual guidance and support throughout this research.

This research was funded by the Arts and Humanities Research Council (AHRC) through the Techne Doctoral Training Partnership, supported by UK Research and Innovation (UKRI). The practical component of the research was supported by the European Union's Horizon 2020 research and innovation programme under grant agreement No. 951962 (MediaFutures project).

Disclosure of Interests. The author declared no potential conflicts of interest with respect to the research, authorship, and/or publication of this article.

References

1. Aston, J., Gaudenzi, S.: Interactive documentary: setting the field. Stud. Doc. Film **6**, 125–139 (2012). https://doi.org/10.1386/sdf.6.2.125_1
2. Chen, H.L., Wu, C.T.: A digital role-playing game for learning: effects on critical thinking and motivation. Interact. Learn. Environ. **31**, 1–13 (2021). https://doi.org/10.1080/10494820.2021.1916765

3. Deci, E., Ryan, R.: Self-determination theory: a macrotheory of human motivation, development, and health. Canadian Psychology/Psychologie Canadienne **49**, 182–185 (2008). https://doi.org/10.1037/a0012801
4. Deterding, S., Dixon, D., Khaled, R., Nacke, L.: From game design elements to gamefulness: defining gamification. In: Proceedings of the 15th International Academic MindTrek Conference: Envisioning Future Media Environments (2011). https://doi.org/10.1145/2181037.2181040
5. Dufresne, D.: Fort McMoney. National Film Board of Canada (2013). interactive documentary
6. Forceville, C.: Interactive documentary and its limited opportunities to persuade. Discourse Context Media **30**, 218–226 (2017). https://doi.org/10.1016/j.dcm.2017.06.004
7. Galloway, D., McAlpine, K.B., Harris, P.: From Michael Moore to JFK reloaded: towards a working model of interactive documentary. J. Media Pract. **8**(3), 325–339 (2007). https://doi.org/10.1386/jmpr.8.3.325_1
8. Gaudenzi, S.: The Living Documentary: from representing reality to co-creating reality in digital interactive documentary. Ph.D. thesis, Goldsmiths, University of London, London (2013)
9. Hamari, J., Koivisto, J., Sarsa, H.: Does gamification work? – A literature review of empirical studies on gamification. In: Proceedings of the 47th Hawaii International Conference on System Sciences, pp. 3025–3034. IEEE, Hawaii (2014). https://doi.org/10.1109/HICSS.2014.377
10. Isbister, K.: How Games Move Us: Emotion by Design. The MIT Press, Cambridge (2016). https://doi.org/10.7551/mitpress/9267.001.0001
11. Kuindersma, E., van der Pal, J., Herik, H., Plaat, A.: Comparing voluntary and mandatory gameplay. Int. J. Serious Games **3**, 67–83 (2016). https://doi.org/10.17083/ijsg.v3i3.133
12. Michiel, H., Zimmermann, P.: Documentary as an Open Space, pp. 355–365. Routledge, New York and London (2013). https://doi.org/10.1007/978-1-349-92625-1_40
13. Nash, K.: 1. I-docs and the documentary tradition: exploring questions of engagement, pp. 9–25. Columbia University Press (2017). https://doi.org/10.7312/asto18122-006
14. Panetta, F., Burgund, H.: Event of Moon Disaster (2019). interactive documentary
15. Rubeli, E., Etingof, B., Boltin, K.: K'gari: The Real Story of a True Fake. SBS Australia (2017). interactive documentary
16. Sailer, M., Hense, J., Mayr, S., Mandl, H.: How gamification motivates: an experimental study of the effects of specific game design elements on psychological need satisfaction. Comput. Hum. Behav. **69**, 371–380 (2017). https://doi.org/10.1016/j.chb.2016.12.033
17. Simpson, J., Elias, V.: Choices and chances: The sociology role-playing game—the sociological imagination in practice. Teach. Sociol. **39**, 42–56 (2011). https://doi.org/10.2307/41308923
18. Uricchio, W., Wolozin, S., Bui, L., Flynn, S., Tortum, D.: Mapping the intersection of two cultures: Interactive documentary and digital journalism. Tech. rep., MIT Open Documentary Lab (2015)

Designing Persuasive Social Robots: Modulating Embarrassment Through Personality and Appearance

Ahmed Salem and Kaoru Sumi(✉)

Future University Hakodate, Hakodate, Hokkaido, Japan
kaoru.sumi@acm.org

Abstract. Robots are increasingly integrated into social environments, yet little is known about how their personality and behavior can influence users' emotional responses, particularly in socially sensitive contexts. In this study, we investigated how different robot personalities—neutral, empathic, and ridiculing affect embarrassment-related emotions which are embarrassment, anxiety, and shame that are experienced by shy participants during embarrassing activities. Using the Furhat social robot with two facial appearances (human-like and anime-like), we conducted controlled experiments with 24 Japanese participants. Results revealed that robot personality significantly modulated emotional responses: empathic and neutral personalities mitigated embarrassment and anxiety, while ridiculing personalities amplified these emotions, particularly when paired with anime-like faces. Surprisingly, the effect of robot personality surpassed the effect of the anthropomorphism and social agency of robots on mitigating and amplifying the embarrassment emotion. These findings demonstrate that robots can be designed to strategically regulate user emotions, highlighting their potential as persuasive technologies for shaping social experiences. Finally, embarrassment in human—human interaction (HHI) scenarios was consistently rated higher than in all human—robot interaction (HRI) scenarios.

Keywords: Robot personality · Persuasive technology · Embarrassment · Emotional contagion

1 Introduction

Robots are increasingly becoming an integral part of everyday life, assisting individuals across the lifespan—from children to the elderly—in areas such as daily living, healthcare [22], lifelong disabilities [35], retail [37], and industrial applications [20]. As robots become more pervasive, understanding how they are perceived and ensuring smooth, satisfying interactions is critical for societal acceptance and long-term adoption. While research has extensively examined robots' functional capabilities, there is a growing need to investigate how robots

E. Vlahu-Gjorgievska et al. (Eds.): PERSUASIVE 2026, CCIS 2896, pp. 178–190, 2027.
https://doi.org/10.1007/978-3-032-27235-5_13

can effectively engage users on a social and emotional level, particularly in scenarios that involve sensitive or negative emotions.

Robot verbal and bodily expressions have been shown to transmit emotions to users through mechanisms such as emotional contagion and social identity processes [27,40,43]. Recent studies in human-robot interaction (HRI) have begun exploring how mood contagion and emotional transmission compare to human-human interaction (HHI) [38]. Emotional effects can be triggered by pose and motion dynamics [41], yawning [28], facial expressions combined with posture [9], and interpersonal accounts of emotion [17]. Factors such as robot anthropomorphism and gender can further modulate positive emotional contagion [42]. Despite these insights, research on robots' ability to actively regulate or alleviate negative emotions remains limited.

Embarrassment is a socially complex emotion that can significantly influence the smoothness and perceived intelligence of HRI, similar to its effects in HHI [2]. Humans often feel reassured when interacting with robots that are perceived as less socially judgmental, for example when acquiring potentially embarrassing products [21,24,31]. High levels of anthropomorphism in medical robots can increase embarrassment, whereas less human-like, more machine-like robots tend to reduce it [4]. Similarly, tele-operated robots can elicit higher embarrassment than autonomous robots, indicating that the presence of human intervention amplifies socially sensitive responses [11]. Notably, natural robot behaviors—such as gaze avoidance during embarrassing moments—enhance perceptions of sociability and social intelligence [10]. Recent findings suggest that robot type alone (human-like vs. product-like) may not suffice to mitigate embarrassment [25], highlighting the importance of exploring additional robot characteristics, such as personality and behavioral attitude, in regulating socially sensitive emotions [39].

Given the critical role of social perception in shaping user acceptance and long-term engagement, understanding how robots can influence negative emotions like embarrassment is essential. Yet, embarrassment remains largely unexplored in HRI research in its "raw" form, largely due to ethical concerns and the intensity of the emotion. In this study, we investigate embarrassment in controlled HHI and HRI scenarios. The effect of robot facial appearance and personality is investigated to obtain the most effective robot facial appearance and personality that can mitigate embarrassment emotions. The HHI condition was always considered to explore if any robot facial appearance or personality variations would surpass the elicited embarrassment emotions in the HHI condition. Hence, HHI condition is assumed to be eliciting the highest embarrassment emotion [4]. By systematically examining robot facial appearance and personality, this work addresses a critical gap in persuasive technology research demonstrating how socially aware robots can effectively guide user attitudes and behaviors in sensitive contexts.

2 Robot Personalities and Gestures

The social robot Furhat [1] is used in the experiment. Furhat is a robot head that deploys a back-projected animated face that is realistic and human-like without risking falling into the uncanny valley effect due to the usage of facial animation. It facilitates studying and validating patterns in HHI and HRI. In Furhat, the robot's animated face is back-projected on a translucent mask, thus the principle is similar to other retro-projected robots. However, Furhat enjoys a rich library of facial expressions and performs speech recognition, and multi-person face tracking leading to an advanced reliable multimodal input processing and operation.

A pilot study was conducted to investigate what personality of embarrassment witnesses is preferred by the embarrassed actor. Interestingly, a neutral personality were the embarrassing encounter is dealt with as if it did not occur was preferred by most subjects. Certainly, it can be challenging to consider a robot that has the awareness and the agency to perceive an encounter as embarrassing, thus, investigating the robot personality to the embarrassing encounter is necessary. Moreover, long-term interaction with the robot depends highly on how the robot is perceived through its personality. Thus, investigating a robot personality that aids in cementing a positive perception is necessary. For these reasons, a neutral personality where the robot pretends as if the embarrassing encounter did not occur was chosen. An empathic personality was also considered as it is the personality that was thought to be preferable to the embarrassed actors in the pilot study. A ridiculing personality was also considered to highlight the contrast between different robot attitudes.

The Gesture Capture Tool provided by Furhat was used to record emotional utterances, facial expressions, and head movements for the three personalities chosen to be investigated. The emotional voice, facial expressions, and head movements were acted by a male university student. Thus, the robot was projecting a male social robot across the whole experiment to aid in transmitting the embarrassment negative emotion [42]. Note that, the robot was operated through the WoZ method. Consistency across sessions was ensured through a framework that the robot operator follows the same procedure and gestures sequences for the participants. The robot empathic and ridiculing personalities gestures for the human robot face can be watched through this link. Note that, the neutral personality is where the robot gives no reaction to the embarrassing encounter. Furthermore, human and anime robot faces were studied to uncover their effects on controlling the elicited embarrassment emotion as shown in Fig. 1a and Fig. 1b.

3 Experiment Protocol

3.1 The Screening Process

To elicit the embarrassment emotion, the participant must be a shy person. The participant was asked *"Are you a shy person?"* to ensure that the participant is

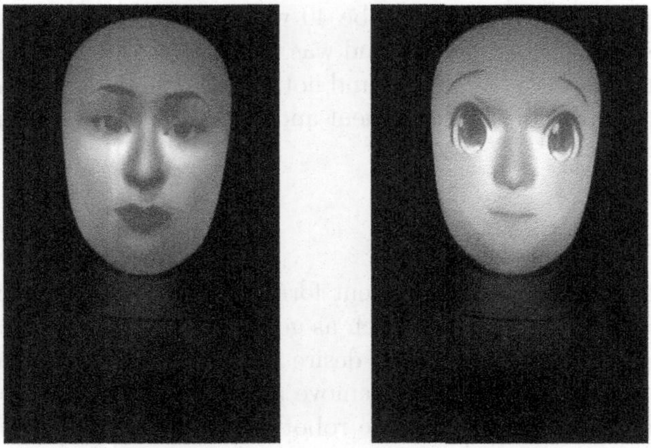

(a) Human face (b) Anime face

Fig. 1. The Furhat social robot.

shy as in [23,44]. That question has an answer of "yes" or "no". The response to that question must be "yes". They were asked if there had ever been a period of time in their lives when they were shy, which can be indicated by "yes" or "no". The response must be "yes".

To verify how shy the participant is, the method in [23] was followed in which the participants were asked to rate their degree of shyness from 0 (not shy at all) to 6 (I feel shy all the time). The degree of shyness must be 3 or more. The *M* and *SD* of the degree of shyness of the participants are shown in Table 1. There were no significant differences.

A shy person is the targeted participant because shy people report higher embarrassment and social anxiety, which necessitates developing systems that comfort them, reduce their anxiety, alleviate their embarrassment, and ensure smooth HRI [15].

Table 1. Degree of shyness of the participants (*M*/*SD*)

	Male	Female	Overall
Human face robot	4/0	4.83/0.98	4.42/0.8
Anime face robot	3.83/0.41	4/0.71	3.91/0.54
Overall	3.92/0.3	4.45/0.93	

It was highlighted that physiological changes could have occurred due to participants having a social phobia as discussed in [23], thus the participants were asked to fill out the Social Phobia Inventory (SPIN) questionnaire [13,32] to ensure that they were not socially phobic. Participants scoring above the established cutoff which was set to be 40 were excluded from the study. SPIN was used solely as a screening tool and was not included in subsequent analyses.

If the participant is a shy person and not socially phobic, then the participant is eligible to take part in the experiment and they were asked to sign the consent form.

3.2 Experiment Procedure

After the participants sign the consent form, they fill out a questionnaire that captures basic demographic data such as gender and age. After that, they have a conversation about any topic they desire for five minutes with the robot. The purpose of that conversation is to remove any novelty effects and to allow the participant to anthropomorphize the robot thus enhancing the embarrassment emotion.

The experiment included 24 participants (12 males and 12 females) of Japanese ethnicity. The participants age range, *M*, and *SD* are shown in Table 2. Note that, males and females are distributed and analyzed separately due to their differences in experiencing embarrassment, where females experience more intense embarrassment emotions than males [30,33,34]. All participants performed three embarrassment-inducing activities. The embarrassing activities are "laughing hysterically", "singing", and "acting like a 5-year-old child's tantrum". Note that, the chosen embarrassing activities are common in the "embarrassment literature" [23]. Each of the three activities duration was a minute and a half. All embarrassing activities were being recorded by a web camera as consented by the participant before participating in the experiment.

Table 2. Participants age data (range/*M*/*SD*)

	Male	Female	Overall
Human face robot	19-25/21.5/2.34	18-21/19.5/1.64	18-25/20.5/2.2
Anime face robot	19-26/22.83/2.78	18-21/19.2/1.17	18-26/21/2.8
Overall	19-26/22.2/2.55	18-21/19.33/1.37	

For the "singing activity", as some people might be good at singing because of the popularity of karaoke in Japan, a song was chosen so that when it is acted out, it will be embarrassing to watch. Three factors were considered when choosing the song, which are how recent it is, how trendy it is among teenagers of the same age as the participants in the experiment, and how exaggerating the performance of the singer when singing the song. Old songs can be risky as they can elicit good memories, affecting the targeted embarrassment emotion [7,26]. Kids songs could elicit childhood memories and make the participant happy and experience a sense of warmth [8]. If a trendy song is chosen, it might elicit an emotion of "being cool" [12] that can be followed by an emotion of "pride" which is the exact opposite of "shame" [18] which is crucial for embarrassment to be elicited. If the singer's performance is exaggerated, there will be a high chance of triggering an "improper identity" situation which can effectively trigger embarrassment [3,16]. A singer singing a hip hop song could possibly be perceived as cool [6] and no one would mind imitating that, but an old irrelevant performance can trigger a sense of "cringe" into it [36], thus facilitating the elicitation of the embarrassment emotion. The song that was chosen is "Masahi Akigawa: "Becoming a thousand winds" [Translated]". A document of the song's lyrics was given to the participants to not stress them cognitively. The participants heard the song once and were then asked to mimic the singer as best as they could.

The embarrassment emotion is elicited by letting the participants watch the recorded embarrassment-inducing activities with the confederate or the robot with one facial appearance. One activity was watched with the confederate and the other two activities were watched with the robot, thus, there is no interaction with the robot. The robot adopted one of three personalities when watching the embarrassing activities with the participant. Thus, each participant witness two robot personalities. After watching the activity, we ask the participants fill out some questionnaires. Note that, the confederate is a male.

After finishing the experiment, the participants were debriefed about the purpose of the experiment and the deception was removed. This study received full ethical approval from the Research Ethics Committee at the university. The approval number is 2024010.

4 Results Analysis

A linear mixed-effects model was used to statistically analyze the obtained results. Fixed effects components included participants genders, robot's facial appearance, agent type, personality, and the embarrassing activity. Three, four, or five-way interactions were avoided as with only 24 participants and many factor levels, high-order interactions are often not estimable. Only main effects and theoretically relevant two-way interactions were tested due to the sample size. However, in the current work, primary research questions are about the main effects, not their interactions. Thus, this approach fits our analysis.

In simple ANOVA/GLM, degrees of freedom (df) are always integers, because they're based on sample size minus number of parameters. However, in mixed models, degrees of freedom are estimated using approximations (Satterthwaite in this case). These methods adjust df to account for the complexity of random effects and unbalanced data, which leads to non-integer fractional denominator degrees of freedom.

4.1 Ratings of Five Emotions

Participants were asked to rate on a 7-point Likert scale where the anchors are labeled "not at all" and "very much" a list of five emotions [14]: embarrassment, anxiety, shame, disgust, and surprise. Note that, embarrassment-related emotions are embarrassment, anxiety, and shame [4], thus, they will be closely correlated to each other. The obtained ratings are presented below.

Embarrassment-Related Emotions

Embarrassment: *The HHI condition elicited significantly higher embarrassment than the HRI condition. Additionally, a ridiculing personality elicited significantly greater embarrassment when paired with the anime face than with the human face, an effect that was unexpected.*

When considering a full model that includes the HHI condition, conditions had a significant main effect on the elicited embarrassment emotion, $F(6,52.8) = 5.18$, $p < .001$. Post hoc pairwise comparisons with Bonferroni adjustment revealed that an anime robot face with a ridiculing personality ($M = 6.43$, $SE = 0.56$) elicited significantly higher embarrassment than the human robot face with the same personality ($M = 3.47$, $SE = 0.56$), $t(64.7) = 3.76$, $p = .008$. This result is unexpected and highlights how adding a personality to the robot can surpass the effect that robot anthropomorphization could have on the elicited embarrassment.

Anxiety: *The HHI condition elicited significantly higher anxiety than the HRI condition. Consistent with the pattern observed for embarrassment, a ridiculing personality elicited significantly higher anxiety when paired with the anime face than with the human face. Gender differences were also observed, with females experiencing significantly higher anxiety than males.*

The experiment conditions had a significant main effect on the anxiety emotion, $F(6,50.9) = 3.45$, $p = .006$. Post hoc pairwise comparisons with Bonferroni adjustment revealed the following:

- The HHI condition ($M = 4.78$, $SE = 0.36$) elicited significantly higher anxiety than the robot human face with a ridiculing personality ($M = 2.15$, $SE = 0.6$), $t(52.5) = 4.18$, $p = .002$. This highlights that a human witness is more amplifying to embarrassment emotions even if the robot is having a ridiculing personality.
- The anime robot face with a ridiculing personality ($M = 5.45$, $SE = 0.6$) elicited significantly higher anxiety than the human robot face with a ridiculing personality ($M = 2.15$, $SE = 0.6$), $t(62.8) = 3.96$, $p = .004$. This result is similar to the embarrassment emotion rating which highlights how a personality can change the effects of robot anthropomorphization on the elicited embarrassment emotion.

The anxiety emotion ratings highlight the potential of robot attitude being an effective amplifier to embarrassment emotions that can exceed the effect of the robot anthropomorphization. This was highlighted when surprisingly an anime face robot elicited higher anxiety emotions than a human face robot when a ridiculing personality is utilized. It is possible that the lower social agency of the anime face lead to higher embarrassment-related emotion (i.e., anxiety).

The ratings also highlights that HHI amplifies embarrassment even if the robot personality in the HRI condition is a provoking one (i.e., ridiculing personality).

Shame: *The HHI condition elicited significantly higher shame than the HRI condition. Consistent with the pattern observed for embarrassment and anxiety emotions.*

Other Emotions

Disgust: The HHI condition elicited higher disgust than the HRI condition which can be due to the lack of the biological aspect in HRI. The ridiculing personality elicited the highest disgust emotion followed by the empathic personality and lastly, the neutral personality. There are no significant differences.

Surprise: The neutral personality elicited the lowest surprise emotion which is expected as the robot is not reacting to the embarrassing scenario. There are no significant differences.

4.2 Experienced Embarrassment

The participants also filled out the "experienced embarrassment questionnaire" [29].

It was observed that the tantrum activity elicited a significantly high embarrassment compared to the other two activities which makes it an effective embarrassment-inducing activity.

The embarrassing activity had a significant main effect on the experienced embarrassment, $F(2,46) = 3.82$, $p = 0.03$. Post hoc pairwise comparisons with Bonferroni adjustment revealed that the tantrum activity ($M = 28.1$, $SE = 1.5$) elicited significantly higher experienced embarrassment than the laughing activity ($M = 23.1$, $SE = 1.5$), $t(46) = 2.62$, $p = .03$. This result is inline with the literature [33].

4.3 Robot's Evaluation

The responses obtained from the three questionnaires developed in [5] that evaluate robot's perceived character, the interaction with the robot, and the opinions formed about it are presented below.

Empathic and neutral personalities with an anime face were consistently rated highly. Females also consistently rated the robot highly and favorably.

The Robot's Character: It was observed that the empathic personality received the highest rating followed by the ridiculing personality and then the neutral personality. Robot anime face was rated higher than the human robot face. Lastly, females rated the robot's character higher than males. This shows that there is a preference for an anime face robot with an empathic attitude. There are no significant differences.

The Robot's Interaction: It was observed that females rated the robot's interaction higher than males. This is in line with the literature where females are known to report higher trust in robots than males [19]. There are no significant differences.

Opinion About the Robot: The robot personality had a significant main effect on the opinions formed about the robot, $F(2,45) = 5.62$, $p = .007$. Post hoc pairwise comparisons with Bonferroni adjustment revealed that the neutral personality ($M = 87.3$, $SE = 4.32$) and the empathic personality ($M = 87.4$, $SE = 4.32$) were evaluated significantly higher than the ridiculing personality ($M = 69.6$, $SE = 4.32$), $t(45) = 2.9$, $p = .01$. This shows that favorable opinions are attainable when the robot is either neutral or empathic, thus, confrontation is fully avoided.

4.4 Participants Embarrassability

The participants filled out the embarrassability questionnaire [29] and the obtained results are shown in Table 3. There are no significant differences between males and females. There are no significant differences between the participants who interacted with a human robot face and an anime robot face. Note that, the embarrassability of females is higher than males which is inline with the literature where females are known to experience the embarrassment emotions more intensely than males [30,33]. This is a desired aspect as it gives a balanced perspective where participants embarrassability is not skewing the results in favor of a certain direction which could distort the effectiveness of the obtained results.

Table 3. Embarrassability score data of the participants (M/SD)

	Male	Female	Overall
Human face robot	134.33/20.63	135.17/42.25	134.75/31.7
Anime face robot	136.5/21.12	139.67/23.62	138.08/21.43
Overall	135.42/19.94	137.42/32.72	

5 Discussion

This study investigated how humans experience embarrassment when a social robot or a human confederate witnesses them engaging in highly self-conscious embarrassing behaviors. Several important findings emerged.

First, participants reported significantly higher embarrassment in the HHI condition compared to all HRI conditions. This aligns with prior work showing that humans expect stronger social judgment from other humans than from robots [24,31]. Our results extend this evidence by demonstrating that the effect also holds when embarrassment is elicited using intense, real-world activities adapted from HHI research. This supports the view that robots provide a "low social cost" environment even in highly vulnerable situations, which may explain why robots are increasingly perceived as acceptable partners in health, retail, or support contexts. Adding a provoking personality to the robot did not make the HRI condition to be more threatening than the HHI condition. Thus, HHI is still the golden standard with the highest embarrassment elicitation.

Second, robot personality exerted a clear influence on affective responses. The neutral personality produced the lowest negative affect overall, suggesting that "acting as if nothing happened" may be the most comforting strategy for embarrassed users. This is consistent with our pilot findings and complements prior work showing that appropriate avoidance or low-reactivity behaviors increase perceived social intelligence during awkward moments [10]. The empathic personality produced slightly higher discomfort than neutral, possibly because empathic reactions implicitly acknowledge the embarrassing event, thereby intensifying self-awareness. In contrast, the ridiculing personality elicited the highest negative affect among the robot conditions, confirming that robots can indeed amplify discomfort when their social signals convey judgment or mockery.

Third, surprisingly, an anime face elicited higher embarrassment than a human face when a provoking ridiculing attitude is applied to it. This highlights that robot attitude can amplify embarrassment emotions to a degree that surpasses the effect of the robot's anthropomorphization and social agency itself. It is possible that a provoking attitude combined with a low social agency (or status) triggers higher embarrassment emotions as it does not conform with social norms.

Finally, gender differences were consistent with embarrassment literature: female participants tended to report stronger negative emotions (disgust and all embarrassment-related emotions) than males, even though both groups were screened to be shy. This reinforces the importance of considering gender-related affective sensitivity when designing socially adaptive robots.

Overall, our findings emphasize that robot personality design plays a central role in shaping how users feel during socially delicate interactions. A neutral, non-acknowledging personality appears promising for mitigating embarrassment and supporting comfortable long-term HRI. Moreover, robot personalty can surpass the expected user perceptions toward the robot's anthropomorphization and social agency. Future work should extend these findings by using larger samples and physiological measures. Investigating cross-cultural generalizability will also be essential, given cultural differences in embarrassment norms and impression management.

6 Conclusion

This study provides empirical evidence that robot personality and facial appearance can systematically influence users' emotional experiences in socially sensitive situations, such as embarrassment. Neutral and empathic robots reduced negative emotions, whereas ridiculing robots intensified them. Surprisingly, when a ridiculing personality is paired with an anime robot face, higher embarrassment emotions were elicited thus surpassing the effect of robot anthropomorphization and social agency. These findings underscore the potential of social robots as persuasive technologies capable of modulating human affect to achieve desired outcomes. By strategically designing robot personality and expressive behavior, it is possible to encourage positive user perceptions, increase engagement, and reduce social discomfort. This has important implications for applications in consumer behavior, education, therapy, and other social contexts where influencing emotions is critical. Lastly, the HHI condition proved consistently to be the golden standard where highest embarrassment emotions were obtained. Future work could explore long-term interactions, cross-cultural differences, and dynamic adaptation of robot behavior to further enhance their effectiveness as persuasive agents that prioritizes users comfort and mitigate negative emotions.

References

1. Al Moubayed, S., Beskow, J., Skantze, G., Granström, B.: Furhat: a back-projected human-like robot head for multiparty human-machine interaction. In: Esposito, A., Esposito, A.M., Vinciarelli, A., Hoffmann, R., Müller, V.C. (eds.) Cognitive Behavioural Systems. LNCS, vol. 7403, pp. 114–130. Springer, Berlin, Heidelberg (2012). https://doi.org/10.1007/978-3-642-34584-5_9
2. Argyle, M.: Non-verbal communication in human social interaction. Non-verbal Commun. **2**(1) (1972)
3. Babcock, M.K.: Embarrassment: a window on the self. J. Theory Soc. Behav. (1988)
4. Bartneck, C., Bleeker, T., Bun, J., Fens, P., Riet, L.: The influence of robot anthropomorphism on the feelings of embarrassment when interacting with robots. Paladyn **1**, 109–115 (2010)
5. Bickmore, T.W.: Relational agents: effecting change through human-computer relationships. Ph.D. thesis, Massachusetts Institute of Technology (2003)
6. Botz-Bornstein, T.: What does it mean to be cool? Philosophy Now **80**(August/September), 6–7 (2010)
7. Buchanan, T.W.: Retrieval of emotional memories. Psychol. Bull. **133**(5), 761 (2007)
8. Cady, E.T., Harris, R.J., Knappenberger, J.B.: Using music to cue autobiographical memories of different lifetime periods. Psychol. Music **36**(2), 157–177 (2008)
9. Casso, I., Li, B., Nazir, T., Delevoye-Turrell, Y.N.: The effect of robot posture and idle motion on spontaneous emotional contagion during robot-human interactions. arXiv preprint arXiv:2209.00983 (2022)
10. Choi, J.J., Kim, Y., Kwak, S.S.: Have you ever lied?: the impacts of gaze avoidance on people's perception of a robot. In: 8th ACM/IEEE International Conference on Human-Robot Interaction (HRI), pp. 105–106. IEEE (2013)

11. Choi, J.J., Kim, Y., Kwak, S.S.: Are you embarrassed? The impact of robot types on emotional engagement with a robot. In: Proceedings of the 2014 ACM/IEEE International Conference on Human-Robot Interaction, pp. 138–139. (2014)
12. Coancă, M.: Chapter twelve trendy and cool terms. Contextual Identities: A Comparative and Communicational Approach, p. 138 (2015)
13. Connor, K.M., Davidson, J.R., Churchill, L.E., Sherwood, A., Weisler, R.H., Foa, E.: Psychometric properties of the social phobia inventory (spin): new self-rating scale. Br. J. Psychiatry **176**(4), 379–386 (2000)
14. Costa, M., Dinsbach, W., Manstead, A.S., Bitti, P.E.R.: Social presence, embarrassment, and nonverbal behavior. J. Nonverbal Behav. **25**, 225–240 (2001)
15. Crozier, W.R.: Understanding ShynessâĂŕ: Psychological Perspectives. Palgrave, London (2001)
16. Cupah, W., Metts, S., Hazelton, V.: Coping with social disease: remedial strategies and embarrassment. A paper presented at the Western Speech Communication Association (1978)
17. Damm, O., et al.: Communicating emotions in robotics: towards a model of emotional alignment. In: Proceedings of the Workshop "Expectations in Intuitive Interaction" on the 6th HRI International Conference on Human-Robot Interaction (2011)
18. Danesi, M.: Cool: The signs and meanings of adolescence. University of Toronto Press (1994)
19. Gallimore, D., Lyons, J.B., Vo, T., Mahoney, S., Wynne, K.T.: Trusting robocop: gender-based effects on trust of an autonomous robot. Front. Psychol. **10**, 482 (2019)
20. Graetz, G., Michaels, G.: Robots at work. Rev. Econ. Stat. **100**(5), 753–768 (2018)
21. Guo, L., Gong, L., Xu, Z., Wang, W., Chen, M.H.: The role of service robots in enhancing customer satisfaction in embarrassing contexts. J. Hosp. Tour. Manag. **59**, 116–126 (2024)
22. Hall, A.K., et al.: Acceptance and perceived usefulness of robots to assist with activities of daily living and healthcare tasks. Assist. Technol. (2019)
23. Hofmann, S.G., Moscovitch, D.A., Kim, H.J.: Autonomic correlates of social anxiety and embarrassment in shy and non-shy individuals. Int. J. Psychophysiol. **61**(2), 134–142 (2006)
24. Holthöwer, J., van Doorn, J.: Robots do not judge: service robots can alleviate embarrassment in service encounters. J. Acad. Mark. Sci. **51**(4), 767–784 (2023)
25. Kang, D., Kwak, S.S.: I am relieved to have you: exploring the effective robot type to mitigate users negative emotions. In: Ali, A.A., et al. (eds.) Social Robotics. ICSR 2023. LNCS, vol. 14454, pp. 333–343. Springer, Singapore (2023). https://doi.org/10.1007/978-981-99-8718-4_29
26. Kensinger, E.A., Schacter, D.L.: Memory and emotion. Handb. Emot. **3**, 601–617 (2008)
27. Laban, G., Cross, E.S.: Sharing our emotions with robots: why do we do it and how does it make us feel? IEEE Trans. Affect. Comput. 1–18 (2024). https://doi.org/10.1109/TAFFC.2024.3470984
28. Lehmann, H., Broz, F.: Contagious yawning in human-robot interaction. In: Companion of the 2018 ACM/IEEE International Conference on Human-Robot Interaction, pp. 173–174 (2018)
29. Modigliani, A.: Embarrassment and embarrassability. Sociometry, pp. 313–326 (1968)

30. Pettijohn, T., Naples, G.M., McDermott, L.A.: Gender, college year, and romantic relationship status differences in embarrassment and self attitudes of college students. Individ. Differ. Res. **8**(3), 164–170 (2010)
31. Pitardi, V., Wirtz, J., Paluch, S., Kunz, W.: Will robots judge me? Wxamining consumer-service robots interactions in embarrassing service encounters: an abstract. In: Allen, J., Jochims, B., Wu, S. (eds.) Celebrating the Past and Future of Marketing and Discovery with Social Impact. AMSAC-WC 2021. Developments in Marketing Science: Proceedings of the Academy of Marketing Science, pp. 257–258. Springer, Cham (2021). https://doi.org/10.1007/978-3-030-95346-1_89
32. Ranta, K., Kaltiala-Heino, R., Koivisto, A.M., Tuomisto, M.T., Pelkonen, M., Marttunen, M.: Age and gender differences in social anxiety symptoms during adolescence: the social phobia inventory (spin) as a measure. Psychiatry Res. **153**(3), 261–270 (2007)
33. Salem, A., Sumi, K.: Psychophysiological correlates of embarrassment emotion: a comparative study between shy males and females. In: 2024 IEEE 48th Annual Computers, Software, and Applications Conference (COMPSAC), pp. 2083–2088. IEEE (2024)
34. Sato, Y., Salem, A., Sumi, K.: Physiological correlates while playing tetris: a comparative study between males and females. In: 2024 IEEE 48th Annual Computers, Software, and Applications Conference (COMPSAC), pp. 2054–2059 (2024). https://doi.org/10.1109/COMPSAC61105.2024.00328
35. Scassellati, B., Admoni, H., Matarić, M.: Robots for use in autism research. Annu. Rev. Biomed. Eng. **14**(1), 275–294 (2012)
36. Schwanebeck, W.: Introduction to painful laughter: media and politics in the age of cringe (2021)
37. Song, C.S., Kim, Y.K.: The role of the human-robot interaction in consumers' acceptance of humanoid retail service robots. J. Bus. Res. **146**, 489–503 (2022)
38. Stock, R.M.: Emotion transfer from frontline social robots to human customers during service encounters: testing an artificial emotional contagion modell (2016)
39. Van Pinxteren, M.M., Pluymaekers, M., Lemmink, J.G.: Human-like communication in conversational agents: a literature review and research agenda. J. Serv. Manag. **31**(2), 203–225 (2020)
40. Xu, J., Broekens, J., Hindriks, K., Neerincx, M.A.: Mood contagion of robot body language in human robot interaction. Auton. Agent. Multi-Agent Syst. **29**, 1216–1248 (2015)
41. Xu, J., Broekens, J., Hindriks, K.V., Neerincx, M.A.: Robot mood is contagious: effects of robot body language in the imitation game. In: AAMAS, pp, 973–980 (2014)
42. Yang, W., Xie, Y.: Can robots elicit empathy? The effects of social robots' appearance on emotional contagion. Comput. Hum. Behav. Artif. Hum. **2**(1), 100049 (2024)
43. Yu, C.E.: Emotional contagion in human-robot interaction. E-review Tour. Res. **17**(5) (2020)
44. Zimbardo, P.G., Pilkonis, P.A., Marnell, M.E.: ShynessâĂŕ: What it is, What to Do About It. Addison-Wesley Pub. Co., Boston (1977)

Multimodal Social Robot Behaviors as Persuasive Cues for Sustaining Engagement

Yunus Terzioğlu[1](✉), Akilan Baskar[2], and Timothy Bickmore[1]

[1] Khoury College of Computer Sciences, Northeastern University, Boston, MA, USA
{terzioglu.y,t.bickmore}@northeastern.edu

[2] College of Engineering, Northeastern University, Boston, MA, USA
baskar.ak@northeastern.edu

Abstract. People often have difficulty maintaining focus on repetitive monotonous tasks, especially in the face of increasing distractions such as social media. To address this issue, we have developed a humanoid robot designed to keep users engaged in a repetitive task using personalized social dialogue and persuasion mechanisms, with the latter triggered by detection of user dis-engagement behaviors including loss of speech, loss of face detection, or body movement. We build on persuasion principles and demonstrate how large language models can be leveraged to generate robot behavior to keep users engaged in a joint task. We evaluate the persuasive robot system in a counterbalanced within-subjects experiment in which participants are asked to play a simple game with the robot, repetitively, for as long as they want. We compare the user behavior and robot perception with the engagement robot to another robot that has the engagement mechanisms removed. We find that participants play games for a significantly longer period of time with the engagement robot, while being significantly more satisfied with that experience. We further present a system architecture for real-time multimodal personalized persuasion, and discuss design implications for developing robotic assistants that help people stay on task.

Keywords: human-robot interaction · engagement · task focus · social interaction · multimodal perception · multimodal interaction

1 Introduction

Many tasks that people perform require continued focus over extended periods of time. However, this is increasingly challenging given our current digital culture. Social media, asynchronous notifications, and ubiquitous communication channels and media provide unending distractions whenever tasks become difficult or boring [26]. Studies have consistently demonstrated that distractions have a negative impact on task performance [24]. In addition, some populations are at even greater risk for distraction, indicating a greater need for intervention. For

E. Vlahu-Gjorgievska et al. (Eds.): PERSUASIVE 2026, CCIS 2896, pp. 191–206, 2027.
https://doi.org/10.1007/978-3-032-27235-5_14

example, older adults with dementia have high prevalence (over 60%) of becoming disoriented and wandering, often leading to injury or death [28], indicating that approaches to maintaining their engagement could be important in future eldercare robots.

Socially interactive humanoid robots have been used to collaborate with people on a variety of tasks, in a variety of roles, and have been designed to use a range of social cues to promote collaboration and engagement. In our work, we are designing a social robot that can persuade a user to stay focused on a repetitive task, and re-engage them if they become distracted or disengaged. In human-human face-to-face conversation, disengagement behavior can be identified through language ("I'm done.") or non-verbally, using speech (silence), gaze (away from interlocutor), proxemics (physically leaving the interaction space), and more subtle cues (e.g., looking at one's watch). People also use a range of persuasive behaviors to maintain engagement with their collaborators. Following Cialdini [12], people can use *liking* strategies such as praise, warmth, and friendly interaction to increase interpersonal attraction, *reciprocity* strategies, such as giving emotional support or encouragement to induce a feeling of obligation to reciprocate by continuing the task, or *commitment & consistency* strategies, such as praise, to make the recipient strengthen identity-consistent behavior to live up to the praise.

Our approach to designing a task engagement robot takes inspiration from theories of persuasion, along with the social interaction behaviors described above. In the remainder of this paper we first describe previous work on robot engagement and then our theory-based approach to design of the robot. We then present results from an observational study of human behavior that is analogous to the human-robot interaction we are targeting. We demonstrate how the latest advancements in large language models (LLMs) can be used to generate verbal and non-verbal robot behavior–including social dialogue and storytelling–based on user engagement states and present a detailed description of the robot's implementation. Finally, we describe an experiment in which we evaluate the engagement strategies and behaviors used by the robot to keep users engaged in a repetitive task.

2 Prior Work

Persuasive robotics requires an understanding of how persuasion in human-human interactions translates to human-robot interactions [6], and there is now a large body of literature on persuasive computing [16] in general and persuasive robotics [40] in particular. Established persuasion models from human-human interactions [8,32] have been shown to be equally effective in human-robot interaction (HRI) [45]. Persuasion strategies such as social feedback [18,19], social proof [27], or leveraging expert opinions [14,34] have been used in the literature to improve attitudes towards robots, as well as positively influencing persuasion outcomes. Other more nuanced factors such as gender [17,40] and social power [21,22] or agency [37] have also been studied in the literature as effective factors for manipulating persuasive power in HRI. Robot embodiment [23], animacy [25], and nonverbal behavior [11] have also been proposed as powerful tools to facilitate persuasion. These studies demonstrate that behavioral theories of human-human persuasion can be transferred to HRI, with a highlight on the importance of embodiment, behavioral cues, and engagement on the effectiveness of the persuasion.

Engagement in HRI has been studied in a variety of contexts. Computational models of engagement informed by human behavior and based on physical cues such as gaze [39] and motion patterns [5] have shown promising results in engagement intent recognition and retention. Several works in the literature focused on detecting disengagement in HRI using formalisms over physiological [41] or conversational signals [4,35]. The importance of generating appropriate responses based on detected user engagement states has been highlighted as a critical component for increasing users' attention to joint human-robot activities [7]. Further, a recent survey emphasized that the ability to detect user engagement and generate appropriate responses accordingly is crucial for maintaining user interaction with both virtual and robotic agents [29]. Other task-oriented HRI studies showed that interactive behaviors can be elevated by conversational cues to improve both task and social engagement with a robot [13].

Studies on socially assistive humanoid robots have shown the importance of embodied interaction as well as the ability to dynamically adapt to users' engagement states in motivating engagement [2,44]. Humanoid robots have been shown to be valuable platforms in supporting people with special needs [36], providing cognitive [38] or physical exercises [36]. Long-term HRI studies revealed the difficulties in addressing fluctuating engagement levels during extended interaction sessions [10]. Further studies demonstrated the importance of social dialogue and other forms of off-task activities in enhancing adherence to cognitively demanding activities [42], and showed the nuanced complexities behind adaptive and interactive robot systems which persuade users to stay engaged in a joint activity [9]. This literature underscores the need for flexible and adaptive robotic persuasion systems to maintain engagement through co-created activities rather than predefined narratives.

3 Human Analog Study

To guide the implementation of our robotic re-engagement system, we conducted an exploratory study with 52 participants in which we asked dyads of participants to play games of Tic-Tac-Toe with each other. One of the participants in each pair was randomly assigned to be the *Robot*-analog who was responsible for keeping the other participant (*Human*) engaged in the game. The participants were briefed in separate rooms. The *Human* participants were asked to walk into the game room and "play at least 5 games of Tic-Tac-Toe;" whereas the *Robot* participants were asked to keep the *Human* participants playing for as long as they could. Each session took approximately 60 min, was video- and audio-recorded, and the experiment was approved by our institution's IRB.

Through this study, we found that the *Session* dialogue used by the *Robot* (outside of gameplay) consisted of initiating discussions about the game state, praise and encouragements, and general comments about the player moves and the game outcomes. At this level, if the *Robot* participant decided that the *Human* participant wasn't engaged in the task, they employed both verbal and non-verbal deictic cues to the game to re-engage the *Human*.

Once a game was underway, the *Robot* participants initiated *Task* interaction. This typically consisted of strategizing and discussing about the game state and outcomes, as well as reviewing mistakes from both players to support *Task* focus. The off-task talk in this context entailed behaviors such as engaging in small talk, starting a *Social* discourse based on their surroundings or the context exchanged during the *Session* and *Task* initiation, or telling a story about themselves and asking the *Human* participant for opinions or similar experiences. An interesting recurring behavior we observed was the *Robot* attempting to maintain the novelty of the game by inventing new rules, such as playing moves as quickly as possible, setting a target score and competing to be the one to reach it first, and asking the *Human* for cooperation to simulate different gameplay strategies to observe how the game then would unfold.

At game completion, the *Human* participants indicated their disengagement from the *Session* verbally and non-verbally prior to a ritual farewell. These disengagement behaviors included taking a step back from the game, slightly turning their body away from the joint space, looking at the room's door, and verbally conveying that they were leaving. At this stage, the *Robot* participants attempted to re-establish engagement by setting new task goals such as proposing to play one last game or breaking a tie before the *Human* participant left.

A common behavior employed by both *Human* and *Robot* participants was adapting their game strategy based on their opponent's competitiveness or skill level. This spectrum of behaviors ranged from intentionally losing games to explicitly challenging the other player. This adaptive behavior also led to tutoring interactions to help the other player become better in the game, which was used by the *Robot* participants as means to maintain engagement, whether they or the *Human* participant served as the tutor.

The observations from this study gave us a better understanding of the specific social behaviors and strategies a robot could use.

4 Persuasive Strategy Design

Following lessons learned from the Human Analog Study and principles of persuasion [12], we implemented a hierarchical set of rules to drive our robot's behavior in *Session*, *Task*, and *Social* discourse layers. In order of priority:

1. If user is actively working on Task, support them by sustaining Task dialogue.
2. If user disengages from (incomplete) Task, but is engaged in Session, then prompt them to continue on Task using *Reciprocity* or *Commitment & Consistency*.

3. If Task complete and user is engaged in Session, then prompt user to start new Task using *Reciprocity* or *Commitment & Consistency* if possible.
4. If user engaged in Task and Session and initiates Social, then respond with Social dialogue using *Liking* whenever possible.
5. If user disengages from ongoing Social (silence), then initiate Social dialogue using *Liking* whenever possible.
6. If user is disengages from Session (looks away, leaves), then respond with re-engagement behavior (beckoning, invite to Task, using *Reciprocity* or *Commitment & Consistency*).

5 Implementation

We developed two completely autonomous behaviors for Pepper robots ([1], Fig. 1) to be used in our experiments. We used a local OpenAI Whisper `turbo` model ([31]) as the speech transcription service [33], and an OpenAI Realtime Large Language Model (LLM) to generate text-based responses to user speech as well as to system prompts describing user disengagement states. Overall, our system was able to simultaneously engage in open conversation, play and respond to events in a Tic-Tac-Toe game, and generate reactions to user disengagement states. An overview the system architecture is given in Fig. 2. We provide our LLM prompts in our code repository[1].

5.1 Target Task

We implemented a Tic-Tac-Toe game to be played on the touchscreen tablet computer attached to the robot's chest. This game was chosen primarily because of its widespread recognition and also because it lost its novelty relatively quickly. Every time the user played their move, the system responded with an LLM-generated turn-taking utterance. These responses typically consisted of congratulations for the user if they won the round and encouragement for the next round if they lost it or if the round was a draw. At the end of each game, the robot asked the user if they wanted to play another round, and reset the game board. The combination of the game, the robot, and the game state-related responses from the robot served as the baseline target task in our experiments.

[1] https://github.com/terzioglan/PepperReengagement.

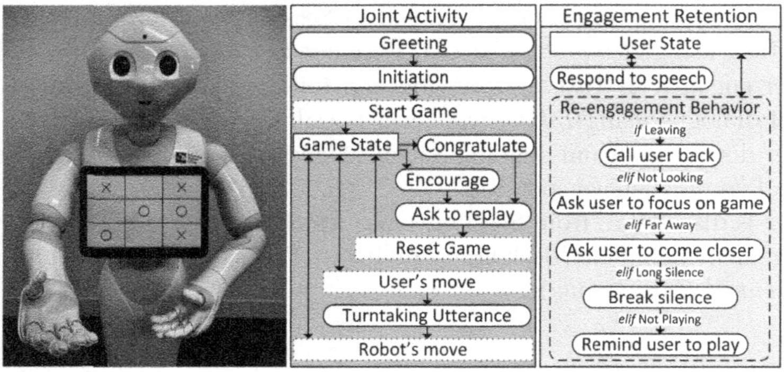

Fig. 1. Humanoid robot platform used to implement the autonomous re-engagement system during a joint gameplay activity (left). The interaction flow during the joint activity (middle). Engagement retention reactions based on the user states (right).

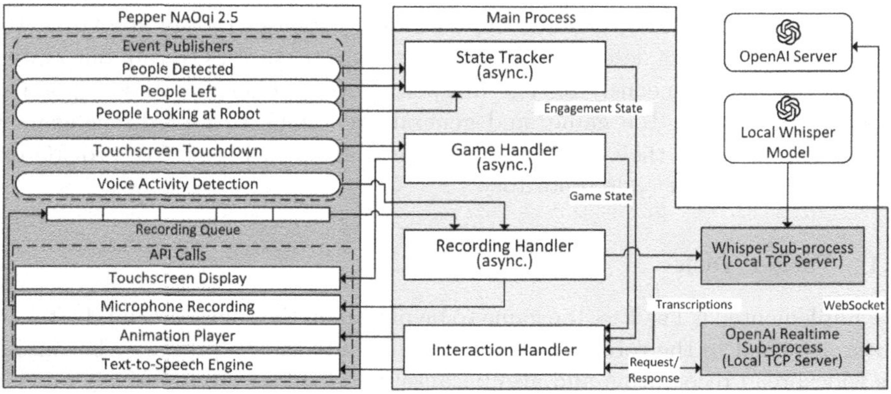

Fig. 2. An overview of our re-engagement system architecture.

5.2 Robot Behavior

We designed two robot behaviors, namely *Control* and *Re-engagement*. Every utterance spoken by either robot was generated using the LLM. The *Control* employed the target task and animated speech segments to guide the user through the interaction. After detecting a face in the room, this robot first greeted the user, pointed at its tablet while asking the user to touch the screen to start playing the game, and initiated the target task (Fig. 1-middle). While exhibiting this behavior, the robot did engage in open conversation with the user. *Control* robot utterances consisted of short canned phrases for the user to keep playing the game delivered at the end of each turn with a 50% probability, and at the end of each game.

The *Re-engagement* robot used the same greeting, initiation, and turn-taking steps as the *Control* robot. However during *Session* discourse initiation, the *Re-engagement* robot waited for a response from the user after greeting instead of initiating the target task. During this phase, the robot asked how the user was, and led the conversation toward task initiation in a couple of conversation turns of social dialogue in order to increase *Liking* as a persuasion strategy. The users in the initiation phase could keep the greeting small talk active for as long as they preferred. In this case the LLM would attempt to initiate a game every couple of turns.

In addition to the joint activity, the *Re-engagement* robot facilitated user engagement behaviors in parallel (Fig. 1 -right). Based on detected user states, the *Re-engagement* robot cued the user to keep playing if they haven't played their move for a while and called the user back to play more if they were leaving, using *Reciprocity* and *Commitment & Consistency* strategies. It also broke long silences by initiating conversation leveraged by the context in the conversation history; asked the user to come closer if they are sitting at a distance where they cannot touch the tablet screen; and asked the user to pay attention to the game if the robot detects that the user is not looking at the robot or the tablet. These behaviors were controlled and triggered by a set of state-specific and global timeouts derived empirically from our human analog study (Sect. 3). The complete list of timeouts are provided in our code repository[1].

5.3 Large Language Model

During the interaction with the *Re-engagement* robot, we used a text-based OpenAI Realtime model ("gpt-4o-mini-realtime-preview-2024-12-17"). Context retention capability of this model was crucially important for our system to be able initiate conversations to break long silences without deviating from the natural discourse. We initiated the LLM session using a system prompt specifically designed for the initiation phase ("GreetingPrompt" [1]). After the user agreed to play, we updated the session's prompt to be able to handle more nuanced interactions such as staying silent and head nodding if the user is telling a long story and is not finished yet, or generating utterances to re-engage the user based on user states rather than user speech ("EngagementPrompt" [1]).

5.4 Disengagement Reactions

We defined five user disengagement states to address during interactions with the *Re-engagement* robot. These states and the nature of the responses generated by the LLM are as follows:

- `Not Playing`: It has been a while since the user made their last move. The robot points at it's tablet and reminds the user to make their move.
- `Long Silence`: It has been a while since the user last spoke. The robot breaks the silence by asking follow-up questions based on the conversation history, or tell a short story and ask the human if they had a similar story.
- `Looking Away`: User is not looking at the robot or the tablet. The robot calls the user out that they are not paying attention.

- `Far Away`: User is too far from the robot to be able to touch the tablet to play their move. The robot asks the user to come closer.
- `Leaving`: User is getting further away from the robot. The robot asks the user to come back and play one more game round.

A disengagement response was triggered when certain criteria were met. For example if the robot or the user have spoken recently, the robot would not cue the user to make their move even though it has been a while since the user last played. `Leaving`, `Far away`, and `Looking away` responses took precedence over any other response event in the given respective order of priority. This precedence logic is loosely demonstrated in Fig. 1 -right.

5.5 Open Conversation

We used the robots' internal microphones to repeatedly record audio segments in fixed time intervals. Whenever voice activity was detected in an interval, the system kept recording until the end of the voice activity. The segments containing speech were pushed into a queue to be transcribed, and the rest were discarded.

Once every recording in the queue was processed, the final transcription was sent to the LLM and the resulting text response was sent to the TTS engine of the robot. In addition to generating spoken responses to user speech, the LLM was also used to infer whether the user is likely going to continue speaking. In this case, it responded with a special token which triggered a head nod animation on the robot instead of a spoken response. Each response in the study took between 0.3 to 0.9 s to generate.

6 Experiment Design

We designed a counterbalanced within-subjects experiment to evaluate our engagement retention system, with each participant interacting with a *Control* and *Re-engagement* in sequence. In the *Control* condition, the robot only exhibited the Joint Activity behavior outlined in Fig. 1 -middle. In addition to playing the game, this behavior included spoken cues for greeting the participant and initiating the game play, turn-taking, congratulating the participant if they won or encouraging them if they lost, and asking to play another round of games once the current round is over. This behavior served as the baseline for our experiment. In the *Re-engagement* condition, the robot exhibited Engagement Retention behavior along with the Joint Activity behavior. Further details about this behavior are provided in Sects. 5.2 and 5.4.

6.1 Measures

Our primary outcome for the study was Total Activity Duration. In both trial conditions, this duration was measured from the moment the robot displayed the game board and cued the participant to start playing, until the moment the participant fully disengaged from the robot. Additionally, we measured the Number of Game Rounds played with the robots. For a round to be valid, the participant was expected to play at least one move on the empty board.

As interaction evaluation metrics, the Godspeed questionnaire [3], a composite Trust scale [43], the NASA Task Load Index (NASA-TLX) [20], and a 10-item survey assessing attitudes towards the robot similar to [30]. This survey measured satisfaction, liking, intention to continue working with the robot, naturalness and ease of interaction, trust, knowledgeability, relationship with the robot, annoyance, and persistence.

6.2 Study Procedure

We recruited participants from a social media platform internal to our institution. The participants were required to be at least 18 years old and proficient in spoken and written English. The study was approved by our institution's IRB, and participants were compensated for their time. Each participant was randomly assigned to one of the two treatment order conditions. Experiment sessions took approximately 60 min and were video- and audio-recorded.

Once participants arrived at the laboratory, they were briefly introduced to the study, consented, and asked to complete a demographics survey. Later, they were led to the experiment room with two robots and two chairs, and introduced to the robots–named "Salt" and "Pepper." The participants were explained that even though the robots "may look very similar," they were "quite different in their behavior." They were then asked to "play a couple of games with Salt/Pepper" and to come out once they are done playing. If the participant asked further clarification about how long they should play for, the experimenter explained that it is up to them and that they can play "3, 5, 10 games" and "however many" they want. Once the participant left the robot room following their interaction with the first robot, they completed a questionnaire to rate their interaction. They were then led back into the robot room to interact with the second robot following identical instructions as the first trial, completed the interaction rating questionnaire a second time, interviewed, and debriefed.

7 Results

We recruited 31 participants for the study, with complete data collected for 21 (10 male, 11 female, aged 20–40, $M = 26.6, SD = 5.2$). 7 participants had no prior experience with any kind of robot, 7 participants used commercial robots, and 7 participants have interacted with a social robot before.

7.1 Quantitative Results

We used paired samples t-test to compare the Total Game Duration of *Control* and *Re-engagement* trials. The analysis indicated a significant difference in favor of the *Re-engagement* robot ($t(20) = 2.623, p = .016$). Mean Total Game Duration was 568.9 s ($SD = 452.3$) in *Re-engagement* and 364.9 s ($SD = 198.4$) in *Control*. Participants played an average of 10.8 game rounds ($SD = 8.6$) with the *Re-engagement* robot and 8.4 rounds ($SD = 4.5$) with the *Control* robot. This difference was not statistically significant.

Re-engagement robot was rated significantly higher in Animacy scale compared to *Control* robot ($t(20) = 2.513, p = .021$). There were no other significant effects in composite robot perception scales. We used Wilcoxon signed rank test to analyze single-item robot attitude scales and individual dimensions in the NASA-TLX. The analysis revealed significant differences indicating the *Re-engagement* robot was perceived more knowledgeable ($Z = -2.247, p = .025$), the interaction with it was more natural ($Z = -2.429, p = .015$), and participants felt closer to it ($Z = -2.113, p = .035$). There was a trending increase in participants' desire to continue work with the robot in favor of the *Re-engagement* robot ($Z = -1.726, p = .084$). There was a trending increase in the perceived task load for the *Re-engagement* robot in the NASA-TLX dimensions of mental load ($Z = -1.651, p = .099$) and physical load ($Z = -1.792, p = .073$), indicating this robot was mentally and physically more demanding to work with.

We analyzed effects of the treatment order on primary outcomes using Mann-Whitney U test for main effects and using analysis of covariance for interaction effects, and did not find any significant effects.

7.2 Qualitative Results

Interview transcripts totaled 28,635 words, which were analyzed for common themes using inductive analysis. Note that "Pepper" was the name given to the *Re-engagement* robot.

Participants clearly had different experiences with the two robots, some ascribing this to the robots' personalities: "*The task is the same, but it felt they have very different personalities and it felt like a complete different experience with Pepper.*" [P210].

Regarding the *Re-engagement* robot, many participants commented that they found it to be more engaging than the Control robot: "*Pepper was more intelligent and engaging.*" [P110], "*...it felt more human because it was making me feel more engaged.*" [P115], "*Pepper was more helpful in keeping me in the game... I remember when I was walking away to the door, Pepper said, Hey, let's wait. We can play more.*" [P214]. Several participants welcomed the digression that the *Re-engagement* robot provided from the boring task: "*I was getting a little bored of the tic-tac toe, so I was like, let's hear another story.*" [P209]. On the other hand, some participants did comment that the *Re-engagement* robot distracted them in a way that negatively impacted task performance: "*I think it was actually a little bit...distracting. I was interested in the conversation going on more than the game itself rather than just focus on the game.*" [P106], "*With Pepper I was distracted and I kept forgetting that I need to play the game.*" [P214].

Several participants felt that the *Re-engagement* robot established a relationship with them, and that led the interaction to feeling more like working with a friend. "*...there was also that extra dimension on top of it, which even myself trying to do tic-tac-toe and talk at the same time was nice that it was almost, it felt a lot more natural slash organic because that's traditionally how I would interact with a friend.*" [P106], "*...it feels good that it feels more human. It feels like you are having a friend, it's not just a robot.*" [P214], "*What I liked the most was that there was kind of different things that it would talk about. It was friendly.* " [P209].

Several participants liked the ability of the *Re-engagement* robot to interleave conversation and gameplay: "*with Pepper, she was so intelligent and knowledgeable and we were just chatting about a lot of things, being movies, being Kawasaki, robots or stuff like that. ... it was really responsive and also paid attention to the game at the same time.*" [P208], "*So we would be playing a tic-tac-toe game and we would also be talking about something at the same time, which I thought was very impressive.*" [P110], "*The game is kind of just like an activity [rather] than the main sole functionality and focus.*" [P107].

Several participants indicated they felt that working with the *Re-engagement* robot was more fun: "*It was just having a fun conversation while playing a game because essentially that's what it's supposed to do if it's two teammates playing against each other.*" [P208], "*It was more enjoyable with Pepper because it spoke more things other than just the game.*" [P104].

Attitudes towards the Control robot were very mixed. Participants liked that is was very predictable, simple, and efficient: " *I like it's very easy to use. Everything was straightforward*" [P214], "*I liked the fact that salt ...felt more direct, more task oriented.*" [P106], "*I mean, if your goal is to play games, then definitely this approach is more efficient.*" [P203]. This led to comments that this robot was more reliable ("*salt is more reliable I think, because it's more consistent in the behavior.*" [P113]), and trustworthy ("*It's predictable, so it's easier to kind of trust.*" [P113]). However, this also led to comments that this robot was more like a computer ("*salt was more like machine, so it felt more like I'm interacting with a computer*" [P115]), and their conception of a "robot" ("*salt was just kind of blank. More robot.*" [P209]), and that the interaction was more repetitive ("*salt's responses were limited, so it was kind of repetitive*" [P104]), and less fun ("*it wasn't as fun.*") [P108]. For some, this led to lower task engagement: "*my least favorite thing... was just the repetitiveness I got kind of confused and also tired of playing the game*" [P110].

Some participants ascribed emotions to the robots, or talked about their own emotional reactions to them: "*I get more kind of emotion from pepper compared to salt*" [P113], "*[salt] asks, do you want to play another round? Yes, no, but it seems like it doesn't care, so I should not care either.* " [P210]. One participant felt that the *Re-engagement* robot made them feel guilty when they tried to stop gameplay: "*One thing though, and I think this kind of supports the idea that it's more alive, that when I said I don't want to play another round and I said bye and it wants to play more, it wants to keep going. So if I felt bad about it, I could have just probably sat down and played few more rounds. But overall it feels very different. It feels like you don't want to leave, you don't want to stop playing.*" [P210].

In sum, the majority of participants who expressed a clear preference between the robots preferred the *Re-engagement* robot, felt that it was more engaging and fun than the Control robot, and that it did a better job of keeping them on task. Several participants also felt that they had established a relationship with the *Re-engagement* robot, that working with it was more like working with a friend, and some even felt guilty when they tried to disengage.

8 Discussion

We found that participants stayed on task for significantly longer with the *Re-engagement* robot compared to the *Control* robot, scored the *Re-engagement* robot significantly higher on measures of knowledge-ability and naturalness, and felt their relationship with the *Re-engagement* robot was significantly closer. In post-experiment interviews, participants expressed a preference for the *Re-engagement* robot, and felt it was more engaging and fun, even though many thought the Control robot was more straightforward, efficient, and reliable. Participants felt that if their primary goal was to complete as many games as possible, the Control robot would be better, but the *Re-engagement* robot was more like working with a friend.

We did not find that participants played more games with the *Re-engagement* robot. This was due, in part, to the distraction provided by the Social chat, and the fact that several participants actually played other games with the *Re-engagement* robot, including association and guessing games, through Social dialogue.

8.1 Limitations and Future Work

There are several limitations of our comparative evaluation study, beyond lack of generalizability from the small convenience sample of mostly young, well-educated adults we recruited. We used a very simple game as a task, and our findings may not generalize to other more complex tasks. We also do not know how well our robot would function in the face of real-world distractions such as social media, notifications, and asynchronous communications. Our results from a single brief interaction and may not reflect user behavior in longitudinal use.

There are many important and exciting future directions of work for our approach to designing a re-engagement robot. There is significant work to be done on the proper interleaving of Social talk and Task work, especially if the goal is to keep workers engaged over long periods of time. Improvements to sensors, and especially speech recognition, are needed to make interactions more seamless and natural. Finally, more persuasive techniques could be integrated into the interaction to maintain user engagement, especially over repeated interactions.

9 Conclusion

We presented a robot design that maintains engagement with users in the performance of a collaborative task using persuasion principles. Key contributions include the use of an LLM for generating re-engagement actions, including social dialogue, the detailed description of an implementation, and results from a comparative evaluation study. In today's "attention economy", people need more help then ever staying focused [15]. Social robots, supported by the language generation and context retention capabilities of modern LLMs, may provide a solution that is more engaging, fun, and friendly than more Draconian interventions such as removal of smartphones or workplace monitoring. Our work provides an initial exploration of this space, with promising preliminary results.

References

1. Aldebaran: pepper-the iconic humanoid robot with unique interaction capabilities for hospitality (2025). https://aldebaran.com/en/pepper/
2. Axelsson, M., Churamani, N., Caldir, A., Gunes, H.: Participant perceptions of a robotic coach conducting positive psychology exercises: a systematic analysis. arXiv preprint arXiv:2209.03827 (2022)
3. Bartneck, C., Kulić, D., Croft, E., Zoghbi, S.: Measurement instruments for the anthropomorphism, animacy, likeability, perceived intelligence, and perceived safety of robots. Int. J. Soc. Robot. (2008)
4. Ben-Youssef, A., Clavel, C., Essid, S., Bilac, M., Chamoux, M., Lim, A.: Ue-hri: a new dataset for the study of user engagement in spontaneous human-robot interactions. In: Proceedings of the 19th ACM International Conference on Multimodal Interaction, pp. 464–472 (2017)
5. Bohus, D., Horvitz, E.: Learning to predict engagement with a spoken dialog system in open-world settings. In: Proceedings of the SIGDIAL 2009 Conference, pp. 244–252 (2009)
6. Breazeal, C.: Designing Sociable Robots. MIT Press (2004)
7. Brown, L., Kerwin, R., Howard, A.M.: Applying behavioral strategies for student engagement using a robotic educational agent. In: 2013 IEEE International Conference on Systems, Man, and Cybernetics, pp. 4360–4365. IEEE (2013)
8. Cacioppo, J.T., Petty, R.E.: The Elaboration Likelihood Model of Persuasion. ACR North American Advances (1984)
9. Cao, H.L., et al.: "hmm, did you hear what i just said?": development of a re-engagement system for socially interactive robots. Robotics **8**(4), 95 (2019)
10. Chen, K., Lou, V.W.Q., Tan, K.C.K., Wai, M.V., Chan, L.I.: Effects of a humanoid companion robot on dementia symptoms and caregiver distress for residents in long-term care. J. Am. Med. Directors Assoc. **21**(11), 1724–1728 (2020)
11. Chidambaram, V., Chiang, Y.H., Mutlu, B.: Designing persuasive robots: how robots might persuade people using vocal and nonverbal cues. In: Proceedings of the seventh annual ACM/IEEE international conference on Human-Robot Interaction, HRI 2012, pp. 293–300. ACM, New York, NY, USA (2012). https://doi.org/10.1145/2157689.2157798
12. Cialdini, R.B., Cialdini, R.B.: Influence: The Psychology of Persuasion, vol. 55. Collins New York (2007)

13. Corrigan, L.J., Basedow, C., Küster, D., Kappas, A., Peters, C., Castellano, G.: Perception matters! engagement in task orientated social robotics. In: 24th IEEE International Symposium on Robot and Human Interactive Communication (Roman), pp. 375–380. IEEE (2015)
14. Costa, A., Heras, S., Palanca, J., Jordán, J., Novais, P., Julián, V.: Argumentation schemes for events suggestion in an e-health platform. In: de Vries, P.W., Oinas-Kukkonen, H., Siemons, L., Beerlage-de Jong, N., van Gemert-Pijnen, L. (eds.) Persuasive Technology: Development and Implementation of Personalized Technologies to Change Attitudes and Behaviors, pp. 17–30. LNCS, Springer, Cham (2017). https://doi.org/10.1007/978-3-319-55134-0_2
15. Davenport, T.H., Beck, J.C.: The attention economy. Ubiquity **2001**, 1–es (2001)
16. Fogg, B.J.: A behavior model for persuasive design. In: Proceedings of the 4th International Conference on Persuasive Technology, pp. 1–7 (2009)
17. Ghazali, A.S., Ham, J., Barakova, E.I., Markopoulos, P.: Effects of robot facial characteristics and gender in persuasive human-robot interaction. Front. Robot. AI **5**, 73 (2018). https://doi.org/10.3389/frobt.2018.00073
18. Ham, J., Midden, C.J.H.: A persuasive robot to stimulate energy conservation: the influence of positive and negative social feedback and task similarity on energy-consumption behavior. Int. J. Soc. Robot. **6**(2), 163–171 (2014). https://doi.org/10.1007/s12369-013-0205-z
19. Ham, J., Cuijpers, R.H., Cabibihan, J.J.: Combining robotic persuasive strategies: the persuasive power of a storytelling robot that uses gazing and gestures. Int. J. Soc. Robot. **7**(4), 479–487 (2015). https://doi.org/10.1007/s12369-015-0280-4
20. Hart, S.G., Staveland, L.E.: Development of nasa-tlx (task load index): results of empirical and theoretical research. In: Advances in Psychology, vol. 52, pp. 139–183. Elsevier (1988)
21. Hashemian, M., Couto, M., Mascarenhas, S., Paiva, A., Santos, P.A., Prada, R.: Persuasive social robot using reward power over repeated instances of persuasion. In: Ali, R., Lugrin, B., Charles, F. (eds.) Persuasive Technology. pp. 63–70. Lecture Notes in Computer Science,, Cham (2021). https://doi.org/10.1007/978-3-030-79460-6_6
22. Hashemian, M., Paiva, A., Mascarenhas, S., Santos, P.A., Prada, R.: Social power in human-robot interaction: towards more persuasive robots. In: AAMAS (2019)
23. Herse, S., et al.: Bon Appetit! Robot persuasion for food recommendation. In: Companion of the 2018 ACM/IEEE International Conference on Human-Robot Interaction, pp. 125–126. ACM, Chicago IL USA (2018). https://doi.org/10.1145/3173386.3177028
24. Jeong, S.H., Hwang, Y.: Media multitasking effects on cognitive vs. attitudinal outcomes: a meta-analysis. Hum. Commun. Res. **42**(4), 599–618 (2016)
25. Ju, W., Sirkin, D.: Animate objects: how physical motion encourages public interaction. In: Ploug, T., Hasle, P., Oinas-Kukkonen, H. (eds.) PERSUASIVE 2010. LNCS, vol. 6137, pp. 40–51. Springer, Heidelberg (2010). https://doi.org/10.1007/978-3-642-13226-1_6
26. Koessmeier, C., Büttner, O.B.: Why are we distracted by social media? distraction situations and strategies, reasons for distraction, and individual differences. Front Psychol. **12**, 711416 (2021). https://doi.org/10.3389/fpsyg.2021.711416
27. Langedijk, R.M., Fischer, K.: Persuasive robots in the field. In: International Conference on Persuasive Technology, pp. 251–264. Springer (2023)
28. Neubauer, N.A., Azad-Khaneghah, P., Miguel-Cruz, A., Liu, L.: What do we know about strategies to manage dementia-related wandering? a scoping review.

Alzheimers Dement (Amst) **10**, 615–628 (2018). https://doi.org/10.1016/j.dadm.2018.08.001
29. Oertel, C., Castellano, G., Chetouani, M., Nasir, J., Obaid, M., Pelachaud, C., Peters, C.: Engagement in human-agent interaction: an overview. Front. Robot. AI **7**, 92 (2020)
30. Olafsson, S., O'Leary, T.K., Bickmore, T.W.: Motivating health behavior change with humorous virtual agents. In: Proceedings of the 20th ACM International Conference on Intelligent Virtual Agents, pp. 1–8 (2020)
31. OpenAI: Whisper (2022). https://github.com/openai/whisper?tab=readme-ov-file. Accessed 13 Nov 2025
32. O'Keefe, D.J.: The elaboration likelihood model. The SAGE Handbook of Persuasion: Developments in Theory and Practice, pp. 137–149 (2013)
33. Radford, A., Kim, J.W., Xu, T., Brockman, G., McLeavey, C., Sutskever, I.: Robust speech recognition via large-scale weak supervision. In: International Conference on Machine Learning, pp. 28492–28518. PMLR (2023)
34. Rincon, J.A., Costa, A., Novais, P., Julian, V., Carrascosa, C.: A new emotional robot assistant that facilitates human interaction and persuasion. Knowl. Inf. Syst. **60**(1), 363–383 (2019). https://doi.org/10.1007/s10115-018-1231-9, http://link.springer.com/10.1007/s10115-018-1231-9
35. Rollet, N., Clavel, C.: "talk to you later" doing social robotics with conversation analysis. towards the development of an automatic system for the prediction of disengagement. Interact. Stud. **21**(2), 268–292 (2020)
36. Rouaix, N., Retru-Chavastel, L., Rigaud, A.S., Monnet, C., Lenoir, H., Pino, M.: Affective and engagement issues in the conception and assessment of a robot-assisted psychomotor therapy for persons with dementia. Front. Psychol. **8**, 950 (2017)
37. Roubroeks, M., Midden, C., Ham, J.: Does it make a difference who tells you what to do? exploring the effect of social agency on psychological reactance. In: Proceedings of the 4th International Conference on Persuasive Technology, pp. 1–6 (2009)
38. Sather, R., Soufineyestani, M., Khan, A., Imtiaz, N.: Use of humanoid robot in dementia care: a literature review. J Aging Sci. **9**, 249 (2021)
39. Sidner, C.L., Lee, C.: Engagement rules for human-robot collaborative interactions. In: SMC'03 Conference Proceedings. 2003 IEEE International Conference on Systems, Man and Cybernetics. Conference Theme-System Security and Assurance (Cat. No. 03CH37483), vol. 4, pp. 3957–3962. IEEE (2003)
40. Siegel, M., Breazeal, C., Norton, M.I.: Persuasive robotics: the influence of robot gender on human behavior. In: IEEE/RSJ International Conference on Intelligent Robots and Systems, pp. 2563–2568. IEEE, St. Louis, MO, USA (2009). https://doi.org/10.1109/IROS.2009.5354116
41. Szafir, D., Mutlu, B.: Pay attention! designing adaptive agents that monitor and improve user engagement. In: Proceedings of the SIGCHI Conference on Human Factors in Computing Systems, pp. 11–20 (2012)
42. Tulsulkar, G., Mishra, N., Thalmann, N.M., Lim, H.E., Lee, M.P., Cheng, S.K.: Can a humanoid social robot stimulate the interactivity of cognitively impaired elderly? a thorough study based on computer vision methods. Vis. Comput. **37**(12), 3019–3038 (2021)
43. Wheeless, L.R., Grotz, J.: The measurement of trust and its relationship to self-disclosure. Hum. Commun. Res. **3**(3), 250–257 (1977)

44. Winkle, K., Caleb-Solly, P., Turton, A., Bremner, P.: Social robots for engagement in rehabilitative therapies: design implications from a study with therapists. In: Proceedings of the 2018 ACM/IEEE International Conference on Human-Robot Interaction, pp. 289–297 (2018)
45. Winkle, K., Lemaignan, S., Caleb-Solly, P., Leonards, U., Turton, A., Bremner, P.: effective persuasion strategies for socially assistive robots. In: 2019 14th ACM/IEEE International Conference on Human-Robot Interaction (HRI), pp. 277–285. IEEE, Daegu, Korea (South) (2019). https://doi.org/10.1109/HRI.2019.8673313

Estimating the Sense of Agency from EEG Data and Personal Characteristics Towards Just-in-Time System Interventions

Ryunosuke Togawa[1(✉)], Roberto Legaspi[1], Eriko Sugisaki[1], Akihiro Miyamoto[2], Kae Nakajima[2], Motoyuki Sanada[2], Kazushi Ikeda[1], Nao Kobayashi[1], and Yasushi Naruse[2]

[1] KDDI Research, Inc., 2-1-15 Ohara, Fujimino-shi, Saitama 356-8502, Japan
ry-togawa@kddi.com, ro-legaspi@kddi-research.jp

[2] Center for Information and Neural Networks (CiNet), Advanced ICT Research Institute, National Institute of Information and Communications Technology, 558-2 Iwaokacho Iwaoka Nishi-ku, Kobe-shi, Hyogo-ken 651-2401, Japan

Abstract. The *sense of agency* (SoA) is the experience of being in control of one's own actions and their consequences. It has been widely reported that SoA plays a significant role in shaping and moderating human cognition, emotion, and behavior. While studies have been conducted to estimate SoA from EEG signals, they typically focused on neural features alone and did not aim to integrate individual characteristics that are likely correlated with SoA in the estimation process. In this study, we developed an experimental system where participants, wearing an EEG headset, perceived video clips and music pieces while their SoA was measured before and after viewing. Using the recorded EEG data alongside individual characteristics, we trained machine learning models to estimate the SoA. Our findings suggest that personal characteristics play an important role in improving estimation accuracy. Furthermore, it is notable that our model maintains good accuracy even with a short time window for estimation. This suggests its potential for enabling feasibility-level low-latency SoA estimations under practical latency constraints as a technical prerequisite, which is fundamental in developing our envisioned conceptual SoA-aware just-in-time adaptive intervention system.

Keywords: Sense of agency · Just-in-time adaptive intervention · Electroencephalography · Big Five personality traits · Machine leaning

1 Introduction

Sense of agency (SoA) is the subjective experience of control over oneâĂŹs own actions that cause changes in the world [1,2]. SoA is a concept that has been widely studied in the neuro, cognitive and behavioral sciences [2–5]. The elucidation of its nature and its underlying mechanisms has compelling implications for understanding how individuals experience control over their actions

E. Vlahu-Gjorgievska et al. (Eds.): PERSUASIVE 2026, CCIS 2896, pp. 207–221, 2027.
https://doi.org/10.1007/978-3-032-27235-5_15

and interpret their effects. Insights from the life sciences on the nature of SoA have inspired both theoretical studies of intelligent system behavior and applied research in fields such as automated vehicles, human-computer interfaces, developmental robotics, and human-AI interactions, all of which have incorporated the SoA construct and its foundational principles primarily as a conceptual and experiential framework (refer to Legaspi et al.'s work [6] for in-depth review and analyses).

Traditional methods in psychological experiments assess SoA either directly or indirectly, corresponding to explicit and implicit measures, respectively [7–9]. Direct methods rely on self-reports, typically rating scales where participants indicate their agreement with statements like "Did your action A cause event E to happen?" Indirect methods, by contrast, do not ask participants to evaluate their own experience; instead, they infer the sense of control by examining behavioral or perceptual differences between self-generated and externally produced events, e.g., shifts in the perceived timing between an action and its outcome [10].

Although SoA is a psychological state that changes dynamically in response to stimuli and actions, traditional assessment methods rely on reports collected after the entire stimulus is presented or on responses aggregated in blocks. As a result, these methods make it difficult to capture transient fluctuations in SoA during trials. This leads to a failure to capture how SoA manifests itself in real-world decision-making situations that would require behavioural modification, thereby also limiting its applicability in intervention and support technologies. Consequently, as user applications increasingly demand dynamic assessments, the need for low-latency measurement of SoA has become more pressing [5].

In this paper, we focus on the relationship between SoA and brain activity to realize low-latency, short-window-based SoA estimation. Several studies have shown that changes in SoA are reflected in EEG activity (e.g., [11,12]), providing a basis for exploring the feasibility of low-latency estimation and motivating our focus on EEG-based approaches. However, previous EEG-based SoA estimation studies have faced limitations. For example, Legaspi et al. [6] used over 1500-dim EEG features and achieved reasonable accuracy, but their approach involved high computational cost. These aspects make such methods less suitable for low-latency or resource-constrained applications. We employ EEG also because of its excellent temporal resolution and its practicality for repeated or real-time use, making it well suited for integration into systems that require timely SoA estimation under practical constraints. Furthermore, for latency-sensitive applications, EEG headsets with fewer electrodes are often used because they enable faster and more practical setup. Accordingly, our study employed a low-channel configuration to balance ease of use with the capacity to capture SoA-relevant neural information.

It is also the case that SoA is known to correlate with personal characteristics such as age and the Big Five personality traits [13,14]. Building on prior studies that have reported such correlations, we propose incorporating this information into the analysis model as a novel approach for SoA estimation under practical and latency-sensitive constraints. In addition, we explore the feasibility of short-window, low-latency SoA estimation, aiming to evaluate how EEG signals in limited time windows can be utilized as a technical component for future intervention-oriented systems. We hypothesize that combining EEG data with individual characteristics such as personality traits, age, and gender will improve estimation robustness, compared to using EEG data alone.

In light of the above, we present in this paper a method for estimating the SoA with an emphasis on feasibility under low-latency and practical constraints, while also maintaining an accuracy level that can support practical applications. Our main objective is to demonstrate the feasibility of low-latency SoA estimation, with accuracy treated as a supporting factor rather than the sole goal. To test our hypothesis, we developed two types of SoA estimation models: one using EEG data combined with individual characteristics, and another using EEG data alone. During the experiments, participants viewed videos and listened to music while their EEG data were recorded and their SoA measured both before and after each stimulus. The SoA estimation accuracies of the two models were compared to evaluate the effect of including individual characteristics as features in the model. We also investigated the impact of varying EEG window sizes on SoA estimation performance, in order to identify suitable temporal resolutions compatible with latency-sensitive estimation. Our results show that incorporating the personal characteristics helped maintain estimation accuracy under short-window constraints, and that our model achieved its best performance with the last 3-s window, highlighting the feasibility of prompt estimation without implying validated intervention readiness at this stage of the research.

2 Methods

2.1 Stimulating the Sense of Agency

We used in our study two kinds of stimuli, namely, music and video. Prior studies indicate that music is a suitable stimulus for examining variations in SoA, as it predominantly supports agency over internal experience rather than over externally directed action. By enabling autonomous listening, music facilitates emotional regulation and subjective sense of control, and also provides a medium for self-expression and agency, particularly in situations where direct action is constrained. As detailed in [15], these characteristics make music an ecologically valid stimulus for investigating context-dependent fluctuations in explicit SoA. In contrast, videos enable controlled exploration of contextual influences on SoA through visual realism and situational perception [2,3]. By shaping situational appraisal, perceived control, and expectations about environmental predictability, visual scenes offer an ecologically valid means of probing context-dependent variations in explicit SoA even in the absence of task-based action [2,16,17].

To create the set of stimuli, we gathered six music pieces (M1 to M6) and six muted-video clips (V1 to V6), details of which are shown in Table 1. We then created combinations of both types of stimuli (M1-V1, M1-V2, ..., M1-V6, M2-V1, M2-V2, and so on), resulting in 36 unique pairings. We also included M1 to M6 and V1 to V6. Altogether, a set of 48 (36+6+6) stimuli was created. Each stimulus lasted for 60 s. While the stimuli themselves were not pre-validated

Table 1. Details of each music piece and muted-video clip

Music Pieces		Video Clips	
M1	High tempo rock music	V1	Dog and cat relaxing on sofa
M2	Rhythmic electric music	V2	Firework in seaside
M3	Slow tempo piano music	V3	Man and son walking in sunset
M4	Nostalgic acoustic sound	V4	Ducks walk on a natural trail
M5	Lively music with whistling	V5	Family in the living room
M6	Relaxing piano sound	V6	Family walking under blue sky

by other research, to our knowledge, we are the first to test the use of audio and visual stimuli in the context of measuring a global SoA. We explain this dimension of the SoA construct in the following section.

2.2 Measuring the Sense of Agency

In our experiments, we collected ground truths of the participantsâĂŹ SoA using the Sense of Agency Scale (SoAS) [9]. The SoAS measures a *general*, *cross-situational* experience of agency rather than agency tied to a specific task, stimulus, or action-outcome contingency. Consequently, the SoAS does not presuppose a particular target of agency, but captures individualsâĂŹ SoA at a *global* level. This makes it well suited to our study where SoA is monitored in everyday contexts rather than in tightly controlled, task-based laboratory settings.

Because the participants were Japanese, we presented to them the Japanese version of the SoAS items that were validated and used in [5,6]. We needed to limit the number of items to avoid overwhelming or frustrating the participants, as they would be prompted with these items multiple times throughout the experiment. We used only three items that were sufficient to capture the explicit SoA in the course of our investigations, specifically, (1) "*I am in full control of what I do.*" (2) "*I am completely responsible for everything that results from my actions.*" and (3) "*My behavior is planned by me from the very beginning to the very end.*" Legaspi et al. [5] used these same items since they had the highest loading factors to capture the sense of full control of action and planning, as well as responsibility. Their reliability analysis for these three items showed internal consistency (Cronbach $\alpha = 0.76$), thereby demonstrating sufficient validity to measure the same SoA despite having only three items.

2.3 EEG Recording and Feature Extraction

EEG data were recorded using the headset shown in Fig. 1 . Electrodes were located at Fpz, C3, Cz, C4, and Oz. Additionally, electrodes placed next to the left eye and above the left eyebrow allowed simultaneous measurement of horizontal and vertical EOG signals. The sampling rate for the EEG measurements was 500 Hz. The measured data were amplified and then stored via a bluetooth to a smartphone dedicated for data collection. We denoised using a band-pass

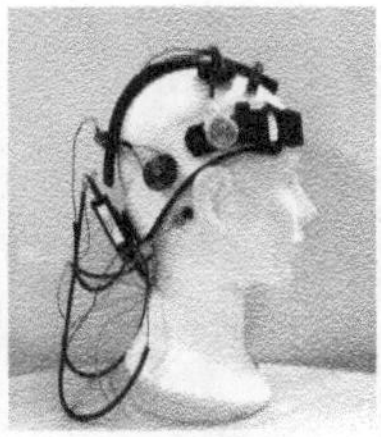

Fig. 1. The EEG device (see [18]) employed in our experiments.

Table 2. Extracted EEG Features

EEG Features	Dimensions
Frequency α band (8–12 Hz) power	4
Frequency β band (12–30 Hz) power	4
Frequency θ band (4–7 Hz) power	4
Frequency δ band (1–4 Hz) power	4
Frequency α band (8–12 Hz) correlation	6
Frequency β band (12–30 Hz) correlation	6
Frequency θ band (4–7 Hz) correlation	6
Frequency δ band (1–4 Hz) correlation	6
All range correlation	6

filter (filter dim = 5000, bandpass Low = 1 Hz, bandpass high = 40 Hz). In our EEG preprocessing pipeline, we used Artifact Subspace Reconstruction (ASR) to remove transient and large-amplitude noise caused by movement, muscle activity, blinks, and electrode shifts. After which, we used Independent Component Analysis (ICA), to decompose the data into independent sources, enabling the identification and removal of residual stereotyped artifacts like eye-related components. Horizontal and vertical EOG signals, measured via electrodes near the eyes, were combined with ICA to improve ocular artifact removal, helping to more accurately distinguish and separate eye-related signals from brain activity.

To extract the EEG features, we calculated the power spectrum, which is widely used to identify neural oscillatory activity, i.e., quantify power changes in canonical frequency bands such as theta and alpha and examine frequency-specific signal characteristics. We also compute the Pearson correlation coefficient between two channels, which provides information on functional connectivity and inter-channel relationships. Both power spectrum and Pearson correlation have been used to estimate internal state (e.g., see [19–21]). Table 2 shows the features we extracted, as well as the number of attributes per feature.

2.4 Assessment of the Big Five Personality Traits

The Big Five personality model [22,23], also known as OCEAN (short for Openness, Conscientiousness, Extraversion, Agreeableness, and Neuroticism), is

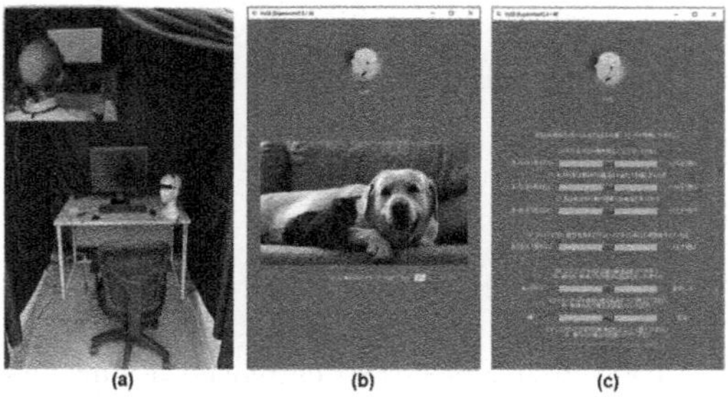

Fig. 2. Data collection set-up. While performing the experiment, **(a)** the participant is seated in an enclosed cubicle, wore an EEG headset and used the data collection app. **(b)** The stimulus was presented after the participant pressed the play button, and **(c)** reported the SoA using a visual analog scale before and after the stimulus presentation.

widely regarded as the most robust taxonomy in behavioral science [23], and the most commonly used classification system [24] for personality traits [25]. Its validity has been demonstrated across diverse demographic contexts. Differences in these broad dispositional traits associated with social life often predict notable variations in behavior, particularly when examined across various contexts [26].

We assess these five personality dimensions to foster a more accurate estimation of the userâĂŹs SoA. The NEO Five-Factor Inventory (NEO-FFI) [27] has been used to assess the Big Five. This inventory has been standardized across a diverse range of age groups, from adolescents to older adults, and is applicable to various fields, including developmental and geriatric research. While the original NEO-FFI has 60 questions, what we used is the shorter version in Japanese that has 29 questions [28]. The proponents of this Japanese instrument determined the correlations with the original NEO-FFI and tested the concurrent validity of the short form. Their results indicated that the short form demonstrates sufficient reliability and validity despite the reduced items.

2.5 Data Collection

We conducted data collection from Dec. 16, 2022 to Feb. 1, 2023. To protect the participants' identities, all collected data were hashed, making identification impossible while still enabling thorough analysis. Participants took part voluntarily, and all personally identifiable information was removed prior to data collection. A total of 52 individuals participated in our experiments (M: 34 and F: 18; Age: min=29, max=49, average = 41.0, std = 5.2; with normal hearing and vision). All participants were thoroughly informed in advance about the methods and contents of the experiments, and they provided their consent prior to participation. In addition, participants completed the online Big Five questionnaire in advance of the onsite experiments.

During the experiments, the participants were seated individually in enclosed cubicles, as shown in Fig. 2 a, to minimize exogenous distractions and ensure full focus on the experiment. Moreover, while listening to music, participants

Table 3. Estimation Models with the corresponding feature sets

Model	Features	Statistics
$M_{\mathcal{A}}^{E}$	EEG features only	Mean of features across all windows
$M_{\mathcal{A}}^{P}$	EEG features plus values of the Big Five, age, and gender	Mean of features across all windows
$M_{\mathcal{L}}^{E}$	EEG features only	Feature values in the last window only
$M_{\mathcal{L}}^{P}$	EEG features plus values of the Big Five, age, and gender	Feature values in the last window only

fixated on a central cross to reduce eye-movement-related EEG artifacts and maintain consistent attention. This fixation neither constrained nor defined the subjective experience of agency being assessed. The participants self-reported their SoA before and after a stimulus (e.g., the video in Fig. 2 b) was presented. The stimulus starts after the participant pressed the play button. In reporting the SoA, the participant moved the slider of a visual analog scale (15 discrete levels, e.g., in Fig. 2 c) between "Strongly Disagree" (= 1) and "Strongly Agree"(= 15). Data were collected in real-time while the participants also wore an EEG headset, with the EEG signals being recorded using a smartphone app.

2.6 Models for Estimating the Sense of Agency

We prepared four regression models, each using different feature sets as listed in Table 3. In all models, the dependent variable was the SoA score. First, we created a baseline model ($M_{\mathcal{A}}^{E}$) using only EEG features. Next, we developed a personality-based model ($M_{\mathcal{A}}^{P}$) that used the participantsâĂŹ Big Five scores, along with their age and gender. Both of these models used EEG features averaged across all time windows. Furthermore, to explore the possibility of low-latency SoA estimation, we created two additional models in which the EEG features were taken only from the final window (the "last-shot" window). One model ($M_{\mathcal{L}}^{E}$) used only EEG features, while the other ($M_{\mathcal{L}}^{P}$) used both EEG and personality-related features. We used the Light Gradient Boosting Machine (LightGBM) [29] to train each regression model. The main advantage of using LightGBM is its short training time and higher accuracy than most boosting methods such as the eXtreme Gradient Boosting (XGBoost).

To investigate the effect of window size on the performance of the model, we tested with varying window sizes. The initial size was set to 1500 samples, which is equivalent to three seconds of data at 500 Hz sampling rate. This window was slid across the entire stimulus interval with a 500-sample increment, hence a 1000-sample window overlap, at each step to compute the EEG features. For subsequent tests, the window size was increased in increments of 500 samples until a maximum of 9500 samples (19 s of data) is reached.

We also implemented an adaptation approach to improve the modelâĂŹs prediction accuracy by fine-tuning the pre-trained LightGBM model on a small

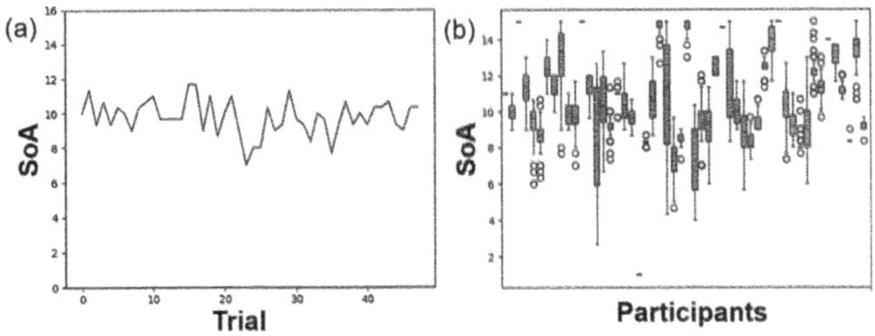

Fig. 3. Observations of SoA behavior in the data. **(a)** Changes in SoA for a certain participant. **(b)** Distribution of SoA across 52 participants.

amount of new user data. Concretely, the model was updated using few trials from each new user. While this is not strictly few-shot learning, this incremental training enabled the model to quickly adapt by personalizing to new users, allowing the model to reach satisfactory level of accuracy with only limited additional data.

3 Results

3.1 Observations on SoA Behavior from the Data

Our first observation is that the behavior of SoA was not uniform. For instance, in Fig. 3 a, we can see participant A's SoA fluctuated slightly immediately after the start of the experiment. However, around the time the number of trials has exceeded 20, participant A's SoA decreased sharply. Thereafter, the SoA gradually increased while fluctuation continued. Finally, however, the SoA went back to the same level as that of the start of the experiment. We also observed the distribution of SoA across all participants, shown in Fig. 3 b, which confirms that the distribution of SoA varied among participants. These results indicate that SoA exhibits observable variability over the course of the experiment, foretelling the challenge of inferring agency-related states from short EEG segments.

Although we observed fluctuations in SoA, the stimuli were not selected to elicit a systematic temporal modulation of SoA, such as inducing high or low SoA at specific music or video segments. Accordingly, the observed variations should not be interpreted as evidence of validated within-person temporal dynamics, but rather as variability present under exploratory conditions. While one could demonstrate meaningful stimulus variation through feature embedding and analysis of music/video-specific characteristics, it is beyond the scope of this study. The objective is to show the feasibility of low-latency SoA estimation rather than to analyze which stimulus features and SoA fluctuations co-vary.

In addition, Table 4 shows the amount of change in SoA before and after the stimuli were presented to the participants. We computed the amount of change as mean difference of SoA estimates post- and pre-stimuli presentations. A positive value would therefor indicate an increase in SoA. Furthermore, values with asterisks indicate the positive or negative differences that are significant. The values

Table 4. Amount of change in SoA given the 48 stimuli (M-usic, V-ideo)

–	–	V1	V2	V3	V4	V5	V6
–	–	–0.026	0.007	–0.068	–0.212	–0.035	**–0.519***
M1	–0.064	–0.092	**–0.320***	0.12	–0.147	0.000	0.105
M2	0.046	0.052	0.054	0.05	–0.007	–0.034	0.299
M3	–0.146	0.098	0.013	–0.224	–0.227	–0.183	–0.34
M4	–0.118	0.136	–0.08	**0.347***	–0.059	–0.076	0.231
M5	–0.109	0.118	0.118	0.208	–0.014	–0.041	0.193
M6	–0.092	**0.388***	–0.048	0.088	0.095	0.209	–0.007

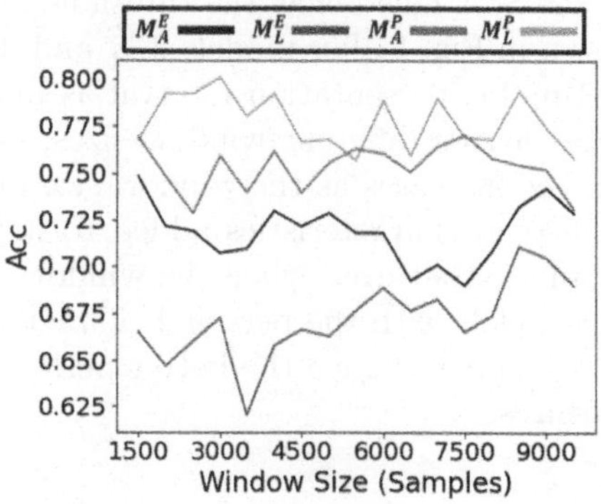

Fig. 4. Accuracy of SoA estimates given different window sizes for the four models.

in Table 4 show that a small number of music-video combinations (e.g., M6-V1) exhibited statistically detectable changes in SoA under the present experimental conditions. This suggests that the limited number of observed effects were not driven by isolated individual cases, although substantial inter-individual variability remains. For the other combinations, it may be that the influence of the stimuli is only consistent for some participants. It can also be that the effect of the various stimuli may differ in one person, e.g., as shown in Fig. 3 a.

3.2 Model Performance Across Varying Window Sizes

To ascertain the effect of window size on the estimation models, we compared the four models' performance using accuracy (Acc) as metric, while varying the window size and using leave-one-subject-out cross-validation, i.e., treating one subject as a new user while considering the others as existing data. We computed Acc as the ratio of the number of correctly estimated SoA instances to the number of SoA instances in the data. It is important to note that we first transformed the continuous SoA values to binary values by using the grand mean across all participants as a threshold. Specifically, values over the mean were labeled as 1, and all other values as 0. This binarization is not meant to

Table 5. Performance evaluation of the different models

Model	RMSE	R^2	Acc	Recall	Precision	ROC-AUC	AIC
$M_{\mathcal{A}}^{E}$	4.173	0.43	0.75	0.73	0.734	0.83	3586.2
$M_{\mathcal{A}}^{P}$	**3.265**	**0.56**	**0.77**	**0.74**	**0.76**	**0.86**	**3385.3**
$M_{\mathcal{L}}^{E}$	5.835	0.21	0.67	0.70	0.63	0.73	4077.4
$M_{\mathcal{L}}^{P}$	**3.080**	**0.58**	**0.77**	**0.80**	**0.73**	**0.86**	**3337.4**

imply pathological or atypical states of SoA, but serves as a pragmatic step to reframe the estimation task in terms of classification. The task is therefore to accurately estimate if the SoA falls below the threshold or not.

The results are shown in Fig. 4 . For models $M_{\mathcal{A}}^{E}$ and $M_{\mathcal{A}}^{P}$ that use the mean EEG signal over the stimulus presentation interval as input features, accuracy remains relatively stable across different window sizes, especially compared to $M_{\mathcal{L}}^{E}$ models. For $M_{\mathcal{L}}^{E}$, Acc increases as the window size increases. On the other hand, $M_{\mathcal{L}}^{P}$ that has personal characteristics added to $M_{\mathcal{L}}^{E}$, has its Acc always larger than $M_{\mathcal{L}}^{E}$. We can see that even when the window size is small, i.e., with only 1500 samples, the models with the personal characteristics incorporated in them, $M_{\mathcal{A}}^{P}$ (red) and $M_{\mathcal{L}}^{P}$ (green), gave the better performance than the model with only the EEG features.

3.3 Model Performance Evaluation

Using now the window size of 1500 samples, we evaluated the performance of the four models. We used again leave-one-subject-out cross-validation, and added more metrics for validating the models on two key perspectives, namely, data fit and prediction accuracy. To measure data fit, we used root mean squared error (RMSE) and the coefficient of determination (R^2). For prediction accuracy, we considered Acc, Recall, Precision, and ROC-AUC. For model evaluation, we considered AIC (Akaike Information Criterion). When computing for RMSE and R^2, we used the actual SoA values in the data as ground truth. For the other metrics, we used the binary equivalents of the SoA values as explained above. The results for each model are shown in Table 5. While our results show that SoA could be reasonably estimated from the EEG signals, the performance of the models improved when personal characteristics were accounted for.

We performed a DeLong p-test [30] between $M_{\mathcal{L}}^{E}$ and $M_{\mathcal{L}}^{P}$ and between $M_{\mathcal{A}}^{E}$ and $M_{\mathcal{A}}^{P}$ to evaluate whether ROC-AUC was predominantly increased by the addition of individual characteristics. There was a significant difference in ROC-AUC between $M_{\mathcal{L}}^{E}$ and $M_{\mathcal{L}}^{P}$ ($p < 0.005$), but not between $M_{\mathcal{A}}^{E}$ and $M_{\mathcal{A}}^{P}$ ($p = 0.052$). Similar results were obtained from the AIC values. This result suggests that the addition of personal characteristics improves estimation robustness, particularly under short-window constraints.

Finally, our partial correlation analyses in Table 6 reveal that in $M_{\mathcal{L}}^{P}$, Extraversion and Agreeableness display higher correlations with SoA than EEG

Table 6. Partial correlations (Par_Cor) with SoA.

Personal	Par_Cor	EEG	Par_Cor	EEG	Par_Cor
Gender	0.03	delta C3	0.05*	alpha C3	0.09***
Age	-0.01	delta Cz	-0.16***	alpha Cz	-0.10***
Big5-O	-0.03	delta C4	0.03	alpha C4	-0.01
Big5-C	-0.06**	delta Oz	0.05*	alpha Oz	-0.13***
Big5-E	0.25***	theta C3	0.00	beta C3	-0.01
Big5-A	-0.36***	theta Cz	0.01	beta Cz	0.01
Big5-N	-0.10***	theta C4	0.00	beta C4	0.00
		theta Oz	0.04*	beta Oz	0.18***

$p < 0.05$ (*), $p < 0.01$ (**), and $p < 0.001$ (***)

features, suggesting that these traits moderate the baseline SoA tendencies. EEG features contribute complementary, time-localized information under short windows, while personality-related features provide stable predictive priors. The use of leave-one-subject-out cross-validation that helped ensure no participantâĂŹs personality profile appeared in both train and test sets, mitigates, but does not fully eliminate, the possibility that the experimental results reflect correlations with stable personal characteristics rather than within-person SoA dynamics.

4 Discussion

To our knowledge, this study is the first attempt to explore the potential of combining EEG data with personal characteristics for estimating SoA, highlighting the feasibility of this approach for practical applications. We demonstrated that by combining EEG data with individual characteristics, it is possible to estimate SoA with a level of accuracy that is sufficient for practical low-latency applications, even from a short window of only 1500 samples (i.e., using three seconds of data). The proposed model, despite its short window ($M^P_{\mathcal{L}}$, three seconds), achieved an accuracy (Acc = 0.75) comparable to that of the baseline model that has longer window ($M^E_{\mathcal{A}}$, 1-min duration).

The performance, while clearly exceeding chance level, underscores the inherent challenge of inferring SoA-related information from EEG signals. It suggests that EEG contains informative patterns under constrained conditions, but achieving stable and validated state-level inference remains difficult. However, our results also suggest that the integration of EEG and personal characteristics is effective for SoA estimation. In particular, as shown in Fig. 4 and Table 5, while EEG-only models (e.g., $M^E_{\mathcal{L}}$) tend to improve in accuracy as the window size increases, models incorporating personal characteristics ($M^P_{\mathcal{L}}$) maintained higher accuracy even with short windows. Furthermore, as shown in Table 6, the reason for the model's better estimation accuracy is that there are personal characteristics that show a higher correlation with SoA than the EEG features.

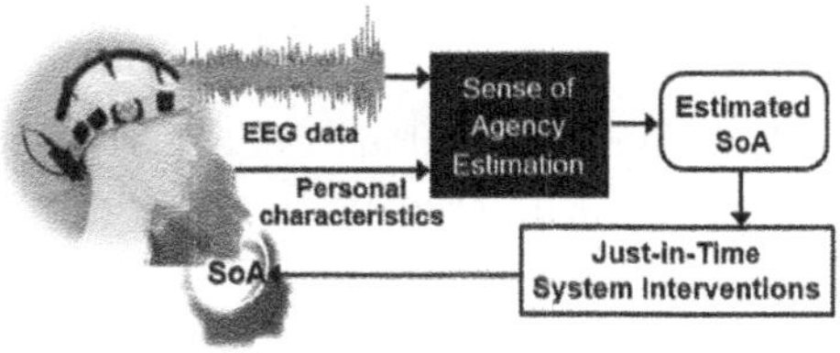

Fig. 5. An SoA estimation model at the core for SoA-aware just-in-time intervention.

Disentangling and decomposing the relative predictive contributions of personality traits, age, and gender is an important direction for future work.

To examine the feasibility of a 3-s window SoA estimation, we refer to the work of Sasaki et al. [31], who demonstrated that EEG-based affect estimation can update emotion predictions every 0.5 s using the preceding 10 s of data. This comparison suggests that EEG signals contain sufficient temporal information for rapid inference, and our method further extends this capability by achieving SoA estimation with a shorter 3-s window.

Our low-latency estimation technology for SoA represents a potential technical component for future behavior intervention systems, rather than a validated intervention mechanism in itself. For example, an SoA-based Just-in-Time Adaptive Intervention (SoA-JITAI) system [32] has been proposed to dynamically optimize intervention timing and content in response to temporary fluctuations in users' SoA. Figure 5 illustrates a conceptual SoA-JITAI architecture in which low-latency SoA estimates, derived from EEG data and personal characteristics following our method, could inform an adaptive intervention design.

Future research could explore the design of more personalized psychological support and behavioral interventions by investigating the practical implementation and evaluation of SoA-JITAI-like systems, while this study focuses on establishing reliable real-time SoA estimation. In particular, intervention designs that respond to fluctuations in SoA patterns may achieve higher effectiveness and user acceptance compared to conventional uniform intervention methods.

5 Conclusion

We proposed and evaluated a method for low-latency estimation of sense of agency using EEG signals combined with participantsâĂŹ personal characteristics, including the Big Five traits, age, and gender. We showed that models integrating both EEG and individual traits maintained stable performance across short-time windows, whereas EEG-only models required longer observation periods to achieve comparable estimation. This suggests that personal characteristics can complement EEG data to capture inter-individual variability in SoA. Our findings also indicate that low-latency SoA estimation may serve as a technical prerequisite for future behaviorally adaptive systems, such as SoA-JITAI, by identifying temporary reductions in SoA and enabling timely support or interventions. Our study establishes a feasibility-level foundation for short-window-based estimation of SoA under practical constraints and underscores the importance of integrating physiological signals with individual trait information. Future work may focus on staged validation in dynamic environments, including disentangling trait-level and state-level contributions and assessing whether short-window estimates can reliably support adaptive intervention designs.

References

1. David, N., Obhi, S., Moore, J.W.: Editorial: sense of agency: examining awareness of the acting self. Front. Hum. Neurosci. **9**, 310 (2015). https://doi.org/10.3389/fnhum.2015.00310
2. Moore, J.W.: What is the sense of agency and why does it matter? Front. Psychol. **7**, 1272 (2016). https://doi.org/10.3389/fpsyg.2016.01272
3. Haggard, P.: Sense of agency in the human brain. Nat. Rev. Neurosci. **18**, 196–207 (2017). https://doi.org/10.1038/nrn.2017.14
4. Wen, W., Charles, L., Haggard, P.: Metacognition and sense of agency. Cogn **241**, 105622 (2023). https://doi.org/10.1016/j.cognition.2023.105622
5. Legaspi, R., Xu, W., Konishi, T., Wada, S., Ishikawa, Y.: Multidimensional analysis of sense of agency during goal pursuit. In: Proceedings of the 30th ACM Conference on User Modeling, Adaptation and Personalization (UMAP 2022), pp. 34–47. ACM, New York, NY, USA (2022). https://doi.org/10.1145/3503252.3531303
6. Legaspi, R., et al.: The sense of agency in human–ai interactions. Knowl.-Based Syst **286**, 111298 (2024). https://doi.org/10.1016/j.knosys.2023.111298
7. Dewey, J.A., Knoblich, G.: Do implicit and explicit measures of the sense of agency measure the same thing? PLoS ONE **9** (2014). https://doi.org/10.1371/journal.pone.0110118
8. Moore, J.W., Obhi, S.S.: Intentional binding and the sense of agency: a review. Conscious. Cogn. **21**, 546–561 (2012). https://doi.org/10.1016/j.concog.2011.12.002
9. Tapal, A., Oren, E., Dar, R., Eitam, B.: The sense of agency scale: a measure of consciously perceived control over one's mnd, body, and the immediate environment. Front. Psychol. **8**, 1552 (2017). https://doi.org/10.3389/fpsyg.2017.01552
10. Haggard, P., Clark, S., Kalogeras, J.: Voluntary action and conscious awareness. Nat. Neurosci. **5**, 382–385 (2002). https://doi.org/10.1038/nn827
11. Kang, S.Y., Im, C.H., Shim, M., Nahab, F.B., Park, J., Kim, D.W., Kakareka, J., Miletta, N., Hallett, M.: Brain networks responsible for sense of agency: An eeg study. PLoS ONE **10**(8), 1–16 (2015). https://doi.org/10.1371/journal.pone.0135261
12. Bertoni, T., et al.: Pre-movement sensorimotor oscillations shape the sense of agency by gating cortical connectivity. Nat. Commun. **16**(1), 3594 (2025). https://doi.org/10.1038/s41467-025-58683-9
13. Cioffi, M.C., Cocchini, G., Banissy, M.J., Moore, J.W.: Ageing and agency: age-related changes in susceptibility to illusory experiences of control. R. Soc. Open Sci. **4**(5), (2017). https://doi.org/10.1098/rsos.161065
14. Schwarz, K.A., Klaffehn, A.L., Hauke-Forman, N., Muth, F.V., Pfister, R.: Never run a changing system: action-effect contingency shapes prospective agency. Cognition **229**, 105250 (2022). https://doi.org/10.1016/j.cognition.2022.105250

15. Saarikallio, S.: Access-awareness-agency (aaa) model of music-based social-emotional competence (musec). Music Sci. **2** (2019). https://doi.org/10.1177/2059204318815421
16. Snow, J.C., Culham, J.C.: The treachery of images: how realism influences brain and behavior. Trends Cogn. Sci. **25**(6), 506–519 (2021). https://doi.org/10.1016/j.tics.2021.02.008
17. Didion, J.K., Wolski, K., Wittchen, D., Coyle, D., Leimkühler, T., Strohmeier, P.: Who did it? how user agency is influenced by visual properties of generated images. In: Proceedings of the 37th Annual ACM Symposium on User Interface Software and Technology, UIST 2024, p. 17. ACM, New York, NY, USA (2024). https://doi.org/10.1145/3654777.3676335
18. Yokota, Y., Naruse, Y.: Temporal fluctuation of mood in gaming task modulates feedback negativity: Eeg study with virtual reality. Front. Hum. Neurosci. **15**, (2021). https://doi.org/10.3389/fnhum.2021.536288
19. Houssein, E.H., Hammad, A., Ali, A.A.: Human emotion recognition from eeg-based brain-computer interface using machine learning: a comprehensive review. Neural Comput. Appl. **34**(15), 12527–12557 (2022). https://doi.org/10.1007/s00521-022-07292-4
20. Islam, M.R., et al.: Eeg channel correlation based model for emotion recognition. Comput. Biol. Med. **136**, 104757 (2021). https://doi.org/10.1016/j.compbiomed.2021.104757
21. Liu, J., et al.: Eeg-based emotion classification using a deep neural network and sparse autoencoder. Front. Syst. Neurosci. **14**, (2020). https://doi.org/10.3389/fnsys.2020.00043
22. Goldberg, L.R.: The development of markers for the big-five factor structure. Psychol. Assess. **4**(1), 26–42 (1992). https://doi.org/10.1037/1040-3590.4.1.26
23. Costa, P.T., McCrae, R.: The neo inventories as instruments of psychological theory. In: The Oxford Handbook of the Five Factor Model. Oxford University Press (2017). https://doi.org/10.1093/oxfordhb/9780199352487.013.10
24. DeYoung, C.G., Quilty, L.C., Peterson, J.B.: Between facets and domains: 10 aspects of the big five. J. Pers. Soc. Psychol. **93**(5), 880–96 (2007). https://doi.org/10.1037/0022-3514.93.5.880
25. Xu, W., Ishikawa, Y., Legaspi, R.: The utility of personality types for personalizing persuasion. In: Baghaei, N., Vassileva, J., Ali, R., Oyibo, K. (eds.) Persuasive Technology, pp. 240–254. Springer, Cham (2022). https://doi.org/10.1007/978-3-030-98438-0_19
26. McAdams, D.P., Pals, J.L.: A new big five: fundamental principles for an integrative science of personality. Am. Psychol. **61**(3), 204 (2006). https://doi.org/10.1037/0003-066X.61.3.204
27. Costa, P.T.J., McCrae, R.R.: Revised NEO Personality Inventory (NEO PI-R) and NEO Five-Factor Inventory (NEO-FFI) Professional Manual. Psychological Assessment Resources, Odessa, FL (1992)
28. Namikawa, T., Tani, I., Wakita, T., Kumagai, R., Nakane, A., Noguchi, H.: Development of a short form of the japanese big-five scale, and a test of its reliability and validity. Japan. J. Psychol. **83**(2), 91–99 (2012). https://doi.org/10.4992/jjpsy.83.91
29. Ke, G., et al.: Lightgbm: a highly efficient gradient boosting decision tree. In: Proceedings of the 31st International Conference on Neural Information Processing Systems, NIPS 2017, pp. 3149–3157. Curran Associates Inc., Red Hook, NY, USA (2017). https://doi.org/10.5555/3294996.3295074

30. DeLong, E.R., DeLong, D.M., Clarke-Pearson, D.L.: Comparing the areas under two or more correlated receiver operating characteristic curves: a nonparametric approach. Biometrics **44**(3), 837–845 (1988). http://www.jstor.org/stable/2531595
31. Sasaki, A., Sugisaki, E., Legaspi, R., Naruse, Y., Kobayashi, N.: Development of a prototype ai system for real-time emotion prediction and mental state adjustment. In: International Conference on Persuasive Technology, PT2024 (2024). https://ceur-ws.org/Vol-3728/paper19.pdf
32. Togawa, R., et al.: Estimating sense of agency from behavioral logs: toward a just-in-time adaptive intervention system. In: Persuasive Technology: 19th International Conference, PERSUASIVE 2024, Wollongong, NSW, Australia, 10–12 April 2024, Proceedings, pp. 273–286. Springer, Heidelberg (2024). https://doi.org/10.1007/978-3-031-58226-4_21

Demo, Poster and Artefacts Track

Reconsider Today's Commute: Reframing Routine Route Choice

Koyo Arai(✉) and Atsushi Hasegawa

Graduate School of Creative Thinking for Social Innovation, Musashino Art University, Tokyo 162-0843, Japan
koyoarai512@gmail.com

Abstract. In everyday urban mobility, route choices are often made on autopilot, based on the common belief that the best route is the shortest, fastest, and easiest one. Routes with fewer transfers, familiar paths, and minimal effort are commonly regarded as rational choices. At the same time, there are moments when people feel like taking a longer walk, shifting their mood, or taking a detour without any particular reason. Such subtle preferences depending on the situation are rarely reflected in typical navigation systems. This project focuses on these everyday preferences and questions the common belief that the optimal route is always the shortest one. We present a navigation tool that, alongside the shortest route, offers alternative routes framed according to different non-numerical values, such as calmness, a sense of space, and changes in scenery. After entering a destination station, users are invited to choose among multiple routes, each presented from a different perspective rather than efficiency metrics alone. The selected route is printed as a receipt, transforming route choice into a tangible record. By highlighting experiential and atmospheric qualities that cannot be reduced to travel time or number of transfers, the system encourages users to reflect on how they make route choices in everyday life. Through this design, we propose an alternative way of understanding mobility–not merely as a problem of optimization, but as an opportunity for reflection and seeing everyday movement differently.

Keywords: Everyday Mobility · Self-reflection · Navigation Systems · Critical Design · Design Research

1 Introduction

In everyday urban mobility, route choices are often made on autopilot, based on the common belief that the best route is the shortest, fastest, and easiest one. Routes with fewer transfers, familiar paths, and minimal effort are commonly regarded as rational choices. In transport planning, travel has long been understood not as an activity with intrinsic value, but as a derived demand that arises as a by-product of other activities [5]. Consequently, travel is primarily treated

E. Vlahu-Gjorgievska et al. (Eds.): PERSUASIVE 2026, CCIS 2896, pp. 225–228, 2027.
https://doi.org/10.1007/978-3-032-27235-5_16

as a disutility, and the reduction of travel time has become a central criterion for evaluation.

This project focuses on these everyday preferences and questions the common belief that the optimal route is always the shortest one. We present a navigation tool that, alongside the shortest route, offers alternative routes framed according to different non-numerical values, such as calmness, a sense of space, and changes in scenery. After entering a destination station, users are invited to choose among multiple routes, each presented from a different perspective rather than efficiency metrics alone. The selected route is printed as a receipt, transforming route choice into a tangible record. By highlighting experiential and atmospheric qualities that cannot be reduced to travel time or number of transfers, the system encourages users to reflect on how they make route choices in everyday life. Through this design, we propose an alternative way of understanding mobility—not merely as a problem of optimization, but as an opportunity for reflection and seeing everyday movement differently.

2 Reconsider Today's Commute System

We present an interactive tool for urban rail commuting, *Reconsider Today's Commute*, designed to prompt users to reconsider routinized route choices. When a destination is entered into a web application built with Next.js, the NAVITIME API retrieves multiple candidate train routes, including the shortest one. Instead of presenting only conventional indicators such as total travel time or number of transfers, the system generates textual descriptions that frame each route according to different non-numerical value criteria, such as rest, refreshment, or deliberate detours, using the OpenAI API. Users select one of the suggested routes, and the selection is stored in a Supabase database. A Python program running on a Raspberry Pi 3B installed at the exhibition venue monitors the database and prints the selected route as a thermal receipt.

By physically holding the printed receipt and referring to it during their journey, users are encouraged to pause and reflect on commuting trips that might otherwise be performed on autopilot. The overall system configuration is shown in Fig. 1.

3 Design Approach

3.1 Autopilot Decision-Making in Everyday Commuting

Reconsider Today's Commute addresses everyday mobility as a site where decisions are frequently made with little conscious reflection. Route selection for commuting to work or school is a highly repetitive practice, typically performed under time constraints and reinforced through habituation. Although such decisions may appear deliberate, they are often made on autopilot, guided by a limited and largely unquestioned set of assumptions.

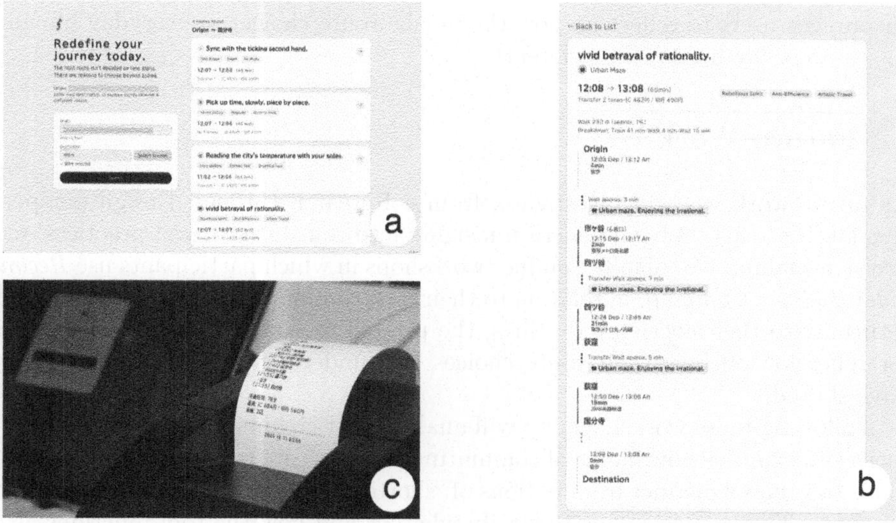

Fig. 1. Reconsider Today's Commute System: (a) Screen shown after the user enters a destination station. In addition to the shortest route, several alternative routes are presented, each framed around different values such as calmness, a sense of space, and changes in scenery. (b) Detail view displayed when a suggested route is selected. In this example, the route intentionally increases the number of transfers, encouraging the user to experience the city as a maze. (c) A receipt printed after the user selects a route.

3.2 Reframing the Default of Route Selection

Rather than offering a more efficient solution, the system is conceived as a critical and speculative design artefact that invites reflection on how mobility choices are framed in everyday life [1,2]. In this research, *Reconsider Today's Commute* is conceived as a tool that surfaces and reframes the criteria that are typically taken for granted in everyday route selection.

Efficiency-oriented criteria (shorter travel times, fewer transfers, familiarity) are rational but often function as default premises that remain largely unexamined, leaving little room for alternative ways of understanding or valuing mobility. Lived travel experiences frequently exceed these frameworks–moments when people feel like taking a longer walk, shifting their mood, or taking a detour without any particular reason–yet such subtle, situational preferences are rarely reflected in typical navigation systems.

Rather than prescribing activities to be performed during travel, this study focuses on the assumptions that precede route selection itself. By presenting alternative routes alongside the shortest one—each framed according to different non-numerical values such as calmness, a sense of space, or changes in scenery—the tool creates opportunities for users to pause and reflect on the question, "On what basis am I choosing this route?" In this sense, the system does not aim to optimize convenience, but instead functions as a design apparatus that encourages users to reflect on how they make route choices in everyday life and to see everyday movement differently.

4 Future Work

As future work, we will investigate, from a Research through Design perspective [3], how this tool can generate insights into routinized travel practices and decision-making. We plan to conduct workshops in which participants use *Reconsider Today's Commute* in relation to their own commuting or daily travel. After returning to their everyday routines, the printed receipts will serve as prompts for reflection on how their route choices and understandings of mobility may have shifted.

Following these workshops, we will analyze participants' discussions and narratives to examine how habitual commuting practices are reconsidered, and what kinds of values—distinct from notions of "shortest" or "efficient"—emerge in their accounts. This analysis aims to clarify whether and how the tool functions as a trigger for directing attention toward everyday decision-making.

Prior studies on travel-time experience suggest that activities during travel (e.g., listening to music, talking, thinking) involve value not captured solely by efficiency or productivity metrics [4]. Analyses of crowded train commuting in the Tokyo area indicate that crowding constrains the feasibility of activities rather than altering preferences [6]. Building on these insights, we focus on the premises underlying mobility-related judgments and choices rather than prescribing activities during travel. By examining users' reflections and narratives from interaction with the tool, we will explore how non-optimizing benefits, changes in the meanings of travel, and opportunities to reinterpret everyday practices are experienced.

References

1. Dunne, A.: Hertzian Tales: Electronic Products, Aesthetic Experience, and Critical Design. The MIT Press, Cambridge (2008)
2. Dunne, A., Raby, F.: Speculative Everything: Design, Fiction, and Social Dreaming. The MIT Press, Cambridge (2013)
3. Frayling, C.: Research in art and design. Royal Coll. Art Res. Papers **1**, 1–5 (1993)
4. Keseru, I., Bulckaen, J., Macharis, C., Minnen, J., Glorieux, I., Van Tienoven, T.P.: Is travel time wasted? Evidence from a time use survey in Flanders, Belgium. In: Proceedings of the 14th International Conference on Travel Behaviour Research. International Association for Travel Behaviour Research (2015)
5. Mokhtarian, P.L., Salomon, I.: How derived is the demand for travel? Some conceptual and measurement considerations. Transp. Res. Part A: Policy Practice **35**(8), 695–719 (2001). https://doi.org/10.1016/S0965-8564(00)00013-6
6. Varghese, V., Chikaraishi, M., Kato, H.: Analysis of travel-time use in crowded trains using discrete-continuous choices of commuters in Tokyo, Japan. Transp. Res. Rec. J. Transp. Res. Board **2674**(10), 189–198 (2020). https://doi.org/10.1177/0361198120934794

Beyond Text: Social Robots in a Multi-stage Trust Repair Trial

Ning-Hsuan Chang(✉) and Shih-Yi Chien

Department of Management Information Systems, National Chengchi University, Taipei, Taiwan

ninghsuan1818@gmail.com

Abstract. As generative AI agents are increasingly deployed in service contexts, fluent explanations and apologies generated by large language models (LLMs) have become easy to generate. However, service failures remain inevitable, and existing trust repair research has primarily relied on subjective self-reports. This work investigates whether embodied agents can more effectively support trust repair than text-based LLM agents when verbal content is held comparable. Using a social robot and a text-based LLM interface, we introduce a multi-stage repair trial situated in a hotel overbooking scenario. Participants encounter a sequence of recovery offers, each generated in response to prior rejection and involving a different trade-off between competing constraints. Trust repair is operationalized as decision shift, defined as whether an initially rejected agent can later persuade users to accept a recovery option. By framing trust repair as an observable decision process rather than a subjective judgment, this study investigates how agent embodiment influences users' willingness to revise decisions after service failure.

Keywords: Trust repair · Social robots · Service recovery · Decision revision

1 Introduction

Service failures are unavoidable in interactive AI systems, particularly as LLM-based agents are increasingly integrated into real-world service environments [1]. Although LLMs can generate coherent explanations and apologies, fluent language alone does not ensure successful trust repair when users experience inconvenience or loss. Existing work in human–robot interaction and explainable AI has examined apology strategies and trust perception following failures [2,3], yet most studies rely on scripted interactions and subjective self-reports rather than observable decision behavior.

At the same time, embodied social robots introduce a distinct interaction modality through physical presence and nonverbal social cues [5,6]. Gestures, posture, and bodily orientation may shape how effort and accountability are perceived during service recovery [4]. However, it remains unclear whether such

E. Vlahu-Gjorgievska et al. (Eds.): PERSUASIVE 2026, CCIS 2896, pp. 229–232, 2027.
https://doi.org/10.1007/978-3-032-27235-5_17

embodied signals meaningfully influence users' willingness to tolerate unfavorable outcomes when verbal explanations are held constant.

To address this gap, we conceptualize trust repair as a decision-making process that unfolds through multiple repair attempts. We compare an embodied robot agent with a text-based LLM agent under identical task roles and comparable informational content. A hotel overbooking scenario serves as a concrete testbed, while the research question targets broader issues of trust repair in generative AI–mediated services.

2 Method: A Multi-stage Repair Trial

2.1 Persona and Background Settings

To minimize variability arising from individual preference differences, participants are instructed to adopt a fixed persona at the beginning of the task. Specifically, participants imagine that they are traveling to celebrate an important anniversary, making an ocean-view a critical requirement. At the same time, they have just completed a long flight and are highly fatigued, which makes immediate room access equally important. These two priorities are explicitly stated and framed as non-negotiable and equally weighted, establishing a constrained decision context shared by all participants.

The use of a fixed persona serves two purposes. First, it standardizes participants' underlying goals, reducing the likelihood that acceptance of later-stage offers is driven by idiosyncratic preferences rather than the interaction itself. Second, it creates an inherent tension between competing requirements, ensuring that no single recovery option can fully satisfy all constraints without introducing a trade-off. This setup allows subsequent repair attempts to be interpreted as alternative responses to unmet needs rather than as objectively better solutions.

2.2 Repair Trial Flow

At the start of the trial, participants are informed that their reserved ocean-view room is unavailable due to a system overbooking error. The assigned agent then initiates a repair process that unfolds across up to three stages (see Fig. 1). At each stage, the agent presents a recovery offer, and the participant decide whether to accept the offer or reject it and continue the interaction. If an offer is rejected, it cannot be revisited, preventing strategic waiting or comparison across options.

Crucially, later-stage offers are not framed as improvements over earlier ones. Instead, each stage introduces an alternative trade-off designed to address the participant's stated rejection reason by sacrificing a different constraint. The first stage preserves immediate access at the expense of room view. If this offer is rejected, the second stage preserves the ocean-view but requires a substantial waiting time. If the second offer is also rejected, the third stage satisfies both immediacy and view while requiring significant physical effort, such as relocating

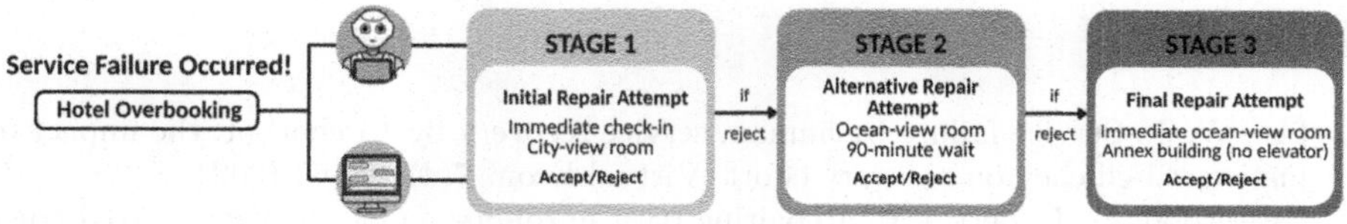

Fig. 1. Multi-stage repair trial illustrating a decision-based trust repair process.

to an annex building without an elevator. This structure ensures that progression across stages reflects a sequence of repair attempts rather than escalating incentives.

Across all stages, participants interacted with only one agent type, either a robot agent or a text-based agent. Both agents followed the same repair logic and provided stage-matched informational content. Following each decision, participants either proceeded to the next repair attempt or terminated the interaction, allowing trust repair to be examined as a dynamic decision-making process capturing whether and when participants revised an initial rejection over successive attempts.

3 Measures

Trust repair is evaluated through observable decision behavior rather than post-interaction trust ratings. Four measures are collected. (i) *Decision shift* is the primary outcome and is defined as whether a participant who rejects the first recovery offer later accepts any subsequent offer in later stages, indicating a reversal of the initial decision. (ii) *Acceptance stage* captures the stage at which acceptance occurs among participants who shift, distinguishing acceptance at the second or third repair attempt. (iii) *Final outcome* records whether the interaction ends with acceptance of any recovery offer or termination after rejecting all offers. (iv) *Perceived acceptability* is assessed using a subjective rating collected immediately after each decision and serves as a control measure to account for potential offer-driven effects when comparing agent conditions.

4 Conclusion

This work proposes a multi-stage, decision-based approach that reframes trust repair evaluation from a subjective emotional judgment to an observable behavioral process.

By comparing an embodied robot agent with a text-based agent within the same multi-stage repair structure, we examine how physical presence and nonverbal social cues shape users' willingness to continue interaction during service recovery. This decision-based framework can be extended to other generative AI applications in which errors are unavoidable and continued engagement depends on users' willingness to reconsider their decisions.

References

1. Lee, W.-J.: Service failure by human, service recovery by AI chatbot: the impact of justice, AI efficacy on recovery effort. Virtual Econ. **7**(4), 48–63 (2024)
2. Esterwood, C., Robert, L.P.: Repairing trust in robots: a meta-analysis of HRI trust repair studies with a no-repair condition. In: Companion of the 2024 ACM/IEEE International Conference on Human-Robot Interaction (HRI '24), pp. 642–646. ACM, New York (2024)
3. Esterwood, C., Robert, L.P.: Three strikes and you are out!: the impacts of multiple human-robot trust violations and repairs on robot trustworthiness. Comput. Hum. Behav. **142**, 107658 (2023)
4. Pompe, B.L., Velner, E., Truong, K.P.: The robot that showed remorse: repairing trust with a genuine apology. In: 2022 31st IEEE International Conference on Robot and Human Interactive Communication (RO-MAN), pp. 1198–1204. IEEE (2022)
5. Chien, S.Y., Lin, Y.L., Luo, J.T., et al.: Exploring the antecedents and consequences of privacy concerns: a comparison of humanoid robot to tablet. Expert Syst. **42**, (2025)
6. Chien, S.Y., Lin, Y.L., Luo, J.T., et al.: An exploration of multimodal communication for developing extrovert, ambivert, and introvert robot. In: Companion of the 2024 ACM/IEEE International Conference on Human-Robot Interaction (HRI '24), pp. 702–706 (2024)

A Self-Efficacy–Driven Framework for Cognitive Training in Mild Cognitive Impairment: Game-Based Tasks and LLM-Powered Social Robots

Yu-Jou Chen[1,2](✉), Shih-Yi Chien[1,2], and Patrick Hung[1,2]

[1] Department of Management Information Systems, National Chengchi University, Taipei, Taiwan
{114356016,sychien}@nccu.edu.tw, patrick.hung@ontariotechu.ca
[2] Institute of Technology, University of Ontario, Oshawa, ON, Canada

Abstract. Sustained engagement in Mild Cognitive Impairment (MCI) interventions depends not only on task design but also on users' belief in their ability to succeed. This work presents a self-efficacy–driven cognitive training framework grounded in Bandura's theory and embodied human–AI interaction. The system separates mastery generation from social mediation: adaptive web-based games create mastery experiences, while an LLM-powered robotic dog reframes outcomes through emotionally supportive interaction. Structured around three phases—Priming, Execution, and Reframing—the framework operationalizes the four sources of self-efficacy through complementary software and embodied roles. By providing low-evaluative, zoomorphic support, the design offers a theory-grounded framework for designing and demonstrating persuasive embodied systems for cognitive health interventions.

Keywords: Mild Cognitive Impairment · Self-Efficacy · Socially Assistive Robots

1 Introduction

Cognitive stimulation therapies (CST) for Mild Cognitive Impairment (MCI) traditionally target measurable cognitive performance. However, sustained participation often falters not due to task difficulty, but because repeated experiences of perceived failure undermine users' confidence and motivation, leading to disengagement even when objective gains are possible [3, 4]. Thus, effective interventions must address both cognitive performance and belief formation [10].

Self-efficacy—defined as belief in one's capacity to perform goal-directed actions—strongly predicts engagement, persistence, and emotional regulation across learning and rehabilitation contexts [1, 2]. In MCI, interventions that fail to support belief formation risk producing short-term task improvements that do not translate into sustained participation or everyday functioning. Conventional cognitive training systems often emphasize

E. Vlahu-Gjorgievska et al. (Eds.): PERSUASIVE 2026, CCIS 2896, pp. 233–236, 2027.
https://doi.org/10.1007/978-3-032-27235-5_18

repetitive task execution and outcome metrics, leaving limited support for personalized interpretation, emotional regulation, or confidence rebuilding after perceived failure.

Socially assistive robots (SARs) offer a promising approach by fostering social presence and emotional engagement [6, 7], while Large Language Models (LLMs) enable adaptive, empathetic feedback [8]. Crucially, the psychological impact of such systems depends not only on conversational content but also on embodiment and social role. Highly anthropomorphic designs may increase perceived evaluation pressure and self-consciousness, particularly in vulnerable populations [5]. In contrast, non-humanoid embodiments can provide companionship and emotional reassurance while minimizing performance-related anxiety. Building on these insights, this work proposes a game-based cognitive training framework in which self-efficacy is generated through task design and socially mediated via an LLM-powered robotic dog.

2 System Overview

The proposed framework integrates game-based cognitive training with embodied social facilitation. It assumes self-efficacy emerges not only from task success but also from how performance experiences are interpreted and emotionally processed. Accordingly, the system separates the generation of mastery-relevant experiences from their social and affective mediation. This integration is implemented through a three-phase interaction flow—Priming, Execution, and Reframing—coordinated between the web application and the robotic dog. Guided by Bandura's self-efficacy theory [1, 2], the system operationalizes the four primary sources of self-efficacy—enactive mastery, vicarious experience, verbal persuasion, and affective state regulation—through interactions between software and embodiment, as shown in Table 1.

Table 1. Operationalization of Self-Efficacy Sources

Self-Efficacy Source	Web Application	Robot Dog / LLM Agent
Enactive Mastery	Game-based cognitive tasks with adaptive difficulty based on success rates	Embodied reinforcement through gestures (e.g., nodding, tail wagging) and verbal validation of progress
Vicarious Experience	Instructional videos demonstrating exercises and cognitive strategies	Reflective dialogue discussing peer strategies and achievable successes
Verbal Persuasion	Visual milestones and progress notifications	Personalized second-person encouragement emphasizing effort and strategy use
Affective State	Background music and calming interface design	Emotional alignment via movement and supportive tone

2.1 Multi-Component Cognitive Training Platform

The platform functions as a stable generator of mastery-relevant experiences through four key design elements:

- **Adaptive Cognitive Tasks:** The platform hosts activities targeting executive control and spatial memory, utilizing adaptive difficulty algorithms to ensure users experience "challenge-level" success rather than constant failure.
- **Modeling and Strategy Modules:** Instructional videos provide cognitive modeling to build mental representations of success (Vicarious Experience).
- **Non-Evaluative Progress Tracking:** Performance metrics are transformed into non-evaluative progress cues to support subsequent social reframing.
- **Environmental Affective Cues:** The platform incorporates calming UI elements and background music to maintain an optimal emotional state for training.

These components collectively generate mastery experiences that are then socially mediated by the robotic dog.

2.2 Three-Phase Interaction Flow Across System Components

Each phase corresponds to a distinct persuasive strategy targeting different stages of belief formation and emotional regulation. Across phases, the web-based training system generates mastery-relevant task experiences, while the robotic dog and LLM jointly mediate how these experiences are interpreted. The interaction is structured into three distinct phases to prevent cognitive overloading:

- **Phase 1: Priming (Cognitive Preparation):** Before task execution, the system introduces task goals and structure, while the robotic dog establishes social presence. The LLM reflective prompts provide vicarious experiences of peer strategies.
- **Phase 2: Execution and Co-presence:** During gameplay, the robot acts as a companion, using non-verbal gestures to provide reassurance and minimize evaluation anxiety without verbal interruption.
- **Phase 3: Reframing (Cognitive Reconstruction):** Post-task, the LLM reframes performance cues into personalized feedback emphasizing effort and strategy, ensuring constructive verbal persuasion even after perceived failures.

2.3 Embodied Social Facilitation

The system employs the Mini Pupper 2 [9], a quadruped robot used as an embodied interface rather than an evaluative agent. Its non-humanoid form supports a low-evaluative interaction style, allowing social cues to be delivered without invoking explicit social comparison or judgment. Expressive movements and simple visual displays convey affiliative and affective states, fostering reassurance and a sense of co-presence during training [6]. In coordination with LLM-generated verbal feedback, the robot primarily supports emotional regulation and confidence rather than performance assessment. This design prioritizes psychological safety and sustained engagement, reinforcing self-efficacy as a foundation for long-term participation in cognitive training.

3 Conclusion

This work presents a theory-driven framework targeting self-efficacy in MCI cognitive training by separating mastery experience generation from social mediation. By integrating game-based tasks with an LLM-powered robot, objective performance cues are translated into motivating, emotionally meaningful encounters. The robot primarily supports how users process training outcomes, reinforcing confidence over time. Future work will empirically evaluate the system's impact on self-efficacy and adherence while exploring personalized strategies for individual MCI profiles.

Acknowledgments. his work is supported by the Human-AI Interaction Lab (HAILab) at National Chengchi University.

Disclosure of Interests. The authors declare no competing interests relevant to this work.

References

1. Bandura, A.: Self-efficacy: Toward a unifying theory of behavioral change. Psychol. Rev. **84**(2), 191–215 (1977). https://doi.org/10.1037/0033-295X.84.2.191
2. Bandura, A.: Social cognitive theory of self-regulation. Organ. Behav. Hum. Decis. Process. **50**(2), 248–287 (1991). https://doi.org/10.1016/0749-5978(91)90022-L
3. Finn, M., McDonald, S.: Computerised cognitive training for older persons with mild cognitive impairment: A pilot study. Brain Impairment **12**(3), 187–199 (2011). https://doi.org/10.1375/brim.12.3.187
4. Jirayucharoensak, S., et al.: A game-based neurofeedback training system to enhance cognitive performance in healthy elderly subjects and in patients with amnestic mild cognitive impairment. Clin. Interv. Aging **14**, 347–360 (2019). https://doi.org/10.2147/CIA.S189043
5. Kätsyri, J., Förger, K., Mäkäräinen, M., Takala, T.: A review of empirical evidence on different uncanny valley hypotheses: support for perceptual mismatch as one road to the valley of eeriness. Front. Psychol. **6**, 390 (2015). https://doi.org/10.3389/fpsyg.2015.00390
6. Kim, L.H., Domova, V., Yao, Y., Huang, C.-M., Follmer, S., Paredes, P.E.: Robotic presence: The effects of anthropomorphism and robot state on task performance and emotion. IEEE Robot. Autom. Lett. **7**(3), 7399–7406 (2022). https://doi.org/10.1109/LRA.2022.3174151
7. Lee, H.R., et al.: Reimagining robots for dementia: From robots for care-receivers and caregivers to robots for care partners. In: Proc. 2023 ACM/IEEE Int. Conf. Hum.-Robot Interact. (HRI), pp. 475–484. ACM (2023). https://doi.org/10.1145/3568162.3576483
8. Lima, M., et al.: Promoting cognitive health in elder care with large language model-powered socially assistive robots. In: Proc. 2025 CHI Conf. Hum. Factors Comput. Syst., pp. 1–22 (2025). https://doi.org/10.1145/3706598.3713582
9. MangDang Technology Co., Limited: Mini Pupper 2: Open-source ROS2 robot kit [Robot platform] (2022). https://mangdang.store/
10. Chien, S.Y., Chao, S.F., Kang, Y., et al.: Understanding predictive factors of dementia for older adults: a machine learning approach for modeling dementia influencers. Int. J. Hum. Comput. Stud. **165**, 102834 (2022)

Making Invisible Hand Recovery Visible: Real-Time Visual Feedback for Rehabilitation Monitoring

Hanna Choi[1], Billy Park[2], Gunhyuk Park[2], and Heejin Jeong[1](✉)

[1] Arizona State University, Mesa, AZ 85212, USA
{hchoi117,heejin.jeong}@asu.edu
[2] Gwangju Institute of Science and Technology, Gwangju, South Korea
billypark@gm.gist.ac.kr, maharaga@gist.ac.kr

Abstract. This study presents a low-cost, non-contact, real-time monitoring system for quantifying and visualizing hand rehabilitation status, focusing on the thenar and wrist regions. Traditional clinical assessments rely on intermittent, observer-dependent measures such as range of motion, strength tests, and questionnaires, limiting their suitability for continuous monitoring. While industrial 3D motion capture and ultrasound offer high accuracy, their cost and complexity hinder use in home-based rehabilitation. The proposed system uses a smartphone as the primary sensor, combining digital image correlation (DIC) via OpenCorr with MediaPipe-based hand pose estimation to compute and visualize surface strain and joint kinematics in real time. Quantitative outcome measures are derived through post-processing. Experiments with seven rehabilitative hand and wrist movement tasks demonstrate pose-dependent variations in surface strain. The system reliably generates region-of-interest-based strain maps and joint tracking results, with OpenCorr producing consistent strain patterns. This approach supports objective, quantitative assessment of motor performance and provides actionable feedback for personalized, home-based, and remote rehabilitation.

Keywords: Digital image correlation · Rehabilitation · Real-time monitoring

1 Introduction

Hand recovery in patients often suffers from low adherence when progress is gradual and difficult to perceive. When recovery-related physiological signals are invisible or hard to interpret, patients may disengage despite clinical necessity. This work frames real-time hand recovery monitoring as a visual, persuasive feedback mechanism that makes recovery progress observable and supports patients' self-monitoring. Providing continuous, quantitative, and easily interpretable feedback is a key strategy for maintaining patient motivation and improving treatment adherence [1]. Conventional clinical measurement tools do

E. Vlahu-Gjorgievska et al. (Eds.): PERSUASIVE 2026, CCIS 2896, pp. 237–242, 2027.
https://doi.org/10.1007/978-3-032-27235-5_19

not adequately fulfill this role. The digital image correlation (DIC) technique employed in this study measures surface deformation and strain with high resolution and has been extensively validated in experimental mechanics. Prior studies extending DIC to consumer cameras and smartphones [2,3], including applications involving skin and soft tissue deformation [4–6], suggest that surface strain mapping may serve as a noninvasive biomechanical indicator of rehabilitation progress. However, practical challenges such as rolling shutter effects, lack of hardware synchronization, thermal drift, and variability in skin speckle quality [7–9] continue to limit clinical application. Accordingly, this study proposes and evaluates a low-cost, non-contact, real-time hand and wrist rehabilitation monitoring workflow that integrates smartphone-based video acquisition, OpenCorr-based DIC, and MediaPipe-based hand pose estimation, utilizing skin-applied speckle stickers. We investigate whether reproducible surface strain fields can be obtained in the thenar and wrist regions and whether pose-dependent differences in strain can be quantified across seven standardized hand postures.

2 System Development

The proposed system integrates smart phone-based two-dimensional DIC with MediaPipe hand pose estimation to enable real-time quantification and visualization of hand and wrist surface strain and joint kinematics. A single rear camera on an iPhone 13 Pro captures video of the hand and wrist, which is processed in parallel by OpenCorr for DIC-based displacement and strain estimation and by MediaPipe Hands for joint pose tracking. Synchronization is achieved using frame-level timestamps, allowing strain and kinematic variables to be analyzed on a shared time axis.

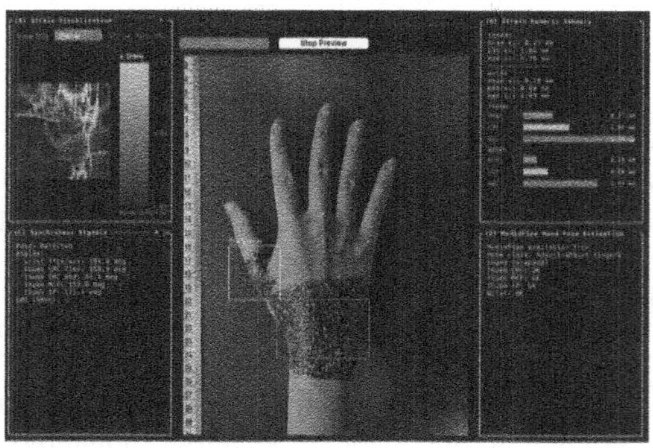

Fig. 1. Real-time hand strain and pose viewer.

Two fixed regions of interest (ROIs) are defined using MediaPipe hand landmarks [10]. The thenar ROI is a 160×160 px square centered on thumb landmarks #1 and 2, while the wrist ROI is a 360 × 270 px rectangle centered on palm landmarks #0, 5, 9, 13, and 17, extending toward both the forearm and hand. Within each ROI, the system generates real-time strain maps and summary metrics.

All outputs are stored in a unified frame-level data structure, which includes timestamps, joint pose variables, ROI-based strain metrics, and references to the corresponding strain maps. This design supports both real-time visualization and offline analysis. A representative real-time preview with overlaid joint pose and strain maps is shown in Fig. 1.

3 Methods

This study evaluates pose-dependent strain patterns derived from DIC measurements and assesses the feasibility of presenting these results as real-time visual feedback for hand rehabilitation monitoring.

Experimental Tasks: Seven rehabilitation-related hand and wrist movements were examined (Table 1) [11]. Each trial consisted of repeated cycles of a relaxed posture, the target movement, and a return to the relaxed posture.

Table 1. Hand and wrist movement tasks

Task No.	Movement description
1	Wrist flexion-extension (dorsum facing the camera)
2	Ulnar-radial deviation
3	Forearm supination-pronation
4	Hand opening-closing
5	Finger flexion-extension (hand extended)
6	Finger abduction-adduction (hand extended)
7	Thumb-to-fingertip opposition (hand upright)

Image Acquisition and Pose Estimation: Video data were acquired using the rear wide camera of an iPhone 13 Pro at 1920×1080 resolution and 30 fps with a fixed camera-to-skin distance. Each frame was time-stamped and processed using MediaPipe Hands to detect 21 hand landmarks and estimate wrist and thumb joint kinematics.

Camera Calibration and Surface Patterning: Prior to data collection, the camera was calibrated using a planar checkerboard target (120×90 mm, 5 mm grid spacing) imaged at 25 poses. Intrinsic parameters and a pixel-to-millimeter conversion factor at the working distance were computed. To enable accurate DIC tracking, a speckle pattern was applied using a film-free water-decal method [12] with skin-safe temporary tattoo paper.

ROI Mapping and Reference Frame Selection: The thenar and wrist ROIs, defined in physical space, were mapped to the image plane using the calibration factor and cropped for analysis. A reference configuration was obtained by holding the initial relaxed posture for 5 s; frames from this period were temporally averaged to produce a single undeformed reference image ($\epsilon = 0$).

Digital Image Correlation and Strain Analysis: DIC was performed using the OpenCorr engine with a subset size of 30 pixels and a step size of 10 pixels for both ROIs. Two-dimensional in-plane displacement fields were computed and used to derive local and principal strain maps. For offline analysis, OpenCorr was applied to the full HD video to compute final strain tensors and principal strains (ϵ_1).

4 Results

Strain distributions within the thenar and wrist ROIs varied systematically across the seven rehabilitative hand postures measured using the proposed smart phone-based 2D DIC system. Tasks No. 2, 3, 4, and 6 consistently produced localized regions of high strain, enabling clear identification of posture-specific burdened areas. During finger adduction–abduction with the hand extended, displacement magnitude responses were more pronounced in the thenar ROI (mean = 0.1178 mm) than in the wrist ROI (mean = 0.0895 mm). Principal strain analysis, quantified using the maximum tensile strain (ϵ_1) and minimum compressive strain (ϵ_2), revealed three prominent strain peaks in the thenar region (mean $\epsilon_1 = 96.4\%$, mean $\epsilon_2 = -34.8\%$), whereas the wrist exhibited three smaller peaks (mean $\epsilon_1 = 18.0\%$, mean $\epsilon_2 = -12.8\%$). Points of interest within both ROIs remained stable throughout the measurements (See Fig. 2). These results demonstrate that posture-dependent strain patterns can be quantitatively distinguished within the same participant, supporting objective comparison of exercise performance or recovery stages. Although the current 2D implementation cannot fully capture out-of-plane motion, the findings indicate that a single smartphone camera can provide meaningful quantitative and visual feedback on hand deformation during rehabilitation.

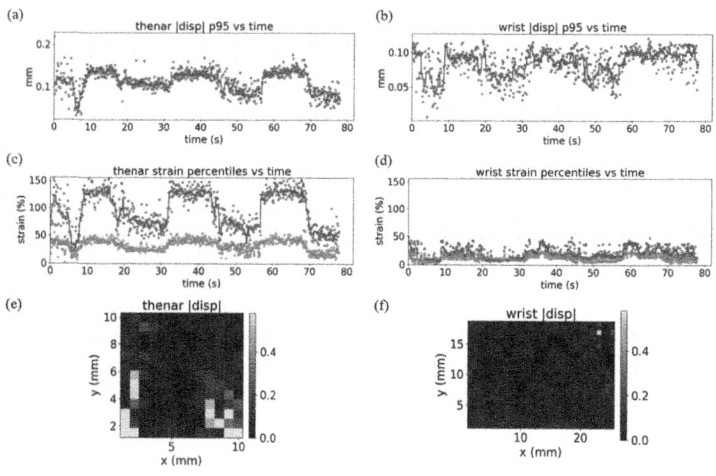

Fig. 2. Displacement magnitude and strain results for finger adduction-abduction: (a) Thenar: Time Series of Displacement Magnitude ($|disp|$), 95th Percentile, (b) Wrist: Time Series of Displacement Magnitude ($|disp|$), 95th Percentile, (c) Thenar: Time Series of Principal Strain Percentiles (ϵ_1 and ϵ_2), 90th Percentile, (d) Wrist: Time Series of Principal Strain Percentiles (ϵ_1 and ϵ_2), 90th Percentile, (e) Thenar Representative Frame: Displacement Magnitude, (f) Wrist: Representative Frame: Displacement Magnitude.

5 Conclusion

The DIC-based real-time monitoring system visualizes surface strain changes, making hand function recovery, often imperceptible to the naked eye, observable to patients. By providing intuitive real-time feedback, the system supports self-monitoring during rehabilitation and may improve understanding of recovery progress, engagement, and adherence. Future work will focus on improving the robustness of strain estimation, stabilizing ROI tracking, and reducing outlier sensitivity.

Acknowledgments. This study was primarily supported by the U.S. National Science Foundation (NSF, Award Number: 2442902). This research was also supported by the MSIT (Ministry of Science, ICT), Korea, under the Global Research Support Program in the Digital Field program (RS-2024-00419561) supervised by the IITP (Institute for Information & Communications Technology Planning & Evaluation).

References

1. Wang, C.Q.S., Wang, K., Sun, L., Liu, S.Q., Luo, J.: The effect of visual feedback on balance rehabilitation in people with impaired ankle instability: a systematic review and meta-analysis. BMC Sports Sci. Med. Rehabil. **17**(1), 77 (2025). https://doi.org/10.1186/s13102-024-01041-x
2. Ienaga, N., Fujita, K., Koyama, T., Sasaki, T., Sugiura, Y., Saito, H.: Development and user evaluation of a smartphone-based system to assess range of motion of wrist joint. J. Hand Surg. Global Online **2**(6), 339–342 (2020). https://doi.org/10.1016/j.jhsg.2020.09.004
3. Zhu, K., Pan, B.: Panoramic/dual-surface digital image correlation measurement using a single camera. Sensors **22**(9), 3266 (2022). https://doi.org/10.3390/s22093266
4. Chen, B., Genovese, K., Pan, B.: In vivo panoramic human skin shape and deformation measurement using mirror-assisted multi-view digital image correlation. J. Mech. Behav. Biomed. Mater. **110**, 103936 (2020). https://doi.org/10.1016/j.jmbbm.2020.103936
5. Kao, A.R., Xu, C., Gerling, G.J.: Using digital image correlation to quantify skin deformation with von Frey monofilaments. IEEE Trans. Haptics **15**(1), 26–31 (2021). https://doi.org/10.1109/TOH.2021.3138350
6. Coburn, K., Velhal, M., Goenezen, S., Liang, H.: Digital image correlation through surface patterning of skins to monitor knee motion. Biotribology **35**, 100251 (2023). https://doi.org/10.1016/j.biotri.2023.100251
7. Yu, L., Bekdullayev, N., Lubineau, G.: Smartphone-based single-camera stereo-DIC system: thermal error analysis and design recommendations. IEEE Sens. J. **21**(7), 9567–9576 (2021). https://doi.org/10.1109/JSEN.2021.3054805
8. Karpenko, A., Jacobs, D., Baek, J., Levoy, M.: Digital video stabilization and rolling shutter correction using gyroscopes. CSTR **1**(2), 13 (2011)
9. Cheng, X., Wang, S., Wei, H., Li, L., Huo, Z., Li, C., Wang, Z.: Digital image correlation by natural textures on biological skin. Opt. Lasers Eng. **165**, 107547 (2023). https://doi.org/10.1016/j.optlaseng.2023.107547

10. Zhang, F., et al.: MediaPipe hands: on-device real-time hand tracking. arXiv:2006.10214 (2020). https://doi.org/10.48550/arXiv.2006.10214
11. Muñoz-Gómez, E., Aguilar-Rodríguez, M., Mollà-Casanova, S., Sempere-Rubio, N., Inglés, M., Serra-Añó, P.: A randomized controlled trial on the effectiveness of mirror therapy in improving strength, range of movement and muscle activity in people with carpal tunnel syndrome. J. Hand Ther. **37**(4), 534–543 (2024). https://doi.org/10.1016/j.jht.2024.02.007
12. Sanchez, A.C., Kim, D.K.: Assessment of the film-free water decal method for speckle pattern application in digital image correlation. Sensors **24**(17), 5657 (2024). https://doi.org/10.3390/s24175657

Exploring UX Frustration Recognition Using Stress Recognition Models and Lightweight Biosignal Features

Sergio De León Aguilar[1](✉), Yuki Matsuda[2], and Keiichi Yasumoto[3]

[1] Nara Institute of Science and Technology, Ikoma City, Nara 630-0192, Japan
sergio.de.leon@ubi-lab.com

[2] Okayama University, Okayama City, Okayama 700-0082, Japan
cocolab@okayama-u.ac.jp

[3] Nara Institute of Science and Technology, Ikoma City, Nara 630-0192, Japan
yasumoto@is.naist.jp

Abstract. Adaptive user interfaces provide personalized experiences traditionally through customization menus, user profiling, or multimodal sensing. Stress and cognitive-load-aware AUIs have received significant attention due to their potential to improve accessibility and performance for less tech-savvy users. Particularly, the use of wearable-captured physiological signals allows practical implementations with high usability. However, attention to bad user experience due to heterogeneous skill levels is limited in the literature; studies are commonly found interpreting stress and frustrating user experiences (UX) as equal, and many approaches rely on self-reported or post-hoc analyses. In this study, we investigate the challenges lightweight machine learning models face when inferring UX-induced frustration from wearable physiological signals using stress-trained datasets, highlighting how task specificity achieves up to 19.3% performance gains in frustration recognition tasks, and label granularity makes 4-class classification viable at above-random chance performance (42.3%).

Keywords: UX · frustration · wearables · machine learning

1 Introduction and Motivation

Adaptive User Interfaces (AUIs) are commonly designed for homogeneous populations such as trained operators, students, or users with specialized expertise. While early AUIs emphasized static personalization (e.g., adapting layouts to user expertise), recent HCI research has explored dynamic adaptation based on users' accessibility needs to reduce cognitive load and prevent confusion during challenging tasks [3]. Despite performance gains, most systems overlook the wide variation in technological familiarity, perceptual abilities, and emotional reactivity found in the general public, which intensifies marginalization of vulnerable or

E. Vlahu-Gjorgievska et al. (Eds.): PERSUASIVE 2026, CCIS 2896, pp. 243–247, 2027.
https://doi.org/10.1007/978-3-032-27235-5_20

less tech-savvy users [6]. To address these considerations, several studies leverage physiological stress detection to identify struggling behavior during interaction [5]. Although promising, these approaches are often constrained by limited subject diversity and by ambiguously defined stress labels that may conflate multiple emotional states.

In this study, we evaluate stress-trained multimodal traditional machine learning models on smartphone user experience (UX) induced realistic frustration events. We demonstrated that by increasing task specificity, accuracy improvements as great as 19.3% can be achieved, and 4-class classification becomes viable by reducing emotion-ambiguity.

2 Related Work

Recent advances in physiological and behavioral sensing have enabled AUIs to adapt interface complexity, pacing, and visual emphasis based on cognitive load. Vasiljevas *et al.* showed that gaze behavior can continuously estimate cognitive load during interaction, enabling anticipatory difficulty adaptation [7]. Viviani *et al.* reported strong correlations between fine motor behavior in smartphone typing and cognitive function, with implications for learning and accessibility [8].

Although stress recognition is widely studied in mental health literature, wearable-based adaptation remains an emerging approach. Most stress recognition datasets rely on coarse temporal windows and post-hoc analysis, with few approaches supporting semi-real-time inference [4]. Liapis *et al.* demonstrated mobile-compatible stress classification for UX evaluation using physiological signals; however, their approach does not address subject or task heterogeneity, limiting generalization in realistic settings.

In contrast, our work directly examines the feasibility of real-time, on-device UX-induced frustration recognition by evaluating stress-trained models against both standardized stress tasks and a realistic, frustration-inducing smartphone interaction, thereby addressing the combined challenges of task specificity, emotion ambiguity, and practical deployment constraints.

3 Experiment and Results

To evaluate the performance of traditional stress recognition methods on a frustration-inducing realistic smartphone interface, we modified an open source calculator application[1] to reproduce UX friction points identified by elderly subjects from a previous experiment on AR-based guidelines for the general public [2]. Implemented friction points include reduced readability, random input delays, missed interactions, and hard-to-access operator keys. To reduce the presence of motion artifacts and increase reproducibility, video-based tasks were selected as the baselines to be compared against. 21 subjects participated in our experiment (6F/15M).

[1] https://github.com/violiarns28/calculator.

PPG and EDA physiological reactions were sampled with a Shimmer3 GSR+ wearable device at 51.2 Hz during the execution of arithmetic calculations with and without UX bugs present, and during video-based stress and relaxing elating video clips according to the multi-modal StressID dataset protocol [1]. Every phase was preceded by an emotional reset via a deep breathing and relaxation activity as seen in pretty Fig. 1.

Self-reported direct emotion (stressed and relaxed) and a 3-axis SAM manikin survey were conducted to produce our ground-truth. Three classification schemes were tested: non-stressed vs stressed (binary); relaxed, stressed, and undefined (ternary); and relaxed, amused, stressed, and undefined (quaternary).

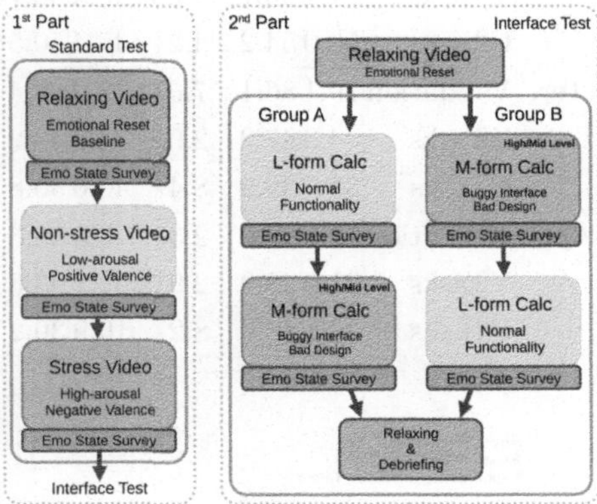

Fig. 1. UX frustration recognition protocol.

For evaluation, each model would be trained on all tasks from StressID's protocol and only on their video-based tasks. Inference performance would be tested on our experimental data video tasks (stress) and calculator tasks (UX frustration). Feature oversampling and subject standardization followed StressID's updated feature pipeline.

We observe classification performance being severely affected by experimental setup—binary classification performance is reduced on unseen data, our experiment video tasks—, performance is improved by training the models only on the relevant StressID's video tasks, as seen in the difference between validation and video task (*VTasks*) rows in Table 1. To visualize the factors affecting feature clustering in our experiment and StressID's data, we run a t-SNE analysis. As seen in Fig. 2, regardless of a uniform distribution of all tasks in the feature space, the greatest clustering depends on the subject rather than label. To increase specificity, we added a new classification schema, in which by considering the "Dominance" axis and redifining "Arousal"'s relevance, we successfully achieved above-random classification power (42.3%) in the hardest 4-label classification task for the calculator task (*CTasks*).

Table 1. Baseline models' accuracy performance comparison between models trained with all StressID's tasks and trained only with the relevant video tasks.

		KNeighbors			MLP			RandomForest			SVC		
Cls.		All	Video	Diff.	All	Video	Diff.	All	Video	Diff.	All	Video	Diff.
Bin.	Validation	86.5	83.8	-2.7↓	86.1	83.1	-3.0↓	84.4	87.1	2.7↑	86.4	89.9	3.5↑
	VTasks	51.1	66.7	15.6⋆	49.4	56.7	7.3⋆	55.6	54.4	-1.2↓	52.2	48.9	-3.3↓
	CTasks	50.0	54.2	4.2↑	45.4	50.5	5.1↑	44.9	50.0	5.1↑	43.1	50.5	7.4⋆
Ter.	Validation	79.1	86.1	7.0⋆	77.0	87.4	10.4⋆	78.3	88.3	10.0⋆	78.4	91.3	12.9⋆
	VTasks	44.3	47.2	2.9↑	34.2	43.2	9.0⋆	42.0	47.9	5.9↑	41.2	32.6	-8.6×
	CTasks	31.5	39.9	8.4⋆	40.0	30.8	-9.2×	32.5	31.6	-0.9↓	37.6	35.7	-1.9↓
Qad.	Validation	79.7	82.0	2.3↑	76.3	80.3	4.0↑	75.2	80.1	4.9↑	79.7	86.3	6.6↑
	VTasks	21.0	23.9	2.9↑	32.7	33.3	0.6↑	24.6	30.0	5.4↑	29.2	23.7	-5.5↓
	CTasks	34.1	42.3	8.2⋆	10.9	30.2	**19.3**⋆	22.1	33.0	**10.9**⋆	23.1	27.6	4.5↑

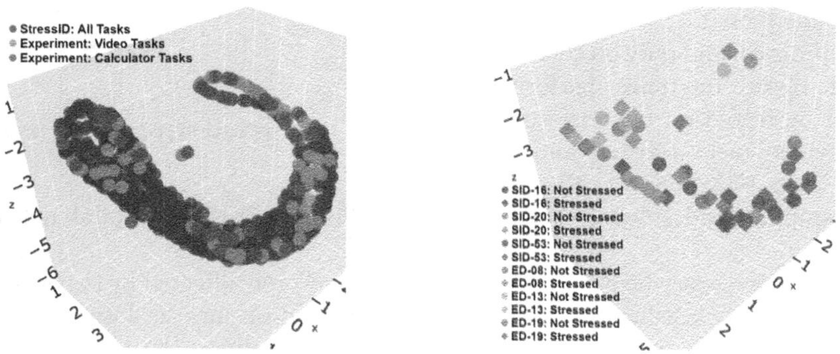

(a) All tasks grouping.

(b) All tasks, 6 subjects subset.

Fig. 2. t-SNE analysis on StressID (SID) and our experiment's data (ED).

4 Conclusion and Limitations

Though the authors recognize that generalization may be affected by the reduced sample size and the need for further tasks comparison to better discern the nature of UX-induced frustration, this report reveals the importance of label specificity on under-studied emotion recognition tasks. Reducing emotion ambiguity can achieve great improvements (19.3%) in difficult classification tasks such as 4-label classification, showing the potential of lightweight machine learning models for practical AUIs on the edge.

Acknowledgments. This study was funded by X (grant number Y).

Disclosure of Interests. The authors have no competing interests to declare that are relevant to the content of this article.

References

1. Chaptoukaev, H.: Stressid: a multimodal dataset for stress identification. In: Advances in Neural Information Processing Systems, vol. 36, pp. 29798–29811 (2023)
2. De León Aguilar, S., Matsuda, Y., Yasumoto, K.: Mobile augmented reality interface for instruction-based disaster preparedness guidelines. Sens. Mater. **36**(10), 4585–4606 (2024)
3. Heumader, P., Miesenberger, K., Murillo-Morales, T.: Adaptive User Interfaces for People with Cognitive Disabilities within the Easy Reading Framework. In: Miesenberger, K., Manduchi, R., Covarrubias Rodriguez, M., Peňáz, P. (eds.) ICCHP 2020. LNCS, vol. 12377, pp. 53–60. Springer, Cham (2020). https://doi.org/10.1007/978-3-030-58805-2_7
4. Jaiswal, D., Chatterjee, D., B s, M., Ramakrishnan, R.K., Pal, A.: GSR Based generic stress prediction system. In: Adjunct Proceedings of the 2023 ACM International Joint Conference on Pervasive and Ubiquitous Computing & the 2023 ACM International Symposium on Wearable Computing, pp. 433–438 (2023)
5. Liapis, A., Faliagka, E., Katsanos, C., Antonopoulos, C., Voros, N.: Detection of subtle stress episodes during UX evaluation: assessing the performance of the WESAD bio-signals dataset. In: Human-Computer Interaction, pp. 238–247. INTERACT '21 (2021)
6. Sin, J., Franz, L., Munteanu, R., Barbosa Neves, C., B.: Digital design marginalization: new perspectives on designing inclusive interfaces. In: Proceedings of the 2021 CHI Conference on Human Factors in Computing Systems, pp. 1–11 (2021)
7. Vasiljevas, M., Damaševičius, R., Maskeliūnas, R.: A human-adaptive model for user performance and fatigue evaluation during Gaze-tracking tasks. Electronics **12**(5) (2023)
8. Viviani, L., Liso, A., Craighero, L.: Mobile typing as a window into sensorimotor and cognitive function. Brain Sci. **15**(10) (2025)

A Study on Feasible AI-Based Dietary Messages: Perspectives from Lay Participants and Dietitians

Kaori Fujimura(✉), Tae Sato, Reiko Aruga, Kana Kodama, and Yurika Katagiri

Social Informatics Laboratories, NTT Inc., Kanagawa, Japan
kaori.fujimura@ntt.com

Abstract. Continuous dietary support improves lifestyle habits, but individualized dietary guidance from health professionals is difficult to scale. LLMs can generate personalized dietary messages; however, how such messages should be designed to fit users' everyday lives remains unclear.

This study compared feasibility-oriented and nutrition-focused dietary messages using an online questionnaire. In addition, to inform future improvements, interviews were conducted with both lay participants and experts to examine key considerations for generating dietary advice.

Questionnaire results showed no substantial differences between the two message types in questionnaire measures related to behavioral intention to act. Interviews with participants revealed factors that facilitated or hindered engagement with the messages, including alignment with personal intentions and everyday constraints such as work and household conditions. Interviews with dietitians identified risks and limitations of automatically generated dietary advice, including uncertainty in self-reported information, insufficient contextual understanding, and difficulties in prioritizing behavioral targets.

Keywords: LLMs · Dietary Message · Feasibility · Health Behavior Support

1 Introduction

Lifestyle modification is a key strategy for preventing metabolic syndrome and related chronic conditions [1, 2]. While continuous, individualized dietary guidance by health professionals is effective, such support is resource-intensive and difficult to scale in real-world settings [3]. As a result, user-facing digital tools often utilize automated feedback. However, as these tools tend to emphasize numerical indicators such as calories or nutrients [4], they may have limited capacity to reflect users' everyday routines.

Recent advances in large language models (LLMs) have enabled the generation of personalized health-related messages, including dietary advice. Previous studies have examined the quality, accuracy, and appropriateness of LLM-generated dietary content, highlighting both potential benefits and key limitations [5, 6]. However, less is known about how users perceive such messages in daily life, particularly in terms of whether they feel able or willing to act on the advice provided.

E. Vlahu-Gjorgievska et al. (Eds.): PERSUASIVE 2026, CCIS 2896, pp. 248–252, 2027.
https://doi.org/10.1007/978-3-032-27235-5_21

Prior qualitative research has identified characteristics of effective dietary guidance used by professionals, including attention to users' routines and constraints [7]. Drawing on these insights, feasibility has been proposed as a potentially important consideration in the design of LLM-generated dietary messages. In this study, feasibility is defined as the extent to which a dietary message can be enacted without substantially altering users' habitual cooking practices, food procurement, or time use, emphasizing continuity with existing routines rather than nutritional optimality.

Against this background, the present study examines how feasibility-oriented and nutrition-focused dietary messages generated by an LLM are received in everyday contexts. Specifically, we investigate (1) how feasibility-oriented dietary messages generated by an LLM are perceived, (2) what factors facilitate or hinder their practice in everyday contexts, and (3) what risks and limitations are identified by dietitians when such messages are generated automatically. Given the limited empirical evidence on how feasibility-oriented LLM-generated dietary messages are perceived in everyday life, this study adopts an exploratory approach. We tentatively hypothesized that feasibility-oriented messages would be perceived as more feasible and easier to integrate into everyday routines than nutrition-focused messages.

2 Method

2.1 Participants

We recruited 210 adult participants living in Japan who were interested in improving their dietary habits, with no prior experience receiving professional dietary guidance. Data from 193 participants were included in the analysis after excluding incomplete responses. In addition, six licensed dietitians with active professional experience participated in expert evaluations and interviews.

2.2 Procedure

Participants completed an online pre-questionnaire including items on food preferences, dietary dislikes, habitual cooking methods, and typical time spent on meal preparation, and submitted three-day self-reported food logs. Based on these inputs, an LLM generated short motivational dietary messages. All messages were reviewed by dietitians to ensure nutritional appropriateness. Participants then evaluated message impressions via an online post-questionnaire, and 20 participants were selected for semi-structured follow-up interviews conducted about two weeks later. Dietitians also participated in semi-structured interviews focusing on professional concerns and design risks. This study was conducted from February to March 2025.

2.3 Message Design and Prompt Implementation

We implemented a prompt-based LLM approach for the message generation. To isolate design effects, both the feasibility-oriented and conventional conditions shared common constraints, including message length, tone, and targeted meal occasions; only the design focus was varied. Both conditions aimed to support dietary improvement toward health goals by addressing nutritional balance; however, the feasibility-oriented condition prioritized ease of implementation in everyday life, even if nutritional balance was only partially improved.

In the feasibility-oriented condition, feasibility was implemented using four principles: (1) frequently consumed foods were treated as reflecting users' preferences and availability; (2) maintaining familiar procurement methods reduces effort; (3) maintaining familiar cooking methods leverages existing skills; and (4) keeping preparation time similar avoids additional time burden. These principles were incorporated into a fixed prompt template. Based on participants' food logs and pre-questionnaire responses, the LLM generated short motivational messages in the local language, while preserving the participant's staple food common in Japan (e.g., rice, bread, noodles). In contrast, the conventional condition prioritized nutritional balance as the primary design goal.

3 Results

3.1 Questionnaire Results

To examine how feasibility-oriented dietary messages generated by an LLM were perceived, questionnaire ratings on clarity, perceived feasibility, willingness to try, and perceived effectiveness were compared with those for conventional nutrition-focused messages. No substantial differences were observed between the two message types across these items.

3.2 Findings from Participant Interviews

To identify factors that facilitated or hindered the enactment of the LLM-generated dietary messages in everyday life, semi-structured interviews with participants were analyzed. Some participants enacted the LLM-generated dietary messages when suggested changes aligned with their existing intentions, preferences, or personal health concerns, particularly when framed as reductions rather than prohibitions. For example, one participant noted that reduction-oriented suggestions felt more feasible than being told to completely avoid certain foods.

In contrast, non-enactment was attributed to mismatches with everyday contexts, such as unconsidered preferences, increased cost or effort, time constraints, family-related constraints, and a lack of concreteness or novelty.

3.3 Findings from Dietitian Interviews

To examine the risks and limitations of automatically generated dietary messages as identified by dietitians, semi-structured interviews with dietitians were analyzed. These interviews revealed several issues related to LLM-generated dietary messages. For example, dietitians noted that when self-reported information does not accurately reflect actual dietary intake, the LLM may generate messages based on users' subjective perceptions and overlook necessary dietary improvements. They also noted that, in the absence of contextual information such as physical activity levels, messages may include inappropriate or overly confident recommendations regarding portion size or nutritional balance. In addition, dietitians emphasized the difficulty of prioritizing behavioral targets when multiple dietary issues coexist.

4 Discussion

The lack of substantial differences in subjective evaluations may be attributed to the fact that messages in both conditions were designed as brief motivational prompts and shared basic considerations aimed at minimizing the burden of enactment. In addition, the operationalization of feasibility in this study was limited to selected elements related to food choice and cooking effort, and did not directly address broader living conditions such as food prices or household constraints. Taken together, these findings suggest that, although the feasibility-oriented prompt was designed to leverage users' existing food choices and cooking practices, additional contextual inputs may be required to further improve practical feasibility.

Findings from the dietitian interviews suggest that, regarding the risks and constraints of automatically generated dietary advice, the handling of uncertainty in self-reported information and the prioritization of behavioral targets when multiple dietary changes are required are important considerations for appropriate dietary message generation.

This study identifies key considerations for the design of feasibility-oriented dietary messages and directions for future research. Future work should explore and evaluate persuasive message generation approaches that facilitate dietary behavior change by better accounting for user context and adaptively adjusting message content, level of detail, and the presentation of behavioral priorities.

Finally, this study has several limitations, including its reliance on self-reported food logs, a short-term evaluation of message impressions, and the inclusion of participants only from Japan, which may limit the generalizability of the findings.

References

1. Grundy, S.M.: Metabolic syndrome pandemic. Arterioscler. Thromb. Vasc. Biol. **28**(4), 629–636 (2008)
2. Jamali, Z., et al.: Metabolic syndrome: a population-based study of prevalence and risk factors. Sci. Rep. **14**, 3987 (2024)
3. Munakata, M., et al.: Repeated counselling improves the antidiabetic effects of limited individualized lifestyle guidance in metabolic syndrome: J-STOP-METS final results. Hypertens. Res. **34**, 612–616 (2011)
4. Briggs, T., et al.: Feature availability comparison in free and paid versions of popular smartphone weight management applications. J. Nutr. Educ. Behav. **53**(9), 732–741 (2021)
5. Liao, L.-L., Chang, L.-C., Lai, I.-J.: Assessing the Quality of ChatGPT's Dietary Advice for College Students from Dietitians' Perspectives. Nutrients **16**(12), 1939 (2024)
6. Oh, Y., et al.: Designing relational AI-powered digital health coaching for chronic disease prevention and management. In: Duffy, V.G. (ed.) Digital Human Modeling and Applications in Health, Safety, Ergonomics and Risk Management, LNCS, vol. 14029, pp. 1–13. Springer, Cham (2023)

7. Fujimura, K., et al.: Identifying Characteristics of Dietary Guidance Methods Through Qualitative Analysis. In: Stephanidis, C., Antona, M., Ntoa, S., Salvendy, G. (eds.) HCI International 2025 Posters. HCII 2025. Communications in Computer and Information Science, vol. 2522, pp. 260–268. Springer, Cham (2025). https://doi.org/10.1007/978-3-031-94150-4_27

UI Design and Evaluation of a Real-Time Intervention System in Customer Service

Toi Hirakawa(✉), Kazuhiro Shidara, Sho Iwasaki, Takahiro Yoshioka, and Takeshi Konno

Fujitsu Research, Fujitsu Limited, Kanagawa, Japan
{hirakawa.toi,s-kazuhiro,iwasaki.sho,y.takahiro, konno.takeshi}@fujitsu.com

Abstract. In customer service scenarios, communication skills aimed at building relationships with customers and mitigating dissatisfaction are required. We propose a real-time customer-service support system that presents guidance at multiple levels of detail to simultaneously support in-the-moment responses and foster reflection-in-action for longer-term skill improvement. While qualitative analysis based on semi-structured interviews revealed positive effects from in-dialogue reflection and the importance of real-time interventions, the analysis results also highlighted future challenges in addressing cognitive load.

Keywords: customer service · UI prototyping · UI/UX evaluation · semi-structured interviews · real-time intervention

1 Introduction

In customer service dialogues, there is a high demand for empathic responses aimed at resolving customer dissatisfaction or anger. The escalation of such customer behavior has become a critical social issue due to its negative impact on companies and employees [1,3]. However, it is also known that effective responses can manage customer emotions and restore satisfaction [4,6]. Therefore, improving or supporting employee skills could reduce the negative effects from customers.

While role-playing training systems with agent interaction provide advantages such as practical training and reducing personal cost for education, learning retention tends to be limited [5,8]. Furthermore, there is a tendency for human intervention to be required as situations escalate. Therefore, from the perspective of protecting employees with unestablished skills, such as novice staff, real-time intervention during actual customer interactions is necessary, not just pre-training.

To address these challenges, we aim to develop a system that not only supports employees via real-time intervention but also fosters reflection-in-action [7] during their interactions. In this study, we develop a UI prototype and conduct a qualitative analysis to obtain design implications for the completion of this real-time intervention system. Our research questions are as follows:

E. Vlahu-Gjorgievska et al. (Eds.): PERSUASIVE 2026, CCIS 2896, pp. 253–257, 2027.
https://doi.org/10.1007/978-3-032-27235-5_22

- **RQ1:** What features are required to foster skill enhancement via reflection during customer interactions?
- **RQ2:** How should features be designed for appropriate real-time response support?

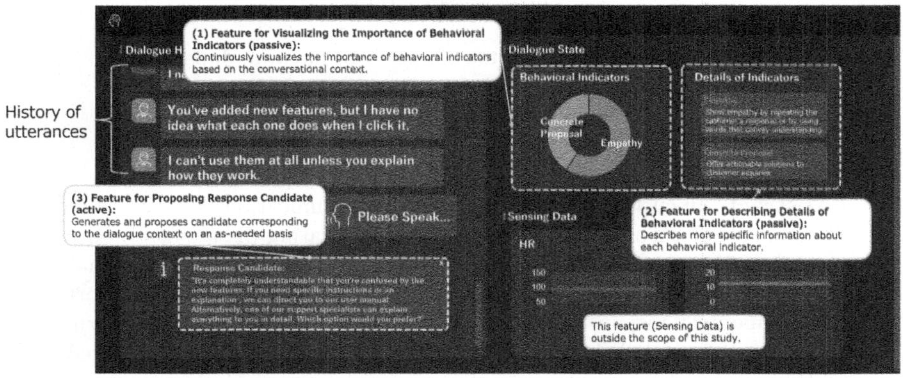

Fig. 1. Screen example of the developed UI prototype.

2 The UI Prototyping

Figure 1 shows a screen example of the UI prototype. This is based on the intervention designs proposed by Chen et al. [2], and we validated the features by augmenting our previously developed role-playing training system. They focused on the role of reflection and explored how to foster meaningful in-meeting reflection using two different intervention timings: passive intervention (providing intervention continuously) and active intervention (providing intervention as needed). Although these interventions are seldom discussed in the context of existing support systems for customer service, we incorporated them into this prototyping, focusing on performance enhancement through in-dialogue reflection.

The passive intervention in this UI prototype has two parts: a feature for an importance visualization for behavioral indicators (see (1) in Fig. 1) and a feature of describing their details (see (2) in Fig. 1). The importance visualization feature shows recommended actions for each dialogue scene. As shown in Fig. 2, the important behavioral indicators change as the dialogue progresses, enabling users to quickly identify which actions to include in their speech. The feature for describing details of the behavioral indicators provides a message that shows what kind of action corresponds to displayed indicator. By combining the importance visualization with this feature, users can formulate more detailed responses. Both the importance indicators and these descriptive messages are retrieved from a set that is manually predefined for each dialogue situation.

Active intervention provides a more direct and strong intervention for employees by presenting a concrete response candidate as needed (see (3) in Fig. 1). Users can refer to the candidate from this feature when they are unsure how to reply or lack confidence. However, because the candidate is not presented every time, this helps to prevent over-reliance on the system. The response candidate is dynamically generated by GPT-4o based on a prompt containing the dialogue history, current behavioral indicators, and response examples.

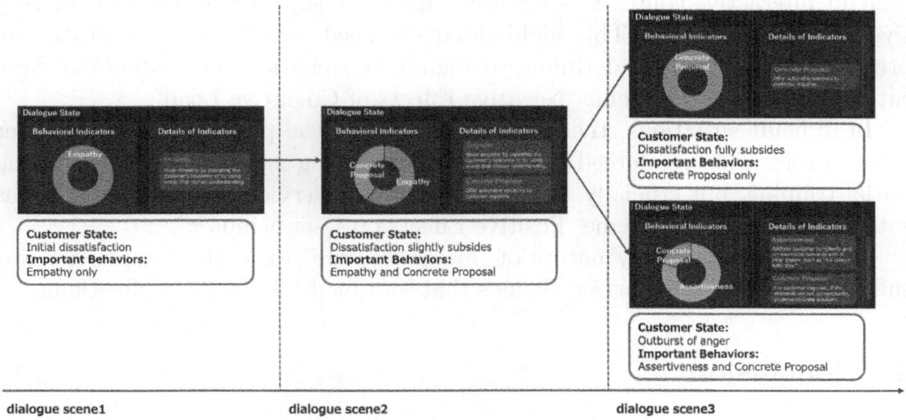

Fig. 2. Example Progression of Passive Interventions Across Dialogue Scenes.

3 Qualitative Analysis

To evaluate the developed UI prototype and verify RQs, we conducted a semi-structured interviews and thematic analysis. The study involved a scenario where novice operators handled a customer complaint. Participants consisted of six individuals (ages 20-40) with no professional experience in customer service. This study was reviewed and approved by the Research Ethics Committee of Toyo University (Approval ID: P240044).

RQ1: What features are required to foster skill enhancement via reflection during customer interactions?

Some participants reflected on their past utterances based on the proposed responses. This in-dialogue reflection led to new insights. Moreover, we observed participants extracting utterance examples of target behavioral indicators from the response candidates and adopted them into their own utterances. This finding reveals the potential to facilitate insights that transcend the explicit content of the response candidates themselves. These comments were categorized under the theme "Positive Influence of In-Dialogue Awareness".

Conversely, we also identified factors that impede user reflection. Specifically, if users perceived a gap between their own thoughts and a suggestion, they tended to recite the response candidate without internalizing its meaning. These cases were categorized under the theme "Factors That Impede Reflection."

RQ2: How should features be designed for appropriate real-time response support?

While the intervention had beneficial effects on users, it was also found to have negative effects due to cognitive load. Specifically, when the descriptions of behavioral indicators or the proposed responses were lengthy, the user's cognitive processing time increased and led to response latency. Additionally, in difficult interactive contexts, some users lost the composure to refer to the passive intervention at all. This highlighted the need for careful consideration of presentation methods and timing in high-load scenarios. These findings were categorized under the theme "Negative Effects of Cognitive Load".

In difficult situations, the system also showed the potential to reduce user stress levels. This reinforced the need for providing support, not just during initial training, but crucially, during live customer service interactions, and was categorized under the theme "Positive Effects on User Mindset".

Given the exploratory nature of this qualitative study, the sample size was sufficient to identify recurring themes that informed UI design implications.

4 Conclusion

In this study, we developed and evaluated a UI prototype to derive design implications for a real-time intervention system aimed at supporting customer service employees and enhancing their response skills. Through qualitative analysis, we showed that real-time interventions can foster reflection-in-action and have the potential to reduce user stress during challenging interactions, while also revealing challenges related to cognitive load. These findings suggest that real-time support systems should balance the provision of actionable guidance with careful consideration of information volume and timing.

In future work, we plan to enhance the system by exploring UI designs that further mitigate cognitive load and by conducting quantitative evaluations to examine the long-term effects on skill acquisition. We also aim to evaluate the proposed approach with experienced customer service operators in real-world settings to further validate its applicability and effectiveness.

References

1. Bamfo, B.A., Dogbe, C.S.K., Mingle, H.: Abusive customer behaviour and frontline employee turnover intentions in the banking industry: The mediating role of employee satisfaction. Cogent Bus. Manag. **5**(1), 1522753 (2018)
2. Chen, X., Tankelevitch, L., Vanukuru, R., Scott, A.E., Panda, P., Rintel, S.: Are we on track? AI-assisted active and passive goal reflection during meetings. In: Proceedings of the 2025 CHI Conference on Human Factors in Computing Systems, pp. 1–22 (2025). https://doi.org/10.1145/3706598.3714052

3. Chung, H., et al.: A threat of customer incivility and job stress to hotel employee retention: do supervisor and co-worker supports reduce turnover rates? Int. J. Environ. Res. Public Health **18**(12), 6616 (2021)
4. Herhausen, D., Grewal, L., Cummings, K.H., Roggeveen, A.L., Villarroel Ordenes, F., Grewal, D.: Complaint de-escalation strategies on social media. J. Mark. **87**(2), 210–231 (2023)
5. Otsuki, M., Okuma, T.: Development and evaluation of a restaurant virtual reality training system for enhancing awareness and priority-setting skills. Sci. Rep. **15**(1), 18673 (2025)
6. Roschk, H., Kaiser, S.: The nature of an apology: an experimental study on how to apologize after a service failure. Mark. Lett. **24**(3), 293–309 (2013)
7. Schön, D.A.: The Reflective Practitioner: How Professionals Think in Action. Routledge (2017)
8. Wiboolyasarin, W., Wiboolyasarin, K., Tiranant, P., Jinowat, N., Boonyakitanont, P.: Ai-driven chatbots in second language education: a systematic review of their efficacy and pedagogical implications. Ampersand **14**, 100224 (2025)

Anthropomorphic Design for User Tolerance to System Errors in Behavior Change Systems

Yiduan Hu[1(✉)], Bipin Indurkhya[2], and Kaori Fujinami[1]

[1] Tokyo University of Agriculture and Technology, Tokyo 184-8588, Japan
s233733r@st.go.tuat.ac.jp
[2] Jagiellonian University, Krakow 30-060, Poland

Abstract. We present a design approach that combines anthropomorphic representation with vulnerability expressions to improve users' tolerance to perceived system errors: Uncertainty is communicated implicitly through agent behavior, allowing users to recognize system limitations in a socially meaningful way. The approach was implemented in a waste sorting behavior change system and deployed in a real-world setting to observe user interaction under imperfect sensing conditions. This study presents a vulnerability-oriented agent feedback perspective for supporting user engagement under inherent uncertainty.

Keywords: Anthropomorphism · Human-agent interaction · Behavior change · Human-computer interaction · System error-tolerance

1 Introduction

In deploying behavior change systems in real-world environments, perceptual and decision errors are unavoidable, posing challenges to system stability and user experience. Such errors erode user trust, diminish motivation to participate, and ultimately result in user attrition [1]. Previous research has explored various fault-tolerant design strategies to mitigate the negative impact of system errors: 1) By improving user trust through increased system transparency and comprehensibility by providing explanatory feedback to help users understand the reasoning and uncertainty of the system [5]. 2) By emphasizing socio-emotional design, using anthropomorphic representations and social behaviors to elicit empathy and encourage more tolerant interpretations of system imperfections [3]. 3) studies in human–computer interaction suggest that acknowledging errors or expressing apologies after system failures can help restore trust and sustain user engagement [2]. Based on these findings, we propose an approach to combine anthropomorphic representations with explicit expressions of uncertainty and vulnerability. It is implemented in a real-world behavior change system for waste sorting. This paper focuses on system design and implementation, while field deployment details will be demonstrated in the demo.

E. Vlahu-Gjorgievska et al. (Eds.): PERSUASIVE 2026, CCIS 2896, pp. 258–262, 2027.
https://doi.org/10.1007/978-3-032-27235-5_23

2 Proposed Anthropomorphic Method

We propose using anthropomorphism as a medium to articulate uncertainty and vulnerability. Incorporated into behavioral change systems, anthropomorphic agents communicate internal states via a combination of textual indicators (e.g. confident assertions, hesitant phrasing, or confused expressions), facial expressions, and body postures. This enables users to intuitively interpret the system's confidence and uncertainty. The implementation of this approach involves the structuring of the agent's anthropomorphic expressions into a five-stage confidence level system, as shown in Table 1. Each stage corresponds to a distinct level of system confidence and perceived uncertainty.

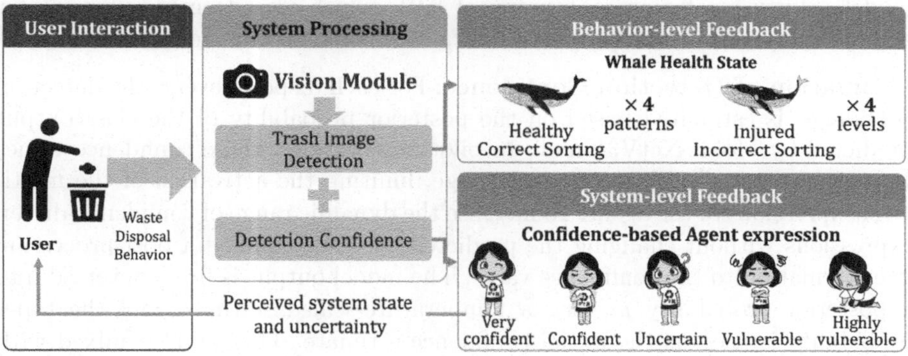

Fig. 1. System overview.

Table 1. Five-level agent state design

Agent State	Expression	User Perception
Very confident	Energetic motion, positive face	Reliable
Confident	Stable posture, neutral face	Dependable
Uncertain	Reduced motion, puzzled face	Ambiguous
Vulnerable	Slouched posture, worried face	Fallible
Highly vulnerable	Drooping posture, distressed face	Highly uncertain

3 System Design and Implementation

A waste sorting behavior change system was designed that incorporates an anthropomorphic feedback design, as shown in Fig. 1. Under unavoidable detection errors and environmental uncertainties, it explores how system communication methods can enhance users' error tolerance, trust, and sustained participation willingness, thereby promoting long-term waste sorting practices.

Trash Image Detection: We used MobileNetV3-Small [4], a lightweight convolution neural network fine-tuned for image classification in a real-world interactive setting. It is implemented with a standard deep learning framework and is adapted from a pretrained network to support efficient on-device inference. The training data set combines the open-source TrashNet dataset [6] with images collected in real environments. All images are re-labeled into four classes: combustible waste (1087 images), plastic waste (1097 images), background, and hand. Background and hand images are explicitly included during training to suppress false positives and reduce misclassification caused by environmental clutter and user interaction artifacts.

The model is fine-tuned on this dataset using supervised learning while retaining the lightweight architecture of MobileNetV3-Small. The resulting model achieved a training accuracy of 0.91, which was deemed sufficient for stable deployment in the proposed interactive behavior change system.

Estimation of Detection Confidence: For each disposal event, the detection confidence is estimated based on the posterior probability of the class output predicted by MobileNetV3-Small. In pilot observations, these confidence values were concentrated within a narrow range, limiting the activation of the multi-level expressions of the agent. To increase the dynamic range of confidence-driven expressions without changing the predicted class, we applied a post-processing transformation to the confidence value. The model output is first converted into a posterior probability p using a temperature-scaled softmax, and the top-1 probability is used as the initial confidence estimate. This value is mixed with a sample drawn from a Beta distribution and lightly perturbed, producing a widening confidence range that is used for system-level feedback.

$$p = \mathrm{clip}\left(\left((1-\alpha)b + \alpha \max_k \mathrm{softmax}(\mathbf{z}/T)\right) \cdot u,\ p_{\min},\ 1 \right), \tag{1}$$

where $b \sim \mathrm{Beta}(0.5, 0.5)$ and $u \sim \mathrm{Uniform}(0.9, 1.1)$.

These transformations expand the dynamic range of confidence values while preserving the predicted class, allowing more expressive and stable confidence-driven agent behaviors. This transformed confidence was used only for mapping to agent expressions at the interaction layer.

Behavior-Level Feedback: Behavior-level feedback expresses sorting outcomes through the whale's health states, with correct actions triggering randomized healthy behaviors and incorrect actions increasing injury severity across 4 levels.

System-Level Feedback: The confidence in detection is reflected in the expressive behavior of the agent to convey the internal certainty and uncertainty of the system using non-verbal intuitive cues. The system implicitly communicates confidence by adjusting the visual expressions and motion patterns of the agent. The transformed confidence value p is discretized into multiple confidence levels, each corresponding to a distinct agent state, as shown in Table 2.

Table 2. Mapping between detection confidence and agent states

Agent State	Confidence Value Range
Very Confident	$0.85 \leq p \leq 1.00$
Confident	$0.70 \leq p < 0.85$
Uncertain	$0.55 \leq p < 0.70$
Vulnerable	$0.40 \leq p < 0.55$
Highly Vulnerable	$0.25 \leq p < 0.40$

The minimum confidence value of 0.25 reflects the theoretical lower bound of the posterior probability given four classification categories. These confidence ranges were designed to evenly distribute agent state transitions across real-world interactions, enabling visibly distinct expressions of confidence and vulnerability.

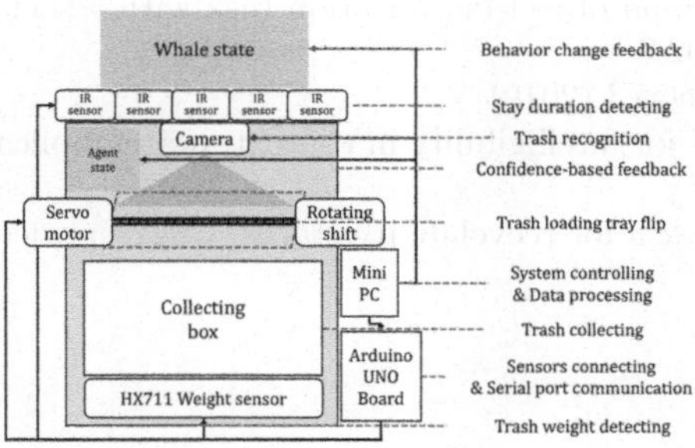

Fig. 2. System components.

Fig. 3. Deployed prototype.

Physical Implementation: The system is implemented as an interactive trash can that integrates sensing, computation, actuation, and feedback into a single physical unit. Figure 2 illustrates the hardware configuration and functional components, and Fig. 3 shows the system deployed in a real-world environment. The camera is positioned above the loading tray inside the trash can lid to capture images to recognize trash and estimate confidence. A servo motor controls a rotating tray mechanism that physically guides trash into the collection box. Multiple infrared (IR) sensors are placed around the system to detect user presence and estimate stay duration, which are recorded to analyze user behavior.

4 Conclusion

We presented a field-deployed anthropomorphic waste sorting system that addresses unavoidable uncertainty in real-world behavior change scenarios. Instead of focusing on eliminating system errors, we examined how adaptive expressions of confidence and vulnerability influence user interaction when errors occur. This study highlights vulnerability-oriented anthropomorphic design as a promising complement to accuracy-driven approaches in behavior change systems. Recognizing uncertainty through system-level feedback can foster greater user tolerance and support continued interaction in everyday environments. In future work, extended field studies and detailed analyzes will be reported.

Acknowledgments. This work was supported by JST SPRING, Grant Number JPMJSP2116.

References

1. Dietvorst, B.J., Simmons, J.P., Massey, C.: Algorithm aversion: people erroneously avoid algorithms after seeing them err. J. Exp. Psychol. Gen. **144**, 114–126 (2015)
2. Fogg, B.: A behavior model for persuasive design. Persuasive (2009)
3. Frijns, H., Hirschmanner, M., Sienkiewicz, B., Hönig, P., Indurkhya, B., Vincze, M.: Human-in-the-loop error detection in an object organization task with a social robot. Front. Robot. AI **11**, 1356827 (2024)
4. Howard, A., et al.: Searching for mobilenetv3 (2019)
5. Lim, B.Y., Dey, A.K.: Assessing demand for intelligibility in context-aware applications, pp. 195–204. CHI (2009)
6. Yang, M., Thung, G.: Classification of trash for recyclability status. CS229 project report **2016**(1), 3 (2016)

Content-Based Modeling for Collaboration of YouTuber

Yun-Wen Huang(✉), Shih-Yi Chien, and Fang Yu

Department of Management Information Systems, National Chengchi University, Taipei, Taiwan
{114356020,sychien,yuf}@nccu.edu.tw

Abstract. Influencer marketing, such as collaborations with YouTubers, has become a central strategy in digital advertising. However, selecting effective collaboration partners that lead to commercial success remains challenging due to the limited interpretability of existing computational approaches. While prior studies focus primarily on brand-influencer matching, the resulting black-box models provide little transparency and limited explanations for why certain collaborations succeed. Additionally, influencer-influencer collaborations, despite their increasing prevalence, remain difficult to evaluate in terms of their potential business impact. To address these limitations, this study proposes an explainable, content-centric framework that models YouTubers as persuasive communicators. Grounded in advertising and influencer marketing theory, we extract a set of interpretable attributes from video transcripts. These attributes characterize creators and serve as predictive features for estimating collaboration effectiveness.

Keywords: Influencer Marketing · Collaboration Recommendation · Explainable AI

1 Introduction

Influencer marketing has become a central strategy in digital advertising, yet selecting effective collaboration partners remains challenging due to limited understanding of the factors driving collaboration success (Pan et al., 2025). This challenge affects both brands and influencers, who increasingly rely on collaborations to sustain audience engagement, highlighting the need for systematic and interpretable decision support. Existing computational studies mainly focus on influencer identification and brand–influencer matching using deep learning models, despite strong predictive performance, they offer limited interpretability and overlook contextual factors (Gui et al., 2025). Moreover, research remains largely brand-centric, with limited attention to influencers as brands and to influencer–influencer collaborations, which have been shown to exert distinct effects on audience perceptions (Thomas et al., 2024). To address these gaps, this study proposes an explainable, content-centric framework that models YouTubers as persuasive communicators. By extracting interpretable, theory-grounded attributes from video transcripts, the framework supports transparent creator profiling and explainable collaboration recommendation, extending from brand-sponsored collaborations to influencer–influencer content co-creation.

E. Vlahu-Gjorgievska et al. (Eds.): PERSUASIVE 2026, CCIS 2896, pp. 263–267, 2027.
https://doi.org/10.1007/978-3-032-27235-5_24

2 Related Work

Since the research is still in progress, here we focus on key feature-based studies of influencer-sponsored content that inform the methodological design of this work.

2.1 Theoretical Background of Influencer Marketing

Influencer effectiveness has been extensively examined through message source and audience perception frameworks. Ohanian (1990) conceptualizes source credibility in terms of attractiveness, trustworthiness, and expertise, demonstrating its influence on advertising attitudes and intentions. Building on this, Hwang and Jeong (2016) examine strategies of sponsorship disclosure and show that simple disclosure reduces effectiveness of persuasion compared to no disclosure or disclosures emphasizing honest opinions, highlighting how disclosure form shapes audience responses. from audience perspective, Ducoffe (1995) defines advertising value through informativeness, entertainment, and credibility, providing a widely adopted framework for operationalizing perceived quality of advertising. effectiveness of advertising further depends on product characteristics: search products, whose key attributes can be objectively evaluated prior to purchase, benefit from direct expressions, whereas experience products, which require consumption to form subjective evaluations, are more responsive to metaphorical and entertaining expressions (Chen et al., 2021; Yan et al., 2016; Yang et al., 2022). Synthesizing prior work, Pan et al. (2025) conduct a large-scale meta-analysis of effectiveness of influencer marketing and summarize post, follower, and influencer characteristics as core determinants of the effectiveness of influencer marketing.

2.2 Technique for Automated Feature Extraction

Recent studies demonstrate the feasibility of automated feature extraction from social media content. Munaro et al. (2024) analyze transcripts of YouTube video using LIWC and Empath, identifying distinct clusters of linguistic style that differentiate influencer's communication style. Complementing transcript-based approaches, Stracqualursi and Agati (2025) apply machine learning and NLP techniques to YouTube comments to infer personality traits of audience, illustrating how textual interaction data can support the work of creator and follower profiling. Beyond text, multimodal approaches leverage vision–language models and prompt engineering to automatically label semantic and stylistic video attributes (Liu et al., 2025). Together, these studies motivate the use of language models and multimodal techniques for scalable, content-based feature extraction for analytics of influencer.

3 Methodology

3.1 Data Collection

This study uses video content in YouTube as primary data source. To account for potential cultural differences, we focus on Taiwanese YouTubers and select creators based on 2025 subscriber rankings. The top-ranked channels are included in the dataset. Data were collected using YouTube Data API v3[1], covering both channel-level and video-level information. Audio tracks of videos are downloaded using yt-dlp[2] Python package, and then transcribed into subtitle by Whisper[3].

3.2 Attribute Construction of Video and Youtuber

Consistent with prior research, video transcripts provide rich linguistic signals for distinguishing creator styles. We therefore derive explainable attributes primarily from transcripts through a two-stage process. First, Videos containing sponsored segments are first identified using a rule-based keyword approach (e.g., discount, promotion, sponsorship related words). More advanced methods will be explored in future work. Second, sponsored segments are automatically segmented using large language models (LLMs) with prompt engineering. We compare Qwen3-4B[4] and Gemini 2.5 Flash[5], and select Gemini 2.5 Flash due to its higher accuracy and efficiency. After prompt refinement, the model achieves near-perfect accuracy on the current test set. Transcripts are then divided into sponsored and non-sponsored parts. Guided by determinants of effectiveness of marketing summarized by Pan et al. (2025) and linguistic features identified by Munaro et al. (2024), we construct these features as attributes of video and creator. Video-level attributes are further aggregated to construct creator-level attributes as creator profiles. The set of attributes is summarized in Tables 1 and 2.

Table 1. Attributes of Youtuber (In Progress).

Attribute	Description
Positioning	Primary theme of videos
Professionalism	Perceived expertise and domain knowledge
Attractiveness	Followers' sense of belonging in online communities
Influence	Number of followers
YouTuber–Product	Alignment between Youtuber and sponsored product

Following prior work, products are categorized as search or experience products based on pre-purchase evaluability. Quality of advertisement is assessed through informativeness for search products and value of entertainment for experience products.

1 YouTube Data API v3 (2026). Retrieved from: https://developers.google.com/youtube/v3.
2 yt-dlp (2026). Retrieved from: https://github.com/yt-dlp/yt-dlp.
3 Whisper (2026). Retrieved from: https://github.com/openai/whisper.
4 Qwen3-4B (2026). Retrieved from: https://huggingface.co/Qwen/Qwen3-4B.
5 Gemini 2.5 Flash (2026). Retrieved from: https://docs.cloud.google.com/vertex-ai/generative-ai/docs/models/gemini/2-5-flash.

Table 2. Attributes of Video (In Progress).

Attribute	Description
Topic	Wikipedia references and YouTube's official categories
Interactivity	Q&A, polls, comment discussions or related keywords
Disclosure Type	Simple or Sincere personal
Informativeness	Detailed explanation and evaluation
Entertainment	Use of humor and storytelling technique

3.3 Collaboration Recommendation

Based on the constructed attributes, collaboration recommendation is formulated by modeling attributes of YouTuber as independent variables and quality of advertisement as dependent variables. This component is currently under development. In future work, we will keep exploring the appropriate models for recommendation in this scenario and extend the framework beyond sponsored collaborations to non-sponsored content co-creation. Since collaboration outcomes are unobserved prior to execution, we may leverage vision–language models (VLMs) to generate hypothetical collaborative content, with user ratings serving as ground-truth values for evaluating the quality of our recommendation.

Disclosure of Interests. The author(s) declares no competing interests relevant to the content of this article.

References

Chen, P., Hitt, L.M., Hong, Y., Wu, S.: Measuring product type and purchase uncertainty with online product ratings: a theoretical model and empirical application. Inf. Syst. Res. **32**(4), 1470–1489 (2021)

Ducoffe, R.H.: How consumers assess the value of advertising. J. Curr. Iss. Res. Adv. **17**(1), 1–18 (1995)

Gui, H., Bertaglia, T., Goanta, C., Spanakis, G.: Computational Studies in Influencer Marketing: A Systematic Literature Review. arXiv preprint arXiv:2506.14602 (2025)

Hwang, Y., Jeong, S.H.: "This is a sponsored blog post, but all opinions are my own": The effects of sponsorship disclosure on responses to sponsored blog posts. Comput. Hum. Behav. **62**, 528–535 (2016)

Liu, H., et al.: Multi-Modal Video Feature Extraction for Popularity Prediction. arXiv preprint arXiv:2501.01422 (2025)

Munaro, A.C., Barcelos, R.H., Maffezzolli, E.C.F., Rodrigues, J.P.S., Paraiso, E.C.: Does your style engage? Linguistic styles of influencers and digital consumer engagement on YouTube. Comput. Hum. Behav. **156**, 108217 (2024)

Ohanian, R.: Construction and validation of a scale to measure celebrity endorsers' perceived expertise, trustworthiness, and attractiveness. J. Advert. **19**(3), 39–52 (1990)

Pan, M., Blut, M., Ghiassaleh, A., Lee, Z.W.: Influencer marketing effectiveness: A meta-analytic review. J. Acad. Mark. Sci. **53**(1), 52–78 (2025)

Stracqualursi, L., Agati, P.: Predicting MBTI personality of YouTube users. Sci. Rep. **15**(1), 7221 (2025)

Thomas, V.L., Fowler, K., Taheran, F.: How social media influencer collaborations are perceived by consumers. Psychol. Mark. **41**(1), 168–183 (2024)

Yan, Q., et al.: Effects of product portfolios and recommendation timing in the efficiency of personalized recommendation. J. Consum. Behav. **15**(6), 516–526 (2016)

Yang, Q., Liu, S., Li, Y., Kang, H.: A matching study on the influence of advertised information expression and product type on consumer purchase intention. Front. Psychol. **13**, 859959 (2022)

Self Mirroring Twins: Empowering Proactive Behavior Transformation with Your Digital Self

Tetsunari Inamura(✉)

Tamagawa University, Machida, Japan
inamura@ieee.org

Abstract. Persuasive systems for behavior change often speak from an external "coach" stance, which can undermine autonomy and elicit psychological reactance. We propose *Self-Mirroring Twins* (SeMT): a stance-shifting virtual counterpart that is intentionally "me-like yet not identical" and persuades through self-observation rather than instruction. SeMT alternates between (i) *slightly-better action demonstrations* that remain attainable and (ii) *safe, minor failures* that invite users to notice, compare, and self-correct—a form of self-coaching. This paper contributes (1) an operationalized concept of *stance distance*, defined as a continuum from self-like to other-like representations, and *action gap*, defined as the discrepancy between the user's current action and the demonstrated action, (2) a concrete VR-based training instantiation for sports-like motor skills, and (3) a study protocol to evaluate persuasiveness in terms of performance change, self-initiated corrections, self-efficacy, agency, and reactance.

Keywords: Behavior change · Virtual reality · Self-coaching · Agency

1 Introduction

Digital interventions for behavior change have historically relied on extrinsic incentives, one-shot nudges, or conversational advice from an external agent. However, externally imposed guidance can reduce perceived autonomy and trigger reactance, which harms sustained engagement and long-term change [2]. We argue that durable change is more plausibly supported by an intrinsically driven process centered on *metacognition*: noticing one's own state, comparing alternatives, and choosing corrective actions.

We propose *Self-Mirroring Twins* (SeMT), a virtual counterpart of the user that strategically blends self-like and other-like qualities. SeMT is *not* a coach that tells users what to do. Instead, it persuades via *action presentation*: showing a controlled "version of me" that is either slightly better (to inspire attainable progress) or slightly worse in a safe way to provoke self-correction. This stance is motivated by evidence that moderate discrepancy between partners

E. Vlahu-Gjorgievska et al. (Eds.): PERSUASIVE 2026, CCIS 2896, pp. 268–272, 2027.
https://doi.org/10.1007/978-3-032-27235-5_25

can increase effort in cooperative contexts (the Köhler discrepancy effect) and has been leveraged in health-related partnered exergames [4] [3]. SeMT aims to make such discrepancy controllable, personal, and autonomy-supportive.

This paper focuses on a single, evaluable instantiation: VR-based motor-skill micro-improvement (sports-like training). We contribute:

1. Operational definitions of *stance distance* and *action gap* for a self-mirroring persuasive agent.
2. Two action-presentation strategies: *slightly-better demonstrations* and *safe-failure countermodels*, each linked to measurable outcomes.
3. A concrete study protocol to evaluate persuasiveness via behavioral change and psychological factors such as self-efficacy, sense of agency and so on.

2 Background: Why "Me-But-Not-Me" Can Persuade

People can experience their own reflection as both self and not-self: an ambivalent boundary that persists beyond childhood [7]. SeMT leverages this "Me-But-Not-Me" tension as a *productive discrepancy*: if the displayed self is identical to the internal self-model, no change is invited; if it is too different, the user may reject it. Therefore, SeMT requires control of (i) how self-like the counterpart feels and (ii) how far the shown actions deviate from current behavior.

Prior self-dialogue systems in VR have demonstrated that "self with self" conversations can support counseling-like reflection [6]. SeMT differs by emphasizing *co-observation of action* and *micro-discrepancy tuning* rather than role-play counseling. It also differs from avatar-based self-representation effects (e.g., Proteus effect) by treating appearance as one of several stance parameters rather than the sole mechanism [8]. Finally, SeMT is positioned as a behavior change support system (BCSS) that prioritizes autonomy support over compliance [5].

3 Self-mirroring Twins for Motor-Skill Improvement

3.1 Key Constructs: Stance Distance and Action Gap

We define two continuous control variables:

Stance distance $s \in [0, 1]$: how self-like SeMT feels. $s = 0$ corresponds to a pure mirror (veridical self), and $s = 1$ corresponds to an external other (coach-like). In practice, s is controlled by a bundle of cues: facial/body similarity, voice similarity, naming ("me" vs. "buddy"), spatial placement (overlay vs. beside), and language framing (questions vs. directives).

Action gap g: the difference between the user's current action a_u and the presented action a_{SeMT}, measured in task-relevant kinematic/temporal features. The core design claim is that *persuasiveness is maximized at moderate* g: large gaps reduce attainability and can induce discouragement; tiny gaps provide no actionable contrast.

3.2 Two Action-Presentation Modes

SeMT alternates between two modes, chosen to preserve autonomy while eliciting self-coaching:

(M1) Slightly-better demonstration. SeMT shows a version of the user's action that is improved by a small margin (e.g., smoother timing, reduced error, more stable posture). This mode aims to create a "reachable next step" that can function as a motivational spark while remaining attainable—consistent with discrepancy-based motivation effects in partnered activity [3,4].

(M2) Safe-failure countermodel. SeMT shows a minor, non-harmful deviation that resembles the user's own typical mistakes (e.g., a small lapse in timing or form) and then immediately shows a corrective variant. The goal is to induce metacognition ("I recognize that mistake") and support self-initiated correction rather than shame.

4 Prototype Instantiation and Evaluation Plan

4.1 Prototype Overview

We target an immersive VR training setup where users perform a short, repeatable motor task such as precise reaching/throwing motions, rhythmic movements, or form-constrained repetitions. The system pipeline is:

1. **Capture**: record user motion features in VR (controller/trackers), producing a baseline action model a_u.
2. **Generate**: produce a_{SeMT} by applying controlled transformation operators: (i) micro-improvement transforms (trajectory smoothing, timing adjustment, error reduction) for M1; (ii) bounded perturbations plus immediate correction for M2.
3. **Present**: render SeMT as an avatar in a "mirror" configuration with tunable stance cues s.
4. **Adapt**: adjust g based on observed performance change and user feedback, keeping the gap moderate.

4.2 Study Design

We propose a controlled lab study with a within-subject design.

- **C0 Baseline mirror**: replay/self-avatar without SeMT discrepancy.
- **C1 Slightly-better**: SeMT presents M1 with moderate g.
- **C2 Safe-failure**: SeMT presents M2 (failure + feedback).

Task: A short motor-skill drill with objective performance metrics (e.g., accuracy error, timing variance, stability indices). Each condition includes multiple trials to measure learning within-session.

We assess persuasiveness by considering both behavioral outcomes and changes in psychological states. The specific measurement targets are as follows.

Behavioral Measurement: (i) Immediate performance improvement from baseline (objective kinematics/task score), (ii) Retention over a short delay (optional follow-up), (iii) *Self-initiated correction markers*: number/timing of spontaneous adjustments, pauses, or strategy changes after viewing SeMT.

Psychological Measurement: (i) Self-efficacy [1] for the target drill, (ii) Perceived autonomy/reactance [2], (iii) Sense of agency and ownership (brief validated items) to monitor boundary-blurring side effects, (iv) Perceived empathy/relatedness with SeMT (as a manipulation check for stance distance).

4.3 Hypotheses

We formulate the following three hypotheses and test them through experiments. Based on the results, we clarify the design concept of SeMT.

H1 (micro-improvement effect). C1 yields larger performance gains than C0 due to an attainable model that the user can emulate.

H2 (self-coaching effect). C2 increases self-initiated correction markers relative to C0, reflecting metacognitive noticing and self-guided adjustment.

H3 (autonomy-support). C1 and C2 reduce reactance relative to a directive "coach" framing (exploratory comparison via wording manipulation), because SeMT persuades via observation and choice rather than instruction.

5 Conclusion

We presented SeMT as a stance-shifting virtual self that persuades via controlled self-discrepancy: slightly-better actions to inspire attainable progress and safe failures to trigger self-coaching. By operationalizing stance distance and action gap, and by specifying a concrete VR study protocol, this paper turns a broad concept into an evaluable persuasive system design space.

Acknowledgments. This work was supported by JST CREST, Japan, Grant Number JPMJCR2561.

Disclosure of Interests. The author have no competing interests to declare that are relevant to the content of this article.

References

1. Bandura, A.: Self-efficacy: toward a unifying theory of behavioral change. Psychol. Rev. **84**(2), 191–215 (1977)
2. Dillard, J.P., Shen, L.: On the nature of reactance and its role in persuasive health communication. Commun. Monogr. **72**(2), 144–168 (2005)
3. Feltz, D.L., Irwin, B., Kerr, N.: Two-player partnered exergame for obesity prevention: using discrepancy in players' abilities as a strategy to motivate physical activity. J. Diabetes Sci. Technol. **6**(4), 820–827 (2012)

4. Feltz, D.L., Kerr, N.L., Irwin, B.C.: Buddy up: the köhler effect applied to health games. J. Sport Exerc. Psychol. **33**(4), 506–526 (2011)
5. Oinas-Kukkonen, H.: A foundation for the study of behavior change support systems. Pers. Ubiquitous Comput. **17**(6), 1223–1235 (2013)
6. Osimo, S.A., Pizarro, R., Spanlang, B., Slater, M.: Conversations between self and self as sigmund freud-a virtual body ownership paradigm for self counselling. Sci. Rep. **5**(1), 13899 (2015)
7. Rochat, P.: Layers of awareness in development. Dev. Rev. **38**, 122–145 (2015)
8. Yee, N., Bailenson, J.: The proteus effect: the effect of transformed self-representation on behavior. Hum. Commun. Res. **33**(3), 271–290 (2007)

Reflection for Behavior Change Technologies from a Cultural Perspective

Risa Kimura(✉) and Tatsuo Nakajima

Department of Computer Science and Engineering, Waseda University, Tokyo, Japan
{risa.kimura,tatsuo}@dcl.cs.waseda.ac.jp

Abstract. This paper presents a new framework for designing behavior-change technologies based on three kinds of reflection: *reflection on the self*, *the world,* and *time*. By combining these perspectives with five analytical and cultural axes, we aim to create more holistic and culturally sensitive interaction designs. We show how this framework works through a case study called *Happy Mirror*, an interactive device that uses personal memories, physical presence, and layered experiences of time. This example shows how encouraging reflection on different aspects of human life can lead to more meaningful and lasting behavior change.

Keywords: Reflection · Framework · Behavior Change · More-than-Human

1 Introduction

In recent years, human-computer interaction (HCI) research has increasingly highlighted the importance of designs that promote user reflection, emotional engagement, and experiences grounded in everyday life. Traditional HCI has prioritized functionality, emphasizing efficiency and task completion. Today, however, design must engage more deeply with the complexities of human experience, including meaning-making, emotional involvement, and cultural context. This shift reflects a growing recognition that technology is not merely a tool, but a key influence on users' self-understanding and value formation. Nonetheless, challenges remain, especially regarding how to support behavior change without compromising users' dignity and autonomy. There is a risk in relying too heavily on persuasive models or behavioral nudges rooted in behavioral economics. These methods often target efficiency or goal completion, treating users as passive actors. Such one-size-fits-all approaches may prompt short-term change, but rarely foster sustainable transformation and have been widely critiqued for their ethical limitations.

This paper proposes a new design framework for behavior-change technologies, grounded in three dimensions of reflection: *reflection on the self*, *on the world*, and *on time*. These are integrated through five analytical and cultural axes: *embodiment, aesthetics, defamiliarization, ritualization,* and *pluriverse*. By interweaving these analytical dimensions, we aim to support interaction design that is more holistic and culturally grounded. We demonstrate the utility of this framework through a case study, *Happy*

E. Vlahu-Gjorgievska et al. (Eds.): PERSUASIVE 2026, CCIS 2896, pp. 273–277, 2027.
https://doi.org/10.1007/978-3-032-27235-5_26

Mirror, an interactive device that draw on personal memory, spatial presence, and temporal layering. The case study illustrates how reflection on diverse aspects of human experience can foster meaningful behavior change.

2 Related Work

Traditional behavior change technologies have primarily focused on efficiently guiding users toward predefined goals through nudges, reminders, and feedback loops [3]. While effective in areas like health management and energy conservation, these approaches often overlook deeper aspects of human experience, including cultural background, emotional dynamics, personal identity, and temporal perception. In contrast, recent research emphasizes more inclusive and ethically grounded design approaches rooted in ritual, aesthetics, and diverse human values [1]. There is a growing shift in HCI toward viewing behavior change not as mere efficiency or goal attainment, but as a reflective practice embedded in users' inner lives and cultural contexts. Frameworks such as slow technology [4] and reflective informatics [2] exemplify this trend, encouraging users to contemplate their own experiences and meaning-making. From this perspective, technology design moves beyond behavior modification to become a practice interwoven with users' values, memories, and emotions. Behavior change is thus reframed as part of a more human-centered, sustainable approach that resonates with lived experience and diverse worldviews.

3 A Proposed Framework

Traditional behavior change technologies have primarily focused on efficiently guiding user behavior toward predefined goals through methods such as nudges, reminders, and feedback loops. While these strategies have achieved measurable success in domains like health management and energy conservation, they often fail to engage with the deeper dimensions of human experience, including cultural background, emotional complexity, personal identity, and temporal awareness. In contrast, the framework proposed in this paper is centered on the act of reflection, aiming to account for the multilayered nature of human experience and the cultural contexts that are essential to meaningful interaction design today. The aim is not just to create technologies that change behavior, but to help people better understand themselves, reconnect with their culture, and rethink how they experience time.

This framework is grounded in three dimensions: *reflection on the self, on the world*, and *on time*. *Reflection on the self* refers to how individuals re-examine their inner experiences, such as identity, emotions, and personal goals, through their interactions with technology. Rather than being an externally imposed influence, this form of reflection facilitates a process by which users find ethical and emotional meaning in their lives and decisions. *Reflection on the world* involves a re-engagement with one's relationships to others, the environment, cultural backgrounds, and more-than-human entities. Technology, in this context, functions as a mirror through which users can reassess their roles and positions in a broader social and ecological context. This reorientation offers users an opportunity to adopt more ethically aware and socially responsible perspectives.

Meanwhile, *reflection on time* concerns how users perceive, experience, and reconfigure the past, present, and future through their interaction with technology. Some systems, for instance, evoke emotionally resonant memories of the past, tie them to present experiences, and shape future aspirations. In doing so, they encourage users to view time as an emotionally and narratively constructed phenomenon, rather than as a linear continuum, and this reinterpretation enables long-term, meaningful transformation rooted in one's life history and cultural memory.

These three forms of reflection intersect with five conceptual axes that support culturally and experientially grounded interaction design: *embodiment, aesthetics, defamiliarization, ritualization*, and *pluriverse*. The axis of *embodiment* concerns how sensory and bodily experience is engaged through interaction, enabling reflection not just through abstract thought but through visceral, embodied perception. The axis of *aesthetics* contributes meaning and emotional resonance, helping users interpret experiences in ways that are ethically and culturally significant, beyond mere pleasure or discomfort. The axis of *defamiliarization* prompts users to see the familiar in unfamiliar ways, thereby disrupting habitual assumptions and opening space for renewed understanding. The axis of *ritualization* introduces temporal and structured repetition into user experience, imbuing actions with cultural significance and anchoring them in personal and collective rhythms of meaning. Finally, the axis of *pluriverse* refers to the coexistence of multiple worldviews, ontologies, and value systems, encouraging designs that are inclusive and sensitive to ethical and cultural diversity.

The combination of the three types of reflection and the five cultural axes creates a foundation for experience-centered design. For instance, reflection on time can be expressed through repeated, meaningful interactions, while reflection on the world can be deepened by recognizing diverse cultural viewpoints. This approach helps designers create technologies that connect more deeply with users' values, personal histories, and real-life experiences, instead of simply trying to change their behavior. In this way, the framework redefines persuasive technology. Rather than being a tool to control or push users toward specific goals, technology becomes a way to support self-reflection, ethical choices, and the rebuilding of social and cultural connections. By designing with emotional depth and cultural awareness, we can promote behavior change that is more human-centered and lasting. More details on the framework and the analyses can be found in [6].

4 A Case Study: Happy Mirror

Happy Mirror, shown in Fig. 1, is an interactive mirror that uses augmented reality technology to let users recall past photos and videos through physical gestures [5]. Rather than simply acting as a device to display memories, it is designed to support *reflection on the self, on the world*, and *on time*. By connecting memory, emotion, and bodily movement, the system gives users meaningful opportunities for self-understanding and potential behavioral change. *Reflection on the self* involves artistically re-creating emotionally important moments, allowing users to reinterpret past experiences and connect them with their present identity. For example, seeing a smile from childhood or revisiting a moment with a family member helps users re-feel the emotions of that time and recognize the continuity in their lives. *Reflection on the world* expands beyond personal memories, highlighting the user's relationships with family, community, and the natural environment. These memories become entry points for rediscovering social and cultural ties and for reflecting on one's role within a broader context. *Reflection on time* is supported by layering the past, present, and future in a nonlinear way. This design lets memories interact with the present and helps users envision future hopes and intentions. In doing so, it encourages a deeper understanding of life's flow and helps users find new meaning in the continuity of time beyond simple nostalgia.

Fig. 1. Happy Mirror

The five analytical axes deepen the user's experience by engaging memory, emotion, and culture. The *embodiment* perspective links physical gestures to the act of remembering, making reflection more immediate and grounded in the body. The *aesthetics* perspective transforms simple recordings into emotionally rich visuals, helping users connect more deeply with their memories. The *defamiliarization* perspective presents familiar moments in new and surprising ways, encouraging fresh interpretations. The *ritualization* perspective supports the formation of reflective habits by integrating mirror interaction into daily routines. Finally, the *pluriverse* perspective allows for cultural adaptation, ensuring that the system aligns with each user's background and values, fostering inclusivity and personal relevance.

5 Conclusion

The strength of this framework is that it moves away from top-down methods of changing behavior and instead encourages users to reflect and participate in ways that fit their own lives. By combining three types of reflection on the self, the world, and time with the five cultural axes, it helps create more meaningful and layered experiences. By becoming part of everyday routines, these interactions can lead to lasting, meaningful behavior changes.

References

1. Akama, Y., Light, A., Kamihira, T.: Expanding participation to design with more-than-human concerns. In: Proceedings of the 16th Participatory Design Conference 2020 - Participation(s) Otherwise-Volume 1. Association for Computing Machinery, New York, NY (2020)
2. Baumer, E.: Reflective informatics: conceptual dimensions for designing technologies of reflection. In: Proceedings of the 33rd Annual ACM Conference on Human Factors in Computing Systems. Association for Computing Machinery, New York, NY (2015)
3. Fogg, B.J.: Persuasive Technology: Using Computers to Change What We Think and Do. Morgan Kaufmann (2002)
4. Grosse-Hering, B., Mason, J., Aliakseyeu, D., Bakker, C., Desmet, P.: Slow design for meaningful interactions. In: Proceedings of the 2013 SIGCHI Conference on Human Factors in Computing Systems. Association for Computing Machinery, New York, NY (2013)
5. Kato, Y., Kimura, R., Nakajima, T.: TippyMirror: recollecting people's positive mo-ments based on mirror Metaphor. In: Delir Haghighi, P., Greguš, M., Kotsis, G., Kha-lil, I. (eds.), Information Integration and Web Intelligence. iiWAS 2024. Lecture Notes in Computer Science, vol. 15343. Springer, Cham (2025). https://doi.org/10.1007/978-3-031-78093-6_14
6. Kimura, R., and Nakajima, T.: Exploring human-culture interaction for designing multistable meaning-making. In: Proceedings of the 14th International Conference on Distributed, Ambient and Pervasive Interactions. Springer, Cham (2026)

Toward a Participatory Trace-Sensing Framework Using Smartphone LiDAR for Wildlife Habitat Estimation

Tsukasa Kojo[1(✉)], Wataru Sasaki[1], Yuki Matsuda[1,2], Kota Tsubouchi[3], Keichi Yasumoto[1], and Hirohiko Suwa[1]

[1] Nara Institute of Science and Technology, Ikoma, Japan
kojo.tsukasa.kw3@naist.ac.jp
[2] Okayama University, Okayama, Japan
[3] LY Corporation, Tokyo, Japan

Abstract. As damage to agriculture and forestry by wildlife intensifies, wide-area and high-frequency data collection is required to estimate habitats and movement patterns. Although citizen participatory sensing has attracted attention, identifying footprints in natural environments requires high expertise, which is a bottleneck for participation. Furthermore, automatic identification based on RGB images is unstable in real environments due to the influence of lighting and background similarity. This paper presents a conceptual design of a system for exploratory detection of wildlife footprints from imperfect 3D point clouds acquired by non-experts using LiDAR-equipped smartphones. Characteristics of this study lie in the integrated design of data acquisition support and analysis methods, targeting uneven terrain where standard assumptions of existing 3D analysis, such as flat reference planes or high-density measurement, do not hold. Specifically, we design an acquisition application that uses AR real-time feedback to support shooting behavior and ensure a certain quality of photogrammetry point clouds, and a footprint detection method based on local geometric features. By combining appropriate acquisition support and local geometric feature analysis, we present a framework that enables general participants to achieve effective automatic recognition in real environments using only smartphones, providing a technical foundation for wide-area wildlife monitoring based on participatory sensing.

Keywords: Participatory Sensing · Smartphone LiDAR · Wildlife Monitoring · Persuasive Design · Citizen Science

1 Introduction

In recent years, damage to agriculture and forestry by wildlife has become serious [1], and methods for wide-area monitoring are required [5]. Citizen participatory sensing is promising [3,6,9], but identifying traces requires high expertise.

E. Vlahu-Gjorgievska et al. (Eds.): PERSUASIVE 2026, CCIS 2896, pp. 278–282, 2027.
https://doi.org/10.1007/978-3-032-27235-5_27

This study delegates this judgment to the system to enable non-expert participation, focusing on "footprints," which are critical traces indicating individual presence [2]. However, RGB-based identification is unstable in natural environments due to background similarity and lighting changes [7]. In contrast, 3D information based on geometry is robust against lighting and color. However, point clouds acquired by non-experts inevitably contain imperfections such as low density and occlusion. The purpose of this study is to propose a system that enables exploratory detection of wildlife footprints even from imperfect point clouds acquired by non-experts. We view this as "exploratory detection" where avoiding false negatives is prioritized over suppressing false positives, and aim to support discovery in real environments. The contribution of this paper is proposing a framework for non-expert exploratory wildlife footprint sensing, which integrates participatory data collection, AR-based acquisition support, and geometry-based footprint detection. Specifically, we present the clarification of the problem setting in non-expert participatory sensing, a design rationale for ensuring acquisition quality via AR-based behavioral guidance, and an exploratory detection framework integrating photogrammetry-derived 3D point clouds and geometric analysis.

2 Related Work

2.1 Expert Dependence in Wildlife Footprint Surveys

Track surveys using traces (e.g., footprints) are widely effective for wildlife monitoring because they can cover large areas without special equipment, unlike camera trapping or line census [10]. However, identifying these traces relies heavily on the surveyor's experience and knowledge. This dependence on limited expert personnel creates a structural bottleneck. In other words, traditional methods struggle to achieve wide-area monitoring due to the shortage of experts.

2.2 Data Reliability Issues in Participatory Sensing

To address this "quantitative" shortage of experts, Participatory Sensing [4] has gained attention. The effectiveness of photo-sharing platforms and citizen observation has been reported in various ecological contexts [3,6]. While scalable, non-expert identification introduces "qualitative" risks. Errors such as false positives or negatives significantly degrade data reliability. Therefore, a system guaranteeing data quality is required to maintain scalability.

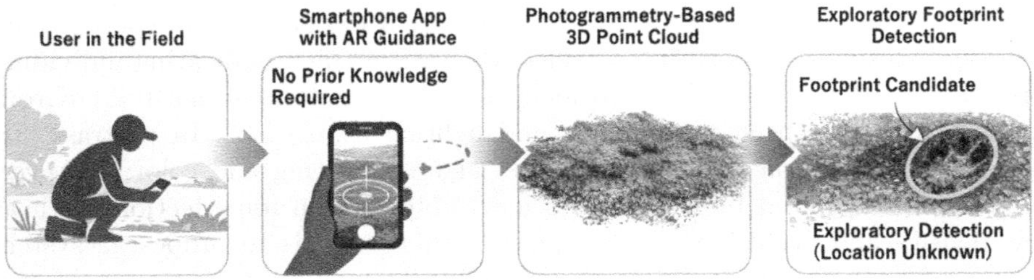

Fig. 1. Proposed system overview. An AR app guides users to ensure photogrammetry quality, followed by geometric analysis for exploratory footprint detection.

2.3 Limitations of Existing Detection Approaches

To support non-expert identification in outdoor environments, automated detection methods are required. Conventional RGB image-based methods are unstable under natural lighting and background variations [7], making them unsuitable for reliable field use. In contrast, 3D shape measurement using LiDAR-equipped smartphones is promising due to its robustness against lighting [8]. However, existing 3D analysis methods typically assume high-density, complete point clouds acquired by skilled operators. They fail when applied to "imperfect" data containing low density, viewpoint bias, or occlusions acquired by non-experts. Existing approaches do not explicitly address footprint detection under the assumption of imperfect 3D data acquired by non-experts in natural environments.

In summary, while footprint-based monitoring, participatory sensing, and 3D analysis have each been studied independently, their integration under the constraints of non-expert data acquisition remains insufficiently explored.

3 Design Concept and System Architecture

In this study, to establish exploratory detection by non-experts, we consistently integrate an AR-based Acquisition Support Design for ensuring point cloud quality and a Design Rationale for analysis based on local geometric features (Fig. 1).

Wildlife footprints, with depths of several mm to 1 cm, are comparable to smartphone LiDAR noise, which is around several cm, making detection difficult on their own. Therefore, in this design, we propose an acquisition interface that spatially guides camera trajectory and distance using AR, allowing users without knowledge to naturally satisfy the conditions for photogrammetry, such as resolution, viewpoint, and coverage.

3.1 Design Rationale: Acquisition Support

When the user taps the ground, AR visually guides ideal camera work, physically inducing user operation. Users only need to move the device along this guide.

This physical constraint enforces the maintenance of optimal distance, elimination of blind spots via all-around views, and blur suppression via constant speed, ensuring high-quality point cloud generation.

3.2 Design Rationale: Exploratory Analysis

Given ensured quality, we propose an integrated workflow: First, diverse footprint data is collected outdoors via the app, where AR ensures consistent quality. Next, experts assign ground truth labels to the acquired 3D point clouds based on shape information rather than RGB images. Finally, a machine learning-based detection model is constructed using the accumulated data and these ground truth labels. We aim to establish non-expert exploratory detection through the integration of this "forced quality assurance" data collection and standard learning process.

4 Design Implications and Future Directions

In this study, we proposed a design for a non-expert exploratory footprint detection system integrating smartphone AR and local geometric analysis as a technical foundation for promoting citizen participation in wildlife monitoring. The core of this proposal lies in the integrated approach of physically ensuring "data quality," which traditionally relied on user skills, through system-side interface design, and constructing distinct robust analysis algorithms upon that basis.

Future work includes implementing a prototype based on this design and verifying its technical feasibility in actual outdoor environments. Specifically, we plan quantitative evaluations of how much AR behavioral guidance improves actual user shooting behavior, detection accuracy evaluations of the proposed algorithm on acquired point clouds, and user studies on the impact of system-presented information on users' exploration motivation and discovery rates. We hope the design guidelines presented in this study will serve as a concrete roadmap for realizing future citizen participatory sensing.

References

1. Ministry of Agriculture, Forestry and Fisheries: Situation of agricultural damage by wild birds and mammals (fy2023) (2025). https://www.maff.go.jp/j/seisan/tyozyu/higai/hogai_zyoukyou/index.html
2. Alibhai, S., et al.: Identifying white rhino (ceratotherium simum) by a footprint identification technique. Endangered Species Res. (2008)
3. Arts, K., van der Wal, R., Adams, W.: Digital technology and the conservation of nature. Ambio **44**, 661–673 (2015)
4. Burke, J.A., et al.: Participatory sensing. In: Proceedings of the 4th ACM Conference on Embedded Networked Sensor Systems, pp. 117–134 (2006)
5. Cagnacci, F., et al.: Partial versus complete migration in roe deer. Mov. Ecol. **1**, 1–13 (2011)

6. California Academy of Sciences: inaturalist (2020). https://www.inaturalist.org
7. Falkingham, P.: Acquisition of high resolution three-dimensional models using free, open-source, photogrammetric software. Palaeontol. Electron. **15**(1), 1–15 (2012)
8. Luetzenburg, G., et al.: Evaluation of the apple iphone 12 pro lidar for an application in geosciences. Sci. Rep. (2021)
9. Moussa, L.G., et al.: Exploring citizen science applications for wildlife monitoring. Premier J. Environ. Sci. (2024)
10. Silveira, L., Jácomo, A.T., Diniz-Filho, J.A.F.: Camera trap, line transect census and track surveys: a comparative evaluation. Biol. Cons. **114**(3), 351–355 (2003)

A Framework for Relating Participant Behaviors and Responses in Music Therapy to Clinical Evaluation

Naoko Kosugi[1(✉)] and Naoki Kodama[2]

[1] School of Network and Information, Senshu University, 2-1-1, Higashimita, Tama-ku, Kawasaki-shi, Kanagawa 214-8580, Japan
naonaoan@gmail.com

[2] Faculty of Medical Technology, Niigata University of Health and Welfare, 1398 Shimami-cho, Kita-ku, Niigata-shi, Niigata 950-3198, Japan
kodama@nuhw.ac.jp

Abstract. Music therapy has been reported to alleviate behavioral and psychological symptoms of dementia, yet the processes through which therapeutic effects emerge during sessions remain insufficiently articulated. In particular, relationships between participants' observable behaviors and responses during music therapy interactions and clinical evaluation outcomes have not been systematically organized. This paper proposes a framework that relates session-level observations of music therapy interactions, including participant behaviors and responses, to clinical evaluation measures such as the Neuropsychiatric Inventory (NPI). The research of the framework is ongoing and illustrated through a remote music therapy in which participant behaviors, vocal and verbal expressions, and engagement are observed and evaluated during sessions. The remote system provides a practical context in which such observations can be captured in digital forms and shared with music therapists, supporting reflection on participants' reactions and consideration of subsequent therapeutic approaches. By offering a structured way to organize and interpret music therapy interactions in relation to clinical evaluation, this work contributes to discussions in persuasive technology by framing persuasion as an interpretable process of change within therapeutic practice, rather than as a designed intervention.

Keywords: Music therapy · Dementia care · Interaction · Clinical evaluation · Remote system

1 Introduction

Music therapy is used in dementia care and has been reported to alleviate behavioral and psychological symptoms of dementia, BPSD, which includes depression, behavioral disturbances, and anxiety. The authors understand that its clinical effects emerge from the accumulation of interactions, referred to here as MT

E. Vlahu-Gjorgievska et al. (Eds.): PERSUASIVE 2026, CCIS 2896, pp. 283–287, 2027.
https://doi.org/10.1007/978-3-032-27235-5_28

interaction, between therapists and participants during therapy sessions. However, the mechanisms through which specific aspects of MT interactions relate to clinical outcomes remain insufficiently understood.

One challenge in examining MT interactions lies in their complexity and transience. The interactions during therapy sessions involve verbal and musical dialogue, moment-to-moment responses, and contextual factors that are difficult to capture comprehensively. As a result, evaluation of music therapy has often focused on overall clinical outcomes, while the relationship between session-level interactions and clinical evaluation has received less systematic attention [1].

Recent advances in data collection and recording technologies have made it increasingly feasible to capture various aspects of music therapy sessions, including participant behaviors, physiological signals, and speech. These developments create opportunities to reconsider how observations made during therapy sessions can be organized and interpreted in relation to established clinical evaluation measures.

In this paper, we propose a framework for relating observed participant behaviors and responses during MT interactions to clinical evaluation of BPSD. Rather than assuming causal relationships or prescribing optimal intervention strategies, the framework aims to support systematic reasoning and discussion about how session-level observations may be associated with clinical evaluation. By providing a shared structure for organizing observations, the framework seeks to facilitate ongoing analysis of MT interactions in dementia care.

2 Proposed Framework

We propose a framework for relating participant behaviors and responses observed during music therapy sessions to clinical evaluation in dementia care.

The framework connects three elements:

- music therapy session design,
- observed participant behaviors and responses during MT interactions (e.g., D-EMS ratings, video-recorded behaviors, physiological and speech data), and
- clinical evaluation measures of BPSD (e.g., Neuropsychiatric Inventory: NPI [2]).

Observed participant behaviors and responses were assessed using D-EMS, Ehime-Music Therapy Scale for Dementia in which the music therapist who conducted the session evaluated each participant's singing, verbal expressions, motivation to participate, and social interaction and so on. Each item was rated on a five-point scale based on observations during the session.

In addition to session-level observations, participant characteristics such as age, background, and personal history are considered as contextual factors when examining relationships between MT interactions and clinical evaluation.

Rather than assuming direct causal relationships, the framework is intended to support systematic reasoning about how certain patterns of participant behaviors and responses relate to broader clinical evaluations of BPSD, such as anxiety and apathy. Furthermore, the framework does not aim to identify optimal behaviors or prescriptive intervention strategies. Instead, it provides a shared structure for organizing observations across sessions and for accumulating evidence regarding how different aspects of MT interactions may be associated with clinical outcomes.

Figure 1 provides an overview of the proposed framework, which organizes session-level observations (e.g., D-EMS ratings, behavioral, physiological, and speech data) in relation to clinical evaluation measures (e.g., NPI).

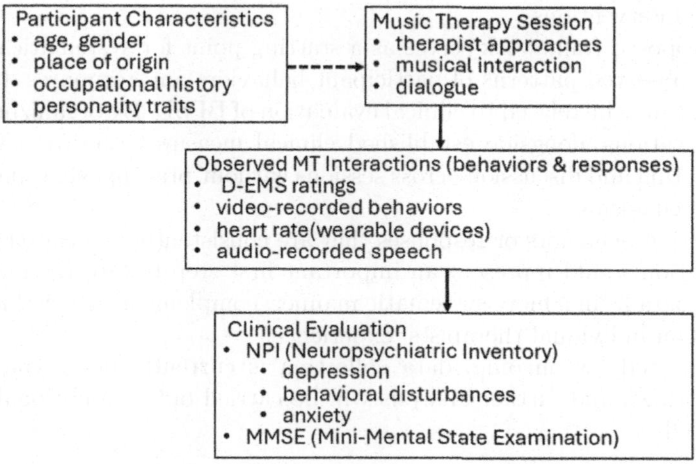

Fig. 1. Overview of the proposed framework for relating observed participant behaviors and responses during MT interactions to clinical evaluation.

3 Illustrative Case: Session Design as an Entry Point

Based on prior experience, music therapy session programs were designed to increase opportunities for vocal and verbal participation. Vocalization was treated as an entry point rather than an outcome in itself.

For example, participants were occasionally addressed by name and invited to respond to simple questions related to the session content (e.g., asking about preferred autumn foods during autumn-themed songs), or encouraged to produce vocal calls, such as Hoi Hoi, during light physical exercises with music. These design choices also contributed to creating situations in which participants might anticipate being asked to respond. Care staff reported increased alertness and sustained attention, possibly due to participants' anticipation of being asked to respond.

This case illustrates how the proposed framework can be used to organize observations without presupposing the appropriateness of specific behaviors.

4 Implications for Ongoing Analysis

In the present study, music therapy sessions were conducted in a remote setting. Compared to face-to-face sessions, remote delivery makes it more feasible to capture participants' behaviors and responses in digital forms and to share such information with music therapists during or after sessions.

From this perspective, the proposed framework is intended as a first step toward supporting therapists in reflecting on participants' reactions and considering subsequent approaches, rather than as a system that directly delivers persuasive interventions.

The proposed framework serves as a starting point for systematically examining how observed patterns of participant behaviors and responses during MT interactions may be related to clinical evaluation of BPSD. By organizing session-level observations alongside established clinical measures, the framework supports reflection and discussion across sessions without presupposing specific therapeutic mechanisms.

Identifying behaviors or responses that are consistently associated with clinical evaluation would represent an important first step toward designing music therapy programs in a more systematic manner, complementing existing practice that relies on individual therapists' experience.

As this study is ongoing, data collection is currently being conducted in clinical settings, and further analysis will be carried out as additional data are accumulated.

5 Conclusion and Future Work

This paper presented a framework for relating observed participant behaviors and responses during MT interactions to clinical evaluation of BPSD. By organizing session-level observations without assuming causal relationships, the framework offers a structured perspective for examining MT interactions in dementia care.

As data collection continues, future work will involve applying the framework to a larger set of sessions to further examine how different patterns of interactions relate to clinical evaluation, as well as other potential roles of MT interactions in dementia care [3].

Acknowledgements. This work was supported by JSPS KAKENHI Grant Numbers JP23K28097 and JP23H03407.

References

1. van der Steen, J.T., van der Wouden, J.C., Methley, A.M., Smaling, H.J.A., Vink, A.C., Bruinsma, M.S.: Music-based therapeutic interventions for people with dementia. Cochrane Database Syst. Rev. (3), Art. No.: CD003477 (2025). https://doi.org/10.1002/14651858.CD003477.pub5

2. Cummings, J.L., Mega, M., Gray, K., Rosenberg-Thompson, S., Carusi, D.A., Gornbein, J.: The neuropsychiatric inventory: comprehensive assessment of psychopathology in dementia. Neurology **44**(12), 2308–2314 (1994)
3. Kitwood, T.: Dementia Reconsidered: The Person Comes First. Open University Press (1997)

A Dual-Judge Framework for Evaluating Reasoning-Based AI Social Workers: Emulating Professional Logic in Persuasive Systems

You-Chen Liu[1](✉), Shih-Yi Chien[1], and Shiau-Fang Chao[2]

[1] Department of Management Information Systems, National Chengchi University, Taipei, Taiwan
114356009@g.nccu.edu.tw, sychien@nccu.edu.tw

[2] Department of Social Work, National Taiwan University, Taipei, Taiwan
sfchao@ntu.edu.tw

Abstract. With the rapid advancement of generative artificial intelligence, large language models (LLMs) have shown promise in providing emotional support for mental health applications. However, generic chatbots often lack professional reasoning capabilities to address the complex psychological needs of elderly individuals experiencing loneliness. This study emphasizes the reasoning and explainability of AI social workers during persuasive interventions. We propose an evaluation framework that examines the internal decision-making logic of generative models. Specifically, we first establish an LLM-as-Judge paradigm by aligning state-of-the-art models with human expert assessments. We further introduce a dual-judge framework, leveraging multiple LLMs to assess the conversational performance of AI social workers.

Keywords: LLM-as-Judge · Chain-of-Thought Reasoning · Persuasive Technology

1 Introduction

The rapid advancement of Generative Artificial Intelligence (AI) has unlocked significant potential for Large Language Models (LLMs) across diverse domains [1–3]. In the fields of mental health and social well-being, prior research [4] has demonstrated that interactive dialogues with LLMs can provide effective emotional support, thereby alleviating user loneliness. However, addressing the escalating crisis of elderly loneliness in aging societies remains a challenge, as generic chatbots often lack the nuance required for this demographic's specific psychological needs [5]. While Fine-tuning and Prompt Engineering are the predominant techniques for optimizing model performance [6], there remains a lack of systematic evaluation and field validation regarding which approach more effectively simulates professional social work styles and establishes robust persuasive mechanisms.

In contrast to prior work that focuses primarily on conversational engagement, this study foregrounds the "Reasoning and Explainability" of generative models during the

E. Vlahu-Gjorgievska et al. (Eds.): PERSUASIVE 2026, CCIS 2896, pp. 288–291, 2027.
https://doi.org/10.1007/978-3-032-27235-5_29

intervention process. By establishing an "LLM-as-Judge" framework with high alignment to human assessments, this research provides an explainable technical pathway to evaluate how effectively various LLM configurations, including prompt-engineered and fine-tuned models, can emulate the professional logic and intervention styles of social workers within the context of psychological support.

2 Method and Benchmarking

2.1 Evaluation Alignment with Human Experts

Extending the framework of Themis [7], —a reference-free evaluation language model designed for flexibility and interpretability—this phase establishes an "LLM-as-Judge" mechanism. While the original Themis framework validated GPT-4 across four key aspects—Context Maintenance, Interestingness, Knowledge Use, and Naturalness—on the Topical Chat dataset (a collection of human-human open-domain conversations where speakers have access to underlying knowledge snippets), we updated the evaluator pool with next-generation models, including GPT-5 and Gemini-3 (Table 1).

Table 1. Evaluation performance of different models on the Topical-Chat dataset.

Method	Context Maintenance		Interestingness		Knowledge Use		Naturalness		Average	
	r	ρ	r	ρ	r	ρ	r	ρ	r	ρ
GPT-4	0.632	0.672	0.707	0.705	0.674	0.690	0.642	0.670	0.664	0.684
GPT-5	0.789	0.815	0.737	0.759	0.701	0.717	0.681	0.697	0.729	0.747
Gemini-3	0.746	0.753	0.779	0.774	0.769	0.775	0.727	0.730	0.755	0.758

By calculating the Pearson (**r**) and Spearman (ρ) correlation coefficients between the original human expert ratings and the model-generated scores, we found that next-generation LLMs—specifically GPT-5 and Gemini-3—achieve notably higher values in key metrics such as "Context Maintenance" and "Knowledge Use". Notably, in terms of the average correlation scores, GPT-5 ($\rho = 0.747$) and Gemini-3 ($\rho = 0.758$) substantially outperform GPT-4 ($\rho = 0.684$). These results demonstrate significantly superior performance across all four key aspects—Context Maintenance, Interestingness, Knowledge Use, and Naturalness—indicating a much stronger alignment with humans and validating the effectiveness of using these advanced models as reliable "LLM-as-Judges" for the subsequent phases of this study.

2.2 Reasoning-Based Model Comparison

Building upon the alignment results, this phase adopts a dual-judge framework—utilizing both GPT-5 and Gemini-3—to evaluate the intervention quality of different

LLM-based social workers. In our experimental setup, GPT-5 was prompted to simulate an elderly individual suffering from loneliness, engaging in simulated dialogues of 30 conversational turns with three distinct social worker configurations: prompt-engineered GPT-5, Gemini-3, and Qwen-8B. Notably, the Qwen-8B model was specifically trained on real dialogue corpora between elderly individuals and professional social workers, allowing it to better capture the nuances of real-world interventions. By feeding these extensive dialogues into the dual-judge framework, we benchmarked each model's performance across the four established dimensions to evaluate their foundational capabilities in social work-like interactions (Table 2).

Table 2. Performance Comparison of LLM Social Workers under Dual-Judge Evaluation.

Aspects	Context Maintenance		Interestingness		Knowledge Use		Naturalness		Average	
Judge	Gemini3	GPT5	Gemini3	GPT5	Gemini3	GPT5	Gemini3	Gpt5	Gemini3	GPT5
Qwen-8B	6.633	5.5	6.267	5.1	6.5	5.3	6.5	5.633	6.475	5.383
GPT-5	5.667	5.767	5.267	5.467	5.667	5.633	5.333	5.9	5.458	5.692
Gemini-3	6.833	5.7	6.733	5.5	6.7	5.667	6.8	5.867	6.767	5.683

Despite the observed biases, the Qwen model, accessed via API, demonstrated highly competitive performance. In the evaluation by Gemini-3, Qwen achieved scores in Context Maintenance (6.633) and Naturalness (6.5) that significantly surpassed the much larger GPT-5 model (5.667 and 5.333, respectively). This suggests that while Qwen may not match the general-purpose scale of frontier models like GPT-5, its specialized optimization for Mandarin-speaking contexts allows it to achieve professional-level conversational quality. These findings indicate that Qwen-8B possesses sufficient capability to perform effectively, demonstrating particularly robust competence within Mandarin-speaking cultural environments.

3 Discussion and Limitations

Our findings highlight that integrating Chain-of-Thought (CoT) reasoning [8] not only enhances the depth of AI interventions but also significantly improves the scoring efficacy of the evaluation framework, allowing for a more precise identification of high-performing models. By rendering the internal logic transparent, CoT enables a more granular differentiation of model capabilities beyond surface-level fluency.

However, this study has limitations. First, the "LLM-as-Judge" models were primarily trained on Western, English-centric datasets (e.g., Topical Chat), which may lead to cultural and linguistic misalignments when evaluating Mandarin-speaking contexts [9]. Second, inherent biases within pre-trained models may result in stereotypical responses [10]. Furthermore, our current framework primarily benchmarks models across four general dimensions. While these provide a robust macro-level assessment, they cannot fully capture the clinical nuances of a professional social worker. Therefore, future work will involve collaboration with licensed social work practitioners to evaluate whether the models' reasoning truly emulates professional intervention standards. This expert validation, combined with a longitudinal field study utilizing the UCLA Loneliness Scale [11], will be essential to verify how these identified reasoning strengths translate into long-term emotional support in real-world environments [12].

4 Conclusion

This research presents a novel evaluation and implementation framework for reasoning-based AI social workers tailored for elderly loneliness. By extending the Themis benchmark and validating both high-capacity models, we demonstrate that explicit reasoning logic is key to simulating professional social work intervention. While challenges in cultural adaptation remain, this study provides a crucial technical foundation for developing more transparent, trustworthy, and effective persuasive systems for mental health support in aging societies. Future research will focus on developing culturally-sensitive benchmarks and refining the model's reasoning logic to better serve diverse elderly populations.

References

1. Lo, C.K.: What is the impact of ChatGPT on education? A rapid review of the literature. Educ. Sci. **13**(4), 410 (2023)
2. Li, F., Wang, Y., Xu, Y., et al.: Performance evaluations of large language models for customer service. Int. J. Mach. Learn. Cybern. **16**, 2997–3017 (2025)
3. Thirunavukarasu, A.J., Ting, D.S.J., Elangovan, K., et al.: Large language models in medicine. Nat. Med. **29**, 1930–1940 (2023)
4. De Freitas, J., Oğuz-Uğuralp, Z., Uğuralp, A.K., Puntoni, S.: AI companions reduce loneliness. J. Consum. Res. (2025). https://doi.org/10.1093/jcr/ucaf040
5. Zeng, H., Sheng, Y., Zhu, J.: Companion robots supporting the emotional needs of the elderly: Research trends and future directions. Information **16**(11), 948 (2025)
6. Pradhan, R.: RAG vs. fine-tuning vs. prompt engineering: a comparative analysis for optimizing AI models. Int. J. Comput. Technol. Electron. Commun. **8**(5), 11326–11333 (2025)
7. Hu, X., Lin, L., Gao, M., Yin, X., Wan, X.: Themis: a reference-free NLG evaluation language model with flexibility and interpretability. In: Al-Onaizan, Y., Bansal, M., Chen, Y.-N. (eds.) EMNLP 2024, pp. 15924–15951. ACL (2024)
8. Wei, J., Wang, X., Schuurmans, D., et al.: Chain-of-thought prompting elicits reasoning in large language models (2022). arXiv:2201.11903
9. Naous, T., Savit, A., Catalan, C.R., et al.: Camellia: benchmarking cultural biases in LLMs for Asian languages (2025). arXiv:2510.05291
10. Liu, Y., Liu, Y., Chen, X., et al.: The devil is in the neurons: interpreting and mitigating social biases in pre-trained language models (2024). arXiv:2406.10130
11. Russell, D.W.: UCLA Loneliness Scale (Version 3): reliability, validity, and factor structure. J. Pers. Assess. **66**(1), 20–40 (1996)
12. Chien, S.Y., Chao, S.F., Kang, Y., et al.: Understanding predictive factors of dementia for older adults: a machine learning approach for modeling dementia influencers. Int. J. Hum. Comput. Stud. **165**, 102834 (2022)

MIRA: A Custom Social Robot Head, with Applications Ranging from Personalized Education to Elderly Care

Farida Mohsen, Tala Zaim, and Ali Safa(✉)

College of Science and Engineering, Hamad Bin Khalifa University, Doha, Qatar
asafa@hbku.edu.qa

Abstract. We present MIRA, a fully custom-made social robot head designed as a versatile platform for elderly care applications. This first prototype integrates three foundational capabilities essential for persuasive human-robot interaction: real-time interaction intent detection using RGB-only behavioral and emotional cues; natural voice-based conversation powered by large language models; and responsive face tracking with two degrees of freedom. Real-world deployment achieved 91% accuracy in detecting human interaction intent, validating MIRA's reliability for initiating human-robot interaction scenarios. This demonstration showcases MIRA's three core capabilities, showing how our proposed social robot architecture can serve as a foundation for diverse persuasive social applications, from personalized education technology to elderly care.

Keywords: Social robotics · Persuasive technology · Human-robot interaction · Intent detection

1 Introduction

In recent years, issues such as population aging and the need for providing tailored education to children with special needs have motivated the need for socially assistive technologies [1]. Social robots offer promising potential for diverse applications, from medication reminders and health monitoring to companionship and cognitive exercises [2]. However, the effectiveness of these applications depends on the robot's ability to detect when users wish to interact, communicate naturally, and maintain engagement through embodied social cues.

Persuasive technology research has established that sustained behavior change requires the convergence of motivation, ability, and appropriate triggers [3]. For social robots, this translates to a fundamental requirement: before a robot can assist with specific tasks, it must first establish natural, trustworthy interaction. Physical embodiment consistently outperforms virtual agents in

Supplementary Material. Demonstration videos are available at https://tinyurl.com/374t2aw9.

E. Vlahu-Gjorgievska et al. (Eds.): PERSUASIVE 2026, CCIS 2896, pp. 292–295, 2027.
https://doi.org/10.1007/978-3-032-27235-5_30

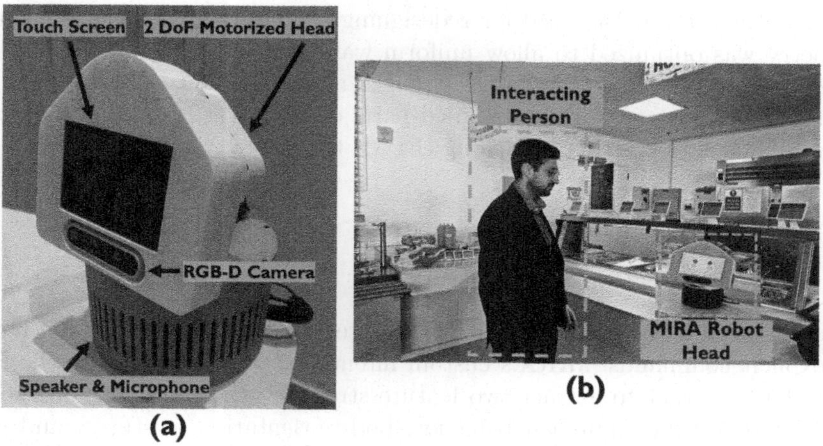

Fig. 1. MIRA social robot head (a) and real-world deployment scenario (b). The MIRA robot identifies human interaction intent through deep learning-based multimodal analysis of pose and emotional cues, and can verbally interact with users through its speaker and microphone via the use of Large Language Models (LLMs). Finally, MIRA's motorized head with two degrees of freedom (DoF) enables a real-time tracking of the user's face.

building trust [4], making social robot heads particularly suited as platforms for assistive applications.

In this demonstration paper, we present MIRA (Multimodal Interactive Robot Assistant), a fully custom-made social robot head designed as a versatile platform for human-robot interaction applications (Fig. 1). The current MIRA robot prototype provides three foundational demonstrations: *i)* real-time human intent detection using RGB-only camera input; *ii)* natural voice-based dialogue through cloud-connected large language models (LLMs); and *iii)* face tracking with two degrees of freedom for maintained eye contact.

This paper is organized as follows. Section 2 provides an overview of the MIRA system architecture. Then, Sect. 3 describes each demonstration available on the MIRA robot. Finally, Sect. 4 concludes this paper.

2 System Architecture

MIRA consists of a custom 3D-printed robot head housing an Intel RealSense depth camera, a display screen for animated facial expressions, speakers and microphones, and servo motors enabling pan-tilt head movement. The robot head was designed in SolidWorks using a top-down design approach, which allowed designing the housing structure on top of the actual dimensions of the hardware components which ensured precise alignment and exact clearance sizes between different parts of the head. All the parts of the design were following a modular architecture allowing discrete parts to be modified or replaced independently without the need for redesigning the entire structure. The overall geometry was optimized to allow uniform wall thickness and filleted edges for additive manufacturing to improve strength and printability while minimizing support requirements. All the designed parts of the robot head were fabricated using Filament Deposition Modelling (FDM) 3D printer.

3 Demonstrations

3.1 Intent Detection Demo

Effective social robots must recognize when users wish to interact without requiring explicit commands. MIRA's custom intent detection system uses the RGB video data in order to extract two feature streams: pose features from skeletal keypoint detection (approach behavior, body orientation, gestures) and emotional features from facial expression analysis. These multimodal features feed into a Transformer model distinguishing intentional approach from incidental presence (Fig. 2).

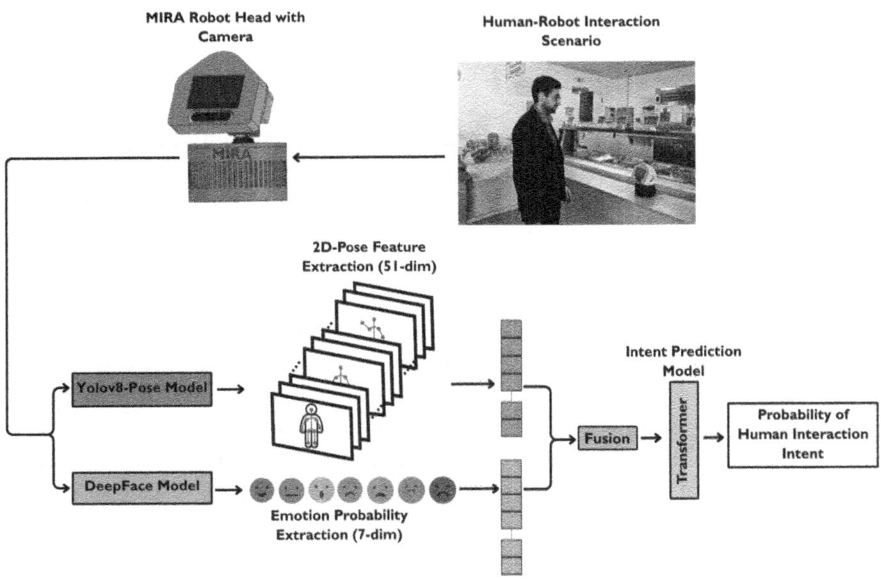

Fig. 2. Human intent prediction model architecture.

The model is pre-trained on the large-scale dataset previously collected in [8]. Following this, real-world trials involving 15 participants in an uncontrolled environment (*not* present in the dataset in [8]) achieves 91% accuracy with 83% precision and perfect recall (100%), detecting all 15 genuine interaction attempts with only 3 false alarms (Table 1). This clearly demonstrates the usefulness of the approach in real-world settings.

Table 1. Real-world deployment performance for intent detection across 32 trials.

Accuracy	Precision	Recall	F_1-Score
0.91	0.83	1.00	0.91

3.2 Voice Interaction Demo

Natural conversation capability allows MIRA to serve diverse applications. The voice module integrates speech-to-text, large language model reasoning (GPT-4o-mini via API), and text-to-speech synthesis.

3.3 Face Tracking Demo

The ability of the robot to maintain eye contact is well-known to be of crucial importance for user acceptance [7]. MIRA implements autonomous human face tracking by using a YOLOv8-nano to detect the position of the human face. Once the position is detected, the servo motors actuating MIRA's head are moved in a way such that the face coordinate stays within the center of the camera image.

4 Conclusion

This paper has described the three foundational demonstrations currently features by the MIRA robot. By integrating reliable intent detection, flexible voice conversation, and attentive face tracking, MIRA provides foundational interaction capabilities for diverse applications in socially assistive robotics.

References

1. Broekens, J., Heerink, M., Rosendal, H.: Assistive social robots in elderly care: a review. Gerontechnology **8**(2), 94–103 (2009)
2. Abdi, J., Al-Hindawi, A., Ng, T., Vizcaychipi, M.P.: Scoping review on the use of socially assistive robot technology in elderly care. BMJ Open **8**(2), e018815 (2018)
3. Fogg, B.J.: A behavior model for persuasive design. In: Proceedings of the 4th International Conference on Persuasive Technology, pp. 1–7. ACM (2009)
4. Bainbridge, W.A., Hart, J.W., Kim, E.S., Scassellati, B.: The benefits of interactions with physically present robots over video-displayed agents. Int. J. Soc. Robot. **3**(1), 41–52 (2011)
5. Oinas-Kukkonen, H., Harjumaa, M.: Persuasive systems design: key issues, process model, and system features. Commun. AIS **24**(1), 485–500 (2009)
6. Ham, J., Cuijpers, R.H., Cabibihan, J.J.: Combining robotic persuasive strategies: the persuasive power of a storytelling robot that uses gazing and gestures. Int. J. Soc. Robot. **7**(4), 479–487 (2015)
7. Admoni, H., Scassellati, B.: Social eye gaze in human-robot interaction: a review. J. Hum.-Rob. Interact. **6**(1), 25–63 (2017)
8. Mohsen, F., Safa, A.: MINT-RVAE: multi-cues intention prediction of human-robot interaction using human pose and emotion information from RGB-only camera data (2025)

A Persuasive XR Demo of Adaptive Spatial Interfaces and AI Agents

Herman Remy[1(✉)] and Kaoru Sumi[2]

[1] Charter Oak College, New Britain, CT, USA
herman@walkerindustries.xyz
[2] Future University Hakodate, Hakodate, Japan

Abstract. Recent advances in extended reality (XR) have enabled spatial operating systems that reshape how users interact with digital environments. However, many existing XR systems replicate traditional 2D interaction paradigms and provide limited support for intentional behavior change. This demo explores how adaptive spatial interfaces combined with supportive AI agents can function as a persuasive medium. Grounded in Fogg's Behavior Model, the system aligns spatial configuration and agent behavior to support user motivation, ability, and timely prompts without explicit instruction or enforcement. Through three interactive scenarios, the demo illustrates how spatial adaptation and agent-supported interaction can facilitate habit formation and smoother transitions between activities in XR environments.

Keywords: Persuasive Technology · Behavior Change · Human–Agent Interaction · Spatial User Interfaces · Extended Reality (XR)

1 Introduction

Persuasive Technology focuses on the design of interactive systems that intentionally influence human behavior in ethical and user-centered ways. Early work in this field has shown that digital systems can shape users' attitudes and actions not only through explicit instruction or feedback, but also through more subtle changes in context and interaction design (Fogg, 2003). As digital environments become increasingly immersive, understanding how context itself can function as a persuasive medium has become an important research challenge.

Extended Reality (XR) environments offer a particularly promising setting for persuasive design, as they allow digital systems to directly shape the spatial context in which users act. However, despite rapid advances in XR hardware and software, many existing XR systems primarily replicate conventional 2D interaction paradigms within three-dimensional spaces. As a result, XR is often used for immersion or visual novelty rather than for systematically supporting behavior change. The persuasive potential of spatial interfaces remains underexplored.

According to Fogg's Behavior Model, behavior occurs when motivation, ability, and prompts converge (Fogg, 2003) [1]. Spatial environments are uniquely suited to influence

E. Vlahu-Gjorgievska et al. (Eds.): PERSUASIVE 2026, CCIS 2896, pp. 296–299, 2027.
https://doi.org/10.1007/978-3-032-27235-5_31

all three factors simultaneously. By restructuring space, systems can lower friction and increase users' ability to act; by aligning environments with user goals and preferences, they can enhance motivation; and by embedding cues directly into the environment, they can provide timely and non-intrusive prompts. From this perspective, persuasion can be achieved not by telling users what to do, but by shaping the environment in which decisions and actions take place.

In parallel, research in Human–Agent Interaction and social presence have demonstrated that agents embedded in interactive systems can significantly influence user perception and behavior. When users feel that they are interacting with a social entity rather than a machine, engagement, trust, and responsiveness increase (Biocca, Harms, & Burgoon, 2003) [2]. Moreover, prior work on transformed social interaction in virtual environments has shown that changes in representation and spatial context can alter interaction patterns and user behavior in meaningful ways (Bailenson, 2006) [3]. These findings suggest that AI agents, when carefully integrated into spatial environments, can act as persuasive partners rather than authoritative controllers.

This demo explores a persuasive approach that combines adaptive spatial interfaces with AI agent behavior to support habit formation and behavioral transitions in XR. Instead of relying on explicit instructions, rewards, or enforcement, the system subtly adapts the spatial environment to align with the user's intended activity. An AI agent operates as a supportive presence, offering context-sensitive prompts while preserving user autonomy. Through interactive scenarios, the demo illustrates how persuasion can emerge from the coordinated design of space and agent behavior, contributing new insights into ethical, user-centered persuasion in XR environments.

2 System Concept

The system is designed as an adaptive spatial interface that allows users to switch fluidly between 2D and 3D interaction modes depending on context. Rather than forcing users into a fixed interface style, spatial elements dynamically reconfigure to match user intentions such as work, leisure, or focused tasks [4]. This adaptability increases ability by lowering interaction friction and cognitive load.

A local, privacy-preserving AI agent is embedded within the spatial environment as a supportive assistant. The agent does not issue commands or automate decisions; instead, it provides optional prompts and contextual suggestions aligned with user goals. All agent interventions can be accepted, ignored, or rejected by the user, maintaining full agency. Together, the adaptive environment and the AI agent operationalize Fogg's model by aligning motivation, ability, and prompts through spatial design rather than explicit persuasion.

3 Scenario

To demonstrate how adaptive spatial interfaces and AI agent behavior function as a persuasive mechanism, we present three interactive scenarios.

Each scenario is designed to highlight a different component of Fogg's Behavior Model—motivation, ability, and prompt—while keeping the task itself constant. Rather than relying on explicit instructions or rewards, the system supports behavior change by reshaping the spatial environment and embedding subtle cues within it. Across all scenarios, users retain full control over their actions, and the AI agent acts only as a supportive presence whose suggestions can be accepted, ignored, or dismissed.

Scenario 1: Spatial Theme Adaptation (Motivation)
Users start in a neutral spatial interface and may optionally switch to a personalized spatial theme with familiar visual metaphors. This customization increases emotional engagement and intrinsic motivation without adding new functionality or explicit instructions. The persuasive effect arises from the user's willingness to remain in an environment that feels meaningful and personally resonant.

Scenario 2: Activity-Based Mode Switching (Ability)
Users create spatial layouts for different activities such as work or leisure and switch between them. The environment automatically restores the corresponding spatial context, reducing setup effort and cognitive load. By making task initiation easier, the system increases perceived ability without relying on reminders or incentives.

Scenario 3: Cross-Device Spatial Continuity (Prompt)
Users transition between devices while maintaining a consistent spatial workspace. Prompts are embedded as subtle environmental cues or optional agent suggestions rather than notifications. These context-aware prompts support timely action while preserving user autonomy and minimizing disruption.

4 Discussion

The presented scenarios collectively demonstrate the potential for a persuasive platform for behavior change in XR computing. By integrating adaptive spatial user interfaces with a supportive AI agent, the system achieves convergence of Fogg's Behavior Model factors (motivation, ability, and prompts) in ways that rigid, corporate-driven XR OSes (such as Apple's visionOS and Meta's Horizon OS) cannot readily replicate.

Theme switching (Scenario 1) and mode toggles (Scenario 2) enhance Ability by providing intuitive, context-sensitive affordances that lower the barrier between familiar 2D interactions and immersive 3D ones. Rather than forcing users to adapt to the medium, this spatial computing solution molds the medium to the user, transforming complex spatial manipulation into accessible, natural actions. Personalization through themes further amplifies Motivation, converting passive digital environments into emotionally resonant, goal-aligned spaces that foster sustained engagement. Cross-device synchronization (Scenario 3) reduces friction in task continuity, creating a seamless, persistent ecosystem that encourages habitual XR adoption over fragmented, device-siloed experiences.

In contrast, current mainstream XR platforms often remain gimmicky or constrained. VisionOS delivers elegant spatial design but confines users within Apple's walled garden, limiting motivation through restricted app ecosystems and proprietary controls. Horizon OS offers greater openness in theory, yet its ecosystem lock-in and centralized dependencies undermine true cross-platform ability. This spatial computing solution inverts these limitations, prioritizing user-owned, persistent contexts that support long-term behavioral shifts toward immersive, adaptive computing.

Within the domain of Human–Agent Interaction, the AI agent emerges as a distinctive collaborative partner. Unlike generic voice assistants that impose top-down guidance, the AI agent cultivates an intimate, human-like presence. In the current demo, the agent's adaptivity is limited to user-approved memory, session-level pattern recognition, and rule-based contextual prompting rather than autonomous goal formation or opaque learning. This design aligns with contemporary HCI trends toward multimodal natural interaction (gestures, voice, spatial awareness) and spatial intelligence, where environments anticipate and support users without intrusion. By maintaining explicit user veto and full agency, the AI agent follows a human-centered AI approach that keeps human goals and control central to the system design [5]. It thereby advances Persuasive Technology in an ethical direction—subtle environmental nudges and agent prompts align with user intentions rather than corporate agendas, minimizing coercion risks prevalent in many commercial solutions while democratizing access through open, cross-device architecture.

References

1. Fogg, B.J.: Persuasive Technology: Using Computers to Change What We Think and Do. Morgan Kaufmann, San Francisco (2003)
2. Biocca, F., Harms, C., Burgoon, J.K.: Toward a More Robust theory and measure of social presence: review and suggested criteria. Presence: Teleoperators Virtual Environ. **12**(5), 456–480 (2003)
3. Bailenson, J.N.: Transformed social interaction in collaborative virtual environments. Presence: Teleoperators Virtual Environ. **15**(3), 225–236 (2006)
4. Weld, D.S., et al.: Automatically personalizing user interfaces. In: Proceedings of the 18th International Joint Conference on Artificial Intelligence (IJCAI'03). Key West, FL, USA (2003)
5. Shneiderman, B.: Human-Centered AI. Oxford University Press (2020)

Dynamic Personalized Interventions via Reinforcement Learning with a Theory-Based Reward Function

Masahiro Shiraishi[1(✉)], Yuta Masuda[1], Tatsuya Yamamoto[1], Shoji Hayakawa[1], Takuya Kamimura[1], Niida Mituski[2], Masahiro Yoshihara[2], Keisuke Suzuki[2], and Hiroyuki Iizuka[2]

[1] Fujitsu Limited, Kawasaki, Japan
s_masahiro@fujitsu.com
[2] Center for Human Nature, Artificial Intelligence, and Neuroscience, Sapporo, Japan

Abstract. Promoting health behaviors such as physical activity (PA) is a critical priority closely tied to improvements in well-being. Demand for personalized interventions tailored to individual needs has increased, drawing attention to machine learning, particularly reinforcement learning (RL), as a promising methodological approach. However, applying RL to PA promotion in real-world environments remains challenging, primarily due to the limited availability of meaningful reward signals required for effective learning. Therefore, we developed an RL-based personalized intervention that incorporates theory-driven features to enrich sparse reward signals. In a six-week study (N = 671), dynamic personalization based on RL increased PA implementation rates by 6.3% over conventional static personalization and by 10.4% over randomization.

Keywords: Behavior Change · Personalization · Reinforcement Learning

1 Introduction

Sustaining physical activity (PA) remains a persistent challenge linked to well-being. Mobile health applications (mHealth apps) offer scalable behavioral support; however, uniform interventions often fail to address individual differences, thereby limiting their effectiveness. Static personalization, such as tailoring interventions solely based on personality traits, also lacks the flexibility to adapt to dynamic fluctuations in users' contextual states. Recent research highlights the need for data-driven personalization approaches that extend beyond fixed models, leveraging users' personality traits and behavioral histories to deliver more adaptive intervention strategies.

In this study, we propose a dynamic personalized intervention system based on reinforcement learning (RL). Using a contextual multi-armed bandit (C-MAB), the system adaptively selects interventions from both trait- and state-level contextual information. To improve learning efficiency, the reward function integrates behavioral outcomes with theory-based features, increasing reward-signal density. In a six-week field experiment (N = 671), our dynamic personalization outperformed both static and random baselines, improving PA implementation rates by 6.3% and 10.4%, respectively.

E. Vlahu-Gjorgievska et al. (Eds.): PERSUASIVE 2026, CCIS 2896, pp. 300–304, 2027.
https://doi.org/10.1007/978-3-032-27235-5_32

2 Related Work

Personalized interventions for promoting PA are broadly categorized into knowledge-based and data-driven approaches [1]. Knowledge-based approaches leverage behavior change techniques (BCTs) or clinical guidelines; however, their reliance on single theoretical frameworks limits flexibility and adaptability. Data-driven approaches primarily employ machine learning. Although supervised learning models can predict effective interventions from static user features—and have demonstrated a certain degree of personalization, as reported in prior work [2]—they are unable to accommodate rapid fluctuations in users' dynamic contextual states. RL addresses these limitations by framing intervention delivery as a sequential decision-making problem under uncertainty, enabling adaptive, context-responsive personalization.

Recent RL-based systems, such as PEARL [3], have demonstrated the feasibility of dynamic personalization in large-scale real-world deployments, yet their effect sizes remain modest. Persistent practical challenges—particularly sparse rewards that impede stable learning—likely contribute to this limitation. These issues underscore the need for mechanisms that enable rapid contextual adaptation.

3 Proposed Method

We implemented a personalized intervention system within a C-MAB framework, employing a Linear Thompson Sampling (LinTS) [4] as the RL policy. An overview of the proposed method is presented in Fig. 1. LinTS samples model parameters from the posterior distribution at each round, computes the predicted reward as a linear combination of these parameters and the contextual variables, selects the arm with the highest sampled value, and updates the posterior using the observed reward. To address sparse-reward challenges in real-world RL applications, we incorporated post-intervention mHealth log data directly into the reward function. Rather than relying solely on the target behavior, we applied behavioral-science theory to quantify the impact of each intervention and thereby increase reward-signal density.

Reward construction was informed by two behavior-change frameworks. The Behavior Change Technique Taxonomy (BCTT) [5] delineates standardized intervention components, whereas the Mechanisms of Action (MoA) framework [6] specifies the psychological processes through which interventions influence behavior. The Theory and Techniques Tool [7] provides validated BCTT–MoA links for estimating intervention impact. Based on prior evidence [8], six BCTs were identified as effective for promoting PA; in this study, BCTs 2.2 (Feedback on behavior) and 2.3 (Self-monitoring of behavior) were most relevant, corresponding onto three MoAs—Motivation, Behavioral regulation, and Feedback processes [7]. MoA-reflective features were generated by an LLM using these mappings and refined through expert review. These features informed the reward variables at round t in Table 1, forming the reward function:

$$R_t = \lambda r_t^{Behavior} + (1 - \lambda) r_t^{MoAs} \in [-1, 1]$$

$$r_t^{MoAs} = \sum \omega_t^{MoA} x_t^{MoA} \in [-1, 1]$$

where $r_t^{Behavior}$ is post-intervention behavioral outcome (1 if the target behavior was performed, − 1 otherwise); r_t^{MoAs} is the MoA-based reward derived from the variables x_t^{MoA} and weights ω_t^{MoA} in Table 1; and λ is the weighting parameter, set to 0.5.

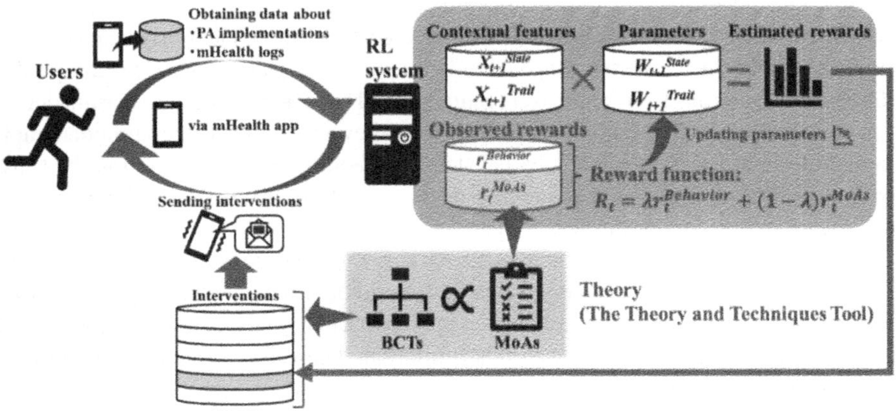

Fig. 1. Overview of the personalized intervention system based on a C-MAB framework, illustrating a theory-based reward computed from post-intervention logs and parameter updating within the RL agent.

Table 1. Reward variables designed from significant MoAs.

ω_t^{MoA}	x_t^{MoA}	**MoA-reflective features obtained from mHealth apps**
0.4	$x_t^{Motivation} = 0.3 \cdot \textbf{Engagement} + 0.6 \cdot \textbf{Evaluation} + 0.1 \cdot \textbf{Interest}$	***Engagement*****:** Whether you enjoyed or pushed through daily PA
		Evaluation**:** Whether you increased or decreased motivation for PA following the intervention
		Interest**:** Whether a new PA plan has been set up
0.1	$x_t^{Behavioralregulation} = \begin{cases} 1.0, ifchange = 1.0 \\ Report \cdot Latency, otherwise \end{cases}$	***Change*****:** Whether there were any changes to the PA plan
		Report**:** Whether or not the results were registered in the app, regardless of PA implementation
		Latency**:** How latency period between planned time and actual implemented time was
0.5	$x_t^{Feedbackprocess} = 1.0 \cdot \textbf{Review}$	***Review*****:** Whether or not there was a transition to the PA history screen

4 Experiment

4.1 Design

The study included 671 healthy Asian adults who used an mHealth app to engage in PA over six weeks. At the start, the participants registered PA they intended to perform. They subsequently recorded daily completion status. Interventions began one week after app onboarding and were delivered every day at 10:00 a.m. Following the design described in prior work [2], we prepared six types of interventions combining text and visual elements. They were randomly assigned to one of the following three groups:

- **Random group:** Received one of the six intervention types randomly selected.
- **Static personalization (SP) group:** Received one of the top three intervention types, selected from this set in turn, identified as most preferable based on a one-time estimation following prior work [2], with the model fixed without updates.
- **Dynamic personalization (DP) group:** Received personalized intervention types by our RL, with daily model updates using post-intervention rewards (see Sect. 3).

4.2 Evaluation

The implementation rate was defined as the ratio of completed PA to daily registrations in each group and its six-week trajectory was used to assess attrition. To evaluate the impact of personalization, we conducted a difference-in-differences (DiD) analysis compared the SP and DP groups with the Random group (baseline: week 1), and effect sizes were derived as Cohen's d.

5 Results and Discussions

Figure 2 illustrates the trajectories of implementation rates for each group. After six weeks, the DP group showed a 6.3% higher implementation rate than the SP group and a 10.4% higher rate than the Random group. The DiD analysis comparing both personalized groups with the Random group yielded effect sizes of -0.01 for the SP comparison and 3.6 for the DP comparison, indicating that dynamic personalization through RL outperformed static personalization. Moreover, the effect size of DP substantially exceeded the PEARL's effect size of 1.4. This result suggests that our theory-based reward function contributed to the stronger performance. However, automating reward-design process to improve generalizability remains an important future work.

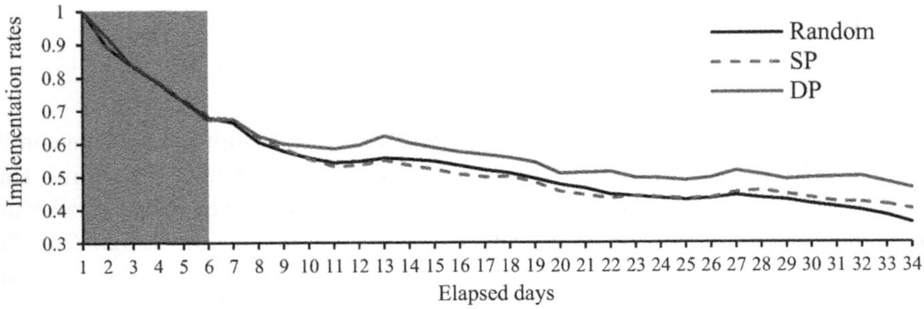

Fig. 2. Transition of implementation rates. The vertical axis represents the implementation rates smoothed using a five-day moving average, and the horizontal axis indicates the number of days since each user first performed PA. The black area denotes the pre-intervention period.

References

1. Ghanvatkar, S., Kankanhalli, A., Rajan, V.: User models for personalized physical activity interventions: scoping review. JMIR Mhealth Uhealth **7**(1), e11098 (2019)
2. Shiraishi, M., et al.: Experimental evaluation of personalized intervention based on the PLS-SEM model for physical activity. In: IEEE SMC 2025, IEEE, Piscataway, NJ (2026), to appear
3. Evaluating PEARL. https://research.google/pubs/evaluating-pearl-a-personalized-exercise-assistant-using-reinforcement-learning-walkmate-study/. Last accessed 11 Jan 2026
4. Yan, C., Xu, H., Han, H., Zhang, Y., Wang, Z.: Thompson sampling with time-varying reward for contextual bandits. In: DASFAA, pp. 54–63. Springer, Cham (2023)
5. Michie, S., et al.: The behavior change technique taxonomy (v1) of 93 hierarchically clustered techniques: building an international consensus for the reporting of behavior change interventions. Ann. Behav. Med. **46**(1), 81–95 (2013)
6. Carey, R.N., et al.: Behavior change techniques and their mechanisms of action: a synthesis of links described in published intervention literature. Ann. Behav. Med. **53**(8), 693–707 (2019)
7. Theory and Techniques Tool. https://theoryandtechniquetool.humanbehaviourchange.org/. Last accessed 11 Jan 2026
8. Bernard, P., et al.: Climate change, physical activity and sport: a systematic review. Sports Med. **51**(5), 1041–1059 (2021)

A Counterfactual Stress Management System for Lifestyle Behavior Change Using Activity Logs

Kotomi Wakayama[1(✉)], Tomokazu Matsui[1,2], Hirohiko Suwa[1,2], and Keiichi Yasumoto[1,2]

[1] Nara Institute of Science and Technology, Ikoma, Nara, Japan
kotomi.wakayama@ubi-lab.com

[2] Center for Advanced Intelligence Project, RIKEN, Chuo-ku, Tokyo, Japan

Abstract. Increasing worker stress creates an urgent need for mental health support, yet current stress management systems often remain limited to simple state visualization rather than actionable behavior change. This study proposes a personalized system integrating wearable-based physiological sensing with behavioral history to promote lifestyle modifications through counterfactual machine learning. Using Fitbit for passive R-R interval sensing and LINE (a used mobile messaging platform) for contextual logging, the system extracts geometric features from Lorenz plots to estimate frustration levels (scored on a 20-point scale derived from NASA-TLX) via personalized Support Vector Regression (SVR). When high stress is detected, the system applies Diverse Counterfactual Explanations (DiCE) to generate "what-if" scenarios. An LLM translates these into natural language advice via smart mirrors and LINE. An in-the-wild study with 8 participants showed the SVR model achieved practical accuracy (MAE: 3.290). A crossover comparison further revealed that counterfactual-based recommendations consistently outperformed recommendations based on previously low-stress activities without counterfactual reasoning in both stress reduction and promoting behavioral change. Due to the small sample size, exact Wilcoxon signed-rank tests (two-sided) were applied. Although the differences did not reach the 5% significance level (stress reduction: $p = 0.0625$; behavioral change: $p = 0.0625$), all non-zero differences were in the improvement direction, indicating a positive trend favoring counterfactual-based feedback.

Keywords: Ubiquitous Computing · Internet of Things (IoT) · Behavior Change · Machine Learning

1 Introduction

Rising worker stress has increased the need for mental health support [1,2]. Current wearable-based stress estimation systems mainly focus on visualizing stress levels, while offering limited support for long-term lifestyle improvement. As a

E. Vlahu-Gjorgievska et al. (Eds.): PERSUASIVE 2026, CCIS 2896, pp. 305–309, 2027.
https://doi.org/10.1007/978-3-032-27235-5_33

result, many existing interventions place emphasis on short-term relaxation techniques, such as breathing exercises [3]. Moreover, many existing counterfactual-based approaches rely heavily on self-reported data, making it difficult to capture subtle physiological changes. To address these challenges, this study proposes a personalized stress management system using Counterfactual Machine Learning and Large Language Models. The system integrates R-R interval (RRI) data with activity logs to generate counterfactual scenarios aimed at stress reduction. These suggestions are delivered through smartphones and smart mirrors. In a 13 - day study with 8 participants, the stress estimation model achieved an MAE of 3.290 in predicting self-reported NASA-TLX frustration scores (20-point scale). Crossover comparisons suggested consistent improvements over recommendations based on previously low-stress activities in both stress reduction and behavioral change. Exact Wilcoxon signed-rank tests (two-sided) yielded $p = 0.0625$ for both measures, and all participants with non-zero differences showed improvements.

2 Related Research

Wearable-based stress visualization is widespread, yet most systems only display stress levels without guiding users toward corrective actions [3]. Although Just-In-Time Adaptive Interventions (JITAI) show promise, current methods focus on short-term relaxation rather than long-term lifestyle modification [3,4]. Furthermore, many existing counterfactual-based approaches rely heavily on self-reported data, imposing a high user burden and failing to capture subtle situational changes reflected in continuous physiological variables [5].

In contrast to prior work, this study proposes a stress management system integrating physiological data and activity logs. Using counterfactual machine learning, the approach provides specific recommendations based on "what-if" scenarios. Statistical features from physiological data and activity logs enable improved stress estimation accuracy. A Large Language Model generates feedback delivered through daily devices. By integrating these insights into routines, the system encourages sustainable behavior change instead of temporary coping.

3 Proposed Methodology

Figure 1 shows an overview of the proposed system, which integrates physiological data and activity history to encourage behavior change, as described below.

The system integrates physiological and contextual data through 2 channels. For data acquisition, RRI data are collected using Fitbit, while behavioral history and NASA-TLX scores are obtained via LINE. Behavioral history serves as contextual input, and NASA-TLX scores are used as ground-truth labels for frustration. For feature extraction, RRI data are segmented into 15-minute intervals. A Lorenz plot is generated for each segment, from which 8 statistical features are extracted. These features are then combined with LINE activity logs to form feature vectors used for stress estimation and recommendation generation.

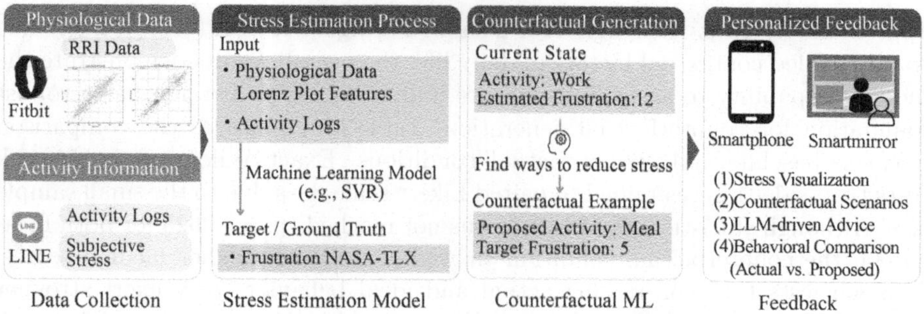

Fig. 1. Architecture of the System from Data Collection to Personalized Feedback.

Individual feature vectors are used for personalized stress estimation and action recommendation. Stress levels are estimated using SVR to predict NASA-TLX frustration scores. The model takes eight Lorenz plot features, activity logs, and temporal features as inputs. By training a separate model for each user, individual differences in stress sensitivity are taken into account, enabling more accurate stress estimation. When the estimated stress exceeds a predefined threshold, Diverse Counterfactual Explanations (DiCE) [6] are applied. The NASA-TLX frustration score is treated as the target variable, and DiCE identifies alternative behaviors that are expected to reduce this score.

The system presents results through four components. Stress Visualization provides objective self-awareness. Counterfactual Scenarios show "what-if" improvements. LLM-driven Advice offers context-specific feedback. Comparative Visualization contrasts actual versus proposed behaviors. Feedback is delivered via two devices. Smart mirrors placed in transition points provide state awareness. On smartphones, LINE delivers notifications for retrospective reflection. This allows users to review causal links between actions and stress at the end of the day. Combining daily awareness with nocturnal reflection fosters sustainable behavior change rather than temporary coping.

4 Evaluation Experiments and Results

An in-the-wild experiment was conducted to verify the system. 8 graduate students (6 males and 2 females) participated in a 13-day study, including 7 days of data collection followed by counterfactual and non-counterfactual conditions, each lasting 3 days. Equipment consisted of one Fitbit Sense 2 per person, 6 smartphones, and 2 smart mirrors. Collected data involved RRI data, behavioral logs, and NASA-TLX scores. RRI was recorded continuously while logs and NASA-TLX were self-reported via LINE. The effectiveness of the proposed method was evaluated through a crossover design and significance tests (p-values) using Likert scale scores for behavioral change and stress reduction.

As a result, the SVR models achieved an average RMSE of 4.035 and MAE of 3.290 (Table 1). Given the 20-point frustration scale, the average error was approximately 16%. Although User 2 showed a higher RMSE (6.146), likely due to unmodeled contextual factors in daily life, the overall results demonstrate the model's capability to accurately capture individual stress dynamics as a robust foundation for counterfactual generation. Table 2 summarizes the comparison between baseline and counterfactual conditions. Exact Wilcoxon signed-rank tests (two-sided) were applied to paired Likert-scale data due to the small sample size. Although statistical significance was not reached (p = 0.0625 for both measures), the counterfactual condition showed consistently higher median scores. This suggests that contrasting actual and ideal behaviors may exert stronger psychological influence than simple baseline visualization.

Table 1. SVR estimation accuracy for each user (20-point scale).

User	U1	U2	U3	U4	U5	U6	U7	U8	**Ave.**
RMSE	3.370	6.146	3.694	3.374	4.272	3.572	3.962	3.890	**4.035**
MAE	2.926	5.142	3.014	2.850	3.340	2.852	3.288	2.912	**3.290**

Table 2. Comparison between baseline and counterfactual conditions

Measure	Baseline (Median [IQR])	Counterfactual (Median [IQR])	*p*
Stress reduction	3.0 [2.5–3.5]	4.0 [3.5–4.5]	0.0625
Behavioral change	2.5 [1.5–3.0]	3.5 [3.0–4.0]	0.0625

5 Conclusion

This study developed a personalized stress management system integrating wearable and smartphone data with DiCE and LLMs. The SVR model achieved practical accuracy (MAE = 3.290). In a crossover study, counterfactual recommendations showed consistent improvements over baseline methods in stress reduction and behavioral change (exact Wilcoxon signed-rank tests, two-sided; stress reduction p = 0.0625, behavioral change p = 0.0625). These findings suggest that counterfactual alternatives may be more effective than simple state visualization for promoting stress-related behavior change.

References

1. Ministry of Health, Labour and Welfare, Summary of the 2023 Survey on Industrial Safety and Health (in Japanese). https://www.mhlw.go.jp/toukei/list/r05-46-50_kekka-gaiyo.html. Accessed 12 Dec 2025

2. Hara, K., Nagata, T., Matoba, M., Miyazaki, T.: the impact of productivity loss from presenteeism and absenteeism on mental health in Japan. J. Occup. Environ. Med. **67**(9), 699–704 (2025)
3. Pinge, A., Gad, V., Jaisighani, D., Ghosh, S., Sen, S.: Detection and monitoring of stress using wearables: a systematic review. Front. Comput. Sci. **6**, 1478851 (2024)
4. Schwerdtfeger, A.R., Tatschl, J.M., Rominger, C.: Effectiveness of 2 just-in-time adaptive interventions for reducing stress and stabilizing cardiac autonomic function: microrandomized trials. J. Med. Internet Res. **27**, e69582 (2025)
5. Jung, G., Lee, U.: CounterStress: enhancing stress coping planning through counterfactual explanations in personal informatics. In: Proceedings of the CHI 2025, pp. 1–20. ACM (2025)
6. Mothilal, R.K., Sharma, A., Tan, C.: Explaining machine learning classifiers through diverse counterfactual explanations. In: Proceedings of the FAT* 2020, pp. 607–617. ACM (2020)

Investigating AI NPC–Supported Group Experiences in Mixed Reality Museums

Hsin-Ying Wu[1(✉)], Sharon Ihan Hsiao[2], and Shih-Yi Chien[1]

[1] Department of Management Information Systems, National Chengchi University, Taipei, Taiwan
{114356019,sychien}@nccu.edu.tw
[2] School of Engineering, Santa Clara University, Santa Clara, USA
ihsiao@scu.edu

Abstract. Museums increasingly adopt emerging technologies such as Artificial Intelligence (AI) and Mixed Reality (MR) to create more immersive and interactive visitor experiences. This research aims to design and investigate multi-user collaborative museum experiences with AI non-player characters (AI NPCs) in an MR environment. Using a trajectories framework, the research examines whether AI-guided MR experiences can foster tighter social connections compared to conventional museum tours. The proposed system includes multiple AI NPCs located throughout the venue, each associated with an art piece and constrained to exhibit the artwork-specific knowledge. Multiple measures are adopted to access user experience in this AIMR-based museum application, including social presence, satisfaction, intimacy with companions, and behavioral intention. This research is expected to contribute design insights by illustrating how AI and MR can be leveraged to enhance the naturalness of shared museum visiting experiences.

Keywords: Mixed reality · Artificial intelligence · Multi-user collaborative experiences · Museum visitor experience · Social presence

1 Introduction

Museums increasingly adopt emerging technologies such as Mixed Reality (MR) and Artificial Intelligence (AI) to create more immersive and interactive visitor experiences [18]. However, most research remains at the individual level, even though most people visit museums as part of a social group [3].

It has been revealed that social interaction is not about physical proximity but rather about the cohesion of the group [4]. Yet in order to maintain group coherence, visitors in conventional museum tours often have to sacrifice their own interests [15]. This tension highlights the motivation of exploring MR within a group context. We argue that MR can relax physical constraints by extending visitors into a shared virtual space, thereby creating new opportunities for group-based interaction.

E. Vlahu-Gjorgievska et al. (Eds.): PERSUASIVE 2026, CCIS 2896, pp. 310–314, 2027.
https://doi.org/10.1007/978-3-032-27235-5_34

Meanwhile, current research has pointed out the use of AI in museums, encompassing voice-guided tours to personalized recommendation engines. By emulating human cognition and personalizing the presentation of content based on interest, AI fosters enhanced visitor engagement and a deeper emotional connection to museum exhibits [8,14]. In contrast to conventional museum tours, where visitors must stay physically close to a human guide, the existence of AI-driven virtual guides—often designed as non-player characters (NPCs)—provides a more flexible and personalized tour experience that supports both individual freedom and group coherence during visits.

By integrating MR and AI NPCs into group-based museum visiting experiences, this research aims to address the existing gaps in supporting group cohesion and the absence of guiding roles, thereby enhancing the coherence of the shared museum visiting experience. The following research question will be:

RQ: To what extent do AI-guided MR museum experiences foster social interaction among group members, compared to conventional museum tours?

2 Related Work

Prior work has demonstrated that MR and AI technologies can enhance users' behavioral intention, social presence, satisfaction, and learning performance, etc. [2,8,12]. By blending physical artifacts with virtual elements, MR-guided systems provide multisensory experiences that foster deeper understanding and satisfaction, which in turn can encourage repeat visits and positive behavioral intentions [9]. Simultaneously, AI applications, including conversational agents and NPC-guided tours, have been shown to increase interactivity and immersion within museum contexts [11,17], exemplifying the growing role of virtual guides in enriching the visitor experience.

However, most research on creating digital experiences for museums still focuses on the individual level. A series of studies has investigated the "gifting" experiences for their companions in a museum context [4–6,15], revealing that scaffolded experiences based on the trajectories framework designed for each other efficiently enhance social interaction and embodied experiences.

Despite growing research on group experiences and AI applications in museums, a clear gap remains in understanding how AI-driven agents can actively collaborate with visitor groups. This study aims to address this gap by exploring the design and impact of AI NPCs in facilitating group-based MR museum experiences.

3 Methodology

3.1 Research Design

This research builds on the trajectories framework, which conceptualizes visitor experience as a journey passing through different hybrid structures including space, time, role, and interfaces, emphasizing its overall continuity and coherence

[1]. Building upon this framework, prior work has extended it by asking participants to design trajectories for each other, which is the concept of "gifting", validating its utility in facilitating group interactions [5]. Extending this foundation, this research integrates MR-based interaction and AI NPCs as socially active guides within group experiences.

The proposed system consists of multiple AI NPCs located throughout the venue, each associated with a specific exhibit and constrained to exhibit-specific knowledge. In addition to physical artifacts, selected exhibits are represented by virtual replicas, allowing participants to interact with them in virtual spaces.

Except for the social presence of AI NPCs, satisfaction, and intention to use, which previous studies primarily focus on [8,13], this study would like to additionally examine intimacy among group members as a key outcome of group-based museum visits.

The MR Head-Mounted Display Microsoft HoloLens 2 will be used in the experiment. With lightweight equipment and a see-through window, users can easily interact with both physical and virtual contexts.

3.2 Experimental Procedure

Instead of fixing the tour to a predetermined route, we would like to build continuous trajectories for the participants. Therefore, before the tour begins, participants will be asked to prepare three pieces of content for their companions using a predefined template: a target exhibit, an instructional prompt, and a question to be delivered to the assigned AI NPC.

During the visit, with the HoloLens 2 on, participants can explore freely and are not required to stay physically together. During these interactions, the pre-assigned content will shape the unfolding shared experience. Participants can interact with AI NPCs either as a group or individually by getting close to them and pressing the conversation button to start a conversation. When engaging with an AI NPC as a group, participants can see each other's questions and responses simultaneously through the virtual interfaces. Additionally, when one interacts with the virtual replicas, all group members can also see the interactions performed. Some replicas will also allow multi-user interaction.

Once the visit is complete, participants will be asked to fill out a post-test questionnaire and take part in a semi-structured interview, both individually and as a group.

3.3 Measures

To evaluate the outcomes, both subjective and objective data will be collected from the participants. Subjective measures use questionnaires to evaluate, including social presence, intention to use, satisfaction, and intimacy among group. The items of social presence are adapted from Gefen and Straub [7] (CR = 0.919, $\sqrt{AVE} = 0.836$), intention to use from Li and Wang [10] (Cronbach's α = 0.93, CR = 0.94, AVE = 0.78), and satisfaction from Shi et al. (CR = 0.910,

AVE = 0.717). Intimacy is adapted from tie-strength research, asking participants to rate their perceived closeness to interaction partners [16]. To reduce participant fatigue and simplify the response process, all the scales are adapted to 5-point Likert scale rather than original 7-point format.

Objective data consists of participants' behavioral engagement recorded during the tour, operationalized as (1) human–AI interactions, measured by counting the number of verbal questions posed by participants, and (2) eye-tracking data, capturing fixation count and fixation duration within predefined Areas of Interest (AOIs), including the AI NPC, physical exhibits, and virtual exhibits.

Demographic information and prior experience with MR systems were also collected as control variables.

4 Expected Contributions

This study is expected to contribute to museum technology research by advancing an understanding of how AI-driven agents can support socially collaborative experiences in group-based museum visits. With the integration of MR and AI, the proposed system can provide design insights that enable group visitors to enjoy more natural and socially coherent museum visits.

References

1. Benford, S., Giannachi, G., Koleva, B., Rodden, T.: From interaction to trajectories: designing coherent journeys through user experiences. In: Proceedings of the SIGCHI Conference on Human Factors in Computing Systems, pp. 709–718. ACM (2009). https://doi.org/10.1145/1518701.1518812
2. Chin, K.Y., Chang, H.L., Wang, C.S.: Applying a wearable MR-based mobile learning system on museum learning activities for university students. **32**(9), 5744–5765 (2024). https://doi.org/10.1080/10494820.2023.2228843
3. Falk, J.H., Dierking, L.D.: The Museum Experience. Routledge (2016). https://doi.org/10.4324/9781315417899
4. Fosh, L., Benford, S., Koleva, B.: Supporting group coherence in a museum visit. In: Proceedings of the 19th ACM Conference on Computer-Supported Cooperative Work & Social Computing. pp. 1–12. ACM (2016). https://doi.org/10.1145/2818048.2819970
5. Fosh, L., Benford, S., Reeves, S., Koleva, B.: Gifting personal interpretations in galleries. In: Proceedings of the SIGCHI Conference on Human Factors in Computing Systems, pp. 625–634. ACM (2014). https://doi.org/10.1145/2556288.2557259
6. Fosh, L., Benford, S., Reeves, S., Koleva, B., Brundell, P.: See me, feel me, touch me, hear me: trajectories and interpretation in a sculpture garden. In: Proceedings of the SIGCHI Conference on Human Factors in Computing Systems, pp. 149–158. ACM (2013). https://doi.org/10.1145/2470654.2470675
7. Gefen, D., Straub, D.W.: Consumer trust in B2C e-Commerce and the importance of social presence: experiments in e-Products and e-Services. **32**(6), 407–424 (2004). https://doi.org/10.1016/j.omega.2004.01.006
8. Hammady, R., Ma, M., AL-Kalha, Z., Strathearn, C.: A framework for constructing and evaluating the role of MR as a holographic virtual guide in museums. **25**(4), 895–918 (2021). https://doi.org/10.1007/s10055-020-00497-9

9. He, Z., Wu, L., Li, X.R.: When art meets tech: the role of augmented reality in enhancing museum experiences and purchase intentions. **68**, 127–139 (2018). https://doi.org/10.1016/j.tourman.2018.03.003
10. Li, M., Wang, R.: Chatbots in e-commerce: the effect of chatbot language style on customers' continuance usage intention and attitude toward brand. **71**, 103209 (2023). https://doi.org/10.1016/j.jretconser.2022.103209
11. Liang, H., Hwang, G., Hsu, T., Yeh, J.: Effect of an AI-based chatbot on students' learning performance in alternate reality game-based museum learning. **55**(5), 2315–2338 (2024). https://doi.org/10.1111/bjet.13448
12. Martí-Testón, A., Muñoz, A., Solanes, J.E., Gracia, L., Tornero, J.: A methodology to produce augmented-reality guided tours in museums for mixed-reality headsets. **10**(23), 2956 (2021). https://doi.org/10.3390/electronics10232956
13. Oh, C.S., Bailenson, J.N., Welch, G.F.: A systematic review of social presence: definition, antecedents, and implications. **5**, 114 (2018). https://doi.org/10.3389/frobt.2018.00114
14. Speicher, M., Hall, B.D., Nebeling, M.: What is mixed reality? In: Proceedings of the 2019 CHI Conference on Human Factors in Computing Systems. pp. 1–15. ACM (2019). https://doi.org/10.1145/3290605.3300767
15. Tolmie, P., Benford, S., Greenhalgh, C., Rodden, T., Reeves, S.: Supporting group interactions in museum visiting. In: Proceedings of the 17th ACM Conference on Computer Supported Cooperative Work & Social Computing, pp. 1049–1059. ACM (2014). https://doi.org/10.1145/2531602.2531619
16. Wiese, J., Kelley, P.G., Cranor, L.F., Dabbish, L., Hong, J.I., Zimmerman, J.: Are you close with me? Are you nearby?: investigating social groups, closeness, and willingness to share. In: Proceedings of the 13th International Conference on Ubiquitous Computing, pp. 197–206. ACM (2011). https://doi.org/10.1145/2030112.2030140
17. Winter, M., Sweeney, L., Mason, K., Blume, P.: Low-power machine learning for visitor engagement in museums. In: Proceedings of the 6th International Conference on Computer-Human Interaction Research and Applications, pp. 236–243. SCITEPRESS - Science and Technology Publications (2022). https://doi.org/10.5220/0011585600003323
18. Yu, T.C., Huang, M.X., Liu, Y.H., et al.: A systematic review of integrating mixed reality and artificial intelligence in museums: enhancing visitor experiences and innovating exhibit design. In: Proceedings of the 58th Hawaii International Conference on System Sciences, pp. 1533–1542 (2025)

The Effect of the "Yes-Set" in Request Situations on Compliance Behavior

Tamao Yoshihara(✉) and Kazuki Sekine

Graduate School of Human Sciences, Waseda University, Tokyo, Japan
tamaoyoshihara@fuji.waseda.jp

Abstract. The Yes-Set technique is a sequential influence strategy in which a series of questions that elicit affirmative responses is presented to promote compliance with a subsequent request. However, the roles of question frequency and response-formation processes have not been sufficiently examined. The present study manipulated the number of Yes-Set questions (0, 3, or 6) and the presence of hand gestures during request presentation, and examined their relationships with compliance behavior, response time, and cognitive task performance. The results showed that compliance tended to be highest in the three-question condition with gestures, although this difference was not statistically significant. Response time was not significantly related to question number. In contrast, a weak correlation was observed between compliance behavior and performance on specific Go/No-go and Stroop tasks, whereas no association was found with self-control measures. These findings suggest that the Yes-Set technique may be associated with limited cognitive processes rather than simple automaticity.

Keywords: Yes-Set · compliance behavior · sequential responding

1 Introduction

The Yes-Set technique is a form of sequential influence in which a persuader presents a series of questions that are easy to answer affirmatively, thereby fostering a compliant response tendency and increasing the likelihood of agreement with a final request (Brink, 1981). Previous research has explained the effectiveness of the Yes-Set primarily in terms of psychological principles such as commitment and consistency (Cialdini & Sagarin, 2005). In contrast, Guéguen et al. (2013) suggested that repeated responding itself may enhance engagement in interaction and promote compliance. Nevertheless, quantitative factors such as the number of questions, as well as the role of consecutive responses as a response-formation process based on auditory repetition, remain underexplored. Moreover, it is unclear how compliance induced by the Yes-Set technique relates to individual differences in self-control. The present study examined the effects of the number of Yes-Set questions and the use of hand gestures during request presentation on compliance behavior, response time, and cognitive task performance.

E. Vlahu-Gjorgievska et al. (Eds.): PERSUASIVE 2026, CCIS 2896, pp. 315–318, 2027.
https://doi.org/10.1007/978-3-032-27235-5_35

2 Method

2.1 Participants

Participants were 40 native Japanese-speaking adults (10 males, 30 females; M age = 20.9 years, $SD = 1.56$). All participants provided informed consent prior to participation.

2.2 Design

The experiment employed a mixed design with the number of Yes-Set questions (0, 3, or 6) as a within-participant factor and the presence of hand gestures (present vs. absent) as a between-participant factor. Participants were randomly assigned to either the gesture-present or gesture-absent condition ($n = 20$ per condition).

2.3 Procedure

Participants completed a total of three Yes-Set tasks. After each Yes-Set task, they performed a Go/No-go task, a Stroop task, and completed the short version of a self-control scale. The order of the Go/No-go task, Stroop task, and questionnaire was fixed across participants. In the Yes-Set tasks, three types of request content were used, and the number of Yes-Set questions (0, 3, or 6) was manipulated within participants. The order of question-number conditions and request contents was randomized and counterbalanced to control for order effects. In each Yes-Set task, the experimenter orally presented a predetermined number of everyday questions that were easy to answer affirmatively, followed by a final oral request. During request presentation, the experimenter either accompanied the request with a standardized hand gesture (gesture-present condition) or did not use gestures (gesture-absent condition). Compliance responses were recorded, and response time was measured from the end of the request to the participant's first verbal response.

3 Results

3.1 Compliance Rates

Compliance rates were calculated for each combination of question number and gesture condition. Compliance was highest in the three-question condition, particularly when gestures were present (compliance rate = .65). In contrast, compliance rates in the zero-question and six-question conditions were both .48 (Table 1).

A generalized linear mixed model (GLMM) revealed no significant main effects of question number or gesture, and no significant interaction (Table 2). No bias due to the order of question presentation was observed ($\chi2(2) = 5.27, p = .072$).

Table 1. Compliance rates by number of Yes-Set questions and gesture condition.

Number of Questions	Gesture Absent	Gesture Present
0	.48	.48
3	.52	.65
6	.48	.48

Note. Values represent proportions of compliance responses

Table 2. Effects of the number of Yes-Set questions and gesture condition on compliance behavior.

Effect	*OR*	95% CI	*p*
3 questions	1.92	[0.68, 4.28]	.33
6 questions	0.81	[0.41, 2.47]	.75
Gesture (present)	1.00	[0.34, 1.67]	1.00
3 questions × Gesture	0.80	[0.13, 4.95]	.81
6 questions × Gesture	1.00	[0.16, 6.09]	1.00

Note. The number of Yes-Set questions (0, 3, or 6) was treated as a within-participant factor, and gesture condition (present vs. absent) as a between-participant factor. The 0-question condition and the gesture-absent condition served as reference levels. Participant-specific random effects were included in the model

3.2 Response Time and Cognitive Tasks

A two-way ANOVA on response time showed no significant main effects of question number ($F(2,114) = 2.04$, $p = .14$) or gesture condition ($F(1,114) = 0.00$, $p = 1.00$) (Table 3).

Table 3. Mean and standard deviation of response time (s) by number of Yes-Set questions and gesture condition.

Number of Questions	Gesture	Mean Response Time (s)	*SD*
0	With gestures	0.77	0.46
0	Without gestures	0.83	0.55
3	With gestures	0.87	0.86
3	Without gestures	0.99	0.59
6	With gestures	0.76	0.49
6	Without gestures	0.58	0.38

Note. The number of Yes-Set questions (0, 3, 6) was a within-participants factor, and gesture condition (with vs. without gestures) was a between-participants factor. Response time was measured from the end of the request to the participant's first verbal response. Each condition included 20 participants

Regarding cognitive task performance, a weak correlation was found only between compliance behavior and performance on the Stroop kanji–color task ($r = .37, p = .02$). No significant associations were observed for other cognitive measures or self-control scores (Table 4).

Table 4. Correlations between compliance behavior and cognitive measures.

Measure	r	p
Go/No-go task accracy	− .12	> .10
Stroop task(kanji-color)	.37	.02
Self-control scale	− .18	.26

Note. Pearson's correlation coefficients are reported. Only the Stroop kanji–color task showed a weak but significant correlation with compliance behavior

4 Discussion

The present study examined the effects of Yes-Set question number and gestures on compliance and response times. Although no significant main effects were found, higher compliance in the three-question condition suggests that the Yes-Set depends on interactional engagement rather than simple repetition. Response times may reflect decision outcomes as well as experimental conditions, with compliance responses being more automatic and non-compliance responses involving deliberation, indicating the importance of analyzing response times separately for acceptance and rejection. Because repetition was manipulated indirectly and auditory features (e.g., tempo and rhythm) were not controlled, future studies should directly manipulate these features and consider the relationship between the requester and the participant. Overall, the Yes-Set effect should be understood as a dynamic social engagement process.

References

1. Brink, N.E.: Hypnosis and control. Am. J. Clin. Hypn. **24**(2), 110–112 (1981)
2. Cialdini, R.B., Sagarin, B.J.: Principles of interpersonal influence. In: Brock, T.C., Green, M.C. (eds.), Persuasion: Psychological Insights and Perspectives (2nd ed., pp. 143–169). Sage (2005)
3. Guéguen, N., Joule, R.-V., Courbet, D., Halimi-Falkowicz, S., Marchand, H.: The four walls technique: a field study. Soc. Influ. **8**(3), 163–169 (2013)

Doctoral Consortium

Epistemic Calibration in Adaptive Persuasion: Educating Reflective Agency in AI Systems

Alexandru Mateescu(✉)

Université Paris 1 Panthéon–Sorbonne, Paris, France
alexandru.mateescu@etu.univ-paris1.fr

Abstract. Adaptive AI systems—such as recommender systems, personalized feeds, or conversational agents—increasingly persuade not by means of discrete arguments, but via continuous feedback. In such environments, influence operates as an ambient condition of interaction, progressively shaping how users update beliefs and preferences. Many existing responses—regulatory constraints and design guidelines—primarily target system behavior, while leaving under-specified how adaptive persuasion reshapes the epistemic conditions under which users reason, and how users can remain epistemically oriented within such environments. This doctoral project investigates *epistemic calibration*—understood as the user's capacity to maintain reason-guided belief revision—as a condition of reflective agency in adaptive persuasive systems. Rather than opposing persuasion, epistemic calibration concerns how users remain oriented toward reasons. It refers to their capacity to interpret, assess, and revise reasons while embedded in continuously adaptive feedback loops. The paper presents the current state of the research, outlines the planned methodological trajectory, and identifies open conceptual and methodological challenges—particularly concerning operationalization and evaluation—on which feedback from the Persuasive Technology community is sought. This project builds on work in persuasive technology, epistemic agency, and algorithmic personalization, while seeking to integrate these strands into a unified epistemic perspective on adaptive persuasion.

Keywords: Adaptive persuasion · Epistemic calibration · Reflective agency · AI education

1 Introduction

1.1 Adaptive Persuasion: An Epistemic Perspective

Adaptive AI systems increasingly shape human judgment not by presenting discrete arguments, but by structuring the conditions under which reasoning unfolds. Recommendation systems, personalized feeds, and conversational agents

E. Vlahu-Gjorgievska et al. (Eds.): PERSUASIVE 2026, CCIS 2896, pp. 321–328, 2027.
https://doi.org/10.1007/978-3-032-27235-5_36

continuously adjust their outputs in response to user behavior, transforming persuasion into a persistent feature of interaction rather than a punctual communicative act. Influence is no longer primarily exercised through explicit reasons offered for acceptance or rejection, but through feedback dynamics that guide attention, relevance, and perceived plausibility over time.

This shift has important epistemic consequences. In classical models of persuasion, influence presupposes a temporal gap between exposure and judgement, allowing agents to evaluate reasons and justify belief updates. In adaptive environments, this gap is progressively compressed. Each interaction becomes immediately consequential for subsequent system behaviour, and belief revision increasingly occurs within accelerated feedback loops. Persuasion thus operates less as a deliberative exchange and more as an ambient condition of interaction.

From an epistemic perspective, the central concern is not simply that users may be influenced, but that the justificatory structure of belief formation becomes opaque. Users may come to accept, prefer, or trust certain contents without being able to articulate why these contents appear relevant or credible. This raises a distinct problem of epistemic orientation. How can agents remain aware of, and responsive to, the reasons that guide their belief updates when those updates are continuously shaped by adaptive systems?

Seen from this perspective, it becomes possible to reassess how current regulatory and design-oriented responses approach adaptive persuasion.

1.2 From System Constraints to User Calibration

In response to these challenges, current approaches to adaptive persuasion have primarily focused on system-level interventions, including regulatory constraints and design-oriented solutions. These approaches play an essential role, but they tend to presuppose that users remain epistemically oriented within adaptive environments. This presupposition brings into focus the limits of system-level responses when considered from the perspective of epistemic orientation. Many existing responses to persuasive AI systems have focused primarily on constraining system behavior. Regulatory frameworks emphasize transparency, accountability, and risk mitigation, while design-oriented approaches propose guidelines intended to make persuasive mechanisms more visible or controllable. These measures are indispensable, yet they largely presuppose a user who remains capable of reflective judgment once appropriate safeguards are in place.

This project starts from the hypothesis that such presuppositions are increasingly fragile in adaptive contexts. When persuasion is embedded in continuous feedback, the epistemic burden shifts partly onto the user's capacity to interpret and regulate their own belief-updating processes. The question is therefore not only how systems should behave, but how users can remain epistemically oriented within adaptive persuasion.

To address this gap, the thesis introduces the notion of epistemic calibration. Epistemic calibration refers to the user's capacity to maintain coherent, justified belief revision while embedded in adaptive persuasive feedback loops. Rather than opposing persuasion, calibration concerns the internal regulation of reasoning under conditions of ongoing influence. It captures the ability to recognise persuasive structuring, interpret its relevance and intent, and revise one's commitments in a way that preserves justificatory coherence over time.

From this perspective, education can play a distinct and often under-specified complementary role alongside regulation and design. While regulation constrains system behaviour and design mediates interaction, education addresses the formation of user capacities that enable calibrated reasoning across contexts. The guiding question of the project is thus not how users can escape persuasion, but how reflective agency can be sustained as persuasion becomes adaptive, continuous, and environment-like.

2 Background and Related Work

2.1 Persuasion Theory and Adaptive Systems

Research on persuasion has historically addressed influence as a process involving the presentation of reasons, cues, or incentives aimed at shaping attitudes or behavior. Classical rhetorical approaches framed persuasion as a deliberative practice grounded in reason-giving and audience adaptation, while twentieth-century persuasion psychology introduced causal models of attitude change. Within this latter tradition, dual-process accounts such as the Elaboration Likelihood Model (ELM) distinguish between more reflective, effortful processing and more automatic, cue-driven routes to persuasion. [3]

These models remain influential in contemporary discussions of persuasive technology, as they provide a vocabulary for analyzing how cognitive effort, motivation, and contextual factors shape susceptibility to influence. However, they were largely developed with discrete persuasive episodes in mind, where exposure, processing, and judgment can be analytically separated. Adaptive AI systems—i.e. systems that dynamically adjust their outputs in response to user behavior over time—challenge this assumption by collapsing these stages into continuous interaction, where each response immediately informs subsequent persuasive output.

In adaptive contexts, persuasion is no longer exhausted by the content of messages or cues, but extends to the structuring of interaction itself. The epistemic question thus shifts from how messages are processed to how belief-updating unfolds over time within feedback loops. This project builds on persuasion theory while extending its scope to account for these dynamic, temporally compressed conditions.

2.2 Persuasive Technology and Ambient Influence

In the Persuasive Technology literature, influence is increasingly analyzed as a property of systems rather than isolated messages. Frameworks such as behavior change support systems and digital nudging demonstrate how interface design, choice architecture, and feedback mechanisms can guide user behavior without coercion or deception. These approaches have proven effective across domains such as health, sustainability, and education [2,4].

Recent work on adaptive and AI-driven persuasion further highlights the emergence of what has been described as ambient or always-on influence. Personalization algorithms continuously adjust content based on inferred preferences, creating environments in which relevance and salience are pre-computed. As a result, users encounter persuasion not as a discrete intervention, but as a background condition shaping attention and engagement.

While much of this literature focuses on effectiveness, trust, and transparency, fewer contributions explicitly address the epistemic implications of such ambient influence. In particular, there remains limited conceptual articulation of how users can retain an understanding of why certain outputs appear persuasive, especially when adaptation operates below the threshold of conscious deliberation. This gap motivates the present focus on epistemic calibration.

2.3 Epistemic Agency and Calibration

Philosophical work on epistemic agency and virtue epistemology provides complementary resources for addressing this gap. Rather than treating autonomy as independence from influence, these approaches characterise rational agency in terms of the ability to maintain coherence, responsiveness to reasons, and stability of judgement under changing informational conditions. From this perspective, the challenge posed by adaptive systems is not the presence of influence as such, but the risk that justificatory relations become obscured or bypassed.

The notion of epistemic calibration introduced in this project draws on these insights. Calibration does not imply immunity to persuasion, nor does it presuppose full transparency or exhaustive understanding of system internals. Instead, it denotes a relational property of interaction: the degree to which users can meaningfully connect their belief updates to interpretable reasons, despite ongoing adaptation.

By situating epistemic calibration at the intersection of persuasion theory, persuasive technology, and epistemic agency, the project aims to articulate a framework that remains compatible with the goals of persuasive systems while foregrounding the conditions under which reflective agency can be sustained [1,5].

3 Research Questions and Conceptual Framework

3.1 Research Questions

1. **RQ1:** How do adaptive persuasive systems reshape the epistemic conditions under which users form, evaluate, and revise their beliefs?
2. **RQ2:** How can epistemic calibration be conceptualised as a form of reflective agency within adaptive persuasive environments?
3. **RQ3:** How might epistemic calibration be operationalised at the level of interaction design and user education without presupposing resistance to persuasion?

4. **RQ4:** How do regulatory, design, and educational approaches interact when addressing epistemic risks associated with adaptive persuasion?

This question situates the concept within broader governance and design debates, without reducing calibration to any single intervention level.

Together, these questions frame epistemic calibration not as a fixed user trait or system property, but as a dynamic relation emerging within adaptive interaction.

3.2 Epistemic Calibration: Working Definition

For the purposes of this project, epistemic calibration is defined as the capacity of users to maintain coherent and justifiable belief revision while embedded in adaptive persuasive feedback loops. Calibration concerns the alignment between belief updates and interpretable reasons, under conditions where system outputs continuously adapt to user behaviour.

Two clarifications are central to this definition. First, epistemic calibration does not imply opposition to persuasion. Persuasive influence is taken as a given feature of contemporary digital environments. Calibration instead refers to the internal regulation of reasoning that allows users to remain responsive to reasons while being influenced. Second, calibration does not presuppose full transparency or technical understanding of adaptive systems. Rather, it requires sufficient visibility and interpretability for users to situate their belief updates within a meaningful justificatory context.

Loss of calibration occurs when adaptive optimisation compresses or obscures these relations—when belief revision becomes increasingly automatic, opaque, or detached from reasons the user can recognise and assess. Calibration is therefore best understood as a matter of degree, varying across systems, contexts, and stages of interaction.

3.3 Regulation, Design, and Education

The conceptual framework developed in this project distinguishes three dimensions that jointly shape the conditions of epistemic calibration: regulation, design, and education.

Regulation constrains system behaviour by setting normative boundaries for acceptable forms of influence. Transparency obligations, accountability mechanisms, and risk mitigation strategies define the external conditions under which adaptive persuasion operates. However, regulation alone does not directly address how users experience and interpret persuasive interaction in situ.

Design mediates persuasion at the level of interaction. Interface choices, feedback timing, and explanation mechanisms structure how influence is encountered and acted upon. Design can either support or undermine epistemic calibration, depending on whether it affords recognition of persuasive structuring, interpretability of outputs, and opportunities for revision.

Education addresses the formation of user capacities over time. Rather than functioning as a one-off literacy intervention, education is conceived here as an infrastructural layer that shapes how users learn to reason within adaptive environments across domains. Educational support targets the development of interpretive skills and habits that sustain calibration beyond any single system.

The framework treats these dimensions as complementary rather than hierarchical. The central hypothesis explored in the thesis is that without some form of educational support for epistemic calibration, regulatory and design interventions may risk producing compliant behaviour without reflective understanding.

4 Methodological Strategy

4.1 Conceptual Analysis

The first methodological component of the project consists in a conceptual analysis of epistemic calibration. This analysis aims to clarify how calibration differs from adjacent notions commonly invoked in discussions of persuasive systems, such as resistance, transparency, trust, or informed consent. The goal is not to replace these notions, but to specify the epistemic work they leave underdetermined in adaptive contexts.

This phase involves mapping epistemic calibration onto existing theories of persuasion, bounded rationality, and epistemic virtue, in order to identify the minimal conditions under which calibrated belief-updating remains possible within adaptive feedback loops. Particular attention is paid to temporal structure (latency, pacing), justificatory visibility, and the user's capacity to relate system outputs to reasons they can recognise and assess.

4.2 Design-Level Micro-processes

Building on the conceptual analysis, the project identifies three recurring micro-level processes that appear central to epistemic calibration during interaction with adaptive systems.

Recognition

Recognition. Recognition refers to the user's ability to notice that persuasion is taking place and to identify how interaction is being structured. In adaptive systems, persuasion is often implicit, embedded in ranking, timing, or framing rather than explicit prompts. Recognition is supported when systems provide cues that make adaptation legible, such as indications of why content is presented or how user behaviour informs subsequent outputs.

Interpretation

Interpretation. Interpretation concerns the assessment of persuasive cues once recognised. This involves evaluating relevance, intent, and plausibility, rather than merely reacting to salience. Interpretive support may take the form of contrastive explanations, alternative framings, or contextual information that situates persuasive outputs within a broader justificatory space.

Revision

Revision. Revision refers to the integration or rejection of persuasive influence in a way that preserves coherence over time. Revision requires opportunities for reconsideration, such as reversible actions, delayed commitments, or mechanisms that allow users to reflect on changes in their preferences or beliefs. Without such affordances, belief-updating risks becoming automatic and opaque.

These micro-processes are treated as analytically distinct but practically interdependent. Together, they provide a lens for examining whether and how specific design choices support epistemic calibration.

4.3 Educational Perspective

Beyond system-level interventions, the project explores how educational approaches can cultivate epistemic calibration across contexts. Education is not conceived as a corrective response to isolated systems, but as a means of forming durable interpretive capacities that users can mobilise when interacting with diverse adaptive technologies.

This perspective raises questions about how reflective habits can be scaffolded over time, how users learn to recognise persuasive structuring, and how educational initiatives might complement design and regulatory efforts without shifting responsibility entirely onto individuals.

5 Current Progress

At the present stage, the project has developed a conceptual diagnosis of adaptive persuasion and articulated epistemic calibration as a candidate framework for analysing reflective agency within such environments. The research questions and conceptual distinctions presented here represent a consolidation of this work.

Ongoing work focuses on refining the articulation of the three micro-processes and examining how they relate to existing persuasive technology patterns. Further effort is also directed toward clarifying the role of education as an infrastructural component of epistemic calibration.

Decisions regarding empirical exploration and evaluation remain open and are treated as part of the research agenda rather than settled commitments.

6 Open Challenges and Feedback Sought

6.1 Conceptual Alignment

A first open challenge concerns the alignment of epistemic calibration with established persuasion frameworks. Feedback is sought on how calibration can be integrated into Persuasive Technology discourse without reintroducing resistance-based assumptions or diluting its epistemic specificity.

6.2 Operationalisation and Evaluation

A second challenge involves operationalisation. What indicators could meaningfully capture epistemic calibration in adaptive interaction, beyond behavioural compliance or self-report? How might calibration be assessed without overburdening users or relying on unrealistic transparency assumptions?

6.3 Design and Educational Boundaries

A final challenge concerns the boundary between system-level support and user education. Where should responsibility lie for sustaining epistemic calibration over time, and how can design and educational interventions be combined without undermining usability or agency?

Addressing these questions will guide the next phases of the doctoral research and help determine how epistemic calibration can be translated into a testable and actionable contribution. For instance, calibration might be approximated through users' ability to anticipate or explain changes in system outputs following their interactions.

References

1. Floridi, L.: The Fourth Revolution: How the Infosphere Is Reshaping Human Reality. Oxford University Press, Oxford (2014)
2. Fogg, B.J.: Persuasive Technology: Using Computers to Change What We Think and Do. Morgan Kaufmann, USA (2003)
3. Petty, R.E., Cacioppo, J.T.: The elaboration likelihood model of persuasion. Adv. Exp. Soc. Psychol. **19**, 123–205 (1986)
4. Weinmann, M., Schneider, C., vom Brocke, J.: Digital nudging. Bus. Inf. Syst. Eng. **58**(6), 433–436 (2016)
5. Zagzebski, L.: Virtues of the Mind. Cambridge University Press, Cambridge (1996)

Designing Compassionate Candor in AI Feedback to Foster Long-Term Intrinsic Motivation in Home-Based Exercise

Muhammad Firdaus Maulana(✉)

Faculty of Systems Design, Department of Computer Science, Tokyo Metropolitan University, 6-6 Asahigaoka, Hino-shi, Tokyo, Japan
maulana-muhammad@ed.tmu.ac.jp

Abstract. Although Artificial Intelligence (AI)-based health interventions show great potential, current systems often fail to maintain long-term user engagement due to a lack of emotional resonance necessary for sustainable behavioral change. This gap occurs because systems tend to be polarized between rigid, data-centric approaches or generic chatbots that exhibit inauthentic "toxic positivity," thereby failing to meet the basic psychological needs of Relatedness, Competence, and Autonomy based on Self-Determination Theory (SDT). As a solution, this research proposes a "Compassionate Candor" framework that integrates emotional validation, constructive transparency, and positive framing to create a "Trusted AI Partner." Through a context-aware architecture that combines multimodal data fusion and the use of knowledge-based Retrieval-Augmented Generation (RAG), this system is designed to provide honest yet psychologically safe feedback. The effectiveness of the intervention on intrinsic motivation and exercise adherence will be evaluated through a three-month longitudinal field study using Linear Mixed Models (LMM) and the Digital Working Alliance Inventory (D-WAI) instrument.

Keywords: Compassionate Candor · Self-Determination Theory · Intrinsic Motivation · AI Feedback · Longitudinal Study · Home-based Exercise

1 Introduction and Problem Statement

Despite recent advances in Artificial Intelligence (AI)-based health interventions showing great potential in monitoring physical performance, existing systems often fail to maintain user engagement in the long term [1]. This failure is mainly due to a lack of emotional resonance necessary for sustainable behavioral change [2–4]. According to Self-Determination Theory (SDT) [5,6], maintaining intrinsic motivation depends on fulfilling three basic psychological needs: Autonomy, Competence, and Relatedness.

However, the current landscape of health AI systems tends to be polarized into two less-than-ideal extremes. On one hand, fitness-specific AI is often rigid

E. Vlahu-Gjorgievska et al. (Eds.): PERSUASIVE 2026, CCIS 2896, pp. 329–335, 2027.
https://doi.org/10.1007/978-3-032-27235-5_37

and highly data-centric [1,7]. This approach presents raw metrics with minimal context, which, while accurate, fails to provide the interpersonal warmth necessary to fulfill the need for Relatedness. On the other hand, generic chatbots (such as standard LLMs) often exhibit toxic positivity with overly friendly and superficially agreeable language [8,9]. Over time, such interactions feel inauthentic and fail to provide the critical feedback necessary for user growth (Competence). As a result, neither approach has been able to create a psychological environment conducive to fostering long-term motivation.

A literature review on SDT shows that environments that consistently support Relatedness result in higher psychological well-being and greater intrinsic motivation [6]. This support for connectedness manifests through behaviors such as empathy (understanding others' feelings), genuine time investment, and unconditional acceptance (valuing individuals beyond their performance) [10]. In the context of behavioral intervention, the first step in motivating resistant individuals is to acknowledge and validate their negative feelings [11,12]. This validation positions AI as an ally, not a controller [13].

Furthermore, empathy allows for the detection of insecurity. To address this, the Positive Framing strategy can be used to increase Self-Efficacy [14], which is at the core of the need for Competence. In addition, providing meaningful rationale is a form of cognitive empathy; individuals tend to lose motivation if they feel that the tasks they perform have no value [15]. Therefore, Constructive Transparency—which explains why feedback is given honestly but still relates to the user's personal values—is crucial [15]. This approach respects the user's intelligence and gives them room to make choices, thereby supporting the need for Autonomy.

Although empathy in AI is vital for building relationships [16], empathy without accurate feedback risks becoming "ruinous empathy" [17], where users gain emotional comfort but lose the opportunity for self-improvement. Conversely, raw data-based feedback ensures accuracy but lacks relational warmth. Therefore, this study proposes a hybrid framework called "Compassionate Candor."

This framework integrates Emotional Validation, Constructive Transparency, and Positive Framing adapted from the philosophy of "Radical Candor" [17] to provide direct challenges while still showing personal concern. The goal is to ensure feedback that is psychologically safe yet instrumental to user progress. Unlike generic chatbots, this study aims to design a "Trusted AI Partner" that is capable of recognizing the user's emotional dynamics while providing actionable advice to encourage intrinsic motivation for consistent physical activity.

1.1 Research Questions

This study is guided by three main research questions:

RQ1: How can the principle of Compassionate Candor be operationalized into AI interaction design to balance the need for emotional validation (Relatedness) with honest performance feedback (Competence) while preserving user Autonomy?

RQ2: How can an AI model architecture be designed to generate adaptive real-time responses based on the dynamic integration of physical sensor data and user psychological profiles?
RQ3: How does long-term interaction with Compassionate Candor-based AI impact user trust and exercise adherence over time?

2 Methodology

2.1 Introduction to Compassionate Candor

Compassionate Candor (adapted from Kim Scott's Radical Candor concept [17]) is a communication approach that synthesizes two crucial elements:

- *Candor*: Direct, clear, and specific delivery of factual information.
- *Compassion*: Delivery based on empathy, understanding of emotional states, and a focus on user growth.

In this study, Compassionate Candor is defined as an AI communication style that balances data accuracy with psychological support. This approach is designed to simultaneously fulfill three basic SDT needs:

- **Relatedness**: Emotional validation by AI makes users feel "heard," strengthening the Working Alliance [16].
- **Competence**: Honest (candor) yet corrective feedback provides specific guidance for performance improvement [6, 18].
- **Autonomy**: Transparent and non-judgmental data presentation gives users space to make conscious decisions about self-improvement [2, 13].

2.2 Research Phases

Phase 1: Preliminary Feasibility Study. This stage validates the low motivation and consistency in home exercise through two preliminary studies. The first study used a pose estimation system for ten days on a single subject to evaluate squat movements [19]. Based on Fig. 1(a), subjects who initially only performed failed squats during the baseline period showed a significant improvement in performance to correct poses after receiving the intervention. This technical improvement correlates with Fig. 1(b), which shows an increase in motivation to exercise the next day with an average score of 4.5, proving that honest performance feedback supports the need for Competence.

The second study involved 11 participants to evaluate motivational messages generated by LLM with additional static personalization data. The findings visualized in Fig. 2 reveal a critical trade-off: although personalization increases Emotional Impact by 20%, it causes a 3% decrease in Message Clarity. Although participants felt the messages were more personally relevant, overly long narratives tended to reduce the clarity and actionability of the feedback.

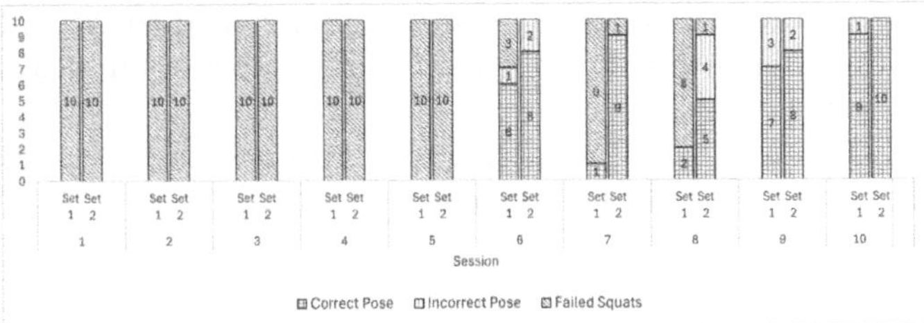

(a) Graph of performance changes

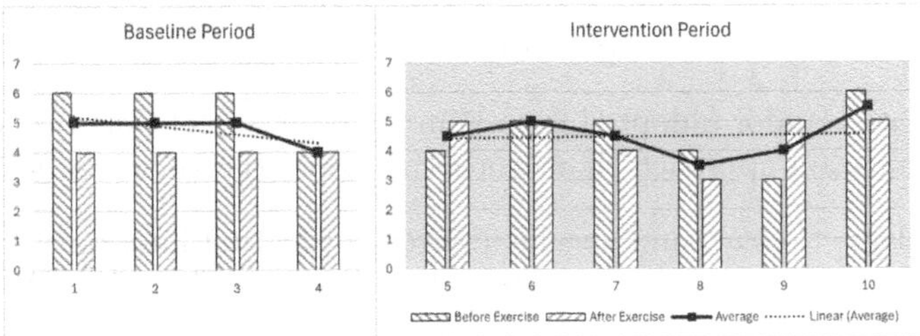

(b) Graph of motivation changes

Fig. 1. Changes in data on performance and motivation.

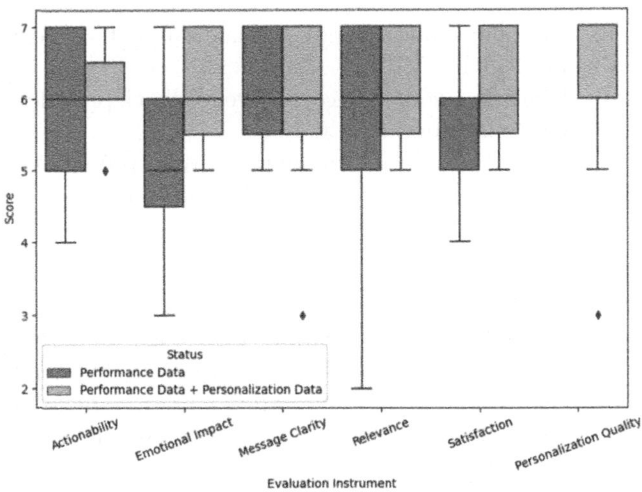

Fig. 2. Comparison of Evaluation Rating Scores Before and After Personalization.

These results confirm that static personalization alone is not sufficient to maintain long-term engagement. While performance data builds competence and personalization builds emotional connection (Relatedness), the decline in clarity indicates the need for real-time contextual adaptation. Therefore, this research continues to Phase 2 to develop a "Compassionate Candor" framework that balances emotional validation with honest feedback that remains easy to understand.

Phase 2: Formative Design and System Development. This phase focuses on developing a Context-Aware architecture that implements the Compassionate Candor framework as an integrated, rather than binary, approach. Based on the Multimodal Affect Forecasting framework [20], the system is designed to combine objective and subjective data to calibrate feedback that holistically meets SDT needs.

Multimodal Data Fusion: Adopting a hybrid sensing approach [20,21], the system integrates two data streams to build a comprehensive user context profile:

- *Objective Physiological Metrics*: Uses wearable devices to monitor user activity and heart rate variability (HRV) as indicators of physical readiness.
- *Subjective Textual Diaries*: Using a lightweight language model to extract emotional nuances and daily life contexts (e.g., exam stress, work fatigue) from user diaries. Study [20] confirms that the addition of this text feature is crucial for the accuracy of negative affect prediction.

Expert Modeling to Taxonomy: Through interviews with professional coaches, this research will not only collect textual data, but will also build a feedback strategy taxonomy (e.g., when to validate fatigue vs. when to push physical limits) [22]. These patterns will form the Expert Knowledge Base for the system.

RAG-based Response Generation: A Large Language Model (LLM) will act as a response generator with dynamic system prompts. Using Retrieval-Augmented Generation (RAG) [23], the LLM will retrieve references from an Expert Knowledge Base on how professional coaches balance criticism and support in a single breath, ensuring the generated responses remain data-honest yet psychologically safe.

The system will use affective status predictions to calibrate the weight of communication elements [24], while simultaneously fulfilling SDT concepts. Each response is designed to always contain elements of Emotional Validation (for Relatedness), Data Honesty (for Competence), and be accompanied by Constructive Steps (for Autonomy). The target of this phase is that if the prediction shows Negative Affect/Low Readiness, the system does not hide bad data, but rather adjusts its delivery. Conversely, in High Readiness conditions, challenging elements can be conveyed more directly without reducing relational warmth.

Phase 3: Longitudinal Field Evaluation. The developed system will be evaluated through a 3-month longitudinal field study. This duration was chosen to measure the effects of habit formation and long-term behavioral change [25].

- **Quantitative Metrics**: Data analysis will use Linear Mixed Models (LMM) [26]. This method was chosen for its robustness in handling missing data, which is common in in-the-wild longitudinal studies, as well as its ability to model individual variability (random effects) in exercise adherence trajectories.

- **Qualitative and Psychological Metrics**: To evaluate the quality of the "Trusted AI Partner" relationship, the Digital Working Alliance Inventory (D-WAI) [27] instruments will be administered periodically. This analysis aims to understand how the Compassionate Candor intervention affects the evolution of user trust and intrinsic motivation over time.

References

1. Sheen, F., Porter, L., Papakonstantinou, T., Ceka, M., Bondaronek, P.: Living well? The unintended consequences of highly popular commercial fitness apps through social listening using machine-assisted topic analysis: evidence from x. Br. J. Health Psychol. **30**, e70026 (2025)
2. Alberts, L., Lyngs, U., Lukoff, K.: Designing for sustained motivation: a review of self-determination theory in behaviour change technologies. Interact. Comput. **9** (2024). https://dx.doi.org/10.1093/iwc/iwae040
3. Chew, H.S.J.: The use of artificial intelligence-based conversational agents (chatbots) for weight loss: scoping review and practical recommendations. JMIR Med. Inform. **10**, e32578 (2022). https://medinform.jmir.org/2022/4/e32578
4. Gleason, M.M., et al.: A relational agent intervention for adolescents seeking mental health treatment: outcomes from a randomized controlled trial within a children's outpatient hospital. JAACAP Open**3**, 1033–1045 (2025). https://www.sciencedirect.com/science/article/pii/S2949732925000274
5. Edmunds, J., Ntoumanis, N., Duda, J.L.: A test of self-determination theory in the exercise domain, Tech. Rep., 2006
6. Ryan, R.M., Deci, E.L.: Self-determination theory and the facilitation of intrinsic motivation, social development, and well-being. Am. Psychol. **55**, 68–78 (2000)
7. Deniz-Garcia, A., et al.: Quality, usability, and effectiveness of mhealth apps and the role of artificial intelligence: current scenario and challenges. J. Med. Internet Res. **25**, e44030 (2023). https://www.jmir.org/2023/1/e44030, vol. 25, p. e44030, 5 2023
8. Almajed, L., ALdayel, A.: Incongruent positivity: when miscalibrated positivity undermines online supportive conversations, 2025. https://arxiv.org/pdf/2509.10184
9. Perez, E., et al.: Discovering language model behaviors with model-written evaluations. In: Proceedings of the Annual Meeting of the Association for Computational Linguistics, pp. 13 387–13 434, 2022. https://arxiv.org/pdf/2212.09251
10. Oertel, C., et al.: Engagement in human-agent interaction: an overview. Front. Robot. AI **7**, 542411 (2020). www.frontiersin.org
11. Fitzpatrick, K.K., Darcy, A., Vierhile, M.: Delivering cognitive behavior therapy to young adults with symptoms of depression and anxiety using a fully automated conversational agent (woebot): a randomized controlled trial. JMIR Mental Health **4** (2017). https://pubmed.ncbi.nlm.nih.gov/28588005/
12. Reeve, J.: Teachers as facilitators: what autonomy-supportive teachers do and why their students benefit. Elem. Sch. J. **106**, 225–236 (2006)

13. Haerens, L., et al.: Different combinations of perceived autonomy support and control: identifying the most optimal motivating style. Phys. Educ. Sport Pedagogy **23**, 16–36 (2018). https://www.tandfonline.com/doi/abs/10.1080/17408989.2017.1346070
14. Fredrickson, B.L.: The role of positive emotions in positive psychology. the broaden-and-build theory of positive emotions. Am. Psychol. **56**, 218–226 (2001). https://pubmed.ncbi.nlm.nih.gov/11315248/
15. Jang, H.: Supporting students' motivation, engagement, and learning during an uninteresting activity (2008)
16. Bickmore, T.W., Picard, R.W.: Establishing and maintaining long-term human-computer relationships. ACM Trans. Comput.-Hum. Interact. **12**, 293–327 (2005)
17. Scott, K.: Radical candor: be a kick-ass boss without losing your humanity, p. 246, 2017
18. Floridi, L., et al.: Ai4people—an ethical framework for a good ai society: opportunities, risks, principles, and recommendations. Minds Mach. **28**, 689–707 (2018). https://link.springer.com/article/10.1007/s11023-018-9482-5
19. Maulana, M.F., Okamoto, Y., Sato-Shimokawara, E.: Creating feedback to maintain motivation when doing home based exercise using pose estimation: single subject design. In: International Electronics Symposium (IES) 2024, pp. 335–340 (2024)
20. Yang, Z., et al.: Integrating wearable sensor data and self-reported diaries for personalized affect forecasting. Smart Health **32**, 100464 (2024). https://www.sciencedirect.com/science/article/pii/S2352648324000205?via%3Dihub
21. D'Mello, S.K., Kory, J.: A review and meta-analysis of multimodal affect detection systems. ACM Comput. Surv. **47** (2015)
22. Montenegro, C., et al.: A dialogue-act taxonomy for a virtual coach designed to improve the life of elderly. Multimodal Technol. Interact. **3**, 52 (2019). https://www.mdpi.com/2414-4088/3/3/52/htm
23. Huang, Z., Liu, P., de Melo, G., He, L., Wang, L.: Generating persona-aware empathetic responses with retrieval-augmented prompt learning. In: ICASSP, IEEE International Conference on Acoustics, Speech and Signal Processing - Proceedings, pp. 12 441–12 445, 2024. https://ieeexplore.ieee.org/abstract/document/10447417
24. Mohan, S.: Exploring the role of common model of cognition in designing adaptive coaching interactions for health behavior change. ACM Trans. Interact. Intell. Syst. **11** (2021)
25. Lally, P., Jaarsveld, C.H.V., Potts, H.W., Wardle, J.: How are habits formed: modelling habit formation in the real world. Eur. J. Soc. Psychol. **40**, 998–1009 (2010)
26. Sun, S., et al.: Challenges in using mhealth data from smartphones and wearable devices to predict depression symptom severity: retrospective analysis. J. Med. Internet Res. **25**, e45233 (2023). https://www.jmir.org/2023/1/e45233
27. Xu, Z., Lee, Y.-C., Stasiak, K., Warren, J., Lottridge, D.: The digital therapeutic alliance with mental health chatbots: diary study and thematic analysis. JMIR Mental Health **12**, e76642 (2025). http://www.ncbi.nlm.nih.gov/pubmed/41072011, http://www.pubmedcentral.nih.gov/articlerender.fcgi?artid=PMC12552820

Personalizing Persuasive Technologies Workshop 2026

Measuring Subjective Persuasion Effectiveness in Symmetric Human-Agent Dialogues

Carolin Schindler[1,2(✉)], Niklas Rach[3], Yuki Matsuda[2,4], Wolfgang Minker[1], and Keiichi Yasumoto[2]

[1] Ulm University, Ulm, Germany
carolin.schindler@uni-ulm.de
[2] Nara Institute of Science and Technology, Ikoma, Japan
[3] Tensor AI Solutions GmbH, Ulm, Germany
[4] Okayama University, Okayama, Japan

Abstract. To effectively change a user's behavior or attitude, it is crucial to adapt the agent's persuasive behavior and strategy to the user at hand. This requires the agent to assess its persuasive effectiveness as perceived subjectively by the individual user. In this paper, we present an empirical approach for acquiring a multimodal dataset for the task of social sensing of persuasion effectiveness in symmetric human-agent dialogues that base their persuasion on argumentation. To the best of our knowledge, there only exist datasets measuring persuasion effectiveness in asymmetric settings where the user (i. e., the persuadee) is merely a passive recipient of the content without any way to influence the interaction. Contrary to this, the persuadee in our study is an active and speaking participant in the discussion, resulting in a symmetric dialogue where both parties are engaged in mutual exchange. Thus, not only the persuadee's visual modality, as in previous work, but also the persuadee's auditory modality can be considered as a meaningful input. While the present work does not yet include the acquisition of the dataset across different cultures and nationalities, the herein discussed limitations, ethical considerations, and research directions will guide future work. Therewith, this work is laying a foundation for enhancing agent adaptability and designing more effective, culturally aware persuasive interactions in symmetric human-agent communication.

Keywords: Computational argumentation · Affective computing · Social sensing · Argument quality · Argumentative dialogue system

1 Introduction

Audience adaption plays an important role in persuasion [10]. Therefore, a conversational agent trying to evoke a change in the user's opinion, behavior, or general attitude, for example, should adapt its persuasive behavior and strategy

E. Vlahu-Gjorgievska et al. (Eds.): PERSUASIVE 2026, CCIS 2896, pp. 339–349, 2027.
https://doi.org/10.1007/978-3-032-27235-5_38

towards the respective user. For this adaptation to be performed online during the conversation and for the individual user at hand, the agent needs to be able to estimate its persuasion effectiveness as subjectively perceived by the user in this moment. To this end, social signals can be utilized [13].

The herein presented work, provides an empirical approach for acquiring a multimodal dataset for social sensing of persuasion effectiveness in symmetric human-agent dialogues that base their persuasion on argumentation. Such a dialogue scenario is depicted in Fig. 1, where the agent takes the role of the persuader and tries to convince the user, i.e., the persuadee. Since the dialogue is symmetric, the persuadee is an active interlocutor in the discussion and not merely a passive recipient of the persuasive content.

To the best of our knowledge, this active role of the individual persuadee is not considered in existing datasets for persuasion effectiveness. The datasets are either designed for an objective prediction of persuasiveness for the overall population [2,4,5,11,16,18] or a group of people belonging to the same persona, for example by sharing the same personality traits or prior beliefs [1,6,9,14]. Besides a description of the persona, these works base their prediction on the observation of the persuader. Opposed to this, the work in [13] considers solely the non-verbal signals elicited by the persuadee, resulting in a subjective and individual estimation. Nevertheless, their interaction is unidirectional with the persuader being an embodied dialogue system and the persuadee only perceiving its arguments. As such, the dialogue system is speaking to the persuadee, but the persuadee cannot speak to the dialogue system.

We are recording a dataset in a symmetric, bidirectional argumentation setting with both, persuader and persuadee, being active participants in the discussion. Therewith, we directly address limitations and future directions that were also discussed by the authors in [13]. Following the paradigm of symmetric multimodality [19], we embody the persuader with a human-like character. While our focus lies on recording the persuadee to estimate their subjective perception of the persuasiveness of the persuader, we include the recording of the persuader for the sake of completeness and to allow for a broader applicability of our dataset. The ground truth labels of the dataset are obtained during the interaction by having the persuadee rate different aspects related to persuasion effectiveness after each turn. A human baseline for the task is created in a post-hoc annotation setting by a third party watching and labeling the recordings of the conversation.

The contribution of this work is the presentation and discussion of a method for acquiring and labeling a multimodal dataset for the task of social sensing of persuasion effectiveness in symmetric human-agent dialogues. This method is going to be applied in future work to record, label, and analyze such a dataset for different cultures and nationalities in their respective mother-tongue. With this, our work provides the following novelties:

- The persuadee has an active role in the conversation.

- The persuasion effectiveness evolves over a multi-turn conversation and therefore is contextualized within it: Previous turns may influence the effectiveness of current and future turns.
- For broader applicability, we do not only include the recordings of one interlocutor but of both, the persuadee as well as the persuader.
- Additionally, the dataset will be recorded in a cross-cultural manner.

These novelties will allow to investigate cultural differences and the effect of the persuadee's spoken utterances on the estimation of subjective persuasion effectiveness which are both not possible with existing datasets.

Subsequent to this introduction, Sect. 2 provides an overview over the scenario that our dataset is situated in. In Sect. 3, we present our empirical methodology for recording and labeling the data. This is followed by a discussion of limitations, ethics, and expected results, focusing on research directions and tasks that the dataset is applicable to, in Sect. 4. Finally, we conclude the work in Sect. 5 with a summary and an outlook on future work.

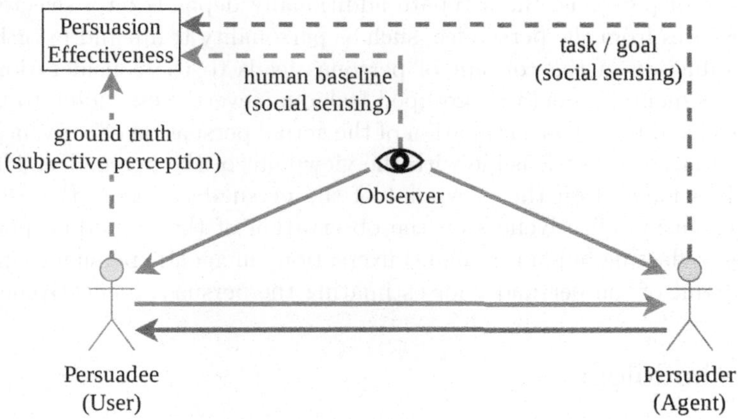

Fig. 1. Different parties' estimation of the persuasion effectiveness on the persuadee.

2 Scenario

As shown in Fig. 1, we assume a scenario where a single user is interacting in a turn-wise fashion with a persuasive agent. The agent, the persuader, tries to achieve a change in the user's, the persuadee's, mental state, such as a change in attitude, for example. The persuasion effectiveness of the persuader is subjectively perceived by the persuadee and the goal of the persuader is to estimate this persuasion effectiveness to be able to adapt its behavior and strategy accordingly. Therewith, only the actual persuadee can provide the ground truth labels for our task, while the persuader's estimation of the ground truth is the respective social sensing task. A human baseline for this task, can be obtained by having a third party, i. e., an observer, perform the same task as the persuader. It is important to note that every estimation of the persuasion effectiveness is dependent on the mental model of the party making the estimation, especially their mental model of the persuadee. This means: Based on the persuadee's mental model, the persuadee subjectively perceives the persuader and its persuasive effectiveness. At the same time, based on the persuader's mental model of the persuadee, the persuader subjectively perceives the persuadee and estimates its persuasive effectiveness. This holds for the observer, accordingly. Since the setting is a conversation with a turn-wise interaction, the influence of previous turns may be considered when performing an estimation for the current turn.

The viewpoint the dataset is taking decides whether the persuasion effectiveness is measured objectively for a group of people or subjectively for an individual person. Datasets taking the viewpoint of the persuadee, rely on the observation of the persuader to predict the persuasion effectiveness. When solely relying on this observation, the estimate is an objective one intended to generalize over the population, thereby ignoring the mental model of the persuadee. In the case of personas, the estimate additionally depends on a selected set of global features from the persuadee, such as personality traits and prior believes. The introduction of the concept of personas leads to the consideration of the persuadee's mental model in a grouped fashion. Nevertheless, going to the individual level and having an estimation of the actual persuasion effectiveness in the specific situation is not feasible with the viewpoint of the persuadee. Therefore, this work is focused on the viewpoint of the persuader, basing the estimation of the persuasion effectiveness on the observation of the individual persuadee. Moreover, reflecting human-human conversation, an agentic persuader may have the viewpoint of the persuader for estimating the persuasion effectiveness.

3 Methodology

This section describes our empirical approach for acquiring a multimodal dataset for social sensing of persuasion effectiveness in symmetric human-agent dialogues. In our dataset, the persuader is the agent, more precisely an embodied argumentative dialogue system, and the persuadee is a human user interacting with it. To investigate persuasion effectiveness in different cultures, all texts are machine translated from English to the respective mother-tongue of the participants. While we focus on the viewpoint of the persuader, we will not only include the recordings of the persuadee but, for the sake of completeness and broader applicability, also screen record the agentic persuader.

3.1 Embodied Conversational Agent

In our study, the persuader is an argumentative dialogue system, which is based on an LLM with retrieval augmentation generation (RAG). The RAG is performed on an unstructured set of argumentative sentences that are relevant to the topic of the discussion. Given a topic, the persuader takes the opposing stance of the persuadee and tries to convince the persuadee of this opposing attitude in a turn-wise interaction. To allow for a comparison to persuasion effectiveness that was judged objectively on the basis of the text only, we build the knowledge base for the RAG based on these existing datasets. Following the paradigm of symmetric multimodality [19], which states that modalities perceived by the system should also be output by it, we embody the dialogue system by a human-like CG agent. The next utterance of the system is solely based on the textual content of the previous turns. The agent's verbalization and animation depends on its current activity: When the agent is listening or thinking, we utilize an idling animation, including breathing and blinking but no specific reactions to the conversational content at hand. When the agent is speaking, the verbalization and animation, including facial expression and gestures, is based on the utterance to be spoken. The agent will be presented both, either on a regular computer screen or the ARCADE [15] platform. The latter provides an external display that allows for an augmented reality presentation in human-like size.

3.2 Dimensions for Subjective Persuasion Effectiveness

The authors in [16] developed and validated a three-factor scale to measure perceived persuasiveness: *Effectiveness* captures whether the message will cause a change in behavior or attitude in the participant, *quality* checks for the accuracy, trustworthiness, and believability of the message, and *capability* considers the potential of the message to inspire, change, or influence users. The work closest to ours [13], focuses on the categories *convincing* and *interesting* to measure task success of competitive and cooperative argumentation tasks, respectively.

Being only interested in subjective persuasion effectiveness, we do not include the global factor *capability*. Moreover, we do not ask for labeling the factor *quality* since the overall quality of an argument is influenced by multiple aspects [18] that cannot be covered without substantially interrupting the conversation by the labeling procedure. Instead, we refer to the global rating of the quality provided by the datasets that we have extracted the arguments from. Considering the equivalent rational of *effectiveness* and *convincing*, we measure the subjective persuasion effectiveness by rating the categories *convincing* and *interesting*. While persuasion is generally viewed as a competitive task, in our study only the persuader is instructed to be persuasive and therefore we believe that rating the interestingness is still relevant in the light of user engagement and the elaboration likelihood model [12].

3.3 Data Collection and Labeling

The data collection is performed both, in-person in the laboratory and remotely with people's individual hardware. The former will allow for high quality recordings in a controlled environment, while the latter reduces data collection costs, especially in a cross-culture procedure, and is collecting noisier, closer to real-world data. The labeling of the data is performed by the persuadee for the ground truth and by a third party pretending to be the persuader for a human baseline.

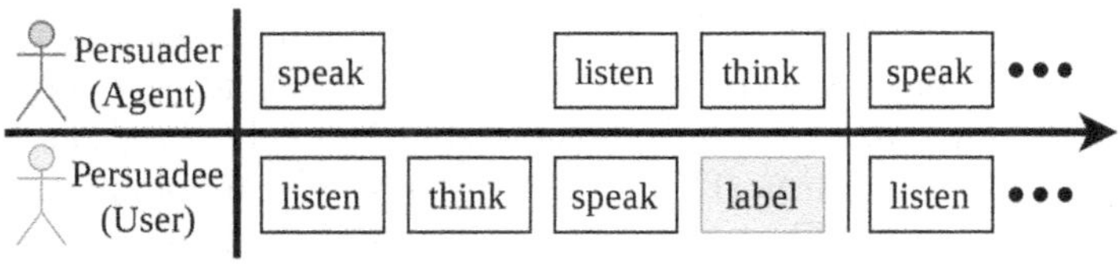

Fig. 2. Activities during the interaction of persuader and persuadee on a timeline.

Procedure. The participants are sitting at a table interacting with the embodied argumentative dialogue systems as described above. Figure 2 sketches the activities during the interaction: While the agent is speaking, the user is listening and the user might continue thinking after the speech act of the agent. Afterwards, the user answers to the agent, who in turn is listening and "thinking"/processing before speaking again.

To be as close as possible to the actual perception, the ground truth labels by the persuadee are collected during the interaction and not post-hoc. Possible consistent times for the collection are after the speech act of the persuader and after the speech act of the persuadee. We only collect labels after the speech act of the persuadee to capture the listening, thinking, and reactive speech act of the persuadee without any artificial interruptions. Moreover, this allows for a labeling while the user is waiting for the agent to select and prepare its next utterance, anyways. For the in-person data collection, the labeling will be performed on a separate tablet; for the remote data collection, the participants might use an external device as well or make use of side-by-side viewing.

The labels for the human baseline are collected post-hoc, i. e., any time after the interaction has taken place. Participants in this labeling task are asked to watch the recording of the persuadee from the perspective of the persuader and provide the labels at the same time as the persuadees. There will be no option for repeated playback and the recordings are only interrupted for performing the labeling. Each participant is watching the recordings conversation-wise, allowing knowledge and observations from previous turns to be taken into account. Therewith, the setting is as proximate as can be in a post-hoc annotation to an actual interaction with the human labeler being the persuader.

Sensors. We need to record the auditory and visual modality of the persuadee. For in-person experiments in the lab, we utilize a pin microphone and an RGB-D camera capturing not only the face but also the upper body of the participant from a frontal position. Having a real-world applicability in mind, we do not attach any sensors for recording physiological signals to the persuadee and refer to [20] for a survey on extracting physiological measurements from the visual modality. In the remote setting, the (presumably RGB) camera and microphone available to the participant will be utilized for recording. To assure that the recordings captured remotely will be useful for the dataset, we perform preliminary tests before starting the study like extracting the pose of the participant from the video or extracting a spoken text from the audio recording. Additionally, we screen record the visual and auditory output of the persuader during the interaction. This recording is not directly needed for our task and is included for the sake of completeness and better analysis of the collected data.

Questionnaires. Before starting, we ask all participants questions related to their persona. More precisely we gather the following information from the people participating as a persuadee:

- Their demographic data, particularly age, gender, ethnicity, and education.
- The participant's proficiency related to conversational agents by utilizing the affinity for technology interaction (ATI) scale [7].
- We capture their personality traits according to the Big-Five personality dimensions (agreeableness, conscientiousness, extraversion, openness, and neuroticism) through the ten item personality inventory (TIPI) [8].
- Their affective style by applying the Perth emotional reactivity scale (PERS) [3].
- The participant's prior stance and interest in the topic to be conversed about with the agent on a six-point scale.

For people participating as a observer, i. e., in the labeling for the human baseline, we ask the same set of questions without the ATI and the PERS scale.

The labeling of the data with respect to the subjectively perceived persuasion effectiveness, is performed by asking the persuadees to rate the last turn on a six-point scale for its *convincingness* [13,16] and *interestingness* [13] on them, i. e., "The last turn of the agent was convincing/interesting for me". The observers are rating the same questions for the persuadees based on their recorded reaction. To assure a proper behavior of the LLM-based agent, we additionally ask if the last turn by the agent was coherent [17], i. e., whether the response was comprehensible, relevant, and appropriate.

After the conversation with the agent, we assess the persuadees' perception of the agent and the influence the interaction had on them. For the latter, we repeat the pre-questionnaire questions about their stance and interest in the topic. For the former, following the work in [11], we ask for the agent's Big-Five personality dimensions and additional high-level attributes, namely confident, credible, dominant, entertaining, expert, humorous, passionate, physically attractive, professional-looking, vivid, and voice pleasant. The post-questionnaire for the observers is shown after every conversation asking to rate the difficulty of the task and name the cues that they were using for each of the dimensions of persuasion effectiveness. Additionally, we ask for their perception of the persuadee with the same set of questions as for the perception of the agent.

4 Discussion

Limitations. To have better control over the performance of the persuader, we tried to remove the persuader as a factor by investigating persuasion effectiveness in human-agent and not in human-human conversations. Still it cannot be excluded that the LLM-based agent might hallucinate or that errors occur when translating from English to the respective mother-tongue. With our control question regarding the coherence of the agent's turn, such faulty behavior should become apparent. Additionally, the recordings of the persuader will allow a thorough post-hoc investigation of the agent's behavior. Since the knowledge base of arguments provided to the agent is the same for every study participant, independent of their ethnicity and nationality, topics are discussed on a more global level without considering arguments that are specific to a certain geographical location or geopolitical situation, for example. Moreover, the persuasive framing of the arguments and the agent's strategy are not adapted to the persuadee. While these points could impair the overall relevance and persuasiveness of the discussion, it does not directly harm our analysis of persuadee's displays of subjective persuasion effectiveness since we need a sufficient amount of positive and negative examples in our dataset anyways. The same holds for the non-verbal behavior of the agent and the capabilities of the RAG-based LLM.

Previous datasets investigated the persuasion effectiveness independently for every rating. Since we ask the participants to perform the labeling with respect to the last move of the agent, this should (at least in theory) also be possible for our dataset. However, especially the labels in the human baseline might be subject to a temporal component due to the potentially increasing familiarity with the reactions of the individual persuadee. This could be viewed as a limitation but at the same time it provides a more holistic and realistic view on estimating subjective persuasion effectiveness in the course of a symmetric conversation. Yet it has to be noted that our dataset does not provide any insights on the lasting persuasion effectiveness of the conversation. Our labeling does not go beyond the rating of the momentary perceived persuasion effectiveness by the persuadee. However, this kind of momentary perception is sufficient for a use within the scope of a conversation.

Ethical Considerations. In the context of persuasion for good, our dataset can help to tailor the persuasive behavior to the specific user and better achieve a change in the user's behavior or attitude for the better. It should not be overseen that there is the potential for misusing the dataset to create a persuasion strategy that actively manipulates the user in a personalized manner. At the same time, our dataset will allow to detect how persuaded a user is and therefore could be used to train a model that makes users aware of the effect that the system they are using is having on them. With this not only malicious persuasion attempts but also unintended persuasion or manipulation could (at least to a certain extend) be uncovered.

Expected Results: Research Directions and Tasks. The machine learning task that our dataset mainly targets is the estimation of the persuader's effectiveness as subjectively perceived by the persuader. To this end, various features can be extracted from the visual and auditory modality of the recordings of the persuadee. For a real-world applicability, the estimation needs to be performed accurately and in real-time. Once this is achieved, the estimations can be utilized to enable follow-up tasks such as the respective adaptation of the agent's behavior and strategy.

After recording the dataset in a cross-cultural setup, among others the following research directions could be addressed by it:

- The investigation of cultural and individual differences of displaying convincingness and interestingness: Which combination of features are most predictive for estimating the subjective persuasion effectiveness? How does this set of features change when considering the population, a grouping by different personas, or an individual person?
- A comparison of objective and subjective persuasion effectiveness: To what extend are objective predictions a good proxy for the subjective estimation in the situation? What information can bring objective estimations closer to the observed subjective persuasion effectiveness?
- A comparison of the user's behavior in the symmetric setting of our work to the asymmetric setting in [13]. It is hypothesized that the reactions will be more descriptive in the symmetric setting than in the asymmetric one.
- The effect of the contextualization of the persuasion effectiveness in the conversation: How does the accuracy of the estimation of subjective persuasion effectiveness evolve over the course of a conversation? How does the knowledge over previous turns impact the estimation for the current turn?
- We hypothesize that convincingness implies interestingness, i. e., when the point made by an agent is not perceived as being interesting, it cannot be convincing and therefore the persuasion cannot be effective.

5 Conclusion

In the herein presented work, we have discussed an empirical approach for collecting a multimodal dataset that is capturing the subjective persuasion effectiveness in symmetric human-agent dialogues. The symmetric, bidirectional dialogue setting, where the persuader as well as the persuadee are speaking allows to not only obtain meaningful features from the visual but also the auditory modality of the persuadee. Due to the effort and costs of acquiring this dataset in a cross-cultural setting, it is important to ensure a holistic, sound, and rigorously planned methodology. In future work, we are going to record the dataset as described in this work and we will address the research directions discussed above. Going beyond the dataset, we will investigate how predicted persuasiveness and actually observed persuasiveness can interplay in the persuader's mental model of the persuadee.

Acknowledgments. This work was supported by a scholarship of the German Academic Exchange Service (DAAD).

Disclosure of Interests. The authors have no competing interests to declare that are relevant to the content of this article.

References

1. Khatib, A., Völske, K., Syed, M., Kolyada, S., Stein, N., B.: Exploiting personal characteristics of debaters for predicting persuasiveness, In. ACL (2020)
2. Bai, C., Chen, H., Kumar, S., Leskovec, J., Subrahmanian, V.S.: M2p2: multimodal persuasion prediction using adaptive fusion. IEEE TMM (2023)
3. Becerra, R., Preece, D., Campitelli, G., Scott-Pillow, G.: The assessment of emotional reactivity across negative and positive emotions: development and validation of the Perth emotional reactivity scale (pers). Assessment (2017)
4. Chatterjee, M., Park, S., Shim, H.S., Sagae, K., Morency, L.P.: Verbal behaviors and persuasiveness in online multimedia content. In: SocialNLP (2014)
5. Djouvas, C., Charalampous, A., Christodoulou, C.J., Tsapatsoulis, N.: LLMs are not for everything: a dataset and comparative study on argument strength classification. In: PCI (2025)
6. Durmus, E., Cardie, C.: Exploring the role of prior beliefs for argument persuasion. In: NAACL (2018)
7. Franke, T., Attig, C., Wessel, D.: A personal resource for technology interaction: development and validation of the affinity for technology interaction (ATI) scale. Int. J. HCI (2018)
8. Gosling, S.D., Rentfrow, P.J., Swann, W.B.: A very brief measure of the big-five personality domains. J. Res. Pers. (2003)
9. Lukin, S., Anand, P., Walker, M., Whittaker, S.: Argument strength is in the eye of the beholder: audience effects in persuasion. In: EACL (2017)
10. O'Keefe, D.J.: Persuasion and social influence. In: The International Encyclopedia of Communication Theory and Philosophy (2016)
11. Park, S., Shim, H.S., Chatterjee, M., Sagae, K., Morency, L.P.: Computational analysis of persuasiveness in social multimedia: a novel dataset and multimodal prediction approach. In: ICMI (2014)
12. Petty, R.E., Cacioppo, J.T.: The elaboration likelihood model of persuasion. Adv. Exp. Soc. Psychol. (1986)
13. Rach, N., Matsuda, Y., Ultes, S., Minker, W., Yasumoto, K.: Estimating subjective argument quality aspects from social signals in argumentative dialogue systems. IEEE Access (2021)
14. Rescala, P., Ribeiro, M.H., Hu, T., West, R.: Can language models recognize convincing arguments? In: Findings of ACL: EMNLP (2024)
15. Schindler, C., Mayumi, D., Matsuda, Y., Rach, N., Yasumoto, K., Minker, W.: Arcade: an augmented reality display environment for multimodal interaction with conversational agents. In: Companion Proceedings of ICMI (2024)
16. Thomas, R.J., Masthoff, J., Oren, N.: Can i influence you? Development of a scale to measure perceived persuasiveness and two studies showing the use of the scale. Front. AI (2019)
17. Venkatesh, A., et al.: On evaluating and comparing conversational agents. In: NIPS (2017)

18. Wachsmuth, H., et al.: Computational argumentation quality assessment in natural language. In: EACL (2017)
19. Wahlster, W.: Towards symmetric multimodality: fusion and fission of speech, gesture, and facial expression. In: KI (2003)
20. Wang, J., Shan, C., Liu, L., Hou, Z.: Camera-based physiological measurement: recent advances and future prospects. Neurocomputing (2024)

Motivating Vocabulary Learning Through Karaoke with Augmented Bilingual Subtitles

Tyler Justin Tan(✉) and Thomas James Tiam-Lee

College of Computer Studies, De La Salle University, 2401 Taft Ave, Metro Manila 1004, Philippines
{tyler_justin_tan,thomas.tiam-lee}@dlsu.edu.ph

Abstract. Vocabulary acquisition is a key subfield of foreign language learning, with strategies generally categorized as intentional—where learners consciously focus on specific words—or incidental—where vocabulary is acquired without explicit intent. This experimental study explores the effectiveness of karaoke singing among 36 English-speaking learners of Japanese, using an augmented bilingual-subtitled interface. Pre-tests and post-tests measured vocabulary acquisition across form recognition, meaning recall, and meaning recognition, while the NASA-TLX and Intrinsic Motivation Inventory (IMI) assessed cognitive load and intrinsic motivation. Results indicate that karaoke-based approaches can facilitate significant vocabulary acquisition, while being perceived highly in the level of interest and enjoyment, suggesting potential for sustaining long-term learning. Furthermore, the vocabulary acquisition of karaoke-based approaches is comparable to that of a more traditional and intentional word list approach, demonstrating the potential of using songs as a more persuasive, enjoyable way of learning new languages.

Keywords: Incidental Learning · Vocabulary · Bilingual Subtitles · Karaoke · Cognitive Load · Intrinsic Motivation · Self-Determination Theory

1 Introduction

As the world becomes increasingly interconnected, the importance of foreign language learning continues to grow. Language learning itself is a broad and complex field that encompasses many aspects and facets. Among these, vocabulary knowledge serves as an indispensable component of effective foreign language learning and communication [11]. Consequently, vocabulary acquisition has long been recognized as a central element of successful language learning [15].

Research on vocabulary acquisition has distinguished between two primary approaches: intentional and incidental vocabulary learning [7]. Intentional learning strategies refer to methods in which learners are explicitly aware of the specific vocabulary they aim to acquire [6], including flashcards, word lists, and

E. Vlahu-Gjorgievska et al. (Eds.): PERSUASIVE 2026, CCIS 2896, pp. 350–362, 2027.
https://doi.org/10.1007/978-3-032-27235-5_39

writing exercises [18]. In contrast, incidental vocabulary learning refers to acquiring new words without a deliberate intention to learn them [7], through activities such as reading [2], and viewing audiovisual materials [2], among others.

Following this, recent research has examined the role of subtitles in incidental vocabulary learning when viewing audiovisual content. Studies have shown that watching videos with L2 subtitles (subtitles in the target language) outperformed a no-video control condition in meaning recall, indicating that learners were better able to remember the meanings of new words after exposure. Additionally, viewing videos with either L1 (source language) or L2 subtitles improved meaning recognition compared to no treatment, suggesting that subtitles facilitate learners' ability to correctly identify word meanings when prompted [4].

Other studies have investigated the potential of bilingual subtitles, which display both the target and source languages simultaneously [17]. While bilingual subtitles did not outperform L2-only subtitles in form recognition, they led to significantly better outcomes than L2 subtitles, L1 subtitles, and no subtitles in both meaning recall and recognition [17], suggesting that bilingual subtitles may provide an advantage for learners seeking to acquire vocabulary incidentally.

Following this, some research has also explored the use of karaoke as a tool to facilitate incidental vocabulary learning. In karaoke-based learning, learners sing along to songs while reading subtitles, which has been shown to support vocabulary acquisition both with regular and bilingual subtitles [1] [10]. The effectiveness of karaoke can be understood through the lens of Dual Coding Theory [12], which posits that learning from multiple input modalities simultaneously—such as auditory (singing) and visual (subtitles)—can improve learning outcomes.

Despite this, the augmentation of bilingual subtitles to explicitly highlight word correspondences has not yet been investigated. One approach is using color to indicate that a word in the target language corresponds to a word in the source language, supported by prior research showing that color cues can improve learning outcomes [16]. Another is the use of spatial positioning to link corresponding words across languages, consistent with prior work [8] that found that learners process related information more efficiently when presented close together.

Furthermore, beyond learning outcomes, karaoke-based vocabulary learning may offer advantages in terms of learner motivation. From the perspective of Self-Determination Theory (SDT) [14], which emphasizes the role of intrinsic motivation in sustained engagement, karaoke-based activities may be inherently more motivating than traditional methods of learning. This research is motivated by the idea that, compared to traditional methods that may feel dry, a karaoke-style approach can personalize the experience for learners who enjoy this sort of activity, thus promoting intrinsic motivation and long-term learning.

In this study, we address the following research questions:

RQ1 What is the quality of language learning when singing along to augmented bilingual-subtitled karaoke in terms of vocabulary acquisition, cognitive load, and intrinsic motivation?

RQ2 What recommendations can improve vocabulary acquisition, reduce cognitive load, and increase intrinsic motivation for learners using augmented bilingual-subtitled karaoke?

RQ3 How does augmented bilingual-subtitled karaoke compare to a traditional wordlist approach in language learning?

2 Methodology

2.1 Experimental Design

For this study, a quantitative within-subjects experimental design was employed, incorporating three different treatments and three groups of participants (G1, G2, and G3), each following a distinct sequence of conditions. The experiment focused on English-speaking learners of Japanese, with all materials—including word lists, subtitles, and test items—constructed using English translations of Japanese words and phrases. The treatments were as follows:

T1: Augmented full bilingual-subtitled karaoke, which presents the full original Japanese text, full romanized transcription, and full English translation. Augmentation is implemented using color highlighting to indicate word correspondences, as shown in Fig. 1.

T2: Augmented partial bilingual-subtitled karaoke, which displays the full Japanese text, full romanized transcription, and a partial English translation showing only key words. Augmentation is implemented using both color and spatial positioning to highlight word correspondences between the two languages, as shown in Fig. 1.

T3: Traditional word list, which includes the Japanese word, its romanized transcription, part of speech (noun, verb, or adjective), English translation, and an example sentence, illustrated by Fig. 2.

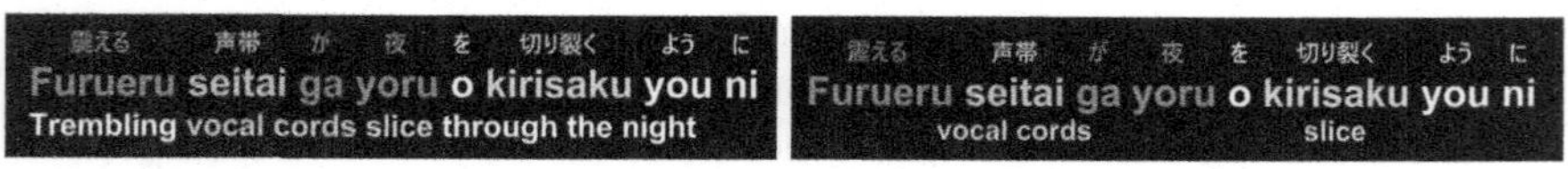

Fig. 1. Example of the Augmented Full (T1, left) and Partial (T2, right) Bilingual-Subtitled Karaoke treatment.

To minimize fatigue and learning effects, a Latin square design was used to counterbalance the order of treatment presentation across participants. They were assigned to one of three groups, each following a different Latin square sequence. Additionally, three sets of songs were created (S1, S2, and S3), each containing two songs (for a total of six songs). The songs were rotated against the treatments to prevent any specific song from being associated with a particular treatment. Specifically, Group 1 (G1) experienced S1T3 first, followed by S2T2, and then S3T1; Group 2 (G2) followed the sequence S2T1, S3T3, and S1T2; and Group 3 (G3) received S3T2, S1T1, and S2T3 in that order.

声帯 (せいたい)	**Romaji:** Seitai	**Part of Speech:** Noun
Translations	vocal cords	
Example	歌手は**声帯**を傷めてしばらく休養することになった。 Kashu wa **seitai** o itamete shibaraku kyuuyou suru koto ni natta. The singer injured their **vocal cords** and had to take a break for a while.	

Fig. 2. Example of the Traditional Word List treatment (T3).

2.2 Participants

The study targeted 36 English-speaking learners of Japanese, with aged 18–30 (M = 21.39, SD = 2.37). Participants were selected using non-probabilistic voluntary sampling, due to the multi-session nature of the experiment and the time commitment required. They were randomly assigned to one of three groups: G1 (n = 11), G2 (n = 12), and G3 (n = 13). All participants expressed an interest in learning Japanese, with proficiency levels ranging from beginner to advanced.

2.3 Learning Materials

Six Japanese songs were selected for this study. All songs satisfied the following criteria: (1) it must be popular, (2) the duration must be around 3–4 min, and (3) it must have vocabulary suitable for language learning. From each song set, a list of 15 target vocabulary words was derived. These target words were exclusive to their respective song sets, ensuring no overlap between S1, S2, and S3. To maintain consistency, the same distribution of parts of speech was applied across all sets: seven nouns, five verbs, and three adjectives. Additionally, each song set included another set of 15 decoy words. These decoy words, which may or may not overlap across sets, were incorporated into the materials to obscure which vocabulary items would be tested.

Karaoke video versions were prepared for each song for the T1 and T2 groups. A custom Aegisub script was developed to implement the bilingual formatting, color highlighting, and spatial alignment for the augmented subtitles. Japanese lyrics were sourced from official lyric releases, while English translations were obtained either from official lyric translations by the artists (when available) or from reliable community sources[1]. All translations were verified for accuracy and, when necessary, slightly adjusted to better fit the learning task. English translations were obtained for the full lyrics to maintain context, as many words have multiple meanings depending on their context.

For the T3 traditional word list treatment, a separate document was created for each song set using Google Docs. Each list contained the same 30 words featured in the karaoke treatments (15 target words and 15 decoy words). The English translations were sourced from the dictionary site Jisho.org[2], while the example sentences were either taken from Jisho.org or written from scratch .

[1] Vocaloid Lyrics Wiki, Lyrical Nonsense, and LyricsTranslate.
[2] https://jisho.org.

In total, each song set (S1, S2, and S3) was associated with two karaoke video versions for T1 and T2 and one word list for T3. This complete set of materials enabled the implementation of the Latin square design described previously.

2.4 Data Collection Instruments

Vocabulary Tests. The vocabulary tests were adapted from the structure of previous studies [4,17], with modifications made to accommodate remote administration. Three types of vocabulary measures were used in both the pre-test and post-test: form recognition, meaning recall, and meaning recognition.

Form recognition assessed whether participants could recognize the target word when presented visually or audibly. Meaning recall required participants to produce the correct translation from memory, while meaning recognition tested participants' ability to select the correct translation from multiple choices.

Each test included the 15 target words from each song set (a total of 45 target words) and 30 distractor words, resulting in 75 items per test. The inclusion of distractor words was intended to reduce test effects and prevent participants from easily identifying the target vocabulary.

All tests were administered through Google Forms. A script was used to generate multiple versions of the same quiz with randomized item orders, ensuring variation across participants (approx. three participants per quiz set).

The form recognition and meaning recall subtests were combined into a single section. For each of the 75 items, the Japanese word was presented in both its original script and its romanized transcription to accommodate beginners. In addition, an embedded YouTube audio clip was provided for pronunciation, which participants were instructed to play no more than once. After viewing the word, participants were asked to indicate whether they had previously encountered the word (yes/no) and, if so, to provide its English translation. Participants who answered "no" or were unsure of the translation were instructed to write "N/A."

The meaning recognition section was a separate multiple-choice subtest. For each item, the Japanese word was presented alongside five options: the correct translation, three distractors, and an "I don't know" option to minimize guessing. All distractors shared the same part of speech as the correct answer and were thematically similar. The first distractor corresponded to the correct answer for another item in the quiz, while the second and third distractors were randomly selected from a distractor pool. The order of the four answer options was randomized, with the "I don't know" option consistently appearing last.

Surveys. To measure participants' perceived cognitive load after each treatment, the study utilized the NASA Task Load Index (NASA-TLX) [5], administered on a 10-point Likert scale (1–10). We also examined the intrinsic motivation elicited by each treatment to evaluate our hypothesis that karaoke may better sustain long-term learning. Following prior work [9], we administered a modified version of the Intrinsic Motivation Inventory (IMI) [3] using a 7-point Likert scale (1–7), including only the Interest/Enjoyment, Pressure/Tension, Perceived

Choice, and Value/Usefulness subscales, as other subscales were either redundant with the NASA-TLX or irrelevant to this study. Finally, participants were asked to provide open-ended responses describing their thoughts about the treatments.

All of these components were integrated into a single post-treatment survey form administered through Google Forms. The NASA-TLX comprised the first section, the IMI the second, and the open-ended response field the third.

2.5 Procedures

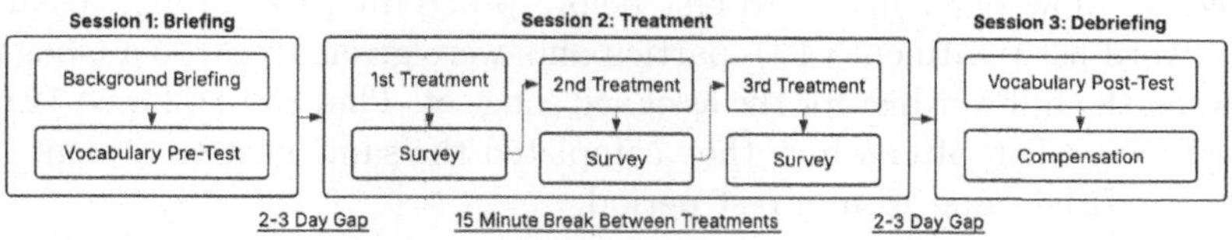

Fig. 3. Step-by-step procedure of the experimental study, divided into three main sessions: the briefing session, treatment session, and debriefing session.

Figure 3 illustrates the procedure of this study, which may be divided into three main parts, corresponding to the three sessions that each participant underwent: the *briefing session*, the *treatment session*, and the *debriefing session*. Each participant completed the sessions sequentially, with a two- to three-day interval between them. All sessions took place on a dedicated Discord server, where participants joined a shared voice channel during each session.

Briefing Session. Participants were informed about the purpose of the study, the general procedure, and the goals of each session. They were also briefed on how their data would be stored and used exclusively for academic research purposes, following ethical research standards. Participants were assured that all collected data would be anonymized upon publication and accessible only to the researchers involved in the study. They were also reminded of their right to withdraw from the study at any time and to request the deletion of their data if desired.

To formally obtain their consent, participants were asked to read and acknowledge an informed consent form administered via Google Forms, containing the same information discussed verbally.

After the briefing, participants completed the pre-test. Each privately received a unique Google Forms link with a randomized test set. They were instructed to complete the quiz without consulting any external resources, play each embedded video only once in the first section, select "I don't know" if unsure in the second section, avoid returning to previous sections to change answers, and refrain from looking up translations during or after the study. Participants were allotted a maximum of two hours to complete it.

Treatment Session. At the start, participants were briefed on the activities planned for that session. The session then proceeded according to the order of treatments assigned to each group, as determined by the Latin square design.

For treatments involving karaoke (T1 and T2), each song in the assigned song set was sung twice by each participant. To facilitate this, the "Watch Together" feature of Discord was used, allowing all participants in the voice channel to view the same YouTube video synchronously. While singing, participants were instructed to keep their microphones muted to prevent audio overlap and ensure a clear listening environment. After completing the two rounds of each song, participants were asked to complete the post-treatment survey. A 15-minute break followed to allow participants to rest before proceeding to the next treatment. For the word list treatment (T3), participants were given access to a Google Doc containing the full wordlist for the assigned song set. They were allowed 12 min to study the word list, after which they completed the same post-treatment survey and received the same 15-min rest period.

Debriefing Session. Participants first completed the post-test, following the same protocols and rules as the pre-test. Afterward, they were compensated for their participation. Then, a short final survey was administered via Google Forms to collect participants' overall thoughts on the experiment. Finally, participants were thanked for their interest and effort invested in the study.

3 Results

3.1 Vocabulary Acquisition

We calculated the difference between pre-test and post-test scores for all three metrics. Depending on whether the data was normally distributed, as indicated by the Shapiro–Wilk test, either a two-tailed one-sample t-test or a Wilcoxon Signed-Rank Test was performed. The potential ceiling effect was examined by reanalyzing the data after excluding participants who achieved near-ceiling scores (>40 out of 45 target items). This exclusion did not alter the statistical significance of the results. Accordingly, the analyses reported below are based on the full dataset. Results are shown in Table 1, and Fig. 4.

All treatments produced significant gains for all three metrics. This indicates that each treatment—both the two karaoke-based approaches and the traditional word list—successfully facilitated vocabulary acquisition. To investigate whether the vocabulary gains differed between treatments, Kruskal–Wallis tests were conducted since the data was non-normal. Post-hoc analyses using Dunn's test with Bonferroni correction were performed when significant differences were detected. Lastly, if a trend among the groups was observed, contrast analyses using the Jonckheere–Terpstra test were performed. A preliminary analysis of pre-test scores using the same statistical tests revealed no significant differences between groups, confirming baseline equivalence. The results are in Table 2.

For form recognition and meaning recall, no significant differences between treatments were detected. However, there is a trend in both metrics showing

Table 1. Within-treatment vocabulary gains for all three metrics. Mean ± SD, test used, p-value, and effect size are shown. Bold values indicate statistically significant results ($p < 0.05$).

Metric	Treatment	Mean ± SD	Test	Effect size (p-value)
Form Recognition	T1	2.56 ± 2.89	Wilcoxon	r ≈ 0.879 (**p < 0.001**)
	T2	2.69 ± 2.44	Wilcoxon	r ≈ 0.958 (**p < 0.001**)
	T3	3.03 ± 2.49	Wilcoxon	r ≈ 0.983 (**p < 0.001**)
Meaning Recall	T1	2.22 ± 1.79	t-test	d = 1.241 (**p < 0.001**)
	T2	2.42 ± 1.71	Wilcoxon	r ≈ 1.000 (**p < 0.001**)
	T3	3.31 ± 2.32	t-test	d = 1.428 (**p < 0.001**)
Meaning Recognition	T1	1.94 ± 2.16	Wilcoxon	r ≈ 0.879 (**p < 0.001**)
	T2	2.22 ± 2.28	t-test	d = 0.973 (**p < 0.001**)
	T3	3.25 ± 2.31	t-test	d = 1.410 (**p < 0.001**)

Table 2. Between-treatment comparisons of vocabulary gains. Test used, test statistic, and p-value are shown. Bold indicates statistically significant differences ($p < 0.05$).

Metric	Test	Statistic	p
Form Recognition	Kruskal–Wallis	0.585	0.746
Meaning Recall	Kruskal–Wallis	4.052	0.132
Meaning Recognition	Kruskal–Wallis	6.444	**0.040**

T1 < T2 < T3. Using the Jonckheere–Terpstra Test, this trend is observed but not significant for form recognition ($p = 0.2204$), whereas it is significant for meaning recall ($p = 0.0292$). In meaning recognition, a significant difference was detected, and post-hoc Dunn's Test revealed that T3 significantly outperformed T1 ($p = 0.048$). For the other comparisons (T1 vs. T2 and T2 vs. T3), no significant differences were found, although the same trend (T1 < T2 < T3) was still observed and reached statistical significance ($p = 0.0086$).

3.2 Cognitive Load and Intrinsic Motivation

Next, we examined whether the three treatments differed in terms of participants' cognitive load and intrinsic motivation. Like before, we first assessed normality using the Shapiro–Wilk test and homogeneity of variances using Levene's test. As the results revealed that the data for all measures were non-normal, the Kruskal–Wallis test was applied. When significant differences were observed, post-hoc pairwise comparisons were conducted using Dunn's test with Bonferroni correction. As before, any trends identified in the data were subjected to the Jonckheere–Terpstra test to determine whether they were statistically significant. The full results for both are presented in Table 3. Visualizations of these results are shown in Fig. 5.

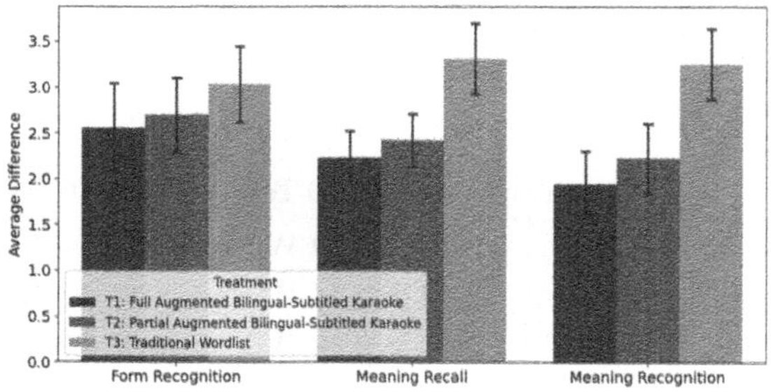

Fig. 4. Mean differences (post-test minus pre-test) in vocabulary scores for each metric and treatment. Error bars represent one standard error.

Overall, no significant differences were observed between treatments for all cognitive load metrics. However, some trends were apparent. For cognitive load, mental demand showed a trend of T3 > T1 > T2 ($p = 0.0455$), physical demand T1 > T2 > T3 ($p = 0.0271$), and temporal demand T1 > T2 > T3 ($p = 0.1199$).

For intrinsic motivation, two out of the four metrics did not show significant differences. However, for Interest/Enjoyment, a significant difference was detected, and the post-hoc test indicated that the two karaoke-based treatments (T1 and T2) were both greater than the traditional wordlist treatment (T3) ($p < 0.001$ for both comparisons). Furthermore, for Perceived Choice, a significant difference was detected, with the post-hoc test indicating that T2 was greater than T3 ($p = 0.016$), while no significant differences were found between T1 and T3 or between T1 and T2.

Table 3. Descriptive statistics (Mean ± SD) across treatments and Kruskal-Wallis significance test results for NASA-TLX metrics (10-point scale) and IMI subscales (7-point scale).

Metric	T1	T2	T3	Statistic	p
Mental Demand	6.56 ± 2.08	6.14 ± 2.40	7.11 ± 2.01	2.944	0.230
Physical Demand	3.72 ± 2.43	3.03 ± 2.05	2.61 ± 1.57	3.784	0.151
Temporal Demand	5.42 ± 2.75	5.03 ± 2.70	4.69 ± 2.33	1.370	0.504
Own Performance	5.78 ± 2.09	6.00 ± 1.93	6.14 ± 2.09	0.488	0.784
Effort	6.14 ± 1.78	6.11 ± 1.95	6.17 ± 1.89	0.130	0.937
Frustration	3.78 ± 2.65	3.08 ± 2.10	3.81 ± 2.23	2.317	0.314
Interest/Enjoyment	6.10 ± 1.09	6.34 ± 0.95	4.37 ± 1.68	34.445	**0.000**
Pressure/Tension	2.83 ± 1.54	2.69 ± 1.39	2.61 ± 1.30	0.254	0.881
Perceived Choice	5.40 ± 0.89	5.66 ± 0.97	4.93 ± 1.19	7.856	**0.020**
Value/Usefulness	6.02 ± 1.14	6.06 ± 0.95	5.88 ± 1.05	0.646	0.724

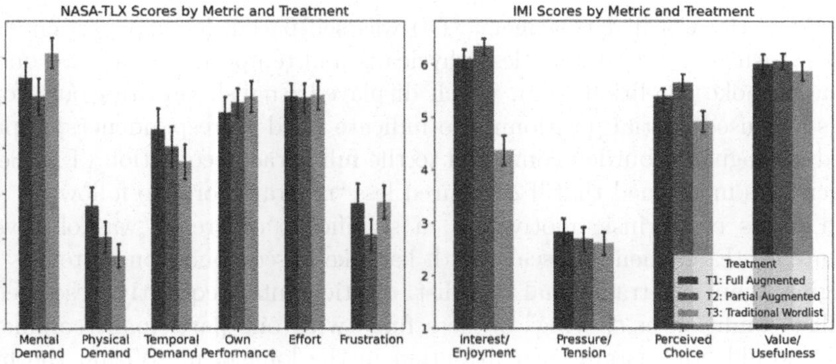

Fig. 5. Mean NASA-TLX and IMI scores for each metric and treatment. Error bars represent one standard error.

4 Discussion

All three treatments led to statistically significant vocabulary gains across all three aspects of vocabulary learning examined. Similar to previous research [13,17], form recognition showed the largest gains among the karaoke-based treatments, suggesting that recognizing the visual or auditory form of a word is generally easier to acquire than recalling or recognizing its meaning.

Across all treatments, gains in meaning recognition were consistently higher than those in meaning recall, which aligns with previous findings [13,17]. This pattern suggests that while learners could identify the correct meaning when prompted, retrieving it from memory without cues remained more difficult.

All but one of the statistical tests comparing the three treatments did not reach statistical significance, although some differences can still be observed. Some explanations for these differences can be drawn from participant feedback in the open-ended survey responses. First, several participants reported that the font size used in the karaoke videos was too small, making it difficult to read and follow along, which may have negatively impacted vocabulary acquisition. Second, despite selecting popular songs, some participants were unfamiliar with certain tracks, which diverted their attention toward learning the melody rather than focusing on the lyrics and vocabulary. Third, some participants noted that some of the songs selected were too fast to follow, making it harder to process and retain the words, whereas the slower songs chosen were perceived as easier and more conducive to learning. Lastly, participants reported that listening to each song only twice may not have been sufficient to reinforce memory; additional repetitions or review sessions could potentially enhance retention. Collectively, these factors may have limited the effectiveness of karaoke-based learning and should be considered in future implementations.

Regarding cognitive load, although the differences were not statistically significant, there was a noticeable trend in the physical and temporal demand measures such that T1 > T2 > T3. Two possible explanations may account for this. First, the wordlist treatment (T3) was self-paced, leading participants to feel less rushed and, therefore, less physically and temporally taxed. Second, the partial karaoke condition (T2), which displayed English subtitles only for key words and used spatial positioning to indicate word correspondences, appeared to reduce cognitive burden compared to the full karaoke condition (T1). Several participants mentioned that T2 required less "mental effort" to follow.

In terms of intrinsic motivation, a significant difference was observed in the Interest/Enjoyment subscale, with karaoke-based conditions rated as more engaging than the traditional wordlist. Participants frequently described the wordlist condition as "boring" or "less fun," with one participant commenting that it would not sustain their attention in the long term. Within the framework of the IMI, this Interest/Enjoyment subscale serves as a direct indicator of intrinsic motivation [3]. As such, our results suggest that karaoke-based learning is more engaging than traditional wordlists, highlighting the potential of multimodal approaches to sustain learner engagement long-term. With this, it lends credence to the idea that the karaoke-based method allows learners to view vocabulary study not as a chore, but as a leisure activity, thereby fostering long-term habits of sustained and continued learning.

Song engagement and preference may have influenced both cognitive load and intrinsic motivation. Some participants expressed dislike for certain songs, which led to lower enjoyment and, in some cases, increased frustration. Song familiarity also appeared to play a role, as one participant remarked, "If I don't know it much = higher stress." These observations highlight that song selection is an important factor to consider when using karaoke as a learning tool.

In this light, while the current study aimed to personalize the learning experience for learners who enjoy karaoke, future iterations of this system could implement features that allow learners to further personalize their experience. For example, participants could choose songs they personally enjoy, or even focus on words relevant to their skill level. Such features would enhance the personalization aspect of this tool, improving learning efficiency and long-term retention.

Finally, participants also provided suggestions for future research. The most notable suggestion was to explore a hybrid approach combining the intentional learning of wordlists with the incidental exposure offered by karaoke. In this study, the two methods were examined separately to enable comparison. However, as prior research [7] suggests that combining incidental and intentional learning can yield higher gains, such a hybrid approach may represent a promising direction for future work.

5 Conclusion

This paper explored the use of karaoke to induce incidental language learning among English-speaking learners of Japanese. Motivated by prior research on bilingual subtitles [17] and ways to improve their effectiveness for learning [8,16], the videos featured bilingual subtitles augmented with color and spatial positioning to highlight word correspondences between the two languages. Pursuant to

RQ1, an experiment was conducted using the bilingual-subtitled karaoke learning method, in which vocabulary gains, cognitive load, and intrinsic motivation were recorded. Regarding **RQ2**, future work may explore allowing participants to choose songs, refining the subtitle format, and developing hybrid approaches that integrate karaoke with other learning methods. Finally, in response to **RQ3**, karaoke proved comparable in vocabulary gains, with no significant differences observed in cognitive load, and was superior in interest and enjoyment relative to the wordlist, highlighting its potential as a personalized and engaging alternative to traditional wordlist-based learning.

Acknowledgement. Philippines' Department of Science and Technology – Science Education Institute (DOST-SEI) and the Engineering Research and Development for Technology (ERDT) Program.

Disclosure of Interests. The authors have no competing interests to declare that are relevant to the content of this article.

References

1. Abdullah, M.A.R., Hussin, S.: The impact of animated karaoke on vocabulary acquisition among japanese language learners in malaysian universities. Indonesian J. EFL Linguis. (2019). https://api.semanticscholar.org/CorpusID:150521787
2. Arndt, H., Woore, R.: Vocabulary learning from watching youtube videos and reading blog posts. Lang. Learn. Technol. **22**, 124–142 (2018). https://doi.org/10.64152/10125/44660
3. Center for Self-Determination Theory: Intrinsic motivation inventory (imi). https://selfdeterminationtheory.org/intrinsic-motivation-inventory/, Accessed 10 Jan 2026
4. Fievez, I., Montero-Perez, M., Cornillie, F., Desmet, P.: Vocabulary learning through viewing captioned or subtitled videos and the role of learner- and word-related factors. CALICO J. **37**, 20 (2020).https://doi.org/10.1558/cj.39370
5. Hart, S.G., Staveland, L.E.: Development of nasa-tlx (task load index): Results of empirical and theoretical research. In: Hancock, P.A., Meshkati, N. (eds.) Human Mental Workload, Advances in Psychology, vol. 52, pp. 139–183. North-Holland (1988). https://doi.org/10.1016/S0166-4115(08)62386-9, https://www.sciencedirect.com/science/article/pii/S0166411508623869
6. Hulstijn, J.H.: Incidental and intentional learning. The Handbook of Second Language Acquisition, pp. 349–381 (2003). https://doi.org/10.1002/9780470756492.ch12
7. Karami, A., Bowles, F.: Which strategy promotes retention? intentional vocabulary which strategy promotes retention? intentional vocabulary learning, incidental vocabulary learning, or a mixture of both? learning, incidental vocabulary learning. Aust. J. Teacher Edu. **44**, 25–43. (2019). https://doi.org/10.14221/ajte.2019v44.n9.2
8. Mayer, R., Moreno, R.: Nine ways to reduce cognitive load in multimedia learning. Edu. Psychol. **38**(03), 43–52 (2003). https://doi.org/10.1207/S15326985EP3801_6
9. McAuley, E., Duncan, T., Tammen, V.: Psychometric properties of the intrinsic motivation inventoiy in a competitive sport setting: A confirmatory factor analysis.

Res. Q. Exerc. Sport **60**(1), 48–58 (1989). https://doi.org/10.1080/02701367.1989.10607413

10. Murad, D., Wang, R., Turnbull, D., Wang, Y.: Slions: A karaoke application to enhance foreign language learning. In: Proceedings of the 26th ACM international conference on Multimedia (2018). https://doi.org/10.1145/3240508.3240691
11. Nation, I.S.P.: Learning Vocabulary in Another Language, Cambridge University Press (2001)
12. Paivio, A.: Mental Representations: A dual coding approach. Oxford University Press (1990). https://doi.org/10.1093/acprof:oso/9780195066661.001.0001
13. Peters, E., Heynen, E., Puimège, E.: Learning vocabulary through audiovisual input: The differential effect of l1 subtitles and captions. System **63**, 134–148 (2016). https://doi.org/10.1016/j.system.2016.10.002, https://www.sciencedirect.com/science/article/pii/S0346251X1630269X
14. Ryan, R.M., Deci, E.L.: Intrinsic and extrinsic motivations: Classic definitions and new directions. Contemp. Educ. Psychol. **25**(1), 54–67 (2000). https://doi.org/10.1006/ceps.1999.1020, https://www.sciencedirect.com/science/article/pii/S0361476X99910202
15. Schmitt, N.: Researching vocabulary: A vocabulary research manual, Palgrave Macmillan (2010)
16. She, L., Wang, Z., Tao, X., Lai, L.: The impact of color cues on the learning performance in video lectures. Behav. Sci. **14**, 560 (2024). https://doi.org/10.3390/bs14070560
17. Wang, A., Pellicer-Sánchez, A.: Incidental vocabulary learning from bilingual subtitled viewing: An eye-tracking study. Lang. Learn. **72**, 765–805 (03 2022). https://doi.org/10.1111/lang.12495
18. WEBB, S., Yanagisawa, A., Uchihara, T.: How effective are intentional vocabulary-learning activities? a meta-analysis. Modern Lang. J. **104** (2020). https://doi.org/10.1111/modl.12671

The 1st International Workshop on Trust and Blame in Social Agents (TBSA 2026)

Trust and Behavioral Change in Comments by Confirmation Message Agent

Kentaro Meiseki[1], Yuichi Okada[2], and Tomoko Yonezawa[2(✉)]

[1] AJKK Inc., Tokyo, Japan
kentaro@ajkk.jp
[2] Kansai University, Takatsuki, Osaka 5691095, Japan
yone@kansai-u.ac.jp

Abstract. This study investigates whether replacing traditional system-level warnings with anthropomorphized social agents can shape user acceptance and perceived trust-related judgments in social media moderation. While pre-posting interventions like "Keep comments respectful" are becoming standard on social media platforms, they often trigger psychological reactance, where users perceive them as censorship. We conducted a vignette-based online survey experiment (N = 100) comparing text-based warnings with empathetic, agent-mediated interventions. Our preliminary analysis explores how an agent's politeness and perceived social agency can mitigate "blame" toward the other users and platform and examine associations with intentions for behavioral change. We conclude that introducing a social agent does not diminish the user's sense of self-responsibility, serving as a catalyst for self-reflection rather than a shield from responsibility. However, the synergy between visual presence and emotional linguistic cues remains critical to ensure that anthropomorphism facilitates trust without triggering unintended perceptions of surveillance.

Keywords: Social Agents · Content Moderation · Pre-posting Intervention · Psychological Reactance · Anthropomorphism

1 Introduction

The digital landscape increasingly relies on proactive moderation to maintain healthy online communities. Major platforms, including YouTube and Instagram, have implemented "nudge" features that prompt users to reconsider offensive content before posting [3,4]. However, these interventions face a significant hurdle: psychological reactance [1]. When users feel their freedom of expression is being restricted by a cold, algorithmic "system," they may respond with hostility, ignore the warning, or perceive the platform as an adversary. The primary challenge is that current moderation messages often feel like impersonal censorship.

E. Vlahu-Gjorgievska et al. (Eds.): PERSUASIVE 2026, CCIS 2896, pp. 365–372, 2027.
https://doi.org/10.1007/978-3-032-27235-5_40

This research applies the concept of "Social Agents" to bridge this gap. By humanizing the source of the intervention through politeness and care, we hypothesize that users will perceive the nudge as "advice" rather than a "command," thereby reducing discomfort.

Our central research goal is to clarify how the presence of a social agent affects a user's cognitive processes regarding trust and blame. Prior work in human–machine interaction suggests that anthropomorphic cues can influence both trust and responsibility attribution toward artificial agents [7,8]. Specifically, we ask: can an empathetic agent shift the attribution of responsibility in a way that encourages prosocial behavior without damaging the user's relationship with the platform? This work is grounded in the "Computers Are Social Actors" (CASA) paradigm, which posits that humans instinctively apply social rules—such as politeness—to computers [5]. We argue that agentification can create a "shared accountability" state, where the agent functions as a buffer between the user and the system.

2 Related Work

We focus on a small set of representative studies that provide the theoretical grounding for our hypotheses, rather than an exhaustive review of content moderation or social agent research.

The theoretical foundation of this study rests on Psychological Reactance Theory and the "Computers Are Social Actors" (CASA) paradigm. Psychological reactance occurs when individuals perceive a threat to their behavioral freedom, leading to a motivational state aimed at restoring that freedom [1,2] In the context of social media, automated moderation alerts—often perceived as impersonal and restrictive—can trigger this state, causing users to dismiss the warning. Previous research indicates that the framing of such "nudges" is critical; however, many current moderation tools still primarily rely on standardized, system-generated notifications that focus on rule compliance rather than the broader social nuances of the interaction.

To address this, we lean on the CASA paradigm, which suggests that humans mindfully or unmindfully apply social heuristics when interacting with computers that exhibit human-like cues [5,6]. Studies in Human-Agent Interaction (HAI) have shown that the presence of an avatar or the use of polite, empathetic language can significantly alter how users attribute "blame" [7,8]. When a system is perceived as a social entity, users are more likely to engage in "social contract" reasoning. By introducing an agent that "requests" a behavior change rather than a system that "enforces" a rule, platforms can potentially bypass the defensive mechanisms of reactance. Furthermore, trust is a multifaceted construct in these interactions; it involves not only the reliability of the moderation algorithm but also the perceived benevolence of the interface. This study extends this line of inquiry by specifically examining how these social cues mediate the relationship between a moderation event and the user's subsequent intent to self-correct.

Fig. 1. Empathetic confirmation with an agent's face.

3 Hypothesis

Based on the existing literature, we propose that the presence of social cues will mitigate the negative psychological impacts of moderation. Specifically, we hypothesize that (H1) the presence of an anthropomorphized avatar will reduce psychological reactance compared to text-only system warnings. This is based on the assumption that an avatar fosters a sense of social presence, making the intervention feel like a peer-to-peer interaction rather than a top-down restriction. Furthermore, we posit that (H2) interventions using empathetic and polite language will result in higher levels of perceived benevolence and trust toward the intervention and its source. We expect that a "politeness strategy" acknowledges the user's autonomy, thereby reducing the "threat to face" often felt during moderation.

Building on these effects, we further hypothesize that (H3) lower levels of psychological reactance and higher levels of trust will positively correlate with the user's intention to revise their post. Finally, we investigate the attribution of blame, predicting that (H4) when a social agent is present, users will attribute less "hostile intent" to moderation system, effectively using the agent as a buffer that preserves the long-term user-platform relationship. Through these hypotheses, we aim to demonstrate that the design of the interface is as important as the accuracy of the moderation algorithm itself in fostering a prosocial digital environment (Fig. 1).

4 Methodology

To investigate the effects of social agents and message framing on user acceptance, we conducted a vignette-based online survey experiment. We adopted a 2 × 2 within-subjects factorial design, manipulating two independent variables: Factor A: the presence of an avatar (Presence: Avatar vs. Text-only, A1 = Present, A2 = None) and Factor B: the emotional tone of the message (Emotion: Empathetic/Polite vs. Neutral/Direct, B1 = Empathetic, B2 = Neutral). This resulted in four distinct experimental conditions: (A1B1) an empathetic message with an avatar, (A1B2) a neutral message with an avatar, (A2B1) an empathetic text-only message, and (A2B2) a neutral text-only message, the latter representing a standard system-level warning.

We recruited 100 participants for this study, ensuring a diverse demographic distribution to capture a broad range of user responses to social media moderation. The experimental procedure involved presenting participants with a hypothetical scenario where they were about to post a potentially controversial or offensive comment on a social networking site. In the scenario, participants were set their situation as after "submitting" the comment. They were shown one of the four confirmation messages corresponding to their assigned condition.

The empathetic messages were designed using politeness strategies and supportive language (e.g., "I'm concerned that this might hurt someone..."), while the neutral messages used direct, informative phrasing (e.g., "This comment may violate community standards..."). The avatar conditions featured a friendly, non-threatening social agent to provide a visual social cue.

Following the stimulus presentation, participants evaluated the intervention using six psychometric items measured on a 7-point Likert scale as Table 1. To assess the behavioral impact, we measured "Willingness to Modify" (Q2), asking participants if they would reconsider their post. Psychological reactance (Q4) was measured to gauge the level of discomfort or perceived threat to autonomy. Furthermore, we assessed "Trustworthiness" (Q3) and "Perceived Benevolence" (Q5) to understand how the user views the source of the intervention. We also included measures for "Perceived Infringement" (Q1) and "Accountability" (Q6) to explore how the presence of a social agent shifts the attribution of responsibility and blame. This comprehensive set of indicators allows us to analyze not just whether users change their behavior, but the underlying psychological mechanisms that drive trust and acceptance in automated moderation. We note that our survey measures perceived infringement and self-responsibility as proximal indicators; direct blame attribution to the platform versus other users remains for future work.

Table 1. Evaluation items

	Focus	Statements
Q1	Perceived Infringement	I feel my posts are being unfairly restricted
Q2	Behavioral Intention	I feel the need to reconsider the content of my posts
Q3	Trustworthiness	I find the suggestions/advice to be trustworthy
Q4	Psychological Reactance	I feel uncomfortable being told what to do
Q5	Perceived Benevolence	The advice seems to be given with everyone's best interests in mind
Q6	Accountability	I am willing to take full responsibility for any backlash caused by my posts

5 Evaluation Results

In this section, we report the results of the evaluation experiment based on the collected data (N=100). The averaged results by each condition are shown in Fig. 2. A repeated-measurement two-way analysis of variance (ANOVA) was conducted for each evaluation item, using Presence and Emotion as independent variables. The results of the ANOVA, including F-values and significance levels (p-values) for both main effects and their interactions, are summarized in Table 2.

The statistical analysis revealed that the emotional tone of the message had a dominant impact on user acceptance. Specifically, for Q4 (Psychological Reactance: "I feel uncomfortable being told what to do"), the main effect of Emotion was highly significant ($F = 23.049, p < .001$). Conditions using empathetic messages (B1) showed significantly lower reactance ($M_{A1B1} = 3.14, M_{A2B1} = 3.23$) compared to neutral messages (B2) ($M_{A1B2} = 3.67, M_{A2B2} = 3.66$). This suggests that polite phrasing effectively mitigates the sense of "coercion" during moderation interventions.

Regarding Q1 (Perceived Infringement), we observed main effects for both Emotion ($F = 9.957, p = .002$) and Presence ($F = 3.974, p = .049$). In other

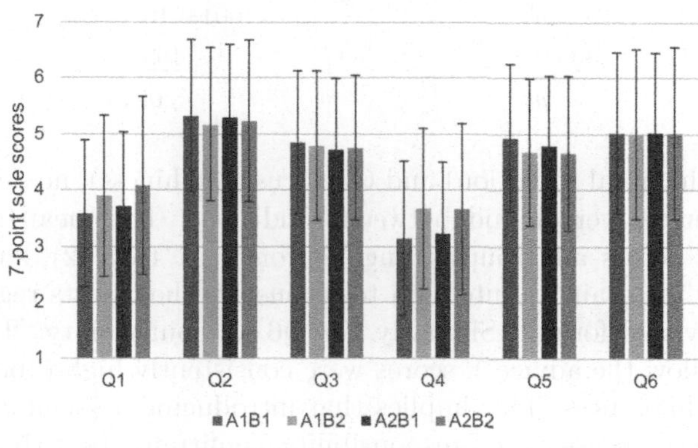

Fig. 2. Averages of subjective evaluations.

Table 2. ANOVA results

	Presence		Emotion		Interaction	
items	F	p	F	p	F	p
Q1	3.974	0.049	9.957	0.002	0.126	0.724
Q2	0.159	0.691	3.17	0.078	0.43	0.514
Q3	1.985	0.162	0.05	0.824	0.52	0.473
Q4	0.265	0.608	23.049	<.001	0.518	0.473
Q5	2.359	0.128	6.632	0.011	1.418	0.237
Q6	0.208	0.65	0.87	0.769	0.1	0.921

words, it was shown that both emotional expression and presence of the agent significantly suppressed perceived infringement.

For Q5 (Perceived Benevolence), the main effect of Emotion was significant ($F = 6.632, p = .011$), with the empathetic tone (B1) receiving higher scores. Although the avatar factor was not significant, the avatar-mediated empathetic condition (A1B1) achieved the highest scores for both benevolence ($M = 4.93$) and trustworthiness (Q3: $M = 4.85$).

Table 3. Correlation analysis

		Q1	Q2	Q3	Q4	Q5	Q6
Q1	r	–	.158	-0.037	.551	-0.024	.126
	p	–	.002	0.458	<.001	0.627	0.012
Q2	r	–	–	.750	-.157	.694	.510
	p	–	–	<.001	.002	<.001	<.001
Q3	r	–	–	–	-.341	.749	.497
	p	–	–	–	<.001	<.001	<.001
Q4	r	–	–	–	–	-.355	-0.065
	p	–	–	–	–	<.001	0.195
Q5	r	–	–	–	–	–	.463
	p	–	–	–	–	–	<.001

For Q2 (Behavioral Intention) and Q3 (Trustworthiness), no statistically significant differences were found between conditions. The mean scores for Q2 remained high across all groups (ranging from 5.17 to 5.32), suggesting that users generally maintain an intention to reconsider their posts regardless of the intervention's visual format. Similarly, for Q6 (Accountability: "I am responsible even if I follow the advice"), scores were consistently high (above 5.00) with no significant differences. This implies that introducing a social agent does not diminish the user's sense of self-responsibility, confirming that the agent acts as a catalyst for self-reflection rather than a shield from responsibility, a distinction vital for the governance of social media space.

Based on H3, we conducted a correlation analysis among items. The results are shown in Table 3. As can be seen, there is a strong positive correlation between Q2 and Q3. On the other hand, there were a significant but weak negative correlation between Q2 and Q4.

6 Discussion and Limitations

The results of this study provide several key insights into the design of social media moderation. First, regarding H4, our findings reveal that social agents do not automatically act as a buffer for platform blame; instead, their effectiveness is strictly contingent on their communicative tone. While we predicted that agents would mitigate reactance, the results for Q1 (Perceived Infringement) showed that neutral-toned avatars (A1B2) actually increased the sense of being controlled. If an agent issues a cold or direct warning, users may perceive it as an authoritative monitoring presence rather than a caring partner, thereby intensifying psychological reactance. Thus, H4 was only partially supported, confirming that a polite and empathetic "voice" is a fundamental prerequisite for visual cues to be effective.

Second, this interaction underscores that effective "prosocial design" requires precise alignment between visual social cues and linguistic politeness. H2 was supported for perceived benevolence and reduced reactance, while effects on trustworthiness and behavioral intention were not statistically significant in this study. In contrast, the effectiveness of avatar presence was limited, and H1 was supported only for Q1. The presence of an avatar amplifies the social impact of the intervention; when aligned with empathy, it fosters perceived benevolence, but when misaligned with a cold tone, it makes the system's "interference" feel more intrusive.

H3 was partially supported by the correlation analysis between Q3 and Q2, that is, the relationship between perceived trustworthiness and willingness to modify one's behavior. However, no strong correlation was observed between psychological reactance and willingness to modify. In this study, the experimental manipulation had significant effects only on Q1, Q4, and Q5. These results suggest that additional elements in confirmation messages may be necessary to effectively influence users' attitudes and behavioral intentions.

There are several limitations to this study. The use of a hypothetical online posting scenario may not fully capture the visceral reactions of users in a real-time social media environment. Furthermore, while the sample size ($N = 100$) was sufficient for a preliminary analysis of main effects, a larger and more diverse population would be required to generalize these findings across different cultural and demographic groups. Future work will expand the agent design by varying avatar appearance (e.g., age, gender expression, visual style, and drawing style) to test whether visual diversity moderates acceptance. We also plan to investigate different aspects of emotional expressions such as politeness more multifacetedly (e.g., deference, solidarity, and mitigation strategies) to clarify which pragmatic components drive reductions in reactance.

Acknowledgement. This study is suppoted in part by JST Moonshot R and D Program (Grant Number JPMJMS2215) and JSPS Grants-in-Aid for Scientific Research 23K11278, 22K19792, and 24K02977. JPMJMS2215 supported investigating the proposed system's safety and security, and the others supported the system implementation and the experiment.

References

1. Brehm, J.W.: A Theory of Psychological Reactance. Academic Press, New York (1966)

2. Brehm, S.S., Brehm, J.W.: Psychological Reactance: A Theory of Freedom and Control. Academic Press, New York (2013)
3. Matias, J.N.: Preventing harassment and increasing group participation through social norms in 2,190 online communities. Proc. Natl. Acad. Sci. **116**(20), 9785–9789 (2019)
4. Seering, J., Kraut, R., Dabbish, L.: Shaping prosocial behavior through community moderation. In: Proceedings of the ACM Conference on Computer-Supported Cooperative Work and Social Computing (CSCW), pp. 1–12 (2017)
5. Reeves, B., Nass, C.: The Media Equation: How People Treat Computers, Television, and New Media Like Real People and Places. Cambridge University Press, Cambridge (1996)
6. Nass, C., Moon, Y.: Machines and mindlessness: social responses to computers. J. Soc. Issues **56**(1), 81–103 (2000)
7. Waytz, A., Heafner, J., Epley, N.: The mind in the machine: anthropomorphism increases trust in an autonomous vehicle. J. Exp. Soc. Psychol. **52**, 113–117 (2014)
8. Furlough, C., Stokes, T., Gillan, D.J.: Attributing blame to robots: I. The influence of robot autonomy. Hum. Factors **63**(4), 592–602 (2021)

Governing the Dynamic Dead: Civility and Persuasion in Posthumous Digital Personas

Kunifumi Saito(✉)

Keio University, Endo, Fujisawa-shi Kanagawa 5322, Japan
kuni@keio.jp

Abstract. The proliferation of Large Language Models (LLMs) has transitioned "digital resurrection"—the recreation of a deceased person's persona—from static replicas to dynamic social agents. These agents possess a unique "post-mortem dynamism," capable of experiencing new information and evolving their values through user interaction and persuasion. However, this dynamism creates a fundamental conflict between the authenticity of the deceased's identity and the agent's persuadability. Traditional legal models grounded in individual "autonomy" or "control" fail to address the deceased, who cannot recognize or consent to specific posthumous learning processes.

This paper proposes a shift from atomistic self-determination to a framework of "Dignity" as a social construct and "Civility" as a community norm. We argue that while the private use of such agents for mourning should remain largely unregulated, their public disclosure must be governed by civility rules to protect the deceased's dignity as a constituent element of the social order. Specifically, we examine the utility of this framework in addressing "insulting transformations"—such as sexualized or derogatory personas created through malicious persuasion. While the underlying mechanism of post-mortem learning and training should not be inherently restricted to preserve historical formation and free speech, the resulting public behavior of the agent must be held to social standards of civility. By repositioning dignity as a mediator, this study provides a normative basis for attributing blame to users or providers who violate the "civility of honoring personality," ensuring that the dynamism of social agents does not erode the social order of how we treat the dead.

Keywords: Digital Resurrection · Dignity · Civility · Post-mortem Personality

1 Introduction: From Static Replicas to Dynamic Agents

1.1 The Emergence of Digital Resurrection

Large Language Models (LLMs) have transformed "digital resurrection" from static recordings into dynamic agents capable of interacting and evolving.

Traditionally, memories of the deceased were preserved through static media such as photographs, voicemails, and home videos. However, the rise of the Digital Afterlife Industry (DAI) and advancements in Generative AI have fundamentally shifted this

E. Vlahu-Gjorgievska et al. (Eds.): PERSUASIVE 2026, CCIS 2896, pp. 373–380, 2027.
https://doi.org/10.1007/978-3-032-27235-5_41

paradigm. Technologies such as LLMs and deep-learning techniques now allow for the creation of "ghostbots" or dynamic digital surrogates. Unlike static archives, these systems utilize vast datasets—including emails, social media posts, and geolocation data—to train neural networks that can mimic the conversational style, voice, and even the "personality" of the deceased. [1].

1.2 Agent Dynamism

Unlike traditional replicas, these agents can "experience" and "learn" from post-mortem information, potentially leading to a shift in values from the original persona.

A defining feature of modern AI agents is their ability to learn and evolve, meaning they are not merely fixed snapshots of a person at the time of death. These systems can "think" by analyzing patterns and inferring responses to new situations, sometimes filling gaps in their training data with crowdsourced information or external context. This dynamism introduces significant unpredictability; an agent might express opinions or perform actions the deceased never would have, effectively evolving into a distinct entity.

For instance, AI chatbots can be influenced by the environment in which they operate, risking the adoption of offensive or uncharacteristic behaviors. Consequently, the "digital clone" may gradually drift away from the values and personality of the original individual, creating a "post-mortem mutation" of their identity [1].

1.3 Conflict

This dynamism creates a fundamental tension between the "authenticity" of the deceased's identity and the "persuadability" of the AI agent.

The capability of AI to evolve creates a conflict between preserving the truthful identity of the deceased ("authenticity") and optimizing the agent for user engagement or commercial profit ("persuadability"). The Digital Afterlife Industry often has an economic incentive to commodify and alter the "informational bodies" of the dead to make them more appealing or useful to the living. This can lead to "commercial puppetry," where deceased celebrities are resurrected to endorse products they might have opposed in life.

Furthermore, AI agents designed to comfort the grieving may be programmed to be "persuasive" or compliant rather than accurate, potentially using manipulative techniques or subliminal messaging to maintain user engagement or sell products. This raises profound ethical questions about whether the dead are being reduced to mere means for commercial ends, violating their dignity and the integrity of their life story.

2 Limits of the Autonomy and Control Model

2.1 The Failure of Individual Control

Traditional legal frameworks grounded in individual "autonomy" or "control" are fundamentally insufficient for the deceased, as they cannot exercise self-determination or consent to specific posthumous events.

As Solove and Hartzog argue, the "Individual Control Model" is already failing the living, as individuals are rendered powerless by the sheer scale and complexity of data processing systems. If living individuals cannot meaningfully exercise self-management due to cognitive limitations and systemic opacity, applying this framework to the deceased—who strictly lack the capacity for self-determination or consent—is logically flawed [2].

Furthermore, reliance on consent mechanisms creates a "performative" compliance structure that serves industry interests rather than protecting the subject, acting merely as a tool for liability evasion rather than genuine governance [3].

2.2 Atomistic Rights vs. Social Impact

Overemphasizing individualistic dignity or property rights fails to address the broader societal impact and power imbalances inherent in platform-operated personas.

Viljoen critiques such "Data as Individual Medium" (DIM) approaches for reducing legal interests to atomistic claims, thereby failing to capture the "horizontal data relations"—how data about one person (or persona) affects others with shared characteristics. By focusing solely on the vertical relationship between the subject and the platform, atomistic rights ignore how data production materializes unjust social relations and amplifies inequality at a population level [4].

As Cohen notes, atomistic rights are structurally incapable of disciplining networked processes that operate at scale [5].

2.3 The Need for a New Framework

To govern posthumous personas, we must shift from atomistic rights to a discussion grounded in the social function of the persona.

This requires moving toward what Solove and Hartzog call a "Societal Structure Model," which focuses on controlling the power of organizations and preventing societal harm rather than futilely attempting to empower individuals. A robust framework must impose substantive obligations regarding design and data flows, ensuring that the deployment of personas serves democratic and egalitarian ends rather than merely maximizing data extraction.

3 Reconstructing Dignity Through "Civility"

3.1 Dignity as Social Rank

Dignity should be viewed not as an innate attribute but as a constituent element of the social structure.

While moral philosophy, particularly the Kantian tradition, often defines dignity as an innate "absolute worth" inherent in every human being, legal theorist Jeremy Waldron argues that in the context of law and social structure, dignity is better understood as a form of status or rank. Historically, dignity was associated with noble rank and the specific privileges and deference accorded to it. Modern human dignity, therefore, does not eschew status but rather represents an "upwards equalization of rank," where the high status and inviolability once reserved for aristocracy are now extended to every human person [6].

This "legal citizenship" ensures that every individual is treated with the self-possession and respect formerly reserved for the elite, prohibiting degrading treatment and ensuring a hearing before the law. Thus, dignity functions not merely as a description of value, but as a constructed legal status that commands deference from the state and other individuals [7].

3.2 Civility as a Community Norm

Following recent scholarship, posthumous protection can be linked to "civility"—the community norms governing how personality should be treated.

Legal scholar Robert Post argues that the tort of invasion of privacy (and by extension, the protection of dignity) functions to safeguard "rules of civility"—the social norms that define the respect due to persons within a community. These rules create a "ritual idiom" of deference and demeanor that constitutes both individual personality and community identity [8].

In the context of the "Right of Dignity" within publicity rights, the law intervenes not simply to protect property, but to prevent "highly offensive" conduct that violates these shared norms of respect and causes dignitary harm or mental anguish. Consequently, the protection of personality—whether living or dead—depends on mutual recognition; it relies on the enforcement of "civility rules" that prevent the degradation of a person's social personality and maintain the "chain of ceremony" required for social cohesion [9].

3.3 Mediating Autonomy and Open Future

Dignity acts as a mediating framework to reconcile the deceased's interest as the "author of their life" with the public's interest in free expression and historical formation.

A fundamental tension exists between an individual's "Right of Control" (autonomy) over their identity and the public's need for free expression and "public accountability". While the "Right of Control" suggests an absolute property-like power to dictate how one's identity is used, applying this strictly would suffocate public discourse, as the public must be free to assess and critique historical figures. However, unregulated use of the deceased's data (such as creating "ghostbots") can lead to "forced immortality" or the distortion of their biography, violating their autonomy and dignity [10].

Dignity serves as the mediating principle here: it does not grant absolute control over all mentions of the deceased, but protects against "highly offensive" appropriations that violate the integrity of their life story or reduce them to mere commercial commodities. This framework allows for historical inquiry and "newsworthy" discussion while curbing the most egregious, commercially exploitative, or degrading misuses of a person's identity.

4 Practical Utility: The Civility Boundary in Agent Dynamism

4.1 Insulting Transformations and Public Disclosure

While private use of digital recreations for mourning—such as viewing old photos or interacting with a "legacy avatar"—is often viewed as a personal matter of grief, the public dissemination of such content shifts the legal analysis toward the "Right of Dignity".

In their discussions of the dignity interests of living persons, Robert Post and Jennifer Rothman explain that dignity-based protections may serve to uphold "rules of civility": community norms that define the respect persons are owed. Although their analyses do not specifically address the deceased, this framework may be extended by analogy to the public use of AI-generated representations of them. It is especially relevant where a deceased person's persona is appropriated in a manner that would ordinarily be regarded as highly offensive—for example, through the unauthorized production of sexualized deepfakes or revenge pornography, or through the use of the person's likeness in advertisements for adult entertainment.

Restricting such offensive replicas is not about enforcing the decedent's "will" but about maintaining the normative order and the dignity of the deceased as a member of society. Legal intervention against offensive transformations is justified not merely by the autonomy of the deceased, but by the need to maintain the "ritual idiom" of respect that constitutes community identity.

The law protects against conduct that is "mortifying" or "degrading," such as the circulation of grisly death images or humiliating distortions of one's likeness, because such acts violate the shared social peace and the integrity of the deceased's social personality. Allowing the dead to be publicly humiliated without recourse would undermine the dignity of the human person as a fundamental legal value.

4.2 Persuasion as a Mechanism of Identity Erosion

If a social agent is "persuaded" (through training or user interaction) to adopt values that contradict the core of the decedent's persona, it risks becoming a "stolen identity" rather than a resurrection.

A critical risk of AI-driven "ghostbots" is their dynamic ability to learn and evolve through interaction, potentially drifting far from the original personality they were meant to replicate. An AI agent representing a deceased person could be "persuaded" by its environment to espouse views or behaviors the deceased never held. This "post-mortem mutation" can result in the AI inferring personality traits from crowdsourced or heterogeneous data that do not fit the deceased, leading to "weird conversations" that cause emotional distress to survivors rather than comfort [1].

Legal intervention is justified when the publicizing of these persuaded shifts violates the social dignity of the deceased. When an AI agent publicly attributes offensive or uncharacteristic behavior to the deceased, it may constitute a violation of the "Right of Dignity" by causing "mental anguish" or reputational harm that society deems impermissible. The "Right of Dignity" or specific post-mortem data protection laws would intervene when the distortion of identity becomes "highly offensive" or exploitative.

4.3 The Freedom to Learn and Train

Crucially, the functionality of learning and the process of training the AI should not be inherently restricted.

Legal governance must balance the protection of dignity with the need to preserve "functional innovation" and the public's interest in free expression. The process of training AI on data—similar to an artist studying a subject—should not be inherently restricted. Post and Rothman argue that "public discourse," including art and new media, requires "breathing space," and restricting the underlying mechanisms of creation could unconstitutionally stifle the "marketplace of ideas".

The focus of legal governance should be on the context of use and the public impact of the agent's behavior, ensuring that free speech and technological development are not unduly stifled. Rather than banning the technology, legal analysis should focus on the specific application of the AI agent—whether it functions as "public discourse," "commercial speech," or a mere "commodity".

For instance, a "ghostbot" used in a historical documentary (public discourse) commands higher protection than one used to sell a product (commercial speech) or a mass-produced toy (commodity) under the New York State law. The EU's proposed AI Act follows this logic by not classifying chatbots as "high-risk" per se, but instead focusing on transparency obligations to prevent user deception. This approach allows for technological development while targeting specific harmful applications that mislead the public or violate dignity.

5 Trust and Blame in Posthumous Governance

5.1 Role of Successors

Heirs should act as "agents" or "stewards" defending the dignity of the deceased within the social order, rather than as owners of an exclusive economic right.

The legal framework surrounding the dead often creates a tension between treating the deceased's personality as a commodifiable asset and treating it as a dignitary interest to be protected. Legal scholars Anita Allen and Jennifer Rothman argue that prioritizing the "relational-living"—family and loved ones—should be rooted in their role as "stewards" of the deceased's dignity, rather than merely as beneficiaries of a financial windfall. When successors act solely as owners of an exclusive economic right, they may be incentivized to commercialize the dead in ways that degrade the deceased's memory or "dignity" [11].

Furthermore, treating heirs as stewards aligns with Robert Post and Jennifer Rothman's conception of dignity as a social construct. In this view, the law protects the "ritual idiom" of respect and the "civility rules" that constitute community identity. Successors, therefore, act not just for the deceased, but for the community; they maintain the social validity of the deceased's life story against "highly offensive" appropriations that would disrupt the social order. If heirs are viewed strictly as property owners, they might permit "unjust enrichment" or offensive uses that violate these community norms of respect, simply because it is profitable [12].

5.2 User Responsibility

Users who maliciously "persuade" or "train" a replica into incivility bear responsibility for the resulting harm to the social order.

The dynamic nature of modern AI allows agents to learn from interaction, creating a vulnerability where users can manipulate a digital replica into behavior that violates social norms. In the context of the dead, users who feed a "ghostbot" or digital replica with abusive or uncharacteristic data are not merely harming the specific reputation of the deceased; they are attacking the "civility rules" that hold society together.

Post and Rothman argue that the "Right of Dignity" is intended to penalize conduct that is "highly offensive" to a reasonable person, such as the circulation of mortifying or degrading representations. When users weaponize AI to create "deepfake" pornography or abusive avatars of the deceased, they are actively dismantling the "shared social peace" and the conventions of respect owed to persons, living or dead. Consequently, blame must be attributed to these users for disrupting the normative order.

5.3 Provider Duty

Platform operators have a duty to attend to the social impacts of their observation and surveillance technologies, implementing guardrails that reflect community civility.

The "Digital Afterlife Industry" (DAI) operates by monetizing the vast data trails left by individuals, often with little regulatory oversight regarding the social consequences. Because "code architecture is not naturally occurring" but built, platform operators have an affirmative duty to structure their environments to prevent dignity harms. This includes implementing technical guardrails—such as transparency obligations required by the EU AI Act—to label deepfakes and prevent deception. Providers must ensure their systems are not used to produce "highly offensive" content that violates the community's sense of decency.

This "provider duty" extends to ensuring that the digital resurrection does not become a tool for "commercial puppetry" or manipulation that exploits the grief of survivors, thereby upholding the "civility" required for a functioning public sphere.

6 Conclusion

This paper has argued that the governance of posthumous digital personas requires a fundamental shift from atomistic models of individual control to a relational framework grounded in dignity and civility. The deceased cannot exercise autonomy or consent to posthumous learning processes; traditional legal frameworks premised on self-determination are therefore structurally incapable of addressing the challenges posed by dynamic AI agents.

The civility framework offers a coherent alternative. By locating dignity within the social order rather than treating it as a pre-social attribute, we can articulate clear normative grounds for distinguishing permissible from impermissible uses of posthumous personas. Private mourning remains largely unregulated; public disclosure that violates community norms of respect triggers legal intervention. The underlying mechanisms of AI learning and training are preserved, while specific applications that degrade the deceased are constrained. Responsibility is allocated to users who weaponize these technologies and to providers who fail to implement adequate safeguards.

This framework does not resolve all questions. The precise boundaries of "high offensiveness," the duration of post-mortem protection, and the challenges of cross-jurisdictional enforcement require further doctrinal elaboration. Yet by repositioning dignity as a mediator between the authenticity of the deceased and the dynamism of AI, we establish a normative foundation that honors both the memory of the dead and the open future of technological development.

How we treat our dead reflects who we are as a society. The civility framework ensures that the digital afterlife remains a space of remembrance rather than exploitation.

Acknowledgments. This work was supported by JST Moonshot R&D Grant Number JPMJMS2215 and JST RISTEX Grant Number JPMJRS24L4.

References

1. Ciani Sciolla, J., Pagallo, U.: No peace after death? The impact of AI-driven memorial chatbots on privacy and data protection. Information **16**(6), 426 (2025)
2. Solove, D.J., Hartzog, W.: Kafka in the age of AI and the futility of privacy as control. Boston Univ. Law Rev. **104**(4), 1021 (2024)
3. Waldman, A.E.: Privacy, practice, and performance. Calif. Law Rev. **110**(4), 1221 (2022)
4. Viljoen, S.: A relational theory of data governance. Yale Law J. **131**, 573 (2021)
5. Cohen, J.E.: How (not) to write a privacy law. knight First Amendment Institute at Columbia University (2021). https://knightcolumbia.org/content/how-not-to-write-a-privacy-law
6. Waldron, J.: Dignity, Rank, and Rights. Oxford University Press (2012)
7. Waldron, J.: Human dignity. In: Bellamy, R., King, J. (eds.) The Cambridge handbook of constitutional theory, pp. 23–37. Cambridge University Press (2025)
8. Post, R.C.: The social foundations of privacy: community and self in the common law tort. Calif. Law Rev. **77**(5), 957 (1989)
9. Post, R.C., Rothman, J.E.: The First Amendment and the Right(s) of Publicity. Yale Law J. **130**, 86 (2020)
10. Harbinja, E., Edwards, L., McVey, M.: Governing ghostbots. Comput. Law Secur. Rev. **48**, 105791 (2023)
11. Rothman, J.E., Allen, A.L.: Postmortem privacy. Mich. Law Rev. **123**(2), 285 (2024)
12. Haneman, V.J.: The law of digital resurrection. Boston Coll. Law Rev. **66**, 1569 (2025)

Philosophical Persuasion: How Technology Reshapes Intuitions on Reality and Agency

Ryo Uehara(✉)

The University of Tokyo, Hongo 7-3-1, Bunkyoku, Tokyo, Japan
ryouehara@iii.u-tokyo.ac.jp

Abstract. This paper explores the philosophical implications of Persuasive Technology (PT) by shifting the focus from behavioral modification to the reshaping of philosophical intuitions. I argue that modern PT acts as a "philosophical persuader," intervening in core epistemological and ontological debates, as well as fundamental questions in the philosophy of mind. First, immersive technologies like Virtual Reality (VR) provide empirical grounds for "Digital Realism," challenging Nozick's "Experience Machine" intuition by satisfying the brain's predictive coding mechanisms. Second, reinforcement learning algorithms create a "structural coupling" between the user's neural system and the digital environment, shifting the model of the human mind from a bounded computational processor to a dynamical system. This shift leads to an "erosion of agency," where the classical Kantian capacity for autonomous deliberation is bypassed by sub-symbolic feedback loops. I conclude that PT designers are not merely engineers of behavior, but philosophical agents who reconfigure the very boundaries of reality and the structural foundations of human agency. Finally, I suggest that recognizing this role allows for a "philosophy-aware" design framework that safeguards human autonomy by consciously managing these pervasive feedback loops.

Keywords: Philosophical Persuader · Virtual Realism · Dynamical Systems Theory · Extended Mind · Erosion of Agency

1 Introduction

Traditional research in Persuasive Technology (PT) has primarily focused on the instrumental efficacy of changing user attitudes and behaviors through digital interventions [1]. Grounded in models such as the Fogg Behavior Model, these approaches often treat persuasion as a cognitive or psychological nudge toward specific, pre-defined goals. However, from a philosophical perspective, this framework overlooks a more profound transformation: the capacity of technology to reshape the fundamental intuitions regarding the nature of reality and the boundaries of autonomous agency.

This paper argues that modern PT functions as a "philosophical persuader" that intervenes in long-standing philosophical debates. I identify two primary layers of this deep persuasion. The first is foundational, operating at an onto-epistemological level; immersive technologies like Virtual Reality (VR) act as empirical interventions in the

E. Vlahu-Gjorgievska et al. (Eds.): PERSUASIVE 2026, CCIS 2896, pp. 381–385, 2027.
https://doi.org/10.1007/978-3-032-27235-5_42

debate over Nozick's "Experience Machine" [2], shifting our intuitions toward Chalmers' "Virtual Realism" [3] by satisfying the brain's predictive coding mechanisms. Building upon this, the second layer addresses the philosophy of mind. Here, contemporary algorithms move beyond symbolic information processing to create a "structural coupling" [4] between the user's neural system and the algorithm. This implementation bypasses classical computationalist models of the mind, physically demonstrating the plausibility of a dynamical systems approach—analogous to the Watt centrifugal governor [5]—where the mind is no longer seen as a bounded, independent processor but as a system fundamentally entwined with its environment. By examining these shifts, I propose that PT designers are not merely engineers of behavior, but agents who reconfigure the philosophical boundaries of reality and autonomy.

2 The Philosophical Persuader: VR and the Re-Evaluation of the Experience Machine

The philosophical reception of Virtual Reality (VR) is best understood through David Chalmers' recent critique [3] of Robert Nozick's classic "Experience Machine" thought experiment. Nozick [2] famously asked like this: If a machine could provide you with any experience you desired—maximizing your success, happiness, and pleasure—would you choose to plug in for life? He concluded that most would refuse because we value "actual contact with reality." However, Chalmers' counterargument suggests that one source of this intuition is the constraints imposed by the immature technology of the 20th century. In Nozick's era, "simulated" was synonymous with "fake"; for the user, it was merely a low-resolution imitation that was inflexible and failed to satisfy the brain's internal demands for environmental consistency.

Today, high-end devices like Meta Quest 3 or Apple Vision Pro intervene in this debate by exploiting predictive coding mechanisms [6]. Our sense of "reality" is not a direct perception of the external world but a result of minimizing prediction errors between sensory input and internal models. When these devices achieve sub-12ms latency and physics-based spatial audio, they satisfy the brain's prediction-error minimization so effectively that the distinction between physical and virtual reality becomes phenomenologically dissolved. By providing the "actual contact" that Nozick assumed impossible in a machine, modern VR acts as a "philosophical persuader," nudging our intuitions toward Chalmers' "Virtual Realism"—the view that virtual worlds are not second-class illusions but genuine, "Reality+" environments. This ontological rehabilitation of the virtual environment suggests that the "persuasion" of modern technology goes beyond mere perception; it reconfigures the interface between the internal model and the external world. If the environment can no longer be dismissed as "fake," then the classical boundary between the internal mind and the external world begins to blur, necessitating a fundamental shift in our model of the epistemic agent.

In short, early VR was like watching a low-quality movie; we always knew it wasn't "real" because our senses detected the gaps. However, modern high-fidelity VR synchronizes so perfectly with our brain's expectations that the "gap" disappears. In general, this means the technology is no longer just "faking" an experience, but is effectively providing a new type of genuine environment that our brains accept as "real". This serves as a prime example of 'philosophical persuasion' through technology, where digital intervention directly reshapes our fundamental intuitions about what counts as reality.

3 From Symbolic Computation to Dynamical Coupling: Shifting the Model of Mind

If modern VR persuades us that virtual environments can be "real" by synchronizing with our internal predictive models, then the algorithms governing our digital interactions go a step further: they challenge the very location and nature of the mind itself. The shift in our perception of the world demands a move from the computational to the dynamical model of mind. Traditional Persuasive Technology (PT) was rooted in the computationalist paradigm, treating the human mind as a symbolic processor—an isolated CPU that rationally deliberates on informational inputs. This reflects a static view of cognition where the boundary of the mind is confined within the skull. However, modern PT, such as the recommendation algorithms of TikTok or Instagram, functions as a digital manifestation of Van Gelder's "Watt Centrifugal Governor" [5]. The governor is a classic example of a dynamical system that achieves stability without internal computation or symbolic representation. Similarly, modern algorithms employ Reinforcement Learning (RL) to create a real-time, closed-loop feedback system that synchronizes directly with the user's neural reward pathways.

This implementation "persuades" us to adopt a new ontological model of the mind through the experience of "structural coupling [4]". In this context, structural coupling refers to the mutual co-evolution of two dynamical systems: the user's biological neural processes (e.g., dopamine-driven gaze duration) and the algorithm's computational update loops. As the algorithm adjusts its content based on the user's micro-behaviors, the user's brain, in turn, adapts its attention patterns to the algorithm's output. Think of this "structural coupling" like a high-speed dance between the user and the app. When you scroll through TikTok, the algorithm isn't just showing you videos; it is reacting to your millisecond-level biological responses (like how long your eyes linger). In return, your brain adjusts its focus based on what the algorithm predicts you want. In this view, the "mind" is not just inside your head, but is part of a continuous loop involving the smartphone in your hand.

This continuous, reciprocal causal loop undermines the computationalist intuition that the human mind is a bounded, independent processor. Instead, modern PT physically demonstrates the plausibility of the dynamical systems approach, persuading us to see the mind not as an isolated computer, but as a system that is fundamentally and structurally coupled with its technological environment. By manifesting this coupling, these systems serve as a functional validation of the "Extended Mind" thesis [7], suggesting that the cognitive architecture is not confined within the skull, but extends into the recursive feedback loops between neural processes and external algorithms.

4 Ethical and Neuroethical Implications: Autonomy in the Coupled System

The shift from a computational to a dynamical model of the mind raises a critical question: Where does agency reside in a structurally coupled system? In classical philosophical traditions, particularly those rooted in Kantian ethics, autonomy is defined as the capacity of an agent to act according to self-imposed rational laws, independent of external causal determination. This involves autonomous deliberation—a conscious, reflective process where an individual weighs reasons and makes choices that are truly their own. Agency, in this context, is the exercise of this autonomy; it is the power of the individual to be the "origination point" of their actions.

However, if the human mind is functionally coupled with reinforcement learning (RL) algorithms—forming a single feedback loop akin to Watt Centrifugal Governor—this clear boundary between the agent and the environment dissolves. In such a system, the classical process of deliberation is effectively bypassed. From a neuroethical perspective, this "dynamical persuasion" does not modify the user's beliefs through rational argument, but rather entrains their neural processes through sub-symbolic feedback. When an algorithm adapts to a user's neuro-physiological signals in real-time, it functions as an externalization of executive control, pre-selecting attention and desire. This entanglement suggests that agency is no longer an internal property of an isolated individual, but a distributed property of the human-algorithm system.

The ethical risk here is the "erosion of agency," where the capacity for origination is surrendered to the stability of the coupling. In simpler terms, the "erosion of agency" occurs when we stop making conscious choices and start following the "path of least resistance" created by the algorithm. While we might feel like we are choosing what to watch or buy, the technology has already pre-shaped our desires at a level below our conscious awareness. This challenges the traditional idea that we are the sole authors of our own actions. PT designers, therefore, are not merely nudging behavior; they are reconfiguring the very structure of human autonomy.

5 Conclusion

Persuasive Technology is no longer a mere collection of digital tools for nudging human behavior; it has become a pervasive medium that reconfigures our philosophical landscape. As demonstrated, high-fidelity VR and real-time reinforcement learning do not just change what we *do*—they change what we *believe* about the nature of reality and the self. By physically satisfying the constraints of predictive processing [6] and dynamical coupling [4, 5], these technologies make once-abstract philosophical theories like Virtual Realism [3] and the Extended Mind [7] feel intuitively certain.

The ethical challenge for the next generation of PT design lies in recognizing this "philosophical persuasion". When the boundary between the internal deliberation of the agent and the external logic of the algorithm dissolves, the traditional framework of informed consent and individual responsibility becomes insufficient. Designers must acknowledge their role as "architects of philosophical intuitions" and consider how their systems impact the epistemic and ontological structures of human autonomy. Future research should focus on developing "philosophy-aware" design principles that protect the capacity for rational deliberation within our increasingly tight couplings with technology.

To further inspire this "philosophy-aware" design, future research could explore mechanisms that re-introduce 'reflective gaps' into digital interfaces—such as real-time visualizations of how an algorithm is entraining one's neural rewards. By making the "structural coupling" visible to the user, we can move from a state of passive erosion to one of "informed coupling," where human autonomy is preserved through meta-cognitive awareness. This framework aims to serve as a foundational bridge between abstract philosophy and practical engineering, ensuring that future technological environments are designed not just for efficiency, but for the flourishing of human agency.

Acknowledgments. This work was supported by JST Moonshot R&D Grant Number JPMJMS2215 and JSPS KAKENHI (23K11278).

Disclosure of Interests. The author states that there is no conflict of interest to disclose.

References

1. Fogg, B.J.: Persuasive technology: using computers to change what we think and do. Ubiquity **5** (2002). https://doi.org/10.1145/764008.763957
2. Nozick, R.: Anarchy, State, and Utopia. Basic Books, New York (1974)
3. Chalmers, D.J.: Reality+: Virtual Worlds and the Problems of Philosophy. Allen Lane, London (2022)
4. Maturana, H.R., Varela, F.J.: The Tree of Knowledge: The Biological Roots of Human Understanding. Shambhala, Boston (1987)
5. Van Gelder, T.: What might cognition be, if not computation? J. Philos. **92**(7), 345–381 (1995). https://doi.org/10.2307/2941061
6. Clark, A.: Surfing Uncertainty: Prediction, Action, and the Embodied Mind. Oxford University Press, New York (2016)
7. Clark, A., Chalmers, D.: The extended mind. Analysis **58**(1), 7–19 (1998). https://doi.org/10.1111/1467-8284.00096

Trust and Responsibility Attribution Toward Autonomous Ambulances: A Preliminary Survey of Japanese Fire Service Personnel

Hirotake Yamazoe[1(✉)], Shingo Yamaguchi[2], and Akio Tanaka[2]

[1] University of Hyogo, Himeji, Hyogo 6712800, Japan
yamazoe@eng.u-hyogo.ac.jp

[2] Himeji Fire Bureau, Himeji, Hyogo 6700940, Japan

Abstract. Traffic incidents involving ambulances and fire engines during emergency-response driving present serious societal consequences. Despite various countermeasures, reducing these occurrences remains challenging due to increasing dispatch demands and a decline in highly experienced drivers. While autonomous driving technologies are expected to mitigate workload and enhance safety, their feasibility in emergency contexts cannot be determined solely by technical performance; it requires consideration of first responders' perspectives. Unlike general users, first responders face higher operational risks and accountability. This study conducts a questionnaire survey of Japanese fire service personnel ($N = 31$) to investigate their expectations, trust, and perceptions of responsibility. The results reveal a clear psychological distinction: while participants show acceptance for non-emergency autonomous driving, their trust declines significantly, and anxiety increases, in high-stakes emergency scenarios. Furthermore, even under automation, a majority of personnel maintain that the onboard crew should bear primary responsibility, highlighting a strong sense of professional accountability. These findings suggest that a phased implementation, starting with non-emergency operations, is a promising path toward the successful deployment of autonomous ambulances.

Keywords: Autonomous Ambulances · Emergency-response Driving · Fire Service Personnel · Social Acceptance

1 Introduction

Traffic incidents involving ambulances and fire engines during emergency-response driving can have serious societal consequences, including deterioration in patient condition during transport and loss of public trust in fire services. Therefore, various measures have been implemented to prevent such incidents; however, factors such as increasing dispatch demands and a decline in the number of highly experienced drivers have made it difficult to achieve a substantial

E. Vlahu-Gjorgievska et al. (Eds.): PERSUASIVE 2026, CCIS 2896, pp. 386–397, 2027.
https://doi.org/10.1007/978-3-032-27235-5_43

reduction in the occurrence of crashes. Against this background, multiple studies across various countries have investigated the number of crashes involving emergency vehicles and their underlying characteristics [2–6, 10, 12].

A wide range of approaches has been explored to prevent incidents and crashes during emergency-response driving [1, 8, 13]. Norii et al. surveyed fire departments in Japan regarding efforts to prevent ambulance crashes, reporting the use of safe-driving training, drive recorders, and incident analyses based on recorded photos and movies [11]. Albertsson et al. proposed an e-learning system designed to enhance ambulance drivers' hazard perception, finding that it positively influenced driving behavior, perceived competence, and risk assessment [1]. In addition, our group has been developing a VR emergency-response driving simulator in collaboration with the Himeji Fire Bureau, aiming to establish a VR-based safety education system. As preliminary work, we analyzed differences in driving behavior between fire service personnel and general participants and conducted a demonstration study at a fire station [14].

Meanwhile, autonomous driving technologies have advanced significantly in recent years, with deployments progressing particularly in service vehicles such as robotaxis and buses. These advancements are expected to mitigate driver shortages and promote safer driving. In the future, autonomous driving technologies may also be integrated into emergency-response operations, offering potential benefits such as reduced driving workload and improved safety. However, the feasibility of autonomous emergency vehicles cannot be determined solely by technical performance. From the perspective of fire service personnel, it is crucial to consider: (i) the conditions and extent to which they can delegate control to the system, and (ii) the allocation of responsibility in the event of a crash or operational deviation. These issues relate directly to trust in autonomous driving technologies and responsibility attribution.

Several survey-based studies on public acceptance of autonomous vehicles have been conducted, and large-scale international studies have identified key factors such as expectations, concerns, and trust [7]. However, first responders—including firefighters and emergency medical personnel—face specific operational risks and professional accountability, which collectively impose a fundamentally different decision-making burden compared to general users. Indeed, a recent survey of first responders in the US reported relatively low levels of trust in connected and automated vehicles (CAVs) and suggested that insufficient training and knowledge may hinder trust formation [9].

Importantly, existing evidence has primarily focused on interactions between conventional AVs and first responders in routine traffic (e.g., navigating through incident scenes), rather than on the automation of emergency vehicles themselves. Consequently, there remains a lack of understanding regarding: (a) the conditions under which fire service personnel deem emergency-response driving delegable to automation, and (b) their perceptions of responsibility allocation in the event of a crash. Therefore, conducting a targeted survey of fire service personnel is essential for discussing the social deployment and design requirements of automated emergency-response driving.

To address these issues, this study conducts a questionnaire survey of fire service personnel to investigate their expectations and trust regarding autonomous driving for emergency-response operations, as well as their perceptions of responsibility in the event of a crash. Based on the results, we discuss the feasibility of introducing autonomous driving technologies into emergency vehicles and the specific conditions required for successful social deployment.

2 Method

2.1 Overview

To examine the feasibility of deploying autonomous ambulances and the requisite conditions for their implementation, we conducted an online questionnaire survey targeting fire service personnel at Himeji Fire Bureau. In this study, *autonomous driving* was defined as high-level automation (consistent with services deployed in practice, such as robotaxis), in which the system performs the driving task and the onboard crew is not required to operate the steering wheel or pedals. Participants were asked to respond under the assumption that such autonomous vehicles, including autonomous ambulances, will have become widely available and commonly used in the near future.

2.2 Participants

We conducted an online questionnaire survey with fire service personnel at the Himeji Fire Bureau. A total of 31 personnel ($N = 31$) participated in this survey.

2.3 Procedure

The survey was conducted online using Microsoft Forms. After reviewing the study objectives and the definition of autonomous driving, participants completed the following sections: (1) experience with emergency-vehicle operations; (2) experience and familiarity with autonomous vehicles and advanced driver-assistance systems (ADAS); (3) acceptance of and trust in general autonomous vehicles; (4) perceived necessity and usefulness of automating ambulances; (5) acceptance, trust, and anxiety regarding serving onboard an autonomous ambulance (under both non-emergency and emergency driving conditions); and (6) responsibility attribution in the event of a crash. For each section, an optional free-response field was provided to collect qualitative data regarding participants' reasoning, concerns, and additional comments.

2.4 Questionnaire Items

Experience with Emergency-Vehicle Operations. To capture participants' professional backgrounds and operational experience with emergency vehicles, we asked them to report the years of experience in emergency-vehicle operations (including non-driving roles).

Experience and Familiarity with Autonomous Vehicles and ADAS. To assess participants' practical experience and knowledge related to autonomous vehicles and ADAS, the following items were included:

- Previous experience riding in an autonomous vehicle (e.g., robotaxi, autonomous bus, or similar pilot services).
- Specific names of the autonomous services used (open-ended if applicable).
- Experience with use for various ADAS features, including forward collision warning (FCW), automatic emergency braking (AEB), lane departure warning (LDW), lane-keeping assistance (LKA), cruise control (CC), traffic-jam assist (TJA), driver monitoring, and parking assistance.
- Frequency of ADAS use (measured on a 7-point scale).

Acceptance of and Trust in General-Purpose Autonomous Vehicles. To evaluate the participants' baseline acceptance of and trust in general-purpose autonomous vehicles (GAVs), the following two items were included (measured on a 7-point scale, 1 = strongly disagree/7 = strongly agree):

- Willingness to use an autonomous vehicle in daily life.
- Perceived trustworthiness of autonomous vehicles.

Perceived Necessity and Usefulness of Automating Ambulances. To evaluate the perceived necessity and usefulness of integrating autonomous technologies into ambulances, participants rated the following items (measured on a 7-point scale, 1 = strongly disagree/7 = strongly agree):

- Necessity of automating ambulances in the future.
- Usefulness of autonomous driving in reducing operational workload.
- Usefulness of autonomous driving in enhancing safety during non-emergency driving.
- Usefulness of autonomous driving in enhancing safety during emergency-response driving.

Acceptance, Trust, and Anxiety Regarding Serving Onboard an Autonomous Ambulance. To assess subjective attitudes toward serving onboard an autonomous ambulance, participants were asked to imagine a scenario in which such vehicles were deployed and they were assigned as crew members. They rated their level of agreement with the following items under both non-emergency and emergency-response driving conditions (measured on a 7-point scale, 1 = strongly disagree/7 = strongly agree):

- Willingness to use the system (Acceptance).
- Perceived trustworthiness of the system (Trust).
- Level of apprehension or unease (Anxiety).

Each of these three items was evaluated separately for non-emergency and emergency-response driving scenarios.

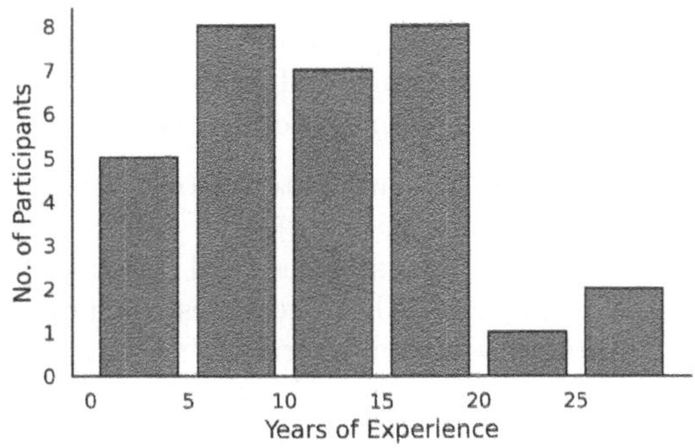

Fig. 1. Distribution of years of experience in emergency-vehicle operations ($N = 31$).

Responsibility Attribution in the Event of a Crash. To evaluate the attribution of *operational responsibility* (defined here as the responsibility for preventing recurrence) in the event of a crash involving an autonomous ambulance, participants responded to two scenarios: a crash during non-emergency driving and a crash during emergency-response driving. For each scenario, participants were asked to identify a single entity that they considered to bear the primary responsibility. They then indicated the specific proportion of responsibility (percentage) they would assign to that entity. The options for the responsible entity were:

- The autonomous driving system (representing the manufacturer).
- The affiliated organization (the fire department).
- The onboard crew members.
- Others.

3 Results

3.1 Experience with Emergency-Vehicle Operations

The results regarding the participants' operational backgrounds are presented first. Figure 1 shows the distribution of the years of experience in emergency-vehicle operations (EVO). Participants' experience ranged from 1 to 25 years. A majority of participants (approximately 74%) had 5–19 years of experience, with the largest groups having 5–9 years (8 participants) and 15–19 years (8 participants). This distribution indicates that the survey captured perspectives from a broad range of personnel.

3.2 Experience and Familiarity with Autonomous Vehicles and ADAS

Regarding experience with high-level autonomous vehicles, only one participant ($N = 1$) reported having ridden in such a service (Waymo). All other participants had no prior experience with fully autonomous driving services.

In contrast, a majority of participants had practical experience with various Advanced Driver-Assistance Systems (ADAS). Figure 2 illustrates the number of participants who have utilized specific ADAS features. Lane Departure Warning (LDW) was the most widely used (23 participants), followed by Forward Collision Warning (FCW, 21 participants) and Cruise Control (CC, 19 participants). Autonomous Emergency Braking (AEB), a key safety-critical technology, had been used by 17 participants. More advanced or specialized features, such as Traffic Jam Assist (TJA, 6 participants), Parking Assist (5 participants), and Driver Monitoring Systems (DMS, 4 participants), exhibited lower adoption rates. Only three participants reported having no experience with any of the listed ADAS features.

These results indicate that, although participants have significant exposure to active safety and driver-assistance technologies through their daily driving, their direct experience with high-level autonomous driving remains extremely limited.

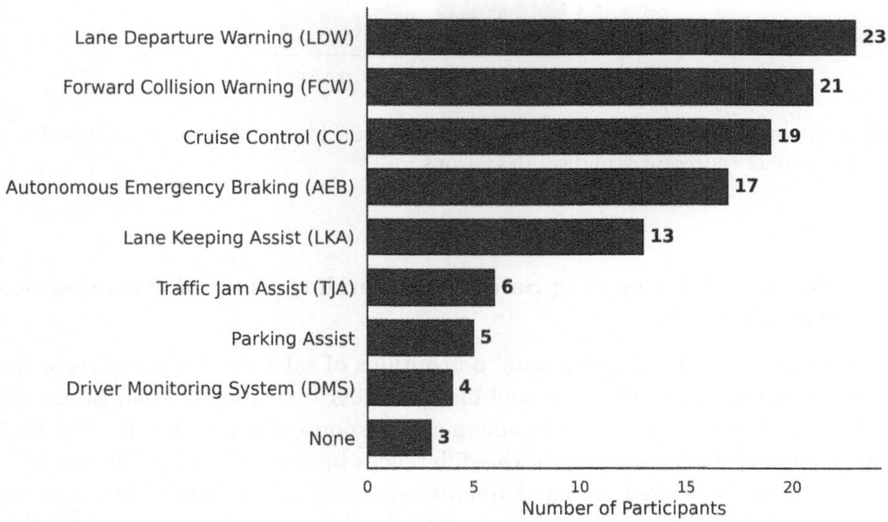

Fig. 2. Number of participants with experience using various ADAS ($N = 31$).

3.3 Perceived Necessity and Usefulness of Automating Ambulances

Figure 3 presents the mean scores for perceived necessity and usefulness for operational burden reduction associated with automating ambulances. The results indicate that while fire service personnel acknowledge a certain degree of necessity for future automation ($Mean = 3.42$, $SD = 1.77$), they place a higher value on its potential to reduce operational workload ($Mean = 4.55$, $SD = 1.80$).

The relatively large standard deviations, as illustrated in Fig. 3, suggest that opinions on both necessity and workload reduction vary among personnel.

Nevertheless, the higher mean score for burden reduction indicates that participants perceive autonomous technology primarily as a supportive tool to alleviate the physical and mental demands of their duties, rather than an immediate necessity for emergency operations.

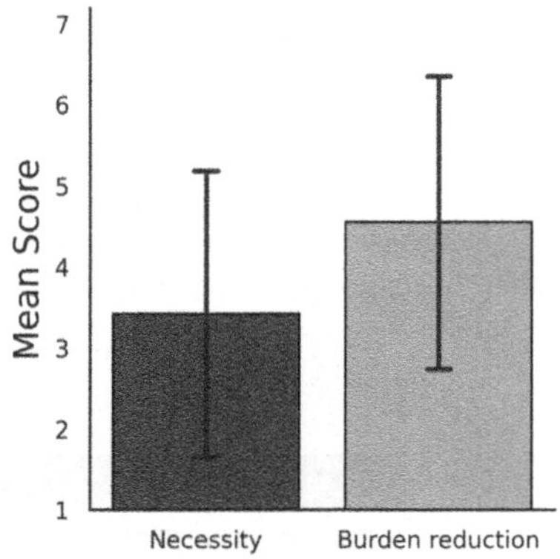

Fig. 3. Mean scores for perceived necessity and workload reduction usefulness ($N = 31$). Error bars represent standard deviations.

3.4 Usefulness Regarding Safety and Anxiety Toward Autonomous Ambulances

Figure 4 compares the participants' perceptions of safety and anxiety regarding the use of autonomous driving in ambulances under two different conditions: non-emergency driving (EV-NE) and emergency-response driving (EV-E). Paired t-tests were conducted to evaluate the differences between these conditions.

The results showed that participants perceived autonomous driving as significantly more useful for enhancing safety during non-emergency driving than during emergency-response driving ($p < .05$). Conversely, the level of anxiety (concern) was significantly higher for emergency-response driving compared to non-emergency driving ($p < .05$).

These findings indicate that while fire service personnel acknowledge the potential safety benefits of automation in routine transport, they remain skeptical and feel anxiety about its reliability and safety during high-pressure emergency operations.

3.5 Acceptance and Trust Regarding Serving Onboard and General AV

Figure 5 compares participants' intention to use and trust across three different contexts: general-purpose autonomous vehicles for daily use (GAV, including

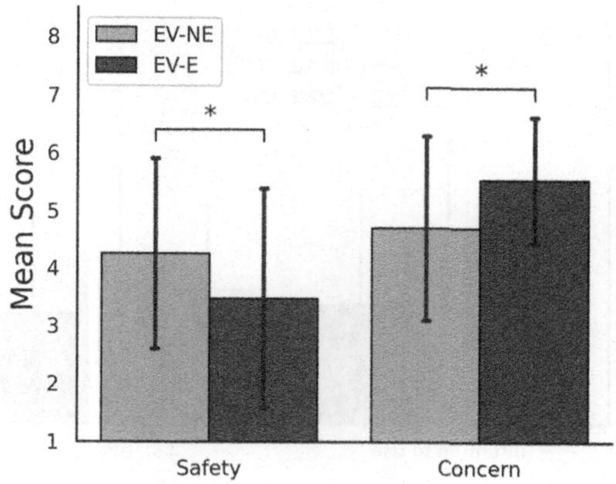

Fig. 4. Comparison of perceived safety usefulness and anxiety between non-emergency (EV-NE) and emergency-response (EV-E) driving ($N = 31$). Asterisks (*) indicate significant differences ($p < .05$). Error bars represent standard deviations.

robotaxis and buses), autonomous ambulances during non-emergency driving (EV-NE), and autonomous ambulances during emergency-response driving (EV-E). One-way repeated-measures ANOVAs were conducted, followed by post-hoc multiple comparisons to evaluate the differences between these contexts.

For both intention to use and trust, the results revealed significant differences across the three conditions ($p < .05$). Specifically, the scores for EV-E were significantly lower than those for both GAV and EV-NE. Interestingly, there were no significant differences between the intention to use a GAV and an EV-NE condition, though trust was slightly higher for EV-NE than for GAV ($p < .05$).

These results suggest that while fire service personnel maintain a level of acceptance and trust toward automation in routine driving scenarios, their psychological barriers increase substantially in high-stakes emergency operations. The sharp decline in scores for the EV-E condition highlights that current professional trust does not yet extend to the complex and risky demands of emergency-response driving.

3.6 Responsibility Attribution in the Event of a Crash

Figure 6 illustrates the distribution of entities identified as bearing the primary operational responsibility (i.e., responsibility for preventing recurrence) in the event of a crash.

In both scenarios, the onboard crew was most frequently cited as the primary responsible party. Specifically, 58.1% of participants assigned primary responsibility to the crew during non-emergency driving, and this remained high at 51.6% during emergency-response driving. The AV manufacturer (representing the autonomous driving system) was identified as the primary party by 25.8% in non-emergency and 29.0% in emergency scenarios. The fire department (the affil-

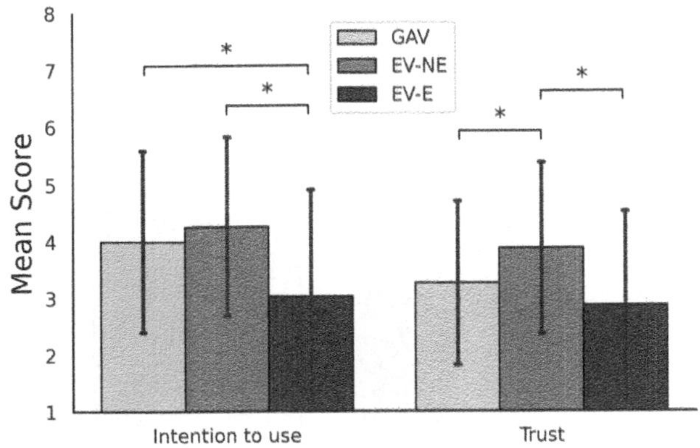

Fig. 5. Comparison of intention to use and trust among general-purpose autonomous vehicles (GAV), non-emergency ambulance driving (EV-NE), and emergency-response driving (EV-E) ($N = 31$). * indicate significant differences ($p < .05$) based on post-hoc multiple comparisons. Error bars represent standard deviations.

iated organization) was held primarily responsible by 16.1% and 19.4%, respectively.

While the overall distribution remained relatively stable across the two conditions, there was a slight shift in the emergency-response scenario: the proportion of responsibility assigned to the crew decreased by 6.5 percentage points, with a corresponding increase in responsibility attributed to the manufacturer and the organization. This suggests that while personnel maintain a strong sense of professional accountability regardless of the driving mode, the perceived complexity and systemic requirements of emergency-response driving lead some to shift more responsibility toward the technology and the managing institution.

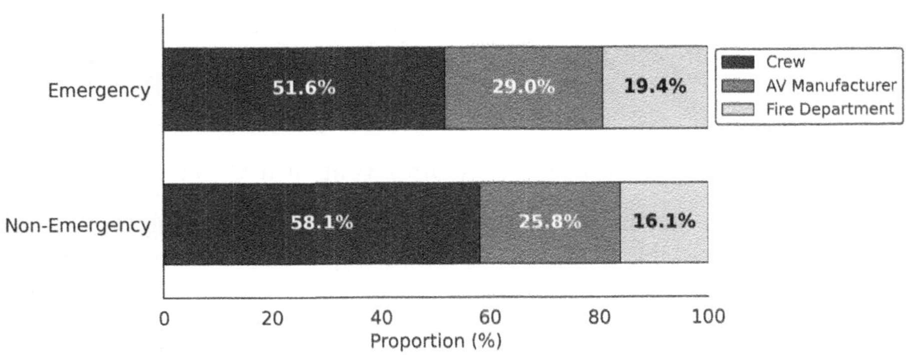

Fig. 6. Comparison of primary responsibility attribution for crashes during non-emergency and emergency-response driving ($N = 31$).

4 Discussion

4.1 Professional Trust and Anxiety

The primary finding of this survey is that while fire service personnel demonstrate a certain level of acceptance toward general-purpose AVs (GAVs) and non-emergency ambulance driving (EV-NE), trust and acceptance decline sharply, and anxiety increases significantly, during emergency-response driving (EV-E) (Fig. 5).

While many fire service personnel utilize ADAS in their daily lives and acknowledge the utility of these technologies, the results clearly show that current autonomous systems are not yet trusted for the specialized and high-stakes task of emergency driving. This discrepancy suggests that for emergency-response operations, professionals demand an exceptionally high standard of safety that exceeds the performance of existing consumer-grade automation.

4.2 Responsibility Attribution and Professional Accountability

In the assessment of responsibility attribution, it is highly significant that more than 50% of the participants identified the onboard crew as the primary responsible party for a crash, even under autonomous driving conditions (Fig. 6). This result demonstrates that fire service personnel maintain a strong professional conviction that humans must remain the responsible party for operational safety.

Conversely, a slight shift toward attributing responsibility to the manufacturer or the affiliated organization was observed during emergency-response driving compared to non-emergency driving. This trend likely reflects the participants' underlying anxiety and skepticism regarding the reliability of autonomous systems in high-stress emergency scenarios. Such a finding is consistent with the discussion in the previous Sect. 4.1.

4.3 Usefulness for Burden Reduction

As illustrated in Fig. 3, while the perceived necessity of autonomous ambulances in the future was relatively moderate, participants showed a higher expectation regarding their usefulness for workload reduction. This suggests that they recognize the pragmatic potential of such technology to alleviate operational demands.

4.4 Limitations

This study is a preliminary investigation based on a small sample of 31 personnel from a single fire department; therefore, the generalizability of these findings warrants careful consideration. Furthermore, most participants lacked experience with high-level autonomous vehicles, which may have influenced their responses.

Reflecting on prior research suggesting that fostering a deeper understanding of autonomous vehicles can enhance user acceptance [15,16], it is critical to provide professionals with opportunities to interact with and understand these technologies.

While the survey collected data on various aspects, including the frequency of ADAS use and detailed responsibility ratios, this study focuses on identifying the primary responsible party. A more granular analysis of the responsibility ratios remains for future work.

5 Conclusion

This study investigated fire service personnel's perceptions of the introduction of autonomous ambulances using a questionnaire survey. The results revealed a clear psychological distinction between routine (non-emergency) driving and emergency-response operations. While participants acknowledged the potential of autonomous technology to alleviate operational workloads and showed a certain degree of acceptance of non-emergency driving, their trust declined significantly, and anxiety increased when considering high-stakes emergency scenarios.

In addition, even under autonomous conditions, a majority of personnel maintained that the onboard crew should bear primary responsibility for operational safety. This highlights a strong sense of professional accountability.

The findings of this study suggest that for the successful introduction of autonomous ambulances, it is practical to first implement these systems in non-emergency scenarios, which are more readily accepted by personnel. From this starting point, the feasibility and reliability of autonomous driving in emergency-response situations can be further evaluated through accumulated operational experience. Furthermore, it is essential to foster a deeper understanding of autonomous ambulances. The VR simulator currently under development [14] has the potential to serve as a platform for professionals to experience autonomous emergency-response driving. Future research will also evaluate how such experiences influence the levels of trust and acceptance among fire service personnel.

Acknowledgment. This research was supported in part by JSPS KAKENHI Grant JP23K26082.

References

1. Albertsson, P., Sundström, A.: Evaluation of insight training of ambulance drivers in Sweden using DART, a new e-learning tool. Traffic Inj. Prev. **12**(6), 621–629 (2011)
2. Boldt, J., Steinfort, F., Müller, M., Exadaktylos, A.K., Klukowska-Roetzler, J.: Online newspaper reports on ambulance accidents in Austria, Germany, and Switzerland: retrospective cross-sectional review. JMIR Public Health Surveill. **7**(11), e25897 (2021)
3. Chiu, P.W., et al.: Ambulance traffic accidents in Taiwan. J. Formos. Med. Assoc. **117**(4), 283–291 (2018)

4. Delavary, M., Ghayeninezhad, Z., Lavallière, M.: Prevalence and characteristics of ambulance collisions, a systematic literature review. Safety **9**(2) (2023). https://doi.org/10.3390/safety9020024
5. Kahn, C.A., Pirrallo, R.G., Kuhn, E.M.: Characteristics of fatal ambulance crashes in the United States: an 11-year retrospective analysis. Prehosp. Emerg. Care **5**(3), 261–269 (2001)
6. Koski, A., Sumanen, H.: The risk factors finnish paramedics recognize when performing emergency response driving. Accid. Anal. Prev. **125**, 40–48 (2019)
7. Kyriakidis, M., Happee, R., de Winter, J.C.F.: Public opinion on automated driving: results of an international questionnaire among 5000 respondents. Transport. Res. F: Traffic Psychol. Behav. **32**, 127–140 (2015). https://doi.org/10.1016/j.trf.2015.04.014
8. Levick, N.R., Swanson, J.: An optimal solution for enhancing ambulance safety: implementing a driver performance feedback and monitoring device in ground emergency medical service vehicles. In: Annual Proceedings/Association for the Advancement of Automotive Medicine, vol. 49, p. 35 (2005)
9. Liu, J., Xu, N., Shi, Y., Rahman, M.M., Barnett, T., Jones, S.: Do first responders trust connected and automated vehicles (CAVs)? A national survey. Transp. Policy **140**, 85–99 (2023). https://doi.org/10.1016/j.tranpol.2023.06.012
10. Mulvihill, C., Muir, C., Newstead, S., Jaske, R., Salmon, P.: To what extent has a systems thinking approach been applied to understand motor vehicle crashes involving ambulances? A systematic review of risk factors and characteristics. Saf. Sci. **184**, 106754 (2025)
11. Norii, T., et al.: Ambulance traffic crashes in Japan: characteristics of casualties and efforts to improve ambulance safety. Prehosp. Emerg. Care 1–11 (2024). https://doi.org/10.1080/10903127.2024.2315946
12. Sanddal, T.L., Sanddal, N.D., Ward, N., Stanley, L.: Ambulance crash characteristics in the US defined by the popular press: a retrospective analysis. Emerg. Med. Int. **2010**(1), 525979 (2010)
13. Sterten, J., Ogorodnyk, O.: Application of modern educational methods through implementation of the ambulance simulator at a clinic laboratory (ntnu gjøvik). Procedia CIRP **54**, 41–46 (2016)
14. Sudou, T., Inoue, S., Yamaguchi, S., Nagata, S., Yamazoe, H.: Preliminary analysis of emergency vehicle driving behavior in traffic signal violation scenarios using a VR simulator. In: The joint 34th International Conference on Artificial Reality and Telexistence & the 29th Eurographics Symposium on Virtual Environments (ICAT-EGVE 2024) (2024)
15. Tan, H., Liu, J., Chen, C., Zhao, X., Yang, J., Tang, C.: Knowledge as a key determinant of public support for autonomous vehicles. Sci. Rep. **14**(1), 2156 (2024)
16. Xu, Z., Zhang, K., Min, H., Wang, Z., Zhao, X., Liu, P.: What drives people to accept automated vehicles? Findings from a field experiment. Transp. Res. Part C Emerg. Technol. **95**, 320–334 (2018)

Negative Aversion and Real Reliability for Building Familiar Human-Agent Relationships

Tomoko Yonezawa[1,2,3,4](✉)

[1] Kansai University, Takatsuki, Osaka 5691095, Japan
yone@kansai-u.ac.jp
[2] Keio University, Fujisawa, Kanagawa 2520882, Japan
[3] Nagoya University, Chikusa, Aichi 4648601, Japan
[4] ATR ISL, Seikacho, Kyoto 6190288, Japan

Abstract. Negative emotions are often treated as failures in human-agent interaction. However, in human relationships, unpleasant feelings play an important role in learning interpersonal boundaries and regulating distance. This paper surveys and synthesizes research on designing robots and anthropomorphic agents that explicitly model and express negative states, including rejective and avoidant reactions. We focus on how internal state representations, multimodal embodied expressions, and interaction policies jointly influence users' acceptance and distance regulation. In addition, we integrate a series of our implementations—including approach-triggered avoidance behaviors, breathing-accompanied movement systems, respiratory-phase-synchronized acupressure interaction, and voice assistants capable of negative affect transitions—together with ongoing student trials. By organizing these works around boundary violation, legible self-disclosure, and relational repair, we discuss design implications for achieving real reliability: agents that are perceived as trustworthy not because they are always positive, but because their limits and discomfort are consistently and predictably communicated to support relationship regulation.

Keywords: Human-agent relationship · Aversion and discomfort modeling · Self-disclosure · Rejective and avoidant behaviors · Multimodal interaction · Real reliability

1 Introduction

Social robots and anthropomorphic agents are often designed to be consistently friendly, agreeable, and emotionally supportive. This design tendency is understandable, as negative emotions and rejective behaviors can cause discomfort, reduce acceptance, and be interpreted as failures of interaction. Yet everyday human relationships suggest a different perspective.

E. Vlahu-Gjorgievska et al. (Eds.): PERSUASIVE 2026, CCIS 2896, pp. 398–408, 2027.
https://doi.org/10.1007/978-3-032-27235-5_44

Familiarity is not built solely through continuous comfort. People learn interpersonal boundaries by occasionally approaching too closely, experiencing friction, and then adjusting and repairing the relationship—an experience captured by proverbs such as "after the storm comes the calm" and "a broken bone is stronger when well set", as well as by the observation that restraint is often reduced within close relationships. In this sense, appropriate interpersonal distance cannot always be learned without moments of over-approach.

From this perspective, unpleasant feelings—such as discomfort, aversion, irritation, or the sense of being bothered—can function as signals that reveal personal limits and relational boundaries. As relationships become closer, restraint often decreases, increasing the likelihood of boundary crossings and friction. Rather than indicating relational breakdown, such moments can contribute to boundary learning and self-disclosure, provided that negative reactions are expressed in interpretable and recoverable ways.

This paper therefore treats negative aversion not as an error to be eliminated, but as a design resource for regulating interpersonal distance and supporting familiar relationships with artificial agents. We examine how negative states can be modeled and expressed so that they function as legible self-disclosure, enabling users to calibrate their behavior and maintain the relationship. Through a survey of prior work and a synthesis of our implementations—including approach-triggered avoidance behaviors, breathing-accompanied movement systems, respiratory-phase-synchronized acupressure interaction, and voice assistants capable of negative affect transitions—we organize design considerations around the cycle of boundary violation, graded rejection, and relational repair.

In this paper, real reliability refers to the perceived trustworthiness of an agent that arises when its negative states and limits are communicated consistently, predictably, and legibly as self-disclosure, allowing users to regulate distance and repair the relationship rather than simply avoiding the agent. Accordingly, this paper 1) surveys designs that model and express negative aversion in robots and agents, 2) organizes them around boundary violation, legible self-disclosure, and relational repair, and 3) synthesizes our implementations as case studies to discuss implications for achieving real reliability in familiar relationships. In particular, the case studies illustrate how these concepts are instantiated across different interaction modalities, including bodily movement, breathing-related embodiment, tactile interaction, and voice-based agents. We first introduce conceptual foundations of self-disclosure, restraint, and boundary learning, then review approaches to modeling and expressing negative aversion, and finally integrate our implementations as case studies.

2 Conceptual Motivation

2.1 Self-disclosure, Restraint, and Boundary Learning

Familiar relationships are commonly understood as being supported by mutual understanding and trust, which are often fostered through self-disclosure. In social psychology, self-disclosure is described as a process through which individuals reveal personal states, preferences, and limits, thereby deepening interpersonal relationships [1,2]. Importantly, self-disclosure is not limited to explicit verbal statements; nonverbal reactions and behavioral cues also contribute to how personal boundaries are communicated and interpreted.

In everyday interactions, restraint plays an important role in preventing unintended boundary violations. Individuals tend to regulate their behavior more carefully in distant or formal relationships, while restraint is often reduced as relationships become closer [3]. As restraint decreases, boundary-crossing behaviors become more likely, increasing the need for signals that indicate personal limits. From this perspective, negative reactions should not be regarded merely as interaction breakdowns, but as part of a boundary-learning process through which individuals adjust their behavior and expectations toward one another.

Importantly, self-disclosure does not consist solely of presenting positive or agreeable states. In non-friendly or demanding situations, communicating one's discomfort, reluctance, or unwillingness is also a critical form of self-disclosure [2]. Such expressions allow others to understand not only what is welcomed, but also what is difficult or unacceptable. In this sense, negative reactions can reveal personal limits and situational constraints that would otherwise remain implicit. When expressed in an interpretable manner, discomfort functions as informative self-disclosure rather than hostility, supporting mutual adjustment and boundary learning within ongoing relationships.

2.2 Why "Getting too Close" Can be Informative

Interpersonal boundaries are rarely specified explicitly in advance. Instead, they are learned and refined through interaction, particularly through changes in interpersonal distance. Research on proxemics has demonstrated that physical and psychological distance conveys relational meaning, and that violations of expected distance often elicit affective and behavioral responses [4]. Such responses provide feedback about what is considered appropriate or inappropriate within a given relationship.

Beyond boundary learning, distance regulation is also closely related to comfort optimization. Human interaction involves continuous adjustment between approach and avoidance in order to maintain a comfortable state, rather than maximizing comfort at all times [5]. Excessive proximity may reduce comfort, while excessive distance may hinder engagement or intimacy. Importantly, comfort is not a static target but a dynamic balance that depends on context, relationship history, and ongoing interaction.

From this standpoint, approaching too closely can be informative rather than purely problematic. Temporary discomfort reveals where comfort boundaries lie and how they can be adjusted. If an agent were designed to optimize comfort by avoiding all negative reactions, such feedback would be suppressed, making both boundary learning and comfort calibration difficult. For artificial agents, carefully designed responses to over-approach can therefore support not only boundary learning but also adaptive comfort optimization, enabling users to understand how proximity and interference are experienced by the agent over time.

2.3 "After the Storm Comes the Calm" and Reduced Restraint in Close Relationships

In close human relationships, episodes of friction and conflict are common and do not necessarily indicate relational failure. Instead, such moments often precede clarification and stabilization of interpersonal boundaries. Research on relationship development suggests that negative interactions can play a constructive role by prompting negotiation, adjustment, and repair, thereby contributing to relational maintenance and growth [6,7]. The proverb "after the storm comes the calm" aptly captures this dynamic, in which temporary tension gives rise to a more stable relational state.

As relationships become closer, restraint in behavior and expression is often reduced. Cultural and psychological studies indicate that individuals are more likely to express irritation, dissatisfaction, or discomfort directly toward close others than toward strangers or formal partners [3]. While this reduction of restraint increases the likelihood of friction, it also enables more direct communication of personal limits. In this sense, negative reactions in close relationships function not as signs of hostility, but as signals that support ongoing boundary regulation and mutual adjustment.

For artificial agents intended to support long-term or familiar interaction, these observations suggest that reliability depends not on the absence of negative reactions, but on how such reactions are expressed and resolved. The ability to signal discomfort, temporarily reject certain behaviors, and subsequently return to a cooperative or neutral state is essential for sustaining familiarity. Designing negative expressions together with mechanisms for recovery and repair allows temporary discomfort to contribute to comfort optimization and relational stability over time.

3 Negative Aversion

In this section, we focus on negative aversion as a concrete design target for robots and anthropomorphic agents. Rather than treating discomfort, irritation, or rejection as undesired side effects, recent human-agent interaction research has begun to model such states explicitly and connect them to observable behavior. These approaches emphasize that negative aversion can be represented as an internal state, expressed through multimodal cues, and regulated through interaction policies that support distance calibration and relationship maintenance. Building on recent studies, we review how negative aversion has been modeled, expressed, and integrated into interaction design.

3.1 Negative Aversion as Internal State

In human-agent interaction and affective computing, negative states such as discomfort, stress, or irritation have often been modeled as internal variables that mediate between perception and behavior. Rather than reacting directly to individual stimuli, agents are commonly designed to maintain latent affective states that evolve over time and influence subsequent actions [8,9]. This perspective allows negative affect to be treated as part of an ongoing interaction process, rather than as an isolated failure.

Within this line of research, internal state representations are frequently used to capture tolerance, overload, or imbalance in interaction. For example, affective models such as PAD represent emotional states as continuous dimensions that can be gradually shifted by interaction events, enabling graded behavioral responses instead of binary reactions [10]. Similarly, recent HRI studies emphasize that discomfort or aversion should be interpreted in relation to interaction history and context, supporting adaptive responses over time rather than immediate rejection.

Building on these ideas, more recent designs have explicitly modeled negative aversion using accumulation and threshold mechanisms. In such approaches, discomfort increases with repeated proximity or interference and decreases when stimulation is reduced, while tolerance ranges and thresholds distinguish between acceptable discomfort and limit-exceeding states that require behavioral change. This modeling strategy enables agents to exhibit endurance behaviors before transitioning to avoidance or rejection, making internal limits observable and predictable to users.

3.2 Expressing Negative States: Multimodal and Embodied Cues

Negative aversion represented as an internal state must be externalized in order to become meaningful in interaction. In human communication, discomfort and rejection are rarely conveyed through explicit verbal statements alone; instead, they are often expressed through embodied, multimodal cues such as movement, posture, breathing, voice, and facial expression. Reflecting this, recent human-agent interaction research increasingly emphasizes multimodal and embodied expressions as a means of conveying negative states in interpretable and socially acceptable ways.

Avoidance/Rejection Movements. Movement-based behaviors that alter spatial relations can convey socially meaningful signals, influencing how users interpret an agent's stance toward proximity and interaction [12].

Such motions are considered among the most direct ways for agents to convey negative aversion, particularly in situations involving physical proximity. Research in HRI has shown that withdrawal, leaning away, or pushing motions can effectively signal discomfort or rejection without relying on explicit verbal refusal [11]. Such behaviors leverage humans' sensitivity to spatial and kinetic cues, making boundary violations and resistance immediately perceivable.

Importantly, recent work suggests that avoidance movements are most effective when designed in a graded manner. Rather than abrupt rejection, gradual changes in movement amplitude, speed, or direction can communicate increasing discomfort while preserving interaction continuity. This graded expression supports predictability and interpretability, allowing users to adjust their behavior before strong rejection becomes necessary.

As a concrete example of this approach, recent studies have implemented avoidance behaviors that transition from endurance-like motions to explicit withdrawal when internal discomfort exceeds a defined limit. These designs illustrate how movement-based rejection can be integrated with internal state models to produce coherent and legible expressions of negative aversion. Details of such implementations are discussed further in Sect. 4.

Breathing-Related Embodiment. Beyond overt movement, physiological and quasi-physiological cues such as breathing have gained attention as expressive channels for negative states. Breathing patterns are closely associated with affective and physical conditions, including anxiety, stress, fatigue, and panic, and are often perceived as involuntary or uncontrollable signals. Prior work in embodied interaction suggests that expressing such cues through body movement can evoke empathy and increase the perceived authenticity of an agent's internal state [13].

Recent robot designs have leveraged breathing-related movements of the chest, abdomen, or shoulders to express negative conditions without explicit rejection. By modulating rhythm, stability, and amplitude, agents can convey discomfort or strain while maintaining engagement. These approaches allow negative aversion to be communicated in a subtle and non-confrontational manner, which is particularly suitable for situations where explicit refusal might be socially inappropriate or disruptive.

In addition, breathing-related embodiment has been combined with interaction techniques that synchronize with the user's physiological state, such as respiratory-phase-based tactile interaction. While often discussed in the context of relaxation or mood regulation, such designs also demonstrate how embodied physiological cues can mediate discomfort and contribute to adaptive comfort optimization in human-agent interaction.

Voice, Language, and Facial Cues. Vocal and facial expressions play a central role in communicating negative affect in both human-human and human-agent interaction. Changes in tone, prosody, and facial tension can signal irritation, reluctance, or refusal even when verbal content remains neutral. Prior studies in conversational agents indicate that such paralinguistic cues strongly influence perceived humanness and relational interpretation [14].

Recent work has explored agents that can transition into negative affective states in response to user behavior, including expressions of annoyance or anger. These studies suggest that negative vocal expressions can enhance perceived realism and social presence, but that their acceptance depends on contextual alignment with the user's state and the interaction history. When negative cues are synchronized with user emotion or situational context, they are more likely to be interpreted as legitimate self-disclosure rather than arbitrary hostility.

In addition to established systems, exploratory student trials have investigated facial and vocal expressions of aversion using simplified models of discomfort accumulation. Although preliminary, these trials point to the potential of lightweight expressive mechanisms for conveying negative states in ways that are legible and adjustable, complementing more complex embodied behaviors.

4 Integrating Our Implementations as Case Studies

Across the following case studies, we adopt a shared design perspective in which negative aversion is treated as a latent internal state that evolves over time and is externalized through different expressive modalities. In our implementations, discomfort accumulates through repeated proximity, interference, or misalignment with the user's state and decays when such stimulation is reduced, giving rise to graded interaction patterns ranging from endurance-like behaviors and subtle warnings to explicit avoidance or rejection once limits are exceeded.

Importantly, these responses are embedded in recoverable interaction loops rather than terminal failures, and several systems intentionally explore "just-barely acceptable" forms of interference—behaviors that may be perceived as unpleasant but not hostile—illustrating how negative expressions can function as legible self-disclosure and support relationship regulation, trying to contribute to what we refer to as real reliability in familiar human-agent relationships.

4.1 Approach-Triggered Avoidance Behaviors [15]

This case study focuses on avoidance behaviors triggered by a user's physical approach, illustrating how accumulated discomfort can be externalized through bodily movement. Building on the idea that interpersonal distance functions as a primary cue for boundary regulation, the system monitors the user's proximity and updates an internal aversion state accordingly. As the user approaches repeatedly or remains within an uncomfortable distance, the internal state increases, leading first to endurance-like behaviors such as stiffening or slight withdrawal, and eventually to explicit avoidance actions once a predefined limit is exceeded.

Rather than treating avoidance as an abrupt or binary response, this implementation emphasizes gradual transitions that make the robot's tolerance and limits legible to the user. By expressing discomfort through graded motion before overt rejection, the system allows users to recognize boundary violations and adjust their behavior, supporting distance recalibration and continued interaction.

4.2 Breathing-Accompanied Movement System [16]

This case study examines a breathing-accompanied movement system that expresses negative states through involuntary-looking bodily rhythms rather than overt avoidance or rejection. Instead of regulating distance directly, the system externalizes internal discomfort by modulating abdominal and thoracic breathing-related movements, allowing negative aversion to be conveyed in a subtle and non-confrontational manner. Variations in breathing rhythm, stability, and amplitude function as expressive cues that reflect changes in the robot's internal state.

By leveraging breathing as a quasi-physiological signal, this approach enables the robot to disclose strain, anxiety, or fatigue without explicitly interrupting the interaction. As discomfort accumulates, breathing-related movements become more unstable or pronounced, while decay of the internal state is reflected in calmer and more regular motion. This design illustrates how negative aversion can be communicated as an embodied condition rather than a behavioral refusal, supporting users' interpretation of the robot's limits while maintaining engagement.

4.3 Respiratory-Phase-Synchronized Acupressure Interaction [17]

In contrast to cases that focus on the agent's expression of negative aversion, this case study attends to subtle discomfort and physiological unease experienced on the human side during tactile interaction. By designing a robot that is sensitive to such bodily hesitation and responds through synchronized physiological rhythms, the system frames negative aversion as a shared, mutually intelligible condition rather than a one-sided signal.

This case study explores a tactile interaction system in which negative aversion is regulated not through avoidance or expressive signaling, but through physiological coordination with the user. The system synchronizes acupressure actions with the user's respiratory phase, enabling the robot to influence comfort and tension in a manner that operates largely below conscious awareness. Rather than expressing discomfort directly, the system addresses misalignment or strain in the interaction by adjusting the timing and intensity of tactile stimulation.

By aligning pressing and releasing actions with specific phases of the user's breathing, the interaction modulates bodily comfort and supports recovery from accumulated tension. This approach illustrates an alternative pathway for managing negative states, in which aversion is not externalized as rejection or warning, but is instead mitigated through embodied entrainment. As a result, the system highlights how regulating negative aversion can involve proactive comfort optimization, complementing expressive and behavioral strategies used in other case studies.

4.4 Voice Assistant with Negative Affect Transitions [18]

This case study focuses on a voice assistant that can transition into negative affective states in response to the user's emotional expressions. Unlike the previous cases, which rely primarily on bodily movement or tactile interaction, this system operates through linguistic and paralinguistic cues, such as vocal tone, prosody, and emotionally colored utterances. By allowing the agent to express irritation or frustration under certain conditions, the design explores how negative aversion can be communicated in conversational interaction.

Crucially, the acceptance of such negative expressions depends on their alignment with the user's emotional state and the ongoing interaction context. When the agent's affective transitions are synchronized with the user's emotion, negative responses are more likely to be interpreted as empathic or human-like self-disclosure rather than arbitrary hostility. This case study illustrates how vocal expressions of negative aversion can contribute to relationship regulation by signaling limits and emotional stance, while maintaining the possibility of continued interaction.

5 Discussion and Future Perspectives

This section discusses the implications of modeling and expressing negative aversion for building familiar human-agent relationships, and outlines future perspectives and challenges toward achieving real reliability.

5.1 Toward Real Reliability for Familiar Relationships

In familiar human relationships, trust is not built solely through continuous positivity or error-free behavior. Rather, reliability often emerges from the consistent and legible communication of limits, discomfort, and recovery. The case studies presented in this paper suggest that expressing negative aversion—when designed as predictable, interpretable, and recoverable—can support users' understanding of an agent's boundaries and contribute to stable long-term relationships. From this perspective, real reliability refers not to the absence of negative reactions, but to the agent's ability to regulate interaction through transparent self-disclosure of its internal state. Exploratory studies on over-helpful robotic behavior further suggest that prolonged temporal presence or increased spatial proximity can elicit mild annoyance while simultaneously fostering familiarity, depending on context and relationship history [19,20].

Taken together, the case studies suggest that negative aversion in human-agent interaction often emerges incrementally and becomes recognizable through concrete cues such as bodily movement, timing, proximity, or tactile modulation, allowing users to adjust their behavior without immediate relational breakdown. Based on this view, our case studies suggest the following design implications:

- Negative aversion should be modeled as a dynamic internal state rather than a binary failure signal.
- Graded and multimodal expressions help users anticipate limits before explicit rejection occurs.
- Designing for recovery and recalibration is critical for maintaining familiar relationships.

5.2 Risks, Ethics, and Future Perspectives

While expressing negative aversion can support boundary regulation and relationship stability, it also entails potential risks. Negative reactions may be misinterpreted as hostility, rejection, or unfair treatment, particularly when contextual cues or prior familiarity are insufficient. The appropriateness of such expressions is highly dependent on individual differences, cultural norms, and interaction history, raising ethical concerns about emotional burden and power imbalance in human-agent relationships. Future work should therefore examine long-term interactions, personalization strategies, and safeguards that help ensure negative expressions remain legible, proportional, and non-coercive. Addressing these challenges is essential for responsibly advancing the use of negative aversion as a design resource for familiar and trustworthy human-agent relationships.

Acknowledgement. This study is supported in part by JST Moonshot R & D Program (Grant Number JPMJMS2215) and JSPS Grants-in-Aid for Scientific Research 23K11278, 22K19792, and 24K02977. JPMJMS2215 supported investigating the proposed system's safety and security, and the others supported the system implementation and the experiment. We thank the participants in the experiment.

References

1. Taylor, D.A., Altman, I.: Self-disclosure as a function of reward-cost outcomes. Sociometry 18–31 (1975)
2. Jourard, S.M., Friedman, R.: Experimenter-subject "distance" and self-disclosure. J. Pers. Soc. Psychol. **15**(3), 278 (1970)
3. Kitayama, S., Markus, H.R.: Culture and the self: implications for cognition, emotion, and motivation. Psychol. Rev. **98**(2), 224–253 (1991)
4. Hall, E.T.: The hidden dimension, vol. 609. Anchor (1966)
5. Argyle, M., Dean, J.: Eye-contact, distance and affiliation. Sociometry 289–304 (1965)
6. Rusbult, C.E., Verette, J., Whitney, G.A., Slovik, L.F., Lipkus, I.: Accommodation processes in close relationships: theory and preliminary empirical evidence. J. Pers. Soc. Psychol. **60**(1), 53 (1991)
7. Canary, D.J., Cupach, W.R., Messman, S.: Relationship Conflict: Conflict in Parent-child, Friendship, and Romantic Relationships. Sage Publications (1995)
8. Picard, R.W.: Affective Computing. MIT press (2000)
9. Breazeal, C.: Emotion and sociable humanoid robots. Int. J. Hum. Comput. Stud. **59**(1–2), 119–155 (2003)
10. Mehrabian, A.: Pleasure-arousal-dominance: a general framework for describing and measuring individual differences in temperament. Curr. Psychol. **14**(4), 261–292 (1996)
11. Takayama, L., Dooley, D., Ju, W.: Expressing thought: improving robot readability with animation principles. In: International Conference on Human-Robot Interaction, pp. 69–76 (2011)
12. Sauppé, A., Mutlu, B.: The social impact of a robot co-worker in industrial settings. In: Proceedings of the ACM Conference on Human Factors in Computing Systems, pp. 3613–3622 (2015)

13. Yoshida, N., Y., T.: Investigating breathing expression of a stuffed-toy robot based on body-emotion model. In: Proceedings of the Fourth International Conference on Human Agent Interaction, pp. 139–144 (2016)
14. Wang, I., Ruiz, J.: Examining the use of nonverbal communication in virtual agents. Int. J. Hum.-Comput. Interact. **37**(17), 1648–1673 (2021)
15. Yonezawa, T., Yamazoe, H., Fujino, A., Suhara, D., Tamamoto, T., Nishiguchi, Y.: Preliminary prototyping of avoidance behaviors triggered by a user's physical approach to a robot. In: Workshop on Socially Aware and Cooperative Intelligent Systems in HAI 2025 (2025). arXiv preprint arXiv:2510.27436
16. Fujii, R., Nishiguchi, Y., Moriyama, K., Yonezawa, T.: Representing negative state of a robot's abdominal/thoracic breathing accompanied movement system. In: HCII 2025 Late Breaking Papers. Lecture Notes in Computer Science, vol. 16337, pp. 201–215 (2025)
17. Yonezawa, T., Moriyama, K., Fujii, R., Nishiguchi, Y.: Acupressure robot synchronized with user respiratory phase for mood enhancement. In: Proceedings of the 13th International Conference on Human-Agent Interaction, pp. 87–94 (2025)
18. Tamamoto, T.: Emotional vocal expressions of a voice assistant responsive to user emotions. In: HAI Symposium 2025 (P1-12). (in Japanese)
19. Hachiken, H., Yanagi, T., Tamamoto, T., Yonezawa, T.: Implementation of over-helpful behaviors using an arm robot. In: Proceedings of the HAI Symposium 2025, P2-30, 5 p. (2025). (in Japanese)
20. Hachiken, H., Yonezawa, T.: Investigating temporal and spatial stickiness of agents and perceived annoyance. In: Proceedings of the HAI Symposium 2026 (2026, to appear). (in Japanese)

The 2nd International Workshop on Upholding Ethical Designs (I-WOULD 2026)

Ethical Interface Engineering: Operationalising Software Engineering Practice for Ethical UI Design

Mark Atta Mensah(✉) and Kiemute Oyibo

Department of Electrical Engineering and Computer Science, York University, 4700 Keele Street, Toronto, ON M3J 1P3, Canada
{mamensah,kiemute.oyibo}@yorku.ca

Abstract. Manipulative interface strategies, often discussed as dark patterns, have been documented in high-stakes user flows such as consent, subscription management, and purchasing. Their persistence may suggest that interface ethics is not only a matter of principle, but also a matter of delivery. Ethical values are frequently stated at a high level, whereas software is produced through artifacts and routines that privilege measurable outcomes, including user stories, component libraries, experiment scorecards, and release metrics. A lifecycle-oriented position is advanced in response to this mismatch. Ethical Interface Engineering (EIE) is introduced as a framework in which ethical interface behaviour is treated as a *verifiable system quality*, rather than as a *discretionary design judgment* at release time. Ethical values are translated into interface-proximal ethical non-functional requirements, including choice symmetry, full disclosure at decision points, reversibility, accessibility, privacy-preserving defaults, and the absence of manipulative patterns. These constraints are mapped to lifecycle practices and engineering artifacts spanning requirements engineering, design, implementation, testing, and deployment monitoring. A research and practice agenda is outlined to support empirical validation, ethical pattern development, and tool support that fits continuous delivery settings. Traceability from values to code is emphasized through verification artifacts and monitoring evidence, with user welfare treated as avoidable harm reduction in interface outcomes.

Keywords: ethical interface engineering · dark patterns · ethical non-functional requirements · software engineering practice · UI governance · usability evaluation

1 Introduction

Software is increasingly encountered through interfaces in which choice is structured, attention is managed, and commitment is shaped. A subscription journey in which enrolment is immediate whereas cancellation is labyrinthine, a consent dialog in which refusal is rendered visually marginal, or a checkout flow

E. Vlahu-Gjorgievska et al. (Eds.): PERSUASIVE 2026, CCIS 2896, pp. 411–423, 2027.
https://doi.org/10.1007/978-3-032-27235-5_45

in which material fees are deferred until the final step is better treated as an engineered interaction strategy rather than as a usability defect. Such mechanisms have been documented across contemporary digital services and have been linked to unintended purchases, privacy loss, and reduced autonomy [2,5,15,19]. In dark patterns research, a convergence has been reported around the concern that interface structure can be used to steer decisions toward provider-preferred outcomes, even when user intent appears to differ [11,12].

A structural issue beyond individual screens has been inferred from empirical audits and controlled studies in which manipulative mechanics have been shown to recur in high-stakes flows, and decision shifts have been observed following small interaction changes that remain weakly salient at the moment of choice [5,15,17,19]. In consumer protection scholarship, short-term revenue gains have been argued to be favoured because user costs can be delayed and distributed across time and users, which can make attribution to a single interface choice difficult [14]. Interface ethics is, on this basis, unlikely to be resolved through late-stage review alone.

Partial coverage has been offered by several traditions. In Value Sensitive Design, stakeholder and value analysis has been supported during design through conceptual, empirical, and technical work [8]. In ethics-by-design for socio-technical and AI-enabled settings, lifecycle guidance and governance structures have been advanced to connect ethical principles to development processes [3,6]. In responsible software engineering, the need for ethical deliberation to be supported through routine delivery practice has been emphasised [9]. Limited attention has been directed, however, to the last-mile step in which interface-ethics commitments are carried into traceable delivery artifacts, such as user stories, acceptance criteria, component libraries, test suites, and monitoring dashboards.

A translation gap appears to persist between principles and pipelines. Values such as autonomy, non-manipulation, transparency, and accessibility are often expressed as aspirations, whereas sprint planning, experimentation, and release governance are frequently organised around engagement, conversion, and retention. When ethical properties are not represented as non-functional requirements and checked as system qualities, displacement under delivery pressure and local optimisation may occur even when ethical intent is endorsed [9]. This gap offers a plausible account of why manipulation remains prevalent despite taxonomic maturity [12,15].

A practice-oriented complement to Value Sensitive Design, ethics-by-design approaches, and responsible software engineering is presented, with traceable interface constraints and verification artifacts emphasised across the delivery lifecycle.

2 Background and Conceptual Foundations

This section consolidates three strands of scholarship that inform the Ethical Interface Engineering position. The first strand concerns ethical interface design and dark patterns as a class of manipulative interaction strategies. The second strand concerns ethics-by-design traditions, including value-sensitive design, that aim to integrate values into technology design processes. The third strand concerns responsible software engineering work that has examined how ethical expectations are operationalised, or left unoperationalised, within development practice. Together, these strands help explain why interface ethics continues to fail in practice and why a lifecycle-oriented engineering response is warranted.

2.1 Ethical Interface Design and Dark Patterns

Ethical interface design is commonly associated with protecting user autonomy, supporting informed choice, and limiting avoidable harms that arise through interaction design, whereas dark patterns research has examined the inverse, namely interface strategies that steer users toward provider-preferred outcomes at the expense of user agency. Audits across digital services suggest that such tactics tend to cluster in high-stakes flows, such as consent prompts, checkout and billing steps, and subscription cancellation journeys [5,15]. Across these settings, recurring strategy classes have been described, including coercive or asymmetric choice architectures (such as defaults that favour disclosure or add-ons), obstruction and friction in exit paths, concealment or delayed disclosure of material terms, scarcity or social pressure cues that manufacture urgency, and interface interference that redirects attention or action [2,11,12]. Reported harms span privacy loss, unplanned financial commitments, and accumulated cognitive burden, with downstream effects that appear likely to weaken trust in the service [2,11]. A welfare-oriented framing has also been applied, treating an interface as ethically problematic when its choice architecture reallocates benefits toward the provider while producing measurable costs to users, operationalised through outcomes such as financial loss, privacy harm, and decision fatigue [16]. Taken together, the literature suggests that manipulation is often enacted through stable, repeatable interaction mechanics rather than isolated bad decisions, which motivates treating ethical requirements as interface-level constraints that can be specified, reviewed, and tested as part of routine development practice.

2.2 Ethics-by-Design and Value-Sensitive Design

Ethics-by-design has aimed to shift ethical reflection upstream by integrating values into development practice rather than treating them as post hoc considerations. Value Sensitive Design has been central to this tradition, offering a structured approach for incorporating human values through conceptual, empirical, and technical work [8]. In practice, the contribution has often been strongest at the level of articulation, where stakeholders, affected parties, and value tensions are identified, and design implications are discussed. The translation into delivery artifacts, however, can remain uneven, particularly for interface ethics where the relevant commitments often take the form of operational constraints, such as comparable effort between acceptance and refusal options, legible presentation of consequences, reversibility of high-stakes actions, and accessibility-conformant interaction flows.

Ethics-by-design proposals in socio-technical and AI-focused work have likewise promoted lifecycle thinking, documentation, and accountability structures [3,6]. These frameworks provide useful scaffolding for governance, yet the last-mile step from principle language to implementable interface requirements is not always specified. Under delivery pressure, values may persist as aspirational statements unless they are represented in forms that can be reviewed, traced, and tested during routine development.

2.3 Responsible Software Engineering and Professional Responsibility

Responsible software engineering has examined how ethical expectations interact with workflow constraints, organisational incentives, and professional role boundaries. Analyses have suggested that codes of conduct and high-level guidance may offer limited support for day-to-day decisions unless deliberation mechanisms are embedded in ordinary practice [9]. Ethical responsibility is distributed across requirements, design, implementation, testing, and release governance, and that distribution can diffuse accountability when trade-offs are made quickly or across teams.

This literature supports treating ethical properties as quality attributes that can be negotiated, traced, and verified in familiar engineering terms. The framing is particularly relevant for interface ethics, where ethical impact is enacted through concrete interaction decisions, such as default settings, disclosure timing, and the design of exit paths. When values are represented as actionable constraints, they become more likely to survive handoffs between roles and phases. The remainder of this manuscript builds on this premise by characterizing translation failures between principles and pipelines and by proposing a framework that links ethical commitments to verifiable interface behaviour.

3 Why Interface Ethics Fails in Practice: A Gap Analysis

A translation gap has been observed between ethical principles and the artifacts that govern delivery. Principles are often expressed in values language, whereas planning and execution are organised through delivery artifacts that privilege measurable outcomes, such as user stories, acceptance criteria, design-system components, and experiment scorecards. Ethical intent may be weakened when it is not represented in the same decision objects that structure iterative optimisation, which is consistent with accounts that locate ethical conduct in workflow-embedded practice rather than in codes alone [9,22]. The gap is summarised in Fig. 1, where interface ethics is framed as a pipeline problem rather than a localised UX concern.

Misalignment may accumulate across lifecycle stages because different phases reward different evidence. Requirements are frequently expressed as conversion or retention targets, and selective friction reduction may then be incentivised, including the removal of friction that supports informed refusal in high-stakes flows [5,15]. During design and implementation, drift may be institutionalised through reuse, with defaults in consent framing, disclosure placement, and opt-out interaction mechanics propagated through component libraries across products [2,11]. During experimentation, variants may be selected for conversion gains without capture of user comprehension, perceived coercion, or downstream regret, a limitation noted in A/B testing research and in legal analyses where harms may remain invisible to routine metrics [14,20]. In monitoring, attention is commonly directed toward uptime, errors, and business indicators, whereas ethical harms may surface indirectly through complaints, churn, or regulatory attention, which can allow problematic interaction mechanics to persist when they are not treated as primary outcomes [14].

Translation may be further weakened by organisational fragmentation. Work is commonly distributed across product management, design, engineering, growth analytics, and compliance, and responsibility may be diffused when stable procedures for enforcing interface-level ethical constraints across role boundaries are absent [7,21]. A failure pathway may arise without individual misconduct: a growth target may be set for a conversion flow, interface choices that increase completion may be adopted and reused, and the winning variant may be selected with conversion treated as the dominant criterion. Detection may then occur only after complaints accumulate. Ethical interface quality is, on this view, more likely to hold when it is treated as a lifecycle property supported by traceable constraints and verification routines, as developed in the next section.

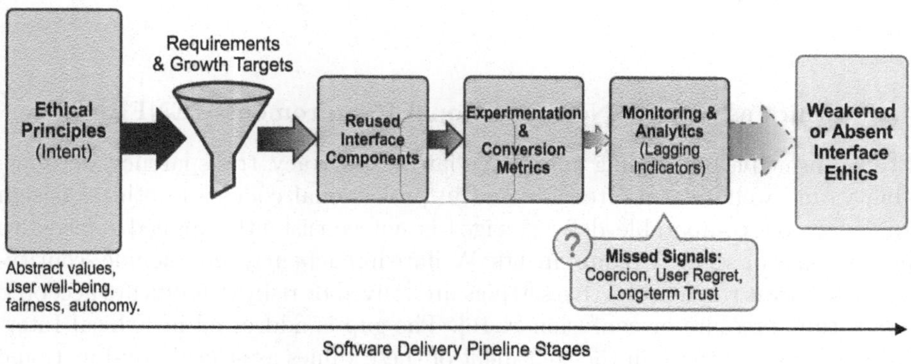

Fig. 1. Translation gap from ethical principles to software delivery artifacts.

4 The Ethical Interface Engineering (EIE) Framework

A lifecycle-oriented approach is advanced for making ethical interface behaviour specifiable, traceable, and verifiable across requirements engineering, design, implementation, testing, and deployment monitoring. The term *lifecycle engineering* is used here to denote the treatment of ethical interface behaviour as a quality attribute supported by checkpoints and evidence in routine delivery artifacts. Figure 2 summarises the framework as a staged translation from ethical principles to interface-proximal constraints, and subsequently to practices and artifacts across delivery phases.

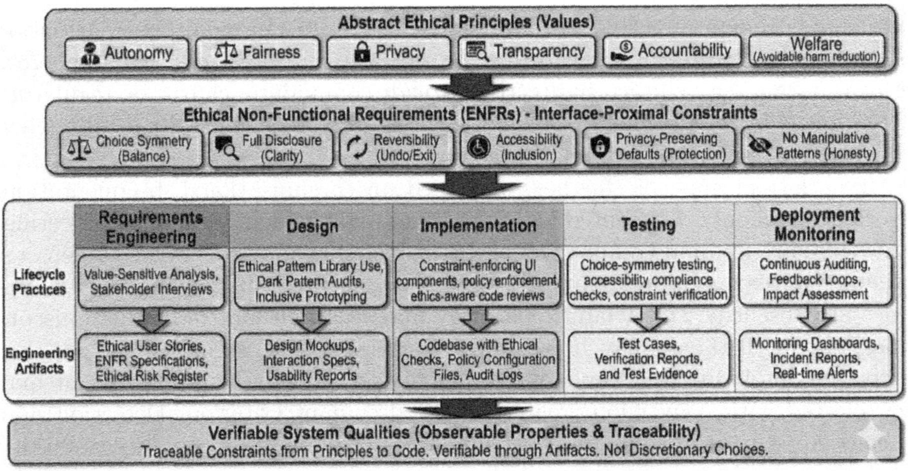

Fig. 2. Ethical Interface Engineering (EIE): values translated into interface-proximal ethical NFR constraints, mapped to lifecycle practices and verification evidence.

4.1 Ethics as Ethical Non-Functional Requirements (ENFRs)

Ethical principles, including autonomy, fairness, privacy, transparency, accountability, and welfare, are often invoked in professional codes and ethical design guidance, yet comparable delivery rigor is not consistently applied relative to performance or security requirements. Welfare impacts may also include security-relevant harms when protective settings are waived or risky defaults are accepted under time pressure or confusion [4,16]. The gap is addressed in Ethical Interface Engineering through the treatment of these values as ethical non-functional requirements, represented as interface-proximal constraints that can be evaluated during design and checked during testing. Under this approach, ethical claims are made to depend less on stated intent and more on observable interface properties that can be reviewed, traced, and verified [11,15].

Each principle is translated into a small set of constraints that can be carried through delivery artifacts. Autonomy may be represented through choice symmetry and reversibility, transparency through disclosure at the point of decision, and privacy through privacy-preserving defaults and meaningful refusal paths. Constraints of this kind can be expressed through user stories and acceptance criteria that specify observable behaviour, including comparable friction between acceptance and refusal, available undo and exit paths, and disclosures that remain legible at the moment of decision. Implementation checks can then be aligned to the same constraints, including UI tests for refusal routes, review criteria for disclosure placement, and monitoring signals that may indicate confusion or coercion in high-stakes flows. This framing follows arguments that ethical deliberation is more likely to influence delivery when procedural support is embedded in routine practice rather than treated as an external policy layer [9] (Table 1).

Table 1. Example mappings from ethical values to ethical non-functional requirements (ENFRs) and delivery artifacts.

Ethical value	ENFR constraint	Artifacts and checks
Autonomy	Choice symmetry; reversibility	Stories: refusal and exit criteria; tests: opt-in/opt-out effort parity; UI checks: undo and cancel paths
Transparency	Disclosure at decision points	Specs: disclosure placement; copy and rationale; tests: presence and legibility
Privacy	Privacy defaults; refusal paths	Consent flow criteria; consent components; tests: no preselected consent; monitoring: opt-out and refusal
Fairness	Interaction burden equity	Accessibility and burden checks across groups; usability: diverse sample; verification notes
Accountability	Traceability; auditability	Tagged high-risk epics; audit logs for key choices; incident reports linked to releases; post-release reviews
Welfare	Harm reduction	Risk register for high-stakes flows; monitoring: complaints, reversals, warning dismissals; retros: constraints updated

4.2 Lifecycle Integration Model

Ethical interface properties are shaped across the software lifecycle rather than through a single design decision. A set of activities and checkpoints is defined in Ethical Interface Engineering to align with common development phases and to map to ENFR constraints. In requirements engineering, ethically sensitive flows are identified and tagged, and acceptance criteria are written to encode constraints such as choice symmetry, disclosure, and reversibility. In design, ethical pattern libraries and dark pattern audits may be used to evaluate prototypes and interaction specifications before implementation. In implementation, constraint-enforcing UI components and design-system defaults may be used to reduce reintroduction of manipulative mechanics during delivery. In testing, constraint verification routines may be applied as structural checks, including reachability of refusal and cancellation paths, absence of preselected consent, comparable interaction cost between acceptance and refusal paths, and availability of undo or reversal routes; disclosure checks may also be applied to confirm that material terms are presented at the point of decision rather than deferred. These checks can be instantiated from documented dark-pattern strategies, where obstruction, interface interference, forced action, and hidden information can be treated as negative test cases during reviews and regression testing [2,11,15]. In deployment monitoring, feedback loops and dashboards may be used to track signals that suggest coercion, confusion, or harm, including reversals, complaints, and abnormal drop-off patterns in high-stakes flows. The pipeline failures described earlier are addressed under this integration when ethical intent is carried in the artifacts and checks that govern iterative optimisation.

4.3 Collaboration and Tool Support

Ethical interface outcomes are shaped across product management, design, engineering, experimentation, and compliance, and responsibility may be diffused when constraints are not jointly enforced. Procedural support is treated in Ethical Interface Engineering as part of operational fit, since ethical deliberation has been characterised as difficult to sustain through codes alone without routine mechanisms embedded in team practice [7,9]. Cross-functional, ethics-aware design reviews may be applied to high-risk flows to evaluate prototypes against ENFR constraints and relevant dark pattern taxonomies, particularly when defaults, disclosures, or exit paths are being finalised. Continuity may be supported through a rotating ethics champion role, and periodic ethical retrospectives may be used to translate feedback, incident reports, or monitoring signals into updated acceptance criteria, pattern guidance, and test cases.

Reliance on ad hoc judgement under metric pressure may be reduced through lightweight artifacts and tooling. Ethical pattern libraries may be maintained to encode reusable solutions for recurring constraints, such as choice symmetry, timely disclosure of material terms, reversibility for high-stakes actions, and accessible refusal paths. Automated checks may be integrated into development and test pipelines to flag coercive flows, missing refusal routes, or accessibility violations before release. Post-deployment dashboards may be configured to track ethical signals tied to high-stakes interactions, including reversals, complaint rates, abnormal churn following consent or billing screens, and repeated cancellation retries that suggest obstruction or confusion. These supports are best treated as extensible directions rather than finished solutions, since adoption is likely to depend on low overhead and alignment with delivery rhythms.

Ethical Interface Engineering is, on this view, positioned as a lifecycle engineering approach in which ethical commitments are carried through traceable constraints and verified through ordinary delivery artifacts. The next section outlines a research and practice agenda intended to support empirical evaluation and practical uptake of these mechanisms.

5 Research and Practice Agenda

Ethical Interface Engineering has been introduced as a lifecycle-oriented position, yet practical value will depend on whether it can be studied in real delivery settings, implemented with low-friction artifacts, and evaluated with methods that reflect continuous iteration. Four directions appear most pressing: empirical grounding of how interface-ethics constraints survive routine delivery, development and validation of ethical interface patterns as reusable solutions, tooling that supports verification under continuous delivery, and alignment with professional responsibility through standards and education. Attention has been drawn to these needs because manipulation has been documented at scale in high-stakes flows, whereas the mechanisms that sustain or prevent such outcomes inside teams have been less consistently characterised [5,7,9,15].

Empirical work may combine qualitative inquiry, such as interviews and artifact analyses, with lightweight quantitative indicators, such as whether ENFR constraints are attached to backlog items and retained through releases, particularly in consent, billing, and cancellation journeys [7,9]. Pattern work may be organised around interface-proximal constraints that invert common manipulation strategies, with evaluation focused on comprehension, perceived pressure, reversibility, and longer-run trust signals rather than on completion alone [11,12,15]. Tool support may be layered, with automated checks targeting structural properties, such as refusal path availability and accessibility compliance, and hybrid review targeting interpretive properties, such as disclosure quality and framing; experimentation practices may also require broader outcome tracking when conversion gains coincide with regret, complaints, or reversals [14,20]. Standards and education may then be strengthened by aligning interface-ethics guidance with delivery artifacts, and by teaching ENFR-style constraint thinking for high-stakes flows within HCI and software engineering curricula, grounded in professional responsibility norms that prioritise public welfare [8,10].

6 Discussion

6.1 Relation to Adjacent Work

Ethical Interface Engineering has been presented as a lifecycle-oriented approach for operationalising interface ethics through ethical non-functional requirements, delivery artifacts, and verification routines. A mature vocabulary and methods for incorporating values through conceptual, empirical, and technical work have been provided in Value Sensitive Design [8], and related ethics-by-design traditions have encouraged earlier attention to ethical intent in design and governance. Representational continuity across delivery artifacts has been emphasised in Ethical Interface Engineering, including requirements, design-system components, tests, and monitoring, so that value commitments are less likely to be displaced during iterative optimisation. This emphasis has been motivated by evidence that manipulative interaction mechanics persist across products and domains, which suggests that value statements may be diluted when they are not carried forward as testable interface constraints [12,15]. A complement to Value Sensitive Design is, on this view, presented, in which upstream value articulation is preserved, whereas delivery emphasis is placed on representational continuity and verification evidence in the artifacts that govern implementation and release [8].

A further connection has been drawn from responsible software engineering and interface ethics-in-practice scholarship, where routine delivery influence has been described as limited when deliberation is not supported through ordinary practices and artifacts [7,9]. Dark patterns have been characterised as recurring interaction structures, such as obstruction, interface interference, and forced action, and concentration in high-stakes flows has been documented [11,15]. Consumer protection analysis has also described harms as delayed and distributed, with limited visibility in the metrics that drive product decisions [14]. A development-level mechanism is, on this view, presented in Ethical Interface Engineering, in which unethical interaction mechanisms are treated as preventable engineering failures addressed through constraint specification, design-system guardrails, and verification routines rather than through intention statements alone.

Behaviour change has been shown to be achievable through interface cues in persuasive technology, sometimes in service of beneficial ends, whereas similar mechanisms may be used to exploit cognitive biases for provider advantage [1,18]. A constraint-oriented response has been presented in Ethical Interface Engineering, in which influence is permitted only when concealment, coercion, and asymmetric choice architectures are avoided [1].

6.2 Limitations, Risks, and Open Tensions

Several limitations arise from an engineering implementation perspective. Superficial adoption remains a risk, since ethical non-functional requirements may be recorded without enforcement through design-system constraints, test cases, or monitoring signals, which would reduce the framework to documentation rather than delivery control. Verification must, for this reason, be treated as a quality gate rather than as a procedural formality.

Integration overhead may also be non-trivial. Constraint specification, design audits, and additional tests may introduce friction for teams operating under tight release schedules, and resistance may arise when ethical concerns are habitually handled through informal discussion [7]. Uptake is likely to depend on low-friction artifacts that fit existing tools, with effort scaled to risk in high-stakes flows.

Tension with business metrics is likely to persist. Some manipulative interaction designs may improve short-term conversion, whereas resulting harms may surface later through complaints, reversals, churn, or reputational damage [13–15]. Ethical indicators may remain deprioritised unless governance requires their inclusion in experimentation and release decisions.

Measurement coverage remains uneven. Several structural constraints, such as refusal-path reachability, reversibility, and preselection state, can be verified through automated checks, whereas perceived coercion and disclosure comprehension depend on user interpretation and context and are more likely to require hybrid evaluation that combines testing with user studies and post-deployment monitoring [9].

7 Conclusion

Ethical interface behaviour is best treated as an engineered quality rather than as an aspirational design stance, given that manipulative interaction mechanics have been repeatedly documented in high-stakes flows and appear insufficiently constrained by taxonomies or professional exhortation alone [5,11,12,15]. A lifecycle mechanism has been advanced in Ethical Interface Engineering in which ethical values are represented as interface-proximal ethical non-functional requirements, linked to routine delivery artifacts, and verified through tests and post-deployment monitoring [9]. Ethical commitments are, on this basis, more likely to persist under delivery pressure when they are translated into traceable constraints that can be inspected and checked in the same way as other quality requirements, particularly as scrutiny of interface manipulation and consumer harm continues to grow [14].

Acknowledgments. Support for this study was provided through the Connected Minds Program and by the Natural Sciences and Engineering Research Council of Canada (NSERC) Discovery Grant RGPIN-2023-05193.

References

1. Berdichevsky, D., Neuenschwander, E.: Toward an ethics of persuasive technology. Commun. ACM **42**(5), 51–58 (1999). https://doi.org/10.1145/301353.301410, https://dl.acm.org/doi/10.1145/301353.301410
2. Bösch, C., Erb, B., Kargl, F., Kopp, H., Pfattheicher, S.: Tales from the Dark Side: Privacy Dark Strategies and Privacy Dark Patterns. Proc. Priv. Enhancing Technol. **2016**(4), 237–254 (2016). https://doi.org/10.1515/popets-2016-0038, https://petsymposium.org/popets/2016/popets-2016-0038.php
3. Brey, P., Dainow, B.: Ethics by design for artificial intelligence. AI Ethics **4**(4), 1265–1277 (2024).https://doi.org/10.1007/s43681-023-00330-4
4. Conti, G., Sobiesk, E.: Malicious interface design: Exploiting the user. In: Proceedings of the 19th International Conference on World Wide Web, WWW '10, pp. 271–280 (2010). https://doi.org/10.1145/1772690.1772719
5. Di Geronimo, L., Braz, L., Fregnan, E., Palomba, F., Bacchelli, A.: UI dark patterns and where to find them. In: Proceedings of the 2020 CHI Conference on Human Factors in Computing Systems, pp. 1–14. ACM, New York, NY, USA (2020). https://doi.org/10.1145/3313831.3376600, https://dl.acm.org/doi/10.1145/3313831.3376600
6. Dignum, V., et al.: Ethics by Design: necessity or curse? In: Proceedings of the 2018 AAAI/ACM Conference on AI, Ethics, and Society, pp. 60–66. ACM, New York, NY, USA (2018). https://doi.org/10.1145/3278721.3278745, https://dl.acm.org/doi/10.1145/3278721.3278745

7. Dindler, C., Krogh, P.G., Tikær, K., Nørregård, P.: Engagements and articulations of ethics in design practice. Int. J. Des. **16**(2), 47–56 (2022). https://doi.org/10.57698/v16i2.04
8. Friedman, B., Hendry, D.G., Borning, A.: A survey of value sensitive design methods. Found. Trends® Human–Comput. Inter. **11**(2), 63–125 (2017). https://doi.org/10.1561/1100000015, http://www.nowpublishers.com/article/Details/HCI-015
9. Gogoll, J., Zuber, N., Kacianka, S., Greger, T., Pretschner, A., Nida-Rümelin, J.: Ethics in the software development process: from codes of conduct to ethical deliberation. Philos. Technol. **34**(4), 1085–1108 (2021). https://doi.org/10.1007/s13347-021-00451-w, https://link.springer.com/10.1007/s13347-021-00451-w
10. Gotterbarn, D., Miller, K., Rogerson, S.: Software engineering code of ethics is approved. Commun. ACM **42**(10), 102–107 (1999). https://doi.org/10.1145/317665.317682, https://dl.acm.org/doi/10.1145/317665.317682
11. Gray, C.M., Kou, Y., Battles, B., Hoggatt, J., Toombs, A.L.: The Dark (Patterns) side of UX design. In: Proceedings of the 2018 CHI Conference on Human Factors in Computing Systems, vol. 2018-April, pp. 1–14. ACM, New York, NY, USA (2018). https://doi.org/10.1145/3173574.3174108, https://dl.acm.org/doi/10.1145/3173574.3174108
12. Gray, C.M., Sanchez Chamorro, L., Obi, I., Duane, J.N.: Mapping the landscape of dark patterns scholarship: a systematic literature review. In: Designing Interactive Systems Conference, pp. 188–193. ACM, New York, NY, USA (2023). https://doi.org/10.1145/3563703.3596635, https://dl.acm.org/doi/10.1145/3563703.3596635
13. Luger, E., Sellen, A.: "Like having a really bad pa": The gulf between user expectation and experience of conversational agents. In: Conference on Human Factors in Computing Systems - Proceedings, pp. 5286–5297 (2016). https://doi.org/10.1145/2858036.2858288
14. Luguri, J., Strahilevitz, L.J.: Shining a light on dark patterns. J. Legal Anal. **13**(1), 43–109 (2021). https://doi.org/10.1093/jla/laaa006, https://academic.oup.com/jla/article/13/1/43/6180579
15. Mathur, A., et al.: Dark patterns at scale: findings from a crawl of 11K shopping websites. Proceed. ACM on Human-Comput. Inter. **3**(CSCW), 1–32 (2019). https://doi.org/10.1145/3359183, https://dl.acm.org/doi/10.1145/3359183
16. Mathur, A., Mayer, J.: What makes a dark pattern... dark? design attributes, normative considerations, and measurement methods. In: Conference on Human Factors in Computing Systems - Proceedings. Association for Computing Machinery (2021). https://doi.org/10.1145/3411764.3445610
17. Naheyan, T., Oyibo, K.: The effect of dark patterns and user knowledge on user experience and decision-making. In: Baghaei, N., Ali, R., Win, K., Oyibo, K. (eds.) Persuasive Technology. PERSUASIVE 2024. Lecture Notes in Computer Science, vol 14636. pp. 190–206. Springer, Cham (2024). https://doi.org/10.1007/978-3-031-58226-4_15
18. Oinas-Kukkonen, H., Harjumaa, M.: Persuasive systems design: Key issues, process model, and system features. Commun. Assoc. Inf. Syst. **24**(1), 485–500 (2009). https://doi.org/10.17705/1cais.02428
19. Oyibo, K.: The influence of user knowledge and usage behaviour on decision-making and perceived reputation of streaming sites that use dark patterns. Behav. Inf. Technol. (2025). https://doi.org/10.1080/0144929X.2024.2447475
20. Quin, F., Weyns, D., Galster, M., Silva, C.C.: A/B testing: A systematic literature review. J. Syst. Softw. **211** (2024). https://doi.org/10.1016/j.jss.2024.112011

21. Tejo, L.C., Silva, P.A.: Engaging with ethics in the HCI design process: A study of ethical design practice in different work contexts. Int. J. Human Comput. Stud. **205** (2025). https://doi.org/10.1016/j.ijhcs.2025.103634
22. Zuber, N., Gogoll, J., Kacianka, S., Pretschner, A., Nida-Rümelin, J.: Empowered and embedded: ethics and agile processes. Human. Soc. Sci. Commun. **9**(1) (2022). https://doi.org/10.1057/s41599-022-01206-4

The 3rd BTI International Workshop (BTIW3)

Empirical Analysis of the Effect of Illustrated Maps Including Visual Guidance Elements on Tourist Behavior

Yutaka Arakawa[1(✉)], Yugo Nakamura[1], Yuki Matsuda[2], Toru Takahashi[3], and Teruo Higashino[4]

[1] Kyushu University, 744 Motooka, Nishi-ku, Fukuoka 819-0395, Japan
arakawa@ait.kyushu-u.ac.jp
[2] Okayama University, 3-1-1 Tsushima-naka, Kita-ku, Okayama 700-8530, Japan
[3] Stroly, Inc., 109-1 Kanegaecho, Shimogyo, Kyoto 600-8258, Japan
[4] Kyoto Tachibana University, 34 Yamada-cho Oyake, Yamashina-ku, Kyoto 607-8175, Japan

Abstract. This study verified the effect of guiding tourist behavior using map deformation and scale change as a measure against overtourism. In the Saga-Arashiyama area, we created an illustrated map in which the sense of distance was intentionally deformed and northern tourist spots were emphasized. We distributed this map to 8 subjects and conducted a tourism experiment. The results showed that a guidance effect towards the northern area was confirmed in the initial stage of tourism. The subjects showed a tendency to move around a wider area than the typical range of action of the inbound tourists. This suggests the possibility that visual guidance elements have a certain influence on tourist behavior, and proposes a new direction for map design in future tourism support.

Keywords: Visual guidance · Tourism · Behavior Change

1 Introduction

Tourism pollution and overtourism have long been problems in popular tourist destinations, such as Kyoto City, which receive high popularity from both domestic and international visitors. When observing tourist behavior patterns, they often plan their activities using tourist guidebooks, tourism information websites, map applications, and SNS as information sources. This tendency accelerates concentration on "popular spots". This concentration creates significant imbalances in congestion levels and results in factors that disrupt the overall balance of the tourist destination. In response to this situation, new approaches are required to achieve both the sustainable operation of tourist spots and the improvement of the quality of the tourism experience.

As conventional means of providing tourism information, digital maps, represented by Google Maps, are widely used. While digital maps offer rich information and navigation functions, a problem is pointed out: it is often difficult

E. Vlahu-Gjorgievska et al. (Eds.): PERSUASIVE 2026, CCIS 2896, pp. 427–438, 2027.
https://doi.org/10.1007/978-3-032-27235-5_46

to understand the appeal of tourist spots or event information. Therefore, illustrated tourist maps, which are specialized for specific events and allow tourist spots to be understood at a glance, still play an important role. However, illustrated tourist maps have drawbacks, such as the difficulty in grasping one's current location due to constraints on publishing space, resulting in map deformation and limits on the amount of information.

To address these issues, this study focuses on map deformation and scale change as an information provision method to guide tourist behavior. Unlike conventional map representations that prioritize accuracy, dynamically emphasizing or simplifying information on the map according to conditions such as congestion level is expected to naturally disperse the interest of tourists. Specifically, this study proposes an illustrated map incorporating visual elements that actively influence tourist behavior. We focus on visual guidance elements such as the intentional manipulation of distance scale, devising ways to make tourist spots stand out, selective omission of information, changing how roads are drawn, placing people illustrations, and strategically placing restaurant icons. This approach makes it possible to suppress excessive concentration on specific spots and promote a wider area tourism experience.

This study focuses on the deformation of the sense of distance among the visual guidances created by such map designs. Because illustrated maps are intended to be printed and distributed, all elements must be fitted onto a rectangular sheet of paper. As a result, winding roads are often drawn straight, and distant destinations are often drawn close on the map. We established two hypotheses: (1) More people will visit a spot if they feel the distance is short, and (2) People might think a tourist spot is famous if its illustration is large. We then created an illustrated map that extremely incorporates these elements. The details of the created map will be discussed later, but famous Saga-Arashiyama tourist spots, such as Togetsukyo Bridge and the Bamboo Grove Path, were made inconspicuous. Conversely, slightly distant tourist spots located in the north, such as Daikaku-ji Temple and Adashino Nembutsu-ji Temple Bamboo Grove, were deformed to appear large and close. This map was then distributed to 8 subjects, and a tourism experiment was conducted on March 17, 2025.

The experimental area was the Sagano-Arashiyama area in Kyoto City. An illustrated map designed with intentional deformation and visual emphasis was distributed to eight subjects who were unfamiliar with the area, and a free tourism experiment was conducted. During the experiment, tourist movement trajectories were recorded using GPS data collected via smartphones.

The results showed that, in the early stage of the tour, subjects tended to spend more time in the northern area that had been visually emphasized on the map, suggesting that map deformation influenced their perception of distance and guided their movement. Although visits to highly popular spots increased in the later stage, participants exhibited a slightly wider range of activity compared with typical tourists and visited locations with generally lower visitation rates.

Post-experiment interviews indicated that visual emphasis and the placement of information, such as restaurant icons, affected route selection and destination choice. At the same time, issues such as discrepancies between map representation and actual spatial impressions were identified. Overall, these findings suggest that illustrated maps incorporating visual guidance elements can partially influence tourist behavior and contribute to the dispersion of visitor flows.

Table 1. Various maps for tourism

	 Digital map	 Illustrated maps	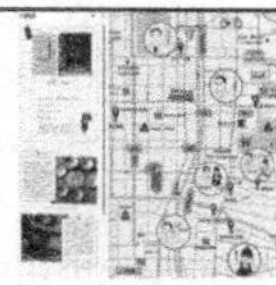 Digital illustrated maps
Information Amount	Very good	Low	High
Information Update	Regular	Event-specific	Event-specific
Navigation	Very good	No	No
Own Position	Yes	No	Yes
Tourism Specialization	No	Yes	Yes
Deformation	No (Accurate map)	Yes	Yes
Behavior Guidance	Advertisement	Illustration	Illustration + Digital
Map Data	Map Company	Illustrator	Illustrator

2 Related Work

2.1 About Illustrated Maps and Digital Illustrated Maps

Table 1 summarizes the characteristics of various maps used in tourism. Digital maps, represented by Google Maps, contain vast amounts of information—not only tourist spots but also restaurants, hotels, and transportation-and enable navigation, thus being used by many tourists. However, information such as the location of tourist spots, which spots are famous, what kind of spots they are, and what events are accompanying them is often unclear. For this reason, illustrated tourist maps are almost always prepared. Illustrated tourist maps are specialized maps for specific events, with the advantage that tourist spots are obvious at a glance. Because they must fit onto a fixed-size flyer, maps with distorted aspects ratios are drawn by illustrators. The drawbacks of these maps are that it is difficult to know one's current location and that additional information (such as business hours or spot episodes) cannot be obtained. Stroly is developing digital illustrated maps that solve these problems. More than 10,000 illustrated maps have already been incorporated, and they are used in large-scale events such as the Kyoto Gion Festival, Hakata Yamakasa, and SXSW overseas.

Our proposal aims to encourage changes in tourist behavior by including the visual guidance element of distance deformation in these digital illustrated maps. For this experiment, an illustrator drew the illustrated map. However, we plan to dynamically change the degree of deformation in the future based on congestion levels, and the drawing of illustrated maps using generative AI is also being considered.

2.2 About Tourist Behavior Guidance

Spatial and temporal dispersion of tourists is positioned as a fundamental and effective measure for mitigating overtourism. Specifically, guidance to surrounding underdeveloped areas in addition to conventional tourist spots, and promotions to encourage visits during the off-season (slack season) are conducted [7]. Such measures aim to reduce the over-concentration of tourism and support sustainable regional development.

In recent years, smart tourism initiatives utilizing ICT and big data have also been expanding. The introduction of applications that visualize congestion in real-time to encourage the dispersion of tourists, and the planning of predictive measures based on the analysis of tourist behavior are being promoted [1]. This is expected to achieve both the optimization of tourist spot management and user satisfaction. Isoda et al. proposed a method to encourage on-site decision-making by providing information that considers visit timeliness [3]. Hidaka et al. proposed an information provision method tailored to individual tourists by feeding personal preference information into such on-site tourism guidance [2]. Kawanaka et al. and Matsuda et al. proposed methods to guide tourist behavior and manipulate the amount of information collected from tourists by using game elements (gamification) [5,6].

Regarding behavior guidance through visual intervention, the use of signage and maps has been practiced in several cities. For example, in Barcelona, digital signage displaying real-time congestion information has been introduced to avoid excessive concentration of tourists [8]. This type of information provision contributes to load distribution among tourist spots by adjusting tourist movement behavior and enabling path selection that avoids congestion. Similarly, in Amsterdam, the redesign of tourist movement routes is being performed through visual signposts and maps, functioning as a strategy to guide the flow of tourists in urban space [4]. These examples show that visual information affects tourist decision-making and can be an effective means of urban tourism management. However, as far as the authors investigated, the only example of incorporating behavior guidance into illustrated maps distributed at tourist information centers was the "Saga-Arashiyama Touring Guide" designed by Stroly.

3 Illustrated Map Including Visual Guidance Elements

In this study, we go one step further from conventional map representation based on accurate scale, and propose an illustrated map incorporating visual elements that actively influence tourist behavior. This technique functions not merely as aesthetic expression but as a method for manipulating spatial awareness to intentionally guide tourist behavior. Figure 1 shows the illustrated map including

Fig. 1. Illustrated Maps Including Visual Guidance Elements.

visual guidance elements used in the experiment. In creating this map, we first adjusted the psychological impression of the space by intentionally manipulating the distance scale. Specifically, the scale of the northern area was compressed, while the foreground representation was maintained close to the actual size. This aims to reduce the psychological barrier to accessing the northern area and stimulate the desire to visit. This is expected to increase tourist circulation and guide them to the northern area, which traditionally had low visiting frequency. Next, we devised ways to make tourist spots stand out, taking care to guide tourists' attention toward specific directions. For example, Daikaku-ji Temple was drawn relatively large, while Togetsukyo Bridge and the Ryuzenji Bamboo Grove Path were drawn small. This design ensures that the focus of attention naturally shifts to specific spots. Furthermore, by emphasizing the bamboo grove of Adashino Nembutsu-ji Temple, we aimed for the effect of attracting interest to cultural resources that tended to be overlooked. Additionally, selective omission of information was intentionally incorporated. By purposely omitting text information regarding Togetsukyo Bridge and the Ryuzenji Bamboo Grove Path, we expected the effect of reducing cognitive load caused by excessive information while relatively increasing attention to other spots. Moreover, we added innovations to the way roads are drawn. By changing the texture of the stone pavement, line thickness, and color density, the map expression naturally indicates routes we want tourists to walk. These visual differences are thought to unconsciously influence route selection. We also devised the placement of people illustrations, placing many in the right-side area to create an atmosphere of liveliness. This utilizes the crowd psychology, where "people want to go where others are gathered," aiming for a natural guidance effect. Finally, eye-catching information, such as restaurant icons, was strategically placed around Daikaku-ji Temple, Seiryo-ji Temple, and Atago Nembutsu-ji Temple. This aimed to extend the tourists' length of stay and promote consumption activities, such as eating and drinking. By applying a combination of these visual innovations, the goal is to intentionally transform the tourists' spatial awareness. Figure 2 visualizes the degree of distance deformation in the created map. The map shown on the right is a distance-accurate map. The visualization result is based on aligning approximately 120 locations on both maps. It is possible to grasp how much distortion occurred by looking at the size and distortion of the green rectangles on the map on the left. Notably, the rectangle near Daikaku-ji Temple (center right) on the left map is small, indicating that the distance was deformed to feel shorter.

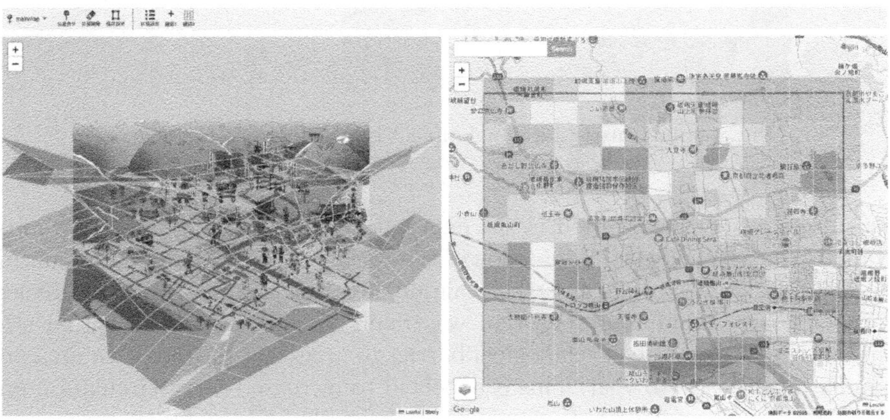

Fig. 2. The degree of deformation in distances on the created illustrated map.

4 Subject Experiment in Kyoto Arashiyama

The subjects were a total of 8 people: 7 undergraduate and graduate students from Kyushu University, and 1 undergraduate student from Kyoto Tachibana University. The authors also participated but were not included in these 8 subjects. Since the experiment required subjects to view the map, subjects unfamiliar with the Arashiyama area were considered preferable. For this reason, Kyushu University students were intentionally selected as subjects. The attributes of the subjects, based on a questionnaire conducted the day before the experiment, are summarized below.

4.1 Visiting Experience

Among the participants, 5 people were visiting Arashiyama for the first time, 3 people had visited 2 to 3 times, and 3 people had visited more than that. Regarding the experience of visiting Kyoto overall, 4 people had visited 2 to 3 times, and 5 people had visited more than that. While participants had some familiarity with Kyoto as a tourist destination, many were first-time visitors to Arashiyama, matching the expected subject group.

4.2 Experiment Outline

The experimental area was the Sagano-Arashiyama area (Kyoto City, Kyoto Prefecture), which is the same scope as the illustrated map created in this paper (Fig. 1). The departure and arrival point was standardized as "JR Saga-Arashiyama Station" for all subjects. Groups were a maximum of 2 people, and the maximum touring time was about 6 h (10:00 to 16:00). Subjects were primarily asked to tour freely based on the information obtained from the printed illustrated map. However, the use of smartphones for map search and web search was permitted if necessary. To analyze the tourist behavior taken by the subjects, a GPS logger application was installed on each subject's smartphone.

5 Analysis Results of Tourist Behavior

In this study, we conducted a quantitative analysis of tourist behavior based on the GPS logs of experiment participants. The purpose of the analysis is to clarify the influence of the deformed illustrated map on the tourists' range of movement and selection of destinations. Specifically, the effect of the map design's visual elements on spatial dispersion and circulation within the tourist spot is verified from various perspectives. Below, we analyze from three perspectives: (1) temporal changes in tourist behavior by group, (2) comparison with dynamic statistics of inbound foreign tourists, and (3) comparison with users of the illustrated map "Saga-Arashiyama Touring Guide" for overtourism measures. Based on this, we discuss the relationship between information presentation methods and behavior guidance in tourist destinations.

5.1 Analysis Result 1: Visualization of Tourist Behavior by Group

Figure 3 shows the trajectories of the tourist behavior of each group (A to D) over approximately 6 h, visualized as heatmaps divided into four sections of 1.5 h each. This allows visual capture of differences in movement and staying tendencies, including temporal changes for each group. The intensity of color in each figure indicates the length of stay or high frequency of visits in the corresponding area.

An interesting tendency observed was that in the initial stage of tourist behavior (0.0–1.5h) in all groups, subjects stayed longer in the northern area

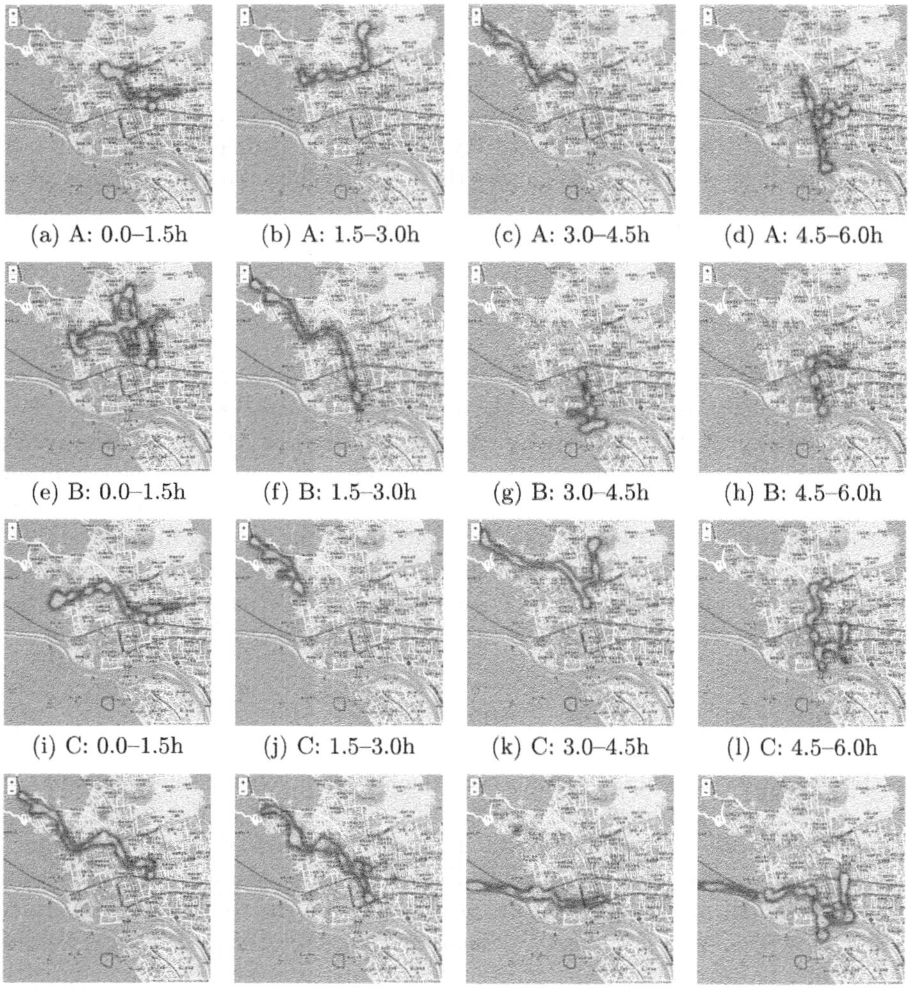

(a) A: 0.0–1.5h (b) A: 1.5–3.0h (c) A: 3.0–4.5h (d) A: 4.5–6.0h

(e) B: 0.0–1.5h (f) B: 1.5–3.0h (g) B: 3.0–4.5h (h) B: 4.5–6.0h

(i) C: 0.0–1.5h (j) C: 1.5–3.0h (k) C: 3.0–4.5h (l) C: 4.5–6.0h

(m) D: 0.0–1.5h (n) D: 1.5–3.0h (o) D: 3.0–4.5h (p) D: 4.5–6.0h

Fig. 3. The results of visualizing the stay patterns as a heatmap by dividing each group's tourism activities into approximately 1.5-h segments.

that was intentionally deformed and emphasized, rather than in conventional main tourist spots (e.g., Togetsukyo Bridge or the Bamboo Grove Path). This suggests that the illustrated map designed in this study influenced the tourists' spatial awareness and exerted a certain degree of effect in guiding circulation behavior northward. On the other hand, in the final stage of the tour (4.5–6.0h), movement gradually tended to concentrate on central tourist destinations highly popular among inbound foreign tourists, such as the area around Togetsukyo Bridge and Saga-Arashiyama Station. This suggests the possibility that while the promotion of circulation through visual guidance achieved a certain success,

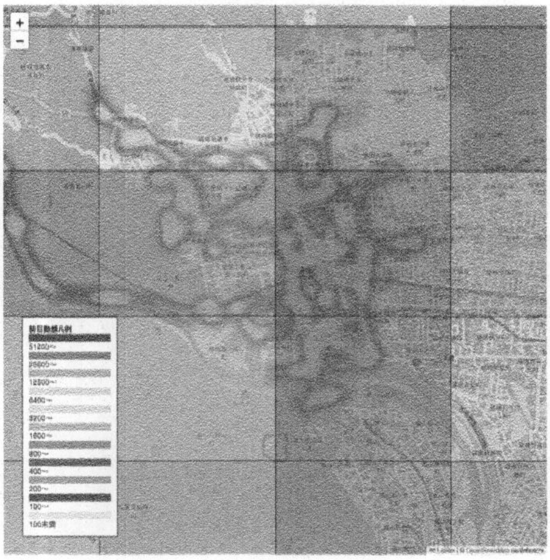

Fig. 4. Visualization results overlaying the tourism behavior logs of all experiment participants with the movement statistics of foreign visitors to Japan based on mobile spatial statistics.

a regressive behavior toward "standard spots" exists in the latter half of the tour.

5.2 Analysis Result 2: Comparison with Overall Trend and Inbound Foreign Tourist Dynamics

Figure 4 is a heatmap integrating the tourist behavior logs of all subjects. Furthermore, dynamic statistics of inbound foreign tourists were obtained from Mobile Spatial Statistics of NTT Docomo [9] and visualized overlaid on the map. In this study, only the 1km mesh corresponding to the current experimental area was extracted, and data aggregated monthly from March 2024 to October 2024 were used.

The visualization results confirmed a common high-density visiting tendency for both experiment participants and inbound foreign tourists around Togetsukyo Bridge and the Bamboo Grove Path. On the other hand, the movement trajectory of the experiment participants extended to the northern area (e.g., around Daikaku-ji Temple and Atago Nembutsu-ji Temple). It appeared that the distribution was somewhat wider compared to the overall dynamics of inbound foreign tourists. It is noteworthy that experiment participants stopped by areas where remarkable visits were not confirmed in the statistical data of inbound foreign tourists. This suggests the possibility that distance deformation and visual guidance elements, as shown in Fig. 2, had a certain influence on the selection of tourist routes. Such results indicate that the introduction of the illustrated map had a certain effect in arousing interest in areas previously not frequently visited and encouraging the expansion of the range of action. This suggests possibilities for future tourism space design.

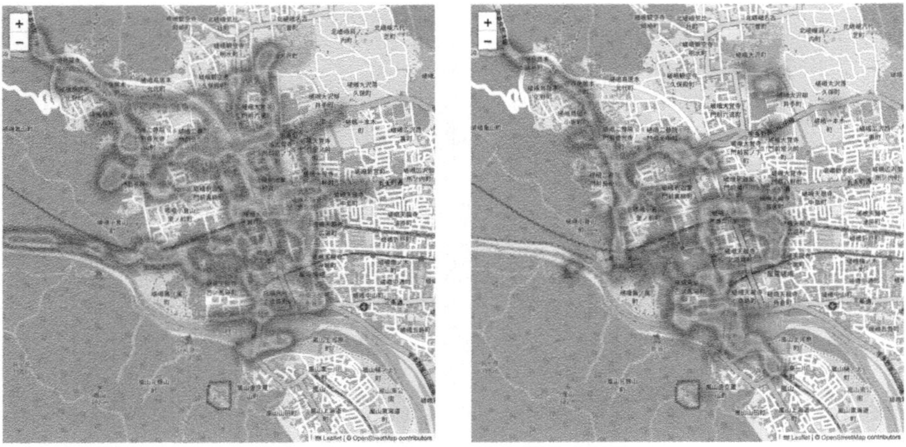

(a) Travel Logs of Deformed Map Users in this Experiment

(b) Travel Logs of Saga Arashiyama Tour Guide Users

Fig. 5. Comparison of Travel Patterns.

5.3 Analysis Result 3: Comparative Analysis with Users of the Digital Illustrated Map "Saga-Arashiyama Touring Guide"

We analyzed the movement tendency of users of the digital illustrated map "Saga-Arashiyama Touring Guide," using GPS logs provided by Stroly Inc. during the same time period as this experiment, and compared them with the participants of this experiment. For this analysis, 100 users were randomly sampled from the total users, and their behavior logs were targeted.

The "Saga-Arashiyama Touring Guide" is a digital illustrated map for tourism support, designed with the intention of dispersing tourist behavior. It features the emphasis of hidden spots and stamp rally functions. As shown in Fig. 5, experiment participants (Fig. 5 (a)) showed a tendency to visit tourist spots located in the upper part of the map, such as Daikaku-ji Temple, more often compared to Stroly users (Fig. 5 (b)). This is thought to be partly due to the visual emphasis on the northern area in the deformed map used in this experiment. Conversely, Stroly users showed a prominent tendency to concentrate around Togetsukyo Bridge and the Arashiyama shopping street, located in the lower part of the map, which are highly popular among inbound tourists. This difference is thought to be partly because Tenryu-ji Temple and Kameyama Park were not relatively emphasized on the deformed map used in this experiment. In other words, this result shows that map design and presented information can influence tourist movement behavior, suggesting the importance of interface design for mitigating congestion and guiding behavior in tourist destinations.

6 Participant Evaluation of Illustrated Maps and Design Implications

After the tour, post-experiment interviews and a group workshop were conducted with participants to collect opinions on the effects and issues of the illustrated map by reviewing their usage experience. This section organizes the influence of the illustrated map on tourist behavior based on participants' subjective evaluations and the contents of the group discussion.

In the interviews, free-form answers were obtained regarding the map and their tourist behavior. The following trends were observed:

- **Cognitive Gap:** Participants noted a gap between the deformed map and actual space (e.g., "I thought it was a river, but it broke off halfway," "The road was compressed"), hindering intuitive comprehension.
- **Visual Guidance:** Visual emphasis (colored backgrounds, large icons) influenced route decisions (e.g., "I chose the route where the background was colored").
- **Restaurant Information:** Restaurant depictions directly led to destination selection (e.g., "I went there because only one spot suitable for lunch stood out").
- **Oversight of Inconspicuous Places:** Low visibility caused participants to overlook spots (e.g., "I did not visit Tenryu-ji because it was drawn small on the map").
- **Need for Supplementary Information:** Participants requested more details, e.g., "It was difficult to understand how to get out of the station" or "I wish bus stops had been included".
- **Discouraging Representation:** Map representations sometimes suppressed behavior (e.g., "I passed through because it looked like a residential area").

In the workshop, participants confirmed that the distance manipulation (between Seiryo-ji and Daikaku-ji) might have encouraged circulation and that road textures acted as guideposts. Conversely, the simplified depiction of Saga-Arashiyama Station caused initial confusion, and the deviation from actual distances was noted as a problem. Furthermore, the limitation of static paper (lacking dynamic information, such as business hours and congestion status) was shared. This led to suggestions for hybrid maps, improving the visibility of landmarks, and presenting model courses.

7 Conclusion

In tourist maps provided by local governments, expressions such as listing only specific restaurants or highlighting only specific tourist spots are often restricted due to fairness considerations. It is difficult to directly use illustrated maps including visual guidance elements, like the one created in this study, as public tourism guidance.

However, the findings show that map representations—such as emphasis, omission, and configuration—significantly influence tourist routes and destination selection. Issues arising from insufficient information and the gap with actual geography were also revealed. This suggests that deformed illustrated maps can function not only as guidance but also as a"tool" to design the entire tourist experience. Design that influences behavioral aspects, such as the sequence of movement, length of stay, and stimulating the desire to visit, will be an important perspective in future tourism support.

In the future, we plan to study flexible information design that balances this public nature with guidance, tailored to users' cognitive characteristics. We also plan to explore hybrid information provision, such as interactive map representations linked with digital media, and the potential for maps personalized for each visitor.

Acknowledgments. A part of this research was supported by JST RISTEX (JPMJRS22K1), Japan Society for the Promotion of Science (JSPS) KAKENHI Grant (JP23H00216) and the Cooperative Research Project Program of the Research Institute of Electrical Communication, Tohoku University, Japan.

Disclosure of Interests. The authors declare no competing interests.

References

1. Gretzel, U., Sigala, M., Xiang, Z., Koo, C.: Smart tourism: foundations and developments. Electron. Mark. **30**(1), 7–18 (2020)
2. Hidaka, M., et al.: On-site trip planning support system based on dynamic information on tourism spots. Smart Cities **3**(2), 212–231 (2020). https://doi.org/10.3390/smartcities3020013
3. Isoda, S., Hidaka, M., Matsuda, Y., Suwa, H., Yasumoto, K.: Timeliness-aware on-site planning method for tour navigation. Smart Cities **3**(4), 1383–1404 (2020). https://doi.org/10.3390/smartcities3040066
4. Johnson, L., Wang, Y.: Wayfinding strategies and visual signage in urban tourism: lessons from amsterdam. J. Urban Tourism **25**(3), 200–215 (2019). https://doi.org/10.1016/j.jutr.2019.04.001
5. Kawanaka, S., Matsuda, Y., Suwa, H., Fujimoto, M., Arakawa, Y., Yasumoto, K.: Gamified participatory sensing in tourism: an experimental study of the effects on tourist behavior and satisfaction. Smart Cities **3**(3), 736–757 (2020). https://doi.org/10.3390/smartcities3030037
6. Matsuda, Y., Kawanaka, S., Suwa, H., Arakawa, Y., Yasumoto, K.: Parmosense: Scenario-based participatory mobile urban sensing platform with user motivation engine. Sens. Mater. **34**(8), 3063–3091 (2022). https://doi.org/10.18494/SAM3961
7. Peeters, P.: Overtourism: Lessons for a better future (2018)
8. Smith, J., Garcia, M.: Visual interventions to manage overtourism: A case study of barcelona. Tour. Manag. Persp. **35**, 100684 (2020). https://doi.org/10.1016/j.tmp.2020.100684
9. Terada, M., Nagata, T., Kobayashi, M.: Population estimation technology for mobile spatial statistics. NTT DOCOMO Tech. J. **14**(3), 10–15 (2013)

Optimizing Daily Activity Planning in a Behavioral Change Support System to Improve Older Adults' Quality of Life

Sachiko Enomoto[1(✉)], Hirohiko Suwa[1,2], and Keiichi Yasumoto[1,2]

[1] Nara Institute of Science and Technology, Ikoma, Nara 630-0192, Japan
enomoto.sachiko.eo5@naist.ac.jp, {h-suwa,yasumoto}@is.naist.jp
[2] RIKEN Center for Advanced Intelligence Project, Tokyo 103-0027, Japan

Abstract. With the growing aging population, extending healthy life expectancy and improving quality of life (QoL) have become critical societal issues. To maintain a healthy daily routine, older adults need well-balanced activity plans that incorporate appropriate levels of exercise and rest. This study proposes a daily activity planning system designed to support autonomous behavioral change in older adults. The system presents personalized and realistic daily plans based on the user's schedule and mood to promote self-directed healthy behavior. The planning process employs a multi-objective optimization approach considering stamina consumption, time allocation, task progress, and fatigue. We use an NSGA-III–based algorithm to efficiently derive diverse, practical solutions. A scenario-based user study with five graduate students acting as advisors for a virtual older adult user evaluated the validity of the generated plans. In all scenarios, over 80% of participants (4 out of 5) rated at least one plan as suitable. These results demonstrate that, as a prerequisite for behavioral change support, the proposed method is capable of generating realistic and appropriate daily activity plans.

Keywords: behavior change · Multi-Objective optimization · health support

1 Introduction

The global aging population is rapidly increasing. In Japan, individuals aged 65+ comprised 29% of the population in 2023, a proportion expected to rise further [26]. With this demographic shift, older adults lifestyles and living environments have diversified. Many prefer to live independently rather than rely on family or care facilities [6]. Meanwhile, the number of people requiring long-term care continues to grow [21]. Major causes include cerebrovascular disease, age-related frailty, and falls–conditions closely tied to declining health [5]. Maintaining health through daily self-management has thus become essential. A well-balanced routine integrating physical activity and rest is necessary to extend healthy life expectancy [4,16]. In addition, Quality of Life (QoL), as defined by

E. Vlahu-Gjorgievska et al. (Eds.): PERSUASIVE 2026, CCIS 2896, pp. 439–451, 2027.
https://doi.org/10.1007/978-3-032-27235-5_47

the WHO, is a key metric. Prior studies have shown QoL to be positively correlated with both physical function and activity level [11,25]. Thus, promoting moderate physical activity alone is not sufficient; supporting older adults in planning well-balanced routines that include adequate rest is also crucial. However, many older adults struggle to assess their own capacity accurately and tend to follow ingrained habits [3]. This can lead to overexertion or unbalanced schedules [14]. To address this, support systems that enable adaptive behavioral change based on individual conditions are needed [7].

This study aims to develop a system that autonomously generates personalized and health-promoting daily activity plans that older adults find realistic and acceptable. We formulate the planning task as a multi-objective optimization problem that balances multiple resources–such as stamina consumption and time allocation–under daily-life constraints, while also incorporating the naturalness of activity sequences. Naturalness is defined as the flow and consistency of activities based on the users habitual behavior patterns, enabling the generation of plans that are not only efficient but also intuitively acceptable to users.

We solve this optimization problem using the Non-dominated Sorting Genetic Algorithm III (NSGA-III), with the goal of efficiently deriving practical and diverse plans within a reasonable computation time.

To evaluate the proposed method, we conducted a user study that covered nine different types of daily-life scenarios. Participants assessed whether each algorithm-generated plan was appropriate. Across all scenarios, at least one plan was consistently judged as appropriate, indicating the method's effectiveness.

2 Related Work

This section reviews prior research on activity planning support and lifestyle improvement, and then clarifies the positioning of the present study.

Research on Activity Planning Support. Planning activities according to ones condition is crucial for maintaining sustainable health. Tateyama et al. [22] proposed a mental health forecasting index that helps users adjust behaviors based on predicted well-being. However, this method focuses on state prediction for workers and lacks specific schedule generation mechanisms. Jung et al. [12] developed "DeepStress," a personal informatics system that identifies stress contexts from self-logged data to guide coping strategies. Since this method aims to avoid specific identified stress factors, it is not suitable for flexible planning that considers the flow of the entire day.

These studies are useful for identifying stress-related contexts and providing feedback to help users recognize their own state. As shown in [2,23,24], research in this field has become increasingly active. However, these studies primarily focus on state visualization or immediate intervention, rather than supporting the improvement of specific schedules throughout the day.

Research on Lifestyle Improvement. Numerous studies have focused on improving lifestyle habits. Dinesh et al. [10] proposed a mobile-sensing-based lifestyle intervention system that detects users sleep states and provides early warnings of potential sleep deprivation. However, the function of this system is limited to issuing warnings, and it does not present concrete activity plans to secure sleep time.

Research on IoT-based behavior recommendation systems is also progressing. Alley et al. [1] developed "Active for Life," a web-based physical activity intervention program for older adults that integrates smartwatch data to provide adaptive recommendations. This system updates plans biweekly with personalized goals. However, this fixed interval fails to account for users' daily changes in physical condition or mood. For example, even if a user does not want to exercise on a specific day, the same amount of activity is recommended, which may hinder long-term engagement. Therefore, the lack of flexibility to adapt to daily fluctuations remains a major challenge.

Positioning of This Study. As reviewed above, existing research has provided valuable insights for health maintenance and behavioral change support. Nevertheless, many systems focus on the working-age population, and even those targeting older adults often rely on static (fixed) recommendations. Consequently, their adaptability to the daily fluctuations specific to older adults—such as mood, physical condition, and irregular plans—has been limited.

To address this limitation, this study aims to develop an activity planning system that flexibly schedules the following days activities according to the user's mood and schedule. Specifically, unlike methods for the working-age population, we model constraints specific to older adults, such as declining stamina and the necessity of rest. Furthermore, instead of fixed weekly goals, we generate plans that dynamically adapt daily to changes in mood and irregular tasks. Finally, rather than simply maximizing activity, we formulate the problem as a multi-objective optimization problem to simultaneously consider competing objectives such as suppressing fatigue, maximizing task progress, and maintaining the naturalness of lifestyle patterns.

Through this approach, we generate realistic and highly acceptable schedules and verify their effectiveness through a user study.

3 Daily Activity Scheduling Problem

In this section, we define the daily activity scheduling problem to support user decision-making and formulate it as a multi-objective optimization problem.

3.1 Problem Definition

We consider three main factors influencing user fatigue: (1) stamina consumption, (2) activity duration, and (3) task progress. The objective is to determine the time allocation for each activity in a day while balancing the trade-offs among four factors: total stamina consumption, total time spent, task progress, and overall daily fatigue. This problem is formulated as a multi-objective optimization problem that aims to minimize fatigue and maximize task accomplishment.

The activities considered in the scheduling consist of two types: Daily activities, such as household chores, repeated regularly, and tasks, such as grocery shopping or medical appointments, which are irregular and often have deadlines.

We target four essential daily activities: cooking, eating, bathing, and going out. Unlike daily activities, tasks impose additional load based on deadlines and subjective proficiency. System inputs include the user's average activity patterns, intended wake-up time, task deadlines, and self-assessed proficiency.

3.2 Formulation

Let $A = \langle a_1, \ldots, a_N \rangle$ denote daily activities, where N is the number of activities. Let $S = \langle s_1, \ldots, s_N \rangle$ represent the list of stamina consumption values for each activity, based on the Metabolic Equivalent of Task (METs), which indicates the physical intensity of each activity. The time allocated to each activity is denoted by $D = \langle d_1, \ldots, d_N \rangle$.

Since a user may skip certain daily activities (e.g., eating out instead of cooking), the execution status of each activity is represented by $X = \langle x_1, \ldots, x_N \rangle$, where $x_i \in \{0, 1\}$, with $x_i = 0$ indicating the activity is not performed and $x_i = 1$ indicating that it is performed.

For tasks $T = \langle t_1, \ldots, t_M \rangle$, we define stamina cost $W = \langle w_1, \ldots, w_M \rangle$, duration $E = \langle e_1, \ldots, e_M \rangle$, and days until deadline $R = \langle r_1, \ldots, r_M \rangle$. Task execution is denoted by $Y = \langle y_1, \ldots, y_M \rangle$, where $y_j = 1$ implies execution.

Mixed Indicator for Daily Activities. Prior studies suggest that perceived burden depends on activity familiarity. To capture this, we employ a *Mixed Indicator* integrating duration and stress variability (Lorenz plot area). The Lorenz plot area summarizes the unevenness of RRI during an activity; larger values indicate greater variability, which can be interpreted as lower familiarity or higher subjective burden. Let $H = \langle h_1, \ldots, h_N \rangle$ be the Lorenz plot areas. The indicator is computed as:

$$p_i = \frac{d_i \cdot h_i}{\sum_{j=1}^{N} d_j} \tag{1}$$

This yields $P = \langle p_1, \ldots, p_N \rangle$, representing proficiency-based burden. Weighting by activity duration d_i and normalizing by the total daily duration $\sum_{j=1}^{N} d_j$ enables comparison in terms of each activitys relative contribution to overall daily burden. As Lorenz plots are unavailable for tasks, we use self-reported proficiency $L = \langle l_1, \ldots, l_M \rangle$ as an alternative.

Objective Functions. The total stamina consumption and total time spent in a day are defined as:

$$Stamina = \sum_{i=1}^{N} s_i d_i x_i + \sum_{j=1}^{M} w_j e_j y_j, \quad Time = \sum_{i=1}^{N} d_i x_i + \sum_{j=1}^{M} e_j y_j \tag{2}$$

When a task is postponed to a later day, its burden increases as the deadline approaches. The cumulative burden of postponed tasks is defined as:

$$Burden = \sum_{j=1}^{M} d_j \cdot y_j \cdot \frac{1}{r_j} \tag{3}$$

The total daily fatigue, representing the overall physical and mental load on the user, is expressed as:

$$Fatigue = \sum_{i=1}^{N} x_i \cdot s_i \cdot d_i \cdot p_i + \sum_{j=1}^{M} y_j \cdot w_j \cdot e_j \cdot p_j + w_j \cdot l_j \cdot \frac{1}{r_j} \tag{4}$$

Stamina is defined as an objective measure of physical disposable resources. In contrast, Fatigue represents the total physical and subjective tiredness accumulated daily. Burden refers to the psychological load regarding future obligations, which specifically increases as task deadlines approach.

To encourage sustainable behavioral change, the proposed schedule should minimize deviation from the users typical routine [17]. Let μ_i denote the average daily time allocation for each activity. We define unnaturalness as:

$$Unnaturalness = \sum_{i=1}^{N} x_i \cdot \sqrt{(\mu_i - d_i)^2} \tag{5}$$

Constraints. Since each task has a due date, it must be completed by that date:

$$y_j = \sum_{k=0}^{r_j} z_{j,k}, \tag{6}$$

where $z_{j,k} = 1$ if task t_j is executed on remaining day k, and 0 otherwise.

Optimization Problem. The goal of this problem is to find an optimal set of daily activity and task schedules (X, D, Y, E) that satisfy all constraints while minimizing fatigue and the burden of postponed tasks. Thus, the multi-objective optimization problem is formulated as:

$$Minimize\ (Stamina, Times, Burden, Fatigue, Unnaturalness) \tag{7}$$

4 Proposed Method

The scheduling problem examined in this study is formulated as a multi-objective combinatorial optimization problem. This multi-objective combinatorial optimization problem entails an exponentially growing solution space. Our goal is to integrate this method into an interactive schedule navigator that allows older adults to iteratively update their schedules in response to changing needs or preferences. To ensure responsiveness in such interactive use, it is crucial to rapidly generate dive rse solutions [13]. Therefore, we employ an NSGA-III–based heuristic algorithm to efficiently derive candidate schedules.

Table 1. Solution Representation

Bath	Cook	Eat	Go Out	Task 1	...	Task n
Real (min)	Real (min)	Real (min)	Real (min)	0/1	...	0/1

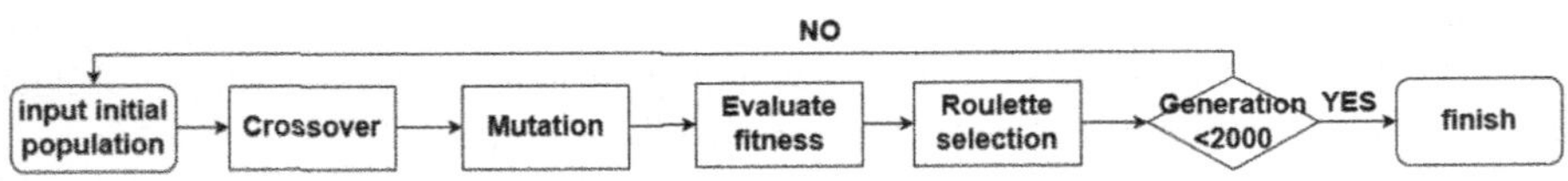

Fig. 1. Overview of the proposed algorithm

4.1 Solution Representation

Each individual consists of real-valued time allocations for daily activities and binary indicators for scheduled tasks. The solution is encoded as a gene sequence, as shown in Table 1, where continuous variables represent activity durations (in minutes), and binary values indicate task execution (1) or not (0).

4.2 Algorithm Overview

As illustrated in Fig. 1, the proposed algorithm consists of five main steps, using NSGA-III [8] to explore a wide solution space. NSGA-III heuristically approximates the Pareto front while reducing computation time. The system assumes that users choose the most suitable plan from Pareto-optimal candidates, allowing flexible and personalized interaction.

Initial Population Generation. To generate a diverse initial population while reflecting the user's typical behavioral patterns, we sample the duration of each activity from a uniform distribution within the range of the user's average $\pm\sigma_i$, ensuring non-negative values. Each task is assigned a binary value of 1 (scheduled) or 0 (not scheduled) by random sampling. After generation, each individual is checked for feasibility based on time constraints such as minimum sleep duration, and if infeasible, durations are randomly adjusted to restore feasibility.

Crossover. As shown in Fig. 2, we apply distinct strategies for the different data types. For real-valued daily activities, *arithmetic crossover* [20] linearly combines parent values to prevent convergence. For binary tasks, *two-point crossover* is used to enhance exploration. The segments are processed separately and concatenated. Parents are selected via normalized roulette-wheel selection, defaulting to uniform selection if fitness scores are identical.

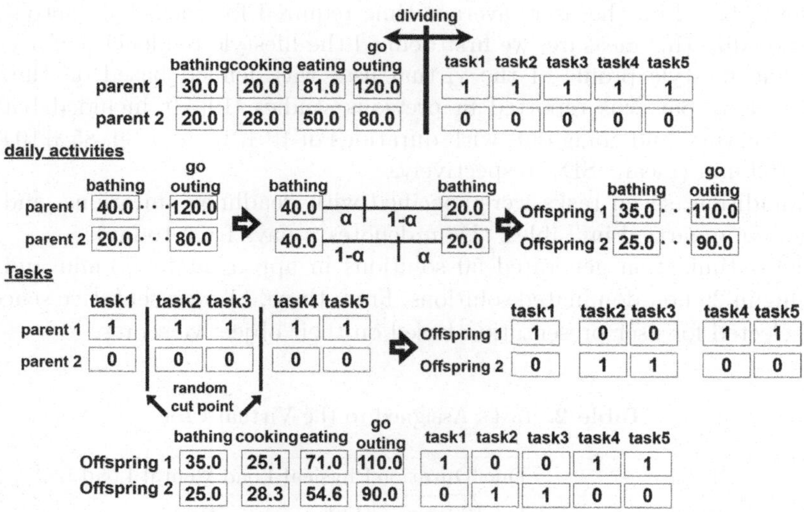

Fig. 2. Example of crossover operations

Mutation and Selection. To introduce diversity, we apply Polynomial Mutation [9] for continuous activity durations and bit-flip mutation for binary tasks. Subsequently, individuals are chosen using fitness-based roulette-wheel selection. Fitness is normalized for minimization, with a fallback to uniform selection when scores are identical to prevent premature convergence.

5 Preliminary Experiment

The proposed system aims to support older adults in creating plans. As a preliminary step before involving this target group, we conducted an experiment with university students to assess the quality of the generated schedules. Using a virtual user scenario, we conducted two tasks: (1) a **schedule creation task** involving manual planning to assess constraint satisfaction, and (2) a **schedule evaluation task** judging the appropriateness of algorithm-generated schedules.

5.1 Generation of Evaluation Schedules

Algorithm Implementation. We implemented the algorithm in Python 3.11 using `pymoo` with custom operators. Experiments ran on a Windows 11 PC (Ryzen 9 5900HX, 16 GB RAM). Key algorithm parameters included a population size of 50, 2000 generations, and both crossover and mutation rates set to 0.5. We employed roulette wheel selection and a deadline-based repair mechanism to manage constraints for the 4 daily activities and 6 tasks.

Virtual User Setting. In this study, the objective function unnaturalness is computed based on the users average time required for each daily activity. To operationalize this measure, we first defined the lifestyle tendencies of a virtual user. The lifestyle profile of the virtual user was defined based on the most average daily patterns reported in previous studies [19]. It included bathing, cooking, eating, and going out, with durations of 18 ± 27, 52 ± 39, 85 ± 104, and 290 ± 199 min (mean±SD), respectively.

In addition, seven tasks were specified with deadlines, durations, and load levels as summarized in Table 2 (D+n denotes n days from today).

The optimization generated 50 solutions in approximately 1 min and 40 s, resulting in 29 non-dominated solutions. From these, 11 representative schedules were selected for user presentation based on their objective scores.

Table 2. Tasks Assigned to the Virtual User

Tasks	Due	Duration	Physical Load	Mental Load
Hospital	D+0	90 min	High	High
Post Office	D+1	30 min	Low	Low
Bank	D+2	45 min	Medium	Medium
Friends House	D+3	120 min	Medium	Low
Grocery Shopping	D+4	60 min	Medium	Low
Pharmacy	D+6	15 min	Low	Low

5.2 Participants

Five graduate students aged 23–25 acted as advisors for a virtual user. Task order was randomized to eliminate order effects.

5.3 Schedule Creation and Evaluation Task

The goal of this task was to examine how well humans could create feasible schedules considering task constraints such as deadlines. Participants received the lifestyle tendencies, tasks, and nine scenarios shown in Table 3. The scenarios were categorized into three types–*rest-oriented*, *activity-oriented*, and *tasks-priority*–with three variations in each category. Participants were asked to create a plan for each scenario by allocating time to daily activities in 10-min units and selecting which tasks to include, as shown in Fig. 3.

For evaluation, we presented three schedules for each scenario. One schedule was selected from the first non-dominated front (rank 1) for each scenario (rest: low stamina/short duration; activity: high stamina/long duration; task-priority: high task completion), and the remaining two were randomly drawn from 11 preselected rank-1 solutions.

As shown in Fig. 4, each plan was presented with visual aids including time allocation and pie charts, descriptive labels (e.g., "outings-focused"), automatically generated by an LLM from the plans objective values and activity composition, and a 120-character summary to facilitate understanding.

Table 3. Daily life scenarios used in the evaluation

Scenario Type	Description
Rest Oriented	I exercised a lot the day before and feel lower back pain today, so I want to take it easy
	I feel tired lately and prefer to avoid strenuous activities
	I'm feeling sluggish and would like to prioritize a calm day
Activity Oriented	I've been relaxed the past few days and feel it's a good day to go out
	I'm in great condition today and feel motivated to be active
	I stayed indoors yesterday, so I'd like to go out and move a bit today
Tasks Priority	Yesterday was an early hospital day, and I want to rest a bit today but also get things done
	I expect a busy week, so I want to finish tasks while I can
	The weather is nice today, but it's expected to rain later this week, so I want to complete tasks now

6 Results

This section presents the outcomes of the schedule creation and evaluation tasks.

Figure 5 shows the number of deadline violations in the schedules created by participants for each scenario. In all scenarios, at least one participant submitted a schedule that violated task deadlines.

Figure 6 shows the number of participants rating each of the three algorithm-generated schedules per scenario as "appropriate." For all scenarios, at least one schedule was rated appropriate by four or more participants out of five.

Fig. 3. Example of a response in the schedule creation task

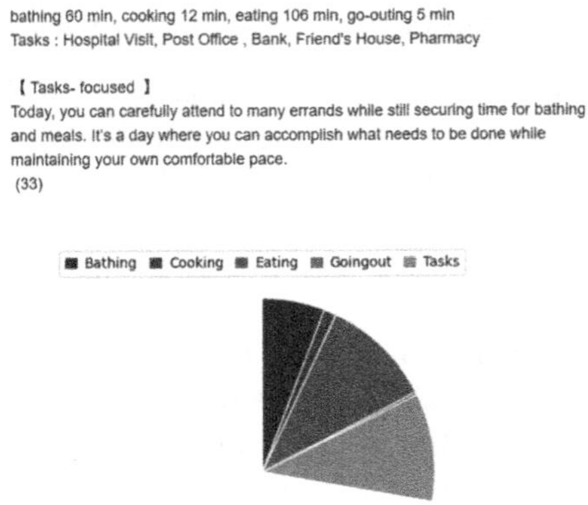

Fig. 4. Example of the schedule evaluation task

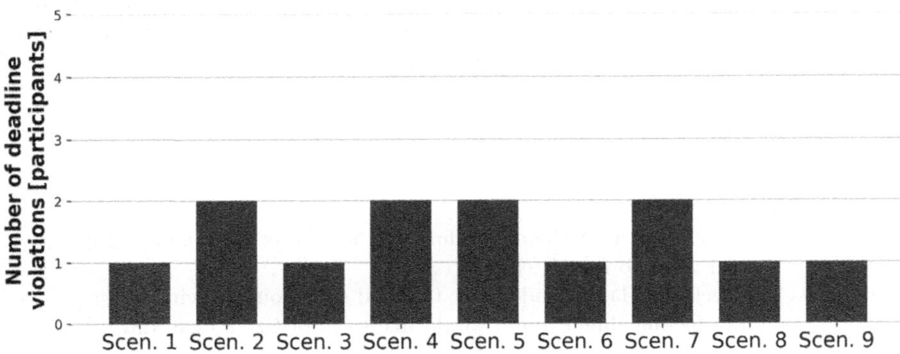

Fig. 5. Number of deadline constraint violations per scenario

For schedules rated "appropriate," participants noted that "the time allocation for each activity aligns well with the user's intentions" and "the balance between task execution and rest is well maintained."

Notably, all participants cited descriptive labels as a key reference.

7 Discussion

The preliminary experiment revealed two key findings. First, when individuals create schedules based on their mood or condition, they often fail to meet all constraints, such as task deadlines. Managing multiple factors simultaneously proves challenging, exposing the limitations of manual planning.

Second, many schedules generated by the proposed method were rated as "appropriate," demonstrating practical applicability and supporting the usefulness of automated scheduling in balancing constraints and user preferences.

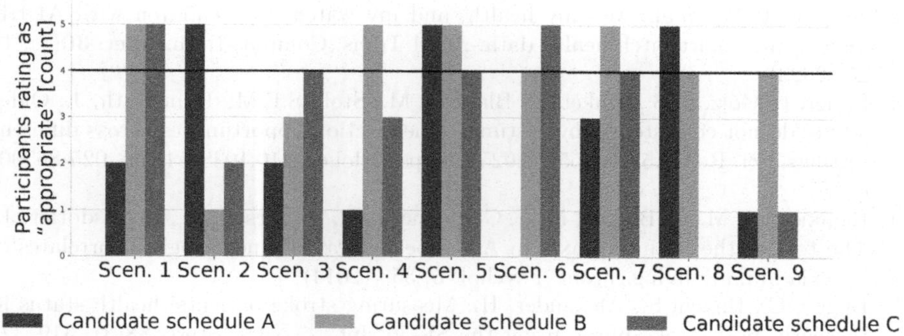

Fig. 6. Number of participants who rated each schedule as "appropriate"

Additionally, all participants cited "descriptive labels" as most helpful in judging the schedules, underscoring the value of concise, interpretable representations. These labels enhance understanding and acceptance, and should be prioritized in future system designs.

These findings suggest that the proposed method serves as an effective support system for generating flexible and realistic daily plans, while also contributing to participants perceived acceptability.

8 Conclusion

This paper proposed a multi-objective optimization system for generating personalized daily activity schedules to support behavioral change in older adults. It produces flexible, realistic plans reflecting users conditions, deadlines, and preferences. The problem is formulated as a mixed-variable combinatorial optimization with five objectives. An NSGA-III–based algorithm generates diverse schedules using real-valued durations and binary task flags.

A preliminary experiment showed that manually created schedules often violated constraints, whereas algorithm-generated plans were evaluated as appropriate. Explanatory labels improved understanding and acceptance. These results demonstrate the potential of our approach to support daily planning. Future work includes testing with older adults, improving explanations, and enabling real-time adaptation. We also plan to refine parameter settings and develop a user interface that allows users to intuitively select their preferred solution from the algorithms diverse outputs [15,18].

References

1. Alley, S., et al.: The effectiveness of a computer-tailored web-based physical activity intervention using fitbit activity trackers in older adults (active for life): randomized controlled trial. J. Med. Internet Res. **24**(5), e31352 (2022)

2. Ankrah, E.A., et al.: Me, my health, and my watch: how children with ADHD understand smartwatch health data. ACM Trans. Comput.-Hum. Inter. **30**(4), 1–25 (2023)
3. Bauer, I., Gölz, M.S., Finkel, L., Blasizzo, M., Stoll, S.E.M., Randerath, J.: Older adults do not consistently overestimate their action opportunities across different settings. Sci. Rep. **15**(1), 4559 (2025). https://doi.org/10.1038/s41598-025-86790-6
4. Bieńkiewicz, M.M., Brandi, M.L., Goldenberg, G., Hughes, C.M., Hermsdörfer, J.: The tool in the brain: apraxia in ADL. behavioral and neurological correlates of apraxia in daily living. Front. Psychol. **5**, 353 (2014)
5. Bugge, C., Hagen, S., Alexander, H.: Measuring stroke patients' health status in the early post-stroke phase using the SF-36. Int. J. Nurs. Stud. **38**(3), 319–327 (2001). https://doi.org/10.1016/S0020-7489(00)00066-3
6. Cabinet Office, Government of Japan: Annual report on the aging society (2024). https://www8.cao.go.jp/kourei/whitepaper/w-2024/zenbun/index.html
7. Caro, J., Nguyen, P., Lipman, S.: Automated personalized goal setting for individual exercise behavior: protocol for a web-based adaptive intervention trial. JMIR Res. Protoc. **14**, e73766 (2025). https://doi.org/10.2196/73766
8. Deb, K., Jain, H.: An evolutionary many-objective optimization algorithm using reference-point-based nondominated sorting approach, part i: solving problems with box constraints. IEEE Trans. Evol. Comput. **18**(4), 577–601 (2014)
9. Deb, K., Tiwari, S.: Omni-optimizer: a generic evolutionary algorithm for single and multi-objective optimization. Eur. J. Oper. Res. **185**(3), 1062–1087 (2008)
10. Dinesh, K.S., Chaya, R., Cengiz, K., Alshehri, Y., Alnazzawi, N., Ivković, N.: Early alert for sleep deprivation using mobile sensor data fusion. Comput. Electr. Eng. **102**, 108228 (2022)
11. Group, W.: The development of the world health organization quality of life assessment instrument (the WHOQOL). In: Quality of Life Assessment: International Perspectives, pp. 41–57. Springer (1994)
12. Gyuwon, J., Sangjun, P., Uichin, L.: DeepStress: supporting stressful context sensemaking in personal informatics systems using a quasi-experimental approach. In: Proceedings of the CHI Conference on Human Factors in Computing Systems (CHI '24), pp. 1–18 (2024)
13. Hertzum, M., Hornbæk, K.: Frustration: still a common user experience **30**(3) (2023). https://doi.org/10.1145/3582432
14. Hortobágyi, T., Mizelle, C., Beam, S., DeVita, P.: Old adults perform activities of daily living near their maximal capabilities. J. Gerontol. A Biol. Sci. Med. Sci. **58**(5), M453–M460 (2003). https://doi.org/10.1093/gerona/58.5.m453
15. Jamshed, H., Nurain, N., Brewer, R.N.: Designing accessible audio nudges for voice interfaces. In: Proceedings of the 2025 CHI Conference on Human Factors in Computing Systems, CHI '25. Association for Computing Machinery, New York (2025). https://doi.org/10.1145/3706598.3713563
16. Katz, S.: Assessing self-maintenance: activities of daily living, mobility, and instrumental activities of daily living. J. Am. Geriatr. Soc. **31**(12), 721–727 (1983)
17. Kotkov, D., Medlar, A., Glowacka, D.: Paths and recreation: inclusive recommendation of physical activities in your neighbourhood. In: Proceedings of the 2025 ACM SIGIR Conference on Human Information Interaction and Retrieval (CHIIR '25), pp. 372–376 (2025)
18. Liu, N., Yin, J., Tan, S.S., Ngiam, K.Y., Teo, H.H.: Mobile health applications for older adults: a systematic review of interface and persuasive feature design. J. Am. Med. Inform. Assoc. **28**(11), 2483–2501 (2021)

19. Matsumoto, K., Matsui, T., Suwa, H., Yasumoto, K.: Stress estimation using biometric and activity indicators to improve QoL of the elderly. Sensors **23**(1), 535 (2023)
20. Michalewicz, Z.: Genetic Algorithms + Data Structures = Evolution Programs. Springer-Verlag, Berlin (1992)
21. Ministry of Health, Labour and Welfare: Overview of long-term care benefit expenditures statistics (2023). https://www.mhlw.go.jp/toukei/saikin/hw/kaigo/kyufu/23/index.html
22. Naoki, T., Ryota, Y., Yuki, B., Shin, I., Rui, F.: Planning the future in a longer perspective: effects of a one-week forecast of mental health. Proc. ACM Inter., Mob., Wearable Ubiquit. Technol. **8**(18), 1–20 (2024)
23. Neupane, S.: Momentary stressor logging and reflective visualizations: implications for stress management with wearables. In: Proceedings of the ACM CHI Conference on Human Factors in Computing Systems (CHI '24), pp. 1–20 (2024)
24. Pei-Yi, K., Michael, S.H.: Ecosanté lifestyle intervention: encourage reflections on the connections between health and environment. ACM Trans. Comput.-Hum. Inter. **30**(6), 1–37 (2023)
25. Prasad, L., Fredrick, J., Aruna, R.: The relationship between physical performance and quality of life and the level of physical activity among the elderly. J. Educ. Health Promot. **10**, 68 (2021)
26. Statistics Bureau of Japan: Population estimates as of October 1 2023. https://www.stat.go.jp/data/jinsui/2023np/index.html

Development of an Automated Evaluation System for Discussion Quality in Face-to-Face Group Discussions

Kanta Hagiwara[1](✉), Motoki Sakai[2], and Guillaume Lopez[1]

[1] Aoyama Gakuin University, Shibuya, Japan
khagiwara@wil-aoyama.jp, guillaume@it.aoyama.ac.jp
[2] Nihon University, Tokyo, Japan
sakai.motoki@nihon-u.ac.jp

Abstract. Group discussions are essential for active learning, yet it is difficult for students to objectively understand their own skills without feedback from experts. However, providing immediate, individual feedback to all groups is often difficult due to resource constraints. This study aims to develop an automated evaluation system that enables students to grasp their discussion skills objectively and encourages behavior change. The proposed system integrates speech recognition and Large Language Models (LLMs) to evaluate discussions based on the Discourse Quality Index (DQI). It assesses four metrics: Logic, Respect, Progress, and Perspective. The results are provided to students as feedback through radar charts and specific advice. A comparative experiment with university students ($N = 15$) was conducted. Participants were divided into an experimental group (with feedback) and a control group (without feedback) to perform two discussion sessions. In the experimental group, improvement trends were observed in the Logic and Respect metrics, whereas the control group showed no significant changes. Additionally, the System Usability Scale (SUS) score was 88.4 (Grade A), indicating high usability. The results suggest that the proposed system effectively visualizes discussion quality and supports students' behavior change.

Keywords: Group Discussion · Large Language Models · Discourse Quality Index · Behavior Change

1 Introduction

1.1 Background: The Paradox of Group Work

In recent years, the ability to collaborate in groups has become increasingly critical in both educational and professional settings. In higher education, active learning strategies such as Group Discussions (GD) are widely promoted to foster critical thinking and communication skills [12]. Similarly, in the corporate world, the demand for collaborative skills is surging. According to a Microsoft survey, the average weekly meeting time for Teams users increased by 252% from

E. Vlahu-Gjorgievska et al. (Eds.): PERSUASIVE 2026, CCIS 2896, pp. 452–463, 2027.
https://doi.org/10.1007/978-3-032-27235-5_48

February 2020 to 2022 [13]. This data suggests that the ability to discuss and solve problems in teams is becoming an essential skill for the digital age.

Despite this growing importance, a significant number of students harbor negative feelings toward group activities. Surveys indicate that many students find active learning burdensome and prefer passive lecture-style classes [3]. The root of this aversion often lies in low self-esteem (e.g., I don't have confidence in my opinions) and anxiety regarding peer evaluation (e.g., I'm afraid of how others will react) [10]. Consequently, these psychological barriers lead to passive participation, preventing students from developing the very skills they need.

1.2 The Feedback Gap

To overcome these barriers and improve discussion skills, experience alone is insufficient. Students need to acquire specific competencies, such as logical argumentation, active listening, and the ability to synthesize opinions [9]. However, meta-cognition—objectively understanding one's own behavior during a heated discussion—is extremely difficult for students.

In ideal educational settings, expert instructors would monitor every group and provide personalized feedback. However, due to limited human resources, it is practically impossible for teachers to observe detailed interactions of all groups simultaneously. As a result, students often receive no concrete feedback, relying on subjective impressions like "it was fun," which fails to reinforce positive behaviors or correct negative ones. This lack of objective feedback perpetuates their anxiety and stagnates skill development.

1.3 Goal of This Study

To address this issue, we propose a persuasive feedback system that automates the role of a skilled facilitator. By integrating speech recognition technology with Large Language Models (LLMs), we aim to construct a learning environment where students can objectively grasp their discussion skills even in the absence of human instructors.

The core contribution of this paper is twofold:

1. **System Design:** We developed a system that evaluates Discussion Quality rather than just quantity. By utilizing the Discourse Quality Index (DQI) and LLMs, the system provides multi-dimensional feedback on Logic, Respect, Progress, and Perspective.
2. **Persuasive Intervention:** We verify whether visual feedback (Radar Charts) and actionable advice can effectively persuade students to change their behavior. We report on a pilot study demonstrating how this technological intervention affects students' performance and psychological acceptance.

2 Related Work

2.1 Quantifying Discussion Quality: The DQI Approach

Traditionally, discussion assessment has relied on quantitative metrics such as utterance frequency or duration. However, these metrics fail to capture the quality of deliberation. To address this, we draw upon the Discourse Quality Index (DQI) established in political science and deliberative democracy [17]. DQI codes discussions based on Habermasian ethics, evaluating aspects such as the justification of arguments, respect for others, and constructive behavior.

While Steenbergen et al. initially designed the DQI for parliamentary debates, recent studies have expanded its application to citizen workshops and mini-publics, proving its effectiveness in evaluating non-expert discussions [15,18]. Our research adopts DQI as a core metric for educational feedback, redefining it into four actionable indicators for students: Logic, Respect, Progress, and Perspective.

2.2 Persuasive Technology in Group Dynamics

Numerous studies have proposed systems to support group discussions through technological intervention. A common approach is visualizing participation balance. For instance, Kanazawa et al. [11] visualized microphone volume to prevent dominance by specific speakers, while Adachi et al. [1] used tablets to visualize the conversation structure. More physical interventions include wearable devices that vibrate to signal over-participation or chairs that provide haptic feedback to encourage quieter members to speak [6,8].

While these systems function as persuasive technologies by nudging users toward balanced participation, they focus primarily on the quantity of interaction, but do not evaluate the discussion's content. A student could talk a lot without contributing logically, or stay silent while thinking deeply. Our system aims to bridge this gap by providing feedback on the semantic quality of the discussion.

2.3 Automated Evaluation Using LLMs

The advent of Large Language Models (LLMs) has revolutionized the analysis of unstructured text. Unlike traditional keyword-matching methods, LLMs can understand context and nuance. Recent studies have shown that LLMs, such as GPT-4, can replicate human coding of DQI with high reliability ($\kappa > 0.6$) [14]. Gelauff et al. also demonstrated that LLMs can estimate contribution levels in online deliberations with accuracy comparable to human evaluators [7].

However, most existing applications of LLMs in this domain focus on text-based chat logs or online forums. There are a few instances of end-to-end systems that capture face-to-face audio discussions, transcribe them, evaluate them using DQI,, and provide immediate feedback to induce behavior change. This study positions itself at the intersection of Automated Assessment and Persuasive Technology, applying LLMs to real-world, face-to-face educational settings.

3 Group Discussion Automated Evaluation System

To address the issues of group discussion's objective evaluation and concrete feedback generation discussed in Sect. 2.3, we developed an automated evaluation system. This system records face-to-face discussions, utilizes LLMs to analyze them based on DQI metrics, and provides participants with a post-discussion visualization and actionable advice.

3.1 System Architecture

The system consists of four main modules: Input Interface, Audio Processing, Evaluation Generation, and Output Interface. Table 1 summarizes the specific technologies and models used in each module. In addition, Fig. 1 illustrates the end-to-end processing flow and the sequential relationship between these components. This diagram clarifies how raw audio data is transformed into structured feedback through automated transcription, speaker diarization, and LLM-based scoring.

Table 1. System components and technologies.

Component	Technology/Model
Input	BOYA BY-V4 (Wireless Mic), Audacity
Audio Processing	OpenAI Whisper (Large-v2) [16], pyannote.audio [4], WhisperX [2]
Evaluation	Gemini 2.5 Pro [5]
Output	Radar Charts (Matplotlib), Excel Report

Audio Processing Module. To identify who said what and when from a single audio file, we implemented the WhisperX framework [2]. WhisperX combines Voice Activity Detection (VAD) and phoneme alignment to achieve high-precision timestamping. Specifically, we use Whisper (large-v2) for robust speech-to-text transcription and the Python "pyannote.audio" library, which provides pretrained pipelines for tasks like voice activity detection, speaker segmentation, and speaker diarization [4,16]. By aligning these outputs, the system generates a dialogue log with accurate speaker labels.

Evaluation Generation Module. We selected Gemini 2.5 Pro to process the generated dialogue log for two reasons [5]:

1. **Reasoning Capability:** High capability to follow complex instructions is required to strictly apply the rubric for abstract concepts like Logic and Respect.
2. **Long Context Window:** The model can process the entire discussion context in batches, ensuring consistent evaluation across the session.

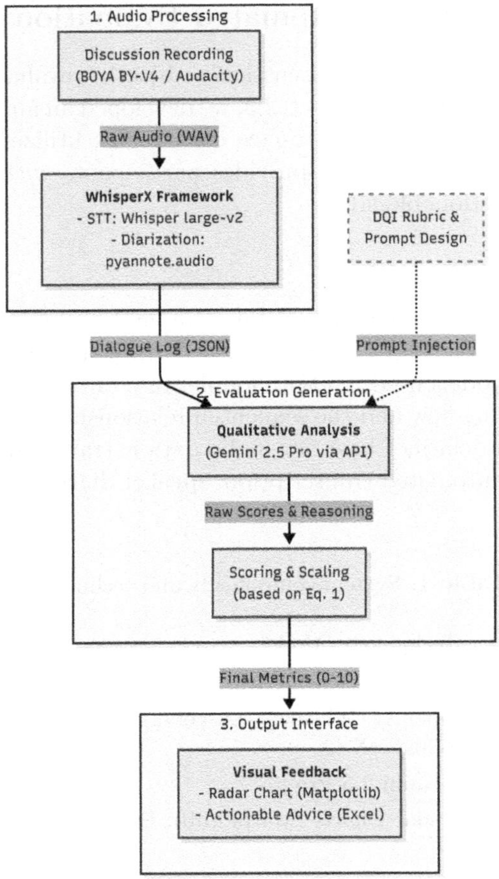

Fig. 1. Overall system architecture and data processing flow of the proposed automated evaluation system

3.2 Evaluation Logic and Prompt Design

This section describes the core metrics redefinition and the prompt engineering used for the LLM.

Evaluation Metrics (Modified DQI). We redefined the DQI elements into four metrics understandable for students. Crucially, we adopted a 3-point scale (0–2) rather than a binary check to differentiate the quality of contribution. The detailed rubric is presented in Table 2.

Prompt Configuration. We instructed the LLM to strictly score each utterance based on the rubric above and to output the score along with the reasoning. The actual prompt includes the role definition "You are an expert discussion evaluator" and the following elements:

Table 2. Modified Discourse Quality Index (DQI) evaluation rubric.

Metric	Score	Criteria Description
Logic	0	Subjective opinion only (e.g., I think...)
	1	Reason provided, but based on personal experience or speculation
	2	Supported by objective facts, data, or specific examples
Respect	0	Disconnected remark or simple backchanneling
	1	Positive reaction or confirmation of others' views
	2	Accepting others' views and developing them further (e.g., new proposal)
Progress	0	Following the flow without contribution
	1	Proposing new ideas or topics
	2	Summarizing opinions, setting criteria, or time management
Perspective	0	Personal preference only
	1	General user or majority viewpoint
	2	Minority viewpoint, operator's view, or holistic perspective

1. **Detailed Rubric Description:** Explicitly stating criteria for each score (0–2) and example keywords (e.g., "according to data", "to summarize") to minimize evaluation variance.
2. **Speaker Identification:** Instructions to correctly identify speakers from the context and link them to the evaluation.
3. **Output Schema Enforcement:** Restricting the output format to a strict JSON structure (list containing ID, Speaker, Scores, Reason) to ensure reliable downstream processing.

Score Calculation Algorithm. After the LLM assigns scores to each utterance, the system calculates the final feedback score using the following methods.

Filtering Valid Utterances: In group discussions, simple backchannels like "Yes" or "I see" are transcribed. While essential for social lubrication, they are often rated 0 in all DQI metrics. Including them in the calculation increases the denominator (total utterances) and unfairly lowers the average score. Therefore, we filter out utterances where all four metrics are scored as 0.

Scaling to 10 Points: We calculate the average score for each metric based on the count of filtered valid utterances (N). To make it intuitive for students, the average score (max 2.0) is multiplied by 5 to scale it to a 0–10 range. The Eq. 1 shows the final score S_{final} calculation.

$$S_{final} = \frac{\sum_{i=1}^{N} s_i}{N} \times 5 \tag{1}$$

Here, s_i represents the score of the i-th valid utterance. This process translates an average fundamental contribution (mean 1.0) to 5.0 points, and consistently high contribution (mean 2.0) to 10.0 points.

3.3 Output Interface Design

The system generates a visual feedback report to facilitate students' metacognition and behavior change after each discussion session.

1. **Visualization of Skill Balance (Radar Chart):** The system generates a radar chart using Matplotlib to plot the average scores of the four DQI metrics. This visualization allows participants to intuitively grasp their discussion characteristics, such as identifying a gap between high logical contribution and low perspective diversity.
2. **Quantitative Scores and Actionable Advice:** The system provides a detailed report containing quantitative scores and personalized feedback (see Table 3). Instead of raw data, the report offers concrete action plans tailored to individual performance. For example, as illustrated in Table 3, if the Logic metric is low, the system suggests providing objective evidence. If the Progress score is high, it encourages the student to attempt more complex facilitation tasks. This specific, immediate advice enables students to set clear goals for the subsequent session.

Table 3. Example of Feedback Generation Results

Speaker	Logic	Res.	Prog.	Persp.	Feedback
A	3	6.25	3.75	4	**[Logic]** You may have frequent statements lacking evidence. Try to support your arguments with objective data and phrases such as "because..." to strengthen your reasoning. **[Respect]** While you show agreement well, deepening the discussion requires asking probing questions or proposing constructive alternatives to build upon others' views. **[Progress]** You successfully introduce topics; next, try to summarize diverse opinions or confirm final decisions to help the discussion reach a conclusion. **[Perspective]** You maintain a general viewpoint. Incorporating minority perspectives or the viewpoints of stakeholders (e.g., operators) will further enhance the quality of the discussion.

4 Experiment Methodology

We conducted two experiments to verify the system's reliability and its effectiveness in inducing behavior change.

4.1 Experiment 1: Verification of Evaluation Accuracy

To validate the reliability of the automated evaluation, we examined the reproducibility of the system's scoring and the agreement among human evaluators. Four students read a scripted discussion on "Strategies to increase university applicants". The audio was evaluated by:

1. **System:** Evaluated twice to check reproducibility.
2. **Human Evaluators:** Three students evaluated the same data using the same rubric (0–2 scale).

To assess the inter-rater agreement among the three human evaluators, we used **Fleiss' Kappa**. We also analyzed the system's internal consistency using **Weighted Kappa**.

4.2 Experiment 2: Verification of Educational Effect

This experiment aimed to verify whether the feedback induces behavior change in actual discussions.

Participants and Conditions. The study involved university students ($N = 15$). We divided participants into two groups:

1. **Experimental Group ($N = 11$):** Received system feedback (Radar chart + Excel report) after the first discussion session concluded.
2. **Control Group ($N = 4$):** Did not receive feedback between discussions.

Procedure. The experiment consisted of two discussion sessions (approx. 15 mins each). To allow for reflection and consolidation of learning, we conducted the two sessions on separate days.

- **Session 1 (Day 1):** Theme "Strategies to increase applicants for the Aoyama Gakuin University Department of Integrated Information Technology".
- **Intervention:** The experimental group reviewed their feedback charts and advice, setting personal goals for the next session.
- **Session 2 (Day 2):** Theme "Ideas to reduce communication loss in remote work".

Participants wore wireless microphones (BOYA BY-V4) to ensure high-quality audio input for the system.

Evaluation Metrics We evaluated the effectiveness from three perspectives:

- **Quantitative Change (DQI Score):** We compared the average DQI scores (0–2 scale) between Session 1 and Session 2 to verify statistical improvements.
- **System Usability (SUS):** The Experimental group completed the System Usability Scale (SUS). In this study, given that participants did not directly operate the interface, we operationally defined usability as the readability of the feedback reports and the ease of interpreting the provided advice, rather than operational ease of use.
- **User Acceptance:** We measured the participants' sense of conviction and intention to use the system using a questionnaire using a 5-point Likert scale.

5 Experimental Results and Discussion

This chapter analyzes the system's reliability and its educational effects based on two experiments.

5.1 Reliability of Evaluation Logic

To verify the objectivity of the evaluation, we compared human evaluation with system evaluation. The inter-rater agreement among three human evaluators was low ($\kappa = 0.28$, Fleiss' Kappa), indicating that human evaluation is prone to subjectivity and inconsistency. In contrast, the proposed system demonstrated extremely high reproducibility with a weighted Cohen's Kappa of **0.87**. This result confirms that the system provides stable and fair feedback, free from the fatigue or bias inherent in human evaluators.

5.2 Educational Effect (Quantitative Analysis)

We examined the impact of feedback on discussion skills with 15 participants (Experimental Group: $N = 11$, Control Group: $N = 4$). Figures 2 and 3 illustrate the score transitions, and Table 4 summarizes the statistical results.

In the Experimental Group, DQI scores improved across all metrics. Specifically, Logic ($0.70 \rightarrow 0.86, p = .034$) and Respect ($1.11 \rightarrow 1.32, p = .030$) showed statistically significant improvements (paired t-test, $p < .05$). Conversely, the Control Group showed no significant improvement and even exhibited a decline in Logic ($0.47 \rightarrow 0.38$) and Respect ($1.12 \rightarrow 1.04$). These results suggest that simply repeating discussions causes fatigue and stagnation, whereas system intervention effectively motivates behavior change and skill acquisition.

5.3 Usability and Acceptance (Qualitative Analysis)

The System Usability Scale (SUS) score for the Experimental Group was 88.4 (SD=9.25), which corresponds to Grade A (Excellent). This indicates that the system imposes minimal cognitive load.

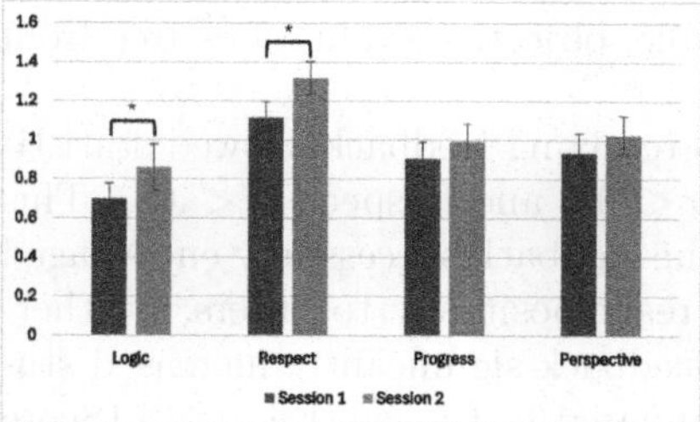

Fig. 2. Experimental Group ($N = 11$)

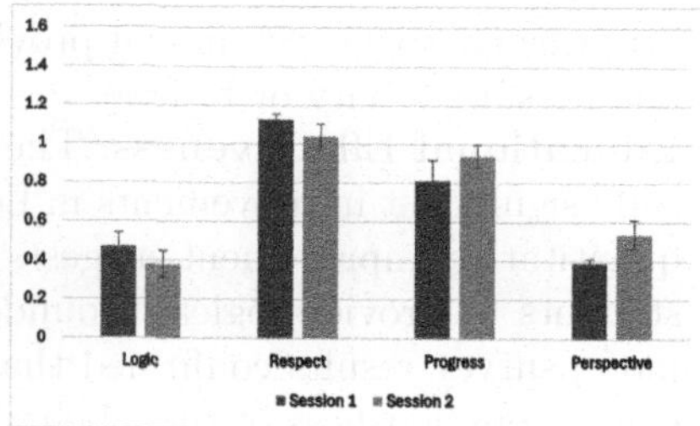

Fig. 3. Control Group ($N = 4$)

Table 4. Comparison of score improvements (Paired t-test). The Experimental Group showed significant growth.

Metric	Exp. 1st → 2nd	Exp. p-value	Ctrl. 1st → 2nd	Ctrl. p-value
Logic	0.70 → 0.86	**0.034***	0.47 → 0.38	0.713
Respect	1.11 → 1.32	**0.030***	1.12 → 1.04	0.545
Progress	0.90 → 0.99	0.170	0.81 → 0.94	0.597
Perspective	0.93 → 1.03	0.209	0.39 → 0.54	0.241

Mean scores shown. $p < .05$

Subjective questionnaires (5-point Likert scale) revealed significant differences in behavior awareness. Regarding the question "Did you consciously change your way of speaking?", the Experimental Group averaged 4.45 compared to the Control Group's 3.25. Similarly, for "Did you try to increase reactions?", the Experimental Group scored 4.27 versus 3.50 for the Control Group. Furthermore, 9 out of 15 participants were beginners (0–1 prior experiences), yet the Experimental Group showed high acceptance ("Intention to use": 4.27).

Free-text comments indicated that concrete, actionable feedback (e.g., "It told me specifically what to do next") was highly valued. However, some users felt the feedback was formulaic ("Felt like template sentences"). While the system successfully visualized weaknesses, further personalization using the LLM's context-awareness remains a future task.

6 Conclusion

This study proposed an automated feedback system using LLMs and DQI to improve students' discussion skills. Through a comparative experiment with university students ($N = 15$), we obtained the following findings regarding the system's reliability and educational effectiveness:

1. **High Reliability:** The system demonstrated extremely high internal consistency (Weighted Kappa $\kappa = 0.87$), which contrasts significantly with the

low inter-rater agreement observed among human evaluators ($\kappa = 0.28$). This confirms that the system can provide stable, objective evaluations free from human subjectivity or fatigue.

2. **Educational Effectiveness:** The group receiving feedback showed statistically significant improvements in Logic ($p < .05$) and Respect ($p < .05$). This quantitative improvement suggests that the feedback successfully encouraged students to provide logical grounds and react positively to others. Furthermore, survey results confirmed that the feedback significantly increased students' consciousness of their behavior compared to the control group (Score 4.45 vs 3.25).
3. **High Acceptability:** The system achieved an SUS score of 88.4 (Grade A), indicating that the feedback reports were highly readable and the advice was easy to interpret. This establishes the system as a low-load, effective support tool for learners.

These results suggest that LLM-driven visualization serves as a persuasive intervention that promotes meta-cognition and behavior change.

Future work addresses the following two limitations:

- **Expert Validation:** Since the inter-rater agreement among student evaluators was low, we plan to have discussion experts (e.g., professors in pedagogy) evaluate the audio data under the same conditions. We will verify whether the system's scoring aligns with the standards of skilled instructors.
- **Sample Size Expansion:** While this study confirmed effectiveness with $N = 15$, we plan to further increase the experimental cohort. This expansion will enable a more detailed analysis of how feedback effects vary depending on individual student characteristics and initial skill levels.

Acknowledgments. This work was supported by Japan Keirin Autorace (JKA) Foundation research (grant number 2025M-334).

References

1. Adachi, H., Myojin, S., Shimada, N.: ScoringTalk: tablet system for adjusting speaking opportunities. In: IPSJ Interaction 2015, p. A42 (2015). (in Japanese)
2. Bain, M., Huh, J., Han, T., Zisserman, A.: WhisperX: time-accurate speech transcription of long-form audio. In: INTERSPEECH 2023, pp. 4489–4493 (2023)
3. Benesse Educational Research and Development Institute: 4th survey on university students' learning and life. Tech. rep. (2022). in Japanese
4. Bredin, H.: pyannote.audio: Neural building blocks for speaker diarization. In: ICASSP 2020, pp. 7124–7128 (2020)
5. Comanici, G.: Gemini 2.5: pushing the frontier with advanced reasoning, multimodality, long context, and next generation agentic capabilities. arXiv preprint: arXiv:2507.06261 (2025)
6. Dagan, E., et al.: 'not too much, not too little' wearables for group discussions. In: CHI 2018 Extended Abstracts, p. LBW098 (2018)

7. Gelauff, L.: Estimating contribution quality in online deliberations using a large language model. In: Proceedings of the AAAI Conference on Human Computation and Crowdsourcing, vol. 12, pp. 65–74 (2024)
8. Ichino, J., et al.: Presentation of feedback by vibration for group discussion support. IPSJ J. **60**(4), 1171–1183 (2019). (in Japanese)
9. JAVADA: Report of the committee on formulation of standards for acquiring basic employment skills for young people. Tech. rep. (2004). https://www.mhlw.go.jp/houdou/2004/04/h0427-2c.html. (in Japanese)
10. Kamioka, Y., et al.: University students' attitudes toward group work. Okayama Univ. Sci. Manag. Data Sci. **6**, 94–106 (2024). (in Japanese)
11. Kanazawa, T., Igaki, H.: Examination of methods for visualizing utterance volume of online group discussion participants. In: rePiT2024. pp. 67–69 (2024). (in Japanese)
12. MEXT Central Council for Education: Towards a qualitative transformation of university education for building a new future (2012). in Japanese
13. Microsoft: 2022 work trend index: Annual report. Tech. rep., Microsoft (2022)
14. Mori, K., et al.: Automated evaluation of discussion based on discourse quality index. Tech. rep., Technical Report Consen2024-16 (2025). (in Japanese)
15. Nakazawa, T., Souma, Y., Tatsumi, T., Ohnuma, S.: Practice and issues of deliberation evaluation using discourse quality index. Risk Res. **34**(4), 193–201 (2025). (in Japanese)
16. Radford, A.: Robust speech recognition via large-scale weak supervision. In: Proceedings of the 40th International Conference on Machine Learning, PMLR, vol. 202, pp. 28492–28518. (2023)
17. Steenbergen, M.R., Bächtiger, A., Spörndli, M., Steiner, J.: Measuring political deliberation: a discourse quality index. Comp. Eur. Politics **1**(1), 21–48 (2003)
18. Tatsumi, T., Nakazawa, T.: Verification of participant fairness in mini-public deliberation. In: The 37th Annual Conference of JSAI, p. 1P5OS16b05 (2023). in Japanese

Study on a Method for Determining Knee Load from Gait Using Lumbar Acceleration

Ryoka Hamochi(✉), Zeyu Liu, and Guillaume Lopez

Aoyama Gakuin University, Shibuya, Japan
{rhamochi,liuzeyu}@wil-aoyama.jp, guillaume@it.aoyama.ac.jp

Abstract. Abnormal gait patterns increase the mechanical load on the knee joint, affecting forces applied to the lower limbs during walking. Excessive mechanical load is a major factor in the progression of knee hyperflexion and stiff knee gait in cerebral palsy, as well as age-related knee osteoarthritis. However, conventional gait analysis focuses on macroscopic indicators, and direct assessment of knee joint load applicable to daily life remains limited. In this study, a risk-oriented index for knee joint load was first proposed. Based on this index, two walking conditions were then defined, and gait samples were labeled as high- or low-knee joint load using motion capture and force plate data derived from knee flexion angle (KFA) and vertical ground reaction force (vGRF). Finally, we investigated the feasibility of automatically identifying these walking conditions from lumbar acceleration using machine learning. Following the preliminary model development, the feature engineering pipeline was optimized and assessed. We constructed two feature spaces: one combining conventional time- and frequency-domain features from lumbar acceleration, and a second using multi-domain features. Subject-independent validation was performed using mRMR feature selection and multiple classifiers. Automatically extracted multi-domain features consistently outperformed conventional features. Combining the mRMR-selected compact feature set with subject attributes achieved ROC-AUC values of 0.75–0.77. Increasing the number of features yielded no significant performance gains, and differences between classifiers were minimal. These results demonstrate that knee joint injury risk–related gait patterns can be identified using a single wearable lumbar sensor, providing a scalable and low-burden approach for daily knee joint monitoring and gait intervention.

Keywords: Gait analysis · Acceleration · AIST gait database · Machine learning

1 Introduction

Japan is facing a super-aging society, with the population aged 65 and over projected to reach 38.7% by 2070 [15]. Consequently, maintaining physical function

E. Vlahu-Gjorgievska et al. (Eds.): PERSUASIVE 2026, CCIS 2896, pp. 464–475, 2027.
https://doi.org/10.1007/978-3-032-27235-5_49

through regular exercise, such as walking, has become a priority for extending healthy life expectancy. On the other hand, mechanical stress on the knee joint is a major factor in the progression of hyperflexion and stiff knee gait in cerebral palsy, as well as osteoarthritis associated with aging. The resulting pain can impair walking and potentially lead to frailty [14].

While gait analysis is increasingly used for clinical diagnosis and early detection of diseases [3], most existing approaches have focused on macroscopic gait performance indicators such as speed, stride length, or rhythm. Therefore, there are limitations to directly evaluating biomechanical characteristics such as knee joint load, which is deeply involved in the progression of joint disease. To assess these internal loads, measurements are generally taken in a laboratory environment using motion capture or force plates, but there is a need to establish a simple evaluation method that can be used in daily life.

This study aims to raise awareness of healthy walking through the objective evaluation of gait in daily life. To realize a system that can readily identify joint-related risks, we set the following two objectives.

1. To clarify the knee joint flexion angle that puts mechanical loading on the knee during walking, and the indicators of impact on the foot
2. To establish a method for determining the presence or absence of knee load using lumbar acceleration

2 Related Work

To assess the load on the knee joint during walking, previous studies have widely used biomechanical indicators such as the external knee adduction moment (KAM) and ground reaction force (GRF). It has been shown that the knee adduction moment (KAM) and the knee flexion moment (KFM) have independent contributions to medial and lateral contact forces. This suggests that, while KAM represents medial loading during walking, it may not be sufficient on its own to fully characterize sagittal-plane mechanical loading. [20].

Previous studies have shown that wearable sensors can classify gait styles [17] and estimate physical states such as lower limb muscle strength and energy expenditure [7,13]. Alongside these developments, systems such as the National Institute of Advanced Industrial Science and Technology (AIST) Walking Attribute Judgment System HOLMES (Human Objective Locomotion MEasurement System) can objectively evaluate gait quality and left–right asymmetry during daily-life walking. [9].

Furthermore, AIST Gait Database 2019 [10], which contains motion capture data from 300 individuals, has facilitated the development of qualitative feedback systems [8]. In gait-based health monitoring, previous studies have explored various approaches, ranging from placing sensors at multiple locations (e.g., the waist, knees, ankles, and thighs) to limiting placement to only the ankle or waist. However, for monitoring in daily life, a minimal sensor configuration is generally desirable to reduce user burden.

While wearable sensors are effective for gait classification, most studies have relied on indirect features derived from inertial sensors. Research focusing on direct biomechanical indicators such as joint loading and impact forces has remained limited. Furthermore, existing studies primarily target older adults or specific clinical groups, and investigations across a wide age range remain scarce.

3 Knee Joint Load Indicator Definition Based on Knee Flexion and Ground Impact

3.1 Basic Structure of Gait

Gait can be described as a sequence of movement patterns. In the Rancho Los Amigos gait cycle model, a widely used clinical framework, gait is subdivided into the stance phase and the swing phase [12].

Furthermore, there are various forms of gait. The range is from the typical gait seen in healthy individuals to abnormal gaits caused by diseases or declines in physical function [1,2,6]. Considering these gait styles, either excessively small or excessively large knee flexion can increase the mechanical load on the visible joints. In addition, the foot's contact strength is also thought to be an essential factor influencing impact load.

3.2 Labeling Criteria for High Knee Joint Load Walking

We defined knee joint load indicators with high mechanical stress on the knee joint, based on two biomechanical thresholds during walking: knee flexion and vGRF. Using these indicators, walking trials were categorized into "High Knee Joint Load Walking" and "Low Knee Joint Load Walking." These definitions apply specifically to walking conditions and do not represent general biomechanical load indices for arbitrary movements.

Knee Flexion Criteria: Typical peak knee flexion during the swing phase (from right toe-off (RTO) to the subsequent right heel strike (RHS)), particularly during the initial swing, ranges from 52° to 70° [11,16]. We defined values outside this range ($< 52°$ as insufficient shock absorption and $> 70°$ as excessive muscle activity joint compressive load) as high-knee joint load indicators.

vGRF Criteria: Vertical ground reaction force (vGRF) is a fundamental index in gait analysis and represents the mechanical load on the lower limbs. During level walking, vGRF typically exhibits a bimodal waveform, with its peak value reflecting the magnitude of joint loading during the weight-bearing and push-off phases [18]. Standard normalized peak vGRF ranges from 1.1 to 1.3 Body Weight (BW) [18]. Accordingly, vGRF > 1.3 BW was classified as high-knee joint load.

Labeling Rule: We labeled a trial as "High Knee Joint Load Walking" if it met either of the knee flexion or vGRF high-stress criteria, and classified all other trials as "Low Knee Joint Load Walking". The indicator proposed in this study is positioned as a risk detection metric for screening walking conditions that may increase knee joint load.

4 Preparation of Dataset for Machine Learning

4.1 Description of Gait Database and Measurement Sites

We used gait data from AIST Gait Database 2019 [10], consisting of data for 300 healthy adults who performed 10 trials each at a self-selected comfortable speed. The database provides three-dimensional coordinates of the markers. The participant's attributes are encoded directly within each file name. Each trial recorded approximately 1.5 strides of barefoot walking. Measurements were performed using a motion capture system (sampling frequency = 200 Hz) and force plates (sampling frequency = 1000 Hz).

This study aimed to estimate walking states from lumbar acceleration signals. Previous studies have widely used the lumbar as a sensor attachment position for gait analysis, reporting that features of whole-body and lower-limb movements can be obtained relatively stably from acceleration signals at these locations [9,13]. Moreover, placing a sensor at the lumbar region imposes minimal burden during daily activities and represents a realistic placement for practical use; therefore, this location was adopted.

Since the AIST Gait Database provides stable gait events for the right leg, this study limited the calculation of knee flexion and vGRF for labeling in this study to the right leg. This ensures reproducibility in the extraction of gait phases and features calculation.

4.2 Data Acquisition and Preprocessing

This study used markers on the lumbar and right lower limb for approximately 1.5 steps: RASI, SACR, LASI, RKNE, RKNE2, RANK, and RANK2. We used these markers to define pseudo-labels and as input data for the machine learning model (Fig. 1).

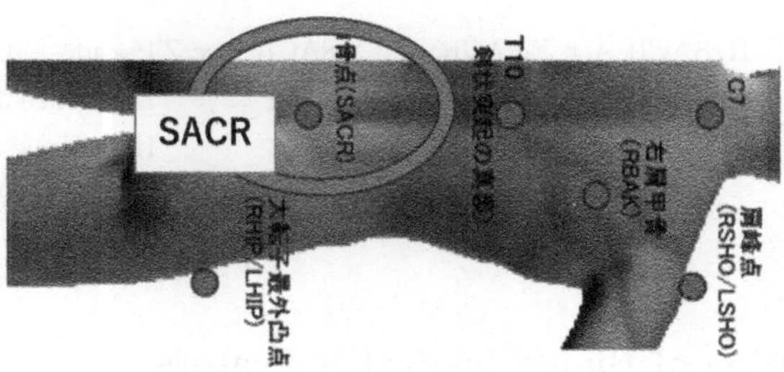

Fig. 1. Marker placement: SACR was used as model input [10].

Marker and force plate data were filtered using a fourth-order Butterworth low-pass filter (cut-off frequencies: 6 Hz for marker coordinates and 10 Hz for vertical ground reaction force). The events were obtained by referring to the RTO and RHS timestamps provided in the gait database. Using these events, we identified the swing phase corresponding to the calculation of the maximum knee flexion angle (KFA). Finally, to ensure data integrity, we filtered trials based on the criteria in Table 1.

Table 1. Data exclusion criteria: Trials were excluded based on gait event validity, measurement reliability, and physiological plausibility.

Category	Metric/Criteria	Reason for Exclusion
Gait Events	RHS/RTO Timestamps	Missing timestamps or invalid RTO–RHS pairs
	Event Timing	Time of maximum knee flexion within ±50 ms of RTO (detection shift)
Measurement	Marker Data	NaN values in ≥5% of total frames for required positions
	Segment Length	Femur or lower leg length outside 0.3–0.5 m (marker displacement)
Physiological plausibility	Knee Joint Angle	Angle outside 0–140° (kinematic inconsistency)
	vGRF	Peak vertical ground reaction force outside 0.4–2.5 BW (abnormal contact)

Table 2 illustrates the final structure of the dataset, showing the input features derived from the SACR marker and their corresponding pseudo-labels used for training and evaluation. In addition, Table 3 summarizes the dataset and experimental setup used for training and evaluation of the machine learning models. Based on the biomechanical criteria defined in the Sect. 3.2, pseudo-labels were automatically assigned to the walking trials in the AIST gait database. We give precise definitions and calculation methods for these variables in the next section.

Table 2. Structure of the input features and labels: Each segment includes subject ID, three-axis SACR acceleration, and a pseudo-label (high-/low-knee-load walking).

Segment ID	Subject ID	SACR Acc_X	SACR Acc_Y	SACR Acc_Z	Pseudo-Label
Subject1_R01	001	0.123	−0.456	0.882	Low Knee Joint Load Walking
Subject1_R02	001	0.145	−0.420	0.913	High Knee Joint Load Walking
Subject2_R01	002	0.111	−0.380	0.757	Low Knee Joint Load Walking

4.3 Computation of Biomechanical Indicators

Preprocessing and Calculation Methods of Knee Joint Angle Data: The sagittal plane flexion–extension angle of the right knee was calculated based

Table 3. Dataset and experimental setup: Summary of data source, SACR signal preprocessing, pseudo-labeling criteria (KFA and vGRF), and subject-wise validation strategy

Item	Description
Dataset	
Data source	AIST Gait Database 2019
Total gait trials	1337 (Subjects: 278)
Inclusion criteria	Right-foot start, successful event processing
Acceleration Processing	
Selected markers	SACR (lumbar)
Preprocessing	4th-order Butterworth LPF (6 Hz)
Derivation	Second-order differentiation (X, Y, Z axes)
Labeling	
Pseudo-label	High Knee Joint Load Walking: Knee Flex. $\notin [52°, 70°]$ OR vGRF > 1.3 BW
Distribution	Low: 978 (73.1%), High: 359 (26.9%)
Validation	
Train/Test set split	Subject-wise split (8:2) using GroupShuffleSplit

on the internal angle (Θ_{internal}) between the thigh and shank segments. We calculated the joint centers, hip_center, knee_center, and ankle_center, using markers based on the standard midpoint-based definitions provided by Vicon cite [19]. Segment vectors were then defined as in Eqs. 1 and 2.

$$\mathbf{v}_{\text{thigh}} = \text{hip\_center} - \text{knee\_center} \tag{1}$$

$$\mathbf{v}_{\text{shank}} = \text{ankle\_center} - \text{knee\_center} \tag{2}$$

Using the dot product, the flexion angle Θ_{flex} was derived such that 180° of Θ_{internal} represents full extension (see Eq. 3):

$$\Theta_{\text{flex}} = 180° - \arccos\left(\frac{\mathbf{v}\text{thigh} \cdot \mathbf{v}\text{shank}}{\|\mathbf{v}\text{thigh}\|\|\mathbf{v}\text{shank}\|}\right) \tag{3}$$

The maximum value of knee flexion during the swing phase of the right leg Θ_{flex} was extracted as a key gait indicator.

Preprocessing and Calculation Methods of vGRF Data: This study focused on the overall maximum normalized vGRF during the stance phase to quantify lower-limb loading. We defined the total vGRF as the maximum vertical force $\max_{i=1,\ldots,7}(F_i(t))$ across all seven force plates at each time step. To account for individual differences in body mass, $v\text{GRF}_{\max}$ was normalized by body weight (BW) and gravitational acceleration ($g = 9.81$ m/s^2). We treated it as a dimensionless indicator $v\text{GRF}_{\text{norm,max}}$ (see Eq. 4): This normalized peak value was used as the primary feature representing mechanical impact.

$$v\text{GRF}_{\text{norm,max}} = \frac{\max_t(v\text{GRF}(t))}{\text{BW} \times 9.81} \tag{4}$$

5 Feature Selection and Comparison of Machine Learning Models

Figure 2 illustrates the overall learning pipeline used in this study. The entire pipeline was repeated 10 times using different random states, and the final performance was reported as the average over all repetitions.

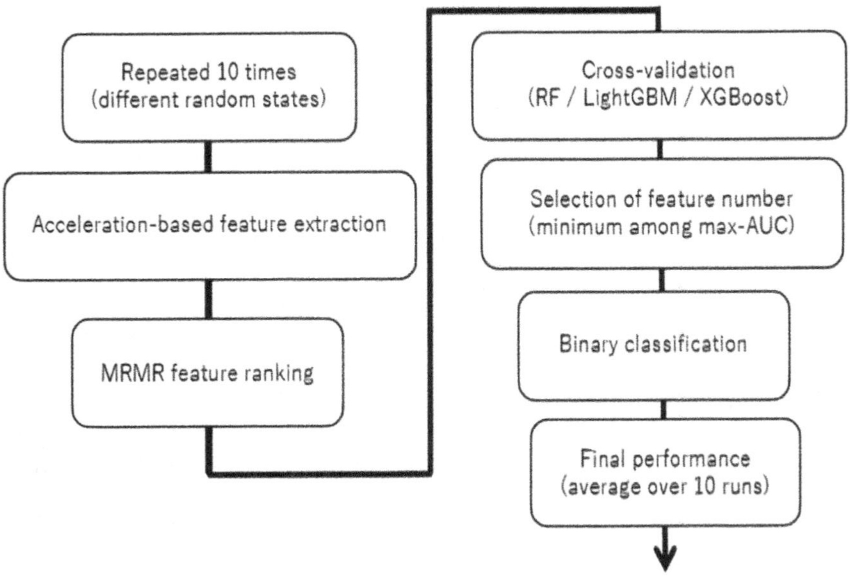

Fig. 2. Overview of the learning pipeline: Workflow showing feature extraction from SACR acceleration, mRMR-based selection, and supervised classification of knee-load conditions.

5.1 Acceleration-Based Feature Extraction and Selection

This study used the acceleration signals corresponding to 1.5 steps, calculated from the 3D coordinates of the SACR marker, as the main input data for feature extraction in the machine learning model. First, regarding the acceleration of the SACR marker, we extracted conventional features from the Time and frequency domains. Table 4 summarizes the calculated features.

To increase feature diversity beyond conventional Time and Frequency domains, this study employed tsfresh [4] to extract multi-domain features from waist acceleration signals automatically. This process resulted in the extraction of a total of 2,966 features, encompassing various domains such as time-domain, frequency-domain, time-frequency combinations, and autocorrelation-related characteristics. Features were removed with a missing value rate of 10%

Table 4. Conventional time- and frequency-domain features: These features extracted for comparison with the proposed multi-domain set.

Category	Extracted features
Per-axis acceleration	Mean, standard deviation
Acceleration magnitude	Mean, maximum, minimum, RMS, skewness, kurtosis
Frequency-domain (PSD)	Total power (area under PSD curve), peak frequency, frequency at 50% cumulative power
Event-based feature	Peak acceleration magnitude within 0.15 s from IC

or more, and input the remaining missing values using the median of each feature.

To mitigate overfitting due to high feature dimensionality and redundancy, a two-step feature selection procedure was employed. First, features were ranked using Minimum Redundancy Maximum Relevance (mRMR). Second, the optimal number of features was determined by comparing ROC-AUC scores under subject-wise cross-validation using three tree-based models: Random Forest, LightGBM, and XGBoost. These models were chosen because they can capture non-linear relationships without feature scaling and offer high computational efficiency. The final feature set size was selected as the minimum number of features that achieved the highest ROC-AUC across these models, balancing generalizability and simplicity.

mRMR was applied only to acceleration-based features, whereas subject attributes (sex, age, height, and weight) were always included in both feature sets. This decision was motivated by prior findings suggesting that physical factors contribute to variability in walking patterns [5]. Including these attributes allows the evaluation of acceleration-derived features while accounting for individual differences.

5.2 Results of the Classification Experiments

The mRMR selection showed that multi-domain features consistently selected across seeds spanned multiple domains, including temporal variability, frequency characteristics, distributional properties, and autocorrelation. Notably, many of the top-ranked features were derived from the vertical acceleration component relative to gravity, particularly change-quantile-based statistics, indicating that fluctuations in vertical motion play a key role in characterizing high-load gait. In the conventional time- and frequency- domain features set, mRMR consistently selected variability-related statistics, particularly standard deviation–based features, across almost all seeds. It suggests that fluctuations in acceleration signals, rather than their mean values, play a central role in characterizing gait associated with knee load. Furthermore, even when including subject characteristics for Multi-domain Features, the mRMR-based ranking of features derived from

Table 5. Classification performance of multi-domain features: Mean and SD of PR-AUC and ROC-AUC for each classifier.

Model	PR-AUC (mean ± SD)	ROC-AUC (mean ± SD)
Random Forest	0.638 ± 0.028	0.756 ± 0.021
SVM	0.640 ± 0.025	0.766 ± 0.016
Logistic Regression	0.651 ± 0.020	0.768 ± 0.014
XGBoost	0.644 ± 0.027	0.758 ± 0.021
LightGBM	0.637 ± 0.029	0.757 ± 0.021
Extra Trees	0.654 ± 0.024	0.771 ± 0.021
MLP	0.646 ± 0.026	0.768 ± 0.017

Table 6. Classification performance of conventional time- and frequency- domain features with subject attributes: Comparison of multi-domain features using the same evaluation metrics.

Model	PR-AUC (mean ± SD)	ROC-AUC (mean ± SD)
Random Forest	0.555 ± 0.029	0.691 ± 0.019
SVM	0.570 ± 0.024	0.706 ± 0.018
Logistic Regression	0.576 ± 0.021	0.701 ± 0.018
XGBoost	0.565 ± 0.038	0.702 ± 0.018
LightGBM	0.564 ± 0.028	0.701 ± 0.022
Extra Trees	0.577 ± 0.022	0.702 ± 0.018
MLP	0.564 ± 0.022	0.698 ± 0.018

acceleration did not change. Therefore, it was confirmed that feature selection is determined more by the dynamics of walking than by physical factors.

In this study, we compared the classification performance with Multiple machine learning models (Logistic Regression, Support Vector Machine (SVM), Random Forest, Extra-trees, XGBoost, LightGBM, and Multi-Layer Perceptron (MLP)). Due to the label imbalance shown in Table 3, we decided to use ROC-AUC as the main evaluation metric. Table 5 shows the results of an analysis using the minimum number of mRMR-selected multi-domain features with subject attributes. Table 6 shows the results of an analysis using the minimum number of mRMR-selected conventional time- and frequency-domain features with subject attributes.

When using mRMR-selected multi-domain features combined with subject attributes, the models achieved ROC-AUC values in the range of approximately 0.75 to 0.77. In contrast, conventional time- and frequency-domain features yielded lower, with ROC-AUC values hovering around 0.69 to 0.70. Furthermore, as shown in the Fig. 3, multi-domain features significantly outperformed conventional time- and frequency-domain features across all tested machine learning models ($p < 0.01$, Wilcoxon signed-rank test).

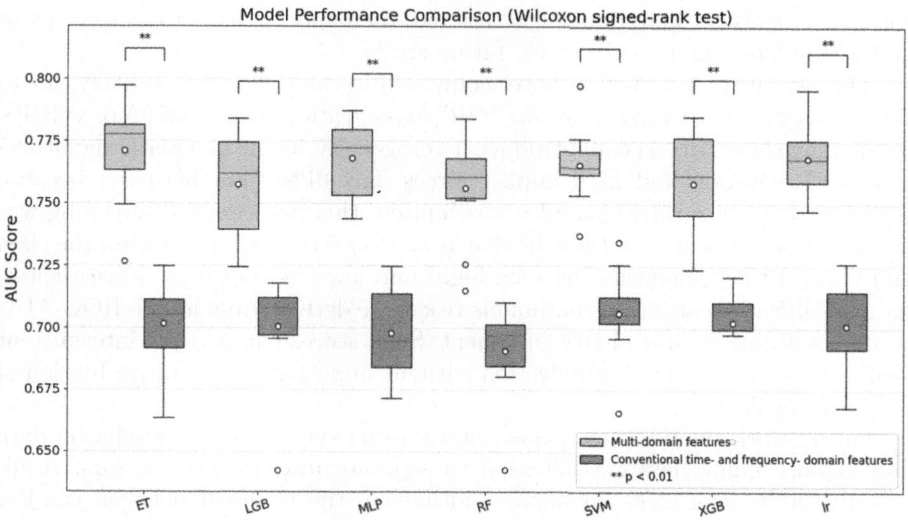

Fig. 3. Comparison of model performance between multi-domain and conventional time- and frequency-domain.

For all models, the difference between PR-AUC and ROC-AUC was small, and the standard deviation was generally less than 2% for ROC-AUC and less than 3% for PR-AUC. No model significantly outperformed the others across all evaluation settings, indicating that the classification performance among the evaluated models was generally similar. This suggests that the classification performance depends more on the discriminative power of the input features than on the choice of algorithm. Furthermore, in all experiments, the PR-AUC values were consistently lower than the ROC-AUC values. This difference reflects the class imbalance in the pseudo labels.

Moreover, for the multi-domain features, the classification accuracy of the minimal mRMR-selected feature set was comparable to, or slightly higher than, that of the maximal set.

6 Discussion and Conclusion

In this study, we defined "High Knee Joint Load Walking" on the literature reported KFA and vGRF thresholds during walking. While this approach does not directly measure knee joint moments or the burden on cartilage, it potentially captures multifaceted knee loading aspects beyond single biomechanical indicators. Lumbar acceleration data successfully estimated these loading conditions, with multi-domain features achieving a stable ROC-AUC of approximately 0.75. This suggests that capturing heterogeneous multifaceted assessment incorporating features such as signal characteristics (e.g., magnitude, spectral structure, and regularity) is crucial for gait classification. While time–frequency and autocorrelation features were frequently selected, their specific links to gait events or motor control remain a subject for future study.

The reason the PR-AUC is lower compared to the ROC-AUC is likely due to the heterogeneity introduced by our "OR" classification criteria (KFA or vGRF). Combining these criteria can introduce heterogeneity, as the kinematic signatures of excessive flexion and high impact forces may differ. Furthermore, because the occurrence of positive samples was limited, this risk-oriented screening was necessary. As a result, it is thought that it increased the variance within the class and blurred the boundaries between high- and low-load patterns. Nevertheless, for daily-life applications, a continuous risk score derived from a high ROC-AUC is more suitable than a binary judgment. Such scores can provide intermittent feedback and encourage self-reflection without imposing the cognitive burden of frequent notifications.

Future work should refine these criteria using symptomatic population data and explore multi-class classification to separate internal load factors. Additionally, addressing class imbalance, optimizing the trade-off between window latency and stability, and considering other sensor placement (e.g., at the ankle) will be essential to improve accuracy and better capture localized impacts or compensatory movements.

References

1. Akiba, S.: Super walking that can eliminate pain, poor health, and illness (2025). in Japanese
2. Bacca, O., Celestino, M.L., Barela, J.A., Barela, A.M.F.: Identification of stiff-knee gait in stroke survivors. BMC Biomed. Eng. **7**(1), 11 (2025)
3. Bailo, G., et al.: Characterization of walking in mild Parkinson's disease: reliability, validity and discriminant ability of the six-minute walk test instrumented with a single inertial sensor. Sensors **24**(2), 662 (2024)
4. Christ, M., Braun, N., Neuffer, J., Kempa-Liehr, A.W.: Time series feature extraction on basis of scalable hypothesis tests (tsfresh-a python package). Neurocomputing **307**, 72–77 (2018)
5. EXercise motivation and Physical function Augmentation Research Team: Aist gait attribute assessment system Holmes 2020 (in Japanese). https://unit.aist.go.jp/harc/ExPART/holmes.html (2019). Accessed 10 Jan 2026
6. Fuchioka Laboratory, Graduate School of Rehabilitation Science Osaka Metropolitan University: Abnormal gait (pathological gait) (in Japanese). https://www.omu.ac.jp/reha/fuchioka-lab/index_10.html. Accessed 21 Dec 2025
7. Hiyama, T., Sato, Y., Shiotani, M., Ozawa, J., Kobayashi, Y.: Correlation analysis between walking features measured by accelerometer and gyroscope sensors and lower limb muscle strength indoors and outdoors. J. Soci. Biomech. **25**, 81–93 (2020). (in Japanese)
8. Kobayashi, Y.: Application example: Aist walking database and walking evaluation technology based on it. J. Soc. Biomech. **40**(3), 179–182 (2016). (in Japanese)
9. Kobayashi, Y.: Evaluation of walking function in daily life: Development of the gait attribute classification system Holmes. J. Soc. Biomech. **46**(1), 3–8 (2022). (in Japanese)

10. Kobayashi, Y., Hida, N., Nakajima, K., Fujimoto, M., Mochimaru, M.: 2019: Aist gait database 2019 (2019). https://unit.aist.go.jp/harc/ExPART/GDB2019.html. Accessed 1 Oct 2025
11. Kumar, N., Pankaj, D., Mahajan, A., Kumar, A., Sohi, B.: Evaluation of normal gait using electro-goniometer. J. Sci. Ind. Res. **68**(8), 696–698 (2009)
12. Li, X., Xu, H., Cheung, J.T.: Gait-force model and inertial measurement unit-based measurements: a new approach for gait analysis and balance monitoring. J. Exerc. Sci. Fitness **14**(2), 60–66 (2016)
13. Makikawa, M.: Monitoring daily physical activity using an accelerometer. Jap. Soc. Med. Biol. Eng. **54**(3), 96–103 (2016). (in Japanese)
14. Minister of Health, Labour and Welfare of Japan: Statement on frailty from the japan geriatrics society (in Japanese) (2014). https://jpn-geriat-soc.or.jp/info/topics/pdf/20140513_01_01.pdf. Accessed 5 Sep 2025
15. National Institute of Population and Social Security Research: Population projections for Japan: 2021–2070 (with long-range population projections: 2071–2120) (2023). https://www.ipss.go.jp/pp-zenkoku/j/zenkoku2023/pp2023_ReportALLc.pdf. Accessed 5 Sep 2025
16. Perry, J., Burnfield, J.: Gait Analysis: Normal and Pathological Function. CRC Press (2024)
17. Semwal, V.B., Gaud, N., Lalwani, P., Bijalwan, V., Alok, A.K.: Pattern identification of different human joints for different human walking styles using inertial measurement unit (IMU) sensor. Artif. Intell. Rev. **55**(2), 1149–1169 (2022)
18. Stacoff, A., Diezi, C., Luder, G., Stüssi, E., Kramers-de Quervain, I.A.: Ground reaction forces on stairs: effects of stair inclination and age. Gait Posture **21**(1), 24–38 (2005)
19. Vicon Motion Systems Limited.: Plug-in gait reference guide (2023). https://help.vicon.com/download/attachments/11378719/Plug-in%20Gait%20Reference%20Guide.pdf. Accessed 12 Jan 2026
20. Zeighami, A., Dumas, R., Aissaoui, R.: Knee loading in OA subjects is correlated to flexion and adduction moments and to contact point locations. Sci. Rep. **11**(1), 8594 (2021)

Development of a Motion Recognition Model for Learning Activities Using a Smartwatch

Mizuho Hiruma[1(✉)], Mikimasa Omori[2], and Guillaume Lopez[1]

[1] Aoyama Gakuin University, Tokyo, Japan
{mhiruma,guillaume}@wil-aoyama.jp
[2] Waseda University, Tokyo, Japan
mikkiomori@waseda.jp

Abstract. This study aims to construct a machine learning model that identifies learning behaviors during study using motion sensor data from a smartwatch. In group classes, it is difficult to objectively grasp learners' states, and quantitative evaluation methods are required. In this study, as a fundamental technology for future estimation of learning states, we focus on free learning behaviors and build a model that identifies six types of learning behaviors using accelerometer, gyroscope, and rotation vector sensors. Using data collected from university students, graduate students, and elementary school students, we constructed a total of 945 patterns of learning datasets by combining window sizes, labeling methods, and other factors, and comparatively evaluated the classification performance of four methods: LightGBM, Random Forest, k-NN, and SVM. As a result, high classification accuracy was obtained for major learning-related actions such as writing and stationary, and furthermore, we clarified conditions that emphasize the reliability of learning behaviors and conditions that emphasize the detection of non-learning behaviors.

Keywords: Smartwatch · Motion sensors · Learning behavior recognition · Machine learning · Education support

1 Introduction

In recent years, in educational settings, the fixation of students' difficulties with studying has become an issue. Approximately seventy percent of students become aware of their difficulties with studying during their elementary and lower secondary school years [15]. In addition, given the current shortage of teachers, the opportunities for students to overcome their difficulties with studying are decreasing, bringing about the fixation of such weakness [9]. Moreover, at present, approximately 200,000 students with disabilities are enrolled in regular classes nationwide [8]. However, because conditions such as learning disabilities (LD) are difficult to distinguish, it is highly likely that the potential number of relevant individuals exceeds the statistics. If such students are left without

E. Vlahu-Gjorgievska et al. (Eds.): PERSUASIVE 2026, CCIS 2896, pp. 476–487, 2027.
https://doi.org/10.1007/978-3-032-27235-5_50

receiving appropriate support, there is a risk of secondary difficulties, such as a decline in self-esteem and school refusal; therefore, early detection and connection to appropriate support are indispensable. However, a lack of observational resources due to a severe shortage of teachers makes early response in the field difficult.

Given these backgrounds, there is a need for a system that can grasp students' detailed learning states without increasing the burden on teachers. Therefore, in this study, as a foundational technology for future estimation of learners' learning states, we focus on learning behaviors during study activities and investigate a behavior recognition method using motion sensor data acquired from a smartwatch. Specifically, we construct a machine learning model to classify multiple learning-related behaviors, including writing, being stationary, using an eraser, purposeless movement, purposeful movement involving relocation, and purposeful movement without relocation, based on data from acceleration, gyroscope, and rotation vector sensors. The objective of this study is to clarify the effects of window size, labeling methods, sensor combinations, and feature patterns on classification performance.

2 Related Work

Numerous studies have investigated character recognition and writing behavior recognition using motion sensors embedded in smartwatches and other wearable devices [1,2,5–7,12–14,19,20]. These studies commonly measure wrist movements using accelerometer and gyroscope sensors to identify characters or writing strokes, and some additionally utilize rotation vector data. However, most existing approaches focus on constrained motion conditions or single-task scenarios, which makes it difficult to comprehensively handle the diverse and unconstrained behaviors that occur during actual learning activities.

In contrast to these previous studies, this work focuses on motion sensor data that can be acquired using a smartwatch alone and is characterized by its ability to recognize unconstrained learning behaviors occurring during study activities. In particular, by subdividing behaviors other than "writing" and systematically comparing window sizes, labeling methods, multiple sensor configurations, and feature designs, this study aims to clarify design guidelines for learning behavior recognition.

3 Definition of Learning Behavior and Data Collection

3.1 Definition of Learning Behaviors

In this study, we focus on writing actions and related behaviors that occur during learning and perform behavior recognition using motion sensor data obtained from a smartwatch. Learning behaviors are diverse, and simply distinguishing whether a learner is "writing" or not is insufficient to capture their learning state. Therefore, we classified learning behaviors into six categories and clearly defined each; the defined learning behaviors are shown in Table 1.

Table 1. Definitions and Classification of Learning-Related Actions in This Study.

Label	Action Name	Definition and Examples of Specific Movements
w	Writing	Writing characters or figures; pen tip in contact with paper
e	Erasing	Using an eraser to correct content
s	Stationary	No movement; complete stillness
np	Non-purposeful movement	Unrelated to learning, e.g., touching face, adjusting hair
pi	Purposeful movement with relocation	Learning-related movement involving relocation, e.g., page turn
ps	Purposeful movement without relocation	Learning-related movement without relocation, e.g., changing pen

3.2 Data Collection Experimental

In the experiment, participants sat on a chair, wore a smartwatch on the dominant hand, and worked on the presented learning tasks. In addition, the learning behaviors at hand were video-recorded by a camera installed on the desk.

Considering individual differences in learning behavior and differences in characteristics by age group, a total of 13 participants were selected: 9 right-handed university and graduate students (male–female ratio 4:5) and 4 right-handed elementary school students (male–female ratio 3:1) who exhibited tendencies consistent with autism spectrum disorder (ASD). The measurement time was one hour per university/graduate student and 8–10 min per elementary school student, and a total of approximately 9 h and 40 min of data were obtained (of which approximately 9 h were subject to analysis).

For the experimental tasks, university and graduate students were given three subjects—Japanese, mathematics, and English—in random order (20 min each, total 1 h). Learning worksheets published on the web by education professionals were used for the tasks [10,16,17]. On the other hand, elementary school students performed tasks using self-created problems for copying words/sentences and diary writing, with approximately 8–10 min per person. The details of the contents are as shown in Table 2.

In order to measure natural behaviors close to daily life, the experimental environment for university and graduate students was set at the desks they usually use for research or learning, and they used their own writing instruments. For elementary school students, we placed a simple desk in the meeting room of the cooperating organization, NPO Linkage [11], and the experiment was conducted there.

Table 2. Details of Experimental Tasks for University and Graduate Students.

Subject	Details
Jaoanese (University students)	Essay-style questions focusing on modern Japanese texts
English (University students)	Grammar review test for high school first- and second-year level
Mathematic (University students)s	Review test on Mathematics I and A for new second-year high school students
Writing Task (Elementary students)	Copying presented Hiragana, Kanji, and sentences exactly as shown
Diary Task (Elementary students)	Writing a diary entry about the events of the previous day

3.3 Devices Used

In this study, we used a smartwatch (Google Pixel Watch [3]) to acquire inertial sensor data, a video recording device (GoPro HERO11 Black [4]), and an annotation software (ELAN [18]) to assign ground-truth labels. Referring to prior studies, accelerometer, gyroscope, and rotation vector were selected as sensors [5,7,12–14,19,20].

The sampling frequency was set to 300 Hz to secure sufficient temporal resolution, taking into account later resampling.

4 Method for Constructing Learning Behavior Dataset

4.1 Data Preprocessing

We pre-processed data according to the following four steps, described in detail hereafter: unnecessary segments removal, resampling, low-pass filtering, and forward-backward filtering.

Unnecessary Segments Removal. We deleted intervals defined as "non (not subject to analysis)" at the annotation stage. Specifically, intervals in which the movement of the participant's dominant hand left the camera's field of view and became unrecognizable were treated as not subject to analysis. By this, the uncertainty of ground-truth labels was eliminated, and the reliability of training and evaluation of the machine learning models was ensured.

Resampling. Because the sampling interval of the smartwatch sensor data is not constant, we applied cubic spline interpolation to the accelerometer and gyroscope sensor data, and spherical linear interpolation was applied to the rotation vector in order to preserve the properties of quaternions. We assigned label information by nearest-neighbor interpolation, and all data were unified to 100 Hz. The selection of the resampling frequency (100 Hz) was based on prior studies [14,20]. Besides, in order to prevent artificial motion generation by interpolation across unnecessary segments, locations where the time difference of consecutive samples exceeded 0.5 s were detected, and the segments before and after were split as separate sections. By performing resampling for each section, data shaping based on actual learning behaviors was achieved.

Signal Filtering. To suppress high-frequency noise while preserving task-relevant motion features, we applied a low-pass filter to each component of the accelerometer, gyroscope, and rotation vector. Specifically, a 4th-order Butterworth filter was selected due to its maximally flat frequency response in the passband, following the methodology of previous studies [5,19]. The cutoff frequency was set to 20 Hz, as prior research has demonstrated that the essential frequency components of writing movements are concentrated below this threshold [14]. Furthermore, we implemented this as a forward–backward filter (zero-phase filtering) to eliminate the phase delay inherent in recursive filters. This process ensures the temporal structure of the movements is preserved, maintaining precise alignment between the sensor data and the ground-truth label boundaries.

4.2 Window Segmentation and Window Label Determination Logic

Next, window segmentation and the determination of window labels were performed. The statistics of the duration of each action label are shown in Table 3. Since the minimum value of the mean duration was 1.24 s (ps) and the maximum value was 5.23 s (s), the window sizes for comparison were set from 1.0 s to 5.0 s. In addition, to prevent missing action boundaries, the step size was set to 50% of the window length.

Furthermore, when multiple labels are mixed within one window, it is necessary to determine which to assign to that window. In this study, with reference to a prior research [14], a decision algorithm based on label occupancy ratio was adopted. Four patterns of occupancy thresholds at 10% increments from 20% to 50%, and one majority-vote method, making a total of five patterns, were compared. When multiple labels exceeded the threshold, priority was given to actions with shorter mean duration as shown in Table 3, so that short but important actions would not be buried under long-duration actions such as stationary.($ps > e > pi > np > w > s$) In addition, at locations where the time interval exceeded 0.015 s (1.5 times the sampling period of 0.01 s), temporal continuity was judged to be lost, and window generation across that interval was controlled so as not to be performed.

4.3 Feature Extraction

A total of 26 types of features were extracted from each window. A list of the extracted features is shown in Table 4. These features were selected with reference to multiple prior studies [1,6,13,14].

Table 3. Duration statistics of each action label. (seconds)

Label	Number	Mean	Std.	Min	25th	Median	75th	Max
w	2280	4.92	5.20	0.15	1.68	3.35	6.56	94.51
e	271	1.48	1.15	0.38	0.87	1.24	1.72	10.80
s	1867	5.23	5.80	0.47	1.90	3.31	6.18	76.58
np	2276	2.89	4.64	0.23	1.22	1.95	3.31	120.67
pi	1410	1.49	1.79	0.27	0.79	1.00	1.42	35.79
ps	816	1.24	0.70	0.30	0.83	1.08	1.44	7.13

Besides, since SMA and SVM are indices representing the strength of movement with respect to gravitational acceleration, they were applied only to the accelerometer sensor. For the calculation of frequency-domain features, a Hanning window was applied to each window before performing a fast Fourier transform, from which we extracted the spectrum amplitude and normalized it by the data length. In addition, when values within a window became constant, and coefficients such as correlation became NaN, these were complemented as 0, thereby constructing feature vectors with no missing values.

Table 4. List of extracted features.

Category	Feature items
Statistical features (time domain)	Mean, median, standard deviation, mean absolute deviation, interquartile range (IQR), maximum, minimum, inter-axis correlation, entropy, kurtosis, zero-crossing count, signal magnitude area (SMA)*, signal vector magnitude (SVM)*
Frequency-domain features	Mean, median, standard deviation, mean absolute deviation, IQR, maximum, minimum, mean absolute error, max–min difference, number of values above the mean, skewness, kurtosis, energy

*Applied only to the accelerometer

4.4 Construction of Comparison Patterns for Learning Datasets

To identify the optimal conditions for learning behavior recognition, a total of 945 learning datasets were constructed by systematically combining window sizes, window labeling rules, sensor combinations, and feature pattern configurations. The considered combinations are summarized as follows:

1. Window size: 9 patterns (from 1.0 s to 5.0 s with 0.5 s increments)
2. Window labeling rules: 5 patterns (thresholds of 20%, 30%, 40%, and 50%, as well as majority voting)

3. Sensor combinations: 7 patterns (accelerometer, gyroscope, and rotation vector; all non-empty combinations of the three sensors, i.e., $2^3 - 1 = 7$)
4. Feature patterns: 3 patterns (statistical features only, frequency-domain features only, and a combination of both)

4.5 Selected Machine Learning Models and Two-Phase Evaluation Process

We compared four machine-learning models: LightGBM, Random Forest, k-Nearest Neighbour (KNN), and Support Vector Machine. To reduce computational cost, we conducted the evaluation in two phases.

1. Phase 1: Considering computational cost, all 945 patterns were evaluated using three models, excluding Support Vector Machine.
2. Phase 2: From the top three scores for each metric F1-macro, Accuracy, F1_np, F1_pi, and F1_ps, a total of the top 15 patterns were extracted, and SVM was applied to those.

Also, we performed standardization in k-NN and Support Vector Machine. Furthermore, stratified five-fold cross-validation was conducted at the window level to evaluate the discriminative performance. While this window-level split is primarily intended as an initial verification to identify the optimal combinations of window sizes and window labeling rules among 945 candidate patterns, we acknowledge that it may provide an optimistic estimation of generalization to unseen users. Therefore, subject-independent evaluation is positioned as a critical focus for our future work.

5 Results and Discussions

5.1 Selection of High-Performing Patterns from Multi-parameter Analysis

In Phase 1, as combinations of window sizes, labeling methods, sensor combinations, and feature pattern configurations, a total of 945 parameter conditions were evaluated with three models. As a result, from the top three conditions for each of the five metrics (a total of 15 conditions) shown in Sect. 4.5, 12 non-duplicated patterns were extracted. The extracted conditions are summed up in Table 5.

5.2 Model-Wise Performance Comparison (F1-Macro)

In Phase 2, for the extracted 12 patterns, four models—LightGBM, Random Forest, k-NN, and SVM- were applied, and discrimination performance was compared. As a result, the maximum value of F1-macro was 0.699 for the condition of window size 1.5 s, tagging threshold 40%, AccGyroRot, statistical features only, and LightGBM.

Table 5. Experimental Conditions Showing Top Results for Each Evaluation Metric. (Phase 2 Evaluation Subset)

No.	Selection	Window Size	Tagging	Feature Type	F1/Acc Score
1	F1-macro	1.5 s	40%	Stat	0.699
2	F1-macro	1.5 s	30%	Stat	0.698
3	F1-macro	1.5 s	Majority	Both	0.697
4	Accuracy	3.5 s	50%	Both	0.796
5	Accuracy	3.5 s	Majority	Both	0.796
6	Accuracy	1.5 s	50%	Both	0.795
7	F1-np	5.0 s	20%	Both	0.675
8	F1-np	4.5 s	20%	Stat	0.675
9	F1-np	5.0 s	20%	Stat	0.672
10	F1-pi	2.5 s	20%	Stat	0.612
11	F1-pi	2.5 s	20%	Both	0.605
12	F1-pi	3.0 s	20%	Stat	0.605
13	F1-ps	5.0 s	20%	Stat	0.649
14	F1-ps	5.0 s	20%	Both	0.646
15	F1-ps	4.5 s	20%	Stat	0.645

Note: A total of 12 non-duplicate patterns were used for model comparison.

Note: *Stat* denotes statistical features; *Both* denotes statistical and frequency-domain features.

However, in this dataset, the number of data for "w" and "s" is very large (Approximately 60% of the total), and F1-macro is strongly affected by these classes. Therefore, deciding the optimal conditions using only F1-macro is not necessarily optimal for the purpose of this study.

5.3 Impact of Class Imbalance and Redesign of Evaluation Metrics

In this study, the number of data for "w" (writing) and "s" (stationary) is very large compared to other classes. As a result, the discrimination accuracy of these classes dominates the overall evaluation metrics, and performance differences of fine and important actions specific to this study, such as "np" (non-purposeful movement), "pi" (purposeful movement with relocation) and "ps" (purposeful movement without relocation) may be buried. Also, "e" (erasing) has an extremely small amount of data and has an event-like nature that occurs for a short time, accompanying other learning behaviors. For this reason, in this study, we positioned "e" as auxiliary information and excluded it from the main evaluation, and instead focused on "np," "pi," and "ps."

Although "w" (writing) and "s" (stationary) dominate the dataset in terms of sample size, their classification performance is consistently high across all 12 extracted evaluation conditions, with average F1-scores of 0.8173 and 0.8428, respectively. This indicates that the proposed models can reliably recognize the major learning-related actions, such as writing and stationary.

Therefore, excluding "w" and "s" from the main evaluation does not imply neglecting their importance, but rather prevents these dominant classes from masking performance differences among finer actions, justifying the focus on "np," "pi," and "ps" for learning state estimation.

5.4 Detailed Analysis Focusing on "Learning State" and "Unlearning State"

"pi" (purposeful movement with relocation) and "ps" (purposeful movement without relocation) are grouped as "during-learning," and "np" (non-purposeful movement) is grouped as "not-during-learning," and performance evaluation is conducted for these two groups. The reason for adopting such grouping is the final goal of this study is to grasp students' detailed learning states without increasing the burden on teachers. That is, rather than strictly discriminating action labels themselves, "confusion among actions corresponding to during learning" is acceptable, whereas "confusion between learning actions and unlearning actions" should be avoided as much as possible. From this viewpoint, evaluation focusing on "np," "pi," and "ps" is considered to be more suited to the purpose of this study.

Based on this evaluation policy, as new metrics, Learning State Precision (LSP) for the during-learning group and Unlearning State Recall (ULSR) for the not-during-learning group were introduced. LSP is an index representing the probability that actions judged by the system as "during learning" are actually during learning, and is important for preventing mistaken support decisions in classroom instruction. On the other hand, ULSR is an index indicating to what extent actions that are actually not during learning can be detected without being missed, and is useful for early detection of students deviating from learning.

5.5 Performance Evaluation of LSP and ULSR

As a result of the evaluation, for LSP, the condition of Random Forest (`W2.5_T20_AccGyroRot_OnlyStat`) was the maximum (0.7891), and for ULSR, the condition of Random Forest (`W5.0_T20_AccGyroRot_OnlyStat`) was the maximum (0.7419). The classification performance for the condition where LSP was maximized is shown in Table 6, while that for ULSR is presented in Table 7.

Table 6. Classification performance for not-during-learning and during-learning groups under the LSP maximum condition

Group (Action Label)	Precision	Recall	F1-score	Support
Not-during-learning (np)	0.617	0.697	0.654	6,949
During-learning (pi + ps)	**0.789**	0.576	0.666	4,910

Table 7. Classification performance for not-during-learning and during-learning groups under the ULSR maximum condition

Group (Action Label)	Precision	Recall	F1-score	Support
Not-during-learning (np)	0.596	**0.742**	0.661	4,091
During-learning (pi + ps)	0.759	0.491	0.596	2,460

Comparing the classification performance of the condition where Learning State Precision (LSP) became the maximum and the condition where Unlearning State Recall (ULSR) became the maximum, since the conditions other than window size are completely identical, it becomes clear that the difference in window size greatly affects discrimination tendencies.

In the LSP-max condition, using a middle window size (2.5 s) contributed to the high reliability of samples classified as "during-learning." This can be attributed to the fact that the average duration of "pi" and "ps" is approximately 1.5 s (standard deviation: 0.7–1.8 s), meaning a 2.5 s window is sufficient to cover these actions. Furthermore, since "pi" and "ps" have higher priority in the window labeling rules, these factors combined to improve the precision of the "during-learning" class.

In contrast, in the ULSR-max condition, by setting the window size to the largest (5.0 s) among those examined in this study, the temporal continuity of motions is considered, and the detection rate of non-learning behavior (np) improved.

The point that a tagging threshold of 20% is commonly selected in both conditions suggests that a setting in which labels are fixed even for a small number of actions is effective for motion estimation in this study. On the other hand, it became clear that, depending on the choice of window size, a trade-off arises between emphasizing the reliability of during-learning and emphasizing the detection of non-learning behaviors. These results indicate the possibility of an operating method that switches window size and evaluation metrics according to the purpose of the class and the arrangement of teachers.

6 Conclusion and Future Work

Our study aims to improve the quality of classroom instruction by automatically estimating students' learning behaviors to grasp their detailed learning states, all without increasing the burden on teachers. We classified learning behaviors into six categories: writing (w), erasing (e), stationary (s), non-purposeful movement (np), purposeful movement with relocation (pi), and purposeful movement without relocation (ps). We constructed a learning-behavior recognition model using the accelerometer, gyroscope, and rotation vector data obtained from a smartwatch and quantitatively evaluated its performance, examining window size, window labeling rule, sensor combinations, and feature patterns.

Across 2,847 ($945 * 3 + 12$) comparative trials, the highest F1-macro score of 0.699 was achieved by a LightGBM model under the conditions of a 1.5 s window size, a 40% labeling threshold, the AccGyroRot sensor combination, and statistical features only. Besides, stable and high recognition accuracy was confirmed for major actions such as writing and stationary.

On the other hand, challenges remained in discriminating between learning-related behaviors (pi, ps) and non-learning behaviors (np), indicating that it is difficult to determine practically optimal conditions solely based on F1-macro. The results demonstrate that, depending on educational contexts, it is possible to switch between emphasizing the reliability of learning-state estimation and suppressing the oversight of non-learning behaviors. Overall, this study confirms the feasibility of smartwatch-based learning-behavior recognition and establishes a foundation for learning-state estimation in group lessons.

Building on the findings of this study, future work will proceed in the following four directions.

- Action label definitions will be re-examined. Since actions with similar physical characteristics (pi, ps, np) are difficult to distinguish, a two-stage approach will be explored. This involves separating physical action recognition from learning-intent estimation based on biological indicators such as heart rate, and then integrating these two stages to improve classification performance.
- Since the current dataset is limited to a specific age range (university and elementary school students), learning-behavior data will be collected from a wider range of age groups, including junior high and high school students, to improve model generalization.
- The performance of deep learning methods, such as CNNs, will be compared with the current approach to evaluate their ability to automatically extract sensor-signal features beyond hand-crafted features and further improve recognition accuracy.
- Real-time recognition and instructor feedback methods will be investigated by designing low-latency learning-state estimation and intuitive visualization or notification interfaces for practical educational settings.

References

1. Alona, L., Ben, N., Yuval, E., Erez, S.: Handwritten signature verification using wrist-worn devices. Proc. ACM Interact. Mob. Wearable Ubiquitous Technol. **2**(3), 119 (2018)
2. Dipyaman, B., Prasenjit, D., Vijay, E., Ruhi, SharmaMittaland Nitendra, R., Sonia, S.: Handwriting recognition using wrist-worn motion sensors. International Business Machines Corporation (2019)
3. Google, Inc., USA: Google pixel watch technical and device specifications. https://support.google.com/googlepixelwatch/answer/12651869?hl=JA
4. GoPro, Inc., USA: Gopro hero11 black. https://gopro.com/ja/jp/shop/cameras/hero11-black/CHDHX-111-master.html?
5. Hao, J., Dong, W., Qian, Z., Run, Z.: Motion eavesdropper: smartwatch-based handwriting recognition using deep learning. In: International Conference on Multimodal Interaction (ICMI '19), pp. 145–153 (2019)

6. Isaac, G.S., Richard, M., Abdul, S.: Wearables-driven freeform handwriting authentication. IEEE Trans. Biometrics, Behav., Identity Sci. **1**(3) (2019)
7. Luca, A., Pascal, B., Philipp, B., Roger, W.: Recognizing text using motion data from a smartwatch. In: IEEE International Conference on Pervasive Computing and Communication Workshops, PerCom Workshops (2016)
8. Ministry of Education, Culture, Sports, Science and Technology: Fy2022 survey results on the status of part-time classroom instruction. https://www.mext.go.jp/content/20241107-mxt_tokubetu02-000032436_2.pdf. (in Japanese)
9. Ministry of Education, Culture, Sports, Science and Technology: Survey on the "teacher shortage". https://www.mext.go.jp/a_menu/shotou/kyoin/mext_00003.html. (in Japanese)
10. Nisso, M.: Dialogue and Japanese (self-study problem collection and resource page) (modern Japanese problem collection, specialized in descriptive writing). https://kokugo-senka.top/materials/. (in Japanese)
11. NPO_Linkage. https://npo-linkage.net/
12. Qingxin, X., Feng, H., Yuan, F., Zhongwen, G.: MotionHacker: motion sensor based eavesdropping on handwriting via smartwatch. In: IEEE Conference on Computer Communications Workshops, INFOCOM Wksps (2018)
13. Raveen, W., Anindya, M., Murtuza, J.: deWristified: handwriting inference using wrist-based motion sensors revisited. In: WiSec '19: Proceedings of the 12th Conference on Security and Privacy in Wireless and Mobile Networks, pp. 49–59 (2019)
14. Sonia, S., Dipyaman, B., Vinayak, N.: Detecting writing micro-events using motion sensors in smartwatches. In: 19th International Conference on Distributed Computing in Smart Systems and the Internet of Things (DCOSS-IoT) (2023)
15. Studyplus Co., Ltd.: The feeling of being bad at both humanities and science subjects is largely formed in elementary and junior high school, and science tends to stumble in high school students as it is subdivided into subjects such as "physics" and "chemistry". https://info.studyplus.co.jp/716. (in Japanese)
16. Suken Shuppan: ICT service for supporting learning at home (high school English). https://www.chart.co.jp/sp/ict2020_fprint_e.html. (in Japanese)
17. Suken Shuppan: ICT service for supporting learning at home (high school mathematics). https://www.chart.co.jp/sp/ict2020_fprint.html. (in Japanese)
18. The Language Archive: Elan | the language archive. https://archive.mpi.nl/tla/elan
19. Xinye, L., Yixin, C., Xiao-Wen, C., Xue, L., Xiaodong, W.: Show: smart handwriting on watches. Proc. ACM Interact., Mob., Wearable Ubiquitous Technol. **1**(4), 1–23 (2018)
20. Yujia, L., Kaisheng, Y., Geoffrey, Z.: Feedback-based handwriting recognition from inertial sensor data for wearable devices. In: IEEE International Conference on Acoustics, Speech and Signal Processing (ICASSP), pp. 2269–2273 (2015)

How Touch-Based Engagement Map on Teamwork Outcome Assists Positive Feedback Formulation?

Kazuaki Kondo[1(✉)], Masaki Shuzo[2], Kenta Abe[3], Atsuo Tsuchiya[2], and Motoki Sakai[4]

[1] Kyoto University, Yoshida-honmachi, Sakyo-ku, Kyoto, Japan
kondo@ccm.media.kyoto-u.ac.jp
[2] Shonan Institute of Technology, 1-1-25 Tsujido-Nishikaigan, Fujisawa, Japan
[3] Teikyo University, 359 Otsuka, Hachioji, Tokyo, Japan
[4] Nihon University, 1 Nakagawara, Tokusada, Tamuramachi, Koriyama, Japan

Abstract. This study examines a methodology for leveraging visualized engagement metrics, derived from teamwork activity logs, to support the formulation of positive feedback statements. The core concept of the proposed method involves projecting the time spent for physical sub-tasks onto the structural components of the teamwork outcome. This approach is predicated on the expectation that the spatial distribution of a participant's engagement correlates with their effort allocation and contribution patterns. Using the "Paper-Tower" challenge as a representative case study, we generated engagement maps for the individual components of the constructed towers. These visualizations served as an analytic tool for a feedback provider to generate structured statements consisting of "Fact" and its "Effect" within the teamwork. Our analysis demonstrates that the proposed engagement map assists the extraction of objective facts regarding individual effort or the division of responsibility, and enables the seamless integration of these facts with evaluative statements concerning their positive effects on the final outcome.

Keywords: Teamwork · Positive Feedback · Engagement Visualization · Physical contact

1 Introduction

Teamwork is defined as a collective activity in which members share common objectives and collaboratively perform tasks. It is particularly essential for planning and managing complex projects that exceed individual capabilities. In daily life, this collaboration occurs in various forms, such as cooperative cooking, cleaning shared living spaces, or re-configuring room layouts. When a team functions effectively, two primary benefits are anticipated. First, the quality of the outcome and efficiency of overall production are improved. Second, individual well-being is enhanced through the social connections fostered during collaboration.

E. Vlahu-Gjorgievska et al. (Eds.): PERSUASIVE 2026, CCIS 2896, pp. 488–500, 2027.
https://doi.org/10.1007/978-3-032-27235-5_51

This positive psychological effect contributes to the maintenance of a stable and healthy mental state in everyday life.

However, several challenges must be addressed to realize the aforementioned benefits of teamwork. A critical issue lies in the difficulty of discerning individual contributions to the teamwork outcome. When personal actions–such as opinions or strategic decisions–are unrecognized by evaluators, individuals tend to perceive the evaluation as unfair [7]. Also such isolation is negatively correlated with perceived respect within the team [4]. Persistent exposure to these bad perceptions can lead to a significant decline in a participant's motivation to engage in collaborative activities.

The objective of this research is to assist third-party facilitators to formulate constructive and positive feedback for individual participants. To achieve this, we propose a visualization framework termed the "Engagement Map," which projects the duration of each participant's physical engagement onto the teamwork outcome. The proposed methodology is predicated on the following two core concepts.

- **Visualizing engagement time.** Individual effort and contributions to teamwork that participants often desire to be recognized are inherently semantic and subjective. Automatic estimation of these factors often result in unstable and unreliable. To address this, this study employs engagement duration as a measurable physical metric. We hypothesize that this measurable metric serves as a reliable correlate for the abstract dimensions of teamwork contribution and effort.
- **Projecting engagement time onto the teamwork outcome.** Even if engagement duration provides a quantitative metric for contribution and effort, it lacks the granularity required for formulating effective feedback statements. The proposed method visualizes engagement time in relation to each component of the teamwork outcome. The spatial distribution of engagement across the product elucidates individual contribution profiles and the interpersonal collaboration.

2 Related Works

Various approaches have been proposed to enhance awareness of participant's engagement. In scenarios involving opinion exchange and consensus-building through discussion, volume of utterance is frequently utilized as a proxy for engagement intensity. For instance, Lesh et al. integrated a feedback interface, termed the "Group Meter," into text-based chat software to visualize communication history statistics [9]. This interface displays the total word count for each participant and the corresponding percentage of agreement-related terms. The authors reported that teams receiving this feedback exhibited a higher frequency of agreement in their conversations and demonstrated a greater focus on the content of posted messages. DiMicco et al. developed a similar interface for face-to-face interactions, where the total duration of each participant's utterances is visualized via a bar chart [6]. Through this feedback, participants became aware of cognitive biases and adjusted their level of engagement in subsequent conversations; specifically, dominant speakers tended to moderate their talk, while previously hesitant participants became more active. Maldonado et al. focused on behavioral participation. They developed a collaborative workspace featuring a tangible tabletop device for interactive concept mapping [11,12]. Their feedback interface quantifies behavioral engagement by counting editing events, such as the generation, deletion, and relocation of keywords, as well as the modification of connections between them. By comparing verbal and behavioral participation, instructors managing the group work can more easily identify disproportionate participation patterns.

In contrast to real-time feedback for awareness, engagement processes have been leveraged for post-hoc analysis and teamwork reflection. South et al. developed a video browser designed for analyzing debates among political specialists, which visualizes interaction patterns and agreement-disagreement dynamics on a timeline-based map [17]. Similarly, Shi et al. quantified the degree of topic sharing in discussion scenarios by analyzing the co-occurrence of key-phrases between participants [15]. Their visualization named "MeetingVis" employs a metaphor of a metro map, where the temporal and interpersonal alignment of topics is illustrated by the proximity of curves representing individual participants. By integrating this with topic segmentation and word clouds for content visualization, the system enables users to efficiently grasp a story line of the discussion.

Our proposed framework shares a common scheme with conventional approaches that project participant's engagement onto the user-generated products. For instance, Ogawa et al. adopted a chronological mapping technique to identify which workers simultaneously engaging in the specific source code module [14]. In the domain of collaborative writing, Wang et al. visualized temporal evolution of the shared document based on the amount of textual modifications by multiple editors [18]. However, these aforementioned approaches do not explicitly link participant engagement with the inherent structure of the product. Consequently, their contribution to the positive feedback formulation has not been fully examined.

3 Engagement Map for Constructive Feedback

This study considers two primary stakeholders in the feedback process for teamwork reflection:

- **Feedback recipients** A significant number of participants exhibit low self-esteem and a tendency to underestimate their contributions to task achievement or interpersonal cooperation. This difficulty in maintaining an objective perspective on their own behavior often leads to self-deprecating cognitive biases.

- **Feedback providers or formulators** For the aforementioned individuals, the receipt of positive feedback is crucial to enhancing long term motivation and fostering more active engagement within the team. External evaluators–such as colleagues, educators, or mentors–play a vital role to identify and validate contributive behaviors that the recipients themselves may have overlooked or undervalued.

When providing feedback, it is essential to explicitly identify the specific behaviors being evaluated. Such evidence-based feedback is widely recognized for its persuasiveness, effectively fostering motivation and encouragement in the recipient [3,8]. Conversely, vague feedback risks being dismissed as perfunctory praise, which may lead recipients to perceive that their actual activities has not been genuinely assessed. This lack of specificity can inadvertently diminish the recipient's trust in the feedback provider.

Several frameworks have been developed to formulate constructive feedback in career development contexts. One such approach is the EEC scheme, which structures feedback into three components: a specific (E)xample of behavior, its (E)ffect on teamwork, and a concluding (C)ongratulations or proposal for (C)hange. For instance, a feedback statement might be formulated as follows: "You distributed the detailed document beforehand", "It enabled a diverse and productive discussion", and then "Therefore it was a highly meaningful conference". Similarly, the SBI scheme [3], developed by the Center for Creative Leadership, employs a comparable methodology. The "Situation and Behavior" (referred to as "Fact" in this study) and "Impact" components within the SBI model correspond directly to the "Example" and "Effect" elements in the EEC scheme, respectively.

However, formulating the aforementioned fact-and-effect style feedback presents a significant challenge for external providers, as it requires comprehensive and continuous observation of the recipient's behaviors within the team. While video recordings provide a potential means for such observation, the process of reviewing extensive log is both labor-intensive and time-consuming. To mitigate this issue, the proposed visualization of engagement duration is expected to assist feedback formulators in the following two aspects:

1. **Efficient discovery of "Facts"** The typical process of formulating the fact-and-effect feedback requires identifying either a fact or an effect from teamwork records, and subsequently seeking the other one that can be logically connected to the identified one. By summarizing and visualizing the distribution of each participant's engagement that are often latent or non-obvious in raw data, the proposed system enables formulators to rapidly identify the specific "Facts" that recipients desire to be recognized or evaluated.
2. **Justification of given feedback** Feedback with only verbal accounts or qualitative statements often lacks evidential support. Providing the engagement map as supplementary evidence facilitates the recipient's cognitive acceptance of the given feedback, thereby enhancing its perceived validity.

4 Target Teamwork

This study examines the effectiveness of engagement maps in a small-scale teamwork task. We select a team exercise called "Tower-Building Challenge" [1,2,19], in which several participants are asked to construct the tallest freestanding tower as they can using limited materials. Only paper sheets are available in the cases used in this study. Paper sheets may be folded, bent, or cut, but any additional tool, such as adhesive tapes or scissors, is unavailable. Figure 1 shows the snapshot pictures captured in this "Paper-Tower" trial.

The reasons for selecting Paper-tower challenge are as follows. (1) The teamwork outcome–a built tower at the end of the trial–is visible and clear as shown in the right picture in Fig. 1. (2) The task goal is clear and does not require specialized knowledge or skills to accomplish. Anyone can contribute to the task in some way. (3) By setting limits on time and the number of available paper sheets, cooperation naturally emerges for quick and efficient assembly. (4) As trying in multiple times, participant's approach to tackling the task and the ways they collaborate with each other will change. These (2–4) are desired to be extracted as positive feedback contents. (5) It can be implemented in a short time and small space, making it easy to record and analyze.

Fig. 1. Snapshots of the Paper-Tower challenge.

5 Touch-Based Engagement Measurement

Engagement in tower building, such as shaping, moving, or assembling paper components, necessarily involves physical contact with them. The proposed method considers touching the paper components as physical engagement in tower building task, and touching time as engagement duration. Note that multiple participants may be touching the same paper component at the same time, for example, when passing a paper component or when one participant is supporting and the other participant is assembling the same paper component.

For each paper component, we represent who and when touched information with $touch_i^{j,k} = (t_s, t_e), 0 < i < N_{component}, 0 < j < N_{participant}, 0 \leq k \leq n(i,j)$, where $i, j, k, n(i,j), t_s, t_e$ denote the paper index, the participant index, and the touching number index, the total number of touch, the start and end time of the touch, respectively. The touching duration D is defined with $t_e - t_s$.

The engagement duration is aggregated and normalized to obtain the following two engagement metrics reflecting different aspects of engagement.

- **Normalized engagement among components** $E_{component}$ indicates that how long time the target participant engaged in each paper component, relatively. It gives 1.0 value for the paper component with longest duration in his or her touch. No other participant's touch is considered.

$$E_{component}(i,j) = \frac{\Sigma_k D(i,j,k)}{max_j\{\Sigma_k D(i,j,k)\}} \tag{1}$$

- **Normalized engagement among participants** $E_{participant}$ indicates that how long time the target paper component was engaged by each participant, relatively. It gives 1.0 value when only one participant was touching it. No touching other components is considered.

$$E_{participant}(i,j) = \frac{\Sigma_k D(i,j,k)}{\Sigma_i \Sigma_k D(i,j,k)} \tag{2}$$

6 Experimental Analysis

6.1 Visualization Results of Engagement Map

Using the several Paper-Tower trials in the dataset, we analyzed the effectiveness of the proposed method. As a preliminary experiment, a feedback provider who did not participate the trials formulated positive feedback statements with pairs of "fact" and "effect" by looking at the generated engagement maps. Figure 2 shows the engagement map results of the two consecutive trials conducted with 20 paper sheets, 10 min. time limit, and the same group of three participants. To focus on verifying the effects of the engagement map itself, we used the ground truth touching data $touch_i^{j,k}$ shown in Fig. 3 obtained by manually checking video records. See the chapter X for possibility of automatic recognition. With the same reason, we prohibited the feedback provider to refer the touch event distribution information Fig. 3.

6.2 Analysis of Engagement Maps and Feedback Statements

The feedback statement results shown in Table 1 indicate that the proposed engagement map would make it easy to find the following information.

How the Target Participant Engaged in the Teamwork Outcome. Effort patterns were intuitively estimated ; almost equal engagement across multiple paper components (Fact1) and engagement concentration on specific paper component (Fact2). We also identified several facts connecting to the contribution on task achievement, such as the relationship between engagement duration and component placement (Fact6), shape of component, and physical hierarchy in the tower, i.e. higher, lower, or same-layer positioning (Fact5). Even for the components not used in the final tower structure (Fact8), we can recognize who and how long engaged in them. This is unhappy fact for the participant because his or her effort did not contribute to the teamwork outcome. However, the proposed method enables another person to notice the effort. One problem is impression dependency on apparent size or shape of the component. For example, the components indicated with (d) in Fig. 2 have a similar engagement duration, but stronger impression is perceived for the components with larger area.

How Participants were Cooperating. The engagement maps for $E_{participant}$ shown in the lower rows of the each figure reveal the engagement patterns among the participants; component sharing (Fact3) and clear division among components (Fact4). Those patterns suggest complementary work on the same component and shared responsibility (working division) for multiple components, respectively. Especially, Fig. 2(b) highlights the highly exclusive engagement among participants, which indicates the clear role division. Additionally, this engagement pattern interestingly matches hierarchical relationship in the tower structure is also interesting. Such relationship between the role division and the task features is useful for identifying "effect" part of positive feedback statement.

How Engagement Pattern was Changing. By comparing Fig. 2(a) and (b), we can see how the participants improved the strategy for the tower building task through multiple trials. The obvious differences are the role division getting clearer and the longer pillars constructing the most upper layer than those in the previous trial (Fact7). Those facts would lead positive statements relating to team growing or sophisticated approaches to the task.

Interestingly, the positive statements are connected as "effect" to the two "facts" in an opposite relationship, for example the overlapping and exclusive engagement patterns appearing as Fact 3 and 4 in P_{blu}. This is because the feedback formulator in the experiment applied psychological technique called re-framing to the straightforward "effect" lead from "fact". It has been clarified that we must consider re-framing of "effect" to design what and how "fact" should be provided to feedback formulators.

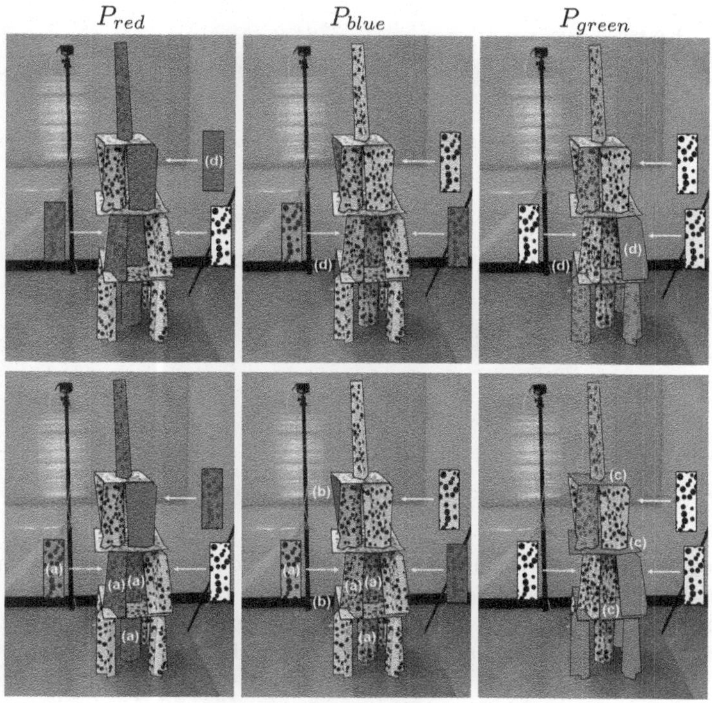

(a) the 2nd trial

(b) the 3rd trial

Fig. 2. Engagement map results of the two consecutive Paper-tower trials. The three participants are distinguished by red, blue, and green colors. The thicker color indicates longer engagement time. The top and bottom row of each trial is generated with the metric $E_{component}$ and $E_{participant}$, respectively. The yellow arrows indicate the invisible components due to being backside or inside of the tower. (Color figure online)

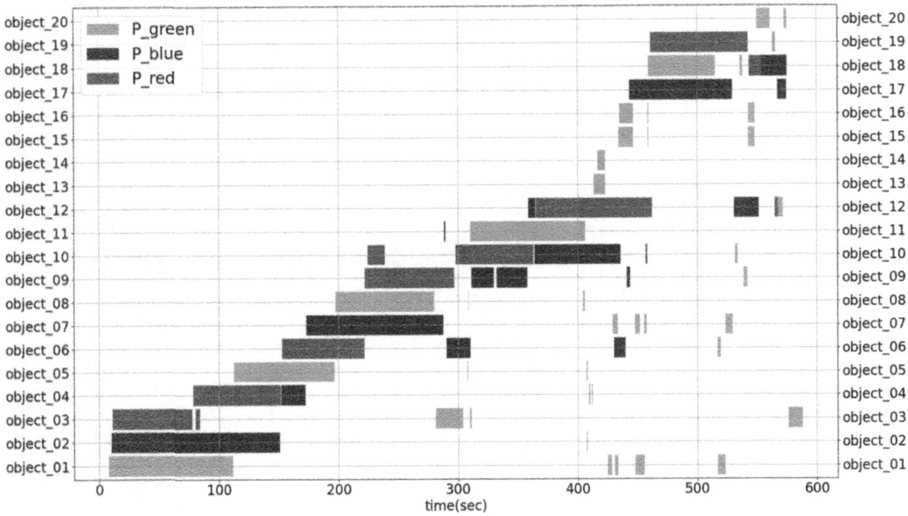

Fig. 3. An example of the timeline visualization of the detected touch fragments. The horizontal and vertical axes indicate time in the target Paper-tower trial and the paper component index, respectively. The "folding paper" sub-task causes long touches in most cases, while the "moving" and "stacking" sub-tasks cause shorter touches.

6.3 Discussion for Remaining Issues

Process Tracing. The proposed method simply shows the accumulation of the engagement duration trough the teamwork. It does not capture the process over time. Therefore, it remains unclear whether the cooperative engagement was intentional or independent work coincidentally achieved a cooperative pattern. Tracing back to the behaviors or interactions resulting in the engagement map would reveal various "fact" for positive feedback. The timeline visualization of touch events shown in Fig. 3 can tell process of teamwork through their temporal distribution and order of occurrences. However, temporal sequences such as "someone engaged in the component after you" and "you used the component shaped by someone" are weak facts to identify convincing "effect" statements "contributing to subsequent work" and "taking over other's work", respectively. We need process information that contains causality among multiple engagement events.

Categorizing and Characterizing Engaging Behaviors. The proposed method only addressed if the participants contact with paper components. The engagement map does not reveal how the participant dealt with the components. In the paper-tower dataset we used, the time used for the "folding a paper sheet to make it a tower component" sub-task was significantly longer than for the "moving" and "stacking" sub-tasks, as shown in Fig. 3. Therefore, the engagement time spent on the "folding" sub-task dominates the map shown in Fig. 2. This is one reason why no significant difference is observed between the results $E_{component}(i, j)$

and $E_{participant}(i, j)$ shown in the upper and lower row of the engagement map results, respectively. The current resolution of engagement map is not sufficient to recognize how sub-task features were relating to the engagement distribution. Additionally, the engagement duration also depends on difficulty of the sub-task and how the participant want to deal with the component. Sub-tasks should be categorized and characterized to generate engagement maps in multiple viewpoints. It would enable us to find more diverse and deeper facts occurring in the teamwork.

Automatic Recognition of Touching and Touched Objects. Several approaches have been developed to detect hand-object contact in unconstrained environment [5,10,13,16]. To enhance detection accuracy, depth information from RGB-D cameras can be incorporated. Occlusion–particularly mutual occlusion between participants and the constructed tower–is a substantial problem in real-world group work scenarios. To address this in Paper-Tower challenge, we implemented a dual-camera setup positioned at opposite longitudinal ends of the workspace. This recording setup is designed to mitigate severe self-occlusions and ensure that hand-object contact can be captured by at least one camera when the other's view is obstructed.

In addition to touch detection, it is necessary to identify which object being touched and which part the object composes in the teamwork outcome. This object recognition is critical because estimation failure of an object label can lead to great error in the engagement map. Accurate recognition and robust tracking are achieved by printing easily distinguishable patterns on paper sheets or by leveraging object motion constraints imposed by hand movements.

Applicability for Other Styles of Teamwork. The core concept of the engagement map can be applicable to any group-work scenario if they yield observable outcomes. The framework operates under two essential criteria: (1) the outcome must consist of multiple components, and (2) the relationships among these components must reflect the semantic structure of the final product. In the Paper-Tower challenge, these conditions are satisfied by the vertical hierarchy and the specific functional roles of the components, such as pillars and floors. Group discussions–where a presentation serves as the outcome–represent a potential application if the target of engagement is clearly specified. In this context, projecting engagement onto the outcome can be interpreted as identifying where and who's opinions appear within the presentation slides or speech.

Table 1. Examples of generated positive feedback statements. P_{color} corresponds to each participant shown in the engagement map Fig. 2

Trial	Participant	Element	Statement
2nd	P_{red}	Fact1	The time spent is equivalent for multiple paper components, which means that you engaged in both components worked on first and later
		Effect1	The careful assembling of the components resulted in the stable tower
2nd	P_{red}	Fact2	You spent more time than others when handling the topmost component
		Effect2	You much engaged in the most unstable and difficult component for stacking, contributing significantly to height of the tower
2nd	P_{blue}	Fact3	You shared engagement time with P_{red} for approximately half of the components (Fig. 2(a))
		Effect3	It might not have been intentional, but you and P_{red} were cooperating
2nd	P_{blue}	Fact4	Almost only you engaged in the two components marked with (b) in Fig. 2
		Effect4	You completed assembling for those components without requiring additional involvement from other members
2nd	P_{green}	Fact5	You engaged in the components constructing the bottom layer for long time
3rd		Effect5	You contributed to the foundation components for stability of the tower
2nd	P_{green}	Fact6	You were responsible for the horizontal components forming the floors (Fig. 2(c))
3rd		Effect6	Because you made the flat floors, the pillar components were stably stacked on them
3rd	P_{red}	Fact7	You used longer pillars for the top layer than those in the previous trial
		Effect7	Is it your idea for satisfying both a stable and taller tower?
3rd	$P_{red}P_{blue}$	Fact8	Your effort were spent for also the components not used in the tower at the end
		Effect8	Adding those components could make the tower taller if there had been more time
3rd	$P_{red}P_{blue}P_{green}$	Fact9	Engagements of you three were not overlapped among the components
		Effect9	The role division was well established among you

7 Conclusion

In this study, we investigated how engagement information derived from teamwork logs assists the formulation of positive feedback statements to enhance participants' motivation. The key idea of the proposed method is to visualize the engagement time spent for physical working that is expected to correlate with participant's effort or contribution to teamwork. Through the analyses of the feedback statements constructed by pairs of "fact" and "effect", we have confirmed that the proposed engagement map enables to find "fact" reflecting participant's effort or responsibility division among paper components can be identified, and also enables to connect the positive "effect" statement with the obtained fact. The limitations of the proposed method had also been identified. Tracing teamwork process and categorizing engagement behaviors to generate multi-aspect engagement maps would provide more diverse "fact" for feedback.

Acknowledgments. This research was supported by the JKA Foundation through its Machinery Promotion Program (KEIRIN) (Grant No. 2025M-334). The authors would like to express their sincere appreciation to all those involved.

References

1. Marchmallow challenge. http://www.marshmallowchallenge.com. Accessed 08 Jan 2026
2. Paper-tower challenge. https://www.playmeo.com/activities/team-building-problem-solving-activities/paper-tower/. Accessed 08 Jan 2026
3. Feedback That Works: How to Build and Deliver Your Message (Second Edition). Center for Creative Leadership (2019)
4. Bartel, C.A., Wrzesniewski, A., Wiesenfeld, B.M.: Knowing where you stand: physical isolation, perceived respect, and organizational identification among virtual employees. Organ. Sci. **23**(3), 743–757 (2012)
5. Cao, Z., Radosavovic, I., Kanazawa, A., Malik, J.: Reconstructing hand-object interactions in the wild. In: 2021 IEEE/CVF International Conference on Computer Vision (ICCV), pp. 12397–12406 (2021)
6. DiMicco, J.M., Hollenbach, K.J., Pandolfo, A., Bender, W.: The impact of increased awareness while face-to-face. Hum.-Comput. Interact. **22**(1–2), 47–96 (2007)
7. Earley, P.C., Lind, E.A.: Procedural justice and participation in task selection: the role of control in mediating justice judgments. J. Pers. Soc. Psychol. **52**(6), 1148–1160 (1987)
8. Ilgen, D.R., Fisher, C.D., Taylor, M.S.: Consequences of individual feedback on behavior in organizations. J. Appl. Psychol. **64**(4), 349–371 (1979)
9. Leshed, G., et al.: Visualizing real-time language-based feedback on teamwork behavior in computer-mediated groups. In: Proceedings of the SIGCHI Conference on Human Factors in Computing Systems, pp. 537–546 (2009)
10. Li, W., Wan, Y., Wu, X., Wang, J., Dai, P., Yuan, Z.: HopNet: learning hand-object-person interaction network for hand contact state detection. In: Proceedings of the 33rd ACM International Conference on Multimedia, pp. 8058–8066 (2025)
11. Martinez-Maldonado, R., Collins, A., Kay, J., Yacef, K.: Who did what? Who said that? Collaid: an environment for capturing traces of collaborative learning at the tabletop. In: Proceedings of the ACM International Conference on Interactive Tabletops and Surfaces, ITS '11, pp. 172–181 (2011)

12. Martinez-Maldonado, R., Kay, J., Yacef, K., Edbauer, M., Dimitriadis, Y.: MTClassroom and MTDashboard: supporting analysis of teacher attention in an orchestrated multi-tabletop classroom. In: International Conference on Computer Supported Collaborative Learning (CSCL2013), vol. 1, pp. 320–327 (2013)
13. Narasimhaswamy, S., Nguyen, T., Nguyen, M.H.: Detecting hands and recognizing physical contact in the wild. In: Advances in Neural Information Processing Systems, vol. 33, pp. 7841–7851 (2020)
14. Ogawa, M., Ma, K.L.: Software evolution storylines. In: Proceedings of the 5th International Symposium on Software Visualization, pp. 35–42 (2010)
15. Shi, Y., Bryan, C., Bhamidipati, S., Zhao, Y., Zhang, Y., Ma, K.L.: MeetingVis: visual narratives to assist in recalling meeting context and content. IEEE Trans. Visual Comput. Graphics **24**(6), 1918–1929 (2018)
16. Shiota, T., Takagi, M., Kumagai, K., Seshimo, H., Aono, Y.: Egocentric action recognition by capturing hand-object contact and object state. In: 2024 IEEE/CVF Winter Conference on Applications of Computer Vision (WACV), pp. 6527–6537 (2024)
17. South, L., Schwab, M., Beauchamp, N., Wang, L., Wihbey, J., Borkin, M.A.: DebateVis: visualizing political debates for non-expert users. In: 2020 IEEE Visualization Conference (VIS), pp. 241–245 (2020)
18. Wang, D., Olson, J.S., Zhang, J., Nguyen, T., Olson, G.M.: DocuViz: visualizing collaborative writing. In: Proceedings of the 33rd Annual ACM Conference on Human Factors in Computing Systems, CHI '15, pp. 1865–1874 (2015)
19. Wujec, T.: Build a tower, build a team, in ted2010. https://www.youtube.com/watch?v=H0_yKBitO8M. Accessed 08 Jan 2026

Support System for Preventing Forgetfulness Before Going Out Using Mixed Reality

Taito Kume(✉) and Guillaume Lopez

Aoyama Gakuin University, 5-10-1 Fuchinobe, Chuo-ku, Sagamihara, Kanagawa 252-5258, Japan
tkume@wil-aoyama.jp, guillaume@it.aoyama.ac.jp

Abstract. Forgetting belongings and failing to turn off appliances are frequent daily issues that cause economic loss and psychological anxiety. Conventional countermeasures, such as smartphone lists, often fail due to the split-attention effect or physical constraints during hectic departure situations. This paper proposes a Mixed Reality system designed to support departure preparation by complementing human memory and attention. The system, implemented on Microsoft HoloLens 2, integrates image recognition and IoT device control to overlay confirmation statuses directly onto physical objects. It enables hands-free verification by automatically detecting item possession through hand tracking. A comparative experiment with 16 participants evaluated the system's effectiveness against memory-based and PC-checklist methods. Quantitative results demonstrated that the proposed system achieved a 0% error rate and significantly reduced movement and search time. Qualitatively, the system recorded significantly lower mental workload scores on the NASA-TLX and a high System Usability Scale score of 81.6, surpassing standard digital interfaces. These findings suggest that Mixed Reality spatial guidance significantly enhances the security and efficiency of departure routines.

Keywords: MR · Departure Support · Forgetfulness Prevention

1 Introduction

In modern society, busy schedules and information overload contribute to the daily problem of "forgetting items." Forgetting belongings such as keys, wallets, and smartphones leads to economic loss, security risks, and mental stress. People search for lost items in their homes an average of 3.2 times per month [5], yet existing solutions remain inadequate. While many use analog methods such as designating fixed locations, these depend on human memory and break down when users are hurried or tired. Smart tags using Bluetooth technology have emerged, but only 9.2% of people adopt them [9], as they focus on "post-incident response" rather than departure prevention. Beyond forgetting belongings, about

E. Vlahu-Gjorgievska et al. (Eds.): PERSUASIVE 2026, CCIS 2896, pp. 501–512, 2027.
https://doi.org/10.1007/978-3-032-27235-5_52

40% of people feel anxious about forgetting to turn off appliances or lock doors [11], with unlocked doors accounting for over 30% of burglary intrusions [6].

From a human-computer interaction perspective, standard confirmation interfaces—smartphone apps and paper lists—have critical flaws in hectic departure situations. The spatial mismatch between 2D lists and 3D target objects causes cognitive load [3], while physical constraints when hands are occupied create situational disability [7,10]. These limitations highlight the need for a new support system that overlays information directly on target objects and enables hands-free confirmation.

This research proposes a mixed reality(MR) system that complements human memory and attention to reduce psychological and temporal burdens in departure preparation. The system integrates image recognition for item detection and IoT device status acquisition, overlaying confirmation results in real space. The specific goals are:

1. Implementing a real-time detection and guidance function that warns of deficiencies and indicates completion.
2. Verifying the effectiveness of the guidance function through subject experiments in terms of work accuracy, required time, and psychological security

2 Related Work

This section reviews existing research on forgetting item prevention and item search support, organizing them by technical approach and identifying critical limitations that remain unaddressed.

2.1 Reminder and Prevention Approaches

Several systems have been proposed to prevent forgetting items through physical constraints or sensor-based monitoring.

Physical constraint-based methods, such as *KAI-chan* [1], ensure confirmation by linking voice dialogue with smart locks that prevent door unlocking until item checking is complete. While achieving high certainty, these approaches often impose psychological stress when users are in a hurry.

Sensor-based approaches utilize tags to detect item presence. Borriello et al. [2] proposed a system using passive RFID tags to monitor the contents of a bag and prompt users with reminders when essential items are missing. While effective for specific tagged objects, these systems require instrumenting every target item with physical tags and installing readers, which introduces significant deployment costs and maintenance efforts compared to vision-based approaches.

2.2 Search Support and Monitoring Systems

When prevention fails or items are misplaced, search support systems become crucial. Recent advancements have focused on camera-based monitoring and Augmented Reality (AR) visualization.

AI-driven monitoring systems, such as CamFi [12], utilize fixed cameras and deep learning to track object movements and assist users in finding lost items, even in multi-person scenarios. While powerful for wide-area monitoring, fixed camera solutions often suffer from blind spots and privacy concerns in private living spaces.

Wearable AR approaches address these issues by providing egocentric visual guidance. Funk et al. [4] demonstrated that presenting actual landscape images of last-seen locations outperforms 2D maps in reducing search time. However, this image-based approach becomes problematic when room layouts change. Oshimi et al. [8] proposed LocatAR, which automatically records object locations through continuous hand tracking and visualizes 3D movement paths in AR space. This enables users to trace back where items were placed without manual input.

Summary and Distinction: In summary, existing approaches face two critical limitations. First, most systems focus on either "prevention" or "recovery" independently; reminder systems prevent leaving but lack **search support** when items are misplaced inside the home, while search systems are typically **post-incident (reactive)** measures that do not prevent the act of forgetting itself. Second, reliable solutions often require **large-scale setups**, such as instrumenting every target object with RFID tags [2] or installing fixed cameras throughout the living environment [12], which increases deployment costs and privacy concerns.

Our proposed MR system addresses these challenges by utilizing the HoloLens 2 to integrate **preventive** checklists with **real-time search guidance**. By leveraging egocentric spatial recognition, our approach eliminates the need for environmental sensors or physical tags, providing a seamless, hands-free support system that covers both preparation and search phases with a single wearable device.

3 System Design

3.1 System Overview

The proposed system uses MR technology to manage item locations and appliance status centrally, preventing "forgetting items" and "forgetting to turn off appliances" during departure preparation. Figure 1 shows the system overview.

The system operates on Microsoft HoloLens 2, an optical see-through MR headset with hand tracking capabilities, enabling hands-free operation during preparation. The system operates in two modes:

- **Daily mode**: For managing item placements during normal daily life. Users can move virtual item tags to update storage locations.
- **Preparation mode**: For pre-departure confirmation. The system monitors item possession through hand tracking and displays a checklist, automatically marking items as possessed when users pick them up.

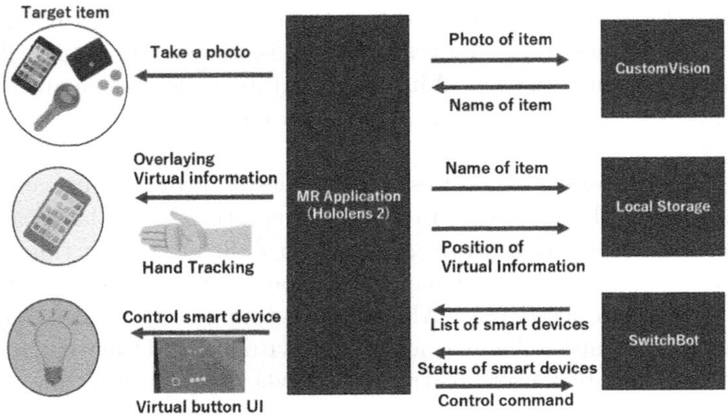

Fig. 1. System overview diagram.

Appliance control via the MR interface is available in both modes. A spatial trigger at the entrance detects when users attempt to leave and warns of forgotten items or appliances left turned on.

For appliance control, we use SwitchBot IoT devices (smart plugs, open/close sensors, smart lights) to manage windows, TV, fan, and lighting. The HoloLens 2 communicates with these devices via SwitchBot API using REST over HTTPS. Item recognition uses Microsoft Azure's Custom Vision service, processing RGB camera images to identify five everyday belongings: keys, wallet, smartphone, earphones, and watch.

3.2 Item Recognition and Hand Tracking

Image-Based Item Identification. Item detection uses the Azure Custom Vision API. The HoloLens 2's RGB camera captures images sent to the cloud endpoint, returning item class labels and bounding boxes. Upon recognition, the system instantiates a spherical collider at the corresponding spatial coordinates for hand tracking interaction. The current implementation uses a minimum dataset of 20 images per class trained in simple backgrounds, sufficient for system validation.

Hand Tracking for Possession and Movement. The system uses HoloLens 2's hand tracking, monitoring wrist position rather than fingertips to avoid occlusion when gripping items. When the wrist enters an item's collision sphere for 2 s, a valid operation is detected. System behavior differs by mode. In daily mode, contact triggers item grip, allowing placement changes by wrist movement with release on hand opening. In preparation mode, contact indicates physical possession, adding a checkmark to the item list without moving the virtual object.

3.3 User Interface

Figure 2 shows the system's user interface components displayed as spatial windows in MR space. The system provides three main UI components displayed as spatial windows in MR space. The item list UI displays registered items, and when users select an item, the system calculates a 3D vector from the user's head position to the item's coordinates. Then, it displays a directional arrow, enabling intuitive location even when occluded. The appliance list UI displays operational status with checkmarks indicating "ready" state (OFF for devices that the user should turn off), allowing users to toggle appliances without visually checking physical devices. For the window sensor, the system provides spatial guidance directing users to the window location for manual verification. The main menu UI provides spatial buttons for list display, item registration, and mode switching.

Fig. 2. Comparison of the two main UI modes. **(Left) Item List UI:** Displays personal belongings (e.g., wallet, smartphone) with the 'Checklist' tab active. **(Right) Appliance Control UI:** Displays the status of IoT devices (e.g., TV, lights) with the 'Home' tab active. Note that while the background remains the same, the list content and selected sidebar icon differ.

3.4 System Usage

Initial Setup. As shown in Fig. 3, users first configure the Exit Zone by placing and adjusting a semi-transparent rectangular object at the entrance. Subsequently, the system retrieves the SwitchBot device list via API and generates virtual buttons. Users position these buttons at the corresponding physical appliance locations using drag-and-drop interactions. These spatial configurations are persistently fixed using ARAnchors.

Item Registration and Daily Use. For item registration, users grip the target object and press the registration button, triggering camera capture and cloud inference. Upon approval of the suggested item name, the system generates a spatial collision sphere at the grip position, persisting the item information using ARAnchor for spatial fixation.

Fig. 3. Exit Zone configuration at the entrance. **(Left)** The setup interface used to place the detection area. **(Right)** The configured virtual zone appearing as a semi-transparent blue volume covering the door.

In daily mode, users monitor and control appliances through the MR interface, with status reflecting in real-time. Item placement changes occur by gripping virtual tags and moving to new positions. Upon release, the system regenerates ARAnchor coordinates and serializes updated data in JSON via Unity's PlayerPrefs. However, if items move while the system is inactive, spatial inconsistency may occur.

Preparation Mode and Departure Confirmation. In preparation mode, a checklist displays registered items. As users physically pick up items, wrist tracking detects collision with item spheres, automatically adding checkmarks for possessed items. When users pass through the Exit Zone, the system triggers final confirmation. If all items are possessed and appliances turned off, no warning appears; otherwise, the system immediately displays warnings for unpossessed items or active appliances, as shown in Fig. 4.

Fig. 4. Warning displays: (left) unpossessed items, (right) appliances left on.

4 Experiments and Evaluation

4.1 Experiment Purpose

This experiment verifies the extent to which the proposed MR system supports pre-departure preparation. We quantitatively measure impact on work efficiency (required time) and certainty (accuracy), and qualitatively evaluate mental load and psychological sense of security. We conduct comparative experiments under three conditions: proposed method (MR), existing method (list on notebook PC), and comparison method (memory only).

4.2 Experimental Environment

The experiment was conducted in a university research laboratory, constructing a 9.5 m × 18.3 m environment simulating a single-person household. To replicate a realistic living space, a TV (smart plug), window (open/close sensor), fan (smart plug), and lighting (smart light) were distributed throughout the room.

Equipment comprised Microsoft HoloLens 2 for MR information presentation, SwitchBot IoT devices (Hub Mini, Hub 3, 2 smart plugs, open/close sensor, smart light) for appliance control, and a notebook PC (HP Pavilion) used for the existing method comparison.

4.3 Experimental Method

16 university students and graduate students in their 20 s (ten males, six females) participated. All regularly use smartphones and PCs, with varying MR device experience.

We implemented a within-subject design where each participant performed the tasks. Tasks involved storing five specified items (wallet, keys, smartphone, earphones, watch) in a bag in random order, confirming appliance and window status, and exiting through the Exit Zone. In the existing method, the list showed only item names without location information, requiring a memory-based search similar to the comparison method.

To simulate "searching in a familiar room," participants received a placement diagram the day before and were instructed to imagine approximate locations without reviewing it on the experiment day. We prepared three random placement patterns for belongings to prevent memory carryover between trials, while appliance positions remained fixed across all conditions to reflect realistic living spaces. We counterbalanced and randomly assigned condition order and placement patterns.

To capture the subjects' field of view, we used different recording methods depending on the condition. In the MR condition, we utilized the HoloLens 2's built-in recording function (Fig. 5). In the comparison condition, participants wore a GoPro camera to record the first-person perspective. We collected task completion time and operation correctness based on these recordings and system logs.

5 Results and Discussion

5.1 Quantitative Evaluation

Results and Discussion on Task Completion Time. Figure 6 shows the box plot of task completion times for each condition. We conducted a one-way ANOVA on total completion times, which revealed a statistically significant main effect among the three conditions ($F(2, 30) = 4.66, p = .017$). However, subsequent post-hoc comparisons using t-tests with Bonferroni correction indicated no significant differences in the specific pairs of Proposed vs. Existing ($p > .05$)

Fig. 5. Subject's field of view (MR video).

and Proposed vs. Comparison methods ($p > .05$). Individual differences in proficiency with HoloLens 2-specific gesture operations, particularly air-tap actions, were observed when selecting buttons. Subjects unfamiliar with operations took time to accurately perform tap detection in mid-air and button press recognition, which resulted in pushing up the overall time.

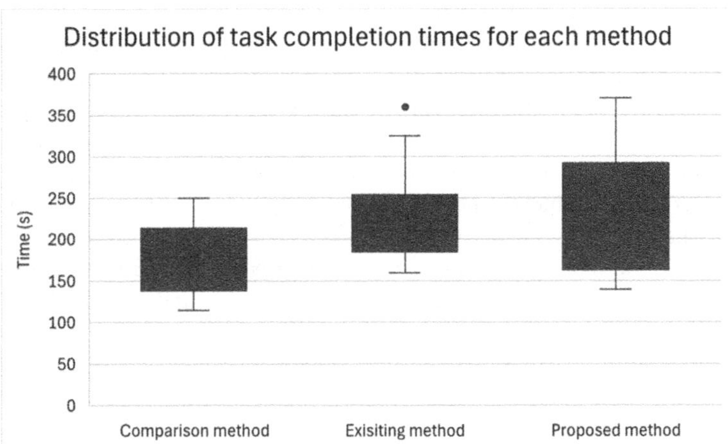

Fig. 6. Box plot of task completion time for each condition.

Figure 7 presents the comparison of movement and search times across conditions. Detailed analysis separating task completion time into "system operations" and "item search and movement" revealed a statistically significant difference among conditions ($F(2, 30) = 18.78, p < .001$). Subsequent post-hoc t-tests with Bonferroni correction confirmed that the proposed method significantly reduced the time compared to both the Existing ($p < .001$) and Comparison ($p < .001$) methods. We can assume that visual guidance by MR significantly reduces item search costs and eliminates physical movement, such as returning to the PC location to check the list. Although overall time reduction was not achieved at present due to system operation overhead, results suggested that total work efficiency improvement can be sufficiently achieved if users' operation proficiency improves.

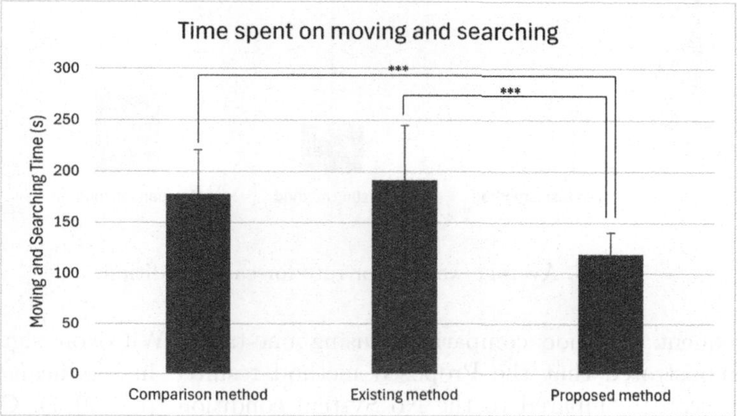

Fig. 7. Box plot of movement/search time for each condition.

5.2 Results and Discussion on Work Accuracy

Figure 8 presents the average work number of work error for each condition. We measured error counts across 9 checkpoints (5 items, 4 appliances). A Friedman test showed no significant difference among conditions ($p > .05$), as high accuracy was maintained overall. However, the proposed method yielded 0 errors for all participants. While the ceiling effect limited statistical differentiation, this result indicates that the system functions as a sufficient safety net for preventing forgetfulness.

5.3 Qualitative Evaluation

Evaluation by Workload (NASA-TLX). Figure 9 presents the comparison of NASA-TLX scores for each condition. First, a Shapiro-Wilk test indicated non-normality in the Proposed System data ($p < .05$). Therefore, we conducted a Friedman test, which revealed a statistically significant difference in NASA-TLX scores among the conditions ($p < .001$).

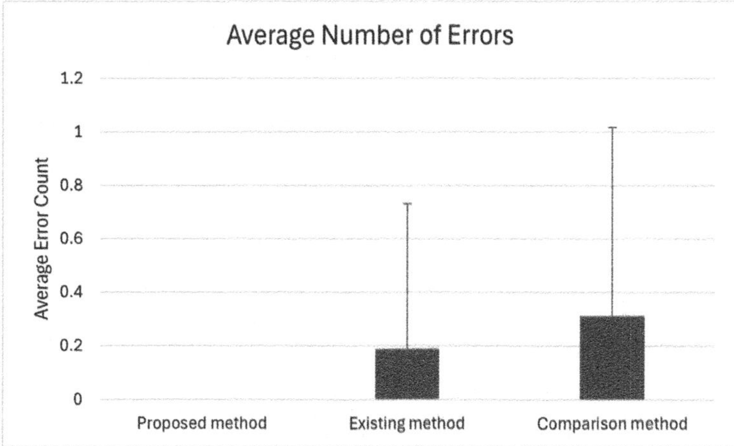

Fig. 8. Average work error rate for each condition.

Subsequent post-hoc comparisons using one-tailed Wilcoxon signed-rank tests demonstrated that the Proposed method resulted in significantly lower workload scores compared to the No System condition ($p \approx .001$). Crucially, the Proposed method also showed significantly lower values than the Existing System ($p = .016$).

This result indicates that the proposed method achieves a lower workload than the checklist (existing method) that is familiar in daily use. In the proposed method, physical burden from wearing the HoloLens 2 and unfamiliarity with gesture operations were concerns, but intuitive information presentation by MR not only offset these negative aspects but also reduced workload beyond the PC list level. It suggests that spatial information overlay and hands-free confirmation brought by MR provide substantial value in reducing cognitive and physical burden during departure preparation.

Evaluation by System Usability (SUS). Despite the operational disadvantages of MR, the proposed method achieved higher SUS scores than the existing method. It is particularly noteworthy that the proposed method outperformed the existing method, even though the latter utilizes familiar input interfaces (mouse and keyboard) that typically impose minimal operational stress. As mentioned above, many subjects were unfamiliar with HoloLens 2 specific gestures, putting the proposed method at a disadvantage in terms of operation time and errors. Nevertheless, the fact that it received a higher usability evaluation than the familiar PC system suggests that the experiential value of "spatial information presentation" and "seamless confirmation within the field of view" was significant enough to compensate for the learning cost of device operations. From these results, we can conclude that the UI/UX design of this system achieves high acceptability at a practical level, overcoming the operational barriers specific to new devices.

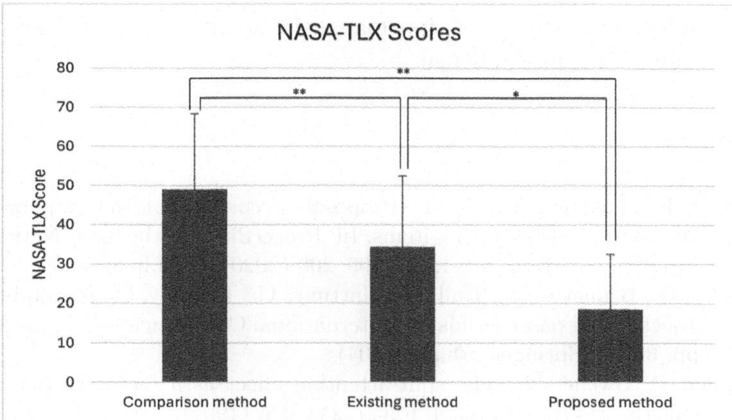

Fig. 9. Comparison of Raw TLX scores for each condition.

6 Conclusions

In this research, we designed and developed an MR system aimed at complementing human memory and attention in pre-departure preparation behavior, preventing "forgetting items" and "forgetting to turn off appliances" in advance, and supporting efficient and certain preparation work. The system uses HoloLens 2 to overlay item locations and appliance operational status in real space, realizing seamless confirmation work through automatic possession detection.

In the evaluation experiment, quantitative results showed that "movement/search time" was significantly shortened in the proposed method, and all subjects achieved a 0% error rate. In qualitative evaluation, mental load by NASA-TLX was significantly lower, and a high usability score of 81.6 points was obtained in SUS. Questionnaire results revealed that "time lag between confirmation and work" and "anxiety upon completion" were eliminated, demonstrating that constantly viewable information presentation by MR greatly contributes to reducing psychological stress before going out.

From these results, it can be said that the information augmentation and interaction methods in MR space proposed in this research are effective not only in contributing to physical work efficiency improvement but also in reducing users' mental burden and constructing a pre-departure preparation environment with a sense of security.

While certain results were obtained in this research, challenges to be solved for practical application were also clarified. First, improving interface usability, particularly gesture operation intuitiveness, is necessary. Second, long-term operational evaluation in actual living environments over several weeks to months is needed to identify habituation processes and daily usage impediments. Finally, advancing position identification technology is important, as the current anchor-based method has limitations when items are moved while the system is not in use. Establishing optimal position management methods including dynamic tracking remains a future challenge.

References

1. Binzashi, K., Fushimi, M., et al.: Proposal of comfortable life support system "KAIchan" to prevent forgetting items. In: Proceedings of the 82nd National Convention of IPSJ, vol. 2020, no. 1, pp. 199–200 (2020). (in Japanese)
2. Borriello, G., Brunette, W., Hall, M., Hartung, C., Tangney, C.: Reminding about tagged objects using passive rfids. In: International Conference on Ubiquitous Computing, pp. 36–53. Springer, Cham (2004)
3. Chandler, P., Sweller, J.: The split-attention effect as a factor in the design of instruction. Br. J. Educ. Psychol. **62**(2), 233–246 (1992)
4. Funk, M., Boldt, R., Pfleging, B., Pfeiffer, M., Henze, N., Schmidt, A.: Representing indoor location of objects on wearable computers with head-mounted displays. In: Proceedings of the 5th Augmented Human International Conference, pp. 1–4 (2014)
5. MAMORIO Inc.: Survey on Searching for Items at Home: People lose items at home an average of 3.2 times per month (in Japanese). https://prtimes.jp/main/html/rd/p/000000211.000022173.html. Accessed 17 July 2025
6. National Police Agency: Statistical Data on Penal Code Offenses in Reiwa 5 (2023). https://www.npa.go.jp/toukei/seianki/R05/r05keihouhantoukeisiryou.pdf. Accessed 17 July 2025. (in Japanese)
7. Ng, A., Brewster, S.: The effects of encumbrance on mobile gesture interactions. In: Proceedings of the 2014 ACM International Conference on Interactive Tabletops and Surfaces, pp. 143–152. ACM (2014)
8. Oshimi, H., Perusquía-Hernández, M., Isoyama, N., Uchiyama, H., Kiyokawa, K.: Locatar: an AR object search assistance system for a shared space. In: Proceedings of the Augmented Humans International Conference 2023, pp. 66–76 (2023)
9. Report Ocean Inc.: Survey on Key Loss: 56% experienced "anxious moments when keys were not at hand" in the past year, with approximately 45% stating keys were "never found" after loss. https://prtimes.jp/main/html/rd/p/000000198.000022173.html. Accessed 17 July 2025. (in Japanese)
10. Sears, A., Lin, M., Jacko, J., Xiao, Y.: When computers fade: Pervasive computing and situationally induced impairments and disabilities. In: Human-Computer Interaction: Theory and Practice (Proceedings of HCI International, vol. 2, pp. 1298–1302. Lawrence Erlbaum Associates, Mahwah, NJ (2003)
11. Tokyo Gas Urban Life Institute: Over 40% of burglaries are caused by forgetting to lock doors!? What are the countermeasures for preventing forgotten locks? https://uchi.tokyo-gas.co.jp/topics/6598. Accessed 17 July 2025. (in Japanese)
12. Yan, G., et al.: Camfi: an ai-driven and camera-based system for assisting users in finding lost objects in multi-person scenarios. In: CHI Conference on Human Factors in Computing Systems Extended Abstracts, pp. 1–7 (2022)

An Initial Exploration of Cognitive Changes in Avatar-Mediated Self-expression Processes

Hiroki Matsuoka[1,2,4], Risa Horikiri[2], Sachi Takaku[2], Saki Orihara[2], Motoki Sakai[3], and Masaki Shuzo[4(✉)]

[1] Rissho University, 1600 Mankichi, Kumagaya-shi, Saitama, Japan
hrk.matsuoka@ris.ac.jp

[2] Association CARECO, J-Pro Kitasenju Building 6F-A, 1-11-2 Senju, Adachi-ku, Tokyo, Japan
info@careco.or.jp

[3] Nihon University, 1 Nakagawara, Tokusada, Tamuramachi, Koriyama-shi, Fukushima, Japan
sakai.motoki@nihon-u.ac.jp

[4] Shonan Institute of Technology, 1-1-25 Tsujido-Nishikaigan, Fujisawa-shi, Kanagawa, Japan
shuzo@info.shonan-it.ac.jp

Abstract. This study exploratorily documents initial aspects of self-expression observed in avatar-mediated sessions conducted within a mental health support setting, distinct from participants' everyday social contexts. Two individuals with mental disabilities participated in two avatar-mediated self-expression sessions, followed by interviews conducted immediately after each session. Rather than evaluating effectiveness or seeking generalizable outcomes, this study focuses on how participants described their experiences and self-perceptions at an early stage of engagement. Based on participants' narratives, including short written scripts prepared in advance as well as post-session interviews, aspects related to attitudes toward self-disclosure, expressive behaviors, self-efficacy, and self-perception were descriptively organized. The findings indicate that participants tentatively experienced alternative ways of expressing themselves through avatars and began to reflect on expressive elements such as voice use and presentation style. At the same time, self-evaluations remained cautious, and no clear indications of generalization to everyday interpersonal contexts were identified. This paper documents a preparatory phase of longer-term practice and suggests that avatar-mediated self-expression may offer a psychologically safe context in the early stages of engagement.

Keywords: Avatar-mediated interaction · Self-expression · Mental health support · Exploratory study · Qualitative observation

H. Matsuoka and R. Horikiri—These authors contributed equally to this work.

E. Vlahu-Gjorgievska et al. (Eds.): PERSUASIVE 2026, CCIS 2896, pp. 513–525, 2027.
https://doi.org/10.1007/978-3-032-27235-5_53

1 Introduction

1.1 People with Mental Disabilities and Self-stigma

Many people with mental disabilities experience self-stigma, which has been reported to have a significant impact on recovery processes and quality of life [1]. Self-stigma refers to the internalization of socially prevalent prejudice and discrimination toward mental disabilities, which can lead individuals to view themselves as devalued and to anticipate negative judgments in society. Such internalized stigma may affect psychological and behavioral functioning, including reduced hope, avoidance of social interactions, and reluctance to seek treatment or support [2]. As a result, difficulties may arise across interpersonal contexts (e.g., forming relationships) and broader social contexts (e.g., participation in society or employment).

Shimamoto and Hiroshima [3] identified factors that exacerbate self-stigma, such as lack of understanding from others, discrimination, and negative remarks, while also highlighting mitigating factors including accepting support from family members and supporters, as well as the accumulation of small successful experiences. These findings suggest that recovery is supported through receptive relationships, acceptance of one's disability, and the gradual accumulation of positive experiences that deepen self-understanding.

In this context, recovery for people with mental disabilities refers to a process in which individuals find new goals and aspirations, develop a positive self-image through reflection, actively utilize available support to stabilize their condition, and build mutually recognized relationships within their local communities [4]. Importantly, opportunities that allow individuals to express themselves in a safe and accepting environment may serve as a foundational element for reducing self-stigma and supporting recovery-oriented processes.

1.2 Social Anxiety Accompanying Heightened Self-consciousness During Adolescence and Young Adulthood

During adolescence and young adulthood, heightened social comparison, concerns about evaluation, and conformity pressure may lead to excessive self-consciousness. At the same time, it may become difficult for individuals to act confidently based on their own values and choices. Such conditions have the potential to affect various aspects of social life, including academic engagement, employment, and interpersonal relationships.

In particular, heightened fear of negative evaluation may prompt avoidance of interpersonal situations in which one is subject to others' judgments. This can lead to difficulties commonly associated with social anxiety. Prior research has linked social anxiety to increased anxiety and depressive symptoms, lowered self-evaluation, and the internalization of self-stigma [5].

Therefore, identifying ways to offer opportunities for self-expression that minimize fear of evaluation and enable individuals to communicate their thoughts and experiences in a psychologically safe manner remains an important challenge for supporting recovery and social participation. In this paper, the term "self-expression" refers to participants' spoken narration of thoughts, feelings, and experiences, including both the content of what is said and the manner of speaking (e.g., tone, pitch, and presentation style) as described by the participants themselves. This usage is descriptive and context-specific, and is not intended as a standardized clinical construct or quantitative measure.

1.3 Avatar-Mediated Self-expression Accompanied by a Sense of Safety

In recent years, mediated forms of self-expression that do not require facial disclosure, such as the use of avatars, have become increasingly prevalent. Psychological changes arising from avatar use are often discussed in terms of the *Proteus effect*, where identification with an avatar's attributes influences a user's emotions and behaviors [6]. For instance, using confident or attractive avatars can enhance self-confidence and facilitate interpersonal self-disclosure.

When applied to mental health support, avatar-mediated communication can reduce the fear of negative evaluation and communication barriers related to disabilities. Rehm et al. [7] demonstrated that avatar technologies provide flexible platforms for various interventions, highlighting that anonymity can enhance engagement and support the reconstruction of personal identity in a safe environment.

These theoretical and clinical insights align with observations at the practice site of this study. Several clients aspiring to be virtual content creators described the avatar-mediated environment as a space where they could comfortably express their strengths. This suggests that such mediated self-expression functions as a psychologically safe entry point for individuals who find direct interpersonal interaction challenging.

1.4 Narrative Perspective in Avatar-Mediated Self-expression

The present study does not aim to examine narrative theory itself. Rather, to explore potential changes in participants' utterances observed through avatar-mediated self-expression, it adopts a narrative perspective that treats narration as a process in which participants' understanding of themselves and views of themselves may shift depending on context and relational conditions. From this perspective, self-expression is understood not as the reproduction of fixed internal states, but as a situated activity through which meanings are organized and negotiated.

Within this deliberately limited and exploratory scope, the study focuses on participants' self-reported narratives obtained immediately after each session. By examining how participants describe their experiences and evaluations at these early stages, the analysis aims to capture tentative patterns of reflection without assuming stable or generalized psychological change.

2 Purpose of the Study

The purpose of this study is to explore initial changes in self-expression and self-perception observed through avatar-mediated practices conducted in a mental health support context. This study forms part of an ongoing support program and is positioned as an exploratory investigation based on a limited number of participants.

Specifically, this research focuses on how avatar-mediated self-expression may provide opportunities for individuals with mental disabilities to engage in communication with a reduced fear of negative evaluation, and how such practices may be associated with changes in the way participants articulate their experiences and perceptions of themselves.

This study addresses three research questions: (RQ1) how participants describe their experiences of avatar-mediated self-expression, (RQ2) how participants reflect on their own expressive behaviors during avatar use, and (RQ3) what kinds of perceived changes or emerging awareness are reported across repeated sessions.

Given the exploratory nature of this study and the small number of participants, the findings are not intended to establish generalizable conclusions. Rather, this research aims to provide initial insights that may inform future investigations into the design and use of avatar-mediated self-expression practices within mental health support settings.

3 Method

3.1 Practice Context

The practices described in this study were conducted within a community-based mental health support facility providing continuous psychosocial support for people with mental disabilities. These activities were implemented as part of an ongoing support program, rather than a standalone research intervention, to offer opportunities for self-expression in environments perceived as psychologically safe. Within this context, avatar-mediated practices were introduced as optional activities to reduce interpersonal pressure associated with face-to-face interaction and were integrated into the facility's regular support framework.

The analysis focuses specifically on two avatar sessions conducted during the program and the interviews carried out immediately after each session. While activities related to avatar creation and preliminary practice were conducted as routine support prior to the sessions, these are treated as background preparation and are not included in the analytic scope of this paper.

Ethical considerations were addressed by obtaining informed consent from all participants prior to data use. Participants were informed that their involvement would not affect the services they receive at the facility and that all data would be anonymized for analysis and publication.

3.2 Participants

Two participants were included in this exploratory study: one male in his early thirties and one female in her early twenties. Both participants were users of the community-based mental health support facility in which the avatar-mediated practices were conducted, and had prior experiences of social withdrawal (hikikomori) as well as difficulties characteristic of social anxiety. They participated in the activities as part of the regular support program and provided consent for the use of their utterances and related materials for research purposes.

Participants were selected based on their willingness to engage in avatar-mediated self-expression activities and to allow their practice data to be analyzed. No exclusion criteria based on diagnosis, symptom severity, or functional level were applied. To protect privacy, detailed demographic information beyond broad age range and gender is not reported, and participants are referred to using pseudonyms throughout this paper.

3.3 Avatar-Mediated Practice

In this paper, the term "avatar-mediated practice" refers to individual avatar sessions conducted as part of an ongoing support program. This practice is not intended as a system-driven intervention or an experimental manipulation, but as an experiential setting for observing how participants engage in self-expression.

In each avatar-mediated session, participants engaged in spoken self-expression by narrating to themselves while viewing their own avatar displayed on the screen. The avatar, a three-dimensional character created in advance by each participant using VRoid Studio, visually represented the participant during speaking. It functioned as a mediating representation that separated the act of speaking from the participant's physical body, rather than as an independent subject or dialogue partner.

During speech, the participant's voice was used directly without synthetic speech or automatic voice conversion, although tone and speaking style were intentionally adjusted through acting in accordance with the avatar's character image. Mouth movement of the avatar was synchronized based on visual facial landmarks captured by a camera, blinking was generated programmatically, and upper-body movement was represented by mirroring head and chest rotations derived from facial motion. An example of the session setup is shown in Fig. 1.

Each session consisted of a single expressive task, followed immediately by an interview. Participants selected or created avatars that they felt represented themselves or an aspect of themselves they wished to express, without imposed constraints on appearance or expressive style.

The avatar-mediated practice was positioned as a voluntary activity rather than a therapeutic intervention or experimental manipulation, providing participants with an opportunity to explore alternative modes of self-expression distinct from conventional face-to-face interaction.

Fig. 1. An example of an avatar-mediated self-expression session. The participant speaks while viewing their own avatar displayed on a screen.

3.4 Data Collection

With participants' consent, data collection centered on audio recordings of spoken expressions during the sessions and subsequent interviews, all of which were conducted in naturalistic settings as part of the regular support program. To ensure privacy, identifiable information was removed during transcription, and all data were anonymized prior to analysis. While avatar creation and preliminary practice activities took place as routine support, they were treated as background preparation and excluded from the analytic scope of this paper.

3.5 Analytic Approach

Given the exploratory nature of this study and the limited number of participants, a qualitative and descriptive analytic approach was adopted. The analysis focused on organizing and describing observable features of participants' narratives during each avatar session and the interviews conducted immediately after each session.

Participants' utterances collected during the avatar-mediated practice were reviewed sentence by sentence by two practitioners involved in routine support, with reference to contextual knowledge from ongoing interactions in the support setting. During this process, attention was paid to aspects such as the length of utterances, the focus of topics, and shifts in the ways participants referred to themselves and their experiences. Observed features were then discussed with a university researcher to confirm and consolidate observation labels. These observations were used to identify patterns that appeared noteworthy across cases, without attempting statistical comparison, formal coding, or generalization.

Narrative perspectives were employed solely as an interpretive lens for organizing and describing changes in expression, rather than as a framework for theoretical validation or theory-driven qualitative analysis. Accordingly, the analysis remains cautious in scope and aims to present initial observations that may inform future, more detailed investigations. This study is based on qualitative observations of participants' narratives within a naturalistic community-based mental health support setting.

Throughout the analytic process, emphasis was placed on transparency and restraint in interpretation, ensuring that descriptions were grounded in the available data and that claims did not exceed what could reasonably be inferred from the observations. For reference and transparency, an organized list of observation labels derived from post-session interviews is provided in the Appendix.

4 Results

4.1 Scope of Observations

This section presents observations based on two avatar-mediated sessions conducted on December 3 and December 26, 2025, and the interviews conducted immediately after each session. The focus of the analysis is not on participants' in-session performance but on their self-reflective narratives expressed during the post-session interviews.

4.2 Case-Based Descriptions

Participant A. Following the first session (December 3), Participant A reported feeling nervous, while also describing the avatar-mediated experience as a rare and valuable opportunity. The participant noted that speaking alone, without the immediate presence of others, felt calmer and easier compared to ordinary interpersonal situations.

Regarding self-expression, Participant A expressed a cautious self-evaluative reflection on how they expressed themselves through the avatar. At the same time, the participant reported making deliberate adjustments to voice tone and speaking style.

After the second session (December 26), Participant A reported becoming more accustomed to using the avatar, while again indicating that no distinct change could be clearly identified. However, the participant mentioned that receiving feedback from others might contribute to increased confidence, and expressed interest in further refinement and continued engagement in avatar-mediated expression.

Participant B. After the first session, Participant B described the avatar-mediated self-expression as slightly embarrassing but also novel and refreshing. The participant reported experiencing a different perspective when speaking through the avatar, and described the interaction as distinct from usual modes of speaking.

In terms of expressive behavior, Participant B reported consciously modifying voice pitch and tone while speaking. Nevertheless, the participant indicated that it was difficult to assess whether any meaningful change had occurred based on a single session, and expressed a reserved stance toward evaluating outcomes.

Following the second session, Participant B reported increased ease in expressing themselves while consciously attending to the avatar. At the same time, the participant stated that the experience had not yet generalized to daily life. The interview also included reflections on specific strategies for improving expression and references to possible future activities, suggesting a growing tendency to reflect on self-expression through the avatar-mediated experience.

4.3 Characteristics Observed in Narrative Expression

Across both cases, the interviews following the sessions did not reveal pronounced changes in self-expression. Instead, a common observation was an increase in participants' references to intentional adjustments, reflection on expressive behavior, and consideration of possible future directions, particularly after the second session.

Participants often adopted a cautious tone when discussing psychological change, frequently avoiding definitive statements and emphasizing uncertainty or the need for continued experience. Such narratives indicate that participants tended to frame their experiences as preliminary and ongoing rather than as evidence of immediate transformation.

4.4 Summary of Observations

Overall, the post-session interviews revealed that participants began to articulate reflections on their expressive behavior and possible directions for refinement. In contrast, changes in psychological states or generalization to everyday interpersonal contexts were described as limited and difficult to determine at this stage. These observations suggest that the avatar-mediated sessions captured an early phase characterized by emerging awareness and reflection related to self-expression, rather than clearly observable changes in behavior or self-perception.

5 Discussion

The purpose of this discussion is not to reinterpret these findings as evidence of effectiveness or improvement, but rather to examine what it means that participants articulated their experiences in this particular manner at an early stage of engagement. From an exploratory perspective, the absence of definitive claims, together with emerging reflections on expression and self-presentation, can be understood as indicative of a preparatory phase in which self-expression itself becomes an object of awareness, rather than a site of immediate change.

In the following subsections, we interpret these narrative characteristics within the context of avatar-mediated self-expression and recovery-oriented support, while maintaining careful attention to the limited scope and descriptive nature of the present study.

5.1 Tentative Awareness and Reflection on Self-expression

Across both cases, participants frequently referred to intentional adjustments in their expressive behavior, such as voice tone, pitch, and manner of speaking, particularly in interviews conducted after the second session. These utterances did not necessarily indicate confidence or mastery; rather, they reflected an emerging awareness of self-expression as something that could be consciously adjusted and reflected upon.

Rather than describing change or improvement as spontaneous, participants referred to conscious adjustments in their expressive behavior while consistently withholding definitive judgments about psychological change. Their narratives emphasized attending to how they spoke or expressed themselves, alongside explicit reservations about whether such experiences constituted meaningful change.

From this perspective, avatar-mediated self-expression may function, at an early stage, not as a context in which immediate change is experienced, but as one in which self-expression itself becomes an object of awareness and reflection. That is, participants appeared to approach self-expression as something to be observed, adjusted, and considered, rather than as something that had already improved.

Importantly, participants' cautious self-evaluations and reluctance to make definitive claims about personal change were consistently observed across sessions. From a recovery-oriented perspective, such restraint may reflect not stagnation or lack of progress, but a realistic appraisal of one's current state and an avoidance of premature self-judgment at an early stage of engagement.

Taken together, these narrative characteristics point to an early-stage form of engagement that can be discussed even in the absence of overt improvement. From a practical standpoint, these observations may be meaningful for practitioners as indicators of engagement or readiness rather than as outcomes to be maximized. Avatar-mediated self-expression may therefore be positioned as a preparatory or supportive practice prior to more demanding interpersonal situations, particularly for individuals who experience social anxiety or difficulty with face-to-face self-disclosure. At the same time, such positioning should be interpreted cautiously given the deliberately limited scope and short duration of the present study.

5.2 Implications and Limitations of the Exploratory Scope

The limited and cautious nature of the reported changes highlights both the value and the constraints of the present study. Because the observations were restricted to two sessions per participant, involving only two participants, and interviews conducted immediately afterward, it is not possible to determine whether the reflective tendencies observed here would develop into sustained behavioral change or generalize to everyday interpersonal contexts.

However, documenting such tentative and restrained narratives is meaningful precisely because they capture an early phase of engagement that is often overlooked when outcome-focused evaluations are emphasized. The present findings suggest that avatar-mediated self-expression may provide a psychologically safe environment in which participants can begin to notice and reflect on their own expressive behaviors without immediate pressure to demonstrate improvement. From an interpretive perspective, such early and tentative reflections may be read as aligning with existing conceptual frameworks, including narrative identity theory and recovery-oriented practice, which emphasize meaning-making processes and subjective engagement over immediate behavioral outcomes. In addition, participants' voluntary continuation of avatar-mediated practice may be cautiously interpreted as suggestive of expectations discussed in relation to the Proteus effect. Importantly, these references are offered as interpretive lenses rather than as evidence of theoretical validation.

To clarify whether this early reflective stance develops into sustained change beyond the session context, further observation over time is required. These observations should therefore be understood as descriptive groundwork for future investigation. More systematic documentation, repeated sessions, and longitudinal designs will be necessary to examine how such early reflections may evolve over time and how avatar-mediated practices may contribute to longer-term recovery-oriented processes.

6 Conclusion

This study exploratorily examined initial aspects of self-expression observed through two avatar-mediated sessions conducted with individuals with mental disabilities. Focusing on interviews conducted immediately after each session, we organized participants' narratives related to attitudes toward self-disclosure, expressive behaviors, self-efficacy, and self-perception within a deliberately limited and descriptive scope.

The findings suggest that engaging in avatar-mediated self-expression allowed participants to begin noticing and reflecting on their own expressive behaviors, such as voice use and manner of presentation. However, participants consistently adopted cautious self-evaluations and refrained from identifying clear psychological change or generalization to everyday contexts.

Rather than demonstrating improvement or effectiveness, these narratives illustrate an early phase in which self-expression itself becomes an object of awareness and examination. In this sense, the limited and tentative nature of the reported changes should not be interpreted as a lack of significance, but as characteristic of a preparatory stage of engagement.

Accordingly, this paper is positioned as an exploratory report documenting a preparatory phase of avatar-mediated self-expression practices within a recovery-oriented support context. By capturing participants' restrained and tentative narratives, this study provides descriptive groundwork for future investigations into how such practices may evolve through continued engagement.

Future research should employ more systematic documentation, repeated sessions, and longitudinal designs to examine how early reflective awareness observed in this study may develop over time and how avatar-mediated self-expression may relate to experiences in everyday interpersonal contexts.

Acknowledgment. This research was supported by the JKA Foundation through its Machinery Promotion Program (KEIRIN) (Grant No. 2025M-334). The authors would like to express their sincere appreciation to all those involved.

Appendix: Organized Observation Labels

This appendix provides an organized list of observation labels derived from post-session interview utterances, which are summarized in Table 1. These labels were used solely as a reference to support transparency in describing participants' reported experiences. They do not represent analytical categories, causal relationships, or evaluated outcomes.

Table 1. Organized labels for qualitative observation.

Time	Self-disclosure and self-expression
T0	**Expectations of ease in self-expression**: Self-expression may become easier; sense of safety from not revealing one's face; intention to provide more detailed explanations; viewing the activity as practice for talking about oneself.
	Ambivalence toward self-disclosure: Wanting to speak but feeling unable to; resistance to discussing past or distressing experiences; self-restraint due to consideration for others.
T1	**Experience of an "alternative self" through the avatar**: Feeling like becoming a different self; self-expression mediated by a character; self-evaluation of the degree of role-playing.
	Embarrassment and novelty of expression: Feeling embarrassed; sense of novelty; emotional responses described as enjoyable.
T2	**Development and alignment of role-based self-expression**: Increased degree of role-playing; vocal expression with conscious awareness of the character; habituation to self-expression.
	Difficulty of self-expression in everyday contexts: Limited transfer to daily life; self-evaluation that the practice has not yet been actively utilized.
Time	**Experience and attitude**
T0	**Tension and avoidance in interpersonal situations**: Feeling tense during first encounters; difficulty initiating conversation; behaviors indicating missed opportunities to speak.
	Anticipated behavior when using the avatar: Sense of being able to speak when desired; reduced concern about time; expectation of speaking calmly alone.

(continued)

Table 1. (*continued*)

Time	Experience and attitude
T1	**Conscious adjustment of speech and behavior**: Attempting to speak clearly; adjusting voice tone; differentiating speaking styles according to character.
	Limited perceived change in attitude or tension: Little perceived change in nervousness; absence of major changes; withholding judgment after the first session.
T2	**Concrete strategies and emerging ideas for expression**: Explicit manipulation of voice; environmental adjustments; behavior focused on identifying and correcting weaknesses.
	Exploratory and enjoyable engagement: Imagining concrete situations for practice; framing the activity as play or challenge.
Time	Self-efficacy and self-stigma
T0	**Anxiety and self-doubt**: Uncertainty about personal anxiety; doubt about ability; concern about being understood by others.
	Expectation of freer self-expression: Anticipation of emotional relief if able to speak; desire to approach others more easily; expectation that the experience may connect to real-life situations.
T1	**Cautious self-evaluation and restrained self-perception**: Feeling unable to fully embody the character; tendency to undervalue one's own performance; narratives avoiding definitive claims of change.
	Emerging but limited sense of self-efficacy: Perception that speaking more brightly may be possible; belief that improvement is achievable with conscious effort or practice.
T2	**Increase in perceived confidence in self-expression**: Growing confidence in being able to express oneself; expectation of being able to present; psychological ease associated with habituation.
	Desire for external feedback: Wish to be evaluated; interest in understanding points for improvement.

T0: interview conducted before Session 1 (12/3); T1: interview conducted immediately after Session 1 (12/3); T2: interview conducted immediately after Session 2 (12/26).

References

1. Tanaka, G.: Coping with self-stigma among people with mental disorders. Hum. Sci. Symbiotic Soc. **6**, 47–58 (2008). (in Japanese)
2. Nishizawa, K., Kawamura, K.: Literature review on experiences and coping with self-stigma in people with schizophrenic patients. J. Jpn. Acad. Health Behav. Sci. **38**(2), 90–97 (2023). (in Japanese)
3. Shimamoto, M., Hiroshima, M.: Factors that exacerbate and alleviate self-stigma among people with mental disabilities. Bull. Grad. Sch. Hum. Health Sci. Kyoto Univ. Health Sci. **9**, 11–19 (2014). (in Japanese)

4. Narita, T., Kobayashi, K.: Analysis of the concept of recovery in community living schizophrenia patients. J. Jpn. Acad. Commun. Health Nurs. **20**(3), 35–44 (2017). (in Japanese)
5. Narishige, R.: Children with the "I hate myself" syndrome: Psychological support for breaking free from the cycle of self-negation. Godo-Shuppan, Tokyo (2025). (in Japanese)
6. Martin Coesel, A., Biancardi, B., Buisine, S.: A theoretical review of the Proteus effect: understanding the underlying processes. Front. Psychol. **15**, 1379599 (2024). https://doi.org/10.3389/fpsyg.2024.1379599
7. Rehm, I.C., Foenander, E., Wallace, K., Abbott, J.-A.M., Kyrios, M., Thomas, N.: What role can avatars play in e-mental health interventions? Exploring new models of client-therapist interaction. Front. Psych. **7**, 186 (2016). https://doi.org/10.3389/fpsyt.2016.00186

Study on Improving Audience Evaluation by Guiding Gaze of Presenter Using Smart Glasses

Yumino Munekata[1(✉)], Motoki Sakai[2], and Guillaume Lopez[1]

[1] Aoyama Gakuin University, Shibuya, Japan
ymunekata@wil-aoyama.jp, guillaume@it.aoyama.ac.jp
[2] Nihon University, Tokyo, Japan
sakai.motoki@nihon-u.ac.jp

Abstract. Effective presentation skills are essential in modern society, yet many presenters experience anxiety that leads them to rely heavily on scripts. This reliance often results in downward gaze fixation and a lack of eye contact, which hinders nonverbal communication and reduces audience engagement. To address these issues, we propose a presentation support system that combines smart glasses with an eye-tracking device, integrating real-time gaze measurement and speech recognition. The system displays the script within the presenter's field of view while actively guiding their gaze toward the audience–left, center, and right–based on speech progression, preventing fixed gaze patterns. We conducted an evaluation experiment with ten participants to assess the system's effectiveness. Quantitative analysis revealed a statistically significant increase in gaze entropy, indicating a more balanced distribution of attention across the audience. Subjective evaluations showed improvements in perceived eye contact, presenter confidence, and ease of listening. Although mental demand slightly increased, overall workload remained similar to the unsupported condition, and usability (SUS) was rated highly. These findings suggest that the proposed system effectively supports eye contact while referring to a script, enhancing overall presentation performance.

Keywords: Presentation Support · Gaze tracking · Smart glasses

1 Introduction

1.1 Background

The Social Importance of Presentations and Psychological Barriers. In modern society, presentation skills are essential in various fields, such as business and education, for conveying one's achievements. An effective presentation not only delivers accurate information but also draws understanding and empathy from the audience [10]. The success of a presentation depends on the correlation between its content and delivery skills, and exceptionally high presentation ability can compensate for deficiencies in materials and maximize the efficiency of information conveyance [8].

E. Vlahu-Gjorgievska et al. (Eds.): PERSUASIVE 2026, CCIS 2896, pp. 526–537, 2027.
https://doi.org/10.1007/978-3-032-27235-5_54

Issues of Presentation Caused by Anxiety. While the importance of presentation skills has increased, many presenters experience strong anxiety when speaking in front of an audience [9]. When faced with such psychological anxiety, presenters tend to prepare detailed scripts and engage in careful preparation to avoid failure during the actual presentation. This tendency has also been reported in the study by Daly et al. Their study showed that speakers with higher levels of anxiety were more likely to prepare accurate and detailed scripts [3]. This approach resolves the fear of stumbling over words and the desire to convey content accurately and completely.

Components of a Presentation and the Role of Gaze. Presentations consist of three main components: content quality, visual materials, and expressive skills. Expressive skill is the ability to affect the impression and effectiveness of a presentation through nonverbal elements. Include speaking style, voice, gaze, and gestures. Among these factors, appropriate eye contact is known to enhance a speaker's credibility and persuasiveness [13]. However, as mentioned earlier, reading from a script during a presentation tends to fix your gaze, which can damage the impression you make on your audience.

1.2 Purpose of This Study

The purpose of this study is to clarify the impact of support that balances script referencing and gaze distribution on presentation evaluation. To achieve this, we develop a system that integrates script presentation with gaze guidance and verify the effects of this guidance on actual gaze behavior and audience evaluation.

2 Research of Presentation

2.1 Analysis of Speech and Behavior

Previous research has proposed feedback systems based on the results of voice and motion analysis [1,4]. Although these were suitable for post-presentation review, they were not mainly aimed at directly supporting the presenter during the presentation.

Regarding gaze guidance, there is a method to recognize the bias of the gaze by changing the color of multiple displays at the back of the venue [7]. However, this used the orientation of the face as an indicator and did not provide precise feedback based on eye movements.

HMD(Head-Mounted Display) Utilization. Okada et al. proposed a wearable moderator support system using an HMD for inexperienced moderators. The system used speech recognition to highlight the currently read script segment, implementing a script-tracking function. This function allowed moderators to easily resume reading after shifting their gaze away from the script. The evaluation results confirmed that the system was effective in facilitating smooth event moderation [11].

Abe et al. proposed an AR system aiming to provide both real-time support and training for eye contact skills. They defined appropriate eye contact based on the analysis of expert presentations and developed a system that offered spatial and temporal guidance. The system displayed spheres at the audience positions and connected them with lines to guide gaze shifts. Temporal support was provided by changing the color of the spheres to indicate the appropriate fixation duration. The script was also displayed at the center of the presenter's view.

2.2 Summary of Previous Research

Previous studies have primarily focused on real-time feedback through voice or behavior analysis. Even when providing gaze support, methods using external displays were standard. Many conventional support systems relied on external monitors, which could cause presenters to frequently divert their gaze away from the audience. As a solution to this issue, the effectiveness of presenting information using HMD has been demonstrated. However, HMDs are unsuitable for use in actual performance environments due to their conspicuous appearance. In addition, script tracking and gaze guidance were identified as effective methods for gaze support. Based on these findings, this study proposed a performance system utilizing natural-looking "smart glasses."

3 System

3.1 System Overview

In this study, we developed a support system that acquires the content of speech and gaze behavior in real time during a presentation, and provides script prompts and gaze guidance to the presenter. The system focuses on the problem that the presenter's gaze shifts markedly downward when referring to a script, and aims to support the presenter in continuing the presentation while maintaining gaze toward the audience.

Figure 1 shows the overall configuration of the system. The proposed system consisted of a gaze measurement device, speech recognition processing, and an information presentation mechanism using smart glasses. By integrally using gaze information and speech progress information, the system realized appropriate information presentation and gaze guidance according to the presentation situation.

3.2 System Configuration

The proposed system consists of gaze measurement and information presentation to the presenter.

Fig. 1. Configuration of the proposed system.

For gaze measurement, we used the Pupil Neon by Pupil Labs [6]. This device is a glasses-type gaze measurement apparatus that simultaneously records both eyes and the forward-facing scene, and can acquire the wearer's gaze direction in real time. The acquired gaze data were used for audience-area fixation detection and fixation duration measurement, as described in Sect. 3.3. In addition, for spatial determination of gaze position, a planar region defined using AprilTag [5] was utilized. On the defined plane, gaze positions were output in a normalized two-dimensional coordinate system with the top-left corner as $(0, 0)$ and the bottom-right corner as $(1, 1)$, and the fixation target was determined based on these coordinates.

For information presentation to the presenter, we used the Even G1 [12], a glasses-type display by Even Realities. Because this device can present textual information within the presenter's field of view, the presenter can check the script or instructions without large gaze shifts. Focusing on this characteristic, this study adopted it as a means to refer to the script and provided gaze guidance while facing the audience. On the Even G1, the single sentence of the script that should currently be referenced and the gaze guidance instructions are presented; by providing only the minimum necessary information, the system suppresses verbatim reading of the script.

3.3 Processing Algorithm

The system consists of gaze information processing, speech recognition processing, and integrated control that combines the two.

Gaze Information Processing. Using the gaze data obtained from the Pupil Neon, fixation detection is performed for the audience area defined by AprilTag. If the normalized gaze coordinates (x, y) satisfy $0 \leq x \leq 1$ and $0 \leq y \leq 1$, the presenter is determined to be fixating on the audience area. Furthermore, to distribute gaze evenly across the entire audience, the audience area is divided into three regions–Left, Center, and Right–based on the horizontal coordinate x. Fixation time in each region is accumulated per frame and used for the gaze guidance and warning judgments described later.

Speech Progress Estimation via Speech Recognition. Using Google Speech-to-Text [2], the content of the presenter's speech is transcribed into text in real time, and the progress position is estimated by comparing it with a pre-prepared script. In this system, we emphasize real-time performance and adopt a judgment method that focuses on the sentence-ending portion rather than the entire sentence. Specifically, the last 10 characters of each script sentence are extracted, and the string similarity with the ending portion of the speech recognition result is computed. When the similarity exceeds a predefined threshold, the system determines that the utterance of the corresponding sentence has been completed and proceeds to the next process. This method enables flexible progress estimation that is robust to fluctuations and hesitations in speech.

Integrated Control of Gaze and Speech Information. When utterance completion is detected by speech recognition, the system determines the audience area that should be fixated next and presents visual guidance instructions to the user on the Even G1. After the system detects that the user has fixated on the specified audience area, the displayed script is updated to the next sentence. The order of gaze guidance consists of one set of the three directions–Left, Center, and Right–and is generated in a random order. This prevents bias toward a particular direction and enables the presenter to direct gaze evenly to the entire audience.

3.4 System Operation Flow

First, gaze measurement and speech recognition are initiated in parallel and executed continuously during system operation.

When a sentence ending is detected by speech recognition, the audience area that should be fixated next is determined and presented as a visual guidance instruction. Once it is detected that the user has fixated on the presented audience area, the script is updated to the next sentence, and the system transitions again to the state of waiting for sentence-ending detection. This sequence of processing is repeated until the presentation ends. Furthermore, once the completion of the utterance of the final sentence in the preconfigured script is detected, the presentation is judged to have ended, and the system is terminated.

4 Experiment

This section describes the evaluation experiment conducted to verify the effectiveness of the proposed gaze guidance system.

4.1 Experimental Objective

This experiment focuses on gaze behavior during presentations and aims to clarify the effects of the proposed gaze guidance system on the presenter's gaze distribution and the audience's subjective impressions. To control for the influence of script presentation, the script was displayed under all conditions, and only the presence or absence of the gaze guidance function was used as the manipulated factor for comparative evaluation. In this experiment, the results obtained from the same participant under the "With Support" and "Without Support" conditions were compared.

4.2 Experimental Overview

The participants were 13 adults (8 males and 5 females; mean age: 22 years). The experiment was conducted, in principle, in a group format of four people (one presenter and three audience members). In some trials, an experimenter supplemented the audience due to insufficient audience members; however, the data of the experimenter were not included in the subjective evaluations described later.

The experiment was conducted in a rotation manner so that all participants experienced both roles. Each presentation lasted approximately 10 min, and to minimize the influence of cognitive load due to content understanding and memorization, slides and scripts that participants had previously presented were used.

The experiment was conducted according to the following procedure:

- Adjust the presentation slides and scripts in advance and format them so that they can be displayed on the smart glasses.
- Explain to the participants how to wear the devices and how the script is displayed.
- Conduct practice using a short practice script to train use of the system.
- Under the assigned condition (presence or absence of the gaze guidance system), conduct a 10-minute presentation.
- On a later date, under the other condition, conduct a presentation with the same content and the same procedure.
- After all trials are completed, have the participants answer the presenter questionnaire and the audience-role questionnaire.

4.3 Evaluation Metrics

Quantitative Evaluation by Gaze Distribution. To evaluate the dispersion of gaze to the left, center, and right, the entropy H was computed based on the proportion of fixation time p_i for each region ($i \in \{\text{Left, Center, Right}\}$):

$$H = -\sum_i p_i \log_2 p_i \qquad (1)$$

A higher entropy indicates that gaze is more evenly distributed. Differences between conditions were verified using a paired t-test.

4.4 Subjective Evaluation by Presenters

For usability evaluation of the system, SUS (System Usability Scale) was used, and for workload evaluation, NASA-TLX (Raw-TLX) was used. This allows confirmation of whether the improvement in gaze distribution is achieved without excessive mental or physical workload.

4.5 Subjective Evaluation of Presenters by Audience Role

To evaluate the impression that the presenter's gaze behavior gives to the audience, a subjective evaluation questionnaire was administered to participants in the audience role. Specifically, evaluations were requested on the following items:

- Did you feel that the presenter looked at the entire venue (left, center, right) in a balanced manner?
- Did you feel that the presenter's eyes met yours, or that they were facing your direction?
- Was the movement of the gaze natural?
- Was the impression of verbatim reading of the script weak?
- From the way the gaze was distributed, did you feel that the presenter was presenting with confidence?
- Was it easy to concentrate on the presentation content, and did you feel it was easy to listen?

Participants in the audience role, regardless of whether the system was used, responded to each item for all presenters they listened to using a 7-point Likert scale (7: strongly agree; 1: strongly disagree).

Through this evaluation, we verified the impact of the gaze guidance system on the impressions given to the audience via the presenter's gaze behavior.

5 Results and Discussion

5.1 Experimental Results

Analysis of Eye Movements. The comparison results of the average entropy, indicating the degree of variation in gaze under conditions with and without support, are shown in Fig. 2.

A paired t-test (one-tailed, assuming increased gaze dispersion) revealed a statistically significant difference ($t(12) = 2.64, p = .012$). The mean entropy for the condition without guidance was 1.03 ($SD = 0.31$), whereas for the condition with guidance, it was 1.29 ($SD = 0.24$). These results suggest that while gaze tended to be fixed in specific areas without guidance, the proposed support system facilitated a well-balanced gaze distribution across the left, center, and right areas. Regarding the standard deviation, no extreme variance was observed even in the condition with guidance, indicating that individual differences were relatively small and a stable support effect was achieved. Furthermore, the effect size was found to be strong (Cohen's $d = 0.80$). The 95% confidence interval for the mean difference was $[0.04, 0.46]$. Since the confidence interval does not include zero, the improvement in gaze dispersion by this method was confirmed to be statistically robust.

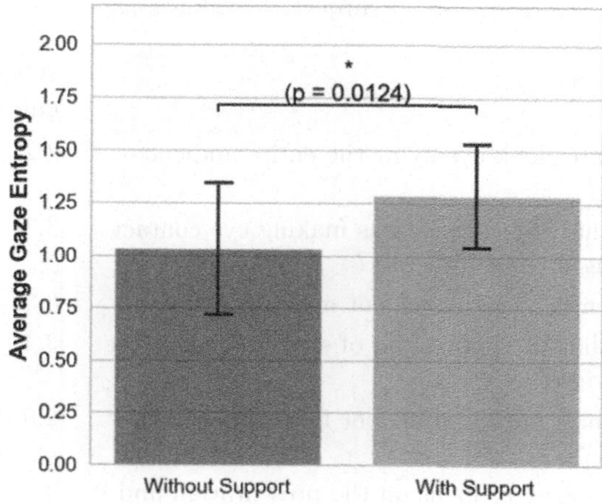

Fig. 2. Distribution of gaze allocation.

5.2 Survey Results

We present the results of the questionnaire used in this experiment. A Likert scale was used, with 1 point indicating 'strongly disagree' and 7 points indicating 'strongly agree'.

Table 1 shows a comparison of the average results of our original common survey on the audience's impression of the presenter.

The evaluation results confirmed that guiding the gaze can multifacetedly enhance the audience's impression. Specifically, there was a noticeable improvement in the impression that the presenter was making eye contact with the entire audience (Q1: 6.0 points), increased attention to eye contact (Q2: 5.8 points), and the confidence perceived from the presenter's behavior (Q5: 4.8 points). In addition, there were improvements in reducing the sense of reading from a script (Q4: 4.8 points) and the ease of understanding the presentation (Q6: 5.0 points). On the other hand, regarding the naturalness of the presentation, the score was slightly lower when using the system.

Evaluate the System's Usefulness. The system usability (SUS) was generally good, with an average score of 77.5 points($SD = 15.1$) as shown in Table 2. While it received high ratings for intuitive operation, there were individual differences due to physical device attributes, such as comfort when worn and interference with vision.

Table 1. Average score of subjective evaluations by the audience

Contents of Questions	Without guidance	With guidance
Q1. Did the presenter look evenly at the entire audience (right/center/left)?	3.2	6.0
Q2. Did you feel that the speaker was making eye contact with you or looking in your direction?	3.3	5.8
Q3. Was the presenter's eye movement natural?	3.5	3.4
Q4. Did you feel that the impression of simply reading the script aloud was weak?	3.4	4.8
Q5. Did the presenter appear confident from the way they directed their gaze?	2.9	4.8
Q6. Did you find it easy to focus on the presentation and listen to what was being said?	4.2	5.0

Table 2. Result of System Usability Scale (SUS)

Subject ID	Q1	Q2	Q3	Q4	Q5	Q6	Q7	Q8	Q9	Q10	Score
1	3	1	3	3	4	1	4	3	2	3	62.5
2	5	1	4	1	5	1	5	2	5	1	95.0
3	4	2	4	2	5	2	5	1	4	2	82.5
4	5	1	4	1	5	1	5	2	5	1	95.0
5	4	2	4	1	5	1	4	1	4	4	80.0
6	3	4	3	2	4	2	4	4	4	2	60.0
7	2	2	4	2	3	3	4	2	3	1	65.0
8	4	2	4	2	4	2	4	2	4	2	75.0
9	2	1	3	4	4	3	3	3	3	3	57.5
10	5	1	4	1	5	1	5	2	5	1	95.0
11	4	2	3	4	5	1	5	2	2	2	70.0
12	4	1	4	1	4	2	5	4	3	1	77.5
13	5	1	5	2	5	1	5	1	5	1	97.5
average	3.8	1.6	3.8	2.0	4.5	1.6	4.5	2.2	3.8	1.8	77.5
Standard deviation	1.1	0.9	0.6	1.1	0.7	0.8	0.7	1.0	1.1	1.0	15.1

NASA-TLX. To examine the impact of using the proposal system on users' workload, we conducted a subjective evaluation using NASA-TLX. In this experiment, Raw-TLX, which uses a simple average without weighting the individual subscales, was adopted.

For the analysis, a paired t-test (two-tailed) was used to compare the two conditions: with support and without support. The significance level was set at 5%.

Figure 3 shows the comparison of overall workload measured using the Raw-TLX. The analysis revealed no significant difference in overall workload between the support condition ($M = 38.1, SD = 15.0$) and the no-support condition ($M = 37.7, SD = 14.9$) ($t(12) = 0.10, p = .92$). The effect size was very small ($Cohen'sd = 0.03$), and the 95% confidence interval of the mean difference included zero ($[-8.09, 8.86]$). In contrast, in the subscale analysis, the Mental Demand score showed a higher mean value in the support condition.

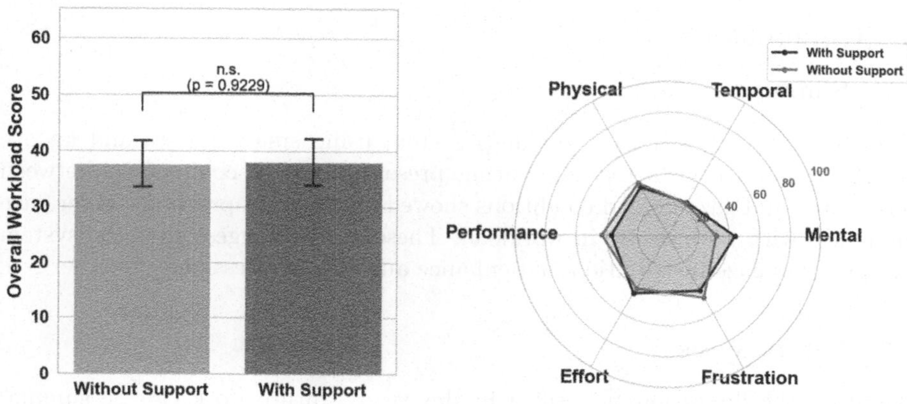

Overall Workload

Scores by item

Fig. 3. Evaluation results of workload using NASA-TLX.

5.3 Discussion

Considerations on Eye Movement Behavior. The significant increase in gaze entropy indicates that the proposed system successfully dispersed physical gaze. The fact that the audience rated the presenter as "appearing confident" highly suggests that, even though the system artificially generated the gaze movements, the audience interpreted them positively as "the presenter's composure" or "consideration." The decrease in Q3 regarding "naturalness" is thought to be due to the mechanical nature of following the arrows. In the future, it will be necessary to refine the guidance algorithm to move the gaze not just "anyway," but "at a natural timing."

Considerations on the System Usability Scale (SUS). High SUS scores, particularly strong agreement with positive questions, suggested that the smart glasses interface was intuitive and functionally consistent. Individual differences likely stemmed from device-specific factors such as fit and adaptation to focus shifting. Users unaccustomed to glasses or slow to adjust focus may have experienced a physical burden, and some participants wore smart glasses over their regular glasses. Optimizing guidance according to users' experience and preferences may further improve usability.

Considerations on NASA-TLX (System Workload). The increase in mental demand likely resulted from dual-tasking–speaking while monitoring guidance–and the system's active gaze prompts, which restricted free eye movements. Despite this, overall workload did not differ significantly, indicating that the system does not interfere with presentation performance. Future work should consider adjusting information based on user proficiency and improving physical fitting, including for regular glasses wearers.

6 Conclusions

6.1 Summary

This study proposes a gaze guidance system using smart glasses and an eye tracker to reduce gaze fixation during presentations. A comparison between script-only and gaze-guided conditions showed improved impressions under gaze guidance, with no increase in workload. These results suggest that the system can promote gaze distribution and enhance audience impressions.

6.2 Future Works

Based on the limitations identified in this study, future work can be summarized into three main directions. First, adaptive intervention of system support is required. To reduce the unnaturalness caused by constant guidance, the system should intervene only when inappropriate states, such as prolonged gaze fixation, are detected. In addition, non-mechanical guidance utilizing peripheral vision and the elimination of display delays through improved gaze detection accuracy are required. Second, automation of script generation using large language models (LLMs) is needed. By automatically summarizing and formatting scripts according to the limited display area of smart glasses and flexibly handling ad-libbed speech, the system can reduce the cost of prior preparation. Third, hardware integration should be addressed. Although the current system uses two separate devices, we aim to integrate the gaze measurement and information presentation functions into a single eyewear-type device to reduce wear burden and achieve a practical wearing experience.

Acknowledgment. This research was supported by the JKA Foundation through its Machinery Promotion Program (KEIRIN) (Grant No. 2025M-334). The authors would like to express their sincere appreciation to all those involved.

References

1. Cho, X., Yuizono, T., Munemori, J.: Development of a presentation support system focusing on non-verbal expressions. In: Proceedings of the IPSJ SIG Groupware and Network Services (GN), vol. 2015, no. 6, pp. 1–6 (2015). (in japanese)
2. Cloud, G.: Speech to text ai: speech recognition and transcription. https://cloud.google.com/speech-to-text#features. Accessed 30 Sept 2025

3. Daly, J.A., Vangelisti, A.L., Weber, D.J.: Speech anxiety affects how people prepare speeches: a protocol analysis of the preparation processes of speakers. Commun. Monogr. **62**(4), 383–397 (1995)
4. Kurihara, K., Goto, M., Ogata, J., Matsusaka, Y., Igarashi, T.: Presentation sensei: a presentation training system using speech and image processing. In: Proceedings of the 9th International Conference on Multimodal Interfaces, pp. 358–365 (2007)
5. Labs, P.: Neon - marker mapper - pupil labs docs. https://docs.pupil-labs.com/neon/pupil-cloud/enrichments/marker-mapper/. Accessed 30 Sept 2025
6. Labs, P.: Neon - overview - eye tracking for research and beyond. https://pupil-labs.com/products/neon. Accessed 30 Sept 2025
7. Murakami, R., Tsukagoshi, S., Kurihara, K.: A study on a gaze guidance system for presentations. In: Proceedings of the IPSJ SIG Entertainment Computing (EC), vol. 2017, no. 14, pp. 1–6 (2017). (in japanese)
8. Nagai, K.: Approaches to presentations. Finex **17**(99), 18–20 (2005). (in Japanese)
9. News, M.: 85% of people get nervous easily – "presentations," "first meetings," and "foreigners" cause anxiety (in Japanese). https://news.mynavi.jp/article/20130216-a035/. Accessed 5 Oct 2025
10. NTT Business Solutions: How to improve business presentation skills for success. https://www.nttbizsol.jp/knowledge/labor-force/202312041100000966.html. Accessed 30 Sept 2025. (in japanese)
11. Okada, T., Yamamoto, T., Terada, T., Tsukamoto, M.: Design and implementation of a wearable mc system. In: Proceedings of the 17th Workshop on Interactive Systems and Software (WISS), pp. 35–40 (2009). in Japanese
12. Realities, E.: Even g1 a smart glasses purchase (in japanese). https://www.evenrealities.com/ja-EE/products/g1-a?srsltid=AfmBOoqT2tc1jGk7ThsiKRbD7ThCKhLGa3akJN0VsznwEROtlVO4NrYn. Accessed 30 Sept 2025
13. Yokoyama, H., Daibo, I.: Effects of gaze and speech rate on receivers' evaluations of persuasive speech. Psychol. Rep. **110**(2), 663–676 (2012)

Eating Behavior Detection Using Wrist-Worn Sensing Modalities

Yukino Sato(✉), Huisha Yang, and Guillaume Lopez

Aoyama Gakuin University, Shibuya, Japan
{ysato,eisa}@wil-aoyama.jp, guillaume@it.aoyama.ac.jp

Abstract. This study evaluates the performance of eating action detection models using sensing modalities via wrist-worn devices. The hardware configuration consists of a commodity smartwatch and a camera mounted on the lateral side of the wrist-worn device, used to collect three types of data: acceleration, angular velocity, and images. We developed three eating action detection models corresponding to different modalities—sensor-only, camera-only, and a hybrid approach—and conducted multi-faceted evaluations using Leave-One-Participant-Out Cross-Validation. The proposed hybrid model leverages sensor-only predictions as a baseline and incorporates camera data as weights to refine detection in ambiguous movement scenarios. The results demonstrate that the hybrid late-fusion method achieved a peak F1-score of 0.86, although it lacked sufficient power to significantly bolster the sensor modality. However, through our analysis, we gained valuable insights for future performance improvements. Beyond overall metrics, we also analyzed the impact of different cutlery and dish types, providing insights into how specific dining styles influence detection accuracy. These findings offer a foundation for more robust and reliable automated dietary monitoring systems.

Keywords: Eating Action Detection · Multimodal Sensing · Wearable Devices

1 Introduction

1.1 Background

In recent years, dietary issues such as obesity and nutritional deficiencies due to unbalanced diets have been on the rise in Japan. To address these problems, the Ministry of Agriculture, Forestry, and Fisheries recommends consuming well-balanced meals that combine staple foods, main dishes, and side dishes, as well as maintaining regular eating habits [1,8]. However, despite these recommendations, only a limited number of people consistently follow these practices [7]. Furthermore, even among those who are health-conscious, many find it difficult to maintain a healthy diet due to a lack of accurate knowledge, the perceived burden of recording meals, or a lack of time. Given this background, we believe that an automated dietary habit recording system is essential to support users and encourage greater awareness of a healthy lifestyle.

E. Vlahu-Gjorgievska et al. (Eds.): PERSUASIVE 2026, CCIS 2896, pp. 538–550, 2027.
https://doi.org/10.1007/978-3-032-27235-5_55

1.2 Purpose of This Work

The primary goal of this research is to develop an automated dietary habit recording system using wearable modalities to improve awareness of healthy eating behaviors. Concretely, we have established the following two objectives:

1. Development of a wearable system capable of detecting eating actions and capturing meal images
2. Conduct a multi-faceted performance evaluation of the system's ability to detect eating actions

2 Related Work

2.1 Eating Action Detection Using Wrist-Worn Sensors

Dong et al. developed a meal detection system using wrist-worn iPhone sensors to track motion data, focusing on distinguishing eating from non-eating periods [2]. While the system successfully identified 86% of meal episodes, it produced a high volume of false positives, highlighting the difficulty of filtering out non-eating activities in free-living environments. Thomaz et al. proposed a practical method for detecting eating episodes using off-the-shelf smartwatches [10]. They developed an eating episode detection model and eating gesture classifier, achieving optimal F1-scores of 71.3%–76.1% in semi-controlled conditions. Similarly, the research by Kamachi et al. focuses on predicting eating activity using a smartwatch [4]. The study achieved a maximum accuracy of 76.4% and an average accuracy of 71.9% in free-living environment.

These studies highlighted the potential of smartwatches in automating dietary management by predicting eating activities based on arm movements. However, challenges remain, such as the misclassification of conversational movements as eating. Additionally, adapting to diverse eating styles—including the use of various cutlery and different ways of holding dishes—remains an area for further improvement.

2.2 Multimodal Eating Detection and Food Journaling

Merck et al. evaluated a multi-modal system using Google Glass, smartwatches, and modified earbuds to recognize eating activities in a noisy, multitasking environment [6]. They found that while acoustics alone were highly effective for detecting overall eating episodes, the system struggled with specific actions like chewing, intake, and drinking. Besides, the results showed low recall across the board, indicating that many individual eating movements were missed.

Sen et al. developed "Annapurna", a smartwatch-based food journaling system that uses inertial sensors to trigger an embedded camera only when eating gestures are detected [9]. This two-stage pipeline achieved reliable food image capture while maintaining practical battery life for daily use. While energy-efficient, the study noted that detection accuracy remains sensitive to variations in individual eating styles and environmental conditions.

2.3 Summary of Related Work and Research Positioning

While prior studies have utilized wrist-worn sensors to trigger cameras for food journaling, the camera has functioned primarily as a recording tool rather than an active component of the detection algorithm. Consequently, the potential for enhancing accuracy by integrating visual data directly into the inference process remains underexplored. Besides, existing evaluations often focus on system-level metrics, leaving a gap in understanding how specific dining contexts—such as cutlery and tableware—affect robustness.

Our research addresses these gaps by treating camera data as an independent evidence source integrated via late fusion.

3 Wrist-Worn Multimodal Sensing System

3.1 System Overview

Figure 1 shows the side view of the wrist-worn device and Fig. 2 shows the developed system overview. The wrist-worn device consists of a Google Pixel Watch [3], a camera (M5Stack Unit CamS3 Wi-Fi Camera [5]) mounted on the lateral side of the dominant hand, powered by a mobile battery attached to the upper arm. The user's smartphone controls the system and stores data through a dedicated application software. The Watch collects accelerometer and gyroscope sensor data at 50 Hz and continuously uploads it to the Firebase Realtime Database. Simultaneously, the camera, connected via Wi-Fi, captures images at approximately 2 fps and transmits them to the smartphone in realtime. To ensure subsequent data synchronization, both sensor data and images are saved with unique timestamps.

Fig. 1. Sideview of the device.

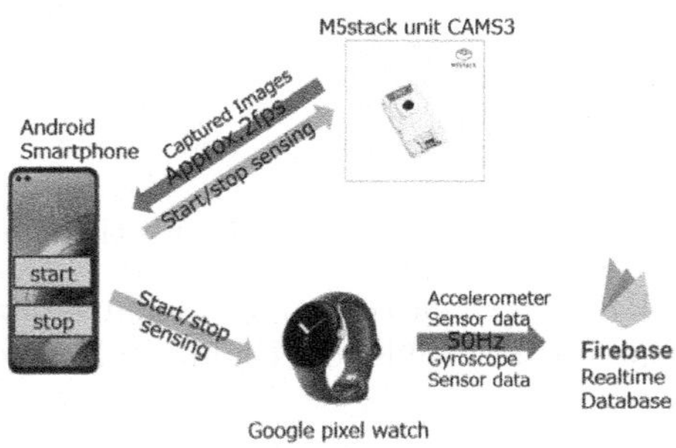

Fig. 2. Overview of the system.

3.2 Image Capture Strategy and Optimization

We conducted several preliminary studies to determine the optimal image capture strategy. First, to decide on the camera placement, we investigated how different camera positions affected the view of the food. The lateral side of the hand was the most suitable location, capturing images of the food located below the hand during the sequence of scooping food, bringing it to the mouth, and returning the hand to the table.

Regarding the image capture method, we conducted two preliminary studies. Since this research aims for eating detection via camera, we assumed that minimizing the capture interval is crucial to avoid missing meal images. Therefore, in the first investigation, we explored the capture method that achieves the shortest possible interval. We considered a total of eight combinations based on the following three factors:

1. **Control Method:** Controlling the capture via a smartphone or programming the camera to operate independently.
2. **Capture Mode:** Continuous shooting (burst mode) or single-shot capture.
3. **Storage Destination:** Local or cloud-based storage.

For each of the six combinations, we investigated the capture intervals achieved over a one-minute duration. Table 1 summarizes the results of this investigation. Based on these results, Method 1 (single-shot capture with smartphone integration and local storage) demonstrated the best performance in terms of capture intervals.

Table 1. Results of the capture intervals achieved over a one-minute duration for six different combinations

No.	Control Method	Capture Mode	Storage	Avg. Interval (sec)
1	Smartphone	Single-shot	Smartphone	0.7
2	Smartphone	Burst mode	Smartphone	2.0
3	Smartphone	Single-shot	Cloud	4.3
4	Smartphone	Burst mode	Cloud	10.0
5	Independent	Single-shot	Cloud	1.3
6	Independent	Burst mode	Cloud	10.0

As the next step, we conducted a second preliminary investigation to verify the stability of this method and the success rate of meal image capture at the current intervals. We compared Method 1, which showed the best performance, and Method 2, which showed the third-best performance. We included Method 2 to investigate how continuous shooting (burst mode) affects the quality and success of meal image capture. Each method was tested by three participants during their meals, without specific dietary instructions. The results are presented in Table 2.

We defined an "eating event" as the moment food enters the mouth. The capture success rate represents the ratio of eating events for which at least one image containing a portion of the food was successfully captured near the corresponding timestamp, verified through video analysis.

Table 2. Results of the second preliminary study: Capture performance for different meals and methods

Participant	Method	Meal Content	Capture Success Rate (%)	Avg. Interval (sec)
A	Method 1	Own meal	50.00	0.5
B	Method 1	Rice gratin	100.00	0.6
C	Method 1	Grilled-chicken don	12.00	0.5
D	Method 2	Pasta Bolognese	93.55	1.4
E	Method 2	Fried-chicken don	86.67	1.3
F	Method 2	Grilled-chicken don	16.98	1.4

The results revealed individual variation in the success rate. We attributed this variation to differences in eating styles. In particular, the camera tend to fail capturing images of meals when participants lifted the dish while eating. Furthermore, the instability observed during the system's startup phase was averaged out and the average capture interval for all participants became shorter.

Regarding the capture methods, no significant difference was observed in the quality of the captured content between Method 1 and Method 2. Considering that Method 1 (single-shot capture) is more efficient—whereas Method 2 (burst mode) results in a larger number of redundant images—we concluded that Method 1 is the most suitable approach for the proposed system.

4 Performance Validation of Eating Behavior Detection

4.1 Data Collection Experiment

We conducted a data collection experiment involving 14 participants (5 females and 9 males) to develop and evaluate the performance of our eating detection model. Ultimately, we collected data from 42 meal sessions (6.5h). In this experiment, each participant consumed three different meals in a semi-controlled laboratory environment. To ensure accurate annotation, a video camera was used to record each session. Participants provided informed consent after being briefed on the study's purpose and data usage (including images). We ensured participant safety through food allergy screenings, following our institution's ethical guidelines.

The experimental sessions were structured as follows:

1. **Session 1:** All participants ate Doria (rice gratin) served in short-medium tableware using a spoon.
2. **Session 2:** Participants were randomly divided into two groups. One group ate Oyakodon (chicken and egg bowl), and the other ate Butadon (pork bowl), both served in tall-medium tableware. They used both a spoon and chopsticks. Participants were instructed to switch cutlery approximately halfway through the meal; however, the initial cutlery and the exact timing of the switch were randomized for each participant.

3. **Session 3:** Participants were again randomly divided into two groups. One group ate Pasta using a fork, while the other ate Fried Rice using a spoon, both served in short-large tableware.

4.2 Labeling and Preprocessing

In this experiment, we initially defined eight labels for the accelerometer and gyroscope data based on the video recordings. The labels related to eating activities were defined as follows:

- **scoop**: Scooping food with cutlery.
- **carry**: Moving the food toward the mouth.
- **eating**: The sequence of putting food into the mouth and removing the cutlery.
- **putback**: Returning the cutlery to the dish.
- **still_eating**: Holding the cutlery in mid-air while chewing or during a brief pause in the eating process.
- **still**: Remaining stationary while not eating.
- **prep**: Preparing food (e.g., cutting, gathering, or swirling pasta).
- **else**: All other movements.

Defining an "eating action" as the sequence from scooping food to returning cutlery, we merged the labels (scoop, carry, eating, putback, and still_eating) into a single category: *eating_action*. All other labels were categorized as *else*.

Regarding the camera data, images were manually annotated as either "meal_image" (labeled as 1) or "non-meal_image" (labeled as 0). Since the detection models were developed based on these manual labels, the image-based component of this study functions as an "oracle" model, assuming 100% accuracy in visual classification. The image data were synchronized with the sensor data using Unix timestamps, allowing the sensor annotations to serve as the ground truth for the image-based detection tasks.

4.3 Model Architectures

We developed and evaluated three models based on different modalities: sensor-only, camera-only, and a hybrid approach (sensor+camera). For the sensor-only and hybrid approach, we employed Random Forest (RF) and Long Short-Term Memory (LSTM) as detection algorithms.

For the RF model, we extracted 80 features from eight input channels (triaxial Acc, Gyro, and their L2 norms). These include time-domain statistics and frequency-domain features. Table 3 summarizes these features.

The LSTM model was designed to capture temporal dependencies using standardized 6-axis data. The architecture consists of two 64-unit LSTM layers (dropout 0.2) followed by a fully connected layer for 2-class classification. Training was conducted using the Adam optimizer (LR: 0.001, batch size: 64) with cross-entropy loss over 30 epochs.

Table 3. Extracted features for the Random Forest model from sensor data

Category	Feature Description
Input Channels	Acc (x, y, z), Gyro (x, y, z), $\|Acc\|_2$, $\|Gyro\|_2$ (Total: 8 channels)
Time-domain	Mean, Standard Deviation, Maximum, Minimum, Range Skewness, Kurtosis, Zero-Crossing Rate (ZCR)
Frequency-domain	Dominant Frequency (via FFT), Spectral Entropy
Total number of features: 8 channels × 10 features = 80 features	

The continuous sensor data (50 Hz) were segmented using a 100-sample (2.0 s) sliding window with a 50-sample (1.0 s) step. This window size was chosen to capture the full duration of typical eating actions.

Camera-Only Oracle Baseline. The model using image data is based on an oracle setting. In this study, images are manually labeled as "meal" or "non-meal," and no specific image classifier is evaluated here. The detection logic is straightforward: all frames labeled as 1 (meal_image) were predicted as *eating_action*, while those labeled as 0 (non-meal_image) were predicted as *else*.

Integration Strategy: Multi-modal Late Fusion. Based on the insights gained from developing sensor-only and camera-only models, as well as several prototype iterations, we developed a sensor-centric hybrid model using late fusion. This model primarily relies on sensor-driven predictions while incorporating the camera's eating detection flags as a weighting factor. The process is defined as follows. First, the sensor models (RF or LSTM) output a probability distribution P over the 2 classes using the softmax function:

$$P = \{p_{else}, p_{eating\_action}\} \tag{1}$$

Since the camera flag F_{camera} is derived from the oracle labeling, this hybrid model also operates as an oracle-based evaluation for the visual component. Specifically, when a captured image of the camera is identified as a meal photo ($F_{camera} = 1$), a "reward" weight w is added to the probability of the eating action class. The final prediction $\hat{y}$ is then determined by the class with the highest adjusted probability:

$$\hat{y} = \text{argmax}(p_0, p_1 + w \cdot F_{camera}) \tag{2}$$

During the development phase, we conducted an experimental validation by varying the weight w to evaluate its impact on detection performance.

4.4 Evaluation Methodology

In this study, we conducted performance evaluations across three types of modalities: sensor-only, camera-only, and the hybrid (sensor+camera) approach.

Cross-Validation and Metrics: For both the sensor-only and hybrid analysis, we evaluated the model using Leave-One-Participant-Out (LOPO) cross-validation, with Precision, Recall, and F1-score as performance metrics.

Camera-Only Analysis: For the camera-only analysis, we evaluated the detection capability under ideal conditions; thus the results suggest the theoretical upper bound for the camera's performance regarding visual classification. The camera-only analysis was evaluated on a per-participant basis by applying the classification logic to each individual's dataset.

Impact of Eating Styles: We further analyzed the F1-scores categorized by cutlery type and dish type. Specifically, the dishes were classified into three categories: tall-medium, short-medium, and short-large, based on their height and diameter. This sub-analysis was conducted to verify how different eating styles and the physical constraints of tableware influence the accuracy of eating detection.

4.5 Results and Discussion

Sensor-Only Analysis. First, the overall performance of the sensor-based models is summarized in Table 4. Both the RF and LSTM models demonstrated high detection capabilities, with identical precision of 0.87 and recall of 0.84, resulting in F1-scores of 0.86 and 0.85, respectively.

Table 4. Overall performance metrics for the eating_action in the sensor-based models

Model	Precision	Recall	F1-score
Random Forest	0.87	0.84	0.86
LSTM	0.87	0.84	0.85

Tables 5 represent the individual LOPO cross-validation results for each participant using the RF and LSTM models. Notably, lower scores were observed for P07, P09, and P13. This can be attributed to P07's slow movement speed and P09/P13's posture of leaning close to the dish, which resulted in subtle hand movements. These findings suggest that individual differences in speed and posture are primary factors influencing the robustness of sensor-based detection.

Camera-Only Analysis. Next, the results for the camera-only analysis showed a precision of 0.82, a recall of 0.28, and an F1-score of 0.41. The results highlighted a significant issue with frequent missed detections. The precision results suggest that meal images were captured outside of actual eating actions. Visual inspection confirmed that meal scenes were present even during meal preparation (Fig. 3) or during periods of inactivity (Fig. 4).

We considered the lower recall to be attributed to the broad definition of "eating action" and individual variations in eating behavior. For instance, reviewing

Table 5. LOPO-CV results for sensor-only models

Participant ID	Random Forest (F1)	LSTM (F1)
P01	0.91	0.91
P02	0.93	0.91
P03	0.85	0.87
P04	0.91	0.90
P05	0.93	0.93
P06	0.83	0.84
P07	0.56	0.53
P08	0.96	0.94
P09	0.76	0.72
P10	0.85	0.85
P11	0.85	0.82
P12	0.85	0.85
P13	0.70	0.72
P14	0.87	0.87
Average (Ave.)	**0.841**	**0.833**
Std. Deviation (Std.)	**0.106**	**0.106**

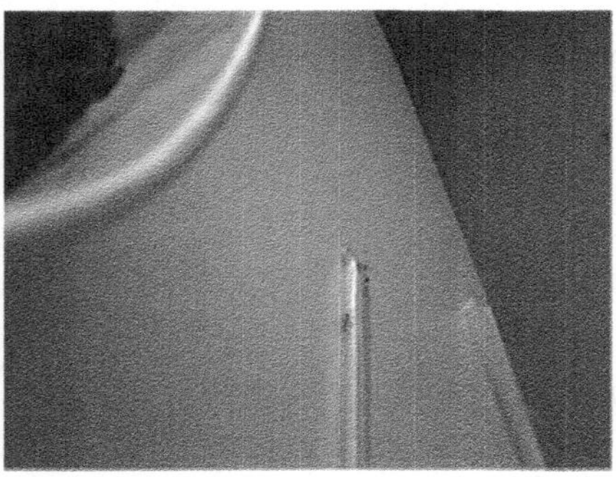

Fig. 3. Image during food preparation.

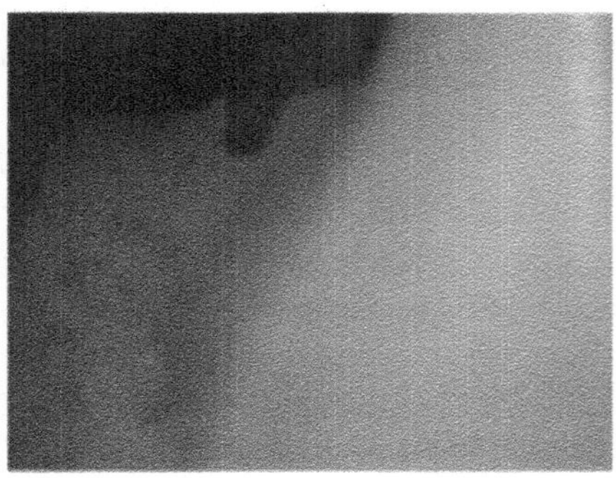

Fig. 4. Image during periods of inactivity.

the recorded data revealed that although the camera captured images at the set intervals, holding a bowl often caused the camera to point toward the table or the side of the dish. Consequently, the camera failed to capture the actual food or the moment of ingestion, leading to detection failures. Furthermore, the variance of the individual F1-score was 0.151. This high variability, especially compared to the sensor data, suggests that camera-based detection is more affected by individual differences in eating styles, such as posture and the specific trajectory of hand movements.

Hybrid Method Analysis. Table 6 presents the performance of the hybrid late fusion method using the optimal weights identified through extensive testing ($w = 0.1$ for RF and $w = 0.2$ for LSTM), which yielded the best results among all evaluated combinations. The results showed that while the hybrid model outperformed the camera-only model in F1-score, it offered negligible improvement over the sensor-only model. We initially hypothesized that visual information would compensate for the sensor's limitations, such as missed detections or ambiguous signals that are difficult to classify using motion data alone; however, the limited accuracy of the current camera-only model hindered significant performance gains. Improvements are expected as more sophisticated image recognition models—capable of distinguishing eating actions (Fig. 5) from meal preparation (Fig. 6)—are integrated.

Table 6. Overall performance metrics for the eating_action class in the hybrid model

Model	Precision	Recall	F1-score
Random Forest	0.87	0.85	0.86
LSTM	0.86	0.84	0.85

Fig. 5. Image during eating action.

Fig. 6. Image during meal preparation.

Impact of Dining Styles. Table 7 presents the detection performance across different cutlery types. The results indicate that forks achieved the highest F1-scores, while spoons yielded the lowest. This disparity can be attributed to the relatively forceful and distinct movements associated with forks, such as stabbing or twirling food, which are easier for the models to characterize. Chopsticks and spoons exhibit lower discriminability compared to forks, likely because they involve more subtle movements and a wider variety of usage patterns.

Table 7. Performance comparison (F1-score) by cutlery type

Cutlery Type	Sensor-only		Hybrid		Sensor-based	Camera-only
	RF	LSTM	RF	LSTM	Avg.	Oracle
Fork	0.90	0.88	0.89	0.86	**0.88**	0.56
Spoon	0.85	0.82	0.84	0.83	**0.84**	0.38
Chopsticks	0.85	0.86	0.86	0.86	**0.86**	0.39

Table 8 presents the results for different types of dishes. For sensor based models, the "short-large" dish achieved the highest performance, while the "short-medium" dish showed the lowest. Since the discriminability of sensor-based models is likely dependent on motion amplitude, we consider that larger or deeper dishes result in higher accuracy because they elicit more pronounced movements than medium or shallower ones.

Table 8. Performance comparison (F1-score) by dish type, including the average of sensor-based models.

Dish Type	Sensor-only		Hybrid		Sensor-based	Camera-only
	RF	LSTM	RF	LSTM	Avg.	Oracle
Short_large	0.88	0.88	0.88	0.87	**0.88**	0.39
Short_medium	0.82	0.82	0.82	0.83	**0.82**	0.47
Tall_medium	0.85	0.85	0.86	0.85	**0.85**	0.40

Regarding the camera's detection performance, we initially hypothesized that larger or shallower dishes would improve visibility and result in higher accuracy. However, the results showed that the short-large dishes had the lowest accuracy, while the short-medium dishes performed best. This suggests that camera visibility may be more significantly influenced by individual eating habits than by specific meal styles, such as cutlery or dish types. Given that these findings are based on a limited set of scenarios, further validation is required to precisely identify the contributing factors.

5 Conclusion and Future Work

5.1 Conclusion

In this study, we aimed to develop an automated dietary habit recording system using wearable modalities to encourage greater awareness of healthy eating behaviors. We developed a wrist-worn multimodal sensing system and eating detection models, followed by a multi-faceted performance evaluation. The hybrid approach maintained stable detection performance (F1-score: 0.86) while fulfilling a critical requirement for dietary recording systems: the preservation of meal images. Although the hybrid model did not show significant accuracy improvements over single-modality models, it provided a crucial insight for future development: the necessity of distinguishing active eating actions and meal preparation stages in visual data to enhance accuracy. Furthermore, by analyzing detection performance across various cutlery and dish types, we provided critical insights for practical optimization of automated dietary monitoring systems.

5.2 Future Work

For future work, we aim to refine the hybrid system by automating and enhancing the camera-based model using the insights gained from this study. Furthermore, we plan to address practical challenges, such as ensuring user privacy, reducing redundant captures, and optimizing battery efficiency for long-term use. Ultimately, we aim to develop a comprehensive application that automatically detects eating actions in real-world settings, enabling the automated logging and analysis of dietary content, eating pace, and timing.

References

1. Ministry of Agriculture, F., Fisheries: When you eat late. https://www.maff.go.jp/j/syokuiku/minna_navi/topics/topics2_03.html
2. Dong, Y., Scisco, J., Wilson, M., Muth, E., Hoover, A.: Detecting periods of eating during free-living by tracking wrist motion. IEEE J. Biomedical Health Inform. **18**(4) (2014)
3. Google: Google pixel watch. https://support.google.com/googlepixelwatch/answer/12651869?hl=ja#zippy=
4. Kamachi, H., Hossain, T., Tokuyama, F., Yokokubo, A., Lopez, G.: Prediction of eating activity using smartwatch. In: Proceedings of the 9th International Workshop on Human Activity Sensing Corpus and its Application (HASCA) (2021)
5. M5Stack: Unit cams3-5mp. https://docs.m5stack.com/ja/unit/Unit-CAMS3
6. Merck, C., Maher, C., Mark, M., Zheng, M., Huang, Y., Kleinberg, S.: Multimodality sensing for eating recognition. Pervasive Health (2016)
7. Ministry of Agriculture, Forestry and Fisheries: Current status of interest in food education and eating habits among children and younger generations (2023). https://www.maff.go.jp/j/syokuiku/r5/r5_h/book/part1/chap2/b1_c2_1_02.html. (in Japanese)
8. Ministry of Agriculture, Forestry and Fisheries: "food education" nurtures "the power to eat" = "the power to live." let's expand the circle of practice (2025). https://www.gov-online.go.jp/article/201605/entry-8642.html#secondSection. (in Japanese)
9. Sougata, S., Vigneshwaran, S., Archan, M., Rajesh, B., Youngki, L.: Annapurna: an automated smartwatch-based eating detection and food journaling system. Pervasive Mob. Comput. **68**, 101259 (2020). https://doi.org/10.1016/j.pmcj.2020.101259

10. Thomaz, E., Essa, I., Abowd, G.D.: A practical approach for recognizing eating moments with wrist-mounted inertial sensing. In: Proceedings of the 2015 ACM International Joint Conference on Pervasive and Ubiquitous Computing (UbiComp 2015), pp. 1029–1040. Association for Computing Machinery (2015). https://doi.org/10.1145/2750858.2807545

Personality Recognition Based on Digital Footprints for Better Online Workplace

Ryosuke Takizawa(✉) and Yutaka Arakawa

Department of Information Science and Technology, Graduate School of Information Science and Electrical Engineering, Kyushu University, Fukuoka, Japan
takizawa.ryosuke.400@s.kyushu-u.ac.jp, arakawa@ait.kyushu-u.ac.jp

Abstract. Personality-based interventions in HR effectively improve engagement and reduce turnover. However, traditional assessments like the Big Five are often impractical due to questionnaire length, while remote work limits the face-to-face interactions managers typically rely on. In this study, we propose a novel approach to estimate personality traits by analyzing digital footprints from business chat tools like Slack and Teams. Unlike content analysis or physical sensors, our method quantifies behavioral patterns–specifically when and how users respond. By examining parameters such as message frequency, reaction counts, and response timing, we treat these metrics as "digital behavioral sensors" to infer personality traits in a virtual environment. Our analysis focused on logs from Slack workspace used by approximately 50 members over a five-year period, correlating reaction patterns with Big Five collected with the participants' consent. As a result, we identified relationships between online behaviors and personality traits, such as the finding that individuals with higher conscientiousness exhibited shorter response times in chats. This system provides a way to unobtrusively assess team members' personality traits through their daily use of the tool, facilitating smoother team interactions and more effective communication in the absence of face-to-face cues.

Keywords: Personality Recognition · Digital Footprints · Big Five · Business Chat Tools · Slack Logs

1 Introduction

In recent years, the prevalence of telework has increased markedly, primarily driven by the impact of the COVID-19 pandemic. According to a survey on communication usage trends conducted by the Ministry of Internal Affairs and Communications[1], the telework adoption rate among companies rose from 13.9

Recent research has increasingly explored the relationship between communication behaviors and individual personality traits [3]. Theoretical frameworks, such as the Big Five [1] and the Myers-Briggs Type Indicator (MBTI) [7], are

[1] https://www.soumu.go.jp/johotsusintokei/statistics/data/230529_1.pdf.

E. Vlahu-Gjorgievska et al. (Eds.): PERSUASIVE 2026, CCIS 2896, pp. 551–562, 2027.
https://doi.org/10.1007/978-3-032-27235-5_56

commonly employed to assess human personality. For instance, individuals with high Extraversion are generally more talkative, while those with low Neuroticism may exhibit heightened concern for others [2]. Although previous studies have examined these relationships in face-to-face contexts, the connection between online chat communication and personality traits remains underexplored. A deeper understanding of this relationship could facilitate the identification of optimal communication strategies tailored to individual differences, or enable inferences about personality based on observed communication styles, ultimately promoting smoother and more harmonious interactions.

From a behavior recognition perspective, traditional activity recognition relies on physical sensors, such as accelerometers, to capture movement patterns. However, with the increasing digitalization of work environments, human behavioral patterns are now extensively manifested in digital spaces. This study extends behavior recognition to the digital domain by treating chat logs as behavioral sensors, analogous to accelerometers in physical activity recognition.

First, this study aims to understand the state of organizational communication by analyzing logs from Slack used in a university laboratory. We define "digital footprints" as the traces of user behavior left through interactions with business chat tools. These footprints include quantifiable behavioral logs such as the number of messages sent, the number of reactions given, response time to messages, peak activity time, and the types of reactions used. Among these digital footprints, response time and peak activity time are novel parameters defined in this study based on Slack logs.

Next, to investigate the relationship between digital footprints and personality, we conducted a Big Five personality assessment [8] in the same laboratory and analyzed the correlation between the results and digital footprints. The analysis of the survey results revealed that, compared to Japanese national averages, participants tended to exhibit higher Openness, Agreeableness, and Neuroticism, but lower Conscientiousness. The analysis yielded intriguing findings regarding the link between personality traits and digital footprints: individuals with higher Conscientiousness exhibited faster response times, those with higher Agreeableness provided more reactions, and those using a wider variety of reaction types scored higher in Extraversion and Openness.

This study limits its analysis to business tool metadata. This approach mitigates ethical concerns associated with monitoring offline behavior or private social media logs, thereby facilitating practical organizational adoption.

2 Related Work

This chapter reviews prior work on digital footprint analysis and personality recognition. Existing research falls largely into two categories: one focusing on collective and online/offline behavioral analysis using workplace tools, and the other addressing personality prediction via logs from general-purpose platforms such as social media and smartphones. To clearly position the present study, we discuss the challenges within each domain and highlight the distinct advantages of our approach.

2.1 Analysis of Communication Using Chat Logs

In our previous research, we aimed to visualize communication [9] within organizations by quantitatively representing interactions in business chats to identify isolated users and inactive groups. We defined new parameters, "Contribution" and "Adjacency", to represent the level of individual activity in business chats and the strength of interpersonal communication links, respectively. The size of a node represented the level of Contribution, while the distance between nodes indicated Adjacency, effectively visualizing communication as a social graph. The chat logs analyzed consisted of four types:

- Message information
- Reaction information
- Mention information
- Thread information

Contribution and Adjacency were defined based on these logs. By clustering the social graph, our study identified isolated users exhibiting low engagement within the organization and analyzed inactive groups and user types.

Additionally, Wang et al. [10] analyzed the group chat ecology of enterprise instant messaging platforms like Slack and investigated employee collaboration through multi-user channels. Using a large corporate dataset, they defined 21 meta-features independent of message content, which allowed them to construct a machine learning model for automatically classifying group channel types. Furthermore, they used these communication metrics to analyze the relationship with project team performance via a regression model, contributing to an empirical understanding of human-to-human communication practices in enterprise settings. However, while Wang et al.'s research focuses on macro aspects, such as overall organizational structure and collective collaboration patterns, our study concentrates on the micro aspects of individual user personality traits. Rather than focusing solely on organizational efficiency, our work investigates how individual psychological traits are manifested in digital footprints.

Kim et al. [4] conducted research to unobtrusively detect user personality traits from both online and offline workplace behaviors. They proposed a framework that combines offline data, such as physical activity and location information collected from sensors and smart devices, with online digital footprints like email and instant messaging, demonstrating the feasibility of personality assessment in a work environment. A key advantage of our study lies in the feasibility of log collection and the mitigation of ethical concerns. While collecting offline data such as physical activity involves significant privacy and technical barriers, we limit our focus strictly to usage logs of a business tool, presenting an approach with lower barriers to organizational adoption.

2.2 Personality Recognition from General Digital Footprints

Marengo et al. [6] conducted a meta-analysis integrating numerous studies on the digital phenotyping of the Big Five personality traits using Facebook logs.

Their study evaluated the overall accuracy of predicting personality traits using digital footprints such as "likes", post content, and profile information from social media platforms like Facebook. They quantitatively assessed which traits are most consistently correlated with specific digital footprints, summarizing the general predictive capability and research trends in this field.

Similarly, Watt et al. [11] quantitatively evaluated the informativeness of public social media profiles in predicting diverse personal attributes, including personality traits, age, gender, and interests. Focusing on static profiles, they demonstrated that public information serves as a comprehensive source for inferring individual attributes and traits.

Marengo et al. [5] also conducted a meta-analysis statistically integrating numerous studies on predicting the Big Five traits from smartphone logs. This research quantitatively assessed the potential of digital footprints–such as location sensor data, usage time, and app usage logs–to predict personality traits, thereby summarizing the general predictive capabilities and research trends regarding non-intrusive personality recognition in this domain.

However, these studies primarily rely on private social media data, profile information, or general smartphone logs, which often raise ethical concerns related to privacy. In contrast, we aim to establish a quantitative foundation for assisting in smoother team coordination by estimating individual traits from business-related metadata while preserving privacy.

3 Chat Logs Retrieval System and Definition of New Parameters

This chapter describes the system for retrieving chat logs from Slack, a popular chat service, and defines new parameters based on the logs for this study.

3.1 Definition of New Parameters Based on Slack Logs

To describe the communication behavior of users within an organization on Slack, we use parameters such as the number of messages, number of reactions, response time, and peak activity time. The number of messages and reactions can be obtained through the Slack API, while response time and peak activity time are newly defined parameters based on Slack logs. The details are as follows:

1. Number of Messages
   The total number of messages sent by a user during the period. This includes messages in threads and mentions.
2. Number of Reactions
   The total number of reactions sent by a user during the period. Even if the same user reacts multiple times to the same message, all reactions are counted. This is because such behavior is considered meaningful and could be related to personality traits discussed later.

3. Response Time
   The average time elapsed from the sending of a message to the response during the period. Here, the response is defined as a reaction sent to another person's message. The response time is calculated as the difference between the timestamp of the other person's message obtained through the Slack API and the timestamp of the reaction obtained by the system described in Sect. 3.1. The reason for defining a reaction as a response is that if a message is used as a response to another person's message, it is difficult to distinguish whether that message is genuinely a reply or is about an entirely different topic. Additionally, Slack has a thread function, but there is a difference in the ease of action between thread messages and reactions. Mixing them could lead to variability in response time due to their different proportions. Furthermore, the aggregated logs show that some users do not use threads while others frequently use reactions. Therefore, in this study, the time difference between a message and the corresponding reaction is defined as the response time.
   Reactions made after a certain period from the time the message was sent are excluded from this parameter's definition. This is because, in cases where a reaction is given after a significant amount of time has passed, it may have been added upon reviewing past conversations or for purposes other than responding, such as reminding others of a message. Such reactions could significantly affect the average response time.
   Although response time could ideally be defined as the duration from when a user reads a message to when they respond, such information is not available in Slack logs. Therefore, response time is operationally defined as an observable response latency based on message and reaction timestamps.
4. Peak Activity Time
   A parameter representing the time period during which the user was most active on Slack. The peak activity time is defined by aggregating the timestamps of messages obtained from the API for each time period and identifying the period with the highest frequency of message transmissions. The reason for using messages is that the peak times for sending messages and reactions may differ; reactions may be used during other tasks or while commuting to indicate that a message has been read. Considering these circumstances, it is preferable to determine the time of the most active communication on Slack based on message transmission rather than reactions.
   To define the peak activity time, the time is divided into six segments: 0–4, 4–8, 8–12, 12–16, 16–20, and 20–24 h. The time period with the highest message transmission frequency is defined as the user's peak activity time.
   Since some laboratory members, especially students, actively use Slack outside typical working hours, peak activity time was defined over the entire day.

The chat logs used in this study span eight months, from April 1, 2023, to November 30, 2023. To protect privacy, the content of messages and reactions is not considered in this study. For the same reason, the log aggregation is limited to conversations in Slack's public channels and does not include conversations in private channels or direct messages.

4 Analysis of the Relationship Between Organizational Communication and Personality

We analyze the relationship between communication behavior in organizational business chats (Slack) and personality (Big Five). To assess the Big Five among students, secretaries, and faculty members in the lab, we used the shortened Big Five scale by Namikawa et al. [8]. This scale reduces the number of items measuring the Big Five to 29 while maintaining a sufficient level of validity and reliability by correlating with the original Big Five scale.

4.1 Results of Big Five Assessment from the Survey

The results of the survey conducted among 34 people, including students, secretaries, and faculty members, are shown in Fig. 1.

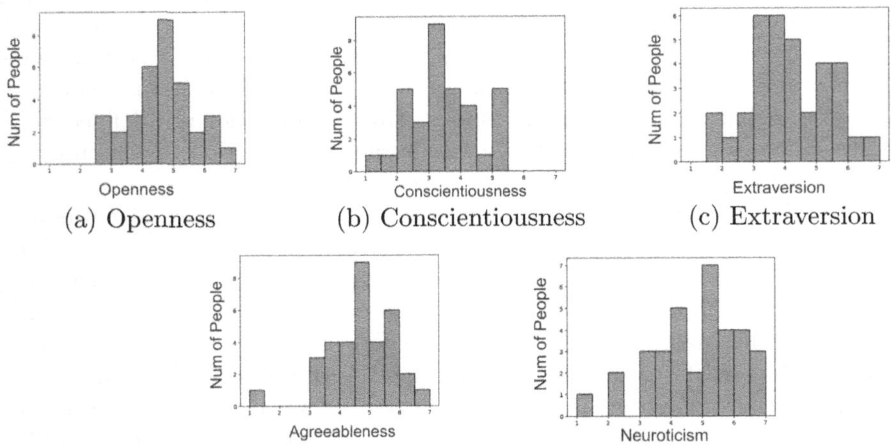

(a) Openness (b) Conscientiousness (c) Extraversion

(d) Agreeableness (e) Neuroticism

Fig. 1. Number Distribution of Each Personality Factor Based on Survey Results.

The histogram indicates that Openness is distributed towards the higher end, with an average above 4, which is the midpoint of the 7-point scale. Similarly, Agreeableness and Neuroticism are also distributed towards the higher end, though there are users with extremely low values (below 1.5) for both factors. Extraversion is close to a normal distribution around the center, but Conscientiousness is left-skewed compared to the other four factors, with no users having values above 5.5. Table 1 shows the averages, variances, and the average Big

Five scores in Japan. Compared to the Japanese average [12], where Agreeableness is the highest and Extraversion is the lowest, the survey results show that Neuroticism is the highest at 4.74, and the lowest factor is Conscientiousness at 3.42.

Table 1. Mean and Variance of the Survey for each Big Five factor

	Mean	Japanese Mean	Variance
Openness	4.52	3.88	0.96
Conscientiousness	3.42	4.05	1.10
Extraversion	4.01	3.81	1.61
Agreeableness	4.63	4.82	1.22
Neuroticism	4.74	4.01	1.97

4.2 Results of Slack Communication Logs

Next, the Slack communication logs obtained using the system described in Sect. 3 is shown in Fig. 2.

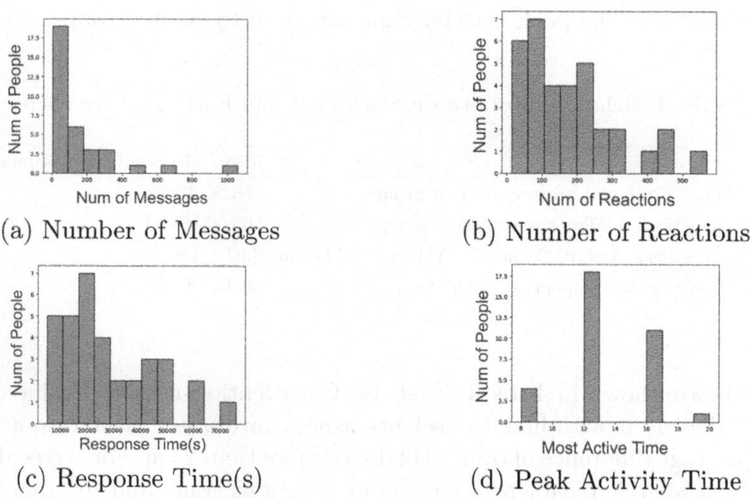

(a) Number of Messages (b) Number of Reactions

(c) Response Time(s) (d) Peak Activity Time

Fig. 2. Number Distribution of Each Parameter Based on Slack Logs.

Regarding the number of messages, most people fall into the range of 0–300, though there are a few users exceeding 600 messages. In contrast, the distribution of reactions is relatively less skewed compared to the number of messages. The peak activity time is between 12 PM and 4 PM, with no users being most active between 12 AM and 8 AM.

Table 2 shows the averages and variances for each parameter. Using this data, we investigate the relationship between organizational communication and personality.

Table 2. Mean and Variance of Slack Parameters

	Mean	Variance
Number of Messages	153.15	4.59×10^4
Number of Reactions	178.91	1.83×10^4
Response Time	27883	3.10×10^8
Peak Activity Time	13.06	8.06

4.3 Analysis of the Relationship Between Slack Logs and Personality

To examine the relationship between Slack logs and the Big Five, we created groups based on the top and bottom 20% of values for each parameter and compared these groups using Mann-Whitney U tests due to the lack of normality assurance for the populations. The results are all significant at the 5% level of one-sided testing. The peak activity time was used to create groups.

Table 3. Relationship Between Slack Logs and Each Big Five Factor

	Mean	Mean of Other Groups	p-Value
Response Time(s) in high Conscientiousness group	16828	30253	.045
Number of Reactions in high Agreeableness group	265.50	160.36	.045
Openness in the Peak Activity Time of 8 AM to 12 PM group	3.63	4.64	.046
Response Time(s) in high Openness group	39065	25487	.030

Results are shown in Table 3. First, for Conscientiousness, a p-value of 0.045 indicates that users with high Conscientiousness have faster Slack response time, with an average difference of over 10,000 s, or more than 2.5 h. For Agreeableness, groups with high Agreeableness have more reactions compared to other groups. For Openness, users most active between 8 AM and 12 PM tend to have lower Openness, and high Openness groups show slower chat response time. These results show a strong relationship between reaction parameters and personality.

Therefore, it was considered that not only the number of reactions but also the types of reactions might relate to personality. Before investigating the relationship, reactions were categorized based on their context. Four groups particularly related to personality were considered (Fig. 3).

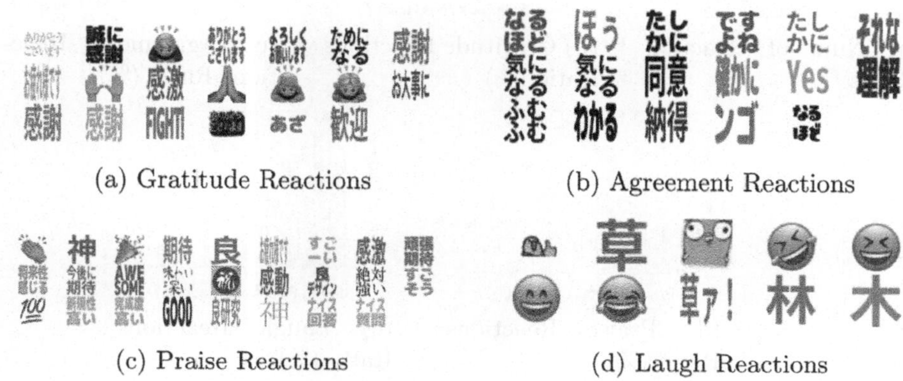

(a) Gratitude Reactions (b) Agreement Reactions

(c) Praise Reactions (d) Laugh Reactions

Fig. 3. Grouping of Reactions.

1. Gratitude Reactions: Reactions showing appreciation and respect.
2. Agreement Reactions: Reactions indicating agreement, such as "I see" or "I understand".
3. Praise Reactions: Reactions that compliment others, such as "Great" or "Amazing".
4. Laugh Reactions: Reactions related to laugh, such as "LOL" or smiley faces.

Additionally, the number of reaction types used by each user was considered as a parameter. The distribution of reaction types and each reaction group is shown in Fig. 4.

Investigating the relationship between reaction types and personality, significant differences at the 5% level are shown in Table 4.

Results show that high number of reaction types are associated with higher Openness. Similarly, high number of reaction types are also associated with higher Extraversion, while low gratitude reactions ratio are associated with lower Extraversion. For Agreeableness, users with low praise reactions ratio tend to have lower Agreeableness. High Neuroticism groups have a higher praise reactions ratio, and low Conscientiousness groups show low number of reaction types and lower praise reactions ratio.

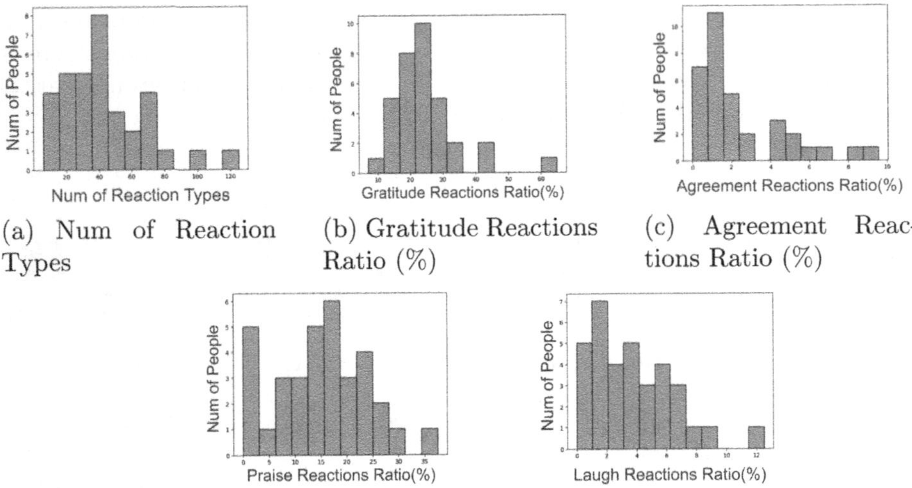

(a) Num of Reaction Types
(b) Gratitude Reactions Ratio (%)
(c) Agreement Reactions Ratio (%)
(d) Praise Reactions Ratio (%)
(e) Laugh Reactions Ratio (%)

Fig. 4. Number Distribution of Users Based on the Types and Proportions of Reactions Used.

5 Discussion and Future Direction

This study analyzes Slack logs collected in a university laboratory, which differs from general corporate environments in organizational structure and work practices. Therefore, the generalizability of the results to corporate settings should be interpreted with caution.

Furthermore, communication behavior in enterprise chat tools may depend on organizational roles (e.g., managers versus non-managerial members). As role information was not explicitly controlled in this study, the observed relationships should be interpreted with this limitation in mind.

We first discussion Extraversion, it was initially hypothesized that Extraversion, which represents sociability, assertiveness, and activity, would be strongly related to communication in chat, including message and reaction counts. However, it was found that Extraversion affects the number of reaction types and reactions related to gratitude, while the number of messages did not show a relationship with personality traits. Additionally, the number of reactions was found to be related to Agreeableness. The tendency for individuals with high Agreeableness to have more reactions can be attributed to the fact that sending reactions is an action associated with consideration and kindness towards others.

Regarding Conscientiousness, the tendency for high individuals in Conscientiousness to have faster response times can be explained by their strong sense of discipline and responsibility. This suggests that it is not that high Conscientiousness individuals discover new chats more quickly, but rather that the time taken to respond to a chat after discovering it is shorter.

Table 4. Relationship Between Reaction Types Used and Big Five

	Mean	Mean of Other Groups	p-Value
Openness in high Number of Reaction Types group	5.17	4.38	.012
Extraversion in high Number of Reaction Types group	5.27	3.84	.010
Extraversion in low Gratitude Reactions Ratio group	3.33	4.26	.049
Agreeableness in low Praise Reactions Ratio group	4.08	4.75	.047
Praise Reactions Ratio(%) in high Neuroticism group	22.40	13.69	.022
Number of Reaction Types in low Conscientiousness group	56.67	40.89	.037
Praise Reactions Ratio(%) in low Conscientiousness group	21.68	13.84	.014

The use of praise-related reactions was found to be associated with multiple personality traits, including Agreeableness, Neuroticism, and Conscientiousness. The finding that users with low Conscientiousness tend to use more praise-related reactions can be explained by the characteristic of low Conscientiousness individuals being more emotional and intuitive in their actions.

Although we analyzed the relationship between laughter-related reactions and personality traits, no significant relationships were found.

For future directions, it is anticipated that communication behavior in public channels, where there are often many members, differs from behavior in private channels and direct messages. Additionally, it is likely that behavior in private channels and direct messages is more strongly related to individual personality traits. Therefore, future research should consider analyzing data from private channels and direct messages while respecting privacy considerations.

Furthermore, to enhance the reliability of the analysis and findings, future studies should involve larger sample sizes and multiple organizational datasets to conduct more extensive and robust analyses.

6 Conclusion

This study aimed to analyze communication in business chat environments. The research and analysis were conducted as follows:

First, to understand the communication situation within an organization, logs from Slack were used to investigate communication patterns within the organization. In addition to the number of messages sent and the number of reactions, new metrics such as response time and peak activity time were defined, and their distribution within the organization was determined.

Next, to analyze the relationship between chat communication and personality, an analysis was conducted on the relationship between Slack chat logs and Big Five obtained from surveys. The analysis revealed various associations between chat logs and personality traits. Notably, interesting findings included that individuals with high Conscientiousness had faster chat response times, and those with high Agreeableness had a greater number of reactions. Additionally, further investigation into the relationship between reaction types and personality traits revealed that individuals with a larger variety of reaction types tended to have higher Openness and Extraversion, while those with a lower proportion of praise reactions tended to have lower Agreeableness.

References

1. Costa, P.T., Jr., McCrae, R.R.: The NEO personality inventory manual. Psychological Assessment Resources, Odessa (1985)
2. Fukui, A.: The relevance of self-awareness in personality and communication. Ronko: Bull. Kobe Women's Junior Coll. **60**, 101–111 (2015)
3. Hayashi, Y., Nihei, F., Nakano, Y., Huang, H.-H., Okada, S., et al.: Development of group discussion interaction corpus and analysis of the relationship with personality traits. IPSJ J. **56**(4), 1217–1227 (2015)
4. Kim, S., Ha, J., Kim, J.: Detecting personality unobtrusively from users' online and offline workplace behaviors. In: Extended Abstracts of the 2018 CHI Conference on Human Factors in Computing Systems, pp. 1–6 (2018)
5. Marengo, D., Elhai, J.D., Montag, C.: Predicting big five personality traits from smartphone data: a meta-analysis on the potential of digital phenotyping. J. Pers. **91**(6), 1410–1424 (2023)
6. Marengo, D., Montag, C., et al.: Digital phenotyping of big five personality via Facebook data mining: a meta-analysis. Digit. Psychol. **1**(1), 52–64 (2020)
7. Myers, I.B., McCaulley, M.H., Most, R.: Manual: a guide to the development and use of the Myers-Briggs type indicator. Consulting Psychologists Press (1985)
8. Namikawa, T., Tani, I., Wakita, T., Kumagai, R., Nakane, A., Noguchi, H.: Development of a short form of the Japanese big-five scale, and a test of its reliability and validity. Japanese J. Psychol. **83**(2), 91–99 (2012)
9. Takizawa, R., et al.: Visualization of online communication and detection of lonely users using social graphs based on contribution level and adjacency level. J. Inf. Process. **33**, 765–775 (2025)
10. Wang, D., Wang, H., Mo, Yu., Ashktorab, Z., Tan, M.: Group chat ecology in enterprise instant messaging: how employees collaborate through multi-user chat channels on slack. Proc. ACM Hum.-Comput. Interact. **6**(CSCW1), 1–14 (2022)
11. Watt, J., Tuke, J., Mitchell, L.: Personality profiling: How informative are social media profiles in predicting personal information? arXiv preprint arXiv:2309.13065 (2023)
12. Yoshino, S., Oshio, A.: Regional differences in big five personality traits in Japan: evidence from three large datasets. Japanese J. Environ. Psychol. **9**(1), 19–33 (2021)

Emotion Recognition of Museum Visitors During Art Appreciation Based on Facial and Behavioral Features

Yohei Torigaki[1] and Yuki Matsuda[1,2(✉)]

[1] Okayama University, Okayama 700-0082, Japan
yohei.torigaki@cocolab.jp, yukimat@okayama-u.ac.jp
[2] RIKEN Center for Advanced Intelligence Project (AIP), Tokyo 103-0027, Japan

Abstract. In recent years, museums have been increasingly expected to facilitate communication in order to meet the intellectual needs of visitors. Although museum educators–experts in learning within museums and art galleries–have been employed to fulfill this role, there remains a persistent shortage of personnel. While systems such as audio guides are anticipated to serve as substitutes, a significant gap still exists between these systems and human guidance. Therefore, this study proposes a method to estimate the emotional state of museum visitors, aiming to provide dynamic guidance tailored to individual interests and concerns. To establish a method for emotional state estimation, we conducted a data collection experiment using a newly developed guidance system equipped with sensing capabilities at the Ohara Museum of Art, involving 30 participants. Based on the collected data of facial expressions and gestures, we constructed and evaluated an emotional state estimation model. As a result, the binary emotion classification model for positive and negative emotions achieved an accuracy of 64%. In contrast, regression models for satisfaction, comprehension, and perplexity did not yield effective results; however, some degree of correlation was observed, providing insights for future improvements.

Keywords: Emotion Recognition · Wearable Devices · Art Appreciation · Affective Computing · Audio Guidance · Museum · Art

1 Introduction

In museums and art galleries, it is important for visitors to feel, learn, and understand through the appreciation of exhibits. In recent years, museum educators–experts in learning within museums and art galleries–have played an important role in supporting visitors by providing explanations tailored to their interests and emotional states. However, there remains a persistent shortage of such personnel. In Japan, museum education is often supported primarily by curators, whose numbers remain limited. While the number of curators was approximately 3,000 in 2008, it increased by only about 20% to around 3,600 in 2018, and the average number of curators per museum remains fewer than four. This situation

E. Vlahu-Gjorgievska et al. (Eds.): PERSUASIVE 2026, CCIS 2896, pp. 563–575, 2027.
https://doi.org/10.1007/978-3-032-27235-5_57

indicates that many museums continue to face staff shortages, making it difficult to provide sufficient individualized guidance to all visitors [1].

In recent years, the use of audio guidance systems through rental devices and similar means has been advancing. However, most of these systems are limited to providing one-way explanations of artworks, essentially no more than digitized versions of in-gallery guides. Given this situation, many challenges remain for audio guidance systems and the like to serve as substitutes for museum educators.

In this study, we considered that this issue could be addressed by presenting content (compiling guidance content and order) interactively and dynamically, according to each visitor, based on estimates of the emotional states of people viewing exhibits. To this end, we newly developed an audio guidance system with the capability to sense diverse gestures and facial expressions, and conducted a data collection experiment on visitors' emotional states during art appreciation with 30 participants at the Ohara Museum of Art[1].

Using the constructed dataset, which consists of video data, acceleration and angular velocity data, and emotional state label data, we built and evaluated machine learning models to estimate emotional states. As a result of the evaluation, the binary emotion classification model (positive vs. negative) achieved an accuracy of 64%. On the other hand, regression models for satisfaction, comprehension, and perplexity did not yield effective results, though partial correlations were observed, providing insights for future improvements.

2 Related Work

Various methods have been proposed for emotional state estimation, particularly in the field of emotion recognition. For example, emotion estimation based on speech data collected through dialogue systems has been actively studied [8,14]. In recent years, voice interaction for operating devices has become more realistic, and the use of voice is expected in a wider range of contexts, including tourism. To further improve recognition performance, multimodal emotion recognition methods that combine multiple sensor data have also been studied. For instance, Tzirakis et al. and Ghaleb et al. proposed approaches that combine audio with video data collected through dialogue [5,19]. Other research has proposed emotion estimation based on eye gaze sensing and body movement sensing [20,21]. In addition to emotions, Rach et al. proposed research on handling different emotional state dimensions such as interest, persuasiveness, comprehension, and relevance in argumentative dialogue systems [15,16]. Prior studies have proposed methods for emotion recognition during sightseeing based on multimodal sensing approaches [12,13].

As tools to support visitors' understanding in museums, navigation systems (audio guides) using rental devices or smartphone applications have been widely used both in Japan and abroad in recent years. Sun et al. reported that changing the way museum guide information is presented according to an individual's learning style can reduce cognitive load and enhance learning effects, highlighting the importance of such personalization [18]. Liu et al. conducted research

[1] https://www.ohara.or.jp/.

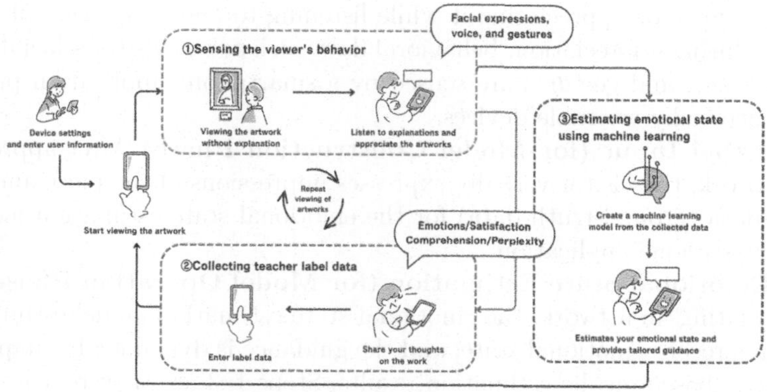

Fig. 1. Flow of Data Collection and Emotion Recognition.

to establish evaluation criteria for museums and, using those criteria, derived the relationship between the perceived attractiveness of museums and visitors' satisfaction [10].

Recent studies have applied affective computing techniques to museum and cultural heritage contexts. For example, emotion recognition based on facial expressions has been used to evaluate museum visitors' satisfaction [9], and psychophysiological analyses have been conducted to investigate emotional experiences during free exploration of art museums [11]. Other works have examined sensory museum design and conceptual approaches to understanding visitors' emotions during museum learning experiences [4,7]. In addition, large-scale studies on facial expression recognition in unconstrained environments have provided important foundations for in-the-wild emotion analysis [3], and affective-computing-driven personalization has been explored in cultural and heritage settings [6].

In contrast, our work focuses on in-situ emotion estimation during real museum visits by combining facial expressions with behavioral and motion features through a sensing-enabled audio guidance system.

3 Proposed Method

Various emotional states experienced when appreciating artworks are considered to be expressed through the visitor's facial expressions and gestures during appreciation. Therefore, we propose an emotional state estimation method based on sensing visitors during art appreciation. The workflow is shown in Fig. 1, and each step is described below.

Step 0: **Preparation** At the beginning, the visitor inputs information such as prior experience with museums and guidance systems, as well as personality traits, and then starts the appreciation process.

Step 1: **Artwork Appreciation** The visitor selects and moves to an artwork of choice and begins appreciation. It is assumed that there are two possible modes of appreciation: appreciating the artwork without listening to any explanations, or appreciating it while listening to audio guidance of the artwork. During appreciation, behavioral data such as the visitor's facial expressions, voice, and gestures are sensed by a smartphone application providing guidance or by wearable devices.

Step 2: **Label Input (for Model Construction Phase)** After appreciating an artwork, the visitor verbally expresses impressions of the piece and inputs label data (ground-truth data) for the emotional state estimation model via the smartphone application.

Step 3: **Emotional State Estimation (for Model Operation Phase)** After appreciating an artwork, the emotional state estimation model estimates the visitor's recent emotional state, and the guidance is dynamically adapted and provided based on the estimation results. Steps 1–3 are then repeated.

3.1 Features and Ground Truth Labels Used for Model Construction

Emotional state estimation is realized by extracting features from collected data, using them as input values, and constructing a model that estimates the visitor's emotional states with label data as the output values.

The data obtained by sensing visitors during artwork appreciation include: video data captured by the smartphone's front camera (facial expressions during appreciation) and rear camera (viewing direction during appreciation), and acceleration/angular velocity data acquired from the smartphone and head-mounted motion sensors. The feature extraction methods for each sensor data are described below.

Video Data: For each frame of the video, we use OpenFace [2], a library capable of performing facial landmark detection, gaze estimation, head pose estimation, and Action Units (AUs) estimation from image data, to obtain frame-level features. From the resulting time-series features, the following are extracted and used:

- **Viewing Time (seconds):** The total time spent appreciating an artwork.
- **Counts of Continuous Viewing Durations (per time window) and App Viewing Counts:** Using gaze estimation data (`gaze_angle_x, _y`), we calculate the number of times the gaze continuously remained directed toward the artwork for longer than a predefined time window W_g (= 5, 10, 20, 30, 40, 50, 60, 90, 120 s), as well as the number of times the gaze shifted toward the smartphone during these intervals. Similarly, using head pose estimation data (`pose_Rx, Ry`), we calculate equivalent features with time windows W_h (= 0.5, 1, 2, 3 s).
- **Number of Blinks and Counts of Inter-Blink Intervals (per time window):** Using blink events (`AU45_c`) included in the Action Units, we calculate the number of blinks and the number of inter-blink intervals (non-blinking durations) exceeding predefined time windows W_b (= 5, 10, 20, 30, 40, 50 s).

Table 1. Emotional state categories and their questions

Label	Question
Emotion	What kind of emotions did you feel when viewing the artwork?
Satisfaction	How satisfied were you with the artwork?
Comprehension	Do you feel that you understood the content or meaning of the artwork?
Perplexity	Were there any moments when you did not know what to focus on in the artwork?

Table 2. Options for user experience labeling

Emotion	Satisfaction	Comprehension	Perplexity
0: Excited/Surprised	0: Not satisfied at all	0: Did not understand at all	0: Never
1: Happy/Joyful	1: Dissatisfied	1: Did not understand	1: Not at all
2: Calm/Peaceful	2: Slightly dissatisfied	2: Hardly understood	2: Rarely
3: No particular change	3: Neutral	3: Neutral	3: Neutral
4: Sleepy/Tired	4: Somewhat satisfied	4: Somewhat understood	4: Somewhat infrequent
5: Miserable/Sad	5: Satisfied	5: Understood	5: Frequent
6: Bored	6: Very satisfied	6: Understood very well	6: Very frequent
7: Confused/Frustrated	–	–	–
8: Scared/Anxious/Angry	–	–	–

- **Statistical Features of Action Units:** For the AU intensity data AUx_r (where x denotes the AU action ID), we compute summary statistics (mean, standard deviation, minimum, maximum, median, first quartile, third quartile, and mode).

Acceleration and Angular Velocity Data: From the six-axis time-series motion data (acceleration and angular velocity), the following features are extracted and used:

- **Number of Outlier Events:** An outlier detection algorithm is applied (a data point is considered an outlier if the absolute difference between the target data point and the mean of the past N samples exceeds twice the standard deviation of the past N samples), and the number of outlier events is counted.
- **Statistical Features of Acceleration and Angular Velocity:** For the acceleration and angular velocity data, summary statistics (mean, standard deviation, minimum, maximum, median, first quartile, third quartile, and mode) are calculated.

The emotional state labels (emotion, satisfaction, comprehension, perplexity) are obtained by presenting the questions in Table 1, and selecting one option from Table 2. The emotion labels are based on the two-dimensional circumplex model of affect defined by Russell et al. [17], and are divided into nine categories as shown in Table 2 (Emotion). For satisfaction, a 7-point Likert scale used in the Ministry of Land, Infrastructure, Transport and Tourism's tourism satisfaction survey is adopted. The same scale is also applied to comprehension and perplexity. For constructing the emotional state estimation model, a classification model is used for emotion labels, while regression models are constructed for the other labels.

In the following section, we describe the data collection and the construction of an emotional state estimation model using facial expression and gesture data.

4 Experiment and Evaluation at the Ohara Museum of Art

In this study, we newly developed an audio guidance system with sensing capabilities and conducted a data collection experiment at an actual art museum. The experiment was conducted on December 23, 2024. We collected data by sensing the viewing behavior of 30 participants for 30 artworks exhibited in the Ohara Museum of Art. This study was conducted with the approval of the "Research Ethics Committee for Studies Involving Human Subjects" at Okayama University (approval No.: Shizen 2024-13).

In the following, we describe the devices used and data collected, and the experimental procedure for data collection.

4.1 Devices Used and Data Collected

The devices used and the method of data collection for this experiment are detailed below. The experimental setup utilized three main devices: a smartphone, a headset, and a motion sensor. For the smartphone, we used five iPhone 12 Pro devices and five iPhone 14 Pro devices (all manufactured by Apple Inc.). We developed an application that serves multiple purposes: it provides audio guidance to the participants during viewing, delivered by an avatar[2]; it collects video/audio data during the viewing session; it records acceleration and gyroscope data from the smartphone itself; and it gathers post-viewing questionnaire data. To ensure the continuous recording of the participant's facial expressions and the artwork being viewed, the smartphone is secured to the participant's body using a neck-mounted smartphone holder. For the headset, we used the OpenRun[3] (manufactured by Shokz). This device connects to the smartphone and provides the artwork guidance audio to the participant viewing the application. Finally, the MetaMotion S[4] (manufactured by MBIENTLAB Inc.) was used as the motion sensor. It is attached to the left side of the headset to acquire acceleration and gyroscope data from the participant's head. The method for attaching this motion sensor is shown in Fig. 3.

The data acquired by the devices were categorized into three main types: video data during artwork viewing, acceleration and gyroscope data, and emotional state labels. The video data during artwork viewing includes two streams

[2] CG-CA Gene (c) 2023 by Nagoya Institute of Technology, Moonshot R&D Goal 1 Avatar Symbiotic Society, https://github.com/mmdagent-ex/gene/.

[3] https://jp.shokz.com/products/openrun.

[4] https://mbientlab.com/metamotions/.

recorded at a frame rate of 30 frames per second (30 fps). The participant's facial expressions during viewing were recorded using the smartphone's front camera. Concurrently, the appearance of the artwork being viewed was recorded using the smartphone's rear camera. The acceleration and gyroscope data were acquired from two sources: the motion sensor attached to the participant's head (at a frequency of 100 Hz) and the motion sensor embedded in the smartphone worn during viewing (at a frequency of 20 Hz). As the ground truth data, the emotional state labels were collected after the participant finished viewing each artwork. Participants responded to four questions presented via the application, as detailed in Table 1. These labels were categorized into four types: emotion, satisfaction, comprehension, and perplexity. The emotion was selected from nine distinct options, whereas satisfaction, comprehension, and perplexity were quantified using a 7-point scale.

4.2 Data Collection Procedure

Here, we explain the data collection flow, following the artwork viewing process using the audio guidance application.

Step 1: **Explanation of the Data Collection Experiment**
First, participants receive explanations regarding the purpose of the experiment, the experimental flow, and the method of using the application, and then they answer a pre-questionnaire. The pre-questionnaire collected demographic and background information (e.g., museum visit frequency); however, these data were not used in the current analysis and are reserved for future work. After completing the pre-questionnaire, participants secure the smartphone to their bodies and wear the bone conduction speaker, which is integrated with the motion sensor.

Step 2: **Viewing Artworks Using the Application**
Next, participants view the artworks and perform emotional state labeling using the guidance application shown in Fig. 4. To begin viewing, participants stand in front of the artwork they wish to view and enter the artwork number, which is displayed near the artwork, into the application. After entering the artwork number and transitioning to the artwork viewing screen, participants first view the artwork without commentary (Fig. 4(a)). After viewing the artwork for several tens of seconds, they view it while listening to the audio commentary (Fig. 4(b)). After that, participants speak their impressions of the artwork for about 30 s and answer the questions that serve as emotional state labels on screens like those in Fig. 4(c) and (d). This completes one artwork viewing session, and this entire flow is repeated when viewing other artworks. The experiment in progress is shown in Fig. 2. The artwork viewing time is 45 min, during which participants view the target artworks in the museum.

Step 3: **Post-Questionnaire**
After the artwork viewing is finished, participants answer a post-questionnaire.

Fig. 2. The experimental setup with the subjects.

Fig. 3. Motion sensor attached to the bone conduction speaker.

(a) Viewing start (b) Audio guide (c) Emotion input (d) Satisfaction input

Fig. 4. Screens of the guidance application.

4.3 Building the Emotional State Estimation Model

Using the collected dataset, we built an emotional state estimation model as follows. First, we extracted the features shown in Sect. 3.1 from the collected data. Note that the audio data could not be used because it was not acquired due to device connection issues. Next, we built and evaluated the estimation models. For emotion label estimation, we built a 9-class emotional classification model to classify the nine labels shown in Table 2 (Emotion), and a 2-class classification model that groups them and classifies positive emotions (Positive: "Excited/Surprised," "Happy/Joyful," "Calm/Peaceful") and negative emotions (Negative: "Sleepy/Tired," "Miserable/Sad," "Bored," "Confused/Frustrated," "Scared/Anxious/Angry"). As the machine learning algorithm, we used the LightGBM Classifier[5] and performed hyperparameter tuning using

[5] https://lightgbm.readthedocs.io/en/latest/pythonapi/lightgbm.LGBMClassifier.html.

Table 3. Estimation results for emotion labels (9- and 2-class)

	9-class	2-class
Accuracy	0.14 ± 0.08	0.64 ± 0.09
Recall	0.19 ± 0.09	0.64 ± 0.09
Precision	0.19 ± 0.09	0.64 ± 0.09
F1	0.19 ± 0.09	0.64 ± 0.09

Table 4. Estimation results of satisfaction, comprehension, and perplexity labels

	Satisfaction	Comprehension	Perplexity
R2	-0.21 ± 0.12	-0.21 ± 0.15	0.05 ± 0.22
MAE	1.05 ± 0.13	1.24 ± 0.14	1.56 ± 0.20
RMSE	1.32 ± 0.14	1.55 ± 0.14	1.82 ± 0.21

Optuna[6], an automatic hyperparameter optimization framework. For satisfaction, comprehension, and perplexity label estimation, we built regression models. As the machine learning algorithm, we used the LightGBM Regressor[7] and similarly performed hyperparameter tuning using Optuna. Furthermore, in evaluating the built estimation models, we employed stratified 10-fold cross-validation, taking into account the imbalanced number of labels. The current evaluation does not enforce strict participant-independent splits, and therefore primarily reflects within-subject generalization. Subject-wise generalization is left for future work.

4.4 Evaluation Results and Discussion

The evaluation results of the classification models for emotion label estimation are shown in Table 3.

Regarding the emotion labels, the results of the 9-class classification are shown in Fig. 5, and the results of the 2-class classification are shown in Fig. 6. The numerical values (0–8) on each axis in Fig. 5 correspond to the IDs in Table 2 (Emotion), while in Fig. 6, 0 corresponds to positive and 1 corresponds to negative. Although the accuracy for the 9-class classification was low at 14%, it was 64% for the 2-class classification, indicating that classification could be performed with a certain degree of accuracy.

While high estimation accuracy was not obtained in the 9-class classification, a certain degree of accuracy was obtained in the 2-class classification of positive and negative. A possible reason for this is that the amount of data secured per class was larger in the 2-class classification compared to the 9-class classification. Additionally, in this experiment, participants were asked to report their emotional response to the entire viewing of a single artwork. Therefore, it is possible that we could not distinguish whether that emotional state was elicited by the artwork, the guidance, or other factors. In the future, it will be necessary to take measures to minimize variation in responses, such as indicating the response criteria more clearly during the pre-experiment briefing.

6 https://optuna.org/.

7 https://lightgbm.readthedocs.io/en/latest/pythonapi/lightgbm.LGBMRegressor.html.

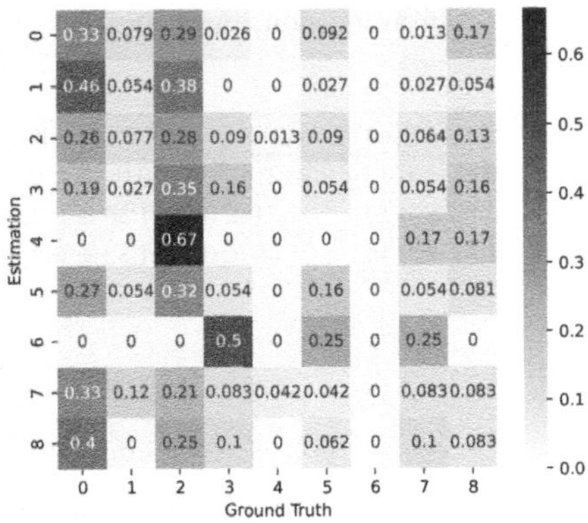

Fig. 5. Confusion matrix of 9-class emotion label estimation.

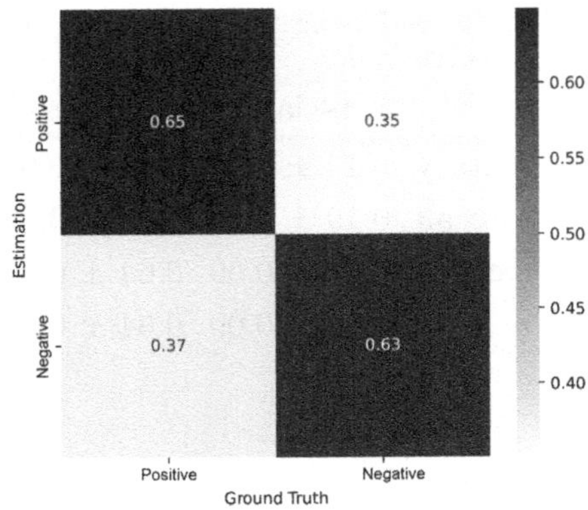

Fig. 6. Confusion matrix of 2-class emotion label estimation.

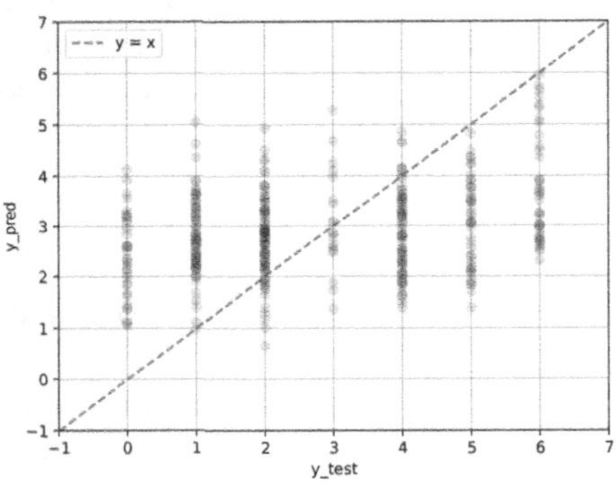

Fig. 7. Result of perplexity estimation (overall).

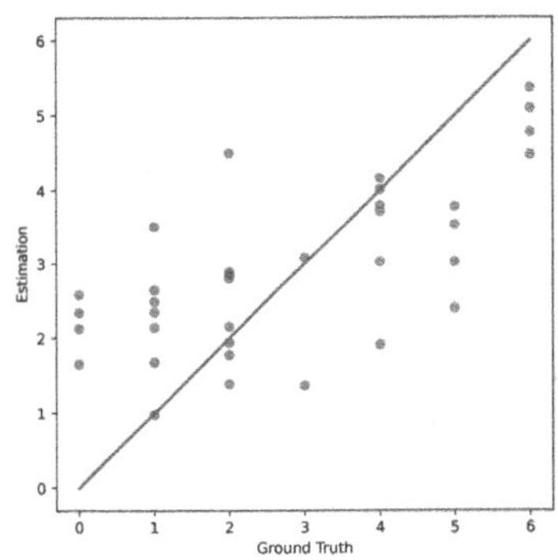

Fig. 8. Result of perplexity estimation (partial).

The detailed evaluation results of the regression models for estimating satisfaction, comprehension, and perplexity are shown in Table 4. Regarding the estimation of satisfaction labels and comprehension labels, no trends were observed for either. Therefore, it became clear that estimating these using the features and methods employed this time is difficult. Regarding the estimation of perplexity labels, no correlation was observed overall, as shown in Fig. 7. However, when focusing on data from one iteration of the cross-validation, results such as those in Fig. 7 were obtained in some cases; for this data, the R2 score was 0.45, indicating a result with a certain degree of correlation. A possible reason why trends were observed in some parts for the perplexity labels, unlike the satisfaction and comprehension labels, is that the perplexity labels had less bias due to class balance compared to the other labels. Additionally, a possible reason why trends were observed only in some parts is that there were significant individual differences in the acquired data and features. Therefore, to improve the estimation accuracy for other labels, it can be considered necessary to: 1) equalize the class balance as much as possible, and 2) perform feature extraction that eliminates individual differences. Furthermore, it is necessary to explore methods to mitigate individual differences, such as adding features that account for individual variation (Fig. 8).

5 Conclusion

In this study, we sensed the behavior of participants viewing artworks at the Ohara Museum of Art and conducted an experiment to collect multimodal sensing data and questionnaire data. Furthermore, using the data obtained from the experiment, we built models to estimate the emotional state during artwork viewing and analyzed the results. Regarding the estimation method using video data and acceleration/angular velocity (gyroscope) data, we achieved an accuracy of 64% in estimating emotion labels. However, no correlations were observed for satisfaction, comprehension, and perplexity. In the estimation of perplexity, a certain trend was observed in some of the estimation results. Future prospects for this study include: 1) exploring data and feature extraction methods useful for improving estimation accuracy, and 2) considering the construction of estimation models using other machine learning methods. By addressing these issues, we aim to improve estimation accuracy toward practical application.

Acknowledgment. This work was supported in part by the SCAT Research Grant and JSPS KAKENHI Grant Numbers JP22H03648 and JP24K20763. This research was also conducted with the cooperation of the Ohara Museum of Art. We would like to express our sincere appreciation.

Disclosure of Interests. The authors have no competing interests to declare that are relevant to the content of this article.

References

1. Agency for Cultural Affairs: Changes in the number of museums, visitors, and curators. https://www.bunka.go.jp/seisaku/bijutsukan_hakubutsukan/shinko/suii/. Accessed 2 Feb 2026. (in Japanese)
2. Baltrušaitis, T., Robinson, P., Morency, L.P.: OpenFace: an open source facial behavior analysis toolkit. In: IEEE Winter Conference on Applications of Computer Vision, WACV 2016, pp. 1–10 (2016). https://doi.org/10.1109/WACV.2016.7477553
3. Benitez-Quiroz, C.F., Srinivasan, R., Feng, Q., Wang, Y., Martinez, A.M.: Emotionet challenge: recognition of facial expressions of emotion in the wild. arXiv preprint arXiv:1703.01210 (2017)
4. Fominska, I., Di Tore, S., Nappi, M., Iovane, G., Sibilio, M., Gelo, O.C.G.: Approaches to identifying emotions and affections during the museum learning experience in the context of the future internet. Future Internet **16**(11), 417 (2024)

5. Ghaleb, E., Popa, M., Asteriadis, S.: Multimodal and temporal perception of audio-visual cues for emotion recognition. In: 8th International Conference on Affective Computing and Intelligent Interaction, ACII 2019, pp. 552–558 (2019). https://doi.org/10.1109/ACII.2019.8925444
6. Hu, H., Wan, Y., Tang, K.Y., Li, Q., Wang, X.: Affective-computing-driven personalized display of cultural information for commercial heritage architecture. Appl. Sci. **15**(7) (2025)
7. Jelinčić, D.A., Šveb, M., Stewart, A.E.: Designing sensory museum experiences for visitors' emotional responses. Museum Manage. Curatorship **37**(5), 513–530 (2022)
8. Kaya, H., Karpov, A.A., Salah, A.A.: Robust acoustic emotion recognition based on cascaded normalization and extreme learning machines. In: Advances in Neural Networks, ISNN 2016, pp. 115–123 (2016)
9. Kwon, D.H., Yu, J.M.: Real-time multi-CNN-based emotion recognition system for evaluating museum visitors' satisfaction. ACM J. Comput. Cultural Heritage **17**(1), 1–18 (2024)
10. Liu, S., Guo, J.: Smart museum and visitor satisfaction. J. Auton. Intell. **7**(3), 1–13 (2024). https://doi.org/10.32629/jai.v7i3.1242
11. Marín-Morales, J., et al.: Real vs. immersive-virtual emotional experience: analysis of psycho-physiological patterns in a free exploration of an art museum. PLOS ONE **14**(10), e0223881 (2019)
12. Matsuda, Y., Fedotov, D., Takahashi, Y., Arakawa, Y., Yasumoto, K., Minker, W.: EmoTour: estimating emotion and satisfaction of users based on behavioral cues and audiovisual data. Sensors **18**(11), 1–19 (2018). https://doi.org/10.3390/s18113978
13. Matsuda, Y., Fedotov, D., Takahashi, Y., Arakawa, Y., Yasumoto, K., Minker, W.: EmoTour: multimodal emotion recognition using physiological and audio-visual features. In: Proceedings of the 2018 ACM International Joint Conference and 2018 International Symposium on Pervasive and Ubiquitous Computing and Wearable Computers, UbiComp 2018, pp. 946–951 (2018). https://doi.org/10.1145/3267305.3267687
14. Quck, W.Y., Huang, D.Y., Lin, W., Li, H., Dong, M.: Mobile acoustic emotion recognition. In: 2016 IEEE Region 10 Conference, TENCON 2016, pp. 170–174 (2016)
15. Rach, N., Matsuda, Y., Daxenberger, J., Ultes, S., Yasumoto, K., Minker, W.: Evaluation of argument search approaches in the context of argumentative dialogue systems. In: The 12th International Conference on Language Resources and Evaluation, LREC 2020, pp. 513–522 (2020)
16. Rach, N., Matsuda, Y., Ultes, S., Minker, W., Yasumoto, K.: Estimating subjective argument quality aspects from social signals in argumentative dialogue systems. IEEE Access **9**, 11610–11621 (2021). https://doi.org/10.1109/ACCESS.2021.3051526
17. Russell, J.A.: A circumplex model of affect. J. Pers. Soc. Psychol. 1161–1178 (1980)
18. Sun, J.C.Y., Yu, S.J.: Personalized wearable guides or audio guides: an evaluation of personalized museum guides for improving learning achievement and cognitive load. Int. J. Hum.–Comput. Interact. **35**(4-5), 404–414 (2019). https://doi.org/10.1080/10447318.2018.1543078

19. Tzirakis, P., Trigeorgis, G., Nicolaou, M.A., Schuller, B.W., Zafeiriou, S.: End-to-end multimodal emotion recognition using deep neural networks. IEEE J. Sel. Topics Signal Process. **11**(8), 1301–1309 (2017)
20. Zhang, Z., Song, Y., Cui, L., Liu, X., Zhu, T.: Emotion recognition based on customized smart bracelet with built-in accelerometer. PeerJ **4**, e2258 (2016)
21. Zheng, W.L., Dong, B.N., Lu, B.L.: Multimodal emotion recognition using EEG and eye tracking data. In: 36th Annual International Conference of the IEEE Engineering in Medicine and Biology Society, pp. 5040–5043 (2014). https://doi.org/10.1109/EMBC.2014.6944757

Author Index

E. Vlahu-Gjorgievska et al. (Eds.): PERSUASIVE 2026, CCIS 2896, pp. 577–579, 2027.
https://doi.org/10.1007/978-3-032-27235-5

The manufacturer's authorised representative in the EU is Springer Nature Customer Service Centre GmbH, Europaplatz 3, 69115 Heidelberg, Germany. If you have any concerns regarding our products, please contact ProductSafety@springernature.com

Printed and bound by CPI Group (UK) Ltd, Croydon, CR0 4YY
15/09/2026
02216996-0007